THE THEORY
OF GOOD AND EVIL

A TREATISE ON MORAL PHILOSOPHY

BY

HASTINGS RASHDALL

D.LITT. (OXFORD), HON. D.C.L. (DURHAM)
FELLOW AND TUTOR OF NEW COLLEGE, OXFORD

SECOND EDITION

VOLUME I

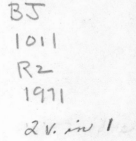

OXFORD UNIVERSITY PRESS

LONDON : GEOFFREY CUMBERLEGE

KRAUS REPRINT CO.
New York
1971

FIRST EDITION 1907
Second edition produced photographically
by the MUSTON COMPANY in 1924
from corrected sheets of the first edition
Reprinted 1938, 1948, photographically
by LOWE & BRYDONE, PRINTERS, LTD., LONDON

L.C. 25-9594

TO THE MEMORY

OF

MY TEACHERS

THOMAS HILL GREEN

AND

HENRY SIDGWICK

PREFACE

THE scope of the present work is perhaps made sufficiently obvious by the title-page. It is an attempt to deal with the chief topics usually discussed in books bearing the title 'Moral Philosophy' or 'Ethics.' It is on a rather larger scale than the books generally described as 'Textbooks,' or 'Introductions,' and is occupied to some extent with difficulties and controversies which can hardly be called 'elementary.' Still, I have in writing it had chiefly before my mind the wants of undergraduate students in Philosophy. I have endeavoured, as far as possible, to assume no previous acquaintance either with ethical or with general Philosophy : but it has not, in all parts of the work, been possible to avoid alluding to the arguments and objections of writers whose systems cannot be fully explained or examined in a book like the present. That is especially the case in Book II, which is largely occupied with replies to objections and with the criticism of views more or less opposed to my own. Even there I have endeavoured to make the drift of my argument intelligible to readers who have not read the works criticized. But those who want a short and fairly elementary treatment of the subject might perhaps read Book I by itself, or pass at once from Book I to Book III. That book deals in part with metaphysical questions which do not admit of an altogether 'popular' treatment ; this section of the work would no doubt be better understood by a student who has read enough to know in a general way the meaning of the metaphysical problem, but I hope it will not be found wholly unintelligible to those who may make their first acquaintance with it in these pages. Advanced students are more likely to complain that I have touched upon many great questions, not specially belonging to the ethical branch of Philosophy, in a way which must appear unsatisfying to those who are well versed in them, and dogmatic to those who do not agree with me. I would venture

1 ∗

in reply to such a criticism to plead that the necessity of touching upon difficult questions without getting to the bottom of them is to some extent inseparable from any treatment of Ethics which does not form part of a complete course or system of Philosophy: and the difficulty is increased when one wishes to avoid allusiveness and technicality of a kind which would necessarily render the book perplexing and uninstructive to a student beginning the subject, or to the general reader who may take some interest in the ethical and religious aspects of Philosophy without wishing to embark upon an elaborate course of Logic, Psychology, and Metaphysic.

The idea prevails among some Philosophers that Moral Philosophy is a particularly ' easy ' branch of Philosophy. I believe that it is easier than other branches of Philosophy in the sense that its more elementary problems can be discussed with less technicality, and can be understood more readily at a first reading by persons of ordinary ability and education. For this reason it seems to me a peculiarly good subject for the student of Philosophy to begin upon, although logically it might well be considered to come rather at the end than at the beginning of a philosophical course. But, though the controversies which range round the words ' Utilitarianism ' and ' Intuitionism ' can be understood and discussed almost without reference to metaphysical problems, the ultimate question of Moral Philosophy— the meaning and nature of the ideas ' good,' ' right,' ' duty '—is after all the ultimate question of all Philosophy, and involves all the others. I am very far from thinking that I have got to the bottom of all the difficulties involved in that fundamental problem: upon some of them I am aware that I have hardly touched in these pages. Nor is there anything very original in such a solution of them as I have been able to offer: and yet I am not aware that, in English at any rate, there is any systematic treatment of them, written from anything like my own point of view, to which I could point as altogether meeting the wants of the class of readers for whom this book is chiefly intended. Neither of the great writers to whom I feel I owe most in the special department of Ethics—the late Professor Sidgwick, and the late Professor T. H. Green whose lectures and private classes I used to attend as an undergraduate—can well be regarded as having said the last word upon the subject by students of a generation later who have profited not merely by the criticism which each of them supplies upon the other, but by the general progress of Philosophy since the first appearance of Sidgwick's *Methods of Ethics* (1874) and of Green's *Prolegomena to Ethics* (1883). Since the last-mentioned date the supposed easiness of this branch of Philosophy, or the superior attractiveness of Logic and Metaphysic, has led perhaps to a certain unwillingness to write separate treatises on Ethics, at least among those who take what one may call a constructive view of the subject[1]. But the period—almost a quarter of a century—which has elapsed since the death of Green has been a period of great philosophical activity, and (I venture to think) of great philosophical progress, and there has been much incidental treatment of ethical questions in the works both of English and of foreign Philosophers. There seems therefore room for a fresh systematic treatment of the main problems of Moral Philosophy in what I will venture to call (in spite of great differences both of opinion and of temperament) the spirit which animated both of them.

Among more recent writers I have learned most perhaps from those from whom I differ most. I have so frequently criticized the writings of Mr. F. H. Bradley that I should like to say that, fundamentally as I dissent from his ultimate position, I believe that no one has a deeper sense than myself of personal obligation to his brilliant writings, or a deeper appreciation of the stimulus which he has given to philosophical progress, not only in his own

---

[1] I should wish to speak with respect of three short English textbooks—Professor Muirhead's *Elements of Ethics*, Professor Mackenzie's *Introduction to Moral Philosophy*, and Bishop d'Arcy's *Short Study of Ethics*; but none of them can be said to represent exactly my own point of view. I feel more sympathy on the purely ethical, though not on the metaphysical, side with a quite recent work—Mr. Moore's very powerful essay, *Principia Ethica*, which appeared when my own work was practically finished. Professor Paulsen's *System of Ethics* is an admirable and very attractive book, which represents on the whole a point of view not unlike my own, but it hardly touches upon many difficulties which have attracted much attention in England.

University of Oxford, but throughout the English-speaking world and beyond it. Unfortunately, Ethics seems to me precisely the side of Philosophy on which his influence has been least salutary. I trust that, while criticizing him with freedom, I have not failed in the respect that is due to perhaps the most original of contemporary thinkers.

With regard to my criticism of the able work of Professor A. E. Taylor (*The Problem of Conduct*), I should wish to explain that the recent number of the *Philosophical Review* in which he withdraws his view about the merely 'apparent' character of evil did not come into my hands till the whole of my criticism was printed and some of it had been finally passed for the press, though I had not failed to notice the change of tone already traceable in his *Elements of Metaphysics*. I can only therefore express my regret for having devoted so much space to the criticism of a position which its author has abandoned.

It is useless for an author to offer apologies for the defects of a book which he is not compelled to write. In explanation of such deficiencies of the present work as may arise from the absence of a more exhaustive knowledge of the literature bearing upon this and cognate subjects, I may, however, be allowed to plead, for the information of persons unacquainted with our English system of University teaching, that Oxford College Tutors are very far from possessing the leisure of a German or an American Professor, and that they have to choose between publishing imperfect work and not publishing at all. They may perhaps console themselves with the reflection that the method of individual teaching by means of essays and conversation gives them opportunities of appreciating the real wants of students which are hardly accessible to teachers who see their pupils only in the lecture-room. I have a strong feeling that the progress of knowledge, especially in the region of Philosophy, is often retarded by an excessive shrinking from criticism, and by an indefinite postponement of publication in the hope of more completely satisfying an author's ideal.

The following articles which have already appeared in various periodicals have been freely made use of with the kind permission of their editors :—' Professor Sidgwick's Utilitarianism '

(*Mind,* 1885) ; 'Dr. Martineau and the Theory of Vocation' (*Mind,* 1888); 'The Theory of Punishment' (*The International Journal of Ethics,* 1891); 'The Limits of Casuistry' (*International Journal of Ethics,* 1894); 'Justice' (*The Economic Review,* 1891, 1892); 'Can there be a Sum of Pleasures?' (*Mind,* 1899); 'The Ethics of Forgiveness' (*International Journal of Ethics,* 1900); 'The Commensurability of all Values' (*Mind,* 1902). Some of the earlier articles have been largely re-written : others are reprinted with little change.

Dr. McTaggart of Trinity College, Cambridge, has kindly read through the whole of my proofs, and I am much indebted to his criticisms and suggestions. For assistance and advice in dealing with parts of the work I am similarly indebted to Mr. C. C. J. Webb of Magdalen College, Oxford, and several other friends, nor must I omit to mention the help of my wife in the final revision.

H. RASHDALL.

The first edition was published in 1907. The second edition is in the main a reprint of the first, but certain corrections, mostly verbal, are incorporated from a copy marked by the author.

ANALYTICAL TABLE OF CONTENTS

VOLUME I

BOOK I. THE MORAL CRITERION

CHAPTER I. INTRODUCTORY

CHAPTER VI. REASON AND FEELING

2

As a matter of abstract right, the answer is 'No,' and at all events there is no way of rewarding superior virtue without rewarding superior capacity; yet it is true that the good ought to be made

CHAPTER IX. PUNISHMENT AND FORGIVENESS

For these reasons I shall make no formal attempt to mark out beforehand the relation of our subject to Philosophy in general or to its other branches. I shall begin by assuming only that we are concerned with the study of human conduct, that we are investigating the meaning of the ideas 'right' and 'wrong' with the object both of arriving at a clearer conception of those ideas in general, and of determining in a more precise manner than is done by ordinary persons in common life what things in particular are right and what are wrong. How far and in what sense such an aim is attainable is one of the things which must be left to appear in the course of our enquiry. And in my treatment of the subject I shall endeavour to follow what is, not indeed always but very frequently, the line of development taken by the mind of students. When first the attempt is made to think out clearly the unanalysed, more or less confused and inconsistent ideas about human conduct with which we all start, the student is very likely to be caught by a theory of extreme simplicity and apparently great scientific completeness and attractiveness—a theory which, as a matter of fact, has always made its appearance at the beginning of every serious historical effort to grapple with the ethical problem. He is very likely to be bitten by the theory which traces all human conduct to the operation of a single motive, the desire of pleasure. If this theory be true, it follows as a matter of course that the only meaning which can be given to the term right is 'conducive to pleasure,' and to the term wrong 'unconducive to pleasure or productive of its opposite, pain.' The commonly received ideas about right and wrong, in so far as they are upon such a view capable of scientific justification at all, have then to be explained by showing that the acts commonly regarded as right are productive of pleasure on the whole to the individual, while the actions commonly accounted wrong are conducive on the whole to pain or loss of pleasure. The examination of this theory, known as psychological Hedonism, will be the starting-point of our investigation, and will occupy the next chapter. If satisfied that pleasure is not always the motive of the individual's own action, the student may still very probably be attracted by other forms of the theory that pleasure in the last resort, either to the individual

or to others, is the sole true and ultimate criterion of human
action. Utilitarianism disconnected from psychological Hedonism
will be the subject of our third chapter. From the Utilitarian
group of ethical theories I shall turn to their extreme opposite,
the theory which asserts in the most uncompromising and unanalysed way the authority, perhaps even the infallibility, of
the individual Conscience and of the judgements about particular
questions of right and wrong which the ordinary Conscience pronounces—the theory commonly known as Intuitionism. I shall
then try to bring together the various elements of truth contained in the conflicting theories, and to arrive at a view which
will embrace and harmonize them, while avoiding the mistakes
and exaggerations which each, taken by itself, can be shown
to involve. I shall then go on to examine more in detail some of
the chief questions of right conduct, the chief commonly recognized virtues and duties or groups of duties, and to show how
they can be explained and co-ordinated, with whatever correction
of popular notions may turn out to be necessary, upon the basis
of the theory which will be adopted.

To arrive at a clearer and more definite conception of the
Moral Criterion—a clearer and more definite answer than is
contained in that common moral consciousness from which we
must all start to the question 'What ought I to do, and why
ought I to do it?' will be the object of our first book. In the
second book I shall enter at greater length into some of the
current controversies connected with our subject, by the examination of which I shall hope further to elucidate and define
the results arrived at in the first book. Most of these controversies may be said to centre round the question of the
relation of the individual and the individual's good to society
and a wider social good. I have therefore styled the book 'The
Individual and the Society.' In the third book I shall deal with
some of those wider philosophical issues which are ultimately involved in any attempt to think out fully and adequately the
meaning of the words 'right and wrong,' 'good and evil'—in
other words with the relation of Morals and Moral Philosophy
to our theory of the Universe in general, to Metaphysic and
Religion, to the theory of Free-will, to the facts of Evolution

and theories of Evolution, and finally to practical life. The subject of this section may be described generally as 'Man and the Universe.' In postponing these more general considerations to the end of our enquiry instead of making them our starting-point, I am once more abandoning what may perhaps be thought the logical order; and adopting the order which will, I hope, be most advantageous for purposes of exposition and dialectical defence, and which will be most convenient for those who may read this book with no previous acquaintance with technical Philosophy or with any of its branches. With regard to the relations between Metaphysic and Moral Philosophy it will be enough to premise this much—that Metaphysic is an enquiry into the ultimate nature of Reality and our knowledge of it; while Moral Philosophy is an enquiry into a particular, though very general and important, department of our knowledge, our ideas of right and wrong [1], that is to say into one particular though very fundamental aspect of Reality, the aspect which is expressed by our moral judgements. To attain some clearer conception as to the relation of these ideas to other ideas, of this aspect of Reality to other aspects, will be one object of our investigation. But, whatever answer may be given to this last problem, it must be possible at least to begin the enquiry as to what we mean by saying that an act is right or wrong, and why we call some actions right and others wrong, without presupposing any more than is presupposed in our common unscientific thinking about the world in general and man's place in it. At a very early stage of our enquiry it may, indeed, be found that we cannot give a satisfactory answer to that question without assuming particular answers to other and more general questions about human knowledge and about the ultimate nature of things—answers which from various philosophical points of view have sometimes been implicitly or explicitly denied. But I shall endeavour, for the

[1] The relation of this question to the wider question 'What is good?' will be dealt with in the sequel; but in modern times Moral Philosophy has grown out of an attempt to answer the question 'What is right?' rather than the question 'What is good?' And this is the essentially ethical question, since, by general admission, Ethics starts with the problem of human conduct, even though it may soon be discovered that that problem involves a wider problem about values in general.

reasons already indicated, to make the first part of our enquiry as purely ethical as possible. If and in so far as it shall be found that to take a particular view about the ideal of human conduct, a view to which we are led purely by the investigation of the actual contents of our ethical consciousness, logically involves us in wider conclusions as to the nature of the Universe and man's place in it, that will be the best way of defending those wider conclusions, and so of exhibiting the true relation between that ethical Science which is the subject of this book and that wider Science of Reality which will be dealt with in these pages only in so far as may be necessary for the purpose of attaining clear ideas about the meaning and end of human life.

CHAPTER II

PSYCHOLOGICAL HEDONISM

I

IN the writings of Bentham [1] and his followers the ethical doctrine that actions are right or wrong according as they do or do not tend to produce maximum pleasure is founded upon the psychological theory that as a matter of fact nothing is or can be desired except pleasure. The most fundamental of all distinctions between ethical systems turns upon the attitude which they adopt towards this theory. It is of course possible for a Moral Philosopher to reject the hedonistic Psychology and still to remain a Hedonist. He may hold that it is, as a matter of psychological fact, possible to desire other things besides pleasure, but that pleasure is the only proper or rational object of desire. It is possible to contend that I may, as a matter of psychological fact, desire other things, but that, if I do so, I am a fool for my pains. On the other hand it is clear that if nothing but pleasure *can* be desired, it is useless, and indeed meaningless, to maintain that something other than pleasure *ought* to be desired. It will be well, therefore, to clear the ground by facing the psychological problem before we attack the ethical questions which depend, to a large extent, upon our answer to that problem.

[1] And earlier of Hobbes, with this difference—that Hobbes defines pleasure in terms of desire ('Whatsoever is the object of any man's appetite or desire, that is it which he for his part calleth good,' *Leviathan*, ch. vi), and then proceeds to define pleasure as 'the apparance or sense of good.' Bentham assumes that we already know what pleasure is, and then proceeds to argue that we desire that and nothing else. The difference might be more important than it is if Hobbes had always remembered it himself. When he identifies the 'iucundum' with 'good in effect, as the end desired,' he practically adopts the position of Bentham.

The plausibility of the doctrine that nothing but pleasure can be the object of desire depends mainly upon a confusion between three different senses in which it may be understood. The proposition that the motive of every. action is pleasure may mean :—

(1) That I always do that which it gives me most pleasure *at the moment* to do ;

(2) That the motive of every action is some *future* pleasure, although that future pleasure is not necessarily the most intense (it being for instance possible to choose the nearer but smaller pleasure in preference to one greater but more remote) :

(3) That the motive of every act is always to get the *greatest quantum of pleasure upon the whole.*

Now the doctrine explicitly maintained by psychological Hedonists is usually the last of these three positions : while its plausibility arises chiefly from its confusion with one or both of the former. The last proposition is, indeed, one of those which would hardly obtain a moment's acceptance but for the supposed consequences of denying it. Let us assume for the moment that nothing ever is desired except pleasure, and ask whether it is always the prospect of *the greatest pleasure* that moves us. That men do not always do that which will as a matter of fact bring them most pleasure will readily be admitted : need we hesitate to assert that the world would be a much better place if they did [1] ? Nor will it be denied that people often do actions which, before the time of acting, they know very well to be contrary to their real interest, understood in the most purely hedonistic sense. The drunkard—the poor drunkard at all events, who suffers from his vices in other than purely physiological ways—knows very well in the morning that he gets more pain than pleasure from his drink : he craves to get rid of the habit, and yet, as a matter of fact, he drinks on. That will be acknowledged,

---

[1] 'The thing to be lamented is, not that men have so great regard to their own good or interest in the present world, for they have not enough ; but that they have so little to the good of others.' Bp. Butler, Preface to *Fifteen Sermons.*

but it may be urged perhaps that *at the moment of action*
such a man has always persuaded himself that the drink will
produce a balance of pleasure on the whole.   Admit, if you
like, that he has.   The question remains : how, on the assumptions of psychological Hedonism, is it possible to account
for such a persuasion ?   Granted that at the time he acts he
does not know that the thing is bad for him, how can a man
who once knew that a thing was bad for himself come, however
momentarily, to believe the contrary ?   Such conduct as that
of the drunkard will hardly be accounted for by mere intellectual
error, mere involuntary lapse of memory.   If a man who in the
morning knew that to drink a whole bottle of gin was not for
his good, comes in the evening to believe the contrary, his
ignorance must be to some extent voluntary : he must, as we
say, have 'persuaded himself' that it will do him no harm.   And
this voluntary ignorance, this bias in his judgement, has to
be accounted for : and on the hedonistic theory (in the form
in which it is now before us), it can be accounted for only
in one way.   On that theory there is only one desire or emotion
that can ever affect the will, and so exercise a distorting influence
upon the judgement, viz. desire for one's greatest pleasure on
the whole.   In the case supposed then desire for his greatest
pleasure on the whole, steadily operating throughout the day,
must somehow have changed the conviction that the man's
greatest pleasure lies in abstinence or moderation into a conviction
that his greatest pleasure lies in drunkenness.   Is this an intelligible piece of Psychology ?

Perhaps the matter may be made plainer by a slightly different
illustration.   If there is a certain piece of hedonistic calculus in
the world, it is that the pleasure of eating something very bad
for one is not worth the indigestion which it causes.   The
pleasure, unlike that of quantitative or qualitative errors in
drinking, is slight and almost momentary : the pain may be
continuous and severe.   Ask a man with a delicate digestion
whether the wise dyspeptic Hedonist will eat lobster salad.
Ask him in the morning, ask him the moment before dinner,
ask him while he is actually tasting his soup, and he will say
emphatically 'No. It has almost always disagreed with me ;

it certainly is not worth the risk of temporary indigestion and the danger of bringing back that chronic indigestion which it took me so long to get over a year ago.' Yet it may be that, as the dinner proceeds and conversation flows and spirits rise, the lobster salad comes round, and he eats. Now I admit that in cases like that it is scarcely possible to account for the man's action without supposing at least a momentary intellectual vacillation. Very likely he does say to himself, 'After all the consequences are not certain: I have upon occasion taken lobster salad without suffering much. I am better now than when I ate it last,' and so on. But the question remains, 'Why should he seek in this way to deceive himself?' Do not these efforts at self-deception imply that the man is not, as the theory supposes him to be, an absolutely impartial judge between the pleasure of the next moment and the pleasure of the next morning or the next week? Were he unbiassed by desire of lobster salad, or of the pleasure attending its consumption, he would unquestionably have retained his well-grounded conviction as to the inadvisability of eating it. Supposing, at the very moment before he took the fatal resolution, he were to be consulted by a no less dyspeptic neighbour, he would have no hesitation whatever about the matter. 'By no means eat lobster salad,' he would have said. And when in his own case he acts differently, it is evident that at that moment he cares more for present pleasure (in so far as his desire is really a desire for pleasure at all) than for his pleasure on the whole. There is a bias in his judgement—a bias derived from desire—which prevents him from correctly balancing present against future pains. He has, in short, other desires besides a desire for the greatest quantum of pleasure, though it may be (for anything we have seen so far) that he still cares about nothing but pleasure. At all events, the nearer pleasure exercises more attractive power than the more remote.

We have seen reason to reject the third interpretation of the hedonistic formula; now let us look at the first. It undoubtedly sounds plausible to say that, if I do a thing, I do it because it pleases me to do it; and from this it does not seem a large step to the admission that, if I prefer one alternative to another,

it is because it pleases me more, and from that to the admission that
I always do that which pleases me most. It might be enough
to point out that we are really misled by an ambiguity of
language. 'It pleases me to do it,' 'it is my pleasure (*placet*)
that it shall be done,' means merely 'I will that it should be
done': as to *why* I will it, the phrase tells us nothing. But
let us admit that we are justified in interpreting this 'placet'
by 'It gives me at this moment more pleasure to do this than
to do anything else [1].' The question still remains 'Why does this
course of action give me so much momentary pleasure as to
determine my will to adopt it?' It certainly cannot always
be the pleasure resulting at the moment of action that moves
me to do it. For the most selfish people clearly do many things
which are painful at the time for the sake of some future end.
Granted that it always gives me most pleasure to do what I have
made up my mind to do, the question remains 'What leads
me to make up my mind?' And this certainly cannot be
the mere momentary pleasure involved in the act itself. If
I thought only of my own momentary sensations while preparing
for a bath on a very cold morning, I certainly should not take it.
Still less, should I go to the dentist when my tooth is not
actually aching. If I do these unpleasant things, it must be
for the sake of something—a feeling of my own or otherwise—
which lies beyond that moment. That brings us to the second
possible sense of the psychological-hedonist doctrine—that I

---

[1] This seems to be very much the position of Sigwart: 'Each end must, if
I am on the whole to will it and to be able to devote my powers to its attainment, be such a one that the attainment of it promises some kind or other
of satisfaction (*Befriedigung*) for me, the thought of which so affects my
feeling, that the expectation of its attainment affords me joy, the fear of the
opposite causes me pain' (Sigwart, *Vorfragen der Ethik*, p. 5). This statement (with others in this remarkably clear and able little work) seems to
me to be not actually erroneous, but to suggest the fallacies of psychological Hedonism, inasmuch as it is not made clear whether the thought of
the action is now pleasant because it will produce in the agent the greatest
possible maximum of pleasant feeling, or because he desires the end and
consequently will find satisfaction in its future accomplishment and in working for its accomplishment in the present. The word 'Gefühl' seems to be
used by Sigwart sometimes in the sense of 'desire,' sometimes of anticipated
pleasure.

always act for the sake of *some* future pleasure [1], though not necessarily for the sake of the greatest quantum of pleasure on the whole.

Why then should one pleasure or sum of pleasures attract me more than another, apart from its being greater in amount ? It may be said that I am more attracted by the nearer than by the remoter pleasure. That is intelligible, and it was admitted by Bentham, who did not see that the admission was fatal to the doctrine, implied if not expressed in the writings of himself and his followers, that what is desired is always the greatest prospective sum of pleasures. Of course in so far as remoteness involves uncertainty, that may logically be taken into account by the hedonistic calculus. But in so far as a remote pleasure is practically just as certain as a nearer one, it ought on Benthamite principles to prove equally attractive. And yet it is matter of experience that it very often does not. And this involves the admission that what I desire in such cases is not pleasure, but immediate pleasure. The pleasure in the hand is treated as if it were worth two in the bush, even when the pleasure in the bush is as certain as that in the hand.

This admission by itself makes a very large inroad into the apparently logical and coherent system of the hedonistic Psychology. Ethically it is of little importance, so long as the only characteristic which can give to one foreseen pleasure an increased attractiveness as compared with some other foreseen pleasure is supposed to be its greater proximity. But the admission may perhaps prepare the way for the recognition of the fact that there are other sources of (so to speak) differential attractiveness in pleasures besides (1) expected intensity and (2) proximity. Let us emphasize the admission that has so far been made. It is admitted, we may assume, that foreseen greater intensity of pleasure does not always carry with it greater constraining power over the will. The human mind is not the mere impartial calculating machine which it is represented to be by the hedonistic Psychology in its most logical form. We have in fact recognized the existence of *passion* in the

[1] Not of course excluding the pleasure of the immediate act which *in some cases* is obviously the prominent element.

human soul, though at present we may be disposed to interpret passion as a mere liability to be more affected by a nearer than by a remoter pleasure. But is that a possible explanation of the extraordinary motive power possessed at certain moments by one pleasure as compared with another which, upon a calm review, would be recognized as being of far greater intensity? Take the case of an angry man. On a calm review of the pleasure of avenging some trifling or imagined slight (at the cost perhaps of some serious and clearly foreseen penalty), the man himself would usually be disposed to admit that the game was not worth the candle. The pleasure, he would admit, would not be worth the sacrifice of even a week's freedom and ordinary enjoyment of life. 'Yes,' it will be said, 'but then the prospect of this pleasure is near, its more clearly perceived intensity triumphs over a chaos of remote, indefinite, and indistinctly envisaged enjoyments such as might be purchased by self-restraint.' Well, at that rate, the offer of some other pleasure more intense and equally near should at once hold back the uplifted hand, and transform the angry countenance. Once assume that the attraction lies wholly in pleasure—that the man is indifferent to the kind of pleasure, except so far as 'kind of pleasure' implies to him a difference of intensity—and this consequence must follow. But does it? The average wife-beating ruffian would probably admit on reflection that the pleasure of beating his wife on one particular occasion was not worth a pot of beer. But tender him the pot of beer when he is angry, and will the uplifted hand inevitably be lowered to grasp it? 'No,' it will be said, 'this is what he would do if he calmly reflected; but at such a moment he does not reflect; his mind is so concentrated upon that one imagined pleasure that the other fails to obtain an entrance.' But why does he not reflect? The determination to reflect or not to reflect is just as much a voluntary action as the determination to strike or not to strike. And, if the hedonistic Psychology is right, this action must be itself determined by a calculation as to the greater pleasantness of reflection or non-reflection. If then a man gets angry and so fails to reflect upon the consequences of what he is doing, that must be, it would seem,

3

because he has come to the conclusion that (in this particular case) non-reflection will be the pleasanter course. But what should lead him to such a conclusion? Experience? Are we then really prepared to say that a hot-tempered man is one who has been taught by experience to believe that at certain moments non-reflection upon the relative value of pleasures, necessarily involving the choice of pleasures which calm reflection would show to be of less intensity, is itself conducive to obtaining the greatest amount of pleasure or at least of immediate pleasure? If any one is really prepared to admit this analysis of passion, there is no more to be said. If he is not, he must concede that, even if we allow the object of choice to be always a pleasure, there is something which causes a man at times to prefer one pleasure rather than another, irrespective of its greater nearness or greater intensity. What is this something? I know of no better way of expressing it than to say that the man *desires* one pleasure (assuming for the moment that it really is pleasure which is desired) rather than another[1]. It is an ultimate fact that one desire is stronger than another[2]. The strength of the desire does not depend wholly upon the intensity of the imagined pleasure. And in so far as it does not depend upon such imagined intensity, it is not really a desire for pleasure *qua* pleasure. If all that is desired is pleasure—as much of it as possible, and for as long as possible—it must be a matter of indifference to the man in what form (so to speak) his pleasure is served up to him, so long as he gets enough of it. But the existence of such passions as we have alluded to is by itself a sufficient proof that it is not pleasure in general but some particular kind of pleasure that is desired in such cases. Now

---

[1] In so far, that is, as his impulses are sufficiently reflected upon to become desires. A large part of our habitual bodily movements are of course due to impulses which cannot be so described. The actions are voluntary only because they can be at once inhibited when any conflicting desire presents itself. Movements which are not voluntary even to this extent are not acts.

[2] Of course the cause may lie in the man's physical constitution or in external influences; but, as *ex hypothesi* we are dealing with *voluntary* actions, these causes lying outside consciousness can only influence him by producing an impulse to act within consciousness, i. e. a desire.

it seems clear that desire for a particular kind of pleasure is not really desire for pleasure and nothing else. Even if we supposed that pleasure was always part of his object, we should have to admit that the man desires not only pleasure but also a particular sort of pleasure, not necessarily thought of as more intense than other pleasures. Desire of pleasure then is not the only motive which is capable of inspiring action.

And having got so far, we may be prepared to go a step further and admit that the desire of pleasure need not really be present at all. At least there need be no desire for anything which would be a pleasure apart from the fact that it is desired. The fact that a thing is desired no doubt implies that the satisfaction of the desire will necessarily bring pleasure. There is undoubtedly pleasure in the satisfaction of all desire. But that is a very different thing from asserting that the object is desired because it is thought of as pleasant, and in proportion as it is thought of as pleasant. The hedonistic Psychology involves, according to the stock phrase, a 'hysteron-proteron'; it puts the cart before the horse. In reality, the imagined pleasantness is created by the desire, not the desire by the imagined pleasantness.

The truth is that to deny the existence of 'disinterested' desires, i. e. desires for objects other than greatest anticipated pleasure [1], destroys the possibility of accounting for nearly all our interests' except those of a purely sensual character [2]. It is admitted on all hands that different people get different amounts of pleasure from the same external sources. Why so? In the case of mere physical sensation we can account for the difference between man and man by differences of physical constitution. Whether a man likes port or champagne depends upon the

[1] The phrase may also be used to mean desires for objects other than one's own *good*, however understood, but I am here arguing with those who would identify good and pleasure. It will be seen below that I regard the Psychology that is egoistic without being hedonistic as open to the same objections as the latter.

[2] Many even of these, as pointed out below, are not originally desires for pleasure, but they may be treated as such for ethical purposes in so far as the impulses or appetites are deliberately acted upon from a conviction of the pleasantness of indulgence.

constitution, as modified by education, of his palate and nervous system. It has nothing to do with the strength of any pre-existing impulse towards the one or the other. His preference is not, in any direct and immediate way, determined by his character. Apart from the anticipated pleasure, he is perfectly impartial or unbiassed in his decision between the two wines. Nothing but experience of their comparative pleasantness determines his judgement as to which of them he will take, so far as no considerations of health, or economy, or the like may dictate the choice of one rather than the other [1]. Suppose a glass of champagne to be administered to a life-long teetotaller and called a glass of lemonade. He may have been wholly innocent of a desire for champagne; he may have habitually denounced it as liquid poison; all his anticipations may have been confined to the unexhilarating lemonade. And yet, given the requisite nervous organization, he will probably exclaim, ' Why, this is the very best lemonade that I have ever tasted in the whole course of my life!' On the other hand, when we turn to moral, intellectual, or other ideal pleasures [2], we find that their attractiveness depends entirely upon their appealing to some pre-existing desire, though no doubt some accidental and undesired experience may sometimes awaken a desire not previously felt. To the mind that does not desire knowledge, knowledge is not pleasant; knowledge compulsorily admitted is often found to be productive of anything but pleasure. Benevolence does not give pleasure to people who are not benevolent. The psychological Hedonist analyses Benevolence into a liking for benevolent

[1] Of course he might be moved by curiosity to desire a wine which he had never tasted; but the pleasure which he got from gratifying his curiosity would be distinguishable from the physical pleasure of drinking. The former would be undiminished should the wine fail to commend itself to his palate.

[2] I am of course far from attempting to draw an absolute line of demarcation between the two classes of pleasure. Pursuits involving a high degree of intellectual activity may often owe some of their pleasantness to some suggestion of sensuous gratification: the desire for power may become fused with the desire for the sensual gratifications secured by power, &c., &c. And on the other hand the sensuous pleasure may be a condition of many others which are not sensuous. Coleridge, for instance, pronounced tea-drinking to be the most intellectual of sensual pleasures.

pleasure. No doubt to the benevolent man Benevolence does give pleasure, but it gives him pleasure only because he has previously desired the good of this or that person, or of mankind at large. Where there is no such desire, benevolent conduct is not found to give pleasure. And so with many bad pleasures: for it is extremely important to insist that disinterested desires are not necessarily good desires[1]. If I have set my heart upon the death of an enemy, it will give me pleasure to kill him. Apart from such a desire, there is nothing in the mere physical process which could possibly account for the pleasure. It would be no pleasure at all to kill some other person by precisely the same means, unless indeed my desire is not a desire for vengeance but a disinterested malevolence towards humanity in general[2]. In all such cases it is a certain idea which is pleasant, the idea of an object which is or may be something quite different from my own sensations, whether of a purely physical character or of any more exalted kind which a hedonistic Psychology may be able to recognize. It is not the representation of my being pleased in the future which makes the idea of the sick man relieved or of the wrong avenged pleasant to me, and so moves my will; my desire is that the actual objective result shall be achieved. Of course if I am to be influenced by such a desire, I must, as we say, 'take an interest' in the desired object. So far every desire might no doubt be called an 'interested' desire. But the

---

[1] The observation of this fact was Bishop Butler's most original contribution to moral Psychology. Aristotle admits that there are desires for objects other than pleasure, but he assumes that these objects are always good objects—Knowledge, Beauty, Virtue, and the like, and thus ultimately admits only two motives, desire of τὸ καλὸν and of τὸ ἡδύ.

[2] The pleasure of sheer cruelty is no doubt less purely 'ideal' than that of vengeance, and may be more correctly represented as a mere desire for a particular kind of physical excitement, which gives pleasure just like any other sensation. It may best be treated as a primitive instinct, just like the impulses commonly described as appetites—a survival in human nature of the brute, in which such an instinct was conducive to survival. But, like these appetites, cruelty of course becomes something different in a man who deliberately makes the satisfaction of the impulse his end. A beast is not capable (strictly speaking) of cruelty any more than it is capable of licentiousness. When deliberately indulged, the impulse or appetite becomes a desire.

question at issue is just this—whether I am capable of taking an interest in other things besides my own sensations, actual in the present or imagined as being enjoyed by me in the future. To deny that I am capable of taking such an interest would make it scarcely possible to explain how anything could please me except purely physical sensations, an interest in which is, so to speak, compulsory. The pleasantness may no doubt be stimulated by an effort of voluntary attention, or diminished by a voluntary effort of abstraction, which will usually take the form of voluntary attention to something else. But it does not rest with us—it does not depend upon our will, or our character, or our desires—whether we shall or shall not feel the sensations and feel them to be pleasant.

It is extremely important to insist upon the full extent of ground covered by this class of 'disinterested desires.' A prejudice is sometimes created against the doctrine of disinterested desires just on account of its ethical import. The greater part of our desires are assumed to be 'interested,' and in asserting some few of them to be 'disinterested,' we are suspected of trying to introduce questionable exceptions in the interests of edification. It is, therefore, desirable to insist that the possibility of being 'interested' in something besides our own sensations is as distinctly implied by the momentary absorption in the plot of a novel, or the most evanescent and morally indifferent sympathy with its characters, as by the most sublime heroism or the most systematic philanthropy. The spectator of a tragedy who had no 'disinterested desires' would simply exclaim, 'What is Hecuba to me, or I to Hecuba, that I should weep for her? Prove to me that my own future pleasures are somehow involved in the fate of Hecuba, and then I shall begin to be interested in her story, but not till then.' No pleasures in short are explicable on the hypothesis of psychological Hedonism except those of a purely sensual character, and I may add, aesthetic pleasures, which after all have a purely sensuous basis, however many higher intellectual activities and sympathies may be involved in them. When a beautiful landscape bursts upon us unexpectedly, the enjoyment of it is not dimmed by the fact that we were not craving for it beforehand. Nor does it appear that a craving for beauty in general precedes or is implied in the first development of the aesthetic faculties; it is rather experience of their pleasantness which begets the love of beauty. For, although beauty is not merely a particular kind of pleasure, the pleasure is certainly an inseparable element of the beauty, and this pleasure does not seem to imply any previous desire [1]. But directly Art begins to involve anything more than the contemplation of immediately beautiful form and colour and sound [2], it interests us only by appealing to desires or interests which are not merely desires for pleasure. A man who cared about nothing but his own sensations might derive pleasure from a beautiful sunset, but he could hardly appreciate a beautiful character or a beautiful plot, and even the appreciation of physical beauty probably has its roots to some extent in a kind of sympathy, however strongly we may repudiate Hume's attempt to analyse away our appre-

[1] There is much truth in Schopenhauer's doctrine that the satisfaction afforded by Art is due (I should say, partly due) to the absorption in mere contemplation which it involves, and so in the temporary suspension of desires.

[2] And even these could not be desired unless they had previously been experienced. There would indeed be a shorter way with psychological Hedonism if we could assume with Prof. A. E. Taylor that 'an appeal to introspection will show . . . that it is impossible to have a representative image or idea of pleasure or pain' (*Problem of Conduct*, p. 113). So far as I have been able to ascertain, Prof. Taylor appears to be alone in this peculiar incapacity for imaging past pleasures and pains. The theory implies so extreme an abstraction of the *content* of the pleasant consciousness from its pleasantness that it hardly requires explicit experience to refute it. If Prof. Taylor cannot remember what the displeasure was like which it gave him to look upon his neighbour's ugly wall-paper, how can he remember even what the paper itself was like? How can he have an idea of the colour and pattern without an idea of its ugliness, and what is an idea of ugliness which does not include unpleasantness? The reason why the more acute physical pains are (fortunately) *less* capable of being represented with distinctness in imagination seems to be that, though assuredly not without content, they have (so to speak) very little content. There are comparatively few distinct kinds of qualities of pain, and still fewer have names; so that the distinction of intensity plays the chief part in our idea of them, and intensity is just the element in which imagination most fails, accurately or fully, to reproduce past sensations, though it reproduces them quite sufficiently to enable a boy to pronounce (when the difference was considerable) which of two floggings hurt most. This is of course quite a different thing from supposing (with Hume) that an 'idea' differs from an 'impression' only in liveliness.

ciation of the elegance of a swan's long neck into sympathy
with its utility to the swan. Any further analysis of aesthetic
pleasure would here be out of place. I merely note that the
aesthetic pleasures, or an element in them, seem to be the most
prominent case of pleasure, not in the ordinary sense purely
sensual, which does not necessarily imply desire for anything
besides the pleasure itself[1].

II

I have so far confined myself to the motives operating upon
the consciousness of adult human beings at an advanced stage of
development. I shall hereafter have to consider how far the
facts of Evolution can throw any light upon our ethical ideas;
and it is of the last importance to keep questions of psychological
fact distinct from questions of psychological origin. The starting-
point of any enquiry into the origin or history or explanation of
our ideas, desires, motives or any other facts of consciousness
must be a clear comprehension of what these facts are now in
that developed human consciousness which alone is accessible to
direct observation. Into questions of origin and history, therefore, I do not propose to enter now in any detail. But it is
hardly possible to deal effectively with the theory of psychological
Hedonism without noticing that its plausibility lies for many
minds in a certain confusion between the question of origin and
the question of actual present fact.

It is constantly assumed as a sort of axiom that 'Altruism'
must have in some way been evolved out of Egoism; and this
assumption often carries with it the further implication that in
some sense Altruism is thereby shown to be Egoism after all, only
more or less disguised. It is not surprising that pre-evolutionary
individualists like John Stuart Mill should have supposed that
primitive men and the lower animals were pure Egoists. But it
is amazing to discover the same delusion more or less underlying
the treatment of this subject by the very writer who, whatever
may be thought of his system as a whole, has at least the merit

---

[1] I do not mean to imply that the value of aesthetic pleasures is to be
estimated merely by their intensity, or that the desire for aesthetic pleasures
(when once aroused) is merely a desire for pleasure as such.

of having been the first among Darwin's disciples to suspect that Darwinian ideas might throw important light upon many psychological and sociological phenomena [1]. If there is one thing which the Darwinian doctrine of Evolution has emphasized in the psychological region, it is the existence in animals and in primitive men of tendencies, impulses, instincts, of whose self-preserving or race-preserving efficacy they themselves are quite unconscious. We have hitherto sought our illustrations of impulses that are not mere desires of pleasure in desires which might be considered as, in a sense, above the moral or at least above the intellectual level of pleasure-seeking. It is quite equally certain that there are in animals, in primitive men, and in infants at an advanced stage of social development (to say nothing of adults), impulses that are below that level [2]. The human or other infant does not suck because experience has convinced it that sucking is a source of pleasure. It does not first suck by accident, and then repeat the action because it has found sucking pleasant, though this last discovery may no doubt aid in inducing it to suck in the right place. It sucks simply because it has an impulse to suck. The Physiologist may know why it sucks; but the child does not. The young bird does not tap the inside of its shell because it has calculated that the breaking of that shell is a condition precedent to the enjoyment of wider pleasures than are possible to it in the limited sphere of its early experiences; it taps for no other reason than that it has an impulse to tap. The beaver that has been in the habit of collecting sticks to build its habitation will go on collecting sticks when its house is ready built for it. The young elephant does not attack the aggressor because experience has convinced it that that is the best way of avoiding aggression, and the painful consequences of aggression, in the future; it attacks because it is angry. No doubt in all these cases the gratification of the impulse does in fact give

[1] The assumption is nowhere distinctly formulated, but it seems to underlie the argument of Mr. Herbert Spencer's *Psychology*, Pt. II, ch. ix, and *Data of Ethics*, ch. v *sq.*

[2] For a fuller refutation of the theory that the lower animals or primitive men or human infants act or behave on egoistic Hedonist principles the reader may be referred to the whole later part of Wundt's *Ethics* and to Prof. James's chapter on 'Instinct' in his *Principles of Psychology* (ch. xxiv.).

pleasure, or at least the resistance to the impulse would be found painful. And the experienced pleasure or relief from pain undoubtedly stimulates the animal to the continued performance of the acts. Moreover, in some cases the impulses which are now blind and unreflecting may have originally in some remote ancestor been purposeful; but the fact remains that the actual stimulus to the present act is not a mere anticipation of pleasure: the pleasure only comes because there is a pre-existing impulse. *Striving* of some kind or other is as primitive a factor in all consciousness as feeling[1]. It is quite true that normally not only is the satisfaction of the impulse itself a pleasure, but the instincts of an animal tend for the most part to prompt actions which are pleasurable on the whole. An instinct which brought immediate pain would *tend* to disappear, and an animal whose instincts on the whole did not bring it pleasure would *tend* to disappear also. But these tendencies are by no means always realized, and require to be stated with many qualifications. The moth would no doubt find it painful to resist the impulse which draws it to the candle: but still it is probable that on the whole it does not find it pleasant to be burned alive. The instinct does not tend to promote survival, and yet the moth survives.

Many of the instincts or impulses of animals are not self-preserving but race-preserving, and these are often sources of immediate pain and danger to the animal itself. The most obvious instance is the maternal instinct which often leads an animal to brave obvious pain or danger for the sake of its young. And among the higher and more gregarious animals there are often found not merely the blind impulses of anger and aggression

[1] Some Psychologists would say more primitive. But I see no advantage in attempting to identify conscious impulses with unconscious tendencies towards an end such as may exist in plants, however decidedly these may differ from merely mechanical processes. Even Mr. Spencer does recognize that race-preserving actions not conducive to the pleasure of the individual are as primitive as individual-preserving actions. That admission cuts away the ground of his assumption that individual-preserving actions are always prompted by a desire of pleasure. To identify 'cravings' with 'discomforts' which inspire a desire for their removal (*Principles of Psychology*, § 123) tends to disguise the *hysteron-proteron* of the Pleasure-psychology.

which do actually preserve individual and race alike, but instincts which lead them to face easily avoidable perils and pains in defence of the herd. How far these instincts are due to 'lapsed intelligence,' how far to natural selection, how far to direct adaptation, how far they may require the hypothesis of a final causality which resists further physiological explanation, are questions with which we are not now concerned. The only point that has here to be emphasized is that the conscious actions of infants or animals are as little explicable by the theory of psychological Hedonism as those of the hero or the saint. The impulses are not desires for a particular imagined pleasure, still less for a greatest possible quantum of pleasure upon the whole. This last aim would imply a power of reflection and abstraction wholly beyond what we have any reason to believe to be possible in an animal or even a not very primitive man. The theory of psychological Hedonism is therefore not entitled to any advantage which it might derive from presenting us with a true account of the historical origin of our present human experience. Altruism was not developed out of Egoism; though, if it were, that would not disprove the existence of Altruism now. Men and animals have always had both race-preserving and self-preserving instincts. Altruism in the developed human beings is evolved out of social and race-preserving instincts: Egoism out of self-preserving instincts. Both in their human form involve an intellectual development of which the lower animals are incapable.

The question may be raised whether these instincts or impulses which we have distinguished from 'disinterested desires' in the stricter sense do not exist even in developed humanity? They certainly exist in the human infant: do they in the adult man? The answer seems to be that these impulses do certainly exist. It is perhaps better not to follow Bishop Butler in classing hunger with such disinterested desires as Benevolence or even Vengeance [1]. Hunger is neither a desire for the pleasure of eating, nor (in its less acute forms) a desire to avoid the pains of

[1] Sidgwick follows him in this view (*Methods of Ethics*, 6th Ed., p. 45). Prof. Mackenzie seems to me right in distinguishing *appetites* from desires (*Manual of Ethics*, 4th Ed., p. 46). See also the chapter in James's *Psychology* already referred to (above, p. 21, *note*).

inanition: but it is not quite the same thing as a disinterested desire of food for food's sake. It is simply an impulse to eat. But then the human being has a power which the animal has not, or a greater power than the animal possesses, of reflecting on these impulses of his, and presenting their satisfaction to himself as an object of thought and of encouraging them or resisting them accordingly. So long as the impulse is a physically irresistible impulse, as when a man closes his eyes or ducks his head to avoid an unexpected missile, that is mere 'reflex action'; that is to say, the act is not in the moral sense of the word an act at all. The impulse is not, properly speaking, a 'motive.' But in so far as the impulse can be inhibited, in so far as the impulse is reflected on and its object deliberately conceived by the understanding and adopted by the will, the mere instinct or impulse passes into what we ordinarily call a desire, and (in so far as the desire is not merely a desire for the imagined pleasure of satisfaction) a 'disinterested desire.' And therefore from an ethical point of view the distinction between appetites and instinctive desires or 'desires of objects' becomes of comparatively little importance— of *comparatively* little importance, though it may for some purpose be important to remember that an action prompted by impulse or appetite or instinct, even where not actually involuntary, may be far less voluntary than one which flows from the conscious and deliberate desire for an object clearly presented to the mind. There are no hard and fast lines to be drawn in this matter. In the developing race and in the growing child reflex action passes by imperceptible gradations into instinctive action, and instinct into voluntary action motived by desire. So in the adult human individual there is every stage between the purely reflex action and the fully premeditated and deliberate act; but it would seem that, though there are instincts, there are here no *purely* instinctive acts in the strict sense of the word except those which are wholly involuntary. The instinct which has been reflected on and has not been inhibited, may be treated as a desire—for pleasure or some other object, as the case may be, and the resulting act is no longer in the strict sense of the word merely instinctive.

III

The course of our argument has already touched upon the question of differences in quality among pleasures. We have already seen that, even upon the assumption that what is desired is always pleasure, it is in many cases clear enough that it is not pleasure in general that is desired but some particular kind of pleasure, and we have already attempted to show that such an admission really surrenders the whole hedonistic doctrine. If people do as a matter of fact desire pleasures for other reasons than their greater intensity, it is clearly possible that the superior ethical quality or rank or dignity of the pleasure may be one of the determining factors in their choice. That this is so has often been admitted by high-minded Hedonists who have not seen how fatal is the admission to the whole doctrine that what they desire is always pleasure as such. We may take for instance the well-known passage of John Stuart Mill :—

' It is quite compatible with the principle of utility to recognise the fact, that some *kinds* of pleasure are more desirable and more valuable than others. It would be absurd that while, in estimating all other things, quality is to be considered as well as quantity, the estimation of pleasures should be supposed to depend on quantity alone.

' If I am asked, what I mean by difference of quality in pleasures, or what makes one pleasure more valuable than another, merely as a pleasure, except its being greater in amount, there is but one possible answer. Of two pleasures, if there be one to which all or almost all who have experience of both give a decided preference, irrespective of any feeling of moral obligation to prefer it, that is the more desirable pleasure. If one of the two is, by those who are competently acquainted with both, placed so far above the other that they prefer it, even though knowing it to be attended with a greater amount of discontent, and would not resign it for any amount of the other pleasure which their nature is capable of, we are justified in ascribing to the preferred enjoyment a superiority in quality, so far outweighing quantity, as to render it, in comparison, of small account [1].'

[1] *Utilitarianism*, pp. 11, 12.

Mill's psychological analysis here leaves little to be desired, but he failed to see that a desire for superior quality of pleasure is not really a desire for pleasure. If I drink a particular wine for the sake of pleasure, I of course care for the quality of the wine—its taste, bouquet, body, exhilarating properties and the like, in so far as these conduce to pleasure. But so far only. I should give it up the moment that I found a pleasanter wine at the same price and with equally hygienic properties, except in so far as occasional variety may be itself a source of pleasure. If, therefore, I care about philanthropic pleasure merely as pleasure, I should necessarily give it up and take to the pleasures of an animal if I were only satisfied of their superior pleasantness. This is just what, according to Mill, the wise man will not do: 'few human creatures would consent to be changed into any of the lower animals, for a promise of the fullest allowance of a beast's pleasures [1].' He admits therefore that such a man desires something other than pleasure. What makes him think the pleasures of the intellect superior to those of a beast is not their intensity as pleasures but their superior nobleness or moral elevation. And that is a consideration which can only appeal to a man who cares about nobleness or moral elevation.

Strictly speaking, pleasures do not differ in quality, but only in quantity. Or, to be entirely accurate, *pleasure* varies only in quantity. In ordinary language we mean by *a* pleasure a total state of consciousness which is pleasant. But no man's consciousness at any one moment can be full of pleasure and nothing else. There must be something there—a taste or a smell, a perception or a thought, an emotion or a volition—to be pleasant. A man who should for a single instant have nothing in his mind but pleasure would be an impossible variety of idiot: for this would imply that he was pleased at nothing at all. The pleasure then of this or that moment of consciousness is an abstraction; it can never exist by itself so long as pleasure is understood to mean the mere quality of pleasing. Very different *contents* of consciousness—the most purely animal sensation or the loftiest moral purpose—may have this common quality of pleasing; but, so long as they are compared merely in respect of this one

[1] l. c., p. 12.

characteristic, they can only differ in one way—in respect of the intensity or quantity of this pleasingness; the pleasure varies in degree, not in kind. All this tends to show how completely the admission of qualitative differences in pleasure abandons the hedonistic point of view. As a popular mode of expression, the doctrine that pleasures differ in kind is a true and useful formula; but it should be recognized that this is not Hedonism. For it means precisely this—that we ascribe value or worth to states of consciousness for other reasons than their pleasantness, although a certain measure of pleasantness might be a characteristic of all states of consciousness which are capable of being desired.

IV

It should be distinctly understood that the question with which we are at present concerned is a purely psychological one. It is a mere question of fact, and can only be answered by each man for himself after careful observation and analysis of what goes on in his own mind, aided by observation of what goes on in other people's minds, in so far as that is revealed by word and act. All that any writer can do towards helping another person to perform this process is (a) to state the question clearly and to warn him against the ambiguities of language which are the main source of error upon such subjects; (b) to remind him of some of the facts which the hedonistic theory has got to explain, and to ask him whether that explanation is adequate; and (c) to state clearly and fully the elements of truth which that theory holds in solution, and to show that a recognition of such elements of truth does not carry with it the inferences which the Hedonist draws from them. I have already attempted to perform the first of these tasks, and have made some suggestions towards the second. But before proceeding to the third, I should like to call attention to some of the more extreme cases of disinterested desire which the theory before us has got to explain away, though I have already tried to show that its failure is quite as apparent in the case of very ordinary impulses to action which are of no special significance from an ethical point of view.

The palmary instance of this failure may perhaps be found in cases where a man labours to accomplish a result which he knows cannot be achieved till he is dead and no longer able to enjoy it. Such instances occur not only in the case of heroic self-sacrifice for a political or religious faith, or the less heroic but no less altruistic efforts of parents to provide for their children, but in the case of many desires which in the ordinary, ethical sense of the word would commonly be described as selfish enough. How is the hedonistic Psychologist to explain the vulgarest desire on the part of some recently ennobled brewer to ' found a family,' or the desire of posthumous fame—say for instance, the kind of literary vanity or ambition which has had so large a share in inspiring the life-work even of men like Hume and Gibbon? It will be urged that the man who is influenced by such motives acts as he does because the thought of being talked about after his death gives him pleasure *now*. Exactly so; the *thought* of it gives him pleasure! But that is just what the hedonistic Psychology declares to be an impossibility. According to this system nothing that is present merely in thought can give pleasure except the thought of a future pleasant state of the man's own consciousness. Being talked about after my death is not a future state of my own consciousness[1]; and therefore the thought of it can, according to the theory, give me no pleasure now. Once again we have the old hysteron-proteron—the cart before the horse. The hedonistic Psychology explains the desire by the pleasure, whereas in fact the pleasure owes its existence entirely to the desire.

The difficulty reaches its climax in the case of an atheistic martyr, who, with no belief in a future life, dies in furtherance of an object which cannot be realized till he will (according to his own view) no longer be able to enjoy it. Or, if we choose (however illogically[2]) to explain his conduct by the desire of enjoying the moments of triumph which may elapse between his

---

[1] In such cases we may ignore the belief in Immortality. Even where such a belief is strong and influential, it probably does not occur to a man to think of himself as hereafter enjoying the contemplation of his great-grandchildren seated on the red benches of the House of Lords, or smiling down upon his own statue in the market-place of his native town.

[2] Since this sense of triumph really implies that he is capable of looking forward with satisfaction to a result other than his own pleasure.

resolution to die and the execution of his sentence, we may put a case where this interval is non-existent. Supposing a condemned man, disbelieving in a future life, to be told that by holding up his finger just before the guillotine fell he would save the life of a dearly loved child or confer some inestimable benefit on the whole human race. On the hedonistic theory even such a minimum degree of benevolence would be a psychological impossibility. For one who knew that the act would be synchronous with the termination of his own consciousness, there would be no future consciousness the imagined pleasantness of which could possibly supply a motive for the present act. If it be contended that the moment of consciousness in which the act is performed is itself pleasant, the whole point is conceded. For it is admitted that volitions are rendered pleasant to us in contemplation, and so are called into actual being, on account of future effects other than a pleasant state of one's own consciousness. The only way of escape would be to contend that the act of lifting up a finger would have seemed pleasant to the man apart from the effects which it was to have after his death. But in normal circumstances the holding up of a finger would give no pleasure at all.

One last skulking-place of psychological Hedonism may be briefly noticed, though this represents a form of the error which rarely imposes upon any but very young students of Ethics. At a certain stage of reflection egoistic Hedonism is often made to present itself in an extremely amiable and even edifying light by including among the pains and pleasures which determine the morality of an action the pains and pleasures of Conscience. Nothing can be more beautiful, it is suggested, than to do my duty simply because I like it. There can be no more efficient sanction and guarantee of Morality than the happiness which experience shows invariably to follow in its train. I will not here examine whether the pains and pleasures of Conscience are as a matter of psychological fact so intense as Moralists have sometimes found it convenient to assume. It is probable that, as regards minor kinds of wrong-doing, in persons of average conscientiousness, the pains of Conscience have been greatly exaggerated. If moral obligation were to be based solely upon this ground, the cynical advice to make one's moral standard as low as possible in order that one may occasionally enjoy the luxury of living up to it would have something to be said for it. But, be this as it may, be the pleasure of right-doing and the pains of wrong-doing great or small, these pleasures and pains are only explicable on the assumption of the existence now or in the past, in the man himself or in others, of desires for something besides pleasure. When the pleasure arises from the person's own purely introspective satisfaction in his own morality or victory over temptation or the like, we have simply another case of the pleasure attending the satisfaction of all desire. The attempt to explain this away is another instance of the old hysteron-proteron. In other cases there may, indeed, be no desire—at least in any conscious and explicit form—for the performance of duty or the happiness of others for its own sake in the individual himself, and yet the doing of the right act may be a source of pleasure or more probably the doing of the wrong one a source of pain. The pleasure in the act, or the pain in its omission, may be due to a habit formed under the influence of other motives. Or pleasure may have come to be associated with the act, and pain with its omission, through the influence of a public opinion which is itself based upon an approval or disapproval not arising from any hedonistic calculus, and which influences the individual quite apart from any anticipated consequences of the public feeling. To attempt to justify (on hedonistic principles) the performance of certain acts commonly called moral by their pleasantness, and then to explain their pleasantness by assuming that they are moral and so sources of conscientious pleasure or means of avoiding conscientious pain, is to argue in a circle. The pleasantness of the act is explained by its morality, and its morality is explained by its pleasantness. It is admitted that the act is often such as could not produce the attainable maximum of pleasure apart from its being regarded as moral ; but, according to the hedonistic Psychology, it could never have come to be regarded as moral except through an experience which showed that apart from the opinion of its morality it was already the way to obtain the greatest maximum of pleasure. The consciousness which can take pleasure in an action because it is right is not a consciousness that cares about nothing but pleasure. If it has not risen to the level of a disinterested love of duty, or of tribe or family or individual person, it must at least be capable of being affected by a desire of social approbation, or other social impulses and interests, which are just as difficult to account for on the hypothesis of egoistic Hedonism as the love of duty for its own sake, and which generally imply more definitely 'disinterested' desires on the part of the community by which the opinion that the act is right has been created. Even if the community is supposed to approve or disapprove merely from self-interest, the community's disapprobation would bring no loss of pleasure to a consciousness that cared not for disapprobation[1]. Moralists like Mandeville, and in a more refined way Hume, have a tendency to reduce the motive of moral conduct to a kind of vanity. But vanity is as good an instance as could be found of a disinterested desire, when it rises above the level of that gregarious instinct which is shared by the lower animals, and which after all is equally proof against the hedonistic analysis.

V

I shall now attempt, even at the risk of some repetition, to state what appear to me the elements of truth contained in the theory of psychological Hedonism, and to guard against some of the exaggerations on the other side which have sometimes helped to secure acceptance for that position.

(1) The gratification of every desire necessarily gives pleasure in actual fact, and is consequently conceived of as pleasant in idea before the desire is accomplished. That is the truth which lies at the bottom of all the exaggerations and misrepresentations of the hedonistic Psychology. The psychological Hedonist explains the martyr's death by a taste for the pleasures of martyrdom. Undoubtedly a martyr must derive pleasure from the thought of dying for a holy cause, and even in the midst of the flames the thought that he is doing something for that cause

---

[1] Of course, when any ulterior consequence of social approbation is to be feared, we should not speak of the person as acting from purely conscientious motives at all.

must, presumably, so long as it actually remains in his consciousness, give him some pleasure.   But you cannot account for his action by that pleasure (waiving for the moment our objection to the hysteron-proteron), unless you contend that the pleasure involved in the gratification of the desire is greater in amount than the pains involved, and foreseen to be involved, in the process of achieving that gratification.   The thought of the purpose accomplished or the cause assisted may no doubt, even in the moment of martyrdom, when abstracted from everything else in the man's consciousness, be pleasant ; but that is a very different thing from saying that the process of being burned alive, taken as a whole, is a pleasant one, and that the man suffers martyrdom because, upon a calm and impartial review, he thinks that the pleasure will predominate over the pain.   His conduct implies that the thought of serving his cause must have had some peculiar attraction for him over and above the pleasantness which it shared with the rejected attractions of a happy and tranquil existence.   Had it ever occurred to him to make the calculation, a man totally indifferent to the source or moral character of his pleasures would surely have found that the pleasures of living were greater than those of martyrdom [1]. Aristotle saw this with peculiar clearness.   The brave man, he tells us, finds pleasure in the exercise of courage ; yet the pleasure is so small in amount, when compared with the attendant pains, that the popular mind hardly notices that there is any pleasure at all in the dying warrior's last moments.   On the whole, such a death seems painful, like the experience of the athlete fighting in the arena, though there too the contemplation of the prize and the glory to be achieved are no doubt sources of pleasure [2].

---

[1] We may here ignore the question of the nearness of the pleasure : for experience seems to show that, even if we grant the delightfulness of looking forward to being burned alive, the prospect does not at all gain in attractiveness when one comes closer to it.

[2] *Ethic. Nicomach.* III. ix. 3 (p. 1117) Οὐ μὴν ἀλλὰ δόξειεν ἂν εἶναι τὸ κατὰ τὴν ἀνδρείαν τέλος ἡδύ, ὑπὸ τῶν κύκλῳ δ' ἀφανίζεσθαι, οἷον κἀν τοῖς γυμνικοῖς ἀγῶσι γίνεται· τοῖς γὰρ πύκταις τὸ μὲν τέλος ἡδύ, οὗ ἕνεκα, ὁ στέφανος καὶ αἱ τιμαί, τὸ δὲ τύπτεσθαι ἀλγεινόν, εἴπερ σάρκινοι, καὶ λυπηρόν, καὶ πᾶς ὁ πόνος· διὰ δὲ τὸ πολλὰ ταῦτ' εἶναι, μικρὸν ὂν τὸ οὗ ἕνεκα οὐδὲν ἡδὺ φαίνεται ἔχειν.   This side

(2) It may be further admitted that this pictured pleasantness of the gratification of a desire, though it will not explain the desire, does greatly add to its strength. The pleasure of getting knowledge cannot be explained without assuming a 'disinterested' love of knowledge. But when, impelled by this desire or assisted by the co-operation of other motives, we do actually acquire some knowledge and find the process more and more delightful, the desire unquestionably becomes stronger; just as, when the anticipated pleasure turns out to be less than was expected, it may be progressively diminished. It would be difficult to say in the former case to what extent the mere love of the experienced pleasure of learning may take the place, as a motive, of all genuine desire for knowledge itself; but certainly it may do so to some extent. The scholar may degenerate into the mere bookworm. And so, on the other hand, the young boy usually begins life with some curiosity to know, but may find his love of knowledge vanish with growing experience of the painfulness of the road to it, or of the greater pleasantness of the athletics and the athletic fame which his schoolfellows, and very probably his schoolmasters, have taught him, by precept and example, to regard as the chief business of life. Here again we have a truth, ignored if not denied by modern Anti-hedonists, which was quite clearly recognized by Aristotle. It is not true, he tells us, as the Platonists maintained, that pleasure 'impedes the activities.' An alien pleasure—the pleasure connected with some other and inconsistent activity—will no doubt do that: the pleasure of eating, for instance, interferes with intellectual activity, and therefore it is when the acting is bad that the eating of sweetmeats goes on most briskly in the auditorium; when the spectators get interested in the play, they stop eating. 'But their own proper pleasure stimulates our activities and makes them better and more sustained[1].' Therefore, as he points out elsewhere, we do best what we do with pleasure.

(3) Still more must this principle be remembered when the

of Aristotle's doctrine is constantly overlooked in stating his view that the virtuous man necessarily acts with pleasure.

[1] ἡ μὲν οἰκεία ἡδονὴ ἐξακριβοῖ τὰς ἐνεργείας καὶ χρονιωτέρας καὶ βελτίους ποιεῖ, αἱ δ' ἀλλότριαι λυμαίνονται. *Ethic. Nicomach.* X. v. 5 (p. 1175 b).

doctrine of disinterested desires comes to be applied, as it was
applied for the first time by Butler, to bad and indifferent as
well as to good desires. Between the desire of an object and the
desire of the pleasure arising from that object it is not possible
to draw an absolutely sharp line of demarcation ; the one is
ever passing into and colouring the other. From the pure desire
of an object for which we should be prepared to sacrifice everything, while feeling all the time that with the personal pleasure
derived from it we could dispense well enough, the mind may
pass by imperceptible transitions to such a desire for the pleasure
as will keep alive an interest in the object entirely for its own
satisfaction—a state of mind well illustrated by the familiar
process of 'riding a hobby.' Although, as we have seen, the
worst passions of human nature (equally with the best) are
properly speaking 'disinterested,' it may be admitted that their
disinterestedness is seldom as pure as that of the highest desires.
For the greatest height of disinterestedness implies that the
desire persists in spite of clear and calm conviction that it is not,
in the hedonistic sense of the word, to one's interest, and this will
seldom be the case with the worst desires. The mere victim of
passion will usually (not perhaps always) 'persuade himself'
that its gratification is hedonistically worth the cost. Moreover,
although the man who indulges to his own loss in what we
commonly call a bad passion does not act merely with a view to
his own pleasure, he does act simply for the gratification of his
own impulses. The outside object—the death of an enemy or
the like—is no doubt desired as an end, but it is merely his own
private and personal desire for it that makes it an end to him ;
and no doubt that desire—though not the result of a comparison
between possible pleasures—is often explicable by association
with other desires and impulses of a more obviously self-regarding,
or a more obviously animal, character—the remembrance of an
injury, instinctive jealousy, or the like. On the other hand, the
self-sacrifice of the good man for the welfare of a stranger or the
triumph of a cause may be produced by purely objective or
rational considerations. The object appeals to or 'interests'
him as a rational and reflecting intelligence, not simply as an
individual being with private passions and impulses which

demand their own gratification.   The bad man may be betrayed by passion into a forgetfulness of his true 'interest on the whole'; but he never wholly forgets himself and his impulses, still less does he 'lose himself' in universal or ideal interests.   There is, therefore, an important psychological as well as an ethical difference between the 'disinterested' impulses of the bad man and the purely 'self-forgetful' Benevolence of the best; and between these two extremes there are of course very many degrees of 'disinterestedness[1].'   If by a disinterested desire we mean the desire of an object not merely as an end which we desire, but as an end in itself which on purely objective

---

[1] Simmel has devoted much space (*Einleitung in die Moralwissenschaft*, 1892, I, Kap. ii) to showing how impossible it is to form any clear conception of pure Egoism or of pure Altruism: he shows how the instincts, desires, and emotions with the satisfaction of which a man identifies his own good or interest or pleasure, always include some which are of social origin and involve a moral element; whilst the most altruistic man is, after all, gratifying impulses in which he finds his own satisfaction.   It seems to me true and important to say that altruistic and egoistic impulses fuse inextricably. Few desires and impulses are wholly altruistic or wholly egoistic: we can only speak of a more or less altruistic or egoistic character in them.   The motives which prompt the average man to devote himself heartily to his profession can as little be represented as pure desire for the public good as they can be represented as merely a desire for his own enjoyment or advancement.   His profession has become to him an end-in-itself, but it has become so because he has both interests which are mainly egoistic and impulses which are mainly altruistic.   At the same time, I do not think we can deny the psychological possibility of the pure Egoist who deliberately gratifies his impulses just so far as he thinks they will yield him pleasure on the whole; this possibility is not affected by the social *origin* or the social *tendency* of some of those impulses.   The pure Altruist who subordinates his own interest entirely to that of others is more difficult to conceive, because the man's very Altruism must produce such an identification of his own interest with that of others that they can hardly be kept absolutely apart in consciousness, except in those cases where there is some absolute and palpable contradiction between the interest of others and what would, but for his Altruism, be conceived of as his own interest.   But where the sacrifice of life, or of all that makes life worth living, is deliberately made, the fact that on reflection the man may recognize the sacrifice as a good for him does not make it impossible to describe the desire as such as altruistic, so long as the object is not desired merely as a means to his own good, whether conceived of as pleasure or something else.   What is true in Simmel's contention is that the normal motives of most men are neither purely altruistic nor purely egoistic.

grounds we conceive of as good, then we must pronounce that such a disinterested desire is possible only in the case of good desires. Bad desires and inclinations may be 'disinterested' in the merely negative sense that they are not desires for pleasure as such. Desires for the good of another person or persons are more 'disinterested' in a stricter sense and a higher degree: while the highest degree of disinterestedness is only reached when a moral or universal element enters into the desired object, when the individual desires the object not merely as a particular individual who chances to have such and such an impulse, but as a reasonable being who aims at what his Reason tells him to be not merely *his* good, but part of *the* good.

(4) It has been implied in what has been said already that pleasure, though not the only object of desire, is nevertheless one possible object of desire, and that desire of pleasure, though incompetent by itself to explain the most ordinary springs of action, is widely operative in human life. If this is not often explicitly denied, there are many Moralists who in their zeal against pleasure seem disposed to ignore or gloss it over. Butler, for instance, appears to ignore entirely the existence of any general desire for pleasure as distinct from (a) particular 'propensions,' or affections, or disinterested desires for objects, and (b) the desire for one's 'interest' on the whole. Whether or not he is right in holding that hunger is a disinterested desire for food, hunger is clearly distinguishable from the desire for gastronomic pleasure. When a City Alderman after satisfying his hunger goes on grossly to over-feed himself, he is surely impelled by a love of pleasure which is as distinct from the passion of hunger as it is from a rational affection towards his own interest on the whole. Indeed, the calculating desire for one's interest on the whole, if 'interest' be understood in the hedonistic sense, is only explicable as the result, in the developed and reflective consciousness, of the desire for present and immediate pleasure. The idea of pleasure on the whole is got by abstraction from a number of particular pleasures each of which the man desires, but which experience shows him cannot be enjoyed all at once.

(5) If modern Anti-hedonists have not explicitly explained

away all desire for pleasure, some of them have categorically and in terms denied the possibility of desiring a 'greatest quantum of pleasure' or a 'sum of pleasures'. The possibility of desiring a sum of pleasures was denied by the late Prof. T. H. Green, but it is difficult to see on what grounds except the obvious but irrelevant fact that pleasures cannot be enjoyed as a sum [1]. Such arguments are surely based upon a mere verbal quibble. You might as well deny that I can desire music because I cannot take in a whole symphony simultaneously, while each separate note, taken by itself, would not be music at all. When I say that I desire a sum of pleasures, I mean of course that I desire to get as much pleasure as possible, i. e. to enjoy pleasure as intense and as lasting as possible. Such an aim seems to me perfectly intelligible and rational as far as it goes. How far such a formulation of the ethical criterion falls short of the real demands of the moral consciousness, we shall have to consider hereafter. It is enough here to say that it is not in my view possible to oppose a hedonistic Ethic on the ground that its end is an impossible or unattainable one, or the hedonistic Psychology on the ground that the motive which it represents as the sole motive of human conduct is an impossible or non-existent motive. The question is, however, of so much importance that I reserve a more full discussion of it for a separate chapter [2].

(6) And here perhaps it may be well to meet an objection which turns upon what is often called the 'paradox of Hedonism.' 'If you aim at pleasure you will not get it,' it is said. 'To get pleasure forget it.' Within certain limits, I quite admit the truth of the experience alleged. It is no doubt a serious argument against the adoption of the hedonistic calculus as our *sole* guide in personal conduct. But to a certain extent it is possible to allow for this fact of experience even in the hedonistic calculus itself. I do not find that I fail to enjoy a holiday because I have carefully considered which of various tours, equally expensive or inexpensive and equally recuperative [3], I should enjoy most,

---

[1] Cf. Sidgwick, *Methods of Ethics*, 6th ed., p. 134. [2] Book II, ch. i.

[3] Even this could not be decided without taking into consideration the pleasure I should get. The hedonistic calculus is as necessary for duty as for pleasure. If the doctrine that pleasure cannot be obtained by contrivance

I should no doubt begin to lose pleasure, if I were always calculating whether the enjoyment had realized my expectations.
But, subject to this consideration, I do not believe that in small
matters—supposing the pursuit of pleasure to be strictly limited
by considerations of duty, so that no latent uneasiness of conscience cleaves to our enjoyment—the alleged paradox holds
good at all. It is not a matter of experience that pleasure is
diminished by being provided and contrived for beforehand [1].
I do not find that the dinner which I have ordered myself
always gives me less pleasure than the dinner which has been
ordered by somebody else. In certain circumstances the previous
contrivance may even become a positive enhancement of the
delight; as when Charles Lamb complained that in his days
of comparative affluence he could not get the pleasure out of his
theatre-goings and occasional holiday-makings which he did
when they had to be anxiously planned and contrived for weeks
beforehand [2].

VI

Before leaving the subject of pleasure I think it desirable
to add a further explanation. It is possible to reject the hedonistic Psychology without admitting the existence of disinterested
desires in the strictest sense of the word. Until recently the
existence of disinterested desires was usually denied (among
modern Philosophers) only by Hedonists. The late Professor
Green agreed with Professor Sidgwick in accepting unreservedly

were true, a Physician would have carefully to conceal from his overworked
or overworried patient the fact that the tonic he was recommending was
simply a dose of pleasure. This may possibly at times be desirable, but not
in the case of persons who have no rooted antipathy to pleasure.

[1] Not only does not the calculation always diminish the pleasure, but a
further pleasure may arise from the satisfaction of the desire for pleasurable
life in general, as has been well pointed out by von Hartmann, who is
assuredly no Hedonist ('eine zweite reflektierte Lust aus der Befriedigung
des eudämonistischen Wollens,' *Ethische Studien*, p. 137). At the same time
he seems to me mistaken, if not inconsistent, in maintaining that all
pleasure arises from the satisfaction of some desire ('dass es keine Lust
giebt, die nicht an die Befriedigung eines Begehrens geknüpft wäre,' l. c.,
p. 143), though he admits that the desire may sometimes be set up by the
mere presence of the means to its satisfaction.

[2] 'Old China' in *The Last Essays of Elia*.

Butler's quite explicit doctrine on this head. At the same time we find in Professor Green's writings, side by side with this view, another which seems to be scarcely consistent with it. He commits himself at times to the doctrine that in every action ' self-satisfaction is sought [1].' His theory of the 'timeless self' no doubt makes it difficult to say in what relation this doctrine of self-satisfaction is supposed to stand to the belief in ' disinterested desires.' Desires are certainly in time, and the object of desire must be conceived of as future. It is, therefore, not easy to see how the satisfaction of a self which is not in time can be made into a motive for conduct, or how we can at a definite moment of time introduce a change into that which is timeless. Here (as so often with theories of this kind) it is difficult not to suspect some confusion between the permanent and the timeless. But, waiving that difficulty, I can only understand the idea of ' aiming at self-satisfaction ' to mean that my motive is a certain future state of my own consciousness. If I am always aiming at a future state of my own consciousness, I cannot be ' disinterestedly ' pursuing the advancement of learning or the good of my neighbour. In that case I should care about my neighbour's good merely as a means to my own ' satisfaction.' The two doctrines are antagonistic and inconsistent. Recent writers of Professor Green's School appear to have recognized the fact, and have explicitly adopted the doctrine of ' self-satisfaction.' They are Egoists without being Hedonists. They admit that every action is properly speaking ' interested,' though my interest is not equivalent to my maximum pleasure. Such a doctrine seems to be no less false psychologically, and ethically scarcely less objectionable, than the hedonistic Psychology itself [2].

Of course there is a sense in which every action is ' interested.' I cannot care for anything—my neighbour's good, the cause

---

[1] *Prolegomena to Ethics*, Book II, ch. ii, and Book III, ch. i.

[2] ' The same analysis which shows me that I do not always aim at my own pleasure, shows me equally that I do not always aim at my own satisfaction. I reject, in the one case as in the other, the conscious egoism of the form in which human choice is conceived—except in the insignificant sense that I am conscious that what I desire and aim at is desired and aimed at by me—a tautological proposition' (Sidgwick, *Ethics of T. H. Green, Mr. Herbert Spencer, and J. Martineau*, p. 103).

of 'learning' or of 'sport' or whatever it may be—unless it interests me. But this has, I suppose, never been denied. It simply amounts to saying that a desire which is to move me must be *my* desire. The question, as I conceive it, is whether the motive of every action is some future state of my own consciousness, or whether it may be some state of some other's consciousness, or some event in the objective world[1]. To assert the former view would amount, as it appears to me, to saying that a man cannot be benevolent simply because he cares about his neighbour for that neighbour's sake, but only because he wants to be a person conscious of his own benevolence. His neighbour's good is regarded not as an end but only as a means —a means to some state of his own soul, however 'spiritual' or exalted that state may be supposed to be. Now such a doctrine seems to be simply a recrudescence of the old 'soul-saving' view of life, which may so easily degenerate into something considerably more nauseous and offensive than an honest egoistic Hedonism which is naked and not ashamed. But the question with which we are now concerned is whether the doctrine is psychologically true. To my own mind it seems open to precisely the same line of objection which its supporters raise in arguing against Hedonism. It involves the same hysteron-proteron. It makes the anticipated 'satisfaction' the condition of the desire, whereas the desire is really the condition of the satisfaction. If I cannot by any possibility be moved by my neighbour's calamity until I have satisfied myself that I shall get myself into a state of desirable moral exaltation by doing so, you cut away all possibility of explaining why such a state should be looked at as desirable or morally exalted. Unless I looked upon my neighbour's good as a thing for which I cared, or which possessed intrinsic value apart from any effect upon me, I should not think it a good state of mind for me to contribute or to have contributed to that good. It is precisely the unselfish-

---

[1] Of course, if such an event is to have real value, it must ultimately have some effect on some consciousness or other, but this need not be distinctly contemplated by the agent. A Samson might well desire the destruction of his enemies and their temple, even at the cost of his own life, without distinctly thinking of the satisfaction to be given to his surviving countrymen.

ness of the action which I find good. If I cared for my neighbour's welfare merely as a means to my own edification, I should not be unselfish. In many cases I cannot doubt that such acts are done entirely without the thought of self, or even of abstract duty : the desire of the other man's good acts as directly and immediately upon the will as the desire of one's own : while, so far as a reflective idea of goodness or duty enters into the motive, the very essence of that ideal of moral goodness or duty for its own sake is precisely this—that the thing should be done simply because Reason approves it, and without calculation as to how it will affect our own future consciousness.

The immediacy with which the conception that a thing is rational acts on the will is best seen perhaps in cases where no very important moral interest is at stake. A man with a taste for 'Bradshaw' sees that certain trains are arranged badly and stupidly. He feels a disinterested aversion to such an irrational arrangement. He proceeds anonymously to write to the papers or to the Company's Traffic Manager. No reputation is to be got by the step, and he never expects to travel that way again. As little is he thinking of any future glow of self-satisfaction or of the improvement of his own character. The mere fact of the thing being irrational and as it should not be is a sufficient reason to a rational being for wanting to put it right. If you say he is 'uneasy' at the thing being wrong and it is the uneasiness that moves him, you are of course falling once again into the hysteron-proteron in the form in which it got hold of Locke [1]. You are explaining the desire (and consequent action) by the uneasiness, whereas it is really the desire that explains and occasions the uneasiness.

No doubt it may be freely admitted that when once an object is looked upon as good, as a thing that interests us, the desire to

---

[1] *Essay*, Book II, ch. xxi, § 40. In so far as Locke actually identifies (as he shows a tendency to do) the 'desire' and the 'uneasiness' he is not open to this criticism, and in fact no one shows more convincingly that it is not 'the greater good, though apprehended to be so' (ib., § 35), which always determines the will ; but in so far as he makes the motive to be 'the removing of pain . . . as the first and necessary step towards happiness '—' that happiness which we all aim at in all our actions ' (ib., § 36)—he is virtually under the influence of the hedonistic Psychology.

attain for ourselves the moral good implied in the promotion of that object supplements, and fuses itself with, the desire that the object should be attained. Just as experience of the pleasure of satisfying a desire reacts upon and reinforces the desire itself, so with those highest desires which consist in devotion to some ideal aim or some form of other people's good the aspiration after goodness for ourselves mingles with and reinforces the desire that others should be benefited or the ideal aim promoted: the desire to *be* good and the desire to *do* good blend into one. The proportion in which the desire for personal holiness on the one hand, and the desire for the promotion of objective interests on the other, enter into the motives of the best lives probably varies enormously even in the noblest characters. And from a practical point of view it is probably desirable that both elements should be present. The man who is only interested in people and causes is apt to be indifferent to aspects and departments of Morality which are really of great social importance ; while the man who thinks only of his own spiritual condition is apt to become unhealthily introspective, if not anti-social. Both types of character are one-sided ; but, if we had to choose between the two, it is hardly to the man who most consciously and deliberately regards his family and his neighbours, the poor and the unfortunate, as the means to his own spiritual advancement, or as supplying occasions for the acquisition of ' merit,' that we should accord the preference. Some of the ethical questions on which we have here touched will demand our attention again. Meanwhile, I content myself with repeating that, as a pure matter of Psychology, the theory that every desire is a desire ' for some form of personal good [1] ' is open to every objection which its exponents have so

---

[1] A few expressions of the doctrine here criticized may be given. Mr. Fairbrother is quite justified in making Green hold (*The Philosophy of T. H. Green*, p. 67) that the end ' is always a " personal good " in some form. . . . Man always is actuated by this conception of himself as satisfied ' ; but he ignores all the passages that have an opposite tendency. The Bishop of Clogher (Dr. d'Arcy) introduces another feature into the doctrine—that ' the end of a desire is not an external thing, but the corresponding activity ' (*Short Study of Ethics*, 2nd ed., p. 158). Somewhat similar, though more vague, is Mr. Bradley's earlier doctrine that ' nothing is desired except that which is identified with ourselves, and we can aim at nothing, except in so far as we aim at ourselves in it ' (*Ethical Studies*, p. 62). Professor Muirhead likewise contends that

convincingly urged against the hedonistic Psychology. The satisfaction of altruistic and other higher desires only comes to be regarded as 'our good' because we care for a good which originally presents itself as a good which is not ours.

'It is only as involved in one's own that one can desire one's neighbour's good: it is only as his good enters into *my* conception of *my* good that I can make it an object of desire and of volition' (*The Elements of Ethics*, p. 154). And again, 'The essential point to note is that all desire, and therefore all will (inasmuch as will depends upon desire), carry with them a reference to self. Their object is a form of self-satisfaction' (ib., p. 50). 'Reference to self' is vague, but appears to be explained by the previous sentence: 'They [the objects of desire] are related to the self, in that it is the realization of them *for a self* that is desired.' Still there is a vagueness which I should like to see cleared up. Does 'for a self' mean (1) that the desire is mine, or (2) that it is my interest in some future state of myself that makes me care to pull my neighbour's child out of the fire? The first doctrine seems to be as unquestionable as it is unquestioned; the latter false. On p. 47 we seem to get an explicit statement that it is always a future state of the self that is desired in the words : 'Desire is a state of tension created by the contrast between the present state of the self and the idea of a future state not yet realised.' Is not this 'tension' very much like Locke's 'greatest present uneasiness,' with the disadvantage of introducing a not very intelligible physical metaphor? I should say that in the case of the anonymous railway reformer contemplated in the text the tension is caused solely by the contrast between the present state of the time-table and the ideal which his reason unfolds to him. If so, the object of his desire, the object for which he cares, is not 'self-satisfaction.' Whatever be the meaning of his earlier and vaguer utterances, I rejoice to find that Mr. Bradley does now repudiate the doctrine which I am attacking. 'It is not true that in volition the idea is always the idea that *I* am about to do something. I cannot admit that the qualification of the change as my act must always in volition form a part of the idea's original content' (*Mind*, N. S., No. 44, 1902, p. 456). It is true that Mr. Bradley is speaking of Will, and in his view 'desire is most certainly not necessary for will' (ib., p. 457), but he elsewhere declares still more clearly that we can desire 'an event outside and quite apart from our psychical existence' (*Mind*, N. S., No. 41, 1902, p. 18). That is exactly the point on which I wish to insist, but it seems to me quite inconsistent with Mr. Bradley's doctrine that the bad man acting (as ordinary people would put it) against knowledge 'is pursuing still and he always must pursue his own good' (*Mind*, N. S., No. 43, 1902, p. 307), and with the whole tendency of that article. Surely 'my good' is not 'an event outside and quite apart from our psychical existence.' Mr. Bradley might reply that to 'desire' and to 'will' are not the same thing, but if a desire (not opposed by some other desire of sufficient strength) does not pass into action, have we not the 'freak of unmotived willing' against which Mr. Bradley very properly protests?

CHAPTER III

RATIONALISTIC UTILITARIANISM

I.

In the last chapter an attempt was made to show that as a matter of psychological fact human nature is capable of desiring other things besides pleasure. To show that something besides pleasure is capable of being desired does not, however, prove that anything besides pleasure is ultimately desirable. It is still quite possible to maintain that pleasure is the only true or rational object of desire. The question remains whether this is actually the case. There are undoubtedly people who on reflection are prepared to declare that they can attach no ultimate value to anything besides pleasure. They may recognize the existence of 'disinterested desires' for knowledge or for power, for wealth or for vengeance, but on reflection it appears to them rational to gratify these desires only in so far as they tend to swell the sum of pleasure—which means, as we have seen, to get as much pleasure as they can for as long as they can. The wise man (it is suggested) will treat the attainment of all other objects as means, not as ends. Other desires will be, so far as possible, gratified or repressed, stimulated or discouraged or transformed in whatever way experience shows to be on the whole conducive to getting as much pleasure out of life as possible.

Now so long as the egoistic Hedonist confines himself to asserting 'I care nothing about anything but my own pleasure, and I propose to gratify my other impulses only in so far as (in the long run) I think it tends to procure for me a maximum yield of pleasure on the whole,' he is inaccessible to logical attack. But very often he does not stop at that. He declares not merely that pleasure is *his* object, but that pleasure is the only reasonable object of desire, that every reasonable man must agree with him in thinking that his own pleasure is to each man the only proper object of pursuit, that any one who pursues any other aim is unreasonable, and makes a mistake. And when that attitude is adopted, it becomes possible to urge that he is implicitly appealing to a universal standard which must be the same for all men. He admits that Reason can pronounce upon the value of *ends*, and that it does so, not from any merely private point of view, but from an objective or universal standpoint. The pursuit of pleasure is approved not merely because it chances to be the end that he prefers, but because in some sense it is the *true* end, the end that ought to be pursued. The champion of pleasure may, indeed, contend that the universal rule which Reason approves, is not that pleasure in general ought to be pursued, but that each man should pursue his own pleasure. But an egoistic Hedonist of this type is liable to be asked on what grounds an impartial or impersonal Reason should take up this position. He may be asked whether, when he condemns the pursuit of ends other than pleasure, he does not imply that the claims of this end are dependent, not upon the individual's chance likings, but upon something in pleasure itself, something which Reason discerns in it, and which every Reason that really is Reason must likewise discern in it. And if that is so, he may further be asked why Reason should attach more importance to one man's pleasure than to another's. If it is pleasure that is the end, it cannot matter, it may be urged, whose pleasure it is that is promoted. The greater pleasure must always be preferable to the less pleasure, even though the promotion of the greatest pleasure on the whole should demand that this or that individual should sacrifice some of his private pleasure. From this point of view it will seem impossible that Reason should approve the universal rule that each should pursue his private pleasure even if a loss of pleasure on the whole is involved. The rational rule of conduct will appear to be that each individual should aim at the greatest pleasure on the whole, and that when a greater pleasure for the whole can be procured by the sacrifice of an individual's private pleasure, the sacrifice should be made. The Egoist's appeal to Reason, the setting up of Egoism as an objectively rational rule of conduct, the condemnation as irrational of those who pursue any other end, seems therefore to react against his own position. The logic of the egoistic Hedonist's position carries him away from egoistic Hedonism and forces him into the adoption of a universalistic Hedonism.

Whatever may be thought of the line of argument which thus attempts to cross the gulf between egoistic and universalistic Hedonism, it is at all events one which has been actually followed more or less consciously and explicitly by many minds. There are many persons who remain Hedonists, who are prepared to declare that all other objects except pleasure should be pursued only in so far as they yield pleasure on the whole, but who are not prepared to say that it is only their private pleasure which should be pursued. Among these desires for objects other than pleasure of which they are conscious, there is one which does present itself to them in a different light from those other impulses which they are prepared to subordinate entirely to the pursuit of private pleasure, and that is the desire for other people's pleasure. For the very principle upon which their own preference of pleasure to all other objects of desire rests, seems to put them under the necessity of approving a similar end for other people. How then can they condemn in themselves an impulse which tends towards the realization of that end for others? To do so would seem to involve inconsistency or self-contradiction. There is of course no contradiction in the mere existence of inconsistent desires in different persons. There is no contradiction in admitting, as a fact, that I may want what my neighbour wants too, and we cannot both enjoy. But it is otherwise when it is a question of approving inconsistent desires. Reason cannot give different answers to the same question. It may of course appear to do so: we may all make mistakes, but when we do so, we acknowledge that it is not really Reason which pronounces. If the Reason of two men tells them opposite things, we necessarily conclude that one of them at least must be wrong. Hence when occasions arise, on which what increases pleasure for me diminishes it for some one else, it is impossible that each can be right in judging his own pleasure to be the more important. By such

a line of thought, the Hedonist who bases his position upon
Reason is driven to recognize that the greatest pleasure on
the whole is from the point of view of Reason the most important
end, no matter whether it is I or some other 'I' that is to enjoy
that pleasure.   No doubt this bare intellectual recognition of
its reasonableness does not by itself lead to altruistic conduct
except where there is either (1) a disinterested desire of other
people's well-being (whether of certain definite individuals or
of humanity at large) or (2) what Professor Sidgwick has called
a 'desire to do what is right and reasonable as such.'   In the
first case, Reason will prevent a man, so to speak, inhibiting
his spontaneous benevolent impulses, as he (more or less frequently) inhibits other impulses when they are shown not
to be conducive to his own interest on the whole; in the second
case, the reasonableness of the conduct will actually become
the motive for its being done, even though (apart from the
verdict of Reason) there should be no spontaneous inclination
towards the conduct which it prescribes.   In this way it is
possible for a mind which starts with a conviction of the
intrinsic reasonableness of the pursuit of pleasure to feel itself
compelled to admit, not only the abstract reasonableness of
unselfish conduct, but also the existence of something within
us which sanctions, prescribes, dictates, a certain course of
conduct quite irrespectively of the individual's interest—in
other words to admit the existence, and the authority of what
is popularly called Conscience, or the 'duty' which Conscience
prescribes—of what in more technical language is styled the
Practical Reason or of the categorical imperative which that
Reason enacts.

   Or if to some minds this language about Reason and im-
peratives carries with it associations which seem to lead them
beyond the point which they have really conceded, we may
put the matter in a slightly different way.   Every one who
ever thinks about conduct at all, who regards the choice of an
end as a matter upon which thinking has got anything to say,
every one who attempts to represent his conduct as capable
of rational justification, gives judgements of value.   The egoistic
Hedonist who says not merely 'I like pleasure and therefore

I intend to pursue it,' but 'the wise man is he who pursues pleasure,' shows that he has this ultimate and unanalysable idea of good or value in his mind as much as the idealizing moralist who says 'Virtue is the true end of human pursuit.' Even though 'that which has value' may be to him coextensive with pleasure, the term 'value' or 'good' does not *mean* merely the same as pleasure. The proposition "my pleasure is good' is not to him a mere tautology. It does not mean merely 'pleasure is pleasant.' Still more obviously is this the case when such a Hedonist recognizes, as I have contended that he is logically bound to recognize, that it is not only *his* pleasure which has value but all pleasure; and that therefore it is rational for him to pursue his neighbour's pleasure as well as his own, and to prefer the larger amount of pleasure to the smaller, even though the larger pleasure be the pleasure of others, and the smaller his own.

After such an admission has been made, the enquirer may still take a utilitarian view of the moral criterion : he may still hold that we find out what it is reasonable to do by asking experience to decide what promotes the greatest happiness on the whole or (less logically) the 'greatest happiness of the greatest number' : but he is no longer a Utilitarian in his view of the ultimate reason for doing what is thus ascertained to be right. In admitting that one course of conduct is rational, another irrational, irrespectively of the individual's 'interest,' he has admitted in effect that one thing is right, another wrong ; he has admitted that the difference between right and wrong is perceived (in a sense) *a priori*[1], and not by experience ; he has admitted the existence of an 'ought' and an 'ought not,' however much he must still protest against what he may be disposed to regard as the mystical character with which the idea of 'ought' or 'duty' or 'moral obligation' has been invested by the traditional schools of anti-utilitarian or 'intuitional' or 'transcendental' Ethics.

[1] This assertion will subsequently be explained and qualified (see below, p. 112, 148, *et passim*).

II

Of the writers who have been led by some such line of thought to attempt the combination of a rationalistic view of the ultimate basis of Ethics with a purely hedonistic criterion of conduct, by far the most important and the most distinguished is the late Professor Henry Sidgwick. To examine the system of 'rationalistic Utilitarianism' with which his writings present us, will be perhaps the best way at once of exhibiting in further detail the argument which has been outlined, and of criticizing the attempt to stop exactly at this point in the dialectic which leads away from Utilitarianism towards what I may be excused for calling by anticipation a higher and deeper Moral Philosophy.

Professor Sidgwick's position in the development of English Utilitarianism may be indicated by saying that he takes up the controversy at the point at which it had been left by Mill. Of John Stuart Mill's attempt to reconcile a theoretical acceptance of the hedonistic Psychology with the practical recognition of an enthusiastic 'Altruism,' and even of a 'disinterested love of Virtue,' almost enough has been said in the last chapter. His expedient is to introduce into the hedonistic calculus differences of kind irresolvable into differences of degree. We have already seen that the desire of a higher pleasure is not really a desire of pleasure: what makes one pleasure 'higher' than another must be something other than its pleasingness. Moreover, when Mill recognizes the possibility of desire for pleasure passing by association into a 'disinterested love of Virtue for its own sake,' even were we to accept the paradoxical allegation that Virtue and pleasure have been invariably associated in our experience, we should still be confronted with the admission that as an actual fact it is possible for me *now* to desire something besides my own pleasure, however I may have come to desire it. Mill's own non-recognition of this consequence was due no doubt to the well-known fallacy of 'mental chemistry'— of supposing that mental states contain within them unaltered the states out of which they may have grown, as a chemical compound still continues to have in it its component elements [1]. But, even were his account of disinterested love of Virtue psychologically tenable, it might still be pointed out that the tendency of Mill's theory is to place the Saint's love of Virtue precisely on a level with the miser's love of money [2]. Granted that both may be accounted for by association, the discovery of the association tends to its own dissolution. When the miser discovers that money is a means and not an end, he will, if he is sensible, cease to love money for its own sake. When the Saint, instructed by the Philosopher, discovers that pleasure is the end and Virtue only the means, he must, one would suppose, cease to desire Virtue for its own sake and cultivate pleasure instead. The more rational he is, the more irrational will he deem it to confuse means with ends. Association of ideas is after all, in such a connexion, only another name for confusion of thought. An ethical system which is based upon confusion of thought surely rests upon a precarious foundation.

Professor Sidgwick [3] completely reverses the mode of expanding in an altruistic direction the Benthamite Hedonism adopted by Mill. It is because he does so that his Utilitarianism is, from an intellectual point of view, so great an advance upon Mill's: though the change of front involves some sacrifice of the peculiar unction which makes Mill's *Utilitarianism* so persuasive a book to young students of Philosophy. Professor Sidgwick sees that the admission of difference in kind among

---

[1] In what sense this assumption of Chemistry is actually true, it is unnecessary here to enquire.

[2] 'To illustrate this farther, we may remember that virtue is not the only thing, originally a means, and which if it were not a means to anything else, would be and remain indifferent, but which by association with what it is a means to, comes to be desired for itself, and that too with the utmost intensity. What, for example, shall we say of the love of money? There is nothing originally more desirable about money than about any heap of glittering pebbles. Its worth is solely that of the things which it will buy; the desire for other things than itself, which it is a means of gratifying. Yet the love of money is not only one of the strongest moving forces of human life, but money is, in many cases, desired in and for itself. . . . Virtue, according to the utilitarian conception, is a good of this description' (*Utilitarianism*, pp. 55, 56).

[3] *The Methods of Ethics*, 1st ed., 1874; 6th ed., 1901.

pleasures is utterly irreconcilable, not only with the hedonistic Psychology which he abandons, but with the hedonistic conception of ultimate good which he retains; while, on the other hand, the 'greatest-happiness principle' defined as 'the creed which holds that actions are right in proportion as they tend to promote happiness, wrong as they tend to produce the reverse of happiness,' is not *prima facie* bound up with the doctrine that all desires are desires of pleasure.

Professor Sidgwick fully admits as a psychological fact the existence of 'disinterested affections,' Benevolence among the number. He rightly, however, distinguishes (with Butler, but in opposition to Shaftesbury and others) between the possibility of action motived by desire for the happiness of others and the reasonableness or obligation of gratifying such a desire in opposition to private interest. In point of disinterestedness Benevolence is on a level with Malevolence. But besides these 'particular affections' (to use Butler's expression) or desires for particular objects, Professor Sidgwick recognizes also the possibility of a 'desire to do what is right and reasonable as such.' And he does not in any way shrink from the admission that such a desire amounts to what Butler would call a desire to do what Conscience prescribes, or what Kant would call a 'respect' for the Moral Law [1]. When a man contemplates himself in his relations to his fellow men and asks what it is reasonable for him to do, he cannot but recognize that he seems 'made,' as Butler would put it, to promote public good. A reasonable man contemplating the world as an impartial spectator, uninfluenced by private desires or passions, would necessarily recognize Benevolence as that affection in the 'œconomy and constitution of human nature' which ought to be gratified in preference to merely self-regarding desires. To the disinterested spectator more good must appear preferable to less good, irrespective of the question whether it is *A* or *B* who is benefited, while the same disinterested Reason will prescribe an equal distribution of good among beings capable of enjoying it. The right course of action is that which would appear reasonable to such a dis-

[1] Von Hartmann uses the expressive term 'Vernunfttrieb' (*Das sittliche Bewusstsein*, pp. 264, 270).

interested spectator, and to the agent himself in so far as his
judgement as a rational being is unbiassed by private desires;
it is the course of action which, if he had to legislate for others
unbiassed by such desires, he would prescribe to all, the course
which as a rational being he recognizes as 'fit to be made law
universal.' In his view of Duty as the reasonable course of
action, and in holding that disinterested love of the reasonable
may be a motive of action, Sidgwick follows Butler and Kant,
who are so far in entire agreement. But Sidgwick (here
identifying himself with Butler more closely than with Kant)
also recognizes that to the rational being placed in the position
of an impartial spectator, it must appear in itself equally
reasonable that each man should pursue his own greatest
happiness. When a man's own greatest happiness would have
to be purchased by the sacrifice of greater happiness on the part
of others, the reasonable course may still seem to be the promotion of the happiness of others at the expense of one's own,
so long as he looks upon the matter from the point of view of
universal Reason; and an impulse more or less strongly
impelling to such a sacrifice is actually felt, at least at times,
by all rational beings. But, all the same, it remains something
apparently unreasonable—something contrary to that order of
things which a perfectly rational being endowed with unlimited
power might be expected to appoint—that the happiness of one
should involve a voluntary deduction by another from his own
in itself no less important happiness. Man is made to promote
public good, but no less evidently is he made to promote private
good. Hence Sidgwick abandons the attempt to find in cases
of collision between the requirements of universalistic and of
egoistic Hedonism any course of action which is completely
reasonable—reasonable from every point of view—without the
admission of theological postulates. Entirely apart from such
postulates, altruistic conduct can be shown to be reasonable: it
is the course which will be chosen, as the more reasonable of the
two alternatives, even in opposition to interest, by the man in
whom the desire to do 'what is right and reasonable as such' is
predominant; but such a course can be shown to be *the one and
only* reasonable course, and the contrary to be completely and

wholly unreasonable, only by the aid of a ' hypothesis unverifiable by experience reconciling the individual with the universal Reason [1],' that the Universe is constructed upon a reasonable basis. And this assumption is one which on the whole the writer seems disposed himself to concede, though, at least in his later editions, he makes no positive assertion to that effect.

The great modern champion of rationalistic or universalistic Hedonism certainly cannot be charged with any desire to conceal the extent of his approximation to the position of Butler and Kant. He is at one with them in the point of view from which he regards the whole subject. He does not look upon the Science of Morals as a branch of Natural History. He gives up altogether the attempt to find the ultimate end of action by ' induction ': he sees that no accumulation of observed sequences, no experience of what *is*, no predictions of what *will be*, can possibly prove what *ought to be*. He neither dismisses the ' ought' as a figment (with Bentham), nor involves the whole discussion in inextricable confusion (with J. S. Mill) by failing to distinguish between the desirable and the desired, and calling a desire for the happiness of others a 'desire for happiness,' a mode of speaking which would allow us to define the passion of revenge as a ' desire for pain, injury, or death.' In one word, Professor Sidgwick shares with the father of Idealism the supreme conviction that νοῦς κρατεῖ πάντα. He recognizes that Morality is based upon rational and *a priori* judgements of value. In so far as the motive of moral action in the individual is concerned, Professor Sidgwick is in fact an ' Intuitionist' or ' Rationalist.' He is a Hedonist only in his view of the nature of ultimate or universal Good, and consequently in his view of the moral criterion. The fundamental question raised by Professor Sidgwick's position is the logical compatibility of a rationalistic theory of duty with a hedonistic conception of

[1] This phrase is taken from the 1st edition (p. 473), but Prof. Sidgwick's statement of the absolute necessity of such a harmony to the construction of a logically coherent Science of Ethics is rather strengthened than weakened in the subsequent editions; though he seems, rather from a desire not to go beyond the province of pure Ethics than from any change of personal opinion, to assert less strongly, or not to assert at all, that the intuitions of Moral Philosophy actually do supply a basis for Theology.

the true good or τέλος of man. Before discussing this question, it will be well to re-state Professor Sidgwick's position in a somewhat more concise form.

Looking upon human nature in Butlerian phrase as 'a system' or 'constitution,' Professor Sidgwick may be said to find in it three distinct groups of 'affections' or 'propensions,' viz. (1) the desire for happiness or private good, or 'self-love'; (2) various disinterested desires for objects, i. e. passions such as Benevolence, hunger, anger, &c.; (3) the desire to do what is right and reasonable as such. In the 'calm moment' when a man, under the influence of this last desire, sits down to ask what it is reasonable for him to do, reflection convinces him, according to Professor Sidgwick :—(a) that for himself (assuming certain postulates which upon the whole he is justified in assuming) it is reasonable to gratify, in cases of collision, Benevolence in preference to self-love, but to make the gratification of all other passions subordinate and instrumental to the promotion of his own interest on the whole ; (b) that in acting for the good of others, it is reasonable to gratify their other desires or passions only in so far as these can be made subservient to the satisfaction of their desire for happiness. In short, in himself he is to recognize Benevolence as having a prerogative over self-love, though both desires are rational ; while in others he is to treat self-love as alone among these desires or propensions entitled to gratification. It is a duty to promote universal good, but universal good is merely pleasure. It is right to promote pleasure, but it is not the individual's own good to do so.

Such a position seems open to the following objections : (1) If we look not so much to the speculative as to the practical side of Sidgwick's Utilitarianism, and put aside certain admissions as to the logical incompleteness of his position, we may say that his attitude towards *duty* was the attitude of Butler or Kant, while his attitude towards the idea of *good* was that of the Hedonist pure and simple. He tells the individual to promote other people's good, but he tells them also that other people's good is pleasure. Reason bids him make duty rather than private pleasure his own end, but in thinking what is the end that he is to promote for other people, it pronounces that end to be pleasure.

He thus assigns a different end to the individual and to the race. Professor Sidgwick in fact proves unfaithful to the principle which he professes to accept from Kant—not, indeed, as an adequate definition, but as a fundamental characteristic of the Moral Law—that it shall be 'capable of serving for law universal.' It is pronounced right and reasonable for. A to make sacrifices of his own happiness to the good of B; yet, in considering what is B's good, he is to treat him as a being for whom it is right and reasonable to live solely for his own happiness, to have no desire gratified but his desire for pleasure. It is a condition of the Moral Law, Professor Sidgwick tells us, that it shall be, in Kantian phrase, 'capable of serving for law universal'; yet that law requires each individual to act upon the hypothesis that he is the only member of the human race subject to it. Reason, we are told, requires us to act at times in a way contrary to our interest from love of the 'right and reasonable as such'; yet we are to treat all other human beings but ourselves as incapable of rational desires, as beings for whom it is reasonable to desire nothing but pleasure. Moral action is rational action; and rational action consists in the gratifying of desires which, it is admitted, become irrational and immoral as soon as they collide with the general interest. Such a consequence can only be avoided by the admission that other people's happiness is only a rational object of pursuit, for them as for me, in so far as it is not inconsistent with their promotion of the general pleasure. The nature of our universal end will then be profoundly modified. The end becomes not mere happiness but a social or moral happiness—a happiness which is consistent with a disposition on the part of each member of the society to promote the happiness of every other in so far as he can do so without sacrificing a greater amount of his own. Morality or Goodness would thus seem to have entered into our practical conception of the end which we are to regard as desirable for human society.

(2) Sidgwick would no doubt have replied to the above objection by frankly admitting the 'dualism of the Practical Reason.' A man may recognize, he wrote in his third edition, that 'There is something that it is reasonable for him to desire, when he

considers himself as an independent unit, and something again which he must recognize as reasonably to be desired, when he takes the point of view of a larger whole ; the former of these objects I call his own Ultimate "Good," and the latter Ultimate Good taken universally ; while to the sacrifice of the part to the whole, which is from the point of view of the whole reasonable, I apply the different term "right" to avoid confusion [1].' It is no doubt quite intelligible that one thing should appear reasonably to be desired from a man's own point of view, and another thing when he takes the point of view of a larger whole. But can both of these points of view be equally reasonable ? How can it be reasonable to take the point of view of the part when once the man knows the existence of the whole and admits that the whole is more important than the part ? Must not the point of the view of the whole be the one and only reasonable point of view ? From the point of view of the whole, the worker for the good of the whole can alone seem reasonable. The only reasonable point of view surely must be the one which recognizes all the facts. From that point of view the promotion of *the* good can alone be the reasonable course of action. The reasonable course is to promote the general good, for the general good is greater than the good of the individual. There is surely no logical contradiction involved in holding that it is intrinsically right and reasonable to promote the good, though such a course will not always be consistent with the individual's own good ; for Reason bids us promote not merely what is good, but the greatest good, and to promote one's own lesser good, just because it is one's own, will be completely and entirely unreasonable.

(3) If the Egoist is pronounced reasonable when he says 'my pleasure is good,' and the universalistic Hedonist equally reasonable when he says 'the general pleasure is good,' does not that show that the terms 'reasonable' and 'good' are really used in different senses ? What is there in common between the 'good for me' and 'objective good taken universally'? The objective universal point of view really implied (by Professor Sidgwick's own admission) in the terms 'reasonable' and 'good,'

---

[1] *Methods of Ethics*, 3rd ed., p. 402.

seems to be forgotten when it is contended that the promotion of
the individual's good, even when inconsistent with the general
good, is nevertheless a reasonable object of pursuit. The writer
seems to be relapsing into that meaning of the term 'reasonable'
which has generally found favour with Hedonists who do not
profess to be 'rationalistic'—that is to say, 'internally self-
consistent' or 'conducive as a means to the end which any one
happens actually to desire.'

(4) The difficulties which have been pointed out might possibly
be evaded by a new mode of statement [1]. But if this were done—if
it were frankly admitted that the Egoist's conduct is not really
reasonable at all—even so the attitude of mind which universalistic Hedonism ascribes to the good man is one which, when
fully realized is, I believe, practically, at least to the great mass
of men, an impossible one. There is no logical contradiction
in telling me to promote other people's good at the expense
of my own, because it is intrinsically and objectively reasonable
so to do. But for me to act on this rational principle there
must be a subjective reason, or motive. Granted that it is
reasonable for me so to act, the question still remains 'Why
should I be reasonable?' The Sidgwickian Moralist might tell
me that I have a desire to act reasonably. I reply: 'Yes, I have
such a tendency, but it is, taken by itself, not a very strong one,
and it is in my power to encourage it or to suppress it. I want
you to give me some reason why, since you say my own true
good is nothing but pleasure, I should pursue an end which
is not my good. An abstract or objective Reason may indeed
condemn me if I do not, but I cannot from my own point of view
condemn myself when I pursue what, as you say, Reason itself tells
me is my own true good, and decline (so far as I can help it) to
trouble myself about an end which is not my good. The whole
force of the subjective hold which the precept "be reasonable"
has exercised over me, so long as I was unacquainted with the

---

[1] The passage just quoted has disappeared from the fourth and subsequent
editions of Sidgwick's great work, and with it some other concessions to the
rationality of Egoism, but not all: see for instance the note on p. 200 of the
4th edition (which has since disappeared), and the concluding paragraph of
the final edition.

teachings of rational Utilitarianism, has lain in its inseparable connexion with another conviction — that it was intrinsically noble for me to act in this way, and that to act in accordance with the reasonable was a good to me, a greater good than I could obtain by pursuing the pleasure which you tell me is the only true good. Destroy that conviction, and I have no motive for trying to cultivate the love of rational action or that love of my neighbour which Reason pronounces to be reasonable. You have convinced me that there is nothing intrinsically good and noble about the promotion of other people's happiness. It is a very nice thing for other people no doubt, but it is not nice for me. It is in vain that you tell me that concentration upon my private happiness is selfish and irrational, for you tell me also that selfishness and irrationality are not bad in themselves, however inconvenient they may be for other people.'

Another way of stating this last difficulty of Sidgwick's position is to say that the internal contradiction which it involves is at bottom not so much formal as material. It may possibly be stated in a form which escapes formal contradiction, though Sidgwick himself does not always succeed in so stating it, but the internal or psychological contradiction remains. The acceptance of rationalistic Hedonism kills and eradicates all those impulses upon which it has to depend for the practical fulfilment of its own precepts, by pronouncing that they have no true worth or value—no less so than Mill's Associationist explanation of the love of Virtue as due to a psychological confusion and muddle-headedness comparable to that of the miser. It tends to reduce the idea of reasonable conduct to the idea of conduct which escapes intellectual contradiction and incompleteness; but the desire to escape such contradiction or one-sidedness is not by itself a very powerful motive of conduct when it is pronounced to have no intrinsic value. For the contradiction, be it observed, involved in bad conduct arises, on the hedonistic view of good, merely when I attempt to justify my conduct. If I say 'it is reasonable of me to be an Egoist,' I can be convicted of self-contradiction. But if I candidly admit 'I know that it is unreasonable to be an Egoist, but I intend to be unreasonable,' the contradiction disappears. When the prohibition of Reason is

held to include a specifically moral condemnation, the idea of
'unreasonable' carries with it the idea, that conduct condemned
is lacking in absolute or intrinsic worth. That idea is lost or
pronounced illusive when to act reasonably is denied to be
good. The whole force which makes Reason appeal to men
as deserving of respect it derives from that conviction of the
intrinsic value or goodness of rational conduct which Reason,
as interpreted by Sidgwick, pronounces to be an illusion. We
are hardly perhaps entitled to say *a priori*[1] that Reason could
not deliver itself of two dogmas, which, though involving no
formal contradiction, tend in their practical effect upon human
life to neutralize one another—the dogma 'it is reasonable to
be altruistic' and the dogma 'to be reasonable is not a good
to him who is reasonable or even intrinsically a good at
all': but it would be strange that that moral consciousness,
which by the rationalistic Hedonist's admission proclaims its
right to govern and control human life, should be so constituted that, in so far as men listen to its voice, its own purposes
are defeated. There is in the last resort no way of refuting the
Sidgwickian or any other Moralist but by showing that he
actually misrepresents the content of the moral consciousness.
And this, I have tried to show, the Sidgwickian Moralist
conspicuously does. He abstracts one half of the moral consciousness as it actually exists, and attempts by the aid of it
to silence and confound the other half. He accepts from the
moral consciousness the abstract idea of value, of intrinsic and
objective worth, and at the same time divorces it from that idea
of the intrinsic worth of promoting what has worth, which is
de facto found in inseparable conjunction with it. The only way
in which this internal inconsistency or discord in the Sidgwickian
system can be cured is by admitting that to act rightly or reasonably possesses value, that to promote the good is a good not
merely to others, but to the individual himself.

(5) But after all, Professor Sidgwick fully admits that he cannot make Reason consistent with itself without the admission of

---

[1] Without assuming the rationality of the Universe. Upon that assumption, which Sidgwick was practically prepared to make, the position to me
becomes unthinkable, as contended in the next paragraph.

theological postulates. 'The negation of the connexion between Virtue and Self-interest,' he tells us, 'must force us to admit an ultimate and fundamental contradiction in our apparent intuitions of what is Reasonable in conduct; and from this admission it would seem to follow that the apparently intuitive operation of the Practical Reason, manifested in these contradictory judgements, is after all illusory [1].' We must, therefore, go on to ask whether, upon Professor Sidgwick's premises, these theological postulates are admissible, and whether (even if admitted) they will suffice to restore the internal self-consistency of the Practical Reason.

The difficulties which the great sum of human and animal suffering presents to the belief in a 'benevolent Author of Nature' ought not to be dissembled by those who believe that Reason warrants the 'venture of faith' and who hold (with Plato) that 'the risk is a noble one [2].' But, on the hedonistic view of the true end of human life, does not the demand made upon faith become absolutely overwhelming? Can a Universe have a rational purpose or constitution in which the end is only pleasure and yet in which Reason daily prompts to the sacrifice of pleasure? Surely the assumption of a 'harmony between the Universal and the Particular Reason' must be pushed a step further. The faith that 'Reason is for us King of Heaven and Earth [3],' never found a more eloquent or a more sober exponent than Professor Sidgwick. But in what sense can it be said that Reason rules in a Universe in which the accomplishment of its true purpose depends upon a systematic concealment of that purpose? It is the sole end or τέλος of man to get as much pleasure as possible: yet in order that he may do so, he is throughout his earthly existence, by way of preparation or discipline for the realization of his true end in another state, to forget that end and live for a totally different one.

So completely does Professor Sidgwick reverse in dealing with the ultimate *ground* of morality the Aristotelian maxim 'that we must look to the end,' upon which he lays so much stress in connexion with the moral *criterion*. We must believe in a future

---

[1] *Methods of Ethics*, 6th ed., p. 506.   [2] Καλὸν τὸ κινδύνευμα.
[3] Νοῦς ἐστὶ βασιλεὺς ἡμῖν οὐρανοῦ τε καὶ γῆς (Philebus, p. 28 c).

life, Professor Sidgwick tells us, because we must believe that the constitution of things is rational. And yet, according to Professor Sidgwick, the Universe is so constituted that the man who most completely succeeds in concealing from himself the true end of his being—or haply in never finding it out—will ultimately realize that end most thoroughly. That the Universe might be so constituted is a proposition which does not involve a logical contradiction, and which is incapable of empirical disproof; but where is the rationality of such a Universe? If we are to make assumptions, let them be such as will satisfy the logical demand on which they are founded. If we are to assume a rational order in the Universe, surely the end prescribed to a man by his Reason must be his highest end. Man is so far a rational being that he is capable of preferring the rational to the pleasant. Surely, then, the reasonableness of such a preference cannot be *dependent* on its ultimately turning out that he has after all preferred the very thing which his love of the reasonable led him to reject. It may be the case that what was rejected had a certain value and would under other circumstances have been good; it may be that it is reasonable to expect the preference of the higher good to be rewarded by the bestowal of the lower also. But surely in a rational Universe that which man, when he is most completely rational, desires most cannot be good merely as a means to what he desires less—in other words, it must have an intrinsic value. Bain's remark that ' " I am to be miserable " cannot be an inference from " I am to be happy," ' is a perfectly fair comment or criticism [1] upon a Theology which is founded upon a purely hedonistic conception of the good. If, however, the end of man be goodness or a happiness of which Virtue is an essential element, then it is not unreasonable that he should be required to undergo sufferings which may be necessary conditions of attaining that end for himself and others. If happiness be the true end, a constitution of things by which the neglect of happiness should be rewarded with happiness and devotion to happiness punished by the loss of it, would be a purely arbitrary, supremely irrational constitution. But if goodness be the end without which the highest happiness is

[1] *Mind*, vol. i, p. 105.

incomplete, if goodness be of the essence of the highest happiness, then it is not inconceivable that the voluntary neglect of a lower good in the pursuit of a higher may be intrinsically necessary to the attainment of that completed state of being, of a life which shall embrace both these concepts of goodness and happiness which Modern Philosophy has been accustomed to separate—the 'Well-being' or εὐδαιμονία of ancient Ethics. If Love be indeed the one element of earthly happiness which is to be permanent, then it is intelligible enough that Self-sacrifice should be a discipline necessary to fit men for its enjoyment.

I will add only one further remark at present on this supreme problem upon which the course of Professor Sidgwick's argument has compelled me to touch. Sidgwick claims Bishop Butler as his predecessor in the doctrine of an 'ultimate dualism' of the Practical Reason. It is true that when Bishop Butler, the thinker who has so profoundly modified Professor Sidgwick's hedonistic tendencies, was engaged in writing Moral Philosophy as the champion of the 'disinterestedness' of virtue against the Hobbist, when he touched upon theological problems only as accessory to moral, he was satisfied with a position very much resembling that of his disciple. Conscience or a 'principle of reflection' prescribed certain conduct as rational irrespectively of the interest of the individual; his highest end was duty. The existence of Conscience was to Butler the basis of Theology, not Theology the basis of Morality. Yet when he wrote the *Sermons*, he still regarded the happiness of the whole as the only conceivable end of the Creator as well as of altruistic conduct in the individual [1]. When he came seriously to face the question of the 'moral government of the world,' the difficulties of such a position were forced upon his notice. The result of the ten years' thought which intervened between the *Sermons* and the *Analogy* were embodied in those chapters of the latter work on human life as 'a state of discipline,' which may still be regarded as (in spite of their rather old-world form and tone) the classical exposition of that one glimpse of a clue to the problem of the origin of evil which is open to those who refuse to be led by a desire for 'reconciliation' or 'unity' and a philosophical horror

[1] See the second paragraph of *Sermon XII* and *Sermon XIII*.

of 'dualism' into some form or other of the denial that evil is evil.

The substance then of my contention is that Professor Sidgwick's attempt to reconcile a hedonistic conception of the 'good,' and consequently a hedonistic criterion of Morality, with an 'intuitional' or rational basis or ultimate ground of Morality breaks down. The 'dualism' of Practical Reason is not bridged over, and cannot be bridged over without the admission of Virtue or character—at least the Virtue or character which consists in the promotion of general pleasure—as an element and the highest element of the 'good' which it is right to promote for the whole human race.

III

At this point it may be well briefly to notice Professor Sidgwick's criticism on the doctrine that character is an end-in-itself. In reference to this view Professor Sidgwick remarks :—

'From a practical point of view, indeed, I fully recognise the importance of urging that men should aim at an ideal of character, and consider action in its effects on character. But I cannot infer from this that character and its elements— faculties, habits, or dispositions of any kind—are the constituents of Ultimate Good. It seems to me that the opposite is implied in the very conception of a faculty or disposition; it can only be defined as a tendency to act or feel in a certain way under certain conditions; and such a tendency is clearly not valuable in itself but for the acts and feelings in which it takes effect, or for the ulterior consequences of these,—which consequences, again, cannot be regarded as Ultimate Good, so long as they are merely conceived as modifications of faculties, dispositions,' &c. [1]

Professor Sidgwick here admits the possibility that the 'acts' in which character or disposition takes effect might conceivably have value. He has nothing to say against such a supposition except that they do not appear to him to have any value. But surely, when it is held that character has value, such 'acts' are included in the idea. And yet the value of the acts cannot be estimated in entire isolation or abstraction from the man's

[1] *Methods of Ethics*, 6th ed., p. 393.

whole inner life. Character does not consist of mere isolated 'acts'—and still less of mere abstract 'tendencies' or 'dispositions.' Not only are the actual volitions involved in the performance of particular good acts parts of consciousness, and not mere possibilities of consequences in the external world, but there is a volitional element running through our consciousness at other times than the particular moment at which we are definitely resisting temptation or making definite acts of moral choice. Attention is an act of the will; even desire involves conation. Emotion, again, is at once a source of action, an accompaniment of moral action, and a consequence and index of the habitual direction of the will. And all these—desire, attention, emotion—are actual elements of consciousness, not mere potentialities which may manifest themselves in future conscious acts. All these are included in what we mean by character. Sometimes no doubt we should further include in the ideal character the intellectual side of the moral life—the ideal that a man sets before himself, the judgements of value which he pronounces, his intellectual interest in the moral life. Professor Sidgwick would hardly have contended that the content of the good man's consciousness does not differ from that of the bad man except at the particular moments in which the former is engaged in performing good actions and the latter bad ones. Character includes, as I have suggested, not merely the actual state of the will, but other elements of consciousness connected therewith. And even if we limit the idea of character to actual volition, volition is an element in the continuous stream of consciousness at all times. Sidgwick himself has told us for instance that 'the adoption of an end as paramount' is 'to be classed among volitions.' A volitional element forms an element of consciousness during the whole—or, to avoid cavil, let me say—nearly the whole of his waking life. And it is upon the nature of this volitional element, upon the nature of the objects to which it is directed, upon the habitual direction of his will, that character primarily depends. It is this that is pronounced to have value when we say that Virtue is a good or end in itself. No doubt we cannot form any conception of character without thinking also of the intellectual and emotional accompaniments of the volition; and it makes little difference whether we do or do not think of these accompaniments as included in the conception of character. For these too have a value which is not to be measured by the amount or intensity of the pleasure which undoubtedly forms an element in them. The important point to insist on is that, when we pronounce character to have value, we are just as emphatically as the Hedonist pronouncing that it is in actual consciousness that value resides, and in nothing else [1]. It is the actual consciousness of a man who loves and wills the truly or essentially good and not mere capacities or potentialities of pleasure-production such as might be supposed to reside in a bottle of old port, which constitutes the 'goodness' or 'virtue' which is regarded as a 'good' or 'end in itself' by the school which Professor Sidgwick is criticizing. A 'virtue' or 'faculty' is, of course (as Professor Sidgwick urges), a mere abstraction, but only in the sense in which pleasure is an abstraction also. A man's consciousness cannot at any one moment be full of nothing but Virtue any more than it can be full of nothing but pleasure. The will must will something if it is to be pronounced virtuous, just as there must be feelings, thoughts, and volitions in a man's consciousness before he can be pleased with them. But for the difficulty which Sidgwick seems to make of the matter, it would have seemed unnecessary to point out that those who make 'virtue' an end mean by virtue 'virtuous consciousness,' just as those who make 'pleasure' an end mean thereby 'pleasant consciousness.' And the virtuous consciousness means a consciousness whose volitions and whose desires are controlled by a rational ideal of life together with the feelings and emotions inseparably accompanying such volitions and desires [2].

[1] We might also criticize Prof. Sidgwick's tendency to ignore the unity and the continuity of the self. No doubt the self cannot be regarded as having value when abstracted from the successive conscious states in which it manifests itself, but it is equally impossible to estimate the value of the conscious states in entire abstraction from the permanent self which is present in all of them.

[2] Modern Psychology is emphatic in rejecting the old sensationalistic view of the content of consciousness as mere feeling, no less than the opposite assumption of the possibility of thought without volition. 'Whenever

It may perhaps be suggested that, when a good state of will is pronounced desirable, or more desirable than a pleasant state of consciousness, the real object of preference is a specific pleasure invariably accompanying volition of a virtuous kind. It is difficult to see what is gained by such a mode of statement for any one who has once parted company with the hedonistic Psychology: but, since some pleasure must undoubtedly accompany consciousness to which the person himself attaches value, no great harm will be done either to ethical theory or to practical Morality by such a way of putting the matter so long as it is clearly understood (1) that the desirability of this specific pleasure does not depend upon any variable susceptibility to it on the part of those for whom it is judged desirable; (2) that the pleasure is not necessarily to those who actually desire it greater in amount or intensity than other pleasures which they forego for the sake of obtaining it. Yet when these admissions are made, it is clear that we no longer really prefer the virtuous direction of the will simply as a source of pleasure. From the point of view of pleasure there seems no reason why this single kind of pleasure should be given so extraordinary a preference. It is one which does not seem to be warranted either by its duration or its intensity. As a matter of experience

we are awake, we are judging; whenever we are awake we are willing' (Bosanquet, *Essentials of Logic*, p. 40). Mr. Bradley has, indeed, maintained the possibility of thought without 'active attention' and so without will (article on 'Active Attention' in *Mind*, N. S., No. 41, 1902), though he admits that it may be that even in the theoretical development of an idea 'the foregoing idea of that development has itself been the cause of its own existence,' and so 'it may indeed be contended that *all* thinking does in the end imply will in this sense '(p. 7). The question is an important one from other points of view, but all that I am protesting against here is the assumption that in estimating the value of consciousness we must necessarily attend merely to the feeling side, and not also to the thinking and willing side of consciousness. That will be equally unreasonable in whatever sense it may be true that we are not always willing. I should myself be disposed to contend that the active attention which is implied in definite efforts to think out a problem differs only in degree from the attention which is implied when 'I passively, as we say, accept the current and course of my thoughts' (ib., p. 6). This very 'passivity' involves a distinct attitude of the will—sometimes a very difficult one, as a man discovers when with a view to going to sleep he tries to think about nothing in particular.

it is found that the pleasures of a good Conscience are not always highly exhilarating: while the pains of a bad one, regarded merely as pains, would in many cases be found tolerable enough. The pain of a small wrong-doing is probably to most men less exquisite than the pain of having made a fool of oneself or committed a gross social blunder. If we regarded the pains of a bad Conscience as merely on a level with the pains of a *gaucherie*, we should try to live down the former as we do the latter. The importance that we attribute to a 'good Conscience' (quite apart from its social effects) cannot possibly be explained on merely hedonistic grounds; the value we attribute to it is not merely the value which it possesses as a source of pleasure, and the pleasures of Conscience themselves spring from and presuppose the consciousness of a value in conscientious conduct which is not measured by its pleasantness.

Sidgwick's arguments against the possibility of regarding truth, beauty, and the like as ends-in-themselves may, as it seems to me, be met in much the same way. He always seems to assume that to assign value to such ends irrespective of their pleasantness [1] is to assign value to them as things existing outside consciousness altogether. It does not seem to make much practical difference whether we say that there are elements in consciousness 'higher' than pleasure, or whether we say that some pleasures are 'higher' than others, so long as no attempt is made to smuggle back the hedonistic Psychology under cover of the latter form of expression. And yet it ought distinctly to be recognized that such preference of higher pleasures as higher is really only a popular way of saying that the true ethical end contains elements other than pleasure. All that is gained by the former way of putting the matter is that it suggests that pleasure is an element of any state of mind which can be regarded as possessing any ultimate value. And this need not be denied, so long as it is recognized that its value is not due solely to the amount or intensity of the pleasure, and that, though such a state may contain some pleasure, it may contain a great deal more pain and so be on the whole painful rather than pleasurable.

[1] But see below, pp. 75-78.

One more of Professor Sidgwick's difficulties may be briefly considered. To the contention that we sometimes prefer what are commonly called higher pleasures to lower ones without necessarily thinking the former more intense than the latter, Sidgwick replies that ' what in such cases we really prefer is not the present consciousness itself, but either effects on future consciousness more or less distinctly foreseen, or else something in the objective relations of the conscious being, not strictly included in his present consciousness [1].' No doubt the pleasure is preferred on account of the person's objective relations : the pleasure abstracted from all knowledge of such objective relations would be pleasure abstracted from most of those characteristics which could make it higher pleasure, from most of the features which could commend it to the Practical Reason as more worthy of a rational being's enjoyment than the lower pleasure. It is just because some knowledge of the ' objective relations ' of his pleasures and of himself as enjoying them always does enter into the consciousness of a rational being enjoying pleasure, that it is impossible for him, desiring as he does other things besides pleasure and recognizing it as ' right ' or ' reasonable ' for him to desire such other objects, to leave them out of account in considering the intrinsic desirability of different kinds of consciousness for himself and other rational beings. For such a being the pleasure itself becomes different in consequence of this knowledge of his own objective relations—different in value even when it is not altered in quantity. The pleasure which a man might take in a cruel entertainment might be harmless enough, if abstracted from his knowledge that the pleasure was won by the sufferings of a fellow creature. The pleasures of sense could not be condemned or disparaged in comparison with more social or more intellectual pleasures, but for the knowledge that the person enjoying them is a member of a society and capable of intellectual activities. The value which a man attaches to his love for wife and children or to the resulting pleasures could not be explained apart from knowledge of the ' objective relations ' implied in marriage or paternity. To ask what is the ultimate good of man apart from his knowledge of

[1] *Methods of Ethics*, 6th ed., p. 399.

the 'objective relations' in which he stands to the world and to his fellow men is really to ask what *would be* the good for man if he were a mere animal.

Sidgwick's unwillingness to recognize Virtue as an end in itself, in spite of his admission that it is reasonable to prefer it to private pleasure, appears to arise largely from an unavowed assumption that there are no other elements in consciousness besides feeling, or at least that no such elements can possibly possess ultimate value. It is impossible to prove that this last is not the case ; we can only ask, 'Is this really what the analysis of the moral consciousness reveals to us; or, if we are disposed to say that it is always the feeling that is ultimately valuable, are not the feelings to which we ascribe such value feelings of a kind which are inseparable from certain volitions and certain thoughts ? And do we not assign a higher value to a rightly directed will, or to the emotions accompanying such a will, than to mere pleasant feeling considered merely as so much pleasant feeling ?'

When all has been done that can be done in the way of developing the difficulties of a Utilitarianism which is at once rationalistic and hedonistic, it must be admitted that it is impossible to convict such a position of *formal* inconsistency, when once it is modified by the admission that Egoism is unreasonable, though there is nothing (on hedonistic grounds) to be said against a man who likes to be unreasonable. It is not the theory that is inconsistent; it is the procedure of Reason which according to the theory is essentially arbitrary and unintelligible. The attitude of Sidgwick's good man, at least when enlightened by Philosophy, may be said to be just this : 'I see that it is reasonable for me to prefer my neighbour's good, but this preference has in it nothing intrinsically desirable or beautiful or noble or worth having for its own sake. Duty is duty, but it is not good. Duty is reasonable, but pleasure is better; what the irrational man secures to himself by selfishness is intrinsically better than what the good man gets by obeying the voice of Reason within him.' And the position of the Sidgwickian Reason does not become more intelligible when we attempt to bridge over the collision between duty and interest by theological assumptions. If Reason, expressing itself in the constitution of the Universe, really does say to the bad man, 'I am sorry that I cannot reward this consistent selfishness of yours as I should like to do; but I am compelled to think of other people besides you, and in their interests I am compelled to punish a course of life and a direction of will which in a better constituted world it would give me the greatest satisfaction to reward,' there is no more to be said.   But does a Universe constructed on such a principle really strike us as a particularly reasonable one?

In the last resort the only way of showing that pleasure is not the true end of life is by an appeal to one's own moral consciousness and that of others so far as it is revealed by word and deed.   Professor Sidgwick, after admitting that a consistent system might be worked out upon the basis of a composite end, i. e. on including both Virtue and happiness, adds: 'I can give a decisive reason for not accepting it myself: viz., that when Virtue and Happiness are hypothetically presented as alternatives, from a universal point of view, I have no doubt that I morally prefer the latter; I should not think it right to aim at making my fellow-creatures more moral, if I distinctly foresaw that as a consequence of this they would become less happy. I should even make a similar choice as regards my own future virtue, supposing it presented as an alternative to results more conducive to the General Happiness [1].'   All that the critic of such a statement can do is to invite the reader to say whether he can accept it as a correct representation of his own moral conscious-ness—or of Henry Sidgwick's.

With the question whether the Virtue either of individuals or of society can ever be antagonistic to the general happiness we are not yet concerned.   My contention so far has been merely this—that as a matter of fact the judgement 'It is right for me to make others happy' is practically inseparable from the judge-

---

[1] *Mind*, No. xiv, 1889, p. 487.   It is observable that Sidgwick shrinks from saying that he would sacrifice his Virtue to his own pleasure if he could do so without loss of pleasure to others.   Whether the sacrifice of happiness to Virtue could ever actually be required by Benevolence I have considered in Book II, chap. ii, § 2.

ment 'It is better for me to do that than to be happy myself at their expense.' Admitting the bare logical possibility of accepting the former judgement while denying the latter, I believe that such a bare speculative admission of the reason-ableness of Altruism would have little or no practical effect upon the majority of minds but for that recognition of its intrinsic goodness by which it is practically accompanied. Reason is reluctant to admit that rationality can ever be a bad thing or even a matter of indifference. No considera-tion of posthumous compensation will ever reconcile Reason to a constitution of things in which it is compelled to pronounce bad, on account of their effects, kinds of conduct which in them-selves it cannot but find very good. The emotions with which we actually contemplate good or bad conduct would droop and wither were we ever once fully persuaded that there is no differ-ence between a good and a bad man except what is constituted by some accidental want of 'adjustment' between the interests of an individual and that of his fellows. Once persuade men that Thrasymachus was right in making Virtue essentially and fundamentally only another man's good, and you will have persuaded them also that it exists by convention and not by nature (νόμῳ, οὐ φύσει)—that it is in short a delusion, not a reality; and with the belief in the intrinsic value of goodness will go the theological beliefs that were based upon it.

IV

Let us see then exactly to what point the course of our argument has carried us. We have felt compelled by the very considerations that led us to regard the preference of other people's well-being to our own as rational, to treat such a preference on our part as intrinsically better even for our-selves. We have in fact (with Kant) recognized the existence of two *prima facie* rational ends—Virtue and Happiness, the latter being treated as part of the true well-being of man only in so far as is consistent with the predominance of Virtue.

It has been objected, indeed, to such a position, both by Professor Sidgwick himself and by others, that such a position involves the admission of two heterogeneous and ' incommensurable' ends—Virtue and happiness. To this we may reply that the very ground on which we have felt bound to recognize Virtue as an end in itself compels us to regard it as an end superior in value to pleasure. Reason pronounces that there is an end which all human acts should aim at promoting, i. e. the general good, and that no state of a rational will can be regarded by Reason as good which is not directed towards that end ; and a will which did not regard the choice of the right as of superior value to pleasure would not be a will directed to that supreme end. The man who acted upon the hypothesis that his own virtue and his own pleasure possessed equal intrinsic value would not really be virtuous at all. The hypothesis is therefore one which contradicts itself. And the principle that the will directed towards the good must be regarded as of more value than the agent's pleasure will equally compel us to regard the pleasure of others as an intrinsically valuable end only in so far as it is consistent with the like preference of the good to the pleasant in those others. In other words, pleasure can only be regarded as intrinsically valuable in so far as it is consistent with Morality. No doubt the 'dualism,' the absolute antagonism between the two ends, the impossibility of fusing them into a harmonious whole in which the sharp contrast between them is lost (so long as all pleasure is put on the same level and is regarded as something which Virtue must simply limit from the outside without modifying and transforming), may be a reason for suspecting that we have not yet reached an adequate and complete view of the elements contained in 'the good.' But there is no absolute logical contradiction involved in such a position ; it is not open to the charge that the two ends or elements of the end are 'incommensurable.'

Now, practically, the introduction of this principle—the principle that Virtue must be regarded as an element, and as the dominant element, in the good—will by itself do much to bring our view of the ethical criterion into harmony with ordinarily accepted moral ideas, and to remove some of the more glaring of the difficulties of Utilitarianism as commonly understood. For (1) the most glaring of all the inconsistencies between Utilitarianism and the deliverances of the ordinary, unsophisticated moral consciousness, lies precisely in its refusal to recognize the intrinsic goodness of Virtue.   (2) The inclusion of Virtue (which for the present we take to mean rational Benevolence [1]) in our conception of the end allows us to exclude from it excessive indulgence in the pleasures which we recognize as good in themselves, and also all pleasures which are inconsistent with the predominance of Benevolence, e. g. the pleasures of cruelty.   We shall not merely disallow them on account of their 'infelicific' effects, but we shall regard them as intrinsically worthless or bad, because they imply an indifference to the good: we shall condemn the man who voluntarily indulges his taste for them, even though accidentally (as in an arena, for instance, in which the combatants were condemned criminals) he might be able to indulge them in a way not immediately inconsistent with the public interest.   (3) We shall attach a high intrinsic value to such pleasures as actually include a benevolent element, and a lower degree of intrinsic superiority to such pleasures as are actually conducive to the public good, though the public good may be no part of the motive of the person indulging in them.   Under the first head we should include the actual pleasures of Benevolence or personal affection, and even to some small extent the pleasures of sociability and friendship in so far as these imply some degree of unselfish good-will to others. Under the second we should include the pleasures of ambition or emulation and the whole range of aesthetic and intellectual pleasures.

In this way it would probably be possible to justify, on the whole, that preference for what are commonly called higher pleasures which is so clear an element of the ordinary moral consciousness; since it will be generally admitted that in the long run indulgence in social and intellectual pleasures is more beneficial in its indirect social effects than indulgence in mere sensual gratification or unintellectual amusement.   But so far we have interpreted Virtue as including nothing but Benevolence, or rather Benevolence and (in due subordination thereto) Prudence; we have admitted no ground for ascribing superior moral

[1] In the sense of 'desire to promote pleasure on the whole, not excluding one's own pleasure in due proportion.'

value to one pleasure over another except its direct or indirect influence on the pleasure of others.   It is now time to ask whether this limitation really corresponds to the deliverances of the moral consciousness.   Is there no element in consciousness to which we should upon reflection ascribe intrinsic value except (1) Virtue in the sense of simple Benevolence and (2) Pleasure with a preference for social useful pleasures?   Is our conception of the *summum bonum* for a rational being limited to these two elements?   If his will invariably prefers (in case of collision) other people's pleasure to his own and if he enjoys as much pleasure as possible, should we say that a human being has all that it is reasonable for him to want?   Would a community of simple people enjoying material plenty and innocent amusements in the utmost degree that is consistent with the predominance of the most intense and most universal love— the life for instance of some rude Moravian Mission Settlement— beautiful and noble as such a life might be, realize to the full our highest ideal of human life?   Would a community devoid of Letters, of Art, of Learning, of any intellectual cultivation beyond that low elementary school standard which might be regarded as absolutely necessary to Virtue and the enjoyable filling up of leisure—would such a state of society realize our ideal?   If it were certain (a by no means extreme supposition) that the communities which have approximated most nearly to this pattern have actually realized a higher average of enjoyment than has ever been attained in more ambitious societies, should we thereupon think it right to adopt an obscurantist policy, to burn down libraries and museums and picture galleries, and to repress all desires for knowledge and beauty which should soar above the standard indicated?   Do we not rather judge that such desires *ought* to be gratified, that in their gratification —nay, in the effort to satisfy desires which grow stronger with every partial satisfaction—lies one large element of true human good, one large source of its nobleness and its value?   And can such a conviction be based upon the extremely dubious calculation that the pleasures resulting from such pursuits or produced by them in others are invariably intenser, when due allowance is made for the increasing susceptibility to pain which they bring with them, than those attainable by the healthy and moderate pursuit of more animal satisfactions in due subordination to the activities of social Morality? Should we really be prepared to condemn any study, say that of pure Mathematics, which could be shown to be less 'felicific' than Sciences and Arts of more immediate and obvious 'utility'? To all these questions I can only answer for myself, 'No.' Argument on questions of ultimate ends is impossible. All that I can do is to trace the further modifications which this admission of other ends besides Virtue and happiness will compel us to make in the system of rationalistic Utilitarianism, from which we have already diverged by making Virtue as well as happiness into an element, and the more important element, in our conception of the ultimate end. The view to which we have been led may be briefly expressed as follows. The human soul is a trinity. Consciousness includes three elements or aspects or distinguishable activities—Thought, Feeling, and Volition or (to use a more general term) Conation, each of which is unintelligible in entire abstraction or separation from the rest. There is a good state and a bad state of intellect, of feeling, and of will. The good consists in a certain state of all three of them. It may be true in a certain rough and popular sense that in thought or even in the good will, if either be taken in abstraction from the two other elements, we could discover no value at all, while in pleasure we could find such a value [1]. That is the assumption upon which all Hedonism is based; and the assumption might perhaps be admitted, though we might refuse to admit the inferences based upon it, if we could attach any meaning to pleasure taken absolutely by itself. But it is often forgotten that there is no such thing as pleasure without a content, and this content, which makes the state of consciousness pleasant or unpleasant, is, at least in rational beings, dependent upon the other two aspects of consciousness. It is no doubt possible by an effort of abstraction to think only of the intensity of our pleasurable feelings without thinking of their content, and to make their value depend upon that intensity, but there is no ground whatever for assuming that

[1] Cf. below, pp. 78, 153.

we actually do so or ought to do so. In judging of the ultimate value of any state of consciousness we think of its content—of the state of desire and of will on the one hand and of intellect on the other, as well as of feeling, and of the content of feeling as well as of its intensity. Sometimes we pronounce a less pleasant state of consciousness to be more valuable than a more pleasant one because it involves an activity of the higher intellectual faculties, or because it represents the direction of the will to a higher good. Sometimes, no doubt, the different parts of our nature represented by the trinity of thought, feeling, and will cannot all obtain equal satisfaction by the same course of action, and then we have to choose between a course which will satisfy one part of our nature and that which will satisfy the other; but the ideal good of men would include all three. It would include truth and activity of thought, pleasantness of feeling, and goodness of will. In what relation the goods predominantly connected with each of these elements of our nature stand to each other, we shall in some general way consider hereafter [1]. It will be enough to say here that we have already recognized the supreme value of the good will, i. e. of the devotion of the will towards that which the moral consciousness recognizes as the good for humanity at large, that in the abstract we recognize the superior value of intellectual activities to mere pleasant feeling, while the superiority of certain states of pleasant feeling to others is largely due to their arising to a greater extent than others from the activity of the two higher elements in our nature, the activity of the good will or of the intellect, or both.

V

If we were to enter at greater length into the relation between the different parts or elements or activities of our nature, with which we have just been dealing, we should find ourselves involved in many difficult and important matters of psychological

[1] It will be fully recognized that no one of them can actually exist in entire abstraction from the other. The good will, for instance, must include some pleasant feeling and some knowledge.

controversy. Such psychological problems I wish in the present
work to avoid in so far as their solution is not directly and
immediately necessary for the purpose of Ethics. But by way
of explaining my use of them, a few remarks may be added.
I do not adopt the usage of those Psychologists who make
feeling equivalent merely to pleasure and pain. Such a usage
seems to imply an abstraction of the pleasure from its content,
which is not what we really mean when we talk about feeling,
and which tends to encourage the idea that we are interested in
nothing but the hedonistic intensity of our consciousness apart
from its content. By Thought or Reason I do not mean merely
discursive thought to the exclusion of immediate perception, but
the whole intellectual side of our consciousness; I include in it
every kind of awareness. Desire I regard as belonging to the
conative or striving side of our nature, though it implies also,
and cannot exist apart from, both the intellectual and the feeling
side of it: we must know in some measure what we desire, and
the desire is itself a state of feeling, though it is more. An
emotion is simply a name for a kind of feeling, but the term is
usually and properly reserved for those states of feeling which
are not, and do not immediately arise from, physical sensations,
but imply the existence of ideas and of those higher desires which
are directed towards ideal objects. It is obvious that in these
distinctions we are concerned with aspects of consciousness
rather than with distinct and separable things or facts or
'states.' In some cases the distinction between them is clear
and capable by an easy abstraction of a pretty sharp differentiation in our thought: in other cases they are simply the same
thing looked at from a slightly different point of view. We
have no difficulty for instance in distinguishing processes of
mathematical calculation from the pleasant feeling by which they
are accompanied in the mathematical mind, or the unpleasant
feeling which those processes create in the unmathematical. On
the other hand a simple perception of colour must be treated as
an intellectual activity when we think of the recognized relation
between the person or subject and his object, as a state of
feeling when we think of it merely as a state of the subject
and from the point of view of his interest in it. Similarly one

and the same desire may be looked upon simply as a particular state of the subject and so as feeling, or as involving the intellectual idea of an end, or again as a conative activity tending to realize that end. Further to illustrate both the distinctions between, and the inter-dependence of, these fundamental aspects of consciousness does not seem necessary to enable us to proceed with our ethical enquiry. All that need here be emphasized is that the value which we recognize in consciousness is not dependent upon any one of these aspects taken in absolute abstraction from another. The extremest Hedonist will find it impossible to attach a clear meaning to the idea of pleasure taken apart from all awareness that one is pleased, or of what one is pleased at; the extremest Rigorist would find it difficult to say what would be the value of a good will which did not know what it willed and did not care whether it willed it or not. And the moral consciousness does not encourage us to approximate to any such feats of abstraction, even in so far as this may be possible. It pronounces its judgement upon the value of consciousness as a whole. For the purpose of weighing one good against another and choosing between them in cases of collision, it may often have to attempt a relatively complete abstraction of one aspect from another; but it does not pronounce that any aspect has exclusive value, or that the value of one aspect is to be estimated entirely without reference to the others, or that *the good* can be conceived of under any one of them. The man is Reason, Feeling, Will; and the ideal state for man is an ideal state of all three elements in his nature in their ideal relation to one another.

At this point it is probable that the reader who is inclined to utilitarian ways of thinking will be disposed to ask 'How do you know that knowledge is good, or (if you like so to express it) that the pleasures attending its pursuit and attainment are intrinsically superior to those of eating and drinking?' The answer must be, 'I do as a matter of fact so judge: I judge it immediately, and, so far, *a priori*: my Reason so pronounces: judgements of value are ultimate, and no ethical position, utilitarian or other, can rest on anything but judgements of value.' What is this, the reader is likely to exclaim, but sheer Intuitionism? How far

I am prepared to accept this identification will appear from the next chapter [1].

[1] The logical contradiction involved in Egoism has been powerfully argued by von Hartmann in his criticism of Nietzsche and Max Stirner (*Ethische Studien*, pp. 33-90). More recently Mr. Moore has incisively expressed the difficulty as follows : ' What Egoism holds, therefore, is that *each* man's happiness is the sole good—that a number of different things are *each* of them the only good thing there is—an absolute contradiction ! No more complete and thorough refutation of any theory could be desired. Yet Professor Sidgwick holds that Egoism is rational,' a conclusion which he proceeds to characterize as ' absurd ' (*Principia Ethica*, 1903, p. 99). I should agree with him that the position is self-contradictory in a sense in which universalistic Hedonism is not, and that with all his subtlety Sidgwick failed altogether to escape what was really an inconsistency in thought, even if he escaped an actual or formal contradiction. But to point out this logical contradiction does not seem to me quite so easy and final a way of refuting Sidgwick's position as it does to Mr. Moore for these reasons : (1) The Egoist with whom Professor Sidgwick is arguing would probably not accept Mr. Moore's (and my own) conception of an absolute objective good, though I should admit and have contended in this chapter that if he fully thought out what is implied in his own contention that his conduct is ' reasonable ' he would be led to that conception. (2) Sidgwick only admitted that the Egoist was reasonable from one point of view—reasonable as far as he goes, i. e. when he refuses to ask whether his judgements are consistent with what he cannot help recognizing as the rational judgements of other men, and limits himself to asking whether he can make his own judgements consistent with themselves from his own point of view. No doubt Sidgwick ought to have gone on to admit that this imperfectly reasonable point of view was not really reasonable at all, and to some extent he has done this in his last Edition. And (3) after all, even if we admit that the Egoist is unreasonable, there remains the question ' Why should he care to be reasonable ? ' It was largely the difficulty of answering this question on universalistic Hedonist principles which drove Professor Sidgwick to admit a ' dualism of the Practical Reason,' and I am not sure that the question has been very satisfactorily answered by Mr. Moore who, though he is no Hedonist, appears to be unwilling to give the good will the highest place in his scale of goods.

CHAPTER IV

INTUITIONISM

I

By Intuitionism is usually understood the theory that actions are pronounced right or wrong *a priori* without reference to their consequences. According to one view it is supposed that Conscience, or whatever else the moral faculty may be called, pronounces on the morality of particular courses of conduct at the moment of action. This form of the doctrine has been styled by Professor Sidgwick unphilosophical Intuitionism, while he gives the name philosophical Intuitionism to the doctrine that what is intuitively judged to be right or wrong is always some general rule of conduct, from which the morality or immorality of this or that particular course of action must be deduced. According to the first view, Conscience is an ever-present dictator issuing detailed injunctions to meet particular cases as they arise : according to the second, Conscience is a legislator, whose enactments have to be applied to particular cases by the same intellectual process as is employed by a judge in administering an act of Parliament [1]. Intuitionists

---

[1] It is probable that many 'Intuitionists' would hold a position midway between these extreme views. They would hold that some rules are intuitively discerned to be of absolute obligation, while in other cases the decision must be left to the intuitive judgement of the moment. It may be asked where we are to find examples of the Intuitionist presupposed by the Utilitarian polemics. To a large extent no doubt he is a man of straw set up to be knocked down again. It will generally be found that most of the writers usually associated with the name make larger admissions than the popular exponents or assailants of this view recognize as to the necessity of considering consequences and the paramount duty of promoting the general good properly understood. But it cannot be denied that Bishop Butler (especially in the *Dissertation of Virtue*) and Reid have approximated to this position. The writer who seems specially to have introduced the term 'intui-

may further be divided into two classes according to the view which they take as to the nature of the faculty by which these *a priori* judgements are pronounced. By some Intuitionists this faculty is supposed to be Reason, by others a 'Moral Sense.' But the nature of the faculty involved in our moral judgements is one which can best be discussed when we have answered the easier preliminary question—'Do we in practice, or can we reasonably, pronounce actions to be right or wrong without regard to their consequences, in so far as such consequences can be foreseen?'

The belief described as unphilosophical Intuitionism in its wildest form is one which can hardly claim serious refutation. If it is supposed that the injunctions of the moral faculty are so wholly arbitrary that they proceed upon no general or rational principle whatever, if it is supposed that I may to-day in one set of circumstances feel bound by an inexplicable impulse within me to act in one way, while to-morrow I may be directed or direct myself to act differently under circumstances in no way distinguishable from the former, then moral judgements are reduced to an arbitrary caprice which is scarcely compatible with the belief in any objective standard of duty; for it will hardly be denied that, if right and wrong are not the same for the same individual on different but precisely similar occasions, they can still less be the same for different persons, and all idea of an objective moral law disappears. It may of course be alleged that the circumstances of no two acts are precisely alike, but they may certainly be alike in all relevant respects. If it be said that Conscience will vary its judgement in accordance with the circumstances of the case, and that other men's Consciences in proportion to their enlightenment will always pronounce the same judgements under

tion' as the note of a School is Richard Price, but that writer's admissions are so ample that he ends by virtually resolving all duties into Benevolence, understood in a non-hedonistic sense, and Justice. His *Review of the principal Questions and Difficulties in Morals* (1769) I regard as the best work published on Ethics till quite recent times. It contains the gist of the Kantian doctrine without Kant's confusions. In this chapter it must be understood that I am criticizing a type of opinion and not any particular writer.

similar circumstances, there must be some rule or principle by which it must be possible to distinguish between circumstances which do and circumstances which do not alter our duty, however little this rule or principle may be present in an abstract form to the moral consciousness of the individual. Granted, therefore, that the moral judgements may as a matter of psychological fact reveal themselves first and most clearly in particular cases (just as we pronounce judgements about particular spaces and distances long before we have consciously put geometrical principles into the form of general axioms), it must still, it would seem, be possible by analysis of our particular moral judgements to discover the general principles upon which they proceed. Analytical thought and philosophical language may be inadequate for the accurate expression of the delicate shades and gradations of circumstance upon which, in complicated cases, our moral judgements actually depend; but some approximation to this, some rough rules or principles of ethical judgement, ought, one would think, to be capable of being elicited from a wide comparative survey of one's own and other people's actual judgements. If this be denied, moral instruction must be treated as absolutely impossible. Now it may be quite true that in many ways 'example is better than precept,' not only on account of its emotional effect but even on account of the intellectual illumination supplied by a good man's conduct in presence of varying practical difficulties. It is true that the contemplation in actual fact or in recorded history of a good life may suggest ideals which no mere system of precepts, abstracted from particular applications, can adequately embody. A general rule is often best embodied in a concrete, typical case. The parable of the Good Samaritan has taught the true meaning of Charity more clearly as well as more persuasively than any direct precept that could be culled from the writings of Seneca or even from the Sermon on the Mount. But still there is a consensus among reasonable men that moral instruction of some kind—however vague, general, and inadequate to the complexities of actual life—is possible, desirable, and necessary. We do not say to a child who asks whether he may pick a flower in somebody else's garden, ' My good child, that depends entirely upon the circumstances of the particular case: to lay down any general rule on the subject would be a piece of unwarrantable dogmatism on my part: consult your own Conscience, as each case arises, and all will be well.' On the contrary, we say at once: 'You must not pick the flower: *because* that would be stealing, and stealing is wrong.' Make any reserves you please as to the inadequacy of the rule, its want of definiteness, its inability to meet many problems of life, the necessity for exceptions and the like; yet it must be admitted that if there be any one point about Morality as to which there is a consensus alike among all plain men and nearly all Philosophers [1] it is surely this—that general rules of conduct do exist. Morality cannot be reduced to copy-book headings, but copy-book headings we do and must have. Now, in proportion as all this is admitted, unphilosophical Intuitionism tends to pass into the philosophical variety of the Intuitionist creed and may be subjected to the same criticism.

The strongest part of Sidgwick's great work consists in its analysis of common-sense Morality. The loose statements of Intuitionists as to the clearness, certainty, adequacy, and self-evidence of the ordinarily received rules of conduct have never been subjected to so searching, so exhaustive, and so illuminating an examination. That task has been done once for all, and need not in detail be done over again. It will be enough in this place to exhibit in the barest outline the difficulties which this mode of ethical thought has to confront:—

(i) Granted the existence of intuitive tendencies to approve action of particular kinds, we may still ask why we should trust to blind unreasoning impulses which refuse to give any rational account of themselves. Granted the existence of such judgements as a matter of psychological fact, whence comes their validity? If it be said 'they are deliverances of moral Reason,' we may ask whether it can be really rational to act without some consideration of consequences? What does rational conduct mean but acting with a clear conception of our ultimate

---

[1] Some of Mr. Bradley's utterances in *Ethical Studies* and elsewhere seem to constitute the only exception known to me. This position will be further discussed in the last chapter of this work.

purpose or aim, and taking the means which seem best adapted
to attain that end? 'Look before you leap' seems to be one
of the clearest of all practical axioms: to act in obedience to
every subjective impulse, even if it be *prima facie* an impulse
arising from the higher part of our nature, would seem very
like adopting as our maxim 'Leap before you look.' Of course
there may be circumstances in which we have to leap after
a very hurried and imperfect survey of the situation under
penalty of being too late to leap at all, but some looking
before leaping is as necessary in the most unexpected and
agonizing crisis of the battle-field or the hunting field as in
the leisured pomp and circumstance of formal athletic sports.

(ii) The moral notions which have seemed equally innate,
self-evident, and authoritative to those who held them have
varied enormously with different races, different ages, different
individuals—even with the same individuals at different periods
of life. It will be unnecessary to illustrate at length the variations of moral sentiment which have formed the main stock-in-
trade of utilitarian writers from the days of John Locke to those
of Herbert Spencer. We have been taught to honour our
fathers and mothers: there have been races which deemed it
sacred duty to eat them. Average Greek public opinion looked
with favour, or at least indulgence, upon acts which are crimes in
most civilized modern communities. Pious and educated Puritans
could see no harm in kidnapping negroes or shooting Irishmen.
The eminent evangelical clergyman John Newton pronounced
the hours which he passed in the captain's cabin of a slaver,
separated by a plank or two from a squalid mass of human
misery of which he was the cause, to have been sweeter
hours of divine communion than he had ever elsewhere known.
Some virtues seem to be of very late development even among
civilized races—religious toleration, for instance, and humanity
towards animals. And so on, and so on.

To beginners in Moral Philosophy these objections to Intuitionism will usually present themselves as the strongest and
most unanswerable. In truth perhaps they are the weakest.
Neither the slow development of the moral faculty nor its
unequal development in different individuals at the same level

of social culture forms any objection to the *a priori* character of moral judgements. We do not doubt either the axioms of Mathematics or the rules of reasoning, because some savages cannot count more than five [1], or because some highly educated classical scholars are incapable of understanding the fifth proposition of Euclid's first book. Some of us will even refuse to allow our belief in the objectivity of aesthetic judgements to be shaken because a Zulu will hold a picture upside down, because an uneducated bargee will often prefer some gaudy sign-board to an old Master, because the taste which pronounced Queen's College the only really satisfactory piece of Oxford architecture does not commend itself to the twentieth century, or because even among the most cultivated art critics of the present day there exist considerable differences of opinion. Intuitionists have no doubt shown a tendency to claim infallibility as well as authority for the moral judgements of the individual: but such a claim is by no means necessary to the extremest view of the arbitrary, unconsequential, isolated character of moral judgements. We may admit the validity of the principles of reasoning and of the axioms of Mathematics, although many men reason badly, and some cannot even count. Men's moral judgements may be intuitive, but they need not be infallible. Self-evident truths are not truths which are evident to everybody. There are degrees of moral illumination just as there are degrees of musical sensibility or of mathematical acuteness. Taken by themselves, the variations of moral judgement form a less serious objection to the intuitional mode of thought than those which follow, although it may be certainly contended that Intuitionism of the cruder kind cannot adequately account for these variations.

(iii) Even when a certain intuition is actually found in all or most men of a certain race and age, the moral rule which it enjoins usually turns out upon examination to be incapable of exact definition. All, or nearly all, detailed moral rules have some exceptions, except indeed when the rule laid down tacitly excludes such exceptional cases. The rule 'Thou shalt do no

[1] Assuming such to be the fact, as is sometimes alleged, though the truth may be that they have no words or other signs for higher numbers.

murder' presents itself no doubt at first sight as a moral rule
admitting of no exception; but that is only because murder
means 'killing except under those exceptional circumstances
under which it is right to kill.' Now, even where there seems
to be the fullest agreement, at least among men of developed
moral nature, as to the main rules, it is frequently found to
disappear as soon as we come to discuss the exceptions; while
even the same individual will often find that at this point
his intuitions become indistinct or fail him altogether. And
in practice it will nearly always turn out that the exception
has been introduced from some consideration of consequences.
Those who are most positive in maintaining a particular moral
rule to be of self-evident and universal obligation independently
of consequences, will generally shrink from applying it in certain
extreme cases. Set forth to the Intuitionist in sufficient detail
the appalling consequences of applying his rule, pile up the
agony sufficiently, and there will almost always come a point
at which he begins to be doubtful as to whether the rule applies,
and a further point at which he is certain that it does not.
'Thou shalt do no murder'; but most men will admit that
there are exceptional cases in which killing is no murder,
and perhaps a very large majority would be got to declare
that their intuitions were clear in excepting self-defence, war
or at least lawful war, and judicial execution. But ask at
what point killing in self-defence becomes lawful, what constitutes war or what constitutes lawful war, for what offences
we may lawfully inflict death, at what point it becomes the
duty of the individual to refuse to take part in an unrighteous
campaign or to carry out an iniquitous sentence—and we find
ourselves once again in a chaos of uncertainties. And observe
exactly the point of the uncertainty: the uncertainty lies
exactly in this—that no clear intuitions are forthcoming as
to the exact moment at which it begins to be legitimate to
take account of consequences. 'Thou shalt not kill except
in self-defence, or by judicial sentence.' So much may perhaps
be pronounced to be self-evident without reference to consequences. But if the established government absolutely refuses
to protect person, property, or Morality, shall we never reach

a state of anarchy such as will warrant the intervention of an extra-legal committee of public safety or vigilance association, and the summary execution of its sentences? If only the foreseen consequences are bad enough, no one but an advocate of absolute non-resistance will fail to relax his severity, and the advocate of unlimited non-resistance is certainly not in a position to claim any general consensus in his favour. Now, if there be any point at which an apparent intuition has to give way before clearly foreseen ill consequences, how can we logically say that it can *ever* be right to exclude consideration of consequences? We must at least examine the probable consequences of an act sufficiently to feel reasonably sure that it will have none of those extreme results which, it is admitted, would have the effect of suspending the moral rule upon which it is proposed to act. The only people who have really carried out the doctrine that apparently self-evident moral rules cannot be modified by the consequences, however socially disastrous, of disobeying them to anything like its logical results, are those who (like Count Leo Tolstoi) preach the doctrine of unlimited submission to force, unlimited giving to mendicants and the like. And here common-sense Intuitionism decidedly declines to follow.

(iv) The above considerations may probably lead on to the reflection that after all some reference to consequences is really included in every moral rule. Indeed, you cannot really distinguish an act from its present or foreseeable consequences. The consequences, in so far as they can be foreseen, are actually part of the act. You cannot carry out any rule whatever without *some* consideration of consequences. You cannot obey the rule of Benevolence without asking whether giving money in the street really is Benevolence; and that depends upon whether it will actually have the effect of doing ultimate good to those to whom you give and others who may be affected by the expectation of similar assistance which your act creates. You cannot obey the command 'Thou shalt not kill' without considering whether the trigger that you pull will actually discharge a bullet, how far the bullet is likely to travel, what it will meet with on the way, and (if it is likely to hit any one) whether that person is on the point of shooting somebody else, or is a peaceable and inoffensive fellow-citizen. What would be the meaning of asking whether drunkenness would be wrong if it did not make a man incoherent in his talk, irrational in his judgements, unsteady in his gait, and irresponsible in his behaviour? Drunkenness taken apart from *all* its consequences would not be drunkenness. Once admit that consequences must be considered at all, and it is arbitrary to stop at any particular point in the calculus of social effects. You are not really in a position to pronounce upon the morality of the act until you have the completest view that circumstances enable you to take of the whole train of events which will be started by your contemplated volition. Until you have formed that estimate of consequences, you do not really know what you are doing: at any point in the vast orbit of changes which spreads from every human action, like the widening ripple that radiates from a stone dropped into smooth water, it is always theoretically possible that some circumstance may be discovered which may remove the case from the category to which your moral rule refers.

No doubt in practice it is often imperative that we should act without this elaborate investigation: but the very enquiry 'how long ought I to deliberate before I act?' is precisely one of those questions upon which it is impossible to discover any intuitive rule containing no reference to the probable consequences—the consequences, that is to say, on the one hand of deliberating too much, and on the other of not deliberating enough. If there are cases in which our moral consciousness clearly bids us do something or other at once without thinking of consequences, it will be found that these cases are precisely those in which excessive deliberation would be likely to lead to harmful results. To stay and reflect upon all the consequences which might be expected to flow from obeying or resisting the impulse to plunge into the water after a drowning man would very rapidly place the former alternative out of the question; to encourage the habit of prolonged deliberation in such cases would be to make gallant attempts at rescues few, and successful rescues fewer. It is therefore considered enough to justify the attempt that a man knows he is a good swimmer, that the sea is not exceptionally rough, and that it is not certain that the attempt will fail. There are, of course, scores of cases in which it is right to act on short deliberation : but it will probably be found, on analysis, that it is some consequence of allowing people to deliberate upon which the judgement is ultimately based. It is a commonplace of utilitarian Ethics that many things must be avoided altogether which might in exceptional cases have good effects just because exceptions, if admitted at all, would have a tendency to become too numerous [1].

(v) Still more obviously does the existence of contradictory moral intuitions compel an appeal to consequences. When the duty of Benevolence collides with the duty of Veracity, or the claim of one individual to immediate relief with the duty of doing what is best for society on the whole, how shall we determine which rule is to take precedence ? It is no use to say with Dr. Martineau ' Act in obedience to the highest motive [2] '; for it is impossible to pronounce one motive higher than another in the abstract, without reference to circumstances. If I were

[1] It is therefore quite reasonable to hold that some acts may properly be forbidden by Morality, just as others are forbidden by law, because (though often harmless) there is a probable balance of harm in allowing the practice at all.   Law forbids my crossing the line except by the bridge (although the practice is quite safe for an able-bodied man in full possession of all his faculties) because my indulging in it has a tendency to encourage imitation in the feeble, the elderly, and the deaf, who are likely to be run over.   It is quite reasonable to urge that even moderate gambling *ought* to be forbidden by public opinion on much the same grounds.   Until public opinion has forbidden it, I am not, indeed, at liberty to treat the man who plays whist for sixpences as a moral offender.   But, if I think that society would do well to adopt as its rule the total condemnation of gambling, it is my duty under ordinary circumstances to abstain from it myself, and to do what in me lies (short of censoriously condemning individuals who differ from me) to bring about the adoption of this rule.   Those who will not under any possible circumstances admit that ' abusus tollit usum ' would find it difficult to justify a whole host of accepted moral rules which rest on this principle.   The whole social code which restricts the time, place, and circumstances of social intercourse between the sexes is based on this principle.   Acts in themselves harmless are forbidden altogether because experience shows that they are liable to lead to bad consequences in some cases.

[2] This doctrine is developed in the first part of the second volume of *Types of Ethical Theory.*

to pronounce Veracity invariably a higher motive than Benevolence, I could never tell a lie or employ a detective to tell one
for me, to avoid the extremest social disaster. If, on the other
hand, I pronounce Benevolence higher than Veracity and every
other possible motive, I have practically adopted the utilitarian
principle, and Veracity would have always to give way to
Benevolence, wherever there was the slightest collision between
them. But neither solution of the problem seems to satisfy the
demands of our moral consciousness. The first view strikes us
as too rigorous, the last as too lax. What our actual moral
judgement seems to say is, that in such collisions it is the
amount of the unveracity or the amount of the inhumanity that
will have to determine which rule is to give way. And this
cannot be ascertained without a calculation of consequences. If
once it be admitted that under any possible combination of
circumstances I may tell a lie (however strongly one may feel
the practical inexpediency of entering upon such a calculation in
all ordinary cases), I must still feel bound to examine the circumstances sufficiently to be pretty sure that there is no probability of this turning out to be one of those extreme or exceptional
cases in which the lie would be warranted. In general, of course,
this hasty survey of the consequences is so instantaneously
performed as to escape notice altogether. A truthful man
acts at once on the general rule unless he detects something
in the circumstances which seems to call for further consideration.

(vi) While the foregoing objections may be urged against
many of the alleged intuitions to which intuitional Moralists
appeal, there are some which do submit to the tests which
have been found fatal to the claim for absolute and final
validity on the part of the rest. The axioms of Prudence,
Rational Benevolence, and Equity do possess the clearness and
definiteness and freedom from self-contradiction which other
alleged intuitions so conspicuously lack. It does on reflection
strike us as self-evident that I ought to promote my own good
on the whole (where no one else's good is affected), that I ought
to regard a larger good for society in general as of more intrinsic
value than a smaller good, and that one man's good is (other

things being equal) of as much intrinsic value as any other man's. But these axioms, so far from throwing any doubt upon the truth of Utilitarianism, are precisely the maxims upon which Utilitarianism itself is founded for those who attempt to base the duty of promoting pleasure upon its intrinsic rightness or reasonableness. In the acceptance of those maxims as genuine moral axioms, Sidgwick has, as we have seen, laid the foundations for a reconciliation between Intuitionism and Utilitarianism. But the acceptance of these axioms does not make in favour of the kind of Intuitionism which it is the object of this chapter to examine; for these are precisely the axioms upon which Utilitarianism itself is based. Such intuitions do not forbid us—on the contrary they expressly require and compel us—to attend to the consequences of actions, and to make our judgement about them depend upon their tendency to promote a universal good.

II

It is perhaps unnecessary to multiply objections to that sort of Intuitionism which declares that certain rules of action are to be followed irrespectively of consequences. It is irrational to judge of the morality of an action without tracing its bearing upon human Well-being as a whole. We are compelled to accept the utilitarian formula in so far as it asserts that conduct is good or bad only in proportion as it tends to promote the Wellbeing of human society on the whole. But we have already seen reasons for rejecting the utilitarian identification of greatest good with greatest pleasure; and we have seen that in the judgements as to the value of different kinds of good we encounter *a priori* or immediate deliverances of the moral consciousness of precisely that kind to which the term Intuition is commonly applied. What then is the difference between the intuitions which we have rejected and the intuitions which we have felt ourselves compelled to accept? The intuitions of the Intuitionist are supposed to lay down invariable *rules* of conduct; the *a priori* or immediate judgements which we have admitted relate to *ends*, to the relative value of different elements in human Well-being or εὐδαιμονία. In other words the intuitions

of the Intuitionist disregard consequences; ours relate precisely
to the value of different kinds of consequence. The Intuitionist
pronounces intuitive judgement upon *acts*; our intuitions relate
to *ends*; his take the form 'this is right,' ours always the form
'this is good.'

A few illustrations will make the contrast plain. The old
intuitive rule of Veracity is supposed to say, 'Do not lie under
any circumstances whatever': our judgement of value gives us
only 'Truth-speaking is good; lying is bad.' And the moment
the intuitive or *a priori* truth is put in this new form, the
irrationality and unworkableness of the old intuitional system
disappears. We are not forbidden to calculate consequences.
Certainly we must trace the bearing of an act upon universal
Well-being; but in our εὐδαιμονία truth-speaking, or rather the
truth-speaking and truth-loving character, finds a place. Supposing the speaking of the truth will in this particular case involve
such and such evils, the question is ' Which is the worse—these
evils or the evil involved in the lie; so much suffering, and suffering caused by my voluntary act, or so much untruthfulness?'
It is impossible, of course, to set forth in detail all the circumstances upon which a right decision of such cases may depend.
But it would be generally agreed that to tell a lie to save somebody from hearing an unpleasant remark, or to save him from
some trifling injury to his pride or self-esteem, would be to choose
the greater of two evils instead of the less. On the other hand,
to save a friend's life at the cost of concealing bad news by a lie
would be a less evil than the voluntary causing of his death by
speaking the truth. Of course, if any one disputes such a view
of the case, we have nothing to say. As in all questions of
ultimate ends, argument is impossible: but so in this particular
case the vast majority of conscientious people judge and act.
And be it observed that on this principle our moral judgements
can never contradict one another. It remains true that truth is
good, and speaking an untruth an evil; but like other goods,
truth may have to give way to greater goods; lying is always
an evil, but it may be the less of two evils. It is evil even
when the justification for the lie is palpable and incontestable.
Where the circumstances are such that the isolated act does not

evidence or encourage an untruthful habit or character, the evil may be very small; but we cannot always secure that the evil shall be a small one. Lying in detectives is necessary and right, but, like some other professional duties, it may not always be good for the character of the person who practises it. It is often necessary to do things which are right for *us*, but which are liable to be imitated by those for whom they are wrong. If the evil of the anticipated imitation be great enough, this may no doubt be a sufficient reason for abstinence, but no sensible man would forbid a father to smoke because the example may fire his youthful son with the ambition to do likewise.

The general result then of our discussion, taken in connexion with preceding chapters, is that the true criterion of Morality is the tendency of an act to promote a Well-being or εὐδαιμονία which includes many other good things besides pleasure, among which Virtue is the greatest. The value of these elements in human life is determined by the Practical Reason intuitively, immediately, or (if we like to say so) *a priori* [1] All moral judgements are ultimately judgements as to the intrinsic worth or value of some element in consciousness or life.

And we may go one step further than this in recognition of the partial truth of Intuitionism. The great objection in many minds to the utilitarian view of Ethics is the element of calculation which it involves. When this objection is made into a plea for acting without regard to consequences, it is (as I have endeavoured to show) completely irrational. But all the same the directness and immediacy which appear to characterize our clearest moral perceptions do seem at first sight an objection to the doctrine that I cannot decide whether a thing is right or wrong until I have worked out all its probable consequences upon so remote and intangible a thing as universal Well-being. And the

---

[1] I wish for the present to avoid as far as possible metaphysical discussion, and therefore content myself with saying that by *a priori* I mean merely that the judgement is *immediate*—not obtained by inference or deduction from something else in the way in which the Utilitarian supposes his judgements to be deductions from rules got by generalization from experience (though, as I have explained, he always assumes the ultimate major premiss ' Pleasure is good '). That in another sense judgements of value are not independent of experience, I shall hereafter strongly insist, especially in the next chapter.

8

difficulty is not fully met by insisting on the fact that on most
of the ethical difficulties of common life the moral consciousness
of the community has already laid down rules which the individual has only to apply to the matter in hand.　For there
are no moral judgements which probably strike those who make
them as more authoritative and self-evident than those by which
a certain act is judged to be wrong in spite of an overwhelming
weight of custom and tradition.　Such a judgement was pronounced,
for instance, when a solitary monk declared that the gladiatorial
combat was a barbarous brutality, though the tradition of ages
and a whole circus-full of professedly Christian spectators pronounced it right, and by a public protest, which cost him his life,
sealed the doom of the whole institution.　And there is no reason
why we should not fully recognize the validity of such judgements
without any surrender of the principles which we have adopted.
For this indefinable Well-being or εὐδαιμονία, which our moral
Reason pronounces to be the ultimate end of all human conduct,
is itself made up of elements of consciousness—feelings, volitions,
emotions, thoughts, activities—each of which is itself an object
of moral valuation.　If these elements were not each of them by
itself [1] the object of a judgement of value, there could be no
judgement of value upon the whole.　Every one would recognize
this as regards acts which cause immediate pleasure or pain.
Nobody supposes that, when I see a man sticking a knife into
another, it is necessary for me to calculate the effect of the act
upon the lives of all human beings, present and future, before
I condemn the proceeding.　I say at once, 'This pain is bad:
therefore the infliction of it is wrong'; and, if I am not a
Hedonist, I may add, 'the character or disposition which this
act shows is worse than the pain which it causes.'　And it is
equally so in many cases where the act has no such immediate
and obvious bearing upon the welfare of human society.　That
a rational being should use his intellect to make things appear
to his brother man otherwise than as they are strikes me at once

---

[1] I speak of course in a rough and relative sense.　We could form no
judgement upon the worth of an act or a state of mind without some general
knowledge of its relation to life as a whole.　The illustrations will, I trust,
sufficiently explain my meaning.

as irrational and evil. I do not want to trace out all the effects of lying upon human society before I say, 'this is a lie and therefore bad.' It is not the existence or even the relative and partial validity of such judgements that is disputed, so much as their finality. In many cases it is practically apparent at the first glance that no possible circumstances could make this act—the cutting or the lying—result in an overplus of good to human society. In many more cases there is a great improbability that any circumstance at present unknown to me will disclose a prospect of beneficial consequences which would reverse my *prima facie* judgement. But, unless I know all the circumstances, it is always *possible* that further knowledge might reveal such a tendency. The man sticking a knife into his fellow with apparently heartless brutality may turn out to be a surgeon performing a salutary operation. The lie which I put down to mere indifference to truth may turn out to be part of a detective's scheme for the capture of a murderer or the protection of an innocent man. It is not always practically necessary to look to the ultimate end before we judge, and act upon our judgement: but, until we have done so, we are never sure that we have reached one of those ultimate moral judgements which represent an immediate deliverance of Reason, and which no further knowledge of facts and no demonstration of consequences can possibly shake. There would be little objection to the claims which the Intuitionist makes for his intuitions, if only he would admit that they are subject to appeal, though it is only an appeal to the same tribunal which pronounced the original judgements—an appeal (to borrow an old legal phrase) *a conscientia male informata ad conscientiam melius informandam.* So long as the intuitive judgement runs in the form, 'This is right,' it is always liable to be reversed on a wider survey of consequences. If it be turned into the form, 'This is good,' it cannot possibly be reversed (supposing that the man's ethical ideal be a true one), though the resulting duty may appear different when this isolated judgement is brought into comparison with other moral judgements affirming the superior goodness of some other end [1]. In Morality, as in other matters,

---

[1] This point has been well put by Dr. McTaggart. 'But is a moral

our judgements require to be correlated and corrected by reference to one another.　Only the judgements that are based upon complete knowledge are final.　The ideal moral judgement implies a conception of the ideal good for society as a whole, but we could have no ideal of what is good for society as a whole unless we had a power of pronouncing that this or that particular moment of conscious life is good or bad.　Our conception of the moral ideal as a whole is built up out of particular judgements of value, though particular judgements of value have to be progressively corrected by our growing conception of the moral ideal as a whole, just as our conception of the laws of nature is built up out of particular perceptions, though when that knowledge is once attained it reacts upon and alters the perceptions themselves.

And by expressing the moral judgement as a judgement of value we get this further advantage.　We emphasize the fact which eudaemonistic systems of Ethics are apt to overlook—that acts are the objects of moral judgements as well as consequences. Because no act can be good or bad without reference to consequences, it does not follow that its morality depends wholly upon those consequences.　To the Hedonist, of course, such a distinction would be meaningless.　For him nothing about an act is of any value or importance besides the consequences.　Whether a poor family economize by infanticide or by curtailing their expenditure is simply a question of profit and loss.　If the sum

criterion,' he asks, 'wanted at all?　It might be maintained that it was not. It would only be wanted, it might be said, if we decided our actions by general rules, which we do not.　Our moral action depends on particular judgements that A is better than B, which we recognize with comparative immediacy, in the same way that we recognize that one plate is hotter than another, or one picture more beautiful than another.　It is on these particular intuitive judgements of value, and not on general rules, that our moral action is based.

'This seems to me a dangerous exaggeration of an important truth.　It is quite true that, if we did not begin with such judgements, we should have neither morality nor ethics.　But it is equally true that we should have neither morality nor ethics if we stopped, where we must begin, with these judgements, and treated them as decisive and closing discussion.　For our moral judgements are hopelessly contradictory of one another.' (*Studies in Hegelian Cosmology*, p. 97.)

of pleasure would be equal in the two cases, it would be a matter of perfect indifference by which machinery the requisite correspondence between food and eaters shall be effected. The inhumanity of the act, the want of self-control which it implies, the temper or character which it expresses and fosters are matters of no importance except in so far as they may result upon the whole in an actual diminution of pleasure or increase of suffering. But, when once it is admitted that the end includes a certain ideal of human character, then the deliberate extinction of children deliberately brought into the world with the intention of so disposing of them will seem a vastly greater evil, to the individuals concerned and to the society which tolerates their conduct, than much poverty with all its physical hardships and privations.

From this non-hedonistic point of view we can no longer recognize an absolute distinction between means and ends. Some means may no doubt have no value beyond that of conducing to a further end; but many, nay most, of the acts which do conduce to further ends have a value (positive or negative) of their own; and this value must be taken into account in estimating the rightness or wrongness of the acts.

It is on this principle that we must deal with most of the *prima facie* collisions between our ordinary moral judgements and the results of eudaemonistic calculation. Nothing but consciousness has value, but volitions and desires, emotions and aspirations and imaginations, are elements in all our consciousness as well as mere pleasures and pains. There are acts so intrinsically repulsive that it strikes us as, on the face of it, impossible that any pleasure which they might yield could be worth the evil which they involve. In this way most people would condemn without further examination proposals for the abolition of marriage or the permission of promiscuous infanticide. But still even in such cases it is not speculatively admissible to say, 'we will not look at the consequences.' Practically, of course, it may often be right to refuse to argue some proposed moral innovation: that must depend upon circumstances. But, if we do argue, if we do want speculatively to get to the bottom of an ethical question, we are bound to look at all the consequences, and pronounce whether, given such and such probable results, they are worth the evil involved in the means taken to gain them. In many cases—where the consequence on the strength of which it is proposed to do some questionable act is not some remote effect but some immediate pleasure—it is convenient to discuss the question as one of higher *versus* lower pleasure, though in strictness this means, according to our view, that the getting pleasure from one source is better than getting it from another, that one kind of pleasant consciousness is intrinsically better than another, though not more pleasant. And, if we treat one pleasure as intrinsically better than another, there is no logical objection to our regarding some pleasures (i. e. the getting pleasure from some things) as intrinsically bad.

It is clear to my mind that there do exist pleasures which are intrinsically bad. On strictly hedonistic principles I fail to understand why we should object to the Spanish or Southern-French bull-fight, to the German students' face-slashing duels, to the coursing and pigeon-shooting which the higher public opinion is beginning to condemn among ourselves, to the wild-beast fights of the Roman amphitheatre, or perhaps even to the gladiatorial combats themselves, at least if the gladiators were justly condemned criminals. Hedonism is not bound to object to all infliction of pain, but only to insist that the pain inflicted shall yield a sufficient overplus of pleasure on the whole. There is no more difficult ethical question than the question of the negative value to be attributed to pain as compared with the positive value to be attributed to pleasure. There is no question assuredly upon which people's actual judgements would differ more. Which would you rather have—some particularly longed for treat, the holiday or the travel that you have set your heart upon + a painful operation without chloroform, or no treat and no operation? Different men would answer such questions very differently[1]. But, to return to our bull-fight, upon any rational

---

[1] It is an extremely difficult question to say how far in such matters Hedonism would be bound to accept the verdict of the persons themselves. For we often deceive ourselves as to the pleasurableness of pleasures not immediately present, even when we have some experience to go upon, and yet such false estimates are causes of further pleasures and pains—pleasures

or intelligible view of the comparative values of pleasure and
pain, the intense pleasure which such spectacles give to thousands
of beholders must surely outweigh the pain inflicted on a few
dozen animals or even a few dozen criminals. If ten thousand
spectators would not be sufficient to readjust the balance, suppose
them multiplied tenfold or one-hundredfold. A humane man
would condemn the spectacle all the same. He will pronounce
such pleasures of inhumanity bad, quite apart from the somewhat dubious calculation that the encouragement of inhumanity
in one direction tends to callousness in another. Experience
does not seem to show that persons habituated to the infliction
of pain in one direction sanctioned by custom are less humane
than other men in other directions. It is possible to question
the morality of many forms of sport without accusing the
average country gentleman of exceptional inhumanity, or doubting the sincerity of the indignation with which he sends a
labourer's boy to prison for setting his dog at the domestic cat.
Another good instance of intrinsically bad pleasures is supplied
by drunkenness. The pleasures of drunkenness strike the
healthily constituted mind as intrinsically degrading and disgusting, though it is probable that occasional acts of drunkenness
are physically less injurious than a course of ordinary dinner-
parties; and we should think the man's conduct in getting
drunk worse instead of better if he had carefully taken precautions which would prevent the possibility of his doing
mischief or causing annoyance to others while under the influence
of his premeditated debauch. Of course in all such cases, where we
pronounce a particular kind of pleasure bad, we must remember
what was said in dealing with the distinction between higher
and lower pleasures. The pleasure taken by itself—in abstraction
from the total content of the consciousness enjoying it—cannot
possibly have anything bad about it. In the night all cows are
black; when we have made abstraction of all that differentiates
one pleasure from another, the abstract remainder must obviously
be identical from a moral as from every other point of view.
It is really the getting pleasure from such and such things that

or pains of expectation, imagination, or retrospect—which must themselves
come into the calculus.

H 2

is pronounced bad in such cases. It is good to be pleased, but not at everything, or under all circumstances, or at all costs.

III

Our examination of the traditional Intuitionism has thus brought us round to the same position which we arrived at by a criticism of the traditional hedonistic Utilitarianism. We found that the Utilitarians were right in saying that actions are right or wrong according as they tend to promote or to diminish universal Well-being, but we found that they were wrong in thinking that the Well-being of a rational creature consists simply in pleasure, and pleasure measured quantitatively. We saw reason to believe that the very choice of the right and rational course for its own sake was itself a good and the greatest of all goods, and that it is impossible logically to establish the duty of preferring the general pleasure to our own without recognizing the intrinsic value of such a preference of universal good both for ourselves and for others. We saw further that besides this preference of the truly good in conduct or character there were many other elements in the ideal state of a human soul other than the Altruism of its volitions and the pleasantness of its sensations; and when we faced the question, how we know these things to be good in various degrees, we were obliged to answer ' We know it intuitively or immediately ; we can give no reason why it should be so except that we see it so to be.' So far we were obliged to admit that the Intuitionists were right. We found, however, that the Intuitionists were mistaken in supposing that the moral Reason on which they rightly base our ethical judgements either lays down fixed and exceptionless laws of conduct, or issues isolated, arbitrary, disconnected decrees *pro re nata* without reference to probable results. We saw that fundamentally these moral judgements were judgements of value: they decide what is good, not immediately and directly what is right. Since *prima facie* it is always right to follow the good, these judgements may often in practice condemn this or that kind of conduct so emphatically that we feel sure that no calculation of consequences is likely to prevent our turning the judgement ' this is

good' into a judgement 'this is right': but we saw that theoretically no single judgement of value can form the basis of
a rule of conduct which admits of no exceptions. For moral
Reason bids us not only seek to realize the good but to realize as
much good as possible, and (if I may anticipate a point which
we have not yet established) to distribute that good justly or
impartially between the various persons who may be affected by
our actions. We have seen reason, while accepting the intuitional
view of the imperativeness of duty and the supreme value of
moral goodness, to hold that the law of duty itself requires us to
consider the consequences of our actions and to seek to promote
for all mankind a εὐδαιμονία or Well-being which shall include
in itself all the various elements to which moral Reason ascribes
value; and include them in such wise that each is accorded
its due value and no more than that value. So far we have
decided nothing as to what these elements are except that Virtue
is the most important of them, that culture or knowledge is
another, and that pleasure has a place among them, although
some pleasures are bad and the relative value of others has to be
determined by a non-hedonistic standard.

We have begun our study of Ethics with the question of the
moral criterion. Logically it might seem that we should have
discussed the theory of duty in general before attacking the
question how we find out what particular acts or classes of acts
are duties. I have adopted the former course because it seemed
the best way of showing how impossible it is for the most
thorough-going Utilitarian to avoid admitting that this simple,
unanalysable notion of duty or the reasonable in conduct does
exist, and of illustrating the impossibility of constructing a
logically coherent system of Ethics without the assumption that
the reasonableness of an act is a sufficient ground for its being
done. Before we go further, however, it may be well to dwell
at some greater length upon the nature of this fundamental
idea; and the best way of doing so will be by a brief examination of the classical exposition of it contained in the system of
Immanuel Kant.

CHAPTER V

THE CATEGORICAL IMPERATIVE

I

WE have seen that there is implied in every ethical judgement the idea that there is something which is intrinsically good, which it is reasonable to do, which is right, which ought to be done. These different modes of expression I regard as alternative ways of expressing the same unanalysable idea which is involved in all ethical judgements—as much in the Utilitarian's judgement that he ought to promote the greatest happiness of the greatest number as in the Idealist's judgement 'I ought to aim at the greatest Virtue or Perfection for myself or for others.' If any one questions the existence of this idea of rightness, no argument can do more than remove some of the misconceptions which may prevent his explicitly recognizing what is really implied in the workings of his own mind. To attempt this task will be the object of the present chapter. If any one denies the authority or validity (as distinct from the existence) of this idea of duty, such a vindication of its validity as it is possible to give belongs to Metaphysic. The relation of Morals to Metaphysic is a subject on which something must be said hereafter : and yet all that even Metaphysic can do in this connexion is to develope the extravagant consequences in which a man becomes involved if he denies the validity of his own thought. To deny the deliverances of our own Reason is to deprive ourselves of any ground for believing in anything whatever. To admit that our Reason assures us that there are some things which it is right to do, and yet to ask why we should believe that those things ought to be done, is to ask why we should believe what we see to be true. Sidgwick's account of this idea of duty is so clear and so entirely dissociated from any metaphysical assumptions which to some minds might seem difficult or questionable, that I cannot do better than quote him at length :—

'It seems then that the notion of "ought" or "moral obligation" as used in our common moral judgements, does not merely import (1) that there exists in the mind of the person judging a specific emotion (whether complicated or not by sympathetic representation of similar emotions in other minds); nor (2) that certain rules of conduct are supported by penalties which will follow on their violation (whether such penalties result from the general liking or aversion felt for the conduct prescribed or forbidden, or from some other source). What then, it may be asked, does it import? What definition can we give of "ought," "right," and other terms expressing the same fundamental notion? To this I should answer that the notion which these terms have in common is too elementary to admit of any formal definition.... The notion we have been examining, as it now exists [1] in our thought, cannot be resolved into any more simple notions : it can only be made clearer by determining as precisely as possible its relation to other notions with which it is connected in ordinary thought, especially to those with which it is liable to be confounded.

'In performing this process it is important to note and distinguish two different implications with which the word "ought" is used; in the narrowest ethical sense what we judge "ought to be" done, is always thought capable of being brought about by the volition of any individual to whom the judgement applies. I cannot conceive that I "ought" to do anything which at the same time I judge that I cannot do. In a wider sense, however,—which cannot conveniently be discarded—I sometimes judge that I "ought" to know what a wiser man would know, or feel as a better man would feel, in my place, though I may know that I could not directly produce in myself such knowledge or feeling by any effort of will. In this case the word merely implies an ideal or pattern which I "ought"—in the stricter sense—to seek to imitate as far as possible. And this wider sense seems to be that in which the word is normally used in the precepts of Art generally, and in political judgements: when

---

[1] In the sentences omitted the writer explains that he does not exclude the possibility that the notion has been gradually developed.

I judge that the laws and constitution of my country "ought to be " other than they are, I do not of course imply that my own or any other individual's single volition can directly bring about the change.   In either case, however, I imply that what ought to be is a possible object of knowledge : i. e. that what I judge ought to be must, unless I am in error, be similarly judged by all rational beings who judge truly of the matter [1].

  ' In referring such judgements to the " Reason," I do not mean to prejudge the question whether valid moral judgements are normally attained by a process of reasoning from universal principles or axioms, or by direct intuition of the particular duties of individuals.   It is not uncommonly held that the moral faculty deals primarily with individual cases as they arise, applying directly to each case the general notion of duty, and deciding intuitively what ought to be done by this person in these particular circumstances.   And I admit that on this view the apprehension of moral truth is more analogous to Sense-perception than to Rational Intuition (as commonly understood): and hence the term Moral Sense might seem more appropriate.   But the term Sense suggests a capacity for feelings which may vary from A to B without either being in error, rather than a faculty of cognition: and it appears to me fundamentally important to avoid this suggestion.   I have therefore thought it better to use the term Reason with the explanation above given, to denote the faculty of moral cognition [2].'

  In claiming for the idea of duty not merely existence but authority, we have implied that the recognition that something is our duty supplies us with what we recognize upon reflection as a sufficient motive for doing it, a motive on which it is psychologically possible to act.   The recognition of the thing as right is capable of producing an impulse to the doing of it.   This impulse need not be strong enough to override other motives, nor need we enter here upon the question in what sense (if any) the choice between this motive of duty and other desires

  [1] As a representation of the present writer's views this statement of the unanalysable character of the right must be taken to be qualified by what follows (below, pp. 137, 138) as to the relation between this notion and the wider concept of ' good.'
  [2] *Methods of Ethics*, 6th ed., pp. 31-34.

or impulses must be held to depend upon the undetermined choice of the individual at the moment of action. It is enough for our present purpose that on reflection we recognize that the seeing a thing to be right is a reason for doing it, and that in some men at some moments the desire to do what is reasonable or right as such causes the action to be done.

Once again I may quote Sidgwick :—

'Further, when I speak of the cognition or judgement that "X ought to be done"—in the stricter ethical sense of the term ought—as a "dictate" or "precept" of reason to the persons to whom it relates; I imply that in rational beings as such this cognition gives an impulse or motive to action : though in human beings, of course, this is only one motive among others which are liable to conflict with it, and is not always—perhaps not usually— a predominant motive. In fact, this possible conflict of motives seems to be connoted by the term "dictate" or "imperative"; which describes the relation of Reason to mere inclinations or non-rational impulses by comparing it to the relation between the will of a superior and the wills of his subordinates. This conflict seems also to be implied in the terms "ought," "duty," "moral obligation," as used in ordinary moral discourse : and hence these terms cannot be applied to the actions of rational beings to whom we cannot attribute impulses conflicting with reason. We may, however, say of such beings that their actions are "reasonable," or (in an absolute sense) "right."

'I am aware that some persons will be disposed to answer all the preceding argument by a simple denial that they can find in their consciousness any such unconditional or categorical imperative as I have been trying to exhibit. If this is really the final result of self-examination in any case, there is no more to be said. I, at least, do not know how to impart the notion of moral obligation to any one who is entirely devoid of it. I think, however, that many of those who give this denial only mean to deny that they have any consciousness of moral obligation to actions without reference to their consequences; and would not really deny that they recognise some universal end or ends—whether it be the general happiness, or well-being otherwise understood—as that at which it is ultimately reasonable to aim. . . . But in this

view, as I have before said, the unconditional imperative plainly
comes in as regards the end, which is—explicitly or implicitly—
recognised as an end at which all men "ought" to aim; and it
can hardly be denied that the recognition of an end as ultimately
reasonable involves the recognition of an obligation to do such
acts as most conduce to the end [1].'

These two positions (1) that the rightness of actions is perceived immediately by the Reason, (2) that this rightness ought
to be and is capable of becoming a motive to the Will, are
embodied by Kant in the two famous phrases, the categorical
imperative and the autonomy of the will. Duty is a categorical
imperative because when a thing is seen to be right, we feel
commanded to do it categorically, absolutely, as a means to no
end beyond itself. If duty meant merely 'Do this if you want
to be happy, or to be perfect, or to go to heaven,' it would be
merely a hypothetical imperative: its obligation would depend
on our happening to desire the end to which we saw the action
in question to be a means. As it is, we feel that the rightness
of doing what we see to be our duty is in no way dependent on
the presence or absence of any desire or inclination towards what
is commanded. It is true that the action cannot be done unless
there is an impulse to do what is right or reasonable on our part,
but such a desire may be created by the Reason which recognizes
the rightness: we desire to do the act commanded (in so far as
we do desire it) because it is commanded; we do not judge that
we are commanded to do the act simply because we chance to
desire it [2]. When then we do a thing because it is right, the will

[1] *Methods of Ethics*, 6th ed., pp. 34-5.

[2] It was partly to avoid this implication that Kant refused to speak of a *desire*
to do one's duty, and partly because, as pointed out below, he erroneously
assumed that every desire was a desire for pleasure. He therefore spoke
of the 'interest' of Reason in the Moral Law or 'respect' for the Moral Law
as the subjective motive of right conduct. But in his eagerness to assert
that Reason immediately moves the will, he has at times the appearance of
forgetting (what Aristotle urges against Plato) that bare thought does not
initiate action (διάνοια αὐτὴ οὐδὲν κινεῖ): that moral choice (προαίρεσις) involves
a desire (ὄρεξις) for the end as well as the intellectual perception that an act
will promote the end. As von Hartmann puts it, 'Das Pflichtgefühl ist selbst
eine Neigung' (*Das sittl. Bewusstsein*, p. 254). Moreover, this habit of speaking as if Reason stepped in (so to speak) and worked the human body without

is autonomous: it is a 'law to itself.' Though the man feels commanded to do the act whether he likes it or not, it is nevertheless the man himself—his own Reason, the highest part of his nature—which issues the command or makes the law. Hence in the highest sense he is most free when most completely the slave of duty[1].

The two positions in which we have taken Sidgwick as a peculiarly lucid exponent of Kant are in the Philosopher's own writings associated with a third in which his utilitarian disciple does not follow him. To Kant the performance of duty is not merely 'right'; it is the highest 'good' of the agent. Here we have already found reason to believe that Kant is right, and can only refer the sceptic to the testimony of his own consciousness. If he denies that he finds in his own consciousness the judgement 'goodness of conduct possesses a higher worth than anything else in the world,' the only way to argue with him would be to try to show that his own actions, or at least his judgements of himself and other men, really imply that he thinks so; that his approval of himself when he does right and disapproval when he does wrong are quite inexplicable upon the assumption that bad conduct is merely conduct which is irrational from the point of view of Society though wholly rational from his own private point of view. For the man who believes it, the judgement 'Morality is good and the greatest of goods' or 'the good will is the most important element in the good' is as much a simple and ultimate deliverance of the moral consciousness as the judgement 'It is right to promote the general good.'

the intervention of any subjective motive, involved him in much unnecessarily mysterious language about the Autonomy of the Will. When Kant said that the will is a 'law to itself' he meant that in right action Reason is a law to the will; in fact, according to Kant, the will is Reason, at least when the will is rightly directed. Wrong acts, it would appear, can only be said to be willed, and so to be free, according to Kant, in so far as Reason might have intervened to stop them and did not. But the Psychology of wrong action is a subject on which Kant is as vague as he is unsatisfactory.

[1] No doubt in Kant's own view this use of the term 'free' (in which it can only be applied to right acts) implies also the opposite of 'determined' or 'necessitated' (see below, Book III, ch. iii, § i). The double sense in which Kant used the term 'free' is very clearly pointed out by Prof. Sidgwick, *Methods of Ethics*, Book I, ch. v and Appendix.

II

So far we may regard Kant as having laid down in the most impressive way the principles which must form the basis of every constructive ethical system [1].   But in Kant's own view these positions are associated with two other doctrines which require further examination.   In the first place he assumed that out of this bare idea of a categorical imperative, without any appeal to experience, he could extract a moral criterion, i.e. that he could ascertain what is the actual content of the Moral Law, what in detail it is right to do.   Secondly, he assumed that, so far as an act is not determined by pure respect for the Moral Law, it possesses no moral value whatever.   Let us examine each of these positions in turn.

The value of Kant's work consisted very largely in supplying a metaphysical basis for Ethics.   So long as it is assumed that all our ordinary knowledge of matters of fact comes from experience of an 'external world,' there is always a sort of suspicion that any kind of knowledge which cannot point to such an origin must be in some sense unsubstantial or delusive.   The Critique of Pure Reason demonstrates that in all our knowledge there is an element which is not derived from experience: all knowledge implies 'forms of perception' and 'forms of understanding' which are *a priori*, part of the constitution of the mind itself, not supplied to it from without.   The matter of sensation is from without, but sense by itself is not thought.   I cannot judge of the size and distance of particular objects without a matter supplied by sensible perception: but I could not build up these data into the conception of a square table of a certain size unless I had already notions of space, of spacial and causal relations, of

<hr/>

[1] Kant was no doubt wrong in supposing that all other systems but his own were based upon 'heteronomy of the Will.'   This is not true of Plato and Aristotle (to say nothing of other ancient writers) whom Kant's education had not qualified him to understand, nor of the Cambridge Platonists and other English Rationalists of whom he appears to have known little or nothing.   It is not true of them unless the doctrine of the categorical imperative is distorted into the precept 'Do your duty without considering whether what you are doing is good for any one or not,' and in that sense the idea of Autonomy is, as contended below, indefensible and absurd

substance and accident and the like which do not come from experience [1]. In all actual knowledge there must be a matter supplied by experience and a formal element which is *a priori*. But in Morality—in the idea of duty—we are presented with a form which needs no filling up from experience, a form which is (so to speak) its own content, since it is an immediate datum of consciousness that this *a priori* concept of duty can supply a motive to the will. Now in this position a very important truth is (as is almost universally admitted by the most Kantian of modern Moralists) confused with a very serious error. That no experience can prove an act to be right, that no accumulation of knowledge as to what *is* can possibly give us an *ought*, is a truth which can only be denied by asserting that there is no meaning in duty or in Morality. Experience of the past may tell us what has been or what will be: it cannot possibly tell us what ought to be. That which ought to be is *ex vi termini* something which as yet is not and which may conceivably never be. In that sense our moral judgements are undoubtedly *a priori* or independent of experience. But that without any appeal to experience we can get at the content as well as the form of the moral law, can easily be shown to be a pure delusion. Let us see how Kant made the attempt.

The rules of action which the categorical imperative is supposed to give us are the following:—

(1) 'So act as if the law of thine action were to become by thy will law universal.'

(2) 'Regard humanity whether in thine own person or in that of any one else always as an end and never as a means only.'

(3) 'Act as a member of a kingdom of ends [2].'

---

[1] This is a very inadequate and popular statement, nor do I mean to assent to Kant's idea of a form derived from the mind and a matter derived from some source outside the mind. I have merely endeavoured to explain for the benefit of any one to whom it is unfamiliar Kant's use of the terms 'form' and 'matter' so far as is necessary for the comprehension of his ethical position.

[2] Kant nowhere explains the relation in which the three rules are supposed to stand towards one another, nor does he ever bring them into close contact with one another; but in different parts of his ethical writings each one of them is treated as the fundamental principle of Morality. In practice

Let us examine the first of these rules—'Act as if the law of thy action were to become by thy will law universal.' Now it is quite true that it does follow from the very idea of there being something which it is right to do irrespectively of inclination that this course must, in the same circumstances, be binding upon every one else. And therefore in a sense it is true that no action can be really a moral rule the principle of which could not be universalized. It is good practical advice to urge that when we have to pronounce upon the morality of a proposed act we should ask ourselves whether it represents a principle which we should think it rational to will as a universal rule of conduct. But this is by itself a merely negative test. It gives us no definite information until we have made up our minds as to what it is which makes conduct rational or irrational. We can, indeed, with a little ingenuity extract from it the all-important axioms of Benevolence and Equity: for, if there is something which it is intrinsically right to do, what is right for me would be right for any one else in the same circumstances [1]: hence it must be right for me to treat every other man as it would be right for him to treat me under similar circumstances [2]. If my good is recognized as something which it is intrinsically right for others to promote, the good of each other individual must also be treated as an end the promotion of which I must look upon as incumbent upon me: hence I am bound to promote the greatest good of humanity collectively (the maxim of rational Benevolence), and to treat each individual's good as of equal value with the good of every other (the maxim of Equity). But these rules by themselves will give us no practical guidance till we know what that good is which ought to be promoted by every rational being for every other.

The Kantian maxim, properly interpreted, thus occupies in

he uses one or the other of them just as may be most convenient for the purpose of proving the particular duty with which he is dealing.

[1] This principle seems to me to require some qualification (see below, p. 116 *note*); and it is obvious that we have not really got this rule out of the form, for without knowing what sort of being the 'other' is, and what 'good' he is capable of, we cannot say what that good is worth.

[2] It is true that we are here assuming, what Kant sometimes ignores— that right conduct must mean the promotion of some end which is intrinsically good.

Ethics the same position which the law of contradiction holds in
Logic[1].   The law of contradiction is a negative test of truth : it
tells us that two judgements which contradict one another cannot
both be true, but as to which judgements in particular are true, it
will give us no information : only, when I know that judgement A
is true, it will tell me that judgement B, being inconsistent therewith, cannot also be true.   In the same way the Kantian rule
tells us that a genuine ultimate rule of conduct must not only be
logically consistent with itself, but also be such as that all its
prescriptions shall be consistent with all other ethical rules.   The
supreme ethical precept must consist of an harmonious and self-
consistent system of precepts.   It need hardly be said that this
by itself is a most important negative test of ethical truth.   It
gives us the principle upon which alone inference or reasoning
(as distinct from immediate judgements of Reason) is possible in
Ethics.   The fact that something is a part of the true ethical
rule supplies, if we assume this principle to be self-evident,
a demonstrative proof that some precept inconsistent with it
cannot be a part of it[2].   But as to what rule of action in
particular is reasonable, it gives us no information whatever.
If we interpret the rule of acting on a principle fit for law
universal as equivalent to Sidgwick's three ethical axioms—of

---

[1] This interpretation of Kant is well insisted on by Sigwart (*Logic*, E. T.,
ii. p. 543 seq.).   Sigwart would call the principle in question a postulate :
I should venture to regard it as both a postulate and an axiom.   It ought
not to be denied by any one who is not prepared to question the validity of
all thinking.   Mr. Bradley is so far consistent that he accuses thought as
well as Morality of internal inconsistency.   Some of his followers (in Ethics)
have been less logical.   Mr. Bradley is only following out his own principle
to its logical conclusion when, in his frequent polemics against Casuistry,
he denies apparently the possibility of any inference whatever in the ethical
sphere (see below, Bk. III, ch. vi).   It is enough for our present purpose to
insist that the self-evident axioms of Ethics and the inferences based upon
them have as much validity as any other parts of our thinking.

[2] It will be observed that I am speaking of elements in the supreme
ethical *rule*, not elements of the *end*.   The end itself must not contain
intrinsically incompatible elements, but in particular circumstances elements of the end are often incompatible : but the ethical rule says 'in
that case promote the good which is of most intrinsic value.'   Even *the* good
may, and obviously does, contain elements which cannot all be enjoyed by
the same persons.

Benevolence, Equity and Prudence—we shall get rules for the promotion and distribution of the good or ultimate end, but no information as to what particular things are good: and, until we know that, we cannot get any principles from which we can deduce the right course of conduct in any one single case. If with Sidgwick (who could quote much in Kant himself to support this interpretation) we made 'good' in this connexion equivalent to 'pleasure,' and interpreted our rule to mean 'promote universal pleasure and distribute it equally,' we should obviously have gone beyond the mere *a priori* formal rule. We should have appealed to experience—an appeal which our categorical imperative was intended by Kant to exclude. The judgement 'Happiness ought to be promoted' is no doubt in a sense *a priori*, but not in the sense that no information derived from experience is necessary to its being made. Kant himself admits that the concept of happiness is of empirical origin [1]. Experience must tell us what happiness is before we can judge happiness to be good. Still more obviously experience is wanted to tell us what particular goods constitute happiness, or what are the means to procure those goods. It might be thought that Kant could get a content for the Moral Law by holding that the true good of man is simply Morality, a concept which might be said to be of purely *a priori* origin, and that we should find out what particular actions are right by considering what actions would promote universal Morality. But here again, if the concept of the end is in a sense purely *a priori*, experience is needed to tell us the means; and Kant has incapacitated himself from adopting this solution of the problem by the exaggerated Libertarianism which made him pronounce an action due to another's influence to be not truly 'free,' and therefore without moral value [2]. Consequently, he pronounced that it was im-

[1] 'All the elements which belong to the notion of happiness are altogether empirical, i.e. they must be borrowed from experience' (*Grundlegung zur Met. d. Sitten*, § 2, translated by Abbot in Kant's *Theory of Ethics*, 4th ed., 1889, p. 35).

[2] *Metaph. Anfangsgründe d. Tugendlehre*, Einleitung, § iv seq. (Abbot, p. 296). But this is qualified (hardly consistently) by the admission of a negative duty towards the moral well-being of others, i.e. not to create temptations (Abbot. p. 304).

possible for one man to make another's moral good his end. Hence if Virtue is by itself to constitute the end, it must be the man's own virtue that he must treat as his end. To tell a man to make his own virtue an end will not tell him what to do until he knows what acts it is virtuous to perform, and as to this the formula that what is right for him is right for others will give him no information whatever. How then did Kant attempt to extract out of the bare form of the Moral Law a knowledge of the particular actions which are right or wrong?

It is impossible to maintain that Kant gives a clear and consistent meaning to his own dictum. Sometimes the irrationality of willing the universal adoption of the immoral course appears to turn simply upon the fact that the social consequences to which the adoption of such a will would lead are consequences which no rational man could regard as good. We cannot will universal promise-breaking because in that case no promises would be made, and at times the irrationality of willing such a consequence seems to turn upon its injurious social effects. Still more clearly when Kant pronounces that we cannot rationally will the non-development of our faculties, the irrationality of such a course is made to depend simply upon the fact that the rational man actually regards this non-development as bad and their development as good[1]. Here the appeal to

---

[1] 'A third' [the first two cases are suicide and breach of promise] 'finds in himself a talent which with the help of some culture might make him a useful man in many respects. But he finds himself in comfortable circumstances, and prefers to indulge in pleasure rather than to take pains in enlarging and improving his happy natural capacities. He asks, however, whether his maxim of neglect of his natural gifts, besides agreeing with his inclination to indulgence, agrees also with what is called duty. He sees then that a system of nature could indeed subsist with such a universal law although men (like the South Sea islanders) should let their talents rust, and resolve to devote their lives merely to idleness, amusement, and propagation of their species—in a word, to enjoyment; but he cannot possibly *will* that this should be a universal law of nature, or be implanted in us as such by a natural instinct. For, as a rational being, he necessarily wills that his faculties be developed, since they serve him, and have been given him, for all sorts of possible purposes ' (*Grundlegung*, § 4 : Abbot, p. 40). I pass over the objections (1) that elsewhere the development of faculties is not regarded by Kant as an ultimate good, the only ultimate goods being Virtue and Happiness; (2) that Kant relies upon teleological assumptions

consequences which can only be known by experience is scarcely disguised: the *a priori* judgement relates simply to the goodness or badness of the end.   But Kant was able to conceal from himself the necessity of this appeal to experience, because in certain carefully selected instances he was able to point to the appearance of *internal* contradiction in the reverse of the accepted rule[1].   We cannot rationally will that men shall break their promises, because in that case no promises would be made; and we cannot rationally will something to be done which will make it impossible to observe the very rule which we will.   In a society in which there were no promises, it would no longer be possible to observe our proposed rule of universal promise-breaking; if no promises are made, none can be broken.   Now even here it is evident that Kant falls back upon his experience of human nature to tell him what will be the consequences of his act: but still he might maintain that, given this much experience, the contradiction is self-evident.   Yet it is easy to show that absence of contradiction, in this sense, would be a very irrational test of conduct.   Kant himself appears to concede that there would be no internal contradiction in willing that all men should leave their faculties undeveloped.   Nor would there be any internal contradiction in adopting as our rule of action the promotion of universal misery, or at least of the maximum of misery which should be consistent with the continued survival of the human race.   That is, indeed, according to some Pessimists, precisely the end which is actually realized in the world as we know it.

And, just as we hold many acts to be wrong which involve no internal contradiction, so there are many things which we pronounce right in spite of such contradiction.   Kant tells us that we cannot rationally will universal promise-breaking, because the universal adoption of such a rule would lead to a state of things in which the rule 'Break your promises' could no longer be observed.   We must not commit suicide, because if every

---

to which he was not entitled: he had no right (from his point of view) to assume that our faculties were 'given' us for any reason whatever.

[1] It is true that even in the selected cases the contradiction is not really internal.   It is the actual structure of human society which makes the suggested rule unworkable.

one did so, there would soon be nobody left to practise the
virtue of suicide. Then are we, it may be asked, to deny that
Philanthropy is a duty because the universal practice of
a reasonable Philanthropy would lead to a state of things in
which there would be no poor upon whom to practise that virtue?
Shall we refuse to bless the peacemaker, because if every one
shared his disposition, there would be no quarrels to adjust?
And then, again, how unreasonable is the alternative with which
we are presented—either to will universal suicide and universal
lying, or to forbid each of these practices in any circumstances
whatever! As reasonably might we pronounce Kant's own
celibacy a crime because universal celibacy would rapidly
extinguish the human race and (consequently) the practice of
celibacy.

It is true that the emergence of an internal contradiction (in
Kant's sense) in any suggested moral rule does show that we
have not reached an *ultimate* principle of conduct. We can,
indeed, put such rules as 'Give to the poor' into a universal
form by making them hypothetical: 'So long as there are any
poor, relieve them;' but so might we say, 'So long as there are
any human beings alive, let them commit suicide.' Still, the
fact that the rule is only applicable to a particular set of circumstances does show that we have not reached an *ultimate*
principle. The rule, 'Be charitably disposed,' may, indeed, be
universally willed: but then Kant's object in applying his test
of fitness for law universal is to supply a guide for the details
of outward conduct, not for mere dispositions and intentions,
and this purpose is not served by such generalities as these.
And even in this case there is really a reference to the physical
constitution of human beings which is known to us only from
experience. We might interpret charity to mean 'a disposition
to promote good,' but the absence of internal contradiction will
not tell us what good is. Moreover, as has already been pointed
out, although an ultimate moral principle must be free from
internal contradiction, it is impossible to deny that many immoral principles might very well be universalized without leading
to any such contradiction. The structure of the Universe and of
human nature is quite as consistent with the non-development

as with the development of human faculties. And if the criterion is not of universal application, how are we to know when to apply it, and when not?

The fact is that Kant appears to have confused two distinct senses of the term 'categorical.' When he sets forth that it is of the essence of every moral law to be categorical, he means that it must admit of no exception due to the subjective disinclination of the individual for the course of action which it prescribes. We must not say, ' I admit Temperance or Veracity to be right in a general way: only I personally happen to have such a rooted antipathy to Temperance or Veracity, or whatever it be, that I must regard myself as an exception to the general rule.' To talk in that way no doubt destroys the very nature of a Moral Law. ' It is an essential characteristic of the Moral Law that whatever is right for me must be right for every man in precisely the same circumstances [1]. But when Kant tries to make out this mere unconditionality of a rule an absolute test of its reasonableness, he has to assume that the categorical character of an imperative excludes the possibility of an exception based not on the mere subjective disinclination of the individual, but on the nature of the case. He does not see that the rule 'Do this except in such and such circumstances' is just as 'categorical' and just as little 'hypothetical' as the rule 'Do this under all circumstances whatever,' so long as the exceptions are recognized as no less universal in their application, no less based upon the reason and nature of things, than the original rule. Kant in fact confuses the inclusion of an exception *in* a moral rule with the admission of an exception *to* a moral rule. He does not recognize that the difference between a rule with an exception and a grammatically categorical rule is often a purely verbal one. The precept 'Do no murder' admits of no exceptions, because 'murder' means 'killing except in such and such circumstances.' The rule 'Thou shalt not kill' has exceptions. So the rule 'Lie not' could be represented as equally

---

[1] That we can only hold this principle by including in the 'circumstances' the man's own character and disposition (other than an indisposition to perform what has once been proved to be his duty), I have contended below in the chapter on 'Vocation' (vol. ii, ch. iv).

'categorical' if there were as clear a usage in favour of the proposition that a legitimate untruth is no lie, as there is in favour of the proposition that in certain circumstances killing is no murder. We are obliged sometimes to express a moral rule in the form of a general command with an exception simply because the enumeration of the circumstances to which the rule is inapplicable is shorter and more convenient than an exhaustive enumeration of all the cases to which it is applicable. And it is clear that every rule, however general, implies some set of circumstances in which alone it is capable of being applied. The duty of not committing adultery is only applicable to the relations between two persons of whom one at least has a lawful spouse, and it is obvious that this term 'lawful' postulates a large number of highly complicated social arrangements, about which there is by no means a universal consensus, and which the most enthusiastic Kantian could hardly attempt to determine on any *a priori* principle. Either, then, we must say that every possible rule really involves a hypothesis under which alone it is applicable; or we may say that every moral law excludes all exception if only you put it into a sufficiently general, and a sufficiently internal, form. 'Kill not' has exceptions: 'Thou shalt love thy neighbour as thyself' (properly understood) has none [1]. But, in whichever way it is put, it is plain that we can get no criterion of Morality out of the presence or absence of exceptions. 'Kill not' has exceptions, and yet (subject to the exceptions) is accounted a good moral principle. On the other hand, 'Thou shalt love thy friend and hate thine enemy' does not appeal to us as the highest morality, in spite of its being quite as categorical as the Christian precept.

Kant's attempt to extract an ethical criterion out of the bare form of the Moral Law is the more remarkable, because he did not hold (as he is sometimes supposed to do) that there is no other rational end of action except the bare performance of duty.

---

[1] 'The Moral Law, we may say, has to be expressed in the form, "Be this," not in the form, "Do this." The possibility of expressing any rule in this form may be regarded as deciding whether it can or cannot have a distinctively moral character. Christianity gave prominence to the doctrine that the true moral law says "hate not," instead of "kill not"' (Leslie Stephen, *Science of Ethics*, 1882, p. 155).

Had he held that view, it would have become fairly impossible
for him even to have persuaded himself that he had discovered
in the bare form of the law any content for the idea of duty [1].
If a man is to perform his duty, he must know what that duty
is; and the mere knowledge that, when he has discovered what
his duty is, it is a thing categorically commanded does not help
to find out what it is. It is impossible, in short, to show the
rationality of one course of action rather than another until we
have admitted that something else besides the performance of
duty—some objective good other than the state of the will—
is a rational end of action or possesses value [2]. And Kant did
admit that there is such another rational end of action—which

---

[1] Dr. Lipps (*Die ethischen Grundfragen*, 1899, p. 158 seq.) has attempted to
clear Kant of the imputation that his categorical imperative has no content
by suggesting that the content is supplied by all our natural desires and inclinations: the moral law simply prescribes the way and extent to which they
should be indulged. I believe that this is very largely the explanation of
Kant's own view of the matter, but it is open to the objection that it allows
all actual tendencies of human nature ('aller möglichen menschlichen
Zwecke') to be indulged in proportion to their actual strength, except in so
far as their indulgence interferes with the indulgence of other such tendencies in ourselves and in other individuals. It is obvious that we should
have to appeal to experience to know what is the relative strength of these
tendencies; and, after all, it supplies us with a very unsatisfactory test of
their relative value. If only the tendency to opium-smoking were sufficiently
strong in a whole community, the Kantian principle (as interpreted by
Dr. Lipps) would make universal opium-smoking a categorical imperative.

[2] Lotze, the last man in the world to sanction vulgar Hedonism, has said:
'There is nothing at all in the world, which would have any value until it
has produced some pleasure in some being or other capable of enjoyment.
Everything antecedent to this is naught but an indifferent kind of fact, to
which a value of its own can be ascribed only in an anticipatory way, and
with reference to some pleasure that is to originate from it' (*Practical
Philosophy*, Eng. Trans. by Ladd, p. 19). I believe this statement might
be defended, since (a) pleasure is an element in all ultimate good. (b) Lotze
has not said that the value lies exclusively in the pleasure abstracted from
the other elements of consciousness, or that it is to be measured by the
amount of that pleasure. But his statement seems to me liable to misunderstanding. On the other hand, it is surprising to find Lotze admitting
that 'the effort to hold fast pleasure, or to regain it, and to avoid pain, are
the only springs of all practical activity' (*Microcosmus*, E. T., i. p. 688), but
here again the taint of Hedonism is removed by a recognition of differences
in the quality of the pleasure.

possesses worth, not indeed 'absolutely and unconditionally,' but
on one condition—that it does not interfere with Virtue. And
that other end is Happiness. From this position it would seem
logically to follow that the true criterion would be the tendency
of an action to promote for all mankind Happiness in so far as
is compatible with Virtue. This would supply us with a quite
intelligible and workable view of the moral criterion, and it
would correspond roughly with the actual deliverances of the
moral consciousness. That it is an inadequate view of the
ultimate end of human life, I have already attempted to show ;
and its deficiencies will be further illustrated when we pass on
to the other mistaken assumption, from which I am anxious to
dissociate Kant's fundamental doctrine of a categorical imperative.

III

That duty should be done for duty's sake we have seen to be
really implied in the very notion of there being such a thing as
duty. But it does not follow that the desire to do one's duty
must always be the sole and exclusive motive of right conduct,
or that conduct not consciously inspired by respect for the Moral
Law as such must possess no moral value at all. Yet such was
the assumption of Kant himself. To Kant the most unselfish [1]
devotion to wife or child, the most ardent patriotism, the most
comprehensive philanthropy, possessed no more moral value than
the purest avarice or the most unmitigated selfishness. Unless
the man loves, or rather behaves as though he loved (since love,
he holds, cannot be commanded) wife, or country, or humanity
simply from an actual, conscious respect for the Moral Law, his
conduct is worthless—not necessarily wrong (for it is not a crime
to promote one's own happiness when duty does not forbid), but
entirely without moral value. The will that wills from pure
love of the brethren is morally on a level with the will that
wills from pure love of self. It is of no more value than the

---

[1] I speak popularly : to Kant there could be no such thing as an
'unselfish' love of anything except duty, and even that could only be
'respected,' not 'loved.' To Kant (in his stricter moments), as to Bentham,
Benevolence not inspired by pure sense of duty was merely a love of
benevolent pleasure.

behaviour of an animal. Such is the revolting and inhuman Stoicism to which Kant's ideal logically leads. It is, as Schopenhauer puts it, the 'apotheosis of lovelessness, the exact opposite, as it is, of the Christian doctrine of Morals[1].' In well-known lines the poet Schiller makes the disciple of Kant complain:

Gladly, I serve my friends, but alas I do it with pleasure.
Hence I am plagued with the doubt that I am not a virtuous person:

in reply to which the answer given is:

Sure, your only resource is to try to despise them entirely,
And then with aversion to do what your duty enjoins you[2].

Nor can it be alleged that Kant has any desire to conceal this result. He holds *ex professo* that all desire is bad. 'The inclinations themselves being sources of want, are so far from having an absolute worth for which they should be desired, that on the contrary it must be the universal wish of every rational being to be wholly free from them[3].' We might ask in what, according to Kant, happiness is to consist? Happiness, as we know it, arises entirely from the satisfaction of desires[4], and happiness is admitted to be a rational end of action; how then can the desires be consistently treated as a mere encumbrance which the rational man would fain be without? But it is enough to point out the utter discrepancy between the Kantian dogma and the strongest moral convictions of mankind. The 'common-sense' philosophy of Bishop Butler is here a far better exponent of the moral consciousness. Insisting as strongly as Kant upon the claims of Conscience, he yet recognizes that Conscience does not prescribe this total suppression of all other 'passions, propensions, or affections.' It rather pronounces that some of the desires ought to be encouraged, some suppressed, others moderated or controlled, and all subordinated to Benevolence and self-love—the two great rational impulses which make for the good of ourselves and our fellow men[5]. And in

---

[1] *Ueber die Grundlage der Moral*, § 6 (*The Basis of Morality*, trans. by A. B. Bullock, 1903, p. 49). He goes on to call it a piece of 'stupid moral pedantry' (*taktlosen moralischen Pedantismus*).

[2] From *Die Philosophen*.   [3] *Grundlegung*, § 2 (Abbot, p. 46).

[4] Including the desire of pleasure.

[5] I do not mean to accept this as a fully adequate account of the matter,

this teaching Butler was only developing the principles of Aristotle who (amid many retrogressions) advanced beyond Plato just by his recognition of the fact that desire is as essential an element of human nature as Reason; that the raw material (so to speak) of the sublimest virtues and of the coarsest vices is the same, that natural impulses are good or evil just according as they are or are not controlled by the ideals which Reason sets up [1]. Granted fully that an act may be done from the bare sense of duty, from a desire which is created solely by our conviction that a certain course is intrinsically right or reasonable, this is not in most cases an adequate analysis of a good man's motives. In most of his acts the good man is doing something towards which he *has* some inclination apart from the consideration that it is his duty. He works for wife and children because he loves them: he speaks the truth because he feels an instinctive repulsion for a lie: he relieves suffering because 'he cannot bear' to see another man in pain. It is rather in the selection of the right one from among the many impulses by which his will is from time to time solicited, and in the reinforcement of it when it is absolutely or relatively too weak, that the 'sense of duty' need come into play [2]. It is only perhaps at rare crises in the moral life, when duty calls for some great sacrifice or commands resistance to some great temptation, that the 'sense of duty' becomes the one all-sufficient motive present to the consciousness. It is no doubt eminently desirable that the sense of duty should be always present in the background or, as the Psychologists have called it, the 'fringe' of consciousness [3]; that Reason should be (so to speak) a consenting party to all our actions, however strongly prompted by natural impulses, and be ready to inhibit even the noblest and most generous of them when it threatens to oppose

unless the idea of Benevolence and that of self-love have been understood in a non-hedonistic sense.

[1] Cf. below, p. 153 *sq.*

[2] Dr. Martineau's Ethics have the merit of developing this idea : but he exaggerates when he denies that the love of duty or desire 'to do what is right and reasonable as such,' can ever be a 'spring of action' at all (*Types of Ethical Theory*, 3rd ed., ii. p. 279 *sq.*).

[3] Cf. James, *Psychology*, i. 258 *sq.*, 471 *sq.*, &c.

itself to duty's call. But, even when this is not the case, even when in a particular act or in the general tenour of a man's life conscious and deliberate respect for the Moral Law as such cannot be said to occupy this paramount and predominant position, we do not in fact regard the act or the character of such a man as entirely destitute of moral value. We may regard his defective sense of duty as a moral defect or shortcoming, but we do not regard him as on a level with the selfish pleasure-seeker. It would be a violent perversion of psychological fact to represent that every man who works hard and resists temptations to self-indulgence from love for his wife and children, or from a zeal for his profession, is inspired by pure respect for the abstract Moral Law; it would be a perversion of moral fact (attested in the only way in which moral fact can be attested, by the evidence of consciousness) to say that such conduct is morally worthless [1]. To do so would involve the denial of moral value not only to much of the normally good conduct of average civilized men, and to all the more elementary morality of children or savages (to whom the idea of a Moral Law or an abstract 'duty' can hardly be said to have occurred), but also to some of the very noblest acts of generous but one-sided and imperfect characters.

The source of Kant's ethical mistake must be sought in his defective Psychology. He assumed, as completely as Hobbes or Locke, that the motive of every action is pleasure except in one case. Reason had, he thought, the power of arbitrarily interposing, and acting directly upon the man's will, by laying upon him a categorical command to do this or abstain from that: but, except when and in so far as the man was influenced by pure respect for such injunctions, his will was always under the influence of pleasure and pain. Apart from the power of interposition accorded to this *deus ex machina*, the categorical

---

[1] It would perhaps be consistent with Kantian principles to say that the act possesses *some* moral value because there is *some* respect for the moral law; but this explanation does not really express the facts. The man is possibly not thinking of the Moral Law *as such* at all (I have explained below that he may nevertheless recognize that there is something intrinsically good in his love for wife and children), and yet we do recognize that the disinterested affection by itself gives the act moral value.

imperative, Kant was a psychological Hedonist. Moreover, he assumed that an action determined by self-interest was completely 'natural,' that the motives of the calculating pleasure-seeker were the same in kind as the mere animal impulses of the savage or even the beast. He would probably have explained the behaviour of animals as due to the pursuit of pleasure. He did not recognize the high degree of abstraction, the high intellectual and moral development, which is implied in the deliberate pursuit of so ideal an object as 'maximum pleasure' or 'happiness' in general. Regarding all desire as desire for pleasure, and the desire of pleasure as merely 'natural,' he was obviously unable to recognize any difference in moral value between one kind of desire and another. Benevolence and malevolence were simply different forms of pleasure-seeking. From the point of view which we have adopted we are able to recognize that the value of the desire depends upon the nature of the objects desired. We can pronounce, and as a matter of fact the moral consciousness does pronounce, that devotion to the family or the tribe is a higher and nobler motive of action than devotion to one's own good, love of knowledge better than love of sensual indulgence, indignation against cruelty or injustice better than resentment provoked by jealousy. We may, therefore, ascribe moral value to a man's acts in proportion as they are inspired by a desire of objects which Reason pronounces intrinsically good, although the man may not pursue them consciously because Reason pronounces those objects to be good—still less because Reason pronounces the acts to be right apart from their tendency to gratify a desire for the objects. In proportion as the moral consciousness is developed, or at all events in proportion as the man's intellectual development allows his morality to become self-conscious and reflective, the intrinsic value of the objects which he pursues is recognized with increasing distinctness and abstractness; and this recognition brings with it reinforcement of the higher impulse as against the competing desires which might otherwise take its place. Some degree of this consciousness of value is no doubt necessary to make it a motive which can fairly be described as a higher desire at all. The most rudimentary family affection implies a certain consciousness (wholly unanalysed no doubt) of the claims or rights or intrinsic worth of other persons, and of the consequent superiority of such an impulse to mere sensual desire—a consciousness which is not present in the maternal impulses of the lower animals, in which naturalistic writers have seen realized their highest ideal of conduct.   But even in highly developed moral natures, and in some of the highest actions of such natures, it is often impossible to discover the conscious presence in any high degree of respect for the abstract idea of duty or the Moral Law as such. The philanthropist is carried away by an enthusiasm of humanity which does not stop to ask whether to relieve suffering or to fight against oppression is or is not contained in the categorical imperative of Reason.   And such zeal for the things contained in the law we certainly pronounce morally good, however little conscious reference there may be to the law which contains them.

IV

And from this point of view the thought may occur to us : ' if good conduct implies only desire for objects which Reason can recognize as good, why do we need the " sense of duty " or the categorical imperative at all ? '   May we not say with Aristotle that a man is not really good unless he likes the things that another may recognize as constituting his duty, or even go beyond Aristotle (who did insist that in developed Morality there should be a conscious recognition that the things desired were good), and say ' It is nobler to be so fired by the thought of tyranny and injustice and suffering, so to feel others' wrongs as though they were one's own, that the question never arises at all whether it is a duty to fight against them, or even whether it be καλὸν to do so?   Would it not show a positive defect in the man's character if he should decline to make a sacrifice which the good of his family demanded till he had calmly reflected that it was a dutiful or a beautiful thing for him to do ?   Is it not better to be socially useful because one loves one's neighbours as oneself than to regard them with indifference, and yet to feed or serve them only because it is one's duty ? '

We are here in the presence of something like an antinomy.

On the one hand, it does seem nobler to love the things contained in the law than to do good things unwillingly because we feel bound to obey the law as such. On the other hand, it seems difficult to admit that there can be any nobler motive than devotion to duty as such, or that there can be a perfect character, or even a perfect act, in the inspiration of which such devotion has no place.

The solution of our difficulty seems to lie in a consideration which we have hitherto neglected. It is quite true that an action may be good which is done from the love of some good object. The poor man who shares his scanty dinner with a still poorer friend has certainly done an act possessing moral worth. The scholar who ' scorns delights, and lives laborious days ' from sheer love of Learning is not to be treated as on a level with the mere sensualist because he is not habitually inspired by reflection on the duty of research, or even because he may be seriously wanting in devotion to many kinds of social good. But love of any particular good object is always liable to interfere with the promotion of some other, and, it may be, more important good. Love of Learning is good, but the scholar in whom that passion extinguishes all others may become selfish and inhuman, if all social impulses are stifled in its pursuit. Nero's love of Art was a redeeming feature in his character, but the fact (if it be a fact) that he ' fiddled while Rome was burning ' was rather an aggravation than an extenuation of his callous indifference to human suffering. Enthusiasm for some particular cause is good, if the cause be a righteous one; but the root of all fanaticism lies in a devotion to some single good which extinguishes all scruple or respect for objects the observance of which is no less essential to human Well-being than Temperance or the influence of the Church or even the conversion of sinners. Unselfish affection or loyalty to particular persons or societies is good; but the morality of the man who surrenders himself to it without restraint may degenerate into mere honour among thieves. Family affection may steel the heart against the claims of a wider humanity. Even a genuine Patriotism may produce absolute blindness to the plainest dictates of Humanity or international Justice. And so on. Now duty means, as we have seen, precisely devotion to the various

10

kinds of good in proportion to their relative value and importance. No one then can be trusted at all times and in all circumstances to attribute to each good precisely its proper degree of worth in whom there is not strong devotion to that supreme good in which all others are summed up. It is not necessary that a man should make the sense of duty the sole motive of all his conduct, provided it is always ready to inhibit an action the moment he sees any reason for believing that it is contrary to his duty. The conscientious man will not seek actually to substitute the sense of duty for other motives of conduct, because he will recognize that many of the commonplace actions of life are better performed from some other impulse, and that the cultivation of altruistic or ideal impulses is actually a part of that ideal of human character which duty bids him promote in himself as in others. He will eat his breakfast from force of habit or because he is hungry; the sense of duty will only be ready, in the background of consciousness, so to speak [1], to stimulate him when appetite fails or to inhibit him when some call of duty demands the suspension or omission of that meal on a particular morning. He will select things to eat and drink because he likes them, provided that he is always ready to modify his choice when there is reason to believe that what he likes is unwholesome or too expensive. He will labour for the good of his family because he cares about it as much or more than he does for his own good, but the sense of duty will always be ready to remind him of the claims of the workmen or the

---

[1] There is considerable ethical importance in the modern Psychologist's recognition that we do not think of one thing or 'idea' at a time, but that while the centre of consciousness may be occupied by some idea, there is a 'fringe' of other ideas present with various degrees of clearness and distinctness (like the object lying on the outside of the fringe of vision, e. g. persons of whose presence we are conscious without actually looking at them sufficiently to know who they are). An idea present in the 'fringe' of consciousness can always become the central object of the mental vision when occasion arises for it. The good man will always have the sense of duty somewhere in the fringe of his consciousness. This view is not inconsistent with the doctrine strongly insisted on by many Psychologists that we can only *attend* to one 'object' at a time; but at all events such an 'object' may include many 'ideas' (in James's sense) which may be the object of different degrees and kinds of attention.

customers whom his methods of business may prejudice. He will throw himself into the work of a profession, because he likes it, because he is ambitious of success, recognition, opportunities of more interesting or more important work and the like; but he will be ready to listen to the faintest whisper of a suspicion arising in his mind that the path of ambition and the path of real social duty have begun to diverge. The Priest will devote himself heart and soul to the good of his parish simply because he wants to see his flock happier and better. He will do his work all the more effectively the more completely he identifies their well-being with his own, the more he takes delight in his occupation; but the sense of duty will always be ready to press upon his attention the more disagreeable or the more unpopular duty, to suggest the claims of study to the unstudious, the claims of his poor to the man whose heart is in books, the claims of rest or reflection or devotion when absorption in work threatens to dry up the foundations of thought and of feeling. In proportion as a man's habitual desires or 'interests' are identified with some wider form or element of human good, the danger of collisions between various forms of good—the difference, so to speak, between devotion to a particular end and devotion to the good in general—may tend to disappear. The sense of duty may be less needed as check or as spur to the man of ardent temperament, absorbed in self-denying philanthropy, than it is to the average man whose habitual energies are divided by a remunerative profession and an affectionate family. But it is unnecessary to illustrate the possibilities of moral aberration which attend upon devotion to every form of good less than the whole.

And where there is devotion to the whole of human good, to the 'matter' of the Moral Law, to every kind of good object in due proportion to its intrinsic worth, need there then be any thought of the 'form' at all? Is the idea of 'duty for duty's sake' part of the highest ideal of character or is it always a note of imperfection? The question is not an easy one, for every term that we use in speaking of such matters is a more or less ambiguous one: but I would suggest the following outline of an answer:—

(1) Goodness in the narrower moral sense—the right direction of the will—is itself the greatest of goods, and must always be paramount in the ideal man; but the ideal man will care about many other things besides the right direction of his own and other people's wills—knowledge, beauty, particular persons, social intercourse, various pleasures in proportion to their intrinsic value. It is scarcely possible that he should acquire this habitual right direction of the will without more or less consciously thinking of it; but, in so far as he does come to love the things prescribed by Reason, respect for duty as such will tend to pass into a sense of the relative value of the goods which he loves, and to lose that abstractness, and also that sense of constraint and obligation, which are elements in the sense of duty as understood by Kant and his followers. At bottom the sense of duty is the due appreciation of the proportionate objective value of ends. In this sense alone is the 'feeling of obligation' an ultimate and indispensable element of the moral consciousness [1].

(2) Since the various ends the promotion of which constitutes the content of the Moral Law are all resolvable into some state of conscious beings, it may be said that an ideal love of mankind would supersede all sense of duty as such, provided that this love of persons be taken to include a desire of various goods for them in proportion to their relative value, and in particular a predominant desire for their moral Well-being. In this sense it may be said that 'perfect love casteth out fear'—even of the Moral Law—and constitutes by itself, in the strictest possible sense, 'the fulfilment of the law.' At its highest the sense of duty is identical with the rational love of persons (including in due measure self-love), and the things which constitute their true good.

(3) For a mind which believes in the existence of a Person whose will is absolutely directed towards the true good, the love of such a Person, the conscious direction of the will towards the end which He wills, absorbs into itself the sense of duty. The love of God is the love of duty with the added intensity both of intellectual clearness and of emotional strength which arises from

---

[1] 'Une conscience morale n'aboutit pas à la formule: *je dois faire ceci*, mais à la formule: *ceci est à faire*' (Rauh, *L'Expérience morale*, p. 32).

the conviction that an ideal is also already real. How far and in what sense the belief in such a Person must be considered as involved or implied in the idea of an objective Morality, is a question which must be considered hereafter. Meanwhile I notice merely as a psychological fact that in the religious consciousness the idea of Duty may lose those aspects and associations which often cause a revolt against the idea of a categorical imperative.

Kant's categorical imperative has been justly (in some of its aspects) ridiculed by Schopenhauer as a mere survival from the lowest form of the 'servile' theological Morality which he professed to have abandoned. 'Whether he calls his fetich categorical imperative or Fitziputzli,' makes no difference [1]. It was the survival of the drill-sergeant Theology of eighteenth-century Prussia with the drill-sergeant turned into an abstraction. In depersonalizing his imperative and cutting it adrift from its connexion with the real world as a whole, life as a whole, good as a whole, he reduced it to something arbitrary, abstract, almost inhuman. Repersonalize it, regard it as the reflex in the human soul of the Will which wills the supreme good of humanity, and the categorical imperative loses all those features which tend to present it as an emotion incompatible with and inferior to the other impulses or emotions which may inspire men to right conduct. To the Christian or the Theist with a worthy idea of God the love of goodness is no longer distinguishable from the love of the concrete good which forms the content of the divine Will as of all good human wills.

V

How far the love of goodness, whether or not embodied in a Person, can supersede in the actual conditions of human life the sense of effort, of struggle, of sacrifice commonly associated with the aspect of Morality embodied in the term Duty, is another question to which we must return hereafter. If the sense of duty be really the sense of the relative value of ends, it is obvious that some sense of constraint or 'obligation' must always be connected with the idea of duty, so long as any of

[1] *Grundlage der Moral*, § 6 (E. T., p. 50).

the ends which we rationally desire are incompatible with the attainment of any other such ends which we either desire or feel that we ought to desire. Meanwhile, I may notice the close connexion between the two great defects in the Kantian ethical system which have been pointed out—the harsh 'dualism' of his view of human good and his erroneous doctrine as to the motives of moral conduct. The ethical criterion to which the Kantian system logically points, and which Kant at moments seems on the verge of deliberately adopting, is the tendency of actions to promote a Well-being or εὐδαιμονία in which there are two elements, (1) Virtue or the performance of duty, (2) Happiness conceived of as mere pleasure. This view has been criticized as inadequate, and it might be possible to enlarge upon the harsh psychological dualism which it involves. It cuts human nature into two halves which have no connexion with, or relation to, or influence on one another. Between these two elements in the ideal human life there seems to be nothing in common: nay, there is at least the appearance of actual irreconcilability between them. In so far as a man succeeds in finding happiness in his work, his Virtue, it might seem, must suffer ('but alas! with pleasure I do it'); in so far as he lives for duty, considered as something opposed to his inclinations, he will tend to be unhappy[1]. Happiness, according to Kant, has value, but no moral value: the work of Virtue on the other hand seems to consist precisely in its tendency to thwart those natural impulses in the satisfaction of which ordinary happiness consists. Now the moment it is recognized that action may be due neither to respect for Moral Law nor to desire for pleasure, but to some other desire, that such desires may have very various degrees of moral value, that Reason does not condemn or supersede but only regulates desire, that pleasure is good or bad according to the nature of the desire from the gratification of which it springs,—both the inadequacy and the dualism disappear. Virtue no longer seems to consist in thwarting all the other impulses of our nature: happiness is no longer destitute of moral value when it arises from the satisfaction in due degree of all the desires which possess an intrinsic worth of their own, a value which may often be superior

[1] No doubt Kant often repudiates this deduction from his principles.

to the value which they possess as mere sources of pleasure. The conditions of human life may prevent the actual attainment of this ideal reconciliation, but there is no necessary or invariable antagonism between the two ends; they tend to pass into a single, internally harmonious and self-consistent, ideal of life.

VI

It may be desirable to add a word about the second of the three moral criteria put forward by Kant—the rule 'Use humanity whether in thine own person or in that of any other always as an end, never as a means only.' It is the principle less frequently insisted on in Kant's own writings, and its relation to the other is not very precisely determined. He uses it chiefly to prove the immorality of suicide and of sexual transgression. There can be no question of the deep moral significance of the principle, but it is too vague to be really of any use as a moral criterion without knowledge of a kind which cannot be extracted out of the formula itself. We must know what is the true end of human life before we can tell whether a certain course of conduct does or does not involve treating humanity only as a means. Now Kant (as we have seen) only recognizes two ends in human life—one primary, i.e. Morality, the other secondary, i.e. happiness. On Kant's view of Free-will it is impossible to make another man immoral or less moral. Hence it would seem that he has no right to condemn conduct towards another for any other reason than its interference with his other end—happiness. And this is clearly not always done by the kind of conduct which he has in mind. Nor, even if this consideration be waived, can he show that the conduct which he condemns involves using the body of another, or one's own, as a means, any more than much conduct which no one could describe as immoral. I am using a porter's body as a means when I employ him to carry trunks for me, and there is nothing immoral in my doing so. I am not using him *only* as a means, if I pay him for his work and treat him as a moral being no less entitled to a share in all the true goods of life than myself. Kant never said anything so absurd (though he is constantly cited as doing so) as that we should never use humanity as a means, but only that we should never use it as a means without using it also as an end, and it is impossible (apart from some conception of a concrete end or good of human life) to show that sexual immorality might not be equally compatible with a like recognition of others' claims. We should only have to insist on just and considerate treatment of those who have been called the 'priestesses of humanity[1].' The one kind of exchange of services is, on Kant's premisses, exactly on a level with the other. Kant's real feeling was no doubt that the conduct in question was inconsistent with a true ideal of the relations between man and woman, but it was impossible for him to prove that inconsistency so long as he narrowed his conception of the ideal human life down to the performance of social duty on the one hand and the indiscriminate enjoyment of pleasure on the other. It is not the treating of humanity as a means that strikes us as wrong (for that might quite well be compatible with recognizing it also as an end), but the treating of humanity as a means *in this particular way*, as a means to such and such a kind of sensual pleasure, to such and such an end in which Reason can find no value. It is only because we have judged already that such treatment is a degradation of humanity that we pronounce it to be using humanity 'only as a means.'

Once again, we see the impossibility of reducing moral judgements to a merely intellectual, non-moral principle; of getting a criterion out of mere formal conceptions, which take no account of the content or intended consequences on which depends all the morality or the immorality of our actions. Mere universality or freedom from contradiction is no test of goodness or badness. The judgement of value cannot be reduced to any other sort of judgement—a judgement of formal consistency or a judgement as to the relation between ends and means, which takes no account of the character of those ends. It

---

[1] Kant has specially in mind the case of certain other kinds of sexual vice, and there his contention would be still more hopeless, if we assume that happiness (= pleasure) is the only end except duty considered simply as the promotion of pleasure for others (*Tugendlehre*, Th. I. § 7, Semple's Translation, 3rd ed., 1871, p. 240).

is only in estimating the value of an end that the moral Reason really comes into play. Abstract the form of the law from the matter of it, and there is nothing left on which a judgement of value can be passed. A rule of action is not moral because it is consistent, unless it consistently conduces to an end in which Reason can recognize value; neither is the making of humanity a means immoral unless the end to which it is a means be one which Reason refuses to recognize as part of the true end for man. The non-recognition of this principle involved Kant in the absurdity of gravely questioning whether it was lawful to cut one's hair, and of solemnly pronouncing the conduct of a woman who cuts off her hair to sell it—irrespectively of the motives for which she wants money—not 'altogether devoid of blame[1].' Such a verdict will probably fail to commend itself to readers of Mr. Marion Crawford's touching 'Cigarette-maker's Romance.'

VII

It has generally been recognized that the best expression of Kant's fundamental ethical principle is to be found in his third rule—'Act as a member of a kingdom of ends': that is to say 'Act in such a way as to treat thyself and every other human being as of equal intrinsic value; behave as a member of a society in which each regards the good of each other as of equal value with his own, and is so treated by the rest,' in which each is both end and means, in which each realizes his own good in promoting that of others. That such an ideal of human Society must, as far as it goes, be approved by the moral consciousness, follows from what has been already said: but, considered as a guide to the details of conduct, it suffers from the same fatal ambiguity as the preceding formulae. There is no sufficient definition or explanation of this good of others which we are to promote. We have still got nothing but a 'form' without any content. If we fill up the deficiency from other parts of Kant's system, and interpret each man's end as 'goodness + happiness,' that (as has been explained) gives us an intelligible, but a rough and inadequate, criterion of Morality: and on that

---

[1] *Tugendlehre*, Th. I. § 6 (Semple, p. 239 *sq.*).

interpretation, which in many passages would appear to be
Kant's own [1], we must cast to the winds the whole of his
elaborate attempt to get at the details of conduct without
appeal to experience or calculation of consequences, and to exhibit that good will as actuated by the mere form of a universal
law without any regard to the content or matter of it.

In truth there run through the whole of Kant's ethical teaching two inconsistent and irreconcilable lines of thought—one
of which is the basis (though only the basis) of all sound
ethical theory; while the other has proved the fruitful parent
of every extravagance, superstition, and absurdity by which
the scientific study of Ethics has been, and still is, impeded.
Every formula of Kant's may be interpreted, and at times
appears to be interpreted by himself, in each of these opposite
ways. 'Duty is a categorical imperative.' That may mean
'there is a right course of action which is intrinsically right
and reasonable for every man whether he likes it or not,' and
that is simply an analysis of what duty means to any one to
whom it means anything at all. Or it may mean 'there are
certain acts which we recognize as being right to do without
thinking of the ends (social or otherwise) which they will tend
to realize,' than which no better definition could be given of
the irrational in conduct. 'Duty for duty's sake' may mean
that 'we should pursue the good or intrinsically valuable end
just because it is good,' or it may mean that we should act
without reference to an end at all. 'Act on a principle fit
for law universal' may mean 'Pursue the ends which Reason

---

[1] 'The realization of the *summum bonum* in the world is the necessary
object of a will determinable by the Moral Law' (*Kritik d. praktischen
Vernunft*, Dialektik, Pt. II, § 4, p. 262, and Abbot, p. 218). 'Now inasmuch
as virtue and happiness together constitute the possession of the *summum
bonum* in a person, and the distribution of happiness in exact proportion to
morality . . . constitutes the *summum bonum* of a possible world; hence
this *summum bonum* expresses the whole, the perfect good' (Dialektik,
Pt. II, Abbot, p. 206). Of course, in so far as Kant did not recognize that
the good will means the will that wills the promotion and just distribution
of happiness, he was still liable to the criticism that he has provided
no means of determining what will is moral: but on the whole it would
seem that in such passages as the above he meant to define virtue as the
willing of acts tending to promote happiness and the just distribution of it.

pronounces to be intrinsically valuable for others no less than for thyself,' or it may mean 'Make the avoidance of internal inconsistency the criterion of thy conduct.' 'Treat humanity as an end and never merely as means' may mean 'Regard the true Well-being of every man as possessing an intrinsic worth,' or it may mean 'Regard it as beneath thy dignity to be of use to the society in which thou livest, and indulge in phantastic scruples about things which do no real harm to thyself or anybody else.' The 'kingdom of ends' represents simply a combination of the two last maxims, and is liable to the same charge of ambiguity ; though of all the formulae employed by Kant it is the one which lends itself most readily to the more rational interpretation.

VIII

One more way of expressing our criticism upon the Kantian system shall be attempted, because it will supply a convenient opportunity of giving a definite answer to an ethical question of fundamental importance—the question which is the logically prior conception, the idea of 'good' or the idea of 'right.' Kant never thoroughly made up his mind about this question. He always started with the idea of 'right'; and all his difficulties arose from the attempt to give a meaning to, and to find a content for, this idea of 'right' without appealing to the idea of 'good.' In our view the idea of 'good' or 'value' is logically the primary conception, though psychologically the idea of 'right' may often in modern men be more explicitly developed. That action is right which tends to bring about the good. There is no attempt here to get rid of the ultimate unanalysable 'ought.' The good is that which 'ought' to be [1].

[1] Such a statement is in no way inconsistent with the doctrine which I fully accept, that the word 'good' is indefinable : we can only bring out the real meaning of the idea by the use of words which equally imply the notion. 'Good,' 'Ought' (when applied to ends), 'Value,' 'the End' I regard as synonymous terms. Mr. Moore, in his recent *Principia Ethica*, has done well to emphasize in a very striking manner that 'good is indefinable'; but when he goes on to say (p. 17) 'and yet, so far as I know, there is only one ethical writer, Prof. Henry Sidgwick, who has clearly recognized and stated this fact,' I cannot admit the historical accuracy of his statement. To say

The difference between the two terms is this : that the term
' right' is applicable only to voluntary actions : the term ' good '
is applicable to many things besides acts. Entirely apart from
the question, ' who caused such things ?' I judge that pain or
discordant music or ugly pictures (i. e. of course the enduring
of pain by conscious beings, the listening to discords or the
contemplation of bad pictures by conscious beings) are bad
things. They seem to me bad whether they arise from chance
or necessity or voluntary action. Only because I have so judged
is there any ground for the judgement ' it is right, in so far as
it is possible, to get rid of these things '; but, whether they can
be got rid of or not, they are equally bad [1]. The will that

nothing of writers who (like Mr. Moore and myself) learned the doctrine
largely from Sidgwick, I should contend that it was taught with sufficient
distinctness by Plato (whatever may be thought of his further attempt to
show that only the good has real existence), Aristotle, and a host of modern
writers who have studied in their school — by no one more emphatically than
by Cudworth. The only criticism which I should make upon Mr. Moore's
exposition of it is that he ignores the other ways in which the same notion
may be expressed, and in particular the correlative notion of 'right' or
'ought.' He is so possessed with this idea that the ' good ' is indefinable that
he will not even trouble to expound and illustrate it in such ways as are
possible in the case of ultimate ideas.

[1] The non-recognition of this principle (so fully admitted, as we have
seen, by Lotze) is to my mind the leading defect in the Bishop of Clogher's in
many respects admirable *Short Study of Ethics* (2nd ed., 1901). Bishop d'Arcy
fully appreciates the defects of Kant's 'formalism,' and of the attempt to
pronounce acts right or wrong without regard to consequences known to us
from experience : yet we find him asserting ' the end, or good, of man is *man
doing*, the concretion of man and the world. This concrete activity is the
only thing which can be called *good* in itself' (pp. 168–9), and ' the only
true good is to be good in the sense of performing the good act ' (p. 277).
Such statements seem to me to imply a reversion to Kant's attempt to say
that to cause toothache is wrong without having first decided whether toothache (however caused) is or is not a bad thing. And it goes beyond Kant in
pronouncing that nothing but a moral act is good at all. Wundt seems to
me equally open to criticism, when he talks about happiness as being ' not
an end in itself, but a by-product of moral effort ' (*Ethics*, Eng. Trans., iii.
p. 90), or about an ' objectively worthless sum of individual happinesses '
(ib., p. 83). It is curious that so modern and 'scientific' a Moralist as
Wundt should be almost the only living thinker of high eminence who out-
kants Kant in his view of the exclusive value of a moral end, which, however, is to him not so much the perfection of individual wills as a vague and
impersonal 'progress of humanity.'

deliberately causes or refuses to fight against such things may be, and I believe is, a worse evil than the pain or the bad music or the ugly pictures. But unless these things were evils, the will that refused to remove them would not be evil either; its acts would not be acts of a wrongly directed will. Kant generally ends by coming round to this view—that the right or rational act is the act which wills the good. Unfortunately he did not see that with that admission his attempt to avoid the appeal to experience completely breaks down. It is possible, though it is irrational, to will particular acts without attending to the consequences which experience shows likely to result from them[1]; it is impossible to pronounce that something is good until one knows what it is. No experience will tell us what is good unless we include in our idea of ' experience ' an un-avowed judgement of value; but without experience of what a thing is it is impossible to say whether it is good or not. It is obvious that this necessity of experience for sound ethical judgements goes a long way to explain the actual divergences of moral codes. When the Caliph Omar (if the story be not a myth) ordered the Alexandrian library to be burned, it is probable that he knew very imperfectly what the Alexandrian library or any other library really was. I do not deny that there might be fanatics who knowing a good deal about the contents of these books would still have ordered them to be burnt; but it is probable that a more extensive acquaintance with their contents would have modified the Caliph's judgement. The consistent Kantian, i. e. a disciple of Kant in his most logical but least rational moments, ought to be able to say whether they should be burned without knowing what sort of books they were or even that they were books at all.

Our moral judgements are ultimately judgements of Value. The fundamental idea in Morality is the idea of Value, in which the idea of ' ought ' is implicitly contained. The advantage in-volved in the use of the term ' value ' lies in its freedom from

---

[1] Strictly no doubt there must be some feature in the act known to us, to account for our choosing it, but the motive might be the simple desire to act without further reflection—the ' pure cussedness ' from which, indeed, it is so hard to distinguish the motive of the ideal Kantian, when Kantism is understood on its irrational side.

many of the exaggerations and mystifications which have sometimes created a prejudice against the term 'ought,' even in
minds which have no prejudice against the reality which it
signifies. The idea of 'good' and the idea of 'right' are, as
it seems to me, correlative terms. It is implied in the idea of
'good' that it ought to be promoted; the idea of 'right' is
meaningless apart from a 'good' which right actions tend to
promote. If, finally, we ask what is the relation of the idea
of value to the idea of 'moral' value, I should answer that all
that has value has moral value, in the sense that it must be moral,
in due proportion to the amount of that value, to promote it; but
by moral value we generally mean the particular kind of value
which we assign to a good character. That value is, as I believe,
the greatest of all values. Pleasure is a good, and it is right for
a man to promote it in himself as in others. We assign value
to the pleasure, but we do not assign any particular value to
the acts or to the character from which it springs, since this
promotion of private pleasure does not necessarily indicate
a good character, and even the promotion of the highest ends
may have no moral value when the promotion of such ends
forms no part of the man's motive; only when we recognize
a man's conduct as exhibiting the preference of the good because
it is the good or the preference of some higher to some lower
good for its own sake do we assign to it the peculiar kind and
degree of value which we usually term moral value [1].

---

[1] I have in this chapter for the most part avoided all criticism of sides of
the Kantian Ethics which could not be discussed without reference to the
defects of the metaphysical system with which they are so closely connected. Even Kant's purely ethical position I have only examined so far as
seemed desirable as a means of helping forward my own argument.

CHAPTER VI

REASON AND FEELING

I

In the preceding chapters I have assumed that Kant is right in making Morality to be essentially rational, in holding that moral approval is a judgement of the Intellect, not a feeling or an emotion. This position seems now to require some further justification than it has yet received, and this justification may perhaps best take the form of a reply to the objections which are commonly made to it. The reply will be one which may be thought to involve considerable qualifications of the creed known as ethical Rationalism as represented by such men as Clarke in the seventeenth century and by Kant and other modern Idealists.

The most obvious form which objections are likely to take will be something of this kind: Does not common opinion recognize that Morality is an affair, not of the head, but of the heart? Are not our moral perceptions attended with a glow and warmth of feeling which is entirely absent from our perception (say) of a mathematical truth[1]? Are not good men very often stupid and bad men often intellectual? If we admit that there is an intellectual element in what is commonly called Conscience, must we not at least say with Bishop Butler that Conscience is neither merely 'a sentiment of the under-standing' nor 'a perception of the heart,' but 'partakes of the nature of both[2]'?

---

[1] Cf. the passage quoted from Martineau, *Types of Ethical Theory*, below, p. 165.

[2] *Dissertation of Virtue.* This change from the more rationalistic position of the Sermons was perhaps due to the influence of Hutcheson. He now uses the term 'moral sense' as a synonym for Conscience.

The common objections seem to imply several misconceptions—misconceptions, however, for which the exaggerations of Kant and other ethical Rationalists are, it must be admitted, largely responsible.   In the first place, when it is held that moral judgements are given by Reason, we do not imply that their rationality is the sole reason for the acts being done.   Undoubtedly it is possible to see that an act is right with absolute clearness and not to do it—nay, to feel practically little or no disposition to do it.   Even when an act is done out of pure ' respect' for a recognized duty, there must at least be present a 'desire for what is right and reasonable as such' (to use Professor Sidgwick's phrase) or the duty will not be done.   And we have seen reason to hold that Kant was wrong in insisting that this rational desire is or ought to be the sole motive which impels us to the performance of good actions. It has been admitted that normally the ends prescribed by the Practical Reason are objects of desire for their own sake, that actions directed towards such ends may possess moral value even when the thought of an abstract law does not enter into the agent's consciousness at all ; and that even the best actions of the best men are commonly influenced by other desires besides bare respect for duty.   Now when Conscience presents itself as partly an ' emotion of the heart,' the term is probably used to include not merely the perception of what is right but also the impulses which cause what is right to be done—to include at least the ' respect' or love for the good and perhaps also the whole of those benevolent or other higher affections and emotions which are approved by the moral Reason as motives to action [1]; while the question at issue between ethical Rationalists and their opponents is simply the question ' by what faculty or part of our nature do we discover that an act ought to be done ?'

It may further be admitted that the judgements of Practical

---

[1] 'The single act of conscience may be a feeling, an emotion, an impulse or a judgment' (Wundt, *Ethics*, Eng. Trans., vol. iii, p. 60).   Wundt is surely wrong in making Conscience or συνείδησις mean originally a ' knowing with God,' instead of an 'inner' or ' self-knowledge.'   The word, it is significant to observe, is first found in the generation immediately after Aristotle— a period of great progress both in ethical feeling and ethical theory.

Reason normally create a more or less powerful impulse towards the performance of what they enjoin; and, in those who are powerfully influenced by such judgements, they are undoubtedly accompanied by an emotion of a kind which is wholly absent from mere mathematical judgements. Still, it is possible to distinguish between the judgement that the act is right and the emotions by which that judgement is accompanied. It will perhaps be contended that in some persons who would commonly be described as very good men emotion of one kind or another is so obviously the main inspirer of their conduct that it is difficult to detect any intellectual judgement at all. And it may be admitted that as a matter of psychological fact the process by which many people come to attach the idea of rightness to particular kinds of conduct is almost entirely an emotional one: but still I should contend that, in so far as the idea of goodness or rightness forms the object of that emotion, the intellectual judgement must necessarily be there. This liability to be influenced or even wholly determined by emotional causes is no peculiarity of ethical judgements. All sorts of psychological causes may be at work in inducing a man to accept a particular theory as to the causes of the French Revolution; but the most prejudiced and passionate view of the matter and the most calm and scientific would be alike impossible to a man whose consciousness did not contain the intellectual concept or category of Causality. Nobody would ever dream of describing such a historical judgement as itself a mere emotion. Just in the same way, emotion may inspire particular judgements of right and wrong, but it could not create the idea of 'right' or of 'good.' Even in those cases where the actual motive is most clearly emotional, some perception of the goodness of the act may be said to enter into the exciting cause of the emotion, or the emotion may be said to be accompanied by a judgement of its own value. A man may devote himself enthusiastically to some philanthropic object, from a passion excited by the abstract idea of Justice, or he may be moved by a pure love of humanity which is nevertheless accompanied by the judgement that it is good to feel such a love. In some cases one, in others the other may seem to be the more

appropriate mode of statement, but the two kinds of judgement—
the judgement which ascribes value to the emotion and the
judgement which ascribes value to an object and by so doing
excites the emotion which leads to action—run into one another.
All that is necessary to contend for at present is that judgement and emotion are logically distinguishable, and that the
judgement of value does more than merely record the fact of
the emotion being felt.

II

When the popular unwillingness to recognize the rational
character of our moral perceptions assumes the form of a philosophical theory, it tends to pass either into the theory of a
'moral sense' or into the theory of a moral 'faculty called
Conscience' which is represented as wholly *sui generis*—distinct
alike from intellectual judgement and from any kind of feeling
or emotion. Let us briefly examine each of these views.

In the writings of John Locke the Rationalism of Cumberland
and the Cambridge Platonists had degenerated into mere theological Utilitarianism. Locke continued to use the old language
about Morality being rational; but in him that language had
come to mean almost the opposite of what it was originally
intended to mean. The appeal to Reason was intended as an
answer to Hobbes, and now Reason was used in a sense in
which Hobbes himself would have had no objection to base
Morality upon it. By Reason was no longer meant a faculty
which originates the idea of something intrinsically good in
itself, and which pronounces what things are intrinsically
good, but merely the faculty which connects ends and means [1].

[1] Exception may be taken in some quarters to the use of the word
'faculty' at all in this connexion. The word has fallen into disfavour
partly because by a certain school it has been used to suggest the idea of
a definite number of mental activities sharply distinguishable from and
independent of each other—planted, as Plato would have said, as it were
'in a wooden horse,' to the ignoring of the unity of self-consciousness, and
partly because the invention of a specific faculty has often taken the place
of logical or psychological analysis of complicated mental processes. I hope
I have sufficiently guarded myself against these mistakes. But to proscribe
altogether the use of the word 'faculty' is to fall into the very superstition
which the denouncers of it have in view. Whatever we do, there must be

To Locke Virtue was rational because it could be demonstrated that without it a man will infallibly go to Hell. Hence in men like Shaftesbury and Hutcheson we find a recoil from a way of thinking which seemed to make Morality a mere matter of selfish calculation. It was thought that Morality would be all the safer if it were removed altogether from the jurisdiction of the intellect, and placed under the control of 'the heart.' Moreover, these men shared, or at least had incompletely shaken off, the metaphysical presuppositions of the Master against whose Ethics they had revolted. Experience, by which was practically meant sensation, was regarded as the sole source of knowledge. If, therefore, Morality was to be shown to be something real, it must, it seemed, be revealed to us by some kind of feeling or sensation. Yet to base Morality upon the deliverances of the ordinary sensibility, upon the pleasures and pains of the bodily senses, meant of course Hedonism pure and simple. To avoid this consequence they invented a special sense which was to be the source of our moral knowledge, just as sight is the source of our colour-perceptions and hearing of our sound-perceptions. Morality was made to rest (like all our knowledge) upon a kind of feeling; only it was a *specific* feeling. Moral approbation was a feeling wholly *sui generis*, arising from the contemplation of good acts; disapprobation a feeling similarly arising from the contemplation of bad acts. Not to insist on the complete want of analogy between the bodily senses and this organless sense of Morality, all such schemes are open to one insuperable objection. If moral approbation is a mere feeling, how can it claim any superiority over other feelings? Granted that it gives me a pleasant feeling to do a kind action, and that it causes me a particular kind of discomfort to tell a lie, that may be a very good reason under normal circumstances for my doing the one and avoiding the other. But supposing I do not happen to be sensitive to this particular kind of feeling, or supposing I am so constituted that a violation of some social conventionality

a faculty or capacity (δύναμις) of doing it. In asking what is the moral faculty, I mean only to ask to which of the distinguishable activities of the single self-conscious self our ideas of right and wrong are to be referred.

shocks me more than a moral offence [1], why should I attach any paramount importance to this particular feeling of moral disapprobation? I may have a certain capacity for the pleasures of whist, but I do not feel bound to play it if I like reading a novel better. If we grant that immorality does normally cause me mental or emotional distress and discomfort of a particular kind; still under particular circumstances Morality may cause me more pain and discomfort of another kind. I may dislike the pains of Conscience much, but I may dislike the thumbscrew more. Why am I bound, if threatened with torture for refusing to reveal a secret which I am bound to keep, or falsely to accuse an innocent man, to prefer the pleasures of an easy conscience to those of a whole skin and easy nerves? To insist on the specific character of the feeling in question is nothing to the point; the pleasures of whist-playing are different from those of touch or taste, but they are not necessarily superior to them. The taste of port is specifically different from that of sherry, but it is not necessarily superior to it. If it be said 'Oh! but you are inwardly conscious that these pleasures are superior in kind, and not merely in quality, to those of sense, that they *ought* to be attended to more than others,' is not that really admitting that we have to do with something more than a mere feeling, with a dictate of Reason or a judgement of value? It is not the feeling which claims obedience, but the judgement which assigns a value to that feeling.

Moreover, not only does a Moral Sense theory fail to supply any reason why the individual should accord to his own moral perceptions a primacy among the feelings and emotions of which his nature is capable, but it is totally unable to assign any

[1] 'The not taking into consideration this authority, which is implied in the reflex idea of approbation or disapprobation, seems a material deficiency or omission in Lord Shaftesbury's *Inquiry concerning Virtue.* He has shewn beyond all contradiction that virtue is naturally the interest or happiness, and vice the misery of such a creature as man, placed in the circumstances which we are in this world. But suppose there are particular exceptions; a case which the author was unwilling to put. . . . Or suppose a case which he has put and determined, that of a sceptick not convinced of this happy tendency of virtue or being of a contrary opinion. His determination is, that it would be *without remedy*' (Butler, Pref. to *Fifteen Sermons*).

universal validity to such moral perceptions. Inconsistent or contradictory feelings, *qua* feelings, are equally true and valid for those who feel them. When the colour-blind man calls the red light green or grey, it really is green or grey to him; his judgement is as true as that of the man who pronounces it red. Feelings as feelings are not 'true' or 'false' at all; while as to the judgements based upon them, the judgement of *A* that he sees red and of *B* that he sees green, these no doubt possess objective validity, but such statements as to what two men actually feel are perfectly compatible with one another. Now, if a good act means simply an act which causes me to experience a particular kind of feeling which I call moral approbation, it is undeniable that such feelings are occasioned in different men by different, and even opposite, kinds of conduct. The pious fraud may occasion no less pleasure to the man brought up to regard such acts as right than a sacrifice made in the cause of truth will cause in the heart of another differently educated. A Spanish bull-fight excites feelings of enthusiastic approval in the minds of most Spaniards and feelings of lively disapproval in most Englishmen. Observe exactly where the difficulty lies. It is not the practical difficulty of ascertaining moral truth. Every ethical system has to admit that the Conscience of the individual is not infallible, that men's ethical judgements do as a matter of fact contradict one another. However strongly I feel that a certain course of conduct is right, I may make a mistake, just as I may make a mistake about a scientific or historical theory to which I may be no less passionately attached. The objectivity of the moral judgement does not mean the infallibility of the individual, or even of a general consensus of individuals at a particular time and place. What is meant is that *if I am right* in my approbation of this conduct, then, if you disapprove of it, you must be wrong. If Morality be a matter of objective truth or falsity, then the Moral Law remains unaffected, though you and I—nay, the whole human race in its present stage of moral development—may have erroneously conceived some of its provisions. But, if the goodness of an act means simply that the act occasions a specific emotion in particular men, then the same act may be at one and the same time good and bad. Moral feelings will have no more objective truth or validity than any other feelings which vary in their nature or intensity with the varying sensibility of different men's skins or sensory nerves. The bull-fight will be neither right nor wrong, but simply right to some people, wrong to others, just as mustard is neither objectively nice nor objectively nasty, but simply nice to some people, nasty to others [1].

It may perhaps be replied, ' These feelings are not what make things right or wrong; they are merely the subjective index by which we recognize the presence of an actual quality in the world of objective fact.' This is no doubt what was really meant by the doctrine of Moral Sense in the hands of constructive Moralists like Hutcheson. A full reply to the objection would involve a discussion of the metaphysical system which it presupposes. No doubt if knowledge of any kind could be explained by mere feeling, Morality so explained would at least possess as much objectivity as the rest of our knowledge. Moral Sense theories are *no more* fatal to Morality than Sensationalism is to Science. I can only point out here that, just as all knowledge implies something more than feeling, so, if Morality is to possess any universal truth or validity, moral perceptions must be regarded as judgements. The specific moral feeling can be at most merely the occasion or index by which we are enabled to make the judgement, it cannot be its sole source; just as I cannot actually make the judgement that this triangle is larger than that without sensible experience, though there is more in the judgement than mere sense. The essential idea of ' good ' cannot come from feeling, though feeling may sometimes be psychologically the cause or occasion of my pronouncing this or that particular act to be right or good.

III

It has been the practice of ethical Rationalists to compare the moral faculty with the faculty by which we immediately appre-

[1] It may indeed be contended that there is an aesthetic, and therefore an objective, element even in gastronomic matters. If so, we must substitute some pleasure of a still more purely sensuous type.

hend mathematical axioms or the laws of thought. I have myself contended that it is possible to discover moral axioms, the truth of which appeals to us very much in the same way as the truth of the axioms 'If equals be added to equals, the wholes are equal' or 'Two straight lines cannot enclose a space.' Such ethical axioms are the three great laws of Prudence, Rational Benevolence, and Equity, which Professor Sidgwick regards as the ultimate basis of Ethics. And I have fully admitted the validity and importance of these axioms. But this comparison of moral to mathematical axioms may be overdone. It may be insisted on in a way which ignores some of the characteristic features of our ethical judgements, and its palpable failure to represent the facts may lead to a reaction against the whole idea of rational Morality. Rationalistic Moralists have not always observed that in themselves there is nothing ethical about these axioms of Prudence, Benevolence, and Equity except the bare formal notion or category of 'the good' which they involve. The axiom of Equity, 'one man's good is of as much intrinsic worth as the like good of another [1],' may, indeed, be reduced to the form of a merely analytical judgement. That which I recognize as having value in one man I must recognize as having the same value in another, provided it is really the same thing that is implied in the assertion that it has value. And the two other axioms—those of Benevolence and Prudence—simply assert that more good is always more valuable than less good. They are not merely comparable to the axioms of Mathematics; they are simply particular applications of those axioms. The judgement that the value of the good of all is greater than of any one man's may be treated as a mere case of the mathematical axiom that the whole is greater than its part. But so far there is nothing really ethical about the judgement except in so far as it involves the ethical proposition that value or good is one of the things which have quantity. Yet, after all, such a way of representing the matter is really superficial; for it is in the conception of value that the whole meaning of the judgement lies. And that conception of value cannot be analysed away

[1] This qualification of the axiom (not recognized by Utilitarians like Bentham or Sidgwick) I shall explain and defend in Chap. viii of this Book.

into the mere statement of an emotional fact. Considered as a mere statement of psychological fact, no assertion could well be more false than that my feeling towards one man, the emotion which I experience in knowing that he is benefited or that he is injured, is the same as that which I should experience in the case of any other. The ethical Rationalists are, it appears to me, quite right in treating these judgements as genuine axioms which are to some extent analogous to the axioms of mathematics; but such axioms are by themselves quite incapable of solving any concrete ethical problem. The really ethical element in them is contained simply in the conception of 'value' or 'good,' and we cannot use them till we have pronounced some concrete thing or experience to be good. They resemble the axioms of Mathematics just because they are purely formal. All that they can do is to direct us as to the way we are to distribute 'the good' when we know what it is. The really ethical judgement lies in the pronouncement that this or that is good. And, when we come to the judgement which pronounces that this or that is good or has value, the judgement assumes a form which seems psychologically much less like the mathematical, and much more like the aesthetic, judgement—a form consequently in which it can with much more plausibility be compared to a mere emotion or even a mere sensation. I can give no reason why I judge one pleasure to be higher than another—that of reading Shakespeare than that of drinking champagne—except that I see it to be so, just as I can give no reason why I know this to be beautiful or that to be square, except that I see that they are so. We naturally express our judgement by saying 'I feel it to be so,' rather than 'I know it to be so.' And that is one reason why they have so often been supposed to be mere feelings. Very often probably this *immediacy* is all that is meant by those who insist on treating them as feelings of a supposed 'Moral Sense.' But only a Sensationalist can suppose that the expression 'I feel *that A is B*' represents a mere feeling. 'I feel' is here merely a loose popular synonym for 'I judge.' Propositions cannot be felt.

Another fact which has favoured the theory is the impossibility

of expressing our real and concrete ethical judgements, as
distinct from the merely formal and abstract axioms just considered, with the scientific accuracy and definiteness characteristic
of other self-evident truths. Although the judgement 'pleasure
is good but not so good as Virtue' is an immediate judgement,
and so far resembles a mathematical axiom, it is one which does
not admit of being expressed with the same precision as mathematical judgements. And still more when we come to particular
applications of our idea of value, when we ask what is the
relative value of this as compared with that pleasure, or what
is the comparative importance for an individual or a nation of
a definite kind of artistic sensibility and of social feeling, we do
not find that consensus among all who barely understand the
meaning of the terms employed which can be claimed for the
axioms of mathematics. And the essence of the really ethical
judgement lies not in general axioms of the type suggested above
but in the concrete judgement 'this particular pleasure or this
kind of knowledge is good or valuable,' 'that kind of pleasure is
bad'; here the immediacy seems to be much more like the
immediacy of the aesthetic appreciation, or even that of a mere
judgement of perception, 'this is green.' All these characteristics
of the ethical judgement tend to win acceptance for the Moral
Sense theory of moral apprehension.

How far the analogy between aesthetic judgements and ethical
can be admitted, must depend upon the view which we take of
the aesthetic judgement itself. The Moral Sense writers have
usually assumed that aesthetic approval is merely a particular
kind of subjective feeling. The judgement 'this picture is
beautiful' means to them merely 'I get from the contemplation
of this picture a particular kind of pleasant feeling.' And, if
that were the case, the relegation of the moral judgement to the
same category as aesthetic appreciation would be fatal to that
authority or universality which we divine to be of its essence. On
the other hand we may be prepared to deny that the judgement
of one man on matters of Art or Poetry is as good as another, as
would undeniably be the case if the aesthetic judgement were
nothing but a matter of feeling. We may maintain that there
is a right and wrong in matters of aesthetic appreciation as well

as in matters of conduct. We may claim for the aesthetic judgement a certain objectivity, and consequently a partly rational character. But Aesthetics is a much more difficult Science than Ethics. The objectivity of aesthetic appreciation is much more difficult to defend, the relation between the rational or intellectual and the merely sensuous or emotional elements in it much more difficult to determine, than is the case with the moral judgement. At all events, the theory of an absolute standard of aesthetic value could not be defended without a more elaborate treatment of the whole subject than would be here in place. Consequently, I dispense myself from any further attempt to define the relations between aesthetic and moral value, and will only point out that the analogy between aesthetic perception and moral may be admitted without giving up the position that there is an element in the moral judgement which cannot be reduced to mere subjective feeling or emotion and which must be regarded as belonging to the rational or intellectual part of our nature.

And when once the rational and objective character of the aesthetic judgement is admitted, we may with great advantage insist upon this rather than upon the mathematical analogy, because the comparison avoids a suggestion which is apt to cleave to the mathematical analogy—the suggestion that these judgements of value can be made prior to and independent of experience [1]. The judgement ' this view is beautiful ' no doubt (in so far as it claims that the man who does not think so makes a mistake) asserts something which is not given in experience, but no one contends that it can be made without looking at the view, or even without the experience of other views and pictures by which the man's aesthetic sensibility has been cultivated. Even the ordinary judgement of perception (' this is a square object ') involves, for those who have learnt the lesson of Kant's Critique, much besides mere sensation—the forms of space and

[1] It is of course admitted by Kant that even the mathematical axioms in point of time are not prior to experience ; his contention is that, when once there has been experience of space or number in general, their truth is seen independently of any particular fact or facts of experience—that the *universal* truth of the principle is implied or presupposed in each particular judgement about space or number.

time, the categories of substance and accident, quantity, &c.
And so the judgement 'this act of charity is good' involves
no doubt experience, for we cannot pronounce that it is good
without knowing what it is, an admission which was, as we
have seen, never explicitly made by Kant himself. But it
remains true (1) that the judgement of value is an immediate
judgement of the Practical Reason, not a mere feeling; (2) that
the essence of the judgement—the idea of value—is a distinct
intellectual concept or category; and (3) that the moral judgement possesses a universality or objectivity which cannot be
ascribed to mere sensations or to the judgements of perception
founded upon them[1]. So much is involved in the very idea
of Morality or duty or moral obligation. The very heart of our
moral conviction is that there is something which every rational
being, in so far as he is rational, must recognize as intrinsically
right, that that something must be the same for all persons
under the same conditions, and cannot be dependent upon the
subjective caprice of particular persons. The Moral Sense
theory, duly realized and thought out, necessarily involves the
admission that that conviction on our part is a delusion. There
is, therefore, no real analogy between an ethical 'perception' (if
the word is to be allowed) and the sensations, perceptions,
or emotions with which they are compared by the Moral Sense
school. So far then ethical Rationalism is right, when once we
have got rid of Kant's attempt to make out that the ethical
judgement is not merely not derived from experience but does
not require as its condition knowledge derived from experience[2].

IV

But there are further elements of truth in the Moral Sense
position to which we have not yet done justice.

[1] Of course there is an objectivity even in the judgement of perception.
My toothache as a feeling is purely subjective in the sense that I alone
feel it. But my judgement 'I have a toothache' claims objectivity. I mean
that the man who denies is in error.

[2] By experience is here meant of course experience in the sense of the
Empiricists—mere sensible experience. There is no objection to saying
that moral judgements are derived from experience if we include in the
term 'experience' the whole of our intellectual as well as our other
psychical activities.

In the first place we must emphasize what is already implied in the admission that experience is necessary to the ethical judgement. This admission implies that the ethical judgement is invariably based upon some fact of feeling; since experience, though it includes more than feeling, does always involve feeling. The ethical judgement pronounces that something has value, and we do not on reflection pronounce that anything can have value except some state of consciousness. I do not, indeed, believe that feeling represents the only element in, or aspect of, consciousness which has value; but feeling is always an element in every state of consciousness, and an inseparable element. And no judgement can be pronounced as to whether a state of consciousness is good without taking the feeling-aspect of it into account. Feeling is therefore always part of the ground on which an ethical judgement is based. This represents the true element in Hedonism. The mistake of Hedonism lies in trying to abstract the feeling side of consciousness from its other sides, and making the whole value of the consciousness to lie in that feeling-aspect, the cognitive and conative elements being deliberately put out of sight; while the value of feeling itself is supposed to reside in the mere abstract pleasantness in respect of which all pleasures are qualitatively alike, and not in the total content which is pleasant. We have already accepted the position that knowledge and goodness are intrinsically valuable elements of consciousness. Yet these things taken apart from feeling are as much abstractions as feeling when taken apart from knowledge and volition. And it is impossible to say what value we should assign to the latter, if they were capable of actually existing apart from the feeling by which they are necessarily and inevitably accompanied. I can, indeed, intelligibly say that knowledge and goodness, even when accompanied by bodily pain, are good; but, even when the pursuit of knowledge or the doing of a good action brings with it a measure of pain, some measure of pleasant feeling normally accompanies those intellectual or volitional states. When I say that the state is on the whole painful, I mean that its pleasantness simply as pleasantness is outweighed by pains of another kind, and yet I may think that it possesses more value than many states which on the whole are pleasant.

We may, indeed, attach value to knowledge even for a consciousness which does not find pleasure in its possession ; but,
if so, we must do so either for its uses or effects or *propter spem*,
as a step to an enjoyment of which the man is capable but to
which he has not yet attained. In a consciousness which was
for ever incapable of feeling the smallest pleasure or interest in
what it knew, it would be difficult to say that knowledge could
be an end-in-itself. Indeed, the very idea of an ' end ' implies
the existence of beings with tendencies, desires, or impulses for
which some kind of satisfaction can be found in that end. This
satisfaction is not the same thing as pleasure, but there can be
no satisfaction without some degree (however low) of pleasure.
' The good ' is an intellectual category, but it is a category which
would be meaningless in a purely knowing consciousness. Hence
it may be doubted whether we could rationally attach any value
even to the good will in a consciousness which not only did not
derive, but was intrinsically and for ever incapable of deriving,
any pleasure or satisfaction from its goodness. We may, indeed,
recognize that the good will has a value, and ought consequently
to be cultivated, in those who, as a matter of present fact, do not
care about goodness and derive no pleasure from it. But then
we should say that they ought to care about it. In so far as it
is possible for a man to do his duty without liking the dutiful
action taken by itself (apart from the pains incidentally involved
in it), we should say that that was because he is not good
enough. The value of goodness does not mean merely its actual
pleasurableness to the agent at this or that moment ; but still
I can as little conceive it psychologically possible for a man to
say ' My whole will is completely devoted to and concentrated
upon the good, but it gives me not the smallest pleasure or
satisfaction to be good ' as I could attach any meaning to the
statement ' I recognize indeed the exquisite beauty of that landscape, but, as far as my own pleasure goes, I would just as soon
gaze at a blank wall ' ; though I can quite intelligibly say ' This
picture gives me more pleasure than that other which I acknowledge to be more beautiful.' Beauty is more than pleasure, but
it is unintelligible without it. Value is not a feeling, but it
cannot be recognized as attributable to anything in consciousness

which can excite no feeling of pleasure in its possessor. The fallacy of Hedonism lies in the attempt to estimate the value of the feeling element in abstraction from the other elements of consciousness. Knowing, feeling, willing are, for us at least, the three inseparable aspects of consciousness. It is upon consciousness taken as a whole that we pronounce our ultimate judgements of value; the nature of its knowledge and its will must necessarily colour and determine the value of the feeling by which in any consciousness they are accompanied.

Invariably, then, moral judgements imply facts of feeling as part of their ground—that is to say either feelings actually experienced or desires which imply feeling in the present as well as feeling in their subsequent satisfaction [1]. Those feelings need not be the feelings of the person making the judgement, and in many cases there is nothing specifically moral about them. I judge that it is wrong for me or any one else to stick pins into a human being, simply because it hurts. If I did not know that it hurts, if I did not know what pain is, I could not judge it to be a bad thing, or the act of causing it wrong. Given that knowledge, I can pronounce the act wrong, quite apart from any sympathetic or other feeling which the act may excite in myself. But sometimes we can recognize a far less superficial truth in the Moral Sense position than this. The actual ground of my judgement may be simply an emotion; and, although an emotion to which I assign value must be to some extent pleasant, I may assign it a value which is not measured by its pleasantness. I may approve of an act not merely on account of the pleasure or pain which it causes, but also on account of the emotion which it excites, the emotion from which it proceeds, or the emotion by which it is accompanied. I may approve of maternal affection not merely on account of the benefit arising to the babe and to society, but for its own sake; and that emotion, though it is a source of pleasure, is assuredly one which also causes much pain. Yet the value which we ascribe to it is certainly not smallest in those cases in which the pain is greatest. Still more closely do we approach to a recogni-

---

[1] What we usually call a desire I take to be a state of feeling and a certain state of will or conation combined.

tion of the specific emotion which the Moral Sense theory
wishes to make the beginning and end of the ethical judgement
when we take into consideration the feelings which the mere
contemplation of some acts excites in a well-regulated mind,
whether the mind be the agent's or that of some 'disinterested
spectator [1] '—say for instance the disgust which is experienced at
an isolated act of otherwise practically harmless drunkenness, or
our feeling about acts of impurity.   It is in cases of this sort
that we can least of all ignore the fact that not merely ordinary
feelings of pleasure but certain specific kinds of higher emotion
do form part of the ground on which our moral judgements are
based.   They are part of what the moral judgement pronounces
to have value.   And they are judgements which could not really
be pronounced by a consciousness which could not experience
those emotions, which knew only on the one hand the data
supplied by the senses and on the other hand the abstract axioms
of the Practical Reason.

But this recognition of the absolute indispensability of certain
specific emotions (in many cases) to our moral judgement does
not in the least invalidate what has already been said as to the
intellectual, rational, objective character of the judgement of
value.   The judgement that a certain emotion has value is
a different thing from the mere emotion itself [2].   Without the

[1] 'For, if we once suppose the general physical basis of animal life to be
seriously altered, it is impossible to say to what extent the types of sentiment and action which, under present conditions, approve themselves as
life-preserving and beneficial to the individual and the species would be
still in place' (Taylor, *The Problem of Conduct*, p. 41). Prof. Taylor's insistence
that the details of duty would be different in different surroundings is quite
justified, but he seems to me to think that this proves more than it does —
that it altogether upsets any claim for objective validity or a 'rational'
character in our moral judgements.   But (1) it is true that I may recognize
that the ferocity of the tiger is as life-preserving and beneficial to its species
as the charity of the Saint ; yet I need not pronounce that it has the same intrinsic value : and (2) though the judgements as to right and wrong for human
nature would be different if our physical constitution were altered, that does
not show that every rational intelligence, in proportion as it is rational,
would not pronounce the same course of conduct to be right for man as he
is.   And this is what we mean by treating the moral judgement as objective.
[2] 'Notre vrai guide n'est ni l'instinct, ni une pensée transcendante, c'est
la réflexion sur l'instinct' (Rauh, *L'Expérience morale*, p. 96).

a priori and purely intellectual idea of value we could never pass from the judgement ' I feel such and such an emotion' to ' it is right for me and others to do the act which excites in me this emotion'; though the judgement could equally little be pronounced by a person incapable of experiencing the emotion, or at least of understanding and respecting its existence in others through the analogy of something more or less similar in his own experience. It is not the existence of the feeling but our judgement that that feeling is good that enables us to say that the act which excites it is right or wrong. It is not merely because it is a feeling excited by conduct that it can claim any pre-eminence over other feelings. If that were so, it would have no validity except for the persons naturally disposed to feel it. But our judgement that certain conduct is wrong does not disappear because as a matter of fact we may know that it excites no such feeling of disgust or repulsion in the person guilty of it. There are doubtless individuals who really do feel no disgust whatever at isolated or even habitual acts of drunkenness (though they are probably fewer than those who merely pretend to feel none): but we do not say that on that account drunkenness is right for such men. On the contrary we say that, if a man has not got such feelings, so much the worse for him: they are feelings which he ought to have. He falls short of the ideal of manhood if he has them not [1] There are other cases where natural feelings of disgust at particular kinds of conduct are pronounced on reflection to have no value whatever—e.g. the young medical student's sensations on first entering a dissecting room. We pronounce that such feelings should simply be got over as quickly as possible. The ultimate truth then which the Moral Sense school distorts is that in some cases a state of feeling is judged to have an absolute value, which, though more or less pleasant, is not measured merely by its pleasantness, and that such states of feeling form in and for themselves, entirely

---

[1] Cf. Aristotle, *Ethic. Nicomach.* III. i. § 13 (p. 1110*b*) Ὁ γὰρ μεθύων ἢ ὀργιζόμενος οὐ δοκεῖ δι᾽ ἄγνοιαν πράττειν ... ἀγνοεῖ μὲν οὖν πᾶς ὁ μοχθηρὸς ἃ δεῖ πράττειν καὶ ὧν ἀφεκτέον, καὶ διὰ τὴν τοιαύτην ἁμαρτίαν ἄδικοι καὶ ὅλως κακοὶ γίνονται· τὸ δ᾽ ἀκούσιον βούλεται λέγεσθαι οὐκ εἴ τις ἀγνοεῖ τὰ συμφέροντα· οὐ γὰρ ἐν τῇ προαιρέσει ἄγνοια αἰτία τοῦ ἀκουσίου ἀλλὰ τῆς μοχθηρίας.

apart from any further consequences, an element in that ideal good which we recognize it as our duty to promote. I shall hereafter give other illustrations of this class of moral judgements [1], but meanwhile I should observe three things about the feelings or emotional states of the kind which I mean:

(1) Although we can give no reason why the feeling, say of human affection, should be better than a feeling of satisfaction in eating except that we judge it to be so, the feelings to which we give this kind of preference are not arbitrarily and capriciously selected. They are intimately connected with our whole conception of the proper relation of man to man—our whole conception of what human life and human society should be. The judgement cannot therefore be reduced to any sort of isolated perception involving no exercise of the percipient's intellect, and no reference or relation to other judgements or ideas. It is impossible to dissociate our condemnation of illicit sexual intercourse from our conception of monogamy as the true type of sexual relation, our approval of which is based upon a great deal besides spontaneous emotions of approval or repugnance. The conception depends upon nothing less than our whole ideal of what constitutes a desirable state of human society and of the individual human soul. We judge that the state of feeling most conducive to the maintenance of the approved type possesses an intrinsic value. We cannot in the ordinary orthodox-utilitarian fashion *prove* irregular sexual relations to be wrong because they tend to prevent marriage and the growth of population; for it depends upon many circumstances whether they have that effect, and whether or not that effect is in itself to be regretted. Our condemnation of fornication, in spite of the diminution of pleasure which its prohibition undoubtedly involves, is not a deduction from a judgement about marriage resting on Utilitarian grounds, but simply one side or aspect of that ideal of life which prescribes both the monogamous marriage and the rule of purity before marriage. That ideal condemns sexual indulgence except where it can be made instrumental and subordinate to higher and more spiritual affections. When certain states of feeling appear to be selected for approval or condemnation by

1 2   [1] See Chap. vii.

a kind of instinct which can give no further account of itself, these are, in so far as they persist after the fullest reflection, not merely isolated feelings of approval or disapprobation such as the deliverances of the Moral Sense are sometimes supposed to be, but feelings which are elements in a single, interconnected, articulated ideal of human life. And ideals are recognized as such by the intellect, however much (in some cases) the existence of certain feelings or emotions may be the condition of such a recognition. So again when I condemn drunkenness, my judgement implies a whole conception of human life—that man is a rational being, adapted for certain ends, responsible for his actions, possessed of a certain worth or dignity, having such and such relations to his fellows, capable of certain intellectual and moral activities, activities which are interfered with and impeded by drunkenness. This whole ideal of what man is and ought to be is implied in my judgement that it is intrinsically degrading and unworthy of a rational being voluntarily to place himself in a state in which he is not master of his own actions, however elaborate the precautions which he may take against doing harm to himself and others when in that condition. The feeling of repugnance to the act is inseparable from a whole complex of judgements about human life and its purposes which are very different from isolated emotions. So again with such an obviously unutilitarian precept as that which condemns cannibalism. Clearly if the victim is not killed on purpose to be eaten, cannibalism under certain circumstances might present itself as an eminently sanitary and economical arrangement. If we judge that man ought to endure considerable privation—some would perhaps say even extreme privation—rather than eat human flesh, it is because we feel that this external reverence to a human corpse is an expression of a reverence for humanity which possesses a higher value than the momentary relief from hunger. It is impossible to isolate our condemnation of cannibalism from our whole ideal of the proper relation of man to his fellow men. The psychologically very similar feeling against dissection which long stood in the way of surgical progress we decline to encourage because it is inconsistent with an enlightened ideal of human life as a whole.

(2) And these considerations do involve the recognition of a principle which is constantly forgotten by Rationalists of the Kantian type. It is quite true that the question of what is moral for man depends upon his actual psychical constitution, including his sensitive, aesthetic, and emotional nature. If it is said that moral judgements are in a sense *a priori*, that must not be taken to mean that we could define the rules of human conduct without an empirically derived knowledge of the actual constitution of human nature, and of human society. That it is right to promote the true good of all that lives and is conscious is, indeed, an *a priori* truth which Reason can recognize without any appeal to empirical knowledge except what is implied in the idea of conscious life: but what actually is for the good of man or any other creature cannot be ascertained without a knowledge of the nature and capacities of that creature. The prohibition of shooting would be irrational among beings who were 'like the air, invulnerable': the law of marriage and all that flows from it presupposes the sexual difference itself—not merely the physical difference, but all the emotional and moral differences—between man and woman. It would be absurd to attempt an answer to the question what would be the best type of sexual union if human beings were not so constituted that man's feelings towards woman are different from those with which he regards his own sex, if men and women were not naturally inclined towards permanent and exclusive unions [1], if emotions of the highest and

---

[1] The researches of Prof. Westermarck (*History of Human Marriage*) tend to confirm Aristotle's dictum that man is τῇ φύσει συνδυαστικὸν μᾶλλον ἢ πολιτικόν. This is proved partly by inference from the fact that the higher apes are monogamous, partly by a wide induction from anthropological and historical facts. Polyandry is a rare, Polygamy a much more common institution, but both are exceptional arrangements due to special circumstances. The later work of Messrs. Spencer and Gillen (*The Native Tribes of Central Australia*) may be held to modify Prof. Westermarck's conclusions, but the most that they point to is a system of group-marriages, not the sheer promiscuity of McLellan's speculations; and after all, even in those marriages, one husband occupies an exceptional position. Even here a *tendency* to Monogamy is discernible. The great difficulty experienced by otherwise successful 'free-love' communities in America is the ineradicable tendency to form exclusive unions. But of course these facts are intended rather as an illustration than as a proof of the position taken up in the text.

purest type were not found to be subtly and inseparably connected with such unions, and so on.

(3) I may add that the passing of judgements of this kind
often demands for its full justification an amount of experience
which is quite beyond the reach of a single individual. The
monogamous ideal of life is based upon the accumulated experience of the human race, not merely the experience of the
numerical majority ; it is doubtful, indeed, whether the independent verdict of the numerical majority, even in those countries
which have not frankly abandoned the Christian ideal in this
matter, would really endorse this judgement, but for the deference
paid to the verdict of the best men which is based upon the results
of all the experience within their reach, experience of themselves
and others, experience of the good results of the observance and
the bad results of the non-observance of the monogamous rule.
But by experience of good and bad results I do not mean, of
course, mere pleasure and pain. It is upon the whole spiritual
condition which results from the control as compared with
the whole spiritual condition which results from the non-
control of these particular passions that the judgement of value
is pronounced. And the dependence of these judgements upon
an experience which cannot well be possessed by the young makes
this department of morality peculiarly dependent in practice
upon respect for moral authority [1]. I shall return to this matter
in a chapter which will be specially devoted to the place of
Authority in Ethics. It is sufficient here to note that there
are many departments of Morality in which it must be recognized
that the judgements of the individual—at least of ordinary
individuals, and of all individuals as regards a large part of
their lives—are and must be largely influenced by Authority.
No prejudice is done by this admission to the final and paramount authority of the moral consciousness : for this authority
to which the appeal is made (when it is rightly made) is simply

[1] This authority is not necessarily or exclusively that of a religious creed,
a religious teacher, or a religious community : but this is the most definite
and conspicuous form which moral authority actually assumes in modern
times. This dependence is, I believe, one explanation of the undoubted fact
that this is a department of morality which is peculiarly liable to suffer from
the decay of religious belief.

that of the moral consciousness in a higher stage of development, or of the moral consciousness working upon an experience which is wider and fuller than that of the isolated average individual.

Two very opposite schools of thought are apt to deny or ignore the truth that the content of our moral judgements is dependent upon the sensitive and emotional as well as the rational nature of man. It is often forgotten by the ordinary Utilitarian. He does not of course refuse to take into account the experience that such and such things bring pleasure, but he does sometimes fail to take into account tendencies to particular emotions, spontaneous tendencies to approve of certain kinds of conduct and to disapprove of others, which rest upon no logical ground, but must simply be taken as data upon which the Practical Reason has to work. The hedonistic assumption that all a man's desires are really desires for pleasure favours the delusion that desires can be created or extinguished or modified at will, if only you can show that good hedonistic results would be attained by doing so. On the other hand the rationalistic Moralist often forgets that the raw material, so to speak, upon which Practical Reason pronounces its judgements of value and which it works up into ideals must always be supplied by the actual experiences, emotions, desires, tendencies and aspirations of human nature. The judgement that the tendency of human nature to find satisfaction in certain kinds of conduct has value is, indeed, an immediate judgement which cannot be derived from experience in the ordinary sense of the word; but we very often cannot say why we should have such a tendency, or deny that in beings differently constituted other kinds of conduct might tend to their highest attainable good [1].

---

[1] Von Hartmann is one of the few idealistic Moralists who have adequately remembered this. Man, according to him, gets his notions of the End 'from the application of Reason to the actual course of events, including the subjective moral motives of men' ('aus der Anwendung der Vernunft auf den gesamten Weltlauf einschliesslich der subjektiven sittlichen Veranlagung der Menschen.' *Ethische Studien*, p. 181). At the same time, when he goes on to call the process of arriving at the ideal end 'inductive,' he seems to ignore the fundamental difference between recognizing a value in the various elements of which the end is made up, and that of merely asserting their actual

The question is raised, for instance, whether the received view of the mutual duties of parents and children, brothers and sisters, can be justified by a purely Utilitarian calculation. Can it be shown to be conducive to the greatest happiness of the greatest number? Waiving the difference between a hedonistic and a non-hedonistic conception of happiness, nothing is easier than to show the practical advantages of the arrangement, if you assume the actual tendency of the human mother to feel for her own offspring the most passionate of human affections, the actual tendency of all human beings to feel a stronger attachment to their own near kin than to strangers, and consequently to recognize a stronger claim upon their Benevolence. Given this tendency, the encouragement of it leads both to unselfishness in parents and to the proper bringing up of

existence. He seems sometimes (ib., p. 192) to fall into the mistake of trying to form a conception of the ethical end by induction from the actual empirically ascertained tendency of the Universe, the fallacy of which has been sufficiently pointed out by Mr. Herbert Spencer's critics. That moral Reason can deal with data which it cannot itself supply or create, no one (among ethical Rationalists) appreciates better than von Hartmann. 'Diese Norm ist ein Produkt der Vernunft, ein Ideal, welches zeigt, wie der Mensch eigentlich sein sollte. Aber dieses Ideal ist nicht ein systematisch aus irgend welchem anderen Prinzip abgeleitetes, sondern ein Komplex von unmittelbaren Gefühls- oder Geschmacksurteilen' (ib., p. 94). He points out too that in time this reasonable criticism of, and selection, among our desires modifies the feelings themselves (ib., p. 199). The only point in this statement to which I should demur is that he seems disposed to identify the 'judgement of taste' with mere feeling, which would leave to the Reason nothing but the function of collecting and combining the actual feelings of the judger—a mode of thought quite inconsistent with the whole of his powerful plea for an absolute or rational standard of Morality. Reason must not merely collect and systematize, but select and value the different elements of human experience.

It is surprising to find how blind naturalistic Moralists continue to be to the fact that the real problem of Ethics is as to how we determine or ought to determine the ultimate end. This problem is wholly ignored in such works as M. Lévy-Bruhl's *La Morale et la Science des mœurs* (1904), the main idea of which is that the Science of the means to the end should be based upon Sociology (or a complex of sociological Sciences): how the end is to be discovered and what are the metaphysical implications of the idea of an 'end' are questions which he does not ask. There is no indication in an otherwise clever work that its author is capable of even understanding their meaning.

children. On the other hand, put out of sight the *de facto* emotional constitution of human nature, and nothing could be easier than to demonstrate the disadvantages arising from these narrow family attachments, and the infinite hedonistic and moral superiority of a society in which all older men should be regarded as fathers, all equals as brothers. So Plato argued, and he was only wrong because he supposed that Reason could pronounce moral judgements without any appeal to the actual emotional tendencies of human nature, or because he supposed that human nature was more modifiable than it is. The Moral Sense school are right in holding that our moral judgements are partly dependent upon the feelings and emotions with which we do naturally regard conduct of various kinds, and that these must be taken account of before we pronounce whether that conduct is to be regarded as right or wrong. It would be impossible to show that it is a more imperative duty to relieve suffering at our own door than suffering at a distance, if it were not an actual tendency of human nature to feel a readier and deeper sympathy with the suffering that one actually beholds: and so on[1]. This last illustration may help to suggest the importance of the opposite side of ethical truth. While Reason must take account of those actual feelings and emotions which form part of our moral nature before pronouncing by what means most good will be realized, we cannot allow the actual strength of the feeling to be the sole test of moral approval or disapproval. Moral progress consists very largely in substituting deliberate thought-out judgements for casual and variable emotions: and the exercise of Reason in time reacts upon the emotions themselves. When we have come intellectually to recognize the claims of suffering which we do not see, we may come to feel for it a sympathy which is something very different from, and very much more powerful as a motive for action than, the bare intellectual recognition that the worth of a human being must

---

[1] Hume was right in insisting that in average human nature (apart from the influence of logical reflection or rational consideration) 'the qualities of the mind are selfishness and limited generosity' (*Treatise*, Book III, Pt. ii, § 2).

be quite independent of geographical considerations or ethnological affinities. Even moral feeling must be guided and controlled by Reason; to a very large extent, indeed, the difference between 'higher' and 'lower' feeling consists precisely in the difference between mere feeling as it exists in merely non-moral natures and feeling in the form which it assumes when guided and controlled by human Reason. The judgement of value which Reason pronounces is not dictated by the feelings, but the actual feelings supply the materials which it uses in building up a consistent and harmonious ideal of human life. Reason cannot invent new feelings, but it can so regulate human conduct as to produce a maximum of those in which it recognizes most value, and that regulation of conduct tends in time to produce actual feeling in accordance with the ideal which Reason sets up.

V

The objections to the Moral Sense view of Ethics are substantially the same as those which must be urged against the systems which represent the moral faculty as something *sui generis*—neither Reason nor feeling. Bishop Butler discerned, as we have seen [1], the fundamental defect of all mere Moral Sense theories—that they could assign no reason why this feeling of the Moral Sense should be accorded any superiority over other feelings. A Moral Sense can have no authority: authority is of the essence of Conscience. To Bishop Butler himself, at least when he wrote his Sermons, the authority of Conscience was, it is probable, simply the authority of Reason. His habitual synonym for Conscience is a 'principle of Reflection': at times he explicitly calls it Reason. But some of his disciples—of whom Dr. Martineau is the most distinguished representative—decline to admit this identification. It is so exceedingly difficult to grasp the idea of a 'faculty' which is neither part of our intellectual nature nor yet any kind of feeling or emotion that the view is not easy to criticize. It may be enough perhaps to quote Martineau's statement of his position and to point out the source of the confusion into which he seems to fall:

[1] See above, p. 144, *note*.

'And when, in order to scrutinise their relation, we lay them side by side and look at their contents, we see at once that the features, present in approval and absent from assent are precisely the whole of the *moral* characteristics, whence the judgement derives its ethical quality. In my assent to the proposition that any two radii vectores of an ellipse, meeting at their peripheral extremities, are together equal to the transverse axis, and my dissent from the assertion that they are always equal to one another, I have none of the self-contentment and of the compunction respectively involved in my right and wrong volitions; I assign no *merit* to the truth, no *demerit* to the error, or to the mind that is subject to them; were my belief rewarded, I should be ashamed of the absurdity: were my misbelief punished, I should resent the injustice. But these experiences, which fail to attend the *Yes* and *No* of Reason, are the sum of the moral sentiments which attend the *Yes* and *No* of Conscience. There is nothing, therefore, in common except the naked fact of acceptance or rejection; the thing accepted or rejected, it is plain, is wholly different [1].'

There is much virtue in that 'nothing except.' All that Dr. Martineau's objections really show is that the moral judgement is an essentially different kind of judgement from any other: they do not show that it is not a judgement. When a piece of conduct is pronounced 'rational' or 'reasonable,' something else no doubt is meant than when a conclusion is pronounced logically to follow from its premisses. If we treat 'reasonable' and 'right' as synonyms, that does not imply that we do not recognize the enormous difference between 'reasonable' or 'reasonable to think' and 'reasonable to be done.' In this sense it is quite true there is an element present in the moral judgement and absent in the mathematical. It does not follow that this element is simply 'the glow of emotion,' though such a glow may be a more or less inseparable accompani-

---

[1] *Types of Ethical Theory*, 3rd ed., vol. II, p. 473. Cf. also the admission 'In one sense, every experience of our nature might be pronounced intellectual. . . . Passion and emotion themselves are, in us, not without thought, and may be always treated as *thought in a glow*' (p. 468). If there is thought in our moral perception, there must be thought about something, and that something cannot be just the fact of the perception itself.

ment of the judgement. Nothing can be more important than to emphasize the *sui generis* character of the moral judgement, that is to say of that idea of goodness or value which forms its essence. But that does not show the necessity for inventing a separate faculty to give such judgements. We are not confusing time with space because we assign to our ideas of both an intellectual origin. We may if we like call Practical Reason a separate faculty from speculative Reason—that is only a question of words. We really mean simply that they are distinguishable aspects of one and the same rational self. The important thing is that we should recognize that moral judgements possess an absolute truth or falsity, which is equally valid for all rational beings [1]; and, if that is recognized, it seems most natural to ascribe them to Reason.

Much the same line of objection to the rationalistic position has been followed in a more recent attempt to rehabilitate the old Moral Sense view of Ethics, or something like it, made by the late Professor Gizycki. His line of argument seems to me to imply the same misunderstandings, and to demand the same concessions, as the old English 'Moral Sense' view and Dr. Martineau's Philosophy of Conscience. But there is one objection made by Gizycki which demands an additional word of explanation. It is really strange to find an eminent Professor of Philosophy solemnly arguing that, if the rationalistic view were true, 'the most intellectual man would be the best morally, and the least intelligent would be the worst [2].' Here in the first place I notice the confusion already pointed out—between what tells a man his duty and what makes him do it. Men of genius may see their duty clearly enough, but they do not always do it. Nobody could discourse more beautifully about Morality than Goethe or Coleridge. But this is not all. It is not even true

---

[1] True for all rational beings, not equally binding on all rational beings. All rational beings must recognize them as binding on beings constituted as man is constituted. The essential principles of morality must no doubt be the same for all such beings, but not its detail.

[2] *An Introduction to the Study of Ethics*, adapted from the German of G. M. Gizycki by Stanton Coit, Ph.D., 1891, p. 87; a work which had already appeared in 1889 under the title 'A Student's Manual of Ethical Philosophy.'

that, on the rationalistic principle, the most intelligent man must know his duty best. For 'intelligence' has many branches or departments, or aspects. The man who has mathematical capacity may be singularly wanting in the gift of language or expression; he may be wholly blind to the beauty of Art or of Poetry; while the Artist and the Scholar may be exceptionally unmathematical. Poets have often been entirely unmusical. Roughly speaking perhaps the possession of superior mental capacity in one direction may be held generally to carry with it something more than average capacity in others; but to this rule there are many exceptions. In the same way it may be roughly—very roughly—true that men of superior ability are on the whole more capable of moral appreciation (and even perhaps more moral in practice) than men of inferior mental capacity. We may distrust the speculations about a distinctly criminal type of brain, but it is certain that professional criminals are usually people of very low mental capacity, though a few are men of great intellectual ability. At the same time it is perfectly possible, and often happens, that the particular capacity for apprehending the distinction between right and wrong may be possessed by persons not otherwise remarkable for intellect; while intellectual persons are occasionally very deficient in this respect. This might be admitted even by the straitest sect of ethical Rationalism. But in these pages it has been further contended that, though the apprehension of moral distinctions is in itself an intellectual act, the exercise of this intellectual capacity is often conditioned by and postulates a certain emotional endowment. Some of our ethical judgements could not be given at all were a certain emotion absent; and, given the emotion, the ethical judgement is often a very simple affair: but intellectual judgements are not the less intellectual because they lie within the capacity of very 'unintellectual' persons. It is much the same, I suppose, with the aesthetic faculty. The intellectual character of the musical faculty—its close connexion with the capacity for the most abstract kind of thinking—is attested by the tendency of musical and mathematical talent to go together. Yet intellect alone will not make a Musician; musical originality or even high musical appreciation presupposes a capacity for certain kinds of emotion, which the Mathematician may lack. So with the moral faculty; it belongs to the intellect, yet it may be paralysed or perverted by want of emotional capacity. This has often been the case probably with enthusiasts and fanatics—men of exceptional sense of duty or exceptional devotion to ideals of one kind or another, but little human affection. Some persons may have little delicacy of moral judgement for want of the original capacity for emotion. Still more often may people who possess perhaps in a high degree all the intellectual capacities required for giving judgements of value exhibit small moral insight in actual life, because through their own personal failure in right willing, or through their unfavourable moral environment, they have not acted up to such light as they had. The Reason that judges and the will that acts are not one and the same thing, but they are only two sides of one and the same self, and they do most powerfully act and react upon one another. The maxim 'obedience is the organ of spiritual knowledge' has been abused in the interests of obscurantism and fanaticism, but it represents nevertheless a most important fact in Moral Psychology [1].

VI

To some minds it will probably appear that I have inadequately stated the intimacy of the connexion between the rational judgement of value and the emotions by which it is normally accompanied. There are Moralists who, agreeing that the idea of value is logically distinguishable from the emotion with which right conduct is contemplated, will insist that *de facto* they are so inseparable that the moral judgement could not be made by, and could have no meaning for, a mind destitute of the specific moral emotion. 'I think,' writes a friend who takes this view [2], 'that the "reason" and "feeling" which are to be found in moral judgments, though no doubt distinguishable, are not only always found together, but each is unintelligible and empty apart from

---

[1] Cf. Aristotle's ἡ κακία φθαρτικὴ ἀρχῆς.

[2] I cannot call to mind any printed expression of this doctrine, though it is taught by high authorities in Oxford—a fact which must be my apology for quoting a private letter.

the other. The judgement "this is right" is not a moral judgement unless one has, more or less, the moral emotion (for in the judgement "this is right," when the ground is any authority, the moral emotion and the judgment proper fall upon the authority, not strictly upon the particular point), nor is it a moral emotion unless it claims universality. This, I think, is the same view as yours, but perhaps you might more carefully avoid the use of language which suggests juxtaposition (reason + feeling); which is surely unsatisfactory, and leads to what one finds inadequate in the language of Hume on one side and Kant on another.' To such a line of criticism I should reply as follows:

(1) With regard to the suggestion about mere 'juxtaposition,' I have very definitely admitted that in all cases some feeling is, in part, the ground of the judgement. That being so, the judgement could not be made without the feeling, but the feeling which is the ground of a moral judgement is, in my view, *not always* any specifically moral or 'higher' kind of feeling. In some cases the judgement implies a particular kind of 'higher' emotion, but not in all. In some cases the only feeling which is implied as the ground of the judgement is simple pleasure and pain, not in ourselves but in others, though without some experience of them in ourselves we should not know what they are in others. To know that this act causes pain in others is all that I want to enable me to condemn it. That pain is the negation of good, and that the good ought to be promoted, are self-evident truths perceivable by the intellect. How far in actual fact there exist persons so constituted as to be capable of seeing that truth without experiencing the smallest emotional repulsion against causing pain, or the smallest inclination to avoid it themselves, is a question of empirical Psychology on which I should not like to pronounce a decided opinion. But I see nothing self-contradictory in the supposition that there may be such persons. There certainly seem to be persons who do make this judgement, but in whom ethical emotion and ethical inclination are so small as in no way to account for the judgement being made.

(2) And even in persons who are not altogether incapable of moral emotion, some moral judgements are not as a matter of

fact accompanied by any emotion at all, though the same judgement may on other occasions call forth emotion of great strength. The proposition that pleasure is good and pain bad—or that some particular trifling pleasure of my own is good and conduct which interferes with it wrong in myself or in another—is one that can be assented to without any emotion whatever; and yet that proposition is the ultimate ground for my condemnation of some act of cruelty which might excite in me feelings of warm indignation. And I regard it as a matter of great theoretical importance to insist that the intellectual categories of good and right are as distinctly present in the cool and calculating judgement that it is unreasonable to throw away a large pleasure for a smaller one (no matter whose that pleasure be), as in our enthusiastic approval of some heroic act of self-sacrifice.

(3) Of course we can, if we choose, include in our idea of good and evil, right and wrong, the emotion which they excite in normally constituted persons, or even all the varieties of emotion that they may excite in abnormally constituted persons. On the principle that we do not know a thing fully till we know all its relations, it may no doubt be said that we do not *fully* understand the meaning of right and wrong unless we do take into account these facts of our emotional nature. To a person incapable of any such emotion the terms would no doubt not mean all that they mean to one who is capable of it. But I am not prepared to admit that it would mean nothing to him. Not only would it mean something to him, but that something is, I should hold, the very essence of the moral judgement, considered simply as a judgement. The ideas of good and evil, right and wrong, seem to be as distinguishable in thought from any emotion accompanying them as the idea of a circle is from the aesthetic feeling which may perhaps be in fact its inseparable accompaniment. To insist upon the greater practical importance of the feeling attending the moral judgement would be wholly beside the point.

(4) The contention that the term 'right' means nothing apart from the emotions by which moral judgements at the higher levels of moral experience are usually accompanied seems to me open to a further objection. I am unable to recognize the

existence of any one particular specifically 'moral' emotion [1]. An intellectual category must be one and the same for all intelligences, though there may be a greater or less degree of clearness, explicitness, and adequacy in the apprehension of it at different stages of intellectual development. But emotion is essentially a variable and subjective thing. And the emotion excited by good or bad conduct, and by the judgements of moral approbation or disapprobation which they call forth, are no exception to the rule. These emotions are different in the case of different races, different individuals, different periods of life. Even in the same individual they vary from day to day with our changing moods and circumstances. The emotions which different kinds of good or bad conduct excite are very different, even when the intellectual approval or disapproval is the same. Few people approve an act of commonplace Justice with the warmth which they bestow on an act of Generosity, and yet Justice is quite as important as Generosity. When I judge a massacre to be wrong, my judgement is exactly the same whether it has been committed by Englishmen on Englishmen in the streets of London, or by Chinamen on Chinamen in the streets of Pekin, but my emotion would probably be very different both in kind and intensity. Even with characters of exceptional moral earnestness, there is every reason to suppose that the emotion accompanying their ethical thinking must be of very different kinds. It is improbable that a mind of John Wesley's severity could ever have felt the tender humanity of St. Francis of Assisi, or that in a man of sympathetic nature like John Stuart Mill the sense of duty assumed the emotional tone with which it was invested in the Philosopher whose personal character has stamped itself for ever upon the doctrine of the 'categorical imperative.' To say that the category of value or of duty was present in the mind of Mill as much as in that of Kant, however little the Metaphysic of the former may have recognized its presence, is an assertion which I understand and accept. Whether the emotional accom-

[1] 'Es giebt demnach nicht ein bestimmtes Gefühl, welches als moralisches Gefühl von allen anderen Gefühlen verschieden wäre, sondern jedes Gefühl entspricht in seiner Tendenz mehr oder minder sittlichen Aufgaben, oder es widerspricht denselben in höherem oder geringerem Grade' (Von Hartmann, Das sittl. Bewusstsein, p. 148).

paniments of their judgements were the same is a psychological question which it would be a piece of the most unwarrantable dogmatism to determine *a priori*. If, therefore, the assertion that a moral emotion claims universality means that the same emotion must be present in all moral persons, I see no ground for the assumption. Nor, indeed, in strictness can I understand the meaning of asserting that any emotion whatever 'claims universality.' That, when I recognize a value in a certain emotion, my judgement claims universality I admit; but I recognize the probability that many different kinds of moral emotion may possess a high degree of intrinsic worth, and I see no reason for selecting one particular type of it as the one and only 'moral emotion,' in the absence of which the judgement could not be moral at all. It may no doubt be urged that the ideal man would feel exactly the same kind of emotion on the same occasions. That would be a somewhat difficult contention, inasmuch as a certain limitation, and therefore a certain individuality, seems essential to a nature that is to be truly human. But, whatever may be thought of this point, the assertion supplies no ground for saying that the judgement is not in thought quite distinguishable from the emotion. The ideal man might be unable to think of universal gravitation without profound 'cosmic emotion,' but that supplies no reason for declaring that a Physicist who has never felt a moment's 'cosmic emotion' in his life must be ignorant of universal gravitation.

(5) It is only, as I have already pointed out, in the case of certain particular ethical judgements (not in all) that they simply cannot be made by a consciousness incapable of certain emotions: here where that is so, the judgements turn upon the actual value of the emotions as elements in human life. A consciousness which was entirely lacking in all the higher feelings—aesthetic, intellectual, social, moral—to which the developed moral consciousness assigns value, would assuredly have a limited and distorted moral ideal, but it does not follow that it would attach no meaning at all to the ideas of right and wrong, or be unable to pronounce correctly upon simple problems of elementary Morality. It might still for instance be able to recognize the wrongness of the individual deliberately preferring his own

interest to that of the community, and to apply that judgement to many particular cases.

(6) It may even be admitted that those judgements which do not psychologically depend upon the presence of emotion are not very likely ever to be made—to say nothing of the respect paid to them—by a mind totally destitute of the emotions which naturally accompany them. If the human mind could ever be a passionless thinking machine, it might indeed be contended that the emotionless man would be a particularly good judge of right and wrong in respect of those questions— questions for instance of Justice in the distribution of pleasure— which lay within its range. But no mind can ever enjoy a passionless vision of Reality. In the mind which is (relatively or absolutely) devoid of moral or social feeling, the place of such feelings is sure to be taken by other feelings, emotions, and desires, which must necessarily distort the moral judgement or totally prevent its exercise. Even our most abstract thinking is dominated by purpose or interest of some kind. Minds which take no interest in Morality do not think about it at all. I see no reason why for instance a person incapable of moral emotion should not be able to recognize the injustice of slavery, though he might have felt no inclination to agitate for its abolition. But we know that as a matter of fact the minds which first pronounced slavery to be wrong were minds dominated by a passion for Justice and an ardent love of Humanity. In minds which have no such passion, indifference may prevent any judgement whatever, or any serious judgement, upon the problem ; interest may suggest wrong judgements.

This doctrine of the inseparability of the moral judgement from one particular kind of emotion seems to me not only unwarrantable in itself, but dangerous in its theoretical tendency : for it obscures the fact that the judgement of value by which I recognize that my own pleasure is a reasonable end of pursuit is exactly the same in its intellectual character as our recognition of an intrinsic value in heroism or saintliness, although the emotional accompaniments of the two judgements may be very different. It is true no doubt that the amount of value which we recognize in the former case is much smaller

than that which we recognize in the latter. To the pleasure
which it is right to pursue we assign value: but we do not
attribute much intrinsic value to the will which wills that
pleasure unless the preference of the pleasure implies devotion
to some higher kind of good, or to the good as such, on the part
of the agent; and this is commonly the case only when the
pleasure aimed at is not the agent's own, since only in this case
is there usually present any strong temptation to pursue some
other end, though we may ascribe some small value to the
preference even of private interest to mere brute passion.
Conduct directed towards the good is right whether it implies
Virtue on the part of the agent or not: but such conduct need
not possess value in any appreciable degree. The value may
often lie in the end or consequences, not in the act itself. And
the term moral value is commonly reserved for the value that
we attribute to character—to the good will or at least to
inclinations and dispositions, desires and emotions, which we
recognize as conducive to or resulting from a settled bent
of the will towards the good[1]. It is important no doubt to
insist on the superior value which we ascribe to such preference
for the good. But the two kinds of value are not absolutely
incommensurable. However much superior the value of a good
act may be to that of a transitory pleasure, we still use the term
'value' of both, and we use it in the same sense: the two kinds
of value differ as being at the top and the bottom of the same
scale, not as representing two totally incommensurable scales.
There can be only one ultimate scale of values, however
heterogeneous the objects which we appraise by that scale.
Thus to the actual relief of pain and healing of wounds which
resulted to the man fallen among thieves from the act of the
good Samaritan we assign value. If it were not good for
wounds to be healed, it would not have been *right* for the good
Samaritan to heal them; but we should not call the injured

[1] Prof. Taylor seems to me to forget this use of the term 'moral value'
when he declares, without qualification, that 'it is quite impossible, after
the fashion of popular philosophy, to draw a line between qualities that are
moral and qualities that are not so. Whatever is felt by men to be *worth*
having at all has, *eo ipso*, moral value, or rather, moral value is a tautologous
expression' (*Problem of Conduct*, p. 297).

man's feeling *morally* good.   On the other hand, to the good Samaritan's act we assign 'moral value,' and we may even assign moral value to the emotion which prompted, or to the pleasure which resulted from the act, even though the emotion and the pleasure may not have been under the immediate control of the will, because it would be an indication of character or of a settled bent of the will.   Such is the ordinary usage of language.   The distinction between 'moral value' and 'value' is no doubt one of great practical importance, inasmuch as it implies a conviction of the supreme and unique value of a rightly directed will.   But there is not the absolute disparity between them that is suggested by the idea of a distinctively moral emotion in the absence of which our judgements as to the value of this or that element of human life could not be moral judgements at all.

It has been contended in this chapter that 'the moral faculty' is essentially Reason.   By that is meant that the ideas of Right and Wrong, Good and Evil, are intellectual concepts or categories which cannot be reduced to any kind or sort of mere feeling.   But it has been fully admitted that practically the power of deciding between right and wrong involves many emotional elements, and these are certainly included in what is popularly spoken of as Conscience.   Conscience or (to speak more scientifically) the moral consciousness may be held to include not merely the capacity of pronouncing moral judgements, but the whole body of instincts, feelings, emotions, desires which are presupposed by and which influence these judgements, as well as those which prompt to the doing of the actions which they prescribe[1].   No more accurate definition can be given, because the 'moral faculty' cannot actually exist apart from the other elements of self-consciousness.   The Practical Reason implies all the other activities of Reason and would be impossible without them; and it implies also, not a mere single specific feeling or emotion, but a whole complex of feelings and

---

[1] Another element in what is commonly called Conscience is simply the individual's consciousness of the fact that he is or is not doing what he himself believes to be right.   'It perceives whether those [actions] it judges right, or those it judges wrong, are actually adopted' (Shadworth Hodgson, *Philosophy of Experience*, vol. IV, p. 86).

emotions upon the value of which the Practical Reason has to pronounce. 'Conscience' or the moral consciousness is a name for a particular aspect of the single self which is thought and feeling and will. Morality would be impossible and meaningless, or at least defective and one-sided, for a being in whom any one of these elements were wanting [1].

[1] It may be broadly stated that all recent moralists who approach the subject from a purely psychological point of view tend to agree with the Moral Sense position in making Morality ultimately to rest upon feeling, though they may be less clear about the specific and distinctive character of the feeling. To Höffding for instance the value-judgement is simply a feeling, arising largely from Sympathy (*Ethik*, pp. 41, 72, &c.); the categorical imperative is 'an instinct' (ib., p. 55). Though quite aware that this position involves the sacrifice of all objective character for moral judgements, he seems to me constantly to use language and to express ideas which imply such an objectivity. Simmel insists strongly on the fact that the 'ought' is an ultimate and unanalysable category of our thought, but makes the whole *content* of the 'ought' come from feeling (*Einleitung in die Moralwissenschaft*, Berlin, 1892, I, pp. 23 *sq.*, 54, 239, &c.). But it is difficult to see how it is possible to assert the validity of a category (and if it is a category of *thought* its validity can hardly be denied) without any power to apply it to a matter or to give it a content. Such an assertion would seem to be like maintaining that we have indeed a category of quantity or number, but are quite incapable of counting. Granted that our judgements in detail are liable to be influenced by all sorts of psychological considerations, just as subjective motives constantly lead to numerical miscalculations (e. g. of the numbers present at a meeting in which we are interested), it is difficult to see how there can be a category which we cannot validly use at all. After all the category of *ought* in general is simply an abstraction got by comparing together actual judgements of value. If what is contended is that we do *think* values but that such judgements possess no objective validity, the reply to it must simply be the general metaphysical reply to all Scepticism. Much of Simmel's polemic against Rationalism in Ethics seems to turn upon the old confusion between Reason and reasoning (e. g. in *Einleitung*, I, pp. 98–99); at the same time he has done a service by pointing out with much acuteness and vivacity some of the psychological causes which as a matter of fact do largely determine our actual moral judgements, e. g. our tendency to assume that the usual or normal conduct of our society is the right course. But it is perhaps a mistake to take Simmel's use of the term 'category' too seriously. It appears that ultimately the category of 'end' (practically identical with that of 'ought') is a merely 'subjective' category (II, p. 347, &c.) which would seem to mean that we have a confused idea of an 'ought' which we take to mean something, but which is of no more objective significance than the idea of 'Kismet' or that of a Centaur, though (like those ideas) it may influence human conduct. But the admission that as a matter

of psychological fact these ideas of 'ought,' 'end,' 'the good,' &c., do exist, and cannot be resolved into something else, represents a great advance on the crude Psychology which simply explained them as 'fear of tribal vengeance,' or the like. When writers like Simmel deny their objective validity, they do so as sceptical or sensationalistic metaphysicians, not as observers of psychological fact. These admissions become particularly valuable when we turn to the philosophical fireworks of such a writer as Guyau (*Esquisse d'une Morale sans obligation ni sanction*), whose original discovery seems to be that any factor of our consciousness which he cannot explain on the assumptions of his own Philosophy may be got rid of by the simple device of calling it 'mystical.'

NOTE ON THE AESTHETIC JUDGEMENT

A chapter on the relation between the moral and the aesthetic judgement might have formed a natural and desirable sequel to the treatment of 'Reason and Feeling' in Ethics, but I do not feel that my acquaintance with Aesthetic Philosophy enables me to undertake it. A few remarks on the subject may, however, be useful with a view to clearing up what has been said in the preceding chapter, and to prevent misunderstanding.

(1) I distinctly recognize an objective element in our aesthetic judgements. That is implied in our strong conviction that there is a right and a wrong about such judgements. They too, like moral judgements, are in a sense judgements of value. But I do not say that they are 'objective' in exactly the same sense and to the same extent as the ethical judgement. For they seem to be more closely connected with the variable physiological organization of individuals than ethical judgements. It has been suggested, for instance, that the restful feeling of green for human beings is due to effects on the human eye and nerves of its frequency in Nature—especially for our arboreal ancestors ; while the effect of red ('like the sound of a trumpet,' to quote the famous remark of a man blind from his birth) is due to its infrequency in Nature. By beings with a different evolutionary history, therefore, a red landscape with a few touches of green would, it may be contended, be pronounced as beautiful, and beautiful in the same way, as we think a landscape of predominant green with a few touches of red. So again the beauty of a Gothic window as compared with a square one may plausibly be connected with the frequency of the Gothic arch in woods and the rarity of square arches in Nature. Even if such theories are well founded, they do not destroy the existence of an objective element in our aesthetic judgements. The perfect intelligence might still pronounce the aesthetic feeling which we experience good, though in beings otherwise constituted other aesthetic experiences might be good also. It may be contended that we have something parallel to this in the moral laws which are obviously applicable only to beings constituted like man, though the good for such beings may be something in which every rational intelligence would recognize value. But then I for one should contend that the

more ultimate of our moral judgements, such as that which recognizes the value of love, are independent of such differences in the structure of individuals or of society (see Bk. III, chap. iii), and represent not merely what all rational beings would pronounce valuable in us, but an element of experience which must exist and have value in all higher minds and in God. It may be that we might say the same of aesthetic judgements— that the value which may be recognized in aesthetic judgements which differ and even contradict one another in detail, might all be referable to some higher principles of aesthetic judgement which would explain them all; but we can form a less distinct conception of such principles than we can of the fundamental moral laws. I cannot undertake to discuss the matter here, but will only notice that aesthetic judgements (as we know them in human beings) do seem to be more intimately connected with, and inseparable from, sensations which presuppose a particular physiological organization than the most fundamental moral judgements, although I do not regard that fact as any reason for denying that they are in a true sense objective.

(2) If the moral judgement is essentially a judgement of value, its sphere must be absolutely all-embracing. There can be no department of human life, no kind of human consciousness or experience, upon which the moral Reason may not pronounce its judgements of value. People in whom aesthetic interests are stronger than ethical interests frequently attempt to set up a sphere of Art to which Morality is supposed to have no relation whatever. Such persons simply show that they have too narrow a view of what Morality is. What they really mean, or ought to mean, is that aesthetic activities or enjoyments have a high value quite apart from any further effects upon conduct in the narrower sense—that it may be morally right to paint and look at pictures which have no tendency to make the artist or the beholder go away and perform his social duties better. That artistic enjoyment has this high value and forms an important element in true human good, I have strongly contended. Our aesthetic objector may, however, mean more than this. He may mean that any amount of aesthetic enjoyment, and all kinds of it, are right, and right in all circumstances. Such a proposition is so extravagant that it could hardly be made by anybody who really contemplated the full consequences of his assertion; but, whether the proposition be true or false, it represents an ethical judgement—as much so as the proposition that the interests of Art must sometimes give way to the claims of social duty, and that there are in the world plays not devoid of aesthetic value which it was morally wrong to write, and which the State is right in not allowing to be acted. The question what kinds of Art it is good to produce, how much time it is right for such and such persons to spend in producing them or in con- templating them, within what limits the aesthetic indulgence should be restrained in the interests of wholesome moral feeling—these and such-like questions are moral questions. Morality deals with ultimate ends or elements in *the* end. No indulgence which does not form part of the true ultimate end can possibly be justified.

(3) The question may then be raised 'what is the relation between the moral and the aesthetic judgement?'

The moral judgement is a judgement of value; but is not, it may be asked, the aesthetic judgement also a judgement of value—at least for those who recognize its objective character and refuse to reduce it to the judgement 'this gives me a particular kind of pleasure'? When I pronounce that a thing is aesthetically 'good,' does not that imply that it is an end which ought to be pursued? Up to a certain point there can be little difficulty in answering the question. We may say that the moral judgement is in all cases the final one, but that the moral judgement must use the data supplied by the aesthetic judgement. The aesthetic judgement tells us 'this is beautiful.' The moral judgement goes on to say 'Beauty, or this particular kind of beauty, has an intrinsic worth, and consequently ought to be pursued.' We may even say that for a consciousness which recognizes the intrinsic value of Beauty, the judgement 'this picture is aesthetically good' practically implies and includes the judgement 'the contemplation of this picture has a certain intrinsic worth,' though other and purely moral judgements will be required to determine its relative worth as compared with other goods.

(4) But what if the moral judgement and the aesthetic judgement actually contradict one another? In ordinary cases of what may be superficially called collisions between the moral and the aesthetic judgements no real difficulty arises. When I say 'this play is aesthetically a good one, but on this particular evening it would be wrong for me to go and see it,' this is merely an ordinary case of the collision between goods. The judgement 'the contemplation of this play has a certain worth' is not rendered untrue by the judgement 'What I should do with my time and money if I did not go to see this play, has a greater worth, and it is my duty not only to seek the good but the greatest good. Hence it would be morally wrong to see the play.'

The real difficulty arises, not when we pronounce merely that what is aesthetically good is yet a good which for certain persons in certain circumstances ought to be surrendered in favour of a greater good, but when we pronounce it to be from a moral point of view actually bad. In some cases it may be possible to isolate and separate the good element from the bad. We may approve a novel as a work of Art, and yet condemn the moral tendency of incidental reflections or remarks by the author, or of certain disgusting episodes which (even if not actually irrelevant to the plot as it stands, as is often the case) may still be regarded as contributing nothing to the aesthetic effect of the piece which could not equally be secured by a somewhat different plot. Here we may say 'the work of Art as such is good; but a novel ought not merely to be artistic but to be decent. What I pronounce morally bad forms no part of what I pronounce aesthetically good.' But in other cases the immoral tendency may be too intimately allied with the artistic effect of the piece to be treated in this way. The particular kind of Art in question may be aesthetically good, and yet by its very nature appeal to passions which had better (from a moral point of view) not be excited, at least in this way and in this intensity. This is particularly the case, I should judge, with certain kinds of Music in their effect upon highly musical natures. But even here is not the case after all only a case of the comparison of values? If we condemn the piece—that is to say, if we judge that it ought not to have been written, or that it ought not to be performed, or that particular persons should not hear it, or that it should not be listened to frequently—we judge that, though the worth which it possesses *qua* work of Art is a real worth, that worth is not so great as the worth of properly regulated passions, and that, if and in so far as the former kind of good cannot be enjoyed without the loss of the latter, that good is one which we should do without.

Of course I need hardly say that we may condemn the moral tendency of a book or a piece of music without necessarily saying that nobody should under any circumstances read the book or hear the music. The good may still—for particular persons and in particular circumstances—outweigh the evil. But that in some circumstances it is a moral duty to abstain from enjoyments which are aesthetically admirable cannot be doubted. In the great majority of cases—at least as regards Literature—the important thing is the relative proportion which the morally stimulating and the morally depressing in our reading bear to each other. Ruskin has remarked that the important thing is not so much what we don't read as what we do read. The properly nourished mind may for a sufficient purpose read, without injury and even with advantage, much which in itself has an immoral tendency, just as the properly nourished physical frame can swallow many germs of disease without deleterious effects. The principle must apply to a greater or less extent to other branches of Art.

(5) Another way of putting the matter is to say that, when we pronounce a particular experience aesthetically good but morally bad, we mean that it appeals to and satisfies a part of our nature, and a part which, when we look at it in abstraction from our nature as a whole, we pronounce good: but that, when compared with our ideal of human nature as a whole, this particular indulgence fails to be approved. To indulge in it—for certain persons, in certain circumstances, or beyond a certain point, or in some cases to indulge in it at all—would be to attach disproportionate value to this side of our nature as compared with others. The case of an aesthetic indulgence given up in deference to moral considerations differs from the case of a banquet condemned and abstained from as too costly or luxurious only in the fact that the good surrendered is, when taken in abstraction from our ideal of human life as a whole, a higher or more valuable good than the pleasures of good eating and drinking.

(6) From the point of view which has now been reached it may be possible to make a further step towards the solution of the difficulties presented by the problem of objectivity in the aesthetic judgement. The difficulty with which we are confronted is that (a) we are unwilling to admit that the judgement (say) of a certain Australian Minister of Education who solemnly pronounced that he had himself examined the works of William Shakespeare and could discover nothing in them but profanity

and obscenity, and that he should therefore discourage their use in schools, is objectively as good as that of the cultivated critics of all nations who regard Shakespeare as the greatest dramatic genius that the world has produced; and yet that (*b*) so many of our aesthetic judgements are so obviously connected with features of our particular human (sometimes even our local or racial) experience which we can perfectly well imagine to be different in another planet. Take for instance the undeniable tendency to regard the usual or normal or typical form of man or any other animal as the more beautiful, and to regard any considerable deviation from it as ugly—even when the individual thereby approximates to a type which in another animal we should think beautiful. We do not like a human face which approximates to the shape which in a horse or a mouse we should think beautiful enough. May it be possible to admit that the question what particular forms or colours give us aesthetic pleasure is largely dependent upon physiological constitution, use and wont, environment, accidental association; but that the objectivity of the aesthetic judgement lies not in the judgement which states the fact that we experience such and such a feeling but in the judgement which ascribes a value to this feeling—that in truth it is not the strictly aesthetic judgement that is objective, but the judgement of value which is pronounced on such and such an aesthetic experience? From this point of view we can admit that aesthetic pleasure is often given to different persons by different experiences; and yet that *in certain cases* there may be no more value in the one state of consciousness than in the other. The pleasure which red trees and a green sunset might give to the inhabitants of another planet might be just as 'true' or 'high' a pleasure as we derive from green trees and red sunset. In a differently constituted planet square arches might suggest feelings of awe and solemnity closely analogous to those which we derive from a Gothic cathedral, and both kinds of emotion might have their value. The negro's ideal of human beauty may include a broader nose and a different shape of head from a European's, but the resulting pleasure might to a perfectly disinterested intelligence appear to possess precisely the same value. But, though this might be so with those particular elements in the aesthetic consciousness which are in this way due to accidental circumstances, it need not be so with all. The Australian statesman mentioned above might have derived some pleasure from the poetry (say) of Longfellow or Mr. Kipling, and the disinterested intelligence would pronounce that that pleasure would have some value, but it would ascribe a higher value to the different pleasure which a more cultivated person would derive from Longfellow or Mr. Kipling, and a still higher value to the pleasure which Longfellow or Mr. Kipling have presumably derived from Shakespeare, but which the illiterate Minister of Education would be incapable of feeling at all. For the different estimate pronounced upon the poets in question would depend not upon mere accidents of physical organization or environment but upon general mental cultivation, upon qualities of intellect and character which to an impartial intelligence would appear to possess very different values,

Here it is not the same pleasure that is caused by different kinds of poetry to different men, but a quite different pleasure. It is true that the capacity for aesthetic appreciation may be dependent upon a delicacy of eye and ear which is purely physical. An unmusical poet may through the structure of his nervous system be incapacitated from deriving pleasure from music without being a man of lower intellect or character than the musician who derives exquisite pleasure from the same sounds, or rather from sounds caused by the same instruments, though they are sounds which the unmusical poet simply does not hear. When the unmusical poet pronounces the music not to be beautiful, his judgement may in a sense possess strictly objective truth: for not only is he right in saying that he gets no aesthetic pleasure from the music, but he is right in saying that no high objective value attaches to what he actually hears—to the sensations, ideas, and emotions which the music actually produces in him. Could the musician share that experience, he would agree with the poet as to its low intrinsic value. The poet is only in error if he denies the objective value of the emotion which the music sets up in souls that possess the musical capacity which has been denied him; or when he supposes that the elementary musical pleasure which he does himself derive from a simple hymn or song is of equal intrinsic worth with the pleasure which Beethoven or Bach gives to the musical. Even where a pleasure is given to some people by what appears to the more cultivated critic absolutely ugly, there may be a worth in the pleasure, though we may say that the uncultivated man is wrong, in a sense, in feeling it because his enjoyment of it implies incapacity for something much better worth enjoying. If we say more than this, if we say that he ought not to go on indulging in his low aesthetic pleasures (even if he cannot school himself into enjoying what the cultivated man enjoys), our judgement is clearly a moral judgement, and not an aesthetic one at all. To distinguish more in detail between the elements of aesthetic appreciation which are due to merely accidental circumstances and which might conceivably vary in differently constituted beings without either of them being in error, and those which are accounted for by incapacities in some beings for kinds of consciousness the value of which could not be denied by any intelligence without error, would involve a treatise on Aesthetic Philosophy which I have no intention of attempting. I merely throw out the suggestion that the really objective element in the aesthetic judgement is the judgement of value which it implies. The judgement of value implied in aesthetic judgement differs from ordinary judgements of value merely in being a judgement as to the value of a particular class or aspect of human experience which requires to be looked at in relation to a whole complex of other judgements of value before it can form a ground for making the avowedly and professedly moral judgement 'this kind of experience ought to be indulged in by A or B or promoted by A or B in C or D at such and such a time and in such and such circumstances.'

(7) The result of this analysis—or mere suggestion of a possible analysis— is not to deny the objectivity of many of our aesthetic judgements, but

to bring the objective element in them into closer connexion with our ordinary judgements of value—the judgements which we usually call distinctively moral judgements. The judgement 'this is beautiful' claims objective validity in the sense that it asserts (a) that in the ideally constituted consciousness, it will produce such and such an aesthetic experience, and (β) that this aesthetic experience possesses such and such a value. There may be cases in which a man might derive an equally valuable aesthetic experience from other external objects, just as one man likes one kind of food and another another without there being any difference of intrinsic value between the two kinds of pleasure : but that is not so always. In other cases the consciousness that thought such and such things beautiful would be pronounced by an omniscient mind to be inferior to the consciousness to which they appeared ugly. At the same time, though aesthetic judgements are (or include) judgements of value, they are value-judgements of a very distinctive and special kind. There will always be this much difference between them and what we usually call moral judgements, (a) that to judge well of the value of various kinds of aesthetic experience requires a different kind of mental capacity from that which is required to judge well of other values, and (b) that the judgement 'this has aesthetic value' cannot pass into a moral judgement, on which any one can be called upon to act, until the value of the aesthetic experience has been compared with the value of other kinds of experience — the value for instance of Love in ourselves and of the pleasure produced by a socially useful action in others, and it is this estimate of *comparative* values which we usually call in a distinctive sense the moral judgement. Many may have a good aesthetic judgement, i. e. are capable of the higher aesthetic experiences and judge rightly of their value, who may have a bad moral judgement, i. e. be incapable of appreciating other kinds of experience at their true value when compared with the higher aesthetic experiences ; others may have a good moral judgement in general, i. e. rightly estimate (say) the superior value of Love and rightly balance the value of other people's pleasure against their own, but may make mistakes in particular cases from want of a developed aesthetic consciousness, i. e. because they do not see that Shakespeare is beautiful or underestimate the true value of the sense of beauty in general.

CHAPTER VII

IDEAL UTILITARIANISM

I

IN previous chapters I have sought to show that the way
to find out whether an action is right or wrong, when we are
forced to consider such a question for ourselves without reference
to some established rule [1], is to consider whether it will tend
to produce for society in general a Well-being or εὐδαιμονία or
good which includes many elements possessing different values,
which values are intuitively discerned and compared with one
another by the moral or practical Reason. The right action is
always that which (so far as the agent has the means of knowing)
will produce the greatest amount of good upon the whole. This
position implies that all goods or elements of the good are in
some sense and for some purposes commensurable. Some of the
objections which may be taken to this position I shall consider
hereafter. In the present chapter I shall aim at illustrating
how the moral judgements implied by the special virtues, and in
particular by those which are *prima facie* most unutilitarian,
are explainable upon the supposition that all moral judgements
are ultimately judgements as to the value of ends. This view of
Ethics, which combines the utilitarian principle that Ethics must
be teleological with a non-hedonistic view of the ethical end,
I propose to call Ideal Utilitarianism. According to this view
actions are right or wrong according as they tend to produce for
all mankind an ideal end or good, which includes, but is not
limited to, pleasure.

A paramount position among our moral judgements is (as we
have seen) occupied by the three axioms of Prudence, Benevo-

---

[1] When we ought to enter upon such a consideration is a question which
I have discussed in Book II, chap. v.

lence, and Equity.   It is self-evident to me that I ought (where
it does not collide with the greater good of another) to promote
my own greatest good, that I ought to prefer a greater good
on the whole to a lesser, and that I ought to regard the good
of one man as of equal intrinsic value with the like good of any
one else.

This last assumption will be further defended and explained
in the Chapter on Justice. Meanwhile, it may be assumed that
the ultimate meaning of absolute Justice is to be sought in this
equal distribution of good.

Such is the meaning, I take it, of ultimate social Justice.
Justice in this absolute sense prescribes the principle, whatever
it be, upon which the good is to be distributed, while Benevolence is taken to mean the promotion of maximum social good
without reference to the question of its distribution. In this
sense even the hedonistic Utilitarian must admit the necessity
of recognizing that Virtue cannot be altogether resolved into
Benevolence, unless the meaning of Benevolence is narrowed
down to a Benevolence which is consistent with Justice. But
it must be admitted that there are many senses of the word
Justice, as popularly used, which do not seem *prima facie*
to have any reference to the question of the distribution of
Well-being or ultimate good. When we say that it is unjust
to punish a man without hearing his defence, or to compel
a man to give evidence against himself, or to punish a man
twice for the same offence, or to make an *ex post facto* law,
or to decide a civil action in favour of the poorer or the more
deserving litigant who has nevertheless the worse case—in
all such cases there seems no obvious or immediate reference
to any principle for the ultimate distribution either of ultimate
Well-being or of its material conditions. In Aristotelian language 'regulative' Justice [1]—the Justice of the law-courts—
seems to be a different virtue from 'distributive' Justice. But in
all these heterogeneous uses of the term Justice there seems

---

[1] The same may be said of his Commercial Justice, or Justice of Exchange.
It assumes the justice of the principle of private property and free barter
in exchange, which a Socialist might regard as intrinsically unjust on account
of the advantage which it gives to the possessor of unearned capital.

to be this much in common; they all prescribe impartiality in
the treatment of individuals; they forbid inequality, or rather
arbitrary inequality—inequality not justified by the requirements of social Well-being, or some other general and rational
principle—in the treatment of individuals. They all involve
the application of some general rule or principle without respect
of persons to particular cases. The question of the justice of
this rule is not, in common discourse, brought into question.
We call a judge unjust who refuses to apply the law impartially,
though we ourselves disapprove of the law and regard it as
essentially unjust. Thus we may say that the word, as used
in ordinary parlance, always denotes impartiality in distribution
upon some condition—assuming some established principle or
rule of the actual social order, which must itself no doubt rest
upon some principle of absolute Justice if it is to be capable of
ultimate justification, but the justice of which is for the moment
assumed. Thus we say that it is unjust to punish one man more
severely than another for the same offence and under precisely
similar circumstances, because here no consideration of social
expediency (that is to say, at bottom no conflicting claims of
other men) can interfere with the general principle that one man
should be treated in exactly the same way as another under exactly
the same circumstances. The principles of absolute Justice cannot
require such unequal treatment: if they did, that would constitute
such a difference of circumstance as might justify the unequal
treatment. But we do not regard it as unjust for the judge to
decide a case in a way which will enrich an already rich man
and beggar a poor man, because we assume the justice of the
laws of property, and regard it as the duty of the judge simply
to administer that law impartially; or for a naval officer
to receive more prize-money than a common sailor, because
on other grounds we assume that social Well-being demands the
adoption of an unequal scale of remuneration for officers and
men, while we should regard it as unjust to give more to one
man than to another of the same rank. It is unnecessary to
multiply illustrations: in all cases the popular usages of the
term Justice, in so far as they are capable of defence, may be
held to imply the due regard of the claim of individuals—not

their intrinsic merit or ultimate claims to Well-being, but their claim according to some established or recognized law or principle of distribution. Varied as are the uses of the term Justice in common language, the underlying idea of all of them seems to be that our accepted principles of social conduct, whatever they may be, should be applied impartially as between different individuals or classes. Sometimes of course when an act or a custom or an institution is pronounced unjust, it is meant that the established principle itself is one which cannot be defended upon any ground of social expediency, that it violates the fundamental principle that the ultimate value of one man's good is equal to that of the like good of another. But this question of absolute Justice raises so many difficult and intricate questions that further explanations must be reserved for a separate chapter.

Subject to due regulation by the rule of Justice or Equity [1], it might seem to follow from the principles which we have hitherto adopted that all virtues could be explained as ultimately resolvable into rational Benevolence or Love. But even the Hedonist must recognize that special names are in practice given to various special kinds of conduct, which are supposed to be conducive in definite and distinguishable ways to human good ; such kinds of conduct, or rather the dispositions to perform them, are called particular virtues. On the view which judges of the ultimate value of goods by other than a hedonistic standard we are able to establish a sharper and clearer distinction between the different duties or the dispositions which lead to their performance, since we can recognize not merely a distinction between different kinds of conduct all ultimately conducive to a single good, but also a real and important distinction between the kinds of good which they tend to promote. Thus even from the hedonistic point of view it is clearly convenient to have a distinctive name for the disposition to observe the rule of truth-speaking, though

---

[1] Which includes Prudence, or the recognition of the due claims of self. That due recognition of the claims of self is a duty is well put by Höffding (*Ethik*, p. 119): 'It follows from the principle of Welfare [or Utility] that the individual is *only* one among many, but it follows also therefrom that the individual really *is* one among many.'

to the Utilitarian truth-speaking is simply one of the particular
rules which the supreme and all-inclusive duty of promoting
human pleasure imposes upon mankind.   From the point of view
of ideal Utilitarianism we may no doubt recognize that devotion
to true human good will include all other virtues, Veracity
among the number: but we shall be disposed to insist more
strongly upon this and other special or particular virtues, because
to us truthfulness of character, in ourselves and others, is a part
of the end or ideal life which the virtuous man will seek to promote, and not merely a means to a good other than itself.   We
shall be less disposed to acquiesce in the disposition to reduce all
the virtues to Benevolence, since in practice ethical teaching
of this kind is pretty sure to obscure or slur over the fact that
the end which the benevolent man is to promote must include
many other kinds of good besides pleasure, many dispositions,
emotions, activities, states of consciousness which are valued for
their own sakes and not merely as a means to some further good.

I do not intend in the present work to attempt any exhaustive
enumeration or description of the particular kinds of conduct,
the particular duties or virtues, which are included in the disposition to promote true human good, or of the various ends or
elements in that good with which these various duties or virtues
are specially concerned.   I shall not attempt to show elaborately
in what ways virtues such as Honesty, Industry, Family Affection,
Kindliness, Compassion, Loyalty (to the State or other social
institutions), Orderliness, Courage (physical and moral) are conducive to the general good.   That they are so is common ground
between the hedonistic and the ideal Utilitarian, though no
doubt it will be possible to find in connexion with all of them
casuistical questions which might have to be differently answered
by those who take and by those who refuse to take a hedonistic
view of human good.   Descriptions or classifications of duties or
virtues are apt to be tedious and useless, unless the details of
duty are discussed with much greater fullness than is compatible
with the scope of the present work.   I propose, therefore, to
confine myself in this chapter to some remarks upon those duties
or virtues which seem at first sight most difficult to reconcile
with the view that all virtue consists ultimately in the promotion

of true social good, and which really are (as it appears to me) incapable of being reconciled with that doctrine, so long as social good is understood in a purely hedonistic sense.

II

In the first place, I must observe that even those virtues which are most obviously altruistic in their tendency are, according to our view, also ends in themselves—having a value independent of, and in some cases much greater than, the mere pleasure which they cause in others. Hence it becomes rational to encourage the cultivation and exercise of these virtues even in ways which cannot always be shown to produce a net gain in pleasure on the whole. I have already illustrated this in the case of Humanity to men and animals. The high value which we assign to all natural kindliness of feeling and to parental affection in particular is, I believe, one of the main grounds for our condemnation of infanticide. The same consideration forbids the extinction of life in the case of the old or the sick or the insane, and generally speaking, persons whose existence is a burden to the community, even should they be willing to consent to the sacrifice. If it be assumed that their lives are a burden even to themselves, then of course the question is complicated with another, the lawfulness of suicide; to which we shall return later on.

It is no doubt quite compatible with this high estimate of the social affections to urge that in certain directions Christian sentiment has been carried to extremes. But here it is important to bear in mind a principle on which we shall have frequently to insist—that we must take into consideration the actual psychological constitution of human nature, and the impossibility of modifying it exactly in the way and to the extent which pleases us. It might be difficult without this principle to justify our absolute condemnation of the extinction of extremely misshapen infants. It would be difficult, that is, to maintain *a priori* that it would not be a gain to society to eliminate the infants most grossly and obviously unfitted for life, were it not for the fact of the horror which the idea actually excites in humane persons. The moral reformer who should feel inclined

1 4

to suggest some modification of the existing custom will, however, reflect on the extreme value of the feelings which such a suggestion would shock, the extreme difficulty of drawing the line between the permitted and the unpermitted elimination, and the impossibility of securing that interference with spontaneous emotions shall stop just where he wants it to stop. He will remember the ease with which the kindly inhibition of an unhappy life might degenerate (in individual parents and in society at large) into a mere selfish repudiation of trouble, privation or anxiety, and the encouragement which any extension of the practice would give to materialistic and hedonistic views of life. We condemn infanticide, because we consider the feelings which the prohibition cultivates to be of more intrinsic worth than the good which it secures. Given the actual psychological constitution of human nature, we may even judge it best that such questions should not be raised at all: but, if they are raised, there is no principle upon which they can be decided but this of the comparative worth of the sentiments and type of character encouraged by that prohibition and of the social advantages which might accrue from its relaxation. While I have no doubt that on the whole the established rule is right, it is possible that in certain extreme cases the Christian sentiment has been pushed too far, and that in the case of actual monsters or beings entirely destitute of human intelligence, in which it is possible to draw a fairly definite line, and in which the life that is preserved is as valueless from a moral as it is from a hedonistic point of view, an exception might be made[1].

[1] It appears that this was the recognized doctrine both for Church and State in Christian countries in the seventeenth century: see constant allusions to it in connexion with the difficulty of defining the term 'man' in the works of Leibniz. In 'Some Remarks on Punishment' in the *International Journal of Ethics* (vol. iv, 1893-4, p. 269 *sq.*), Mr. Bradley assumes the whole of the modern aversion to infanticide to be due to what he would regard as a pure superstition about the taking of human life. That the feeling of the sanctity of life, assumed to be prescribed by direct divine revelation, has historically exercised some influence in this direction can hardly be denied; but that so deeply-seated and widely-spread an ethical change should be due entirely to 'superstition' or to *merely* theological ideas (reasonable or unreasonable) is a view which will probably commend itself only to anti-Christian fanaticism. The Buddhistic feeling against the taking

Another possible case in which a valuable sentiment has been indulged to an exaggerated extent may perhaps be found in the practice of preserving, at immense risk to warders and doctors, the lives of homicidal maniacs.

III

I pass on to consider some other of the less obviously utilitarian virtues and duties. Through all of them there seems to run the general principle that a higher value should be attributed to the exercise and cultivation of the higher—that is to say, of the intellectual, æsthetic, and emotional—faculties than to the indulgence of the merely animal and sensual part of our nature. We regard knowledge, culture, enjoyment of beauty, intellectual activity of all kinds, and the emotions connected with these things, as having a higher value than the pleasures arising from the gratification of the mere animal propensities to eating and drinking or physical exercise or the like [1]. What

of life, however little in its exaggeration capable of rational defence, is at all events sufficient to show that the sentiment with which we have to deal is not the mere influence of a supposed divine command inherited by Christianity from Judaism. Moreover, it is worthy of note that the practice advocated by Mr. Bradley was condemned by the best pagans. Even Plato, to whom Mr. Bradley appeals, did not approve of the deliberate bringing into existence of children expressly designed for the slaughter-house; he sanctioned infanticide only in case of children born of parents who had passed the prescribed age; while Aristotle condemned infanticide for the mere purpose of reducing population, and allowed it only in the case of misshapen infants. For a sanction to 'social surgery' of the wholesale type advocated by Mr. Bradley we must descend below the level of the 'higher Paganism.'

[1] We may legitimately attribute a higher value to athletic enjoyment than to mere gratification of the senses because (a) athletic exercises (especially in the form of games) in moderation are as conducive to the due activity of the intellect as in excess (an excess very soon reached) they are detrimental to it, (b) because (especially in men of small moral or intellectual capacities) they supply a useful antidote to still more animal propensities, (c) because they do cultivate some moral and intellectual qualities. I might say more on this side of the matter if it were not for the enormous exaggeration of the moral value of athletics which is popular at the present moment, and which is threatening the higher life of the nation no less than the prestige of our commerce and the efficiency of our army. The fallacy of the arguments commonly used by those schoolmasters who encourage the

is the relative value of these things as compared with activities of a directly social character, is a question on which we may have to say something hereafter. It is not necessary to deny that the encouragement even of such intellectual pursuits as are of the least direct and obvious social utility does lead to an increase of pleasure on the whole, but our feeling about them is not based upon any such doubtful calculations : and assuredly there are many cases where an individual would find it difficult to justify the devotion of his whole time to pursuits which bring pleasure only to himself, and perhaps a very small circle of other people, when it might be bestowed upon work which would undoubtedly bring pleasure or a saving of pain to large numbers, if he thought that all pleasure was of equal worth, that nothing was of any value but pleasure, and that conduct was right only in so far as it tends to increase of pleasure.

This general principle of the superiority of certain parts of our nature to others—the more purely human to the more animal—is the root of two sets of virtues :—

1. Of those virtues (though moderns are not much in the habit of thinking of them as virtues at all) which consist in the exercise of the higher intellectual and æsthetic faculties :

2. Of the virtues which consist in the due control or subordination of the lower or more animal impulses.

Of the first we need not speak more at length, except in one connexion. This seems to be the place to say a word about the source of our respect for Truth. Granted the great social utility of being able to take a man's word (say in commercial transactions), it is obvious, to my mind, that upon hedonistic assumptions the exceptions would be much more numerous than would commend themselves at least to a well-brought-up Englishman. There would be no reason why we should resist that tendency to say (in matters of no importance),

exaggerations of Athleticism seems to lie chiefly in assuming (1) that the qualities undoubtedly cultivated by games cannot be cultivated in any other way, (2) that the resource, initiative, self-control, habit of co-operation, prompt action, &c., cultivated in one particular way will transfer themselves to other spheres. Experience does not seem to favour either assumption. A football player who excels in ' combination ' is quite as likely as other men to play for his own hand in real life.

at any expense to Truth, what would be agreeable to the hearer which is, indeed, almost sanctioned by the current morality of some civilized nations. It is of course possible to enumerate many inconveniences—particularly what we may call moral inconveniences, loss of any opportunities of learning our defects and the like—which result from such a toleration of minor lying. But, entirely apart from all such considerations, I believe that we do on reflection recognize something intrinsically fitting in the rule which prescribes that a rational being, endowed with faculties which enable him to pursue, to communicate, and to love the truth, should use those faculties in that way rather than for the purpose of making things appear otherwise than as they are. So much appears to me to be the clear result of introspection, and to be implied in the strongest moral convictions of other men. But, it is equally easy to show that to erect the principle of Veracity into a hard and fast rule admitting of no exceptions is out of harmony with the belief and the practice of the most conscientious persons. Where some conventional use of language is sufficiently recognized, formal untruths may no doubt be removed from the category of lies proper by the principle that words must be taken to mean what they are commonly understood to mean. In this way we may defend the formal 'not at home,' the usual forms of social and epistolary salutation, the hyperboles of courtly compliment, though in proportion as these latter pass beyond the minimum of fixed convention their justification becomes more precarious. But this principle is inapplicable to the actual deception practised by detectives, or by private persons towards a brigand inquiring the whereabouts of his victim, or to the denial of bad news to sick persons, or to lies told for the preservation of important secrets, or to the employment of ancient formulae (a political oath, a declaration imposed by some ancient Statute, or a confession of faith [1]), which nobody takes quite literally, but with respect to which the limits of permissible latitude are not definitely fixed by universally under-

---

[1] I have discussed this particular application of the principle in an article in the *International Journal of Ethics*, 'Prof. Sidgwick on Religious Conformity,' vol. III (Jan. 1897).

14 ★

stood and accepted custom. Of course, in proportion as these exceptions to the rule of truth-speaking are generally recognized, part of the moral objection to them disappears. Though they in some cases deceive for the moment the particular person to whom they are addressed, they do not to any important extent tend to weaken respect for truth, the habit of telling the truth, and the general confidence in other people's statements.

It is no doubt much to be desired that a general understanding should be arrived at about such matters. But as a matter of fact no such general understanding does exist, and the absence of such an understanding forms an insuperable objection to finding even in the case of Veracity—the stronghold of popular Intuitionism—the case of an intuitively discerned rule of conduct, universally binding without any consideration of consequences. From our point of view we have no difficulty in reconciling the ' intuitive ' basis of the virtue with the occurrence of exceptions based upon consideration of consequences. Truth-speaking is a good, and so (still more) is that inward love of truth of which truth-speaking is the expression and the guarantee. It *is* almost invariably right to speak the truth, because it is morally good both for ourselves to speak it and for others to hear it, even when it is unpleasant to both parties. But there are other goods besides truth-speaking and truth-loving: and sometimes Truth must be sacrificed to the more imperative claims of Humanity or of Justice. In each case we must decide which is of the greatest worth—the speaking of truth and the habit of speaking it which my lie would tend to discourage, or the life which my lie will save, the injustice that it will prevent, the practical good which it will enable me to do, the greater truth which it will enable me to diffuse. There are even cases in which a lie has to be told in the interests of Truth itself. An untrue statement must be made to one man in order to keep a secret which one has promised to respect ; a statement literally untrue must be made that a higher truth may be taught or real liberty of thought and speech advanced [1].

[1] This is admirably put by Höffding (*Ethik*, p. 178) : ' The duty of speaking the truth amounts to this, the duty of promoting the supremacy of the truth

It will be observed that I have drawn no hard and fast distinction between the duty of Veracity and the duty towards Truth in a wider and more speculative sense. And it seems to me of great practical importance to insist that the social duty of Veracity and the duty of scientific enquiry ultimately spring from the same root, though in the case of Veracity the duty is more directly and immediately dependent upon our social relations. We ought not to lie one to another (as was recognized by St. Paul), because we are 'members one of another,' because we do not like to hear lies told to ourselves, and ought not to like them even when they are pleasant. Deception implies want of respect for the personality of others. But, after all, the distinction is only one of degree, for there is some social reference even in the duty of seeking speculative truth. It is under ordinary circumstances best for ourselves and for others that we should seek and make known the truth in matters of Religion and of Science as well as about the facts of common life. It is important to insist upon the close connexion between a very practical duty and one which is intimately associated with the highest intellectual aspirations for two reasons. It emphasizes the fact that the social duty is not confined to the mere abstinence from false statements (though of course the negative rule is capable of more exact definition and admits of fewer legitimate exceptions than the

("die Wahrheit zur Herrschaft zu bringen"): the end may, however, often be interfered with by speaking the truth.' So Sir Leslie Stephen: 'The rule, "Lie not," is the external rule, and corresponds approximately to the internal rule, "Be trustworthy." . . . Truthfulness is the rule because in the vast majority of cases we trust a man in so far as he speaks the truth : in the exceptional cases the mutual confidence would be violated when the truth, not when the lie, is spoken' (*A Study of Ethics*, p. 208). So the insistence upon a strict and literal interpretation of political or religious formulae is often opposed to the interests of Truth. The man too scrupulous to join a party, some part of whose programme does not express his real mind, or to subscribe a creed details of which are obsolete, often does less than he might do to propagate the truth. Such protests often have their value, but it is perhaps the tendency of conscientious persons to over-estimate this negative devotion to Truth. In the case of the actual 'pious fraud' or γενναῖον ψεῦδος it is most commonly the minor, not the major premiss of the moral syllogism which is questionable. Such frauds would be justifiable if (when *all* their consequences are considered) they were socially beneficial.

positive), and it further illustrates how the admission of exceptions is compatible with the fullest recognition of an 'intuitive' basis for the duty. It may be recognized as a general principle that it is a duty to seek for and to reveal the truth in spite of the fact that its discovery often seems to weaken or to shatter beliefs, institutions, habits, traditions of high social utility. Even in the most modern times I believe that this duty is inadequately recognized, at least by those who are in the habit of attaching most value to what are commonly called moral considerations in the narrower sense of the word. There is probably, in this country at least, too much, not too little, unwillingness to communicate to the ignorant and the young the results of Science or of scientific Theology, for fear they should weaken the reverence and the Morality which have in the past been associated with beliefs no longer tenable. And yet those who put the duty highest acknowledge that it has at times to give way to others more imperative still. No one but a fanatic thinks it a duty to proclaim the truth on every subject, at all times and under all circumstances—in omnibuses and railway trains, before old and young, simple and learned, on suitable occasions and unsuitable—with equal openness and equal insistence. Some respect we all recognize it as right to show to the known convictions, the sympathies, the limitations, the prejudices of our hearers; to the social convenience of the principle that there is a time and place for all things; to a host of conventions, traditions, and understandings. The principle that all moral judgements are judgements of value, while all value is comparative, supplies us with an unfailing means of reconciling the highest reverence for Truth with the limitations which all sensible and right-feeling persons recognize to the duty of actively proclaiming it; although it does not (any more than any other ethical principle) supply us with an infallible mode of discerning what is right in difficult cases of ' conflicting duties [1].'

[1] Of course in the strictest sense there can be no ' conflict of duties.' It is no doubt true that the duty only begins when the conflict of traditional rules or of real moral principles has been decided. If one supposed 'duty' is overruled by another, the former is not really a duty. But the expression is a natural and convenient one.

IV

The due subordination of the appetites, their control in such a way as is most favourable to the activity of the higher part of our nature, constitutes the virtue of Temperance in that wider sense indicated by the Greek σωφροσύνη, translated by the Schoolmen *temperantia*, but for which modern languages have no single comprehensive name. In some ways the circumstance is regrettable, as it tends to oblivion of the fact that the same consideration which dictates the control of the sexual impulse dictates also moderation not only in drinking but in eating and (it may be added) in respect of all the lower and more animal pleasures. On the other hand it has the advantage of emphasizing the fact that in the degree and kind of control which the highest Morality imposes upon the sexual appetite we have advanced beyond the mere moderation which commended itself to the average Greek mind in the time of Aristotle.

It is in dealing with the virtue of Purity as it has been understood by the Christian consciousness, and the higher religious consciousness even outside the limits of Christendom, that hedonistic-utilitarian explanations of Morality break down most hopelessly. It is in reference to this virtue that the developed moral consciousness does seem most nearly to assume the form which Intuitionism gives to all ethical precepts— that of a prohibition to do certain acts, a prohibition which gives no further account of itself, and which positively forbids any calculation of consequences or admission of exceptions. While strongly insisting that the moral consciousness in its highest development does condemn all sexual indulgence outside monogamous marriage, I should contend that this prohibition admits of being stated in the form of a judgement as to the ultimate value of an end. It is a certain state of feeling which is pronounced to be of intrinsic value—a state of feeling which the clearest moral insight and the highest spiritual experience of the race have decided to be incompatible with sexual indulgence outside a relatively permanent monogamous union. If the moral consciousness here *seems* to forbid all calculation

of consequences, or comparison of values, it is because from
the nature of the case it is practically impossible that considerations of social well-being should ever prescribe a departure
from the rule.   I will not attempt to discuss the wholly abnormal
circumstances in which it might be possible to conceive that
some great advantage, whether for country or for humanity,
might be obtained by submission to a single act of impurity
at the behest of a tyrant or the like.   Without positively
denying that such exceptions might conceivably be found, I will
only point out that even the absolute refusal to relax the
rule in however extraordinary a case would be quite compatible
with the doctrine that the morality of acts depends upon their
consequences, for it may be held that such a refusal (when we
take into account its tendency to secure respect for the principle
in the eyes of others) is so great a good as to be worth any
sacrifice which has to be paid for it in any particular combination
of circumstances.   The man or the woman who brought suffering
on family or country by heroism of this kind would not be
setting up an arbitrary categorical imperative against the true
interests of the human race, but simply interpreting the true
interests of the race by a non-hedonistic standard of value.

I have said that the law of Purity is the moral precept which
admits of the most exact definition and which gives rise to the
smallest possibility of exceptions of a kind which will appeal to
men of highly developed moral nature in modern Christendom.
But it is worth pointing out that there is a side on which the
law is less capable of exact and universally accepted definition,
and on which it involves questions obviously incapable of settlement without reference to social consequences.   There is a consensus, within the limits indicated above, that sexual indulgence
must be limited to monogamous marriage.   But as to the exact
conditions which constitute a lawful monogamous marriage the
consensus is certainly much less complete—in particular upon
two points, upon the question of prohibited degrees and the
question of divorce.   With regard to prohibited degrees, nothing
much need be said, since it is generally admitted by those
who do not feel that society is bound for all time by the
decision of the early Church, or of Roman Emperors and their

ecclesiastical advisers, that the limits must be determined by considerations of social convenience in the ordinary sense of the term. The only way in which the adoption of a non-hedonistic standard will be likely to modify our attitude towards the question will be in reinforcing the demand that the higher moral aspect of marriage shall be allowed due weight as well as the question of mere materialistic convenience. We shall ask not merely whether the prohibition of marriage with a deceased wife's sister is most conducive to the convenience and enjoyment of widowers and their families, but whether the principle that marriage-relationship shall be regarded as equivalent to blood-relationship tends to heighten the general ideal of the marriage bond. I do not contend that this consideration will practically be likely to modify the decision to which we should have come on other grounds. On the question of divorce, however, this aspect of the matter becomes of paramount importance.

Those who take the highest view of the marriage-tie—for practical purposes, we may as well say, those who adopt the Christian view of marriage—are agreed in insisting that it is part of its ideal that such unions shall be permanent. The *ideal* of marriage is a spiritual union of a kind which absolutely forbids any voluntary termination of it, even independently of the interests of children, which are also no doubt best secured by the greatest attainable permanence. The question whether under particular circumstances, when this ideal has not been reached, the dissolution of the marriage with liberty to marry again is or is not the less of two evils involves precisely the same kind of comparison of goods—in this case of very heterogeneous goods—which we have seen to be necessary in every ethical judgement. Here, as usual, the comparison is not wholly a balancing of higher good against lower: there are moral advantages and moral disadvantages on both sides. On the one hand there is the moral advantage of insisting upon the idea of permanence, in forcing people to enter upon marriage with the deliberate intention of doing all that in them lies to make it a permanent and a spiritual union and not a mere partnership based upon interest and terminable at pleasure : on the other hand there are the obvious moral objections to the prohibition of re-marriage where cohabitation has become impossible. The question does not seem to be one which admits of any universal solution without regard to circumstances of time and place: and it is to be observed that the moral problem is here not precisely the same as the political problem. It is one question whether people aiming at the highest ideal of life ought to marry again in certain circumstances: it is another question whether, if people wish to do so, the State should prevent them. The question is, therefore, one to which the State may quite intelligibly give one answer, and the Church, which is a voluntary society for the promotion of the highest life, a somewhat different one. On the other hand any appearance of discord between the morality of the Church and the morality of the State is itself a grave source of moral perplexity and relaxation: on such matters the State, at least in Protestant countries and with the majority of their inhabitants, is a more powerful moral educator than the Church. I will leave the subject with the remark that on this question there is likely to be a grave difference between the solutions offered by hedonistic and by non-hedonistic Utilitarianism. The logical Hedonist will attach much greater importance than the ethical Idealist to the hardship involved in the prohibition of re-marriage to an offending party [1], and much less to the social importance of inculcating, even at the cost of real hardship to individuals, a high and spiritual ideal of marriage.

Another question connected with the definition of Purity is raised by the change which is actually passing over the morality of Europe with regard to the relation of the sexual instinct to the procreation of children. The subject deserves a passing mention because we have here a great unsettled problem of Ethics in which differences of ethical theory may have a vital bearing upon practical questions of immense moment: and it is good even from the most purely theoretical point of view to bring our ethical theories into contact with real practical

---

[1] I regard the prohibition of marriage even by the Church to the innocent party in the case of adultery as clearly incapable of rational justification (whatever may be thought about the question of the guilty party): the Eastern Church has always observed this distinction.

problems. In Christian countries there has been a tendency
until recently to condemn all restriction, even of the most purely
negative kind, to the number of births, and to represent it as
a moral duty for married persons to bring into the world the
largest number of children that is physically possible.   The time
is past when such a precept would have been defended on the
ground that a maximum increase of population is in itself, in all
circumstances, a desirable end ; though our solution of the
problem may be seriously affected by our view of the degree
of urgency which the population question has reached. Every one
but a Pessimist will admit that the population of a country
ought to be kept up or even (so far as this can be done without
lowering the quality of its life) to increase ; and that therefore
it is a moral duty on the part of married persons to be willing
to undertake the responsibilities of parentage : that is part of the
ideal of marriage. It does not follow that it is desirable that
population should increase with a maximum rapidity : if that
were so celibacy would be immoral.   But even apart from the
population question, there are many considerations which may
reasonably be urged against the assumption that large families
are always a good thing : and these considerations are not
all of a hedonistic or materialistic character.   There is the
wife's health, the interference with other than purely domestic
employments, the loss of educational advantages which the
increase of family may entail upon every member of it.   Of
course if it is considered desirable that the increase of families
should sometimes be restrained by rational considerations, the
morality of such restraint may depend much upon the method
adopted.   Methods which involve ' interference with nature '
are open to objections which cannot be urged against the method
which involves nothing but self-restraint during certain periods.
The question is one which cannot be discussed in detail here,
though it is one which urgently demands free and candid
examination.   My object here, as throughout this chapter, is not
so much to discuss and to settle detailed questions of Casuistry as
to point out the method by which they ought to be solved.   In
this, as in other cases, if we are not to prove unfaithful to the
method we have adopted, we must not fall back upon the short

and easy method of saying that we have an intuition that all
such methods are wrong. We must fairly estimate on the one
hand the evils of all sorts, moral, intellectual, hedonistic, which
are imposed by the over-multiplication of families on the individuals primarily concerned and on the community, on the other
the goods which may be secured by the absence of birth-
restriction, and compare them with the good and evil involved in
the restriction of births—the value or unvalue which we attribute
to the act in itself and to its subsequent effects upon health,
upon character, and upon the whole ideal of life which it expresses and tends to foster. We must pronounce on the side
on which we judge the balance of ' good ' to lie.

The other branch of the Greek self-control ($\sigma\omega\phi\rho\sigma\sigma\acute{\nu}\nu\eta$) is the
one to which the term Temperance has generally been confined
by modern usage. There is a disposition to narrow it still
further to the duty of moderation in drinking, which has nearly
succeeded in eliminating from modern Morality the idea that
there is anything disgraceful in what medieval Ethics styled
' gulosity '—over-eating or excessive addiction to the ' pleasures
of the table ' at whatever expense of money or (what is the same
thing) of human labour. When taken in the narrower sense
of moderation in drinking, there is undoubtedly no duty that
can be more easily or convincingly inculcated on the most purely
hedonistic grounds, so long as it is understood to forbid merely
habitual excess in the use of alcohol or similar stimulants. And
of course occasional excess may be condemned on account of the
great probability that it will lead to more frequent acts of
the same kind. Nevertheless, the question of the immorality
of occasional drunkenness is one upon which there will be,
as it seems to me, a real difference between the verdict of hedonistic and of ideal Utilitarianism. The hygienic ill-effects of
getting drunk once a month are probably not so bad (for many
men) as the taking of two glasses of port every day after dinner.
For some men the former are in all probability a negligible
quantity, while the two glasses of port would mean certain gout
or chronic dyspepsia. On hedonistic principles an occasional act
of drunkenness would only be condemned because it might lead,
in the man himself and others, to habits of excess which would

not be innocent, and under many circumstances there is little risk [1] that such an act will lead to habitual excess. And yet the healthy moral consciousness does condemn as intrinsically degrading even the most occasional act of deliberate drunkenness. On the method of ideal Utilitarianism such a condemnation will be justified without any elaborate attempt to prove the existence of remoter social ill consequences. We see the act to be intrinsically disgusting, and there is an end of the matter [2].

It will be observed that in some of the obligations usually included under the name of Purity and in the duty of Temperance we have clear instances of self-regarding duties. It is true no doubt that no kind of wrong-doing is without social ill effects, but in some cases the social ill effect may be simply the encouragement of the like violations of self-regarding duty in others. There would be no objection to such encouragement unless the act were wrong in the individual case. The duty of Self-culture —of developing one's intellectual and aesthetic capacities in so far as is compatible with the fulfilment of social obligations— is another self-regarding duty. On the method of hedonistic Utilitarianism a man on a desert island would have no duty except to get as much pleasure as possible, and perhaps to preserve his capacity for future service in the event of his rejoining society. The latter contingency being, in the case supposed, highly problematical, it might be urged that an Alexander Selkirk would best observe the precepts of the Utilitarian creed by seeking to increase his pleasure to a maximum point, even though the effect of such indulgence would be to incapacitate himself for future service, and to hasten his end. 'A short life and a merry one' would be the aim of any

---

[1] I do not say none. The loss of self-respect which arises from a first act of drunkenness may involve grave consequences, but this is so just because the man does not really believe that drunkenness is only wrong so far as it diminishes pleasure.

[2] Of course by drunkenness I mean the voluntary extinction of consciousness and self-control for no purpose but momentary pleasure or satisfaction of impulse. If alcoholic poisoning were a suitable anaesthetic for medical purposes, its use might undoubtedly be as justifiable as that of chloroform. In normal circumstances it is obvious that there can be no remoter good effects to outweigh the immediate evil.

such consistent Utilitarian who thought that a longer life of higher pursuits would not so effectually extinguish the misery of solitude as 'the short vehemence' of some carnal pleasure. On our theory it would be the duty, even of the man accidentally separated from society and little likely to rejoin it, to cultivate the higher part of his nature and with that view to moderate his indulgence in such lower pleasures as might be open to him.

V

Among the virtues which are based upon the principle of the due subordination of lower to higher impulses may perhaps be included the virtue of Humility. This virtue is unlike the various forms of Temperance inasmuch as the impulse which is subordinated is not of a purely animal character : pride or the high estimation of self is a feeling which, though it may have no doubt an instinctive and almost animal impulse as its basis, arises in its human form from desires peculiar to a rational nature. There is no passion, I may remark in passing, which more obstinately refuses to be resolved into a desire of pleasure on the one hand or into any other impulse, such as love of power, on the other. The love of power is no doubt closely connected with the tendency to self-estimation and self-assertion, but it is not the same thing. Love of power is itself a very clear instance of a 'disinterested desire,' though the fact is often forgotten by Hedonists owing to the plausibility of the attempt to resolve it into love of the pleasures which power will bring. But love of power is not the same thing as pride : it has a closer affinity with vanity. The pleasure of self-approbation can only be explained on the supposition that there is already a love of self-approbation which cannot be resolved into a desire for the pleasure.

The virtue of Humility seems to call for some further examination because it is often brought forward as a palmary instance of the non-utilitarian, and even the non-teleological character, of our highest ethical judgements. From the point of view of hedonistic Utilitarianism the approval of Humility could hardly be justified except on the ground that most people are prone to an over-estimation of self (which involves obvious social inconveniences), and that it is therefore desirable to aim at the opposite state of feeling in the hope of reaching the desirable mean. But it is not only from a hedonistic point of view that we may feel a difficulty in admitting that there can be anything virtuous in an untruthful estimate of one's own powers, attainments, or achievements, whether in the moral, the intellectual, or any other sphere. The Idealist will feel bound, more even than the Hedonist, to aim at Truth; and it may be doubted whether the undiscriminating exaltation of Humility, considered as an under-appreciation of self, is the best means of attaining this end. It might be urged that it is more likely to lead to profession, on occasions when such profession will be belauded, of an estimate which is not really entertained. And yet it can hardly be seriously maintained that there is nothing of permanent worth in the Christian ideal of Humility beyond a common-sense precept that it is well to think rather less of oneself than one is naturally inclined to do for fear of thinking too much. The frequent exaggerations and occasional gross aberrations of Christian sentiment on this matter may be admitted: and yet we have only to think of Aristotle's revolting picture of the high-souled man ($\mu\epsilon\gamma\alpha\lambda\acute{o}\psi\nu\chi os$)[1] to realize that even the least Christian modern Moralist will recoil from that proud insistence upon one's own merits which is more or less the tendency of all pagan thought, at least till the second century of the Christian era, upon this matter. The solution of the difficulty seems to be that we should approve a truthful estimate of one's own powers and merits as being most favourable to moral progress, to intellectual self-development, and to social usefulness; but that we should disapprove of any habitual dwelling with satisfaction upon one's own capacities or one's own merits for two reasons. Any true or worthy conception of the moral ideal places too great a gulf between that ideal and the actual performance (in his own view) even of a good man to permit him any great self-complacency at the thought that he is better than the majority of his neighbours.

[1] *Ethic. Nicomach.*, IV, § 3 (p. 1123 b). Of course I am aware of the explanations by which all superior people are accustomed to defend the Aristotelian ideal.

In most men at least this feeling will be strengthened by the recognition that the difference between themselves and their fellows is largely due to the influence of others in the present or the past, and not to any efforts which begin exclusively with themselves. To use theological language, the good man will ascribe his goodness to ' grace,' recognizing that his good qualities are due in the first instance to parentage, influence, example. social tradition, education, community, Church, and ultimately, if he is a religious man, to God : he will care for goodness too much for its own sake to treat it as a ground for self-satisfaction at his own achievement as compared with that of others.[1] And that brings us to the second ground upon which the high ethical value of the Humility may be considered to rest. The good man cares too much for others to derive pleasure from the thought that they are worse than himself. His highest goodness is too much pervaded by the impulse of self-communication to be regarded as a private possession which is enjoyed because it is he that has it rather than some one else. The Saint cannot help being aware that he has certain qualities of character which many men lack, but so far from wishing to keep his virtues to himself he will wish that they were common as the air of heaven, that ' all the Lord's people were prophets.' He will, moreover, recognize in others goodness, or at least capacities of goodness, which will prevent his treating the worst of men with anything

---

[1] It may be objected that if a man is to ascribe his virtues (in a sense) to God or the Universe, so may he his vices. Humility will be saved at the expense of Remorse. In so far as this difficulty is theological or metaphysical, I shall deal with it in the chapter on Free-will (Book III, chap. iii) : from the merely ethical point of view I should contend that, just as the consideration I am insisting on is not inconsistent with a due approval of and satisfaction in one's own good qualities, so the reflection that a man did not make his own original bad tendencies will not be inconsistent with disapproval of those tendencies and dissatisfaction with himself so long as he yields to them. The same consideration will condemn an exaggerated contemplation of one's own original bad tendencies no less than exaggerated self-complacency at one's good ones. If the good man will be more disposed to dwell upon the share of other persons or of the Universe in the production of his good qualities than upon their share in the production of his bad ones, that is because it is morally healthier, more conducive to moral progress, to do so.

approaching contempt. When those capacities are unrealized, he will feel sorrow and pity rather than smug self-complacency. It is not so much by his opinion of himself that the Aristotelian 'magnanimous man' disgusts us as by his contempt for other people. Humility then turns out to be no separate, distinct, isolated, non-social virtue [1]—a sort of arbitrary appendix to the code of duty to one's neighbour introduced (as seems to be suggested in some quarters) by special divine decree for the express purpose of showing the inadequacy of all rational principles of Morality. The duty flows directly from the general principle of the individual's subordination to the whole society. Any attempt to cultivate the virtue in and for itself is likely to be suicidal: it is simply one particular aspect of the ideal attitude towards the moral ideal on the one hand and towards one's neighbour on the other. Pride means self-absorption; Humility is simply the consequence of absorption in something higher and something wider. Just as true Benevolence does not involve absolute forgetfulness or neglect of self, so true Humility does not demand a voluntary ignorance of one's real capacities or character, or forbid the assertion of one's claims in ways consistent with due respect for the claims of others. Humility only involves a due subordination of self-love to those social impulses in the satisfaction of which alone the true or higher self-love can attain its end. True Humility is but an aspect of true love of one's neighbour.

VI

The question of Suicide is one of so exceptional a character that a writer on Ethics may fairly be asked how he proposes to deal with it. It will be unnecessary to enlarge upon the various utilitarian reasons against suicide in the vast majority of cases. Even if life be hedonistically not worth living, it

---

[1] That Humility is really a kind of Charity is well recognized by St. Thomas Aquinas, who is entirely free from the medieval tendency to encourage excessive self-debasement. He condemns 'Pusillanimitas' as severely as Aristotle. In principle he exactly hits the weak points of the Aristotelian ideal when he condemns the vainglorious man, because 'appetitum gloriae suae non refert in debitum finem, puta ad honorem Dei, vel proximi salutem' (*Summa Theol.*, II, Pt. ii, Q. 132).

is possible to do something to diminish its miseries. Only if there were reason to hope that the practice could be largely imitated, would a pessimistic Hedonism include suicide among its duties. It is only when a man's life becomes burdensome to others as well as to himself that the hedonistic Utilitarian would seem logically bound to sanction it. When, however, life is looked upon as possessing value on other than hedonistic grounds, it can no longer be pronounced to have lost that value the moment it ceases to yield a balance of pleasure on the whole either to the individual or to society. This consideration is amply sufficient to condemn the act in a vast number of cases in which it might seem rational enough on hedonistic grounds. It would not tend to a right estimate of the relative importance of the higher and lower goods for a man to give up the struggle to live nobly the moment he begins to doubt whether it is hedonistically worth the pain that it costs, or for society to allow him to do so as soon as his services cease to bring it a net gain of pleasure. It may be thought, however, that even allowing its due weight to this consideration, there are extreme cases in which it becomes difficult to defend the peremptory rule of modern Christianity when once it is admitted that pain is an evil. There are times when life seems to have lost its value from an intellectual and a moral point of view as well as from a hedonistic one. When life has reduced itself to a slow and painful process of dying, why, it may be thought, should we prolong a useless agony which seems to be as incompatible with moral effort as with enjoyment of life? On this question I will only make the following remarks, premising that they are not intended as a full and adequate discussion of the subject:

(1) It is impossible, as I have several times remarked, to construct *de novo* an ideal of human life without taking into consideration the actual constitution of human nature, including feelings about conduct which from a purely rational point of view seem difficult to account for. I do not regard the existence of such feelings as final arguments for or against particular kinds of conduct. They cannot dispense us from the necessity of passing upon them our judgements of value. It is always possible that such feelings, however strong and widely diffused, may

in some cases be feelings which Reason must disregard. But when in a general way the feeling commends itself to us as possessing high moral value, or as intimately associated with what possesses high value, the wise man will hesitate to defy it in particular cases, even though *a priori* he might have been inclined to doubt whether its value is great enough to overbalance what is sacrificed to it.

(2) Although the value of the higher life is not dependent upon its duration, the comparative valuation of higher and lower goods may be considerably affected by the answer which is given to the question how long the consequences of moral effort may be expected to last. There are many cases in which I should myself be unable to regard as rational the prohibition of suicide without admitting the postulate of Immortality. The good will is possible even in extremest agony, but the good will is not all that is necessary for Well-being; and it does not seem possible to decide whether the continuance of moral discipline is worth the prolongation of an existence from which all else that gives value to life has departed without asking what are to be the fruits of this moral discipline, whether it is rational to hope for another state in which the character thus formed may have further opportunities of expressing itself in moral activity and of producing that happiness without which all other good must be incomplete. I may add that this is almost the only case (unless we include also the somewhat parallel question of infanticide) in which the answer to any detailed question of Ethics can rationally be affected by the answer that is given to a theological problem [1]. Our attitude towards Morality in general—the whole tone and temper of our ethical life—is likely to be profoundly modified by our acceptance or rejection of fundamental theological ideas; but I hardly know of any other detailed question of Casuistry (except of course those connected with what may be called in the narrower sense religious or ecclesiastical duties), about which what is the rational solution for a Christian or a Theist could be pronounced irrational for one who does not think it reasonable to entertain even the hope of Immortality.

[1] The question is theological in so far as the belief in Immortality rests on Theism: it is of course possible to believe in Immortality without believing in God.

(3) We shall hereafter have to consider the weight which an individual ought to attach to those ethical judgements of other men which have taken shape in established rules and institutions, and in particular to the ethical judgement of the best men—in a word the place of Authority in Ethics. This is precisely a case in which the wise man will feel bound to remember the great weight of authority to which the absolute rule against suicide may appeal [1]. A strong feeling against suicide seems to be the spontaneous deliverance of the moral consciousness, wherever the Christian view of life, with its ideas of discipline, education, or moral probation, and its sense of responsibility to a divine Father, is accepted. It was the acceptance of this faith by a society in which suicide was one of the commonest ways of quitting life which created the modern tradition on the subject. The strength of the feeling is the more remarkable in the entire absence of any express prohibition either in the Jewish or the Christian scriptures. Any one who sympathizes with this general view of life will give its due weight to this accumulation of authority before he proceeds

---

[1] No doubt it may be urged that there may be just as many possible opportunities of moral discipline in another life as there are in this, and that we might as reasonably refuse to inoculate against small-pox, on account of the moral discipline which small-pox may involve, as refuse to cure a diseased life by a voluntary death. (Cf. Hume's *Essay on Suicide*.) I should submit that the two cases re not parallel. We do know tolerably well the consequences of curing disease or refusing to cure it, and we judge that, though there is some good to be got by voluntary endurance of pain, there is more good to be got on the whole by fighting against it, and using one's life for work and for enjoyment. In the case of Suicide we do not know enough about the consequences of the two alternatives to make such a comparison of moral advantages and disadvantages. We do not know whether, if opportunities of moral discipline and self-improvement are voluntarily thrown away here, other such opportunities will be afforded in another life. I freely admit, however, that such merely negative considerations would not be sufficient to condemn Suicide, but for the strong moral instinct against it which seems to accompany a certain stage of moral development— an instinct so strong that it supplies (for those who believe that the course of things is directed by Reason towards an End) a presumption that it has a purpose in the economy of the Universe. I admit that such instincts and the presumptions founded upon them are not final : but a man ought to be very sure of his ground before he overrules them.

to introduce either in theory or practice an exception to this rule, even in those extreme cases where his own unassisted moral consciousness might have felt disposed to do so.

I have been speaking of the general rule.   There are no doubt exceptional cases in which suicide, or something which it is difficult to distinguish from suicide, would be generally approved. Where a sufficient object is to be attained by it, the voluntary courting of death becomes the sublimest heroism: and, if it be held that only the actual wielding of the weapon or voluntary swallowing of the poison constitutes suicide, a little ingenuity might possibly reveal exceptional cases where an unselfish object of great importance could only be achieved by such an act of self-slaughter.   The strong feeling against multiplying such cases or accustoming men even to contemplate their possibility is, as I have contended, a healthy one.   I will only venture to suggest a doubt whether the idea that it is an absolute duty, under all circumstances, to prolong life to the last moment at which medical skill and care can prolong it is not sometimes carried to extremes.   It is a remarkable fact that when it was rumoured that the imprisoned Europeans in Pekin had determined in the last resort to shoot themselves and their wives, rather than face certain torture and dishonour at the hands of the barbarians, not a word was heard in condemnation of that resolve.   When the alternative between a more or a less painful form of death is brought about by disease and not by human agency, are we bound to choose the more painful?   May it not at least be said that, when disease has reached a certain point, the Physician may frankly recognize that his primary aim should be to save pain, even though this should involve some shortening of life?   And perhaps this is not going much beyond the actual practice of the medical profession in recent times.

I cannot but feel that in my treatment of this question I may seem to some to be hesitating between a frank acceptance and a thorough-going rejection of what are commonly called ' Intuitions.'   But the reason for this is, I believe, to be sought in the nature of things, in the real difficulty of distinguishing mere feelings or aversions which may be only prejudices due to inheritance or environment or superstition from real judgements of value [1]. And yet I am clear that the two things must be distinguished. Incest is not wrong simply because it shocks me, but because I judge that the feeling which revolts from incest is one which deserves respect. The idea of eating rat's flesh inspires me with horror, but under some circumstances I am clear that it would be a duty to eat it. There are cases where it is less easy to discriminate between pathological aversion and moral condemnation. The only approach to a test by which to effect such a discrimination that I can suggest is to put the question—does the spontaneous aversion or apparent intuition disappear after full reflection upon the act itself as well as upon all circumstances and consequences? If an intuition—an apparently unaccountable repugnance to some kind of conduct—persists after a due consideration of all the consequences of yielding to it, it may probably be taken to represent not merely a feeling, but a feeling to which the moral Reason attributes intrinsic value. If it disappears, it may be dismissed as a pathological affection, due to mere education or environment, which it is rational to ignore. The aversion to cruelty remains even when we have satisfied ourselves that coursing causes an amount of pleasure to some Englishmen and bull-fighting to most Spaniards which greatly outweighs the pain caused

[1] 'As knowledge arises unperceived from the excitations of experience, it develops a host of prepossessions, partly true, partly erroneous. . . . Just in the same way there arise from the original nature of the mind and the silently working influences of circumstances many prepossessions, some true and some erroneous, concerning what we ought to do; if we examine ourselves, we find that at first it is only belief in Duty in general and in binding laws of action that stands out with clearness and self-evidence; but what these laws are, and how far we can comprehend them in their purity, depends partly upon the influence of external conditions of life, which moderate or excite our blind impulses, partly upon the accuracy with which, in reflection, we separate the general commands of Conscience from the individual forms in which, as applicable to the particular circumstances of our own life, they first press themselves upon us' (Lotze, *Microcosmus*, E. T., I, pp. 710-1). How far a study of the psychological and evolutionary origin of our moral intuitions or instincts may assist the process of discrimination between permanently valid moral judgements and inherited prejudices or survivals of an earlier morality, I have considered in a later chapter (Book III, chap. iv).

to hare and bull and horses. On the other hand a Jew or an eastern Christian probably experiences no less horror at the thought of eating blood-pudding, and a strictly educated Scotchman at the thought of Sunday music. But in these cases, when the man learns the history of the traditions about Sabbath-observance and the eating of blood, he ceases to attach any moral value or authority to the scruple, though for a time the mere subjective feelings may retain something of their old intensity.

In most cases it is possible in this way to break up an intuitive moral feeling into the feeling and the judgement that accompanies it. But in other cases this analysis is by no means easy. I do not believe that there is any infallible logical or psychological process for distinguishing between real judgements of value and mere prejudices or valueless instincts, any more than there is any infallible receipt for correct reasoning. If there were, the difficulties both of ethical speculation and of practical life would for the most part disappear. But the difficulty of the process, of which such a case as that of suicide may be considered the extremest illustration, contains in it nothing to make us doubt :—(1) that Morality ultimately rests upon immediate judgements of value ; (2) that a feeling—whether the feeling arises from the contemplation of the act or from the act itself—can legitimately be a ground of action only when approved by a judgement of value ; (3) that no moral judgement can be considered final in which the moral Reason has not contemplated all the foreseeable consequences of an action before passing its judgement of value.

VII

So far it has been assumed that the moral criterion is constituted by the effect of the action upon the good of mankind. It seems unnecessary at every turn to add 'and of animals in so far as their good can be promoted by human action' : but in strictness (as was contended by John Stuart Mill), this ought, I believe, always to be included. The idea of taking into consideration the good of animals will no doubt seem to many

† 1

extravagant. A disposition to minimize the intelligence of animals, and the importance of their sufferings, is a traditional prejudice of the metaphysical mind. The prejudice was no doubt inherited from Theology, but prejudices of theological origin often continue rampant in the philosophical field long after Theology, more in touch with changes of popular sentiment, has got rid of them. Philosophers will not now, like the Cartesian who denied feeling to the brutes or Spinoza who admitted it [1], boldly pronounce that we may do what we like with the animals. But still there is an unwillingness to admit that the sufferings of animals really matter. It is, we are told by writers of the school of Green, not in the interest of animal well-being, but in that of our own humanity that we ought to avoid causing them unnecessary suffering. I have already dwelt upon the illogicality of this position in speaking of the question whether pleasure is part of the end for mankind. The same considerations which apply to the case of human pleasure apply also to that of animals. If the suffering of animals is no evil, it cannot be inhumane in me to cause it. If it is an evil, it must be my duty to prevent it. The well-being of animals then—whatever well-being they are capable of—seems to me quite distinctly to possess some value, and therefore to form part of that good which constitutes the ethical end. From a practical point of view no doubt the duty becomes very much more of a negative than a positive one. For it rarely happens in practice that we can do much

---

[1] 'Nec tamen nego bruta sentire: sed nego, quod propterea non liceat nostrae utilitati consulere et iisdem ad libitum uti, eademque tractare, prout nobis magis convenit; quanloquidem nobiscum natura non conveniunt et eorum affectus ab affectibus humanis sunt natura diversi ' (*Ethica*, P. IV, Prop. XXXVII, Schol. I). Such is Spinoza's quite logical deduction from the theory which bases my neighbour's claims simply upon the fact that my good and his are ' a common good,' and not on the fact that each has value. Perhaps the first Philosopher to assert strongly the duty of humanity to animals was Schopenhauer, who condemns Kant for resting it merely upon the tendency of cruelty to spread from beast to man, instead of treating animals as (in their way) ends in themselves (*Die Grundlegung d. Moral.*, § 8, E. T., p. 94). The claims of animals are fully recognized by Höffding (*Ethik*, pp. 172, 173): 'That the beast is not to be treated as a mere means, follows at once from his capacity for pain.'

to promote the positive well-being of animals, at least of animals not in a state of captivity; and, although we do assign some value to the well-being of domestic animals, it is, we think, of very small value in comparison with that which we set upon human well-being. While, therefore, we should condemn the infliction of needless torture upon the brutes, we should generally condemn any large expenditure of human energy in ministering to their comforts and luxuries. What is the comparative value of animal pleasure or of the avoidance of animal suffering as compared either with human pleasure and pain or with the higher good of man is a question on which wide differences of opinion exist, as is shown by the much-debated question of Vivisection. I do not propose now to discuss that problem in detail. I will merely say that from the point of view which I have taken up it is not possible either to deny that it may sometimes be right to inflict unmerited suffering upon an animal or to declare that no amount of animal suffering can be of any importance when compared with the smallest amount of human convenience or the smallest accession to human knowledge. The whole question is one of comparative value: and that is one which no formula can settle [1].

It will be observed that I have assumed that the sole good of which animals are capable is pleasure, and that for them there exists no evil but pain. Such is the only hypothesis on which, in our profound ignorance of animal minds, it seems reasonable to act. No doubt it would be difficult to deny that the domestication or education of animals, in some cases amounting almost to their participation in human friendship, may constitute a sort of higher good, and may be looked upon as possessing something more than a merely hedonistic value: but I cannot follow an enthusiastic writer in the *International Journal of Ethics* who has lately contended that animals have a right not merely to pleasure but to 'self-realization [2].'

[1] The only adequate and philosophical discussion of the question which I have seen is to be found in Edmund Gurney's essay in *Tertium Quid*. He decides for a moderate and strictly regulated permission of Vivisection.

[2] *The Rights of Animals*, by Henry S. Salt (Jan., 1900).

VIII

The view of Ethics which has now been sketched lacks a recognized name, and it is a misfortune that it does so: for modes of thought which have no names often fail to obtain the currency of those which have. The term Utilitarianism is irretrievably associated with Hedonism; and the word Intuitionism, which is commonly used to denote the opposite of Utilitarianism, is inevitably suggestive of the crude and absurd theory that the morality of an act can be determined apart from its consequences. And yet the view expounded in this chapter has been widely held. It is the view of Plato and of Aristotle, though in them there is always a tendency to make Morality consist in the pursuit of the individual's own well-being, unhedonistically understood, strongly as it was asserted, especially by Plato, that the individual's own good was essentially bound up with that of his society. It was the view of all the older English Moralists, in whom Platonic and Aristotelian traditions were universalized by Christianity—the view of Cumberland, of the Cambridge Platonists, and (substantially) of Clarke. It was equally the view of the Moral Sense school, which arose when in Locke the rationalistic tendency had sunk back into Theological Hedonism: for Hutcheson, the author of the famous 'greatest happiness of the greatest number[1]' formula, recognized the superior 'dignity' of some pleasures and of some persons as compared with that of others. It was very seldom, indeed, that the proposition that Morality consists in promoting the true well-being of human society was ever formally denied before the time of Butler in England[2] and of Kant in Germany[3]. The ethical system of Kant

---

[1] Hutcheson actually used the phrase 'for the greatest numbers.'

[2] And by him explicitly only in the *Dissertation*. In the *Sermons* he still often adopts the Utilitarian test, though he treats conscience as a sort of magical key to Utility.

[3] I do not say that the proposition was always positively asserted. This was prevented partly by the influence of ideas of Natural Rights derived from the conception of Natural Law and partly by the idea of particular

(assisted in England by the influence of Butler and his followers) has produced a hopeless confusion between the question whether Morality consists in promoting an end and the question what that end is. From that confusion Moral Philosophy has hardly yet emerged : and we still occasionally find eminent writers arguing that Morality consists in doing certain things that one feels a mysterious prompting to do without knowing why one does them or seeking to harmonize and co-ordinate the isolated, instinctive, unanalysed deliverances of the individual moral consciousness. But there is observable a very general tendency to come back to the view of the older seventeenth-century writers, and to assert that Morality consists in the promotion of true human good, but a good of which pleasure is only an element. Janet in France, in Germany Lotze (though he has hardly elaborated a Moral Philosophy), and more recently Paulsen, may be mentioned among the writers who have contributed to this tendency[1]. If it is not the view of Hegel, in whom Moral Philosophy is practically merged in political Philosophy, it is at least the view of many who call themselves his disciples[2]. And yet the system remains without a name. Non-hedonistic Utilitarianism might serve the turn, though a definition by negation is unsatisfactory. Idealistic Utilitarianism would do better, though the term is too apt to suggest a metaphysical, instead of a purely ethical, position. Professor Paulsen has suggested that 'teleological' Ethics should be contrasted with unteleological or 'formalistic' Ethics[3]. This is an excellent classification, but unfortunately we still lack a neat and recognized term to denote the view of Ethics which is at once teleological and anti-hedonistic. On the whole, perhaps, the term 'ideal Utilitarianism[4]' seems the best that is available. Eudae-

precepts not discoverable by Reason but enjoined by express divine Revelation.

[1] Lotze often approaches very near to the position of pure Hedonism, but he is saved from it by his admission of a qualitative difference in pleasure.

[2] Notably Dr. McTaggart, if we are to include that very original thinker among 'Hegelians.' I may also mention Mr. Moore's *Principia Ethica* as a striking expression of the same view of Ethics.

[3] *A System of Ethics*, Eng. Trans., by Prof. F. Tilly, 1899.

[4] In so far as he is teleological and not hedonistic, I might include among

monistic Ethics might better serve to distinguish such a view from the rigorist or ascetic theory which refuses even to include pleasure in its conception of the end ; but (through the persistent misrepresentation of certain writers) the term Eudaemonism has become too much confused with Hedonism to be wholly free from ambiguity. The term Utilitarianism will perhaps sufficiently suggest that we do estimate actions by their tendency to promote human good, and 'Utility' will always carry with it some suggestion of pleasure ; while the qualification 'ideal' will remind us that the good for which we seek is not a conception got by abstraction from a number of empirically given experiences of pleasure or pain, but an ideal set up by rational judgements of value passed upon all the elements of our actual experience.

the supporters of 'Ideal Utilitarianism' the distinguished German thinker, Eduard von Hartmann, whose writings appear to me to be the most important of recent contributions to the subject. But von Hartmann insists that the true end, and consequently the true Ethic, is not positively but negatively Eudaemonistic ('privativ-eudämonistische'). This seems to imply three differences from ordinary Hedonism : (1) Inasmuch as positive happiness or good of any kind is unattainable, the object of the moral man must be to diminish the evil of the Universe, partly for the sake of the persons immediately affected, and partly with a view to assist the efforts of the Absolute to reach the one ultimately desirable good (all consciousness being necessarily attended with more pain than pleasure)—a relapse into its original state of Unconsciousness ; (2) the true ethical end must include other elements of Value besides pleasure ('Unter dem Gesichtspunkte eines ethischen Zweckes ergeben sich andere Wertbestimmungen für alle Dinge und Seelenvorgänge als unter dem Gesichtspunkte des ästhetischen, religiösen, eudämonistischen, intellektualischen.'—*Ethische Studien*, p. 128); (3) Morality, though an end-in-itself to us, is from the point of view of the Universe merely a means to a further end (as to this see below, Bk. III, chap. ii). It is clear that the first and the third modifications are dictated by a pessimistic system of Metaphysics which I do not share, and seem to have no necessary connexion with the second, which is not at all suggested by the term 'negative Eudaemonism.' With this reservation his view of the relation to each of the various elements in the end—hedonistic, intellectual, moral— seems to me peculiarly well balanced, except that his desire to show the unattainability of positive Well-being makes him exaggerate the difficulties and underestimate the utility (restricted as I myself believe it to be) of the 'hedonistic calculus.' All these difficulties would equally have to be met in determining how to attain a minimum of pain.

IX

Some of the objections most frequently urged against such a view of Ethics will be considered in our later books. But there is one to which I may briefly reply at once. The view that we have arrived at is that the morality of our actions is to be determined ultimately by its tendency to promote a universal end, which end itself consists of many ends, and in particular two—Morality and pleasure. Against this position it may be objected that if two (or more) goods are brought together, neither of them will remain unaltered. The different ends cannot simply exist side by side: the difference between them must be ' transcended.' 'That two elements should necessarily come together, and at the same time that neither of them should be qualified by this relation, or again that a relation in the end should not imply a whole which subordinates and qualifies the two terms— all this in the end seems unintelligible [1].' I have alluded to this objection here because it seems to be directed against an ethical position more or less resembling my own. It is easy enough to expose any system to ridicule when the critic deliberately introduces into the statement of it features which have no place in the minds or the writings of those whom he criticizes, and ignores much which they both think and say. I do not know any writer who has maintained that the good consists of two elements—happiness and virtue—which are unaltered by their relation to each other. At all events, in these pages nothing has been said, and nothing is implied, about the different elements in the end not being qualified by the relation in which they stand to one another: and much has been said of a directly opposite tendency. I have insisted that the recognition of differences among pleasures means the qualification of pleasure by other elements in consciousness— knowledge or virtue or whatever it is, and that, on the other

[1] Bradley, *Appearance and Reality*, 2nd ed., p. 426. The criticism is indeed directed against the idea of a good consisting of only two ends—happiness and goodness—for which the present writer does not contend, but in principle the objection might equally be brought against any view which recognized a good consisting in a number of goods.

hand, the idea of pleasure is so intimately bound up with all that
we call good that it is impossible to form any conception of an
ideal Virtue or contemplation of Beauty which includes no kind
or degree of pleasure. We can give no account of 'the good'
without breaking it up into various 'goods'; and yet no one
element in the good can be unaffected by the relation into which
it is brought in the consciousness of the person enjoying it with
the other elements in that good. In particular, the value which
is set upon the good will determines the kind of pleasure
which can be regarded as good by the good man. What the
benevolent man regards as good for self is a different thing from
what a selfish man regards as his good. The pleasure which
is derived from culture is a different thing from the pleasure
which comes from other sources just because the goodness of
culture does not lie solely in its pleasantness. For the ideal man
placed in favourable circumstances it will be impossible to draw
a sharp line between the good for himself and the good for
others : for he finds his good largely in activities useful to
others, and the indulgences which apart from their bad effects on
others he might enjoy he can enjoy no longer when he knows
those effects. The ideal end or good for man is not a number of
goods lying side by side and having no relation to one another,
but a particular kind of life in which various elements are
harmoniously combined. Undoubtedly the elements are altered
by their relations, just as the notes of a chord or the instruments
of an orchestra produce together an effect which is different from
what each of them produces by itself. But there could be no
musical notation unless we could distinguish these elements and
speak of the whole—the chord or the harmony—as produced by
their combination. That the whole is the sum of the parts is
true, though it is not the whole truth : for it is equally true that
the whole is more than that sum. Every attempt to distinguish
the elements of which the ideal good is made up involves some
abstraction. But, as no one has taught us more convincingly
than Mr. Bradley himself, all thought involves abstraction. We
could give no intelligible account of the good except by regarding
it as a combination of goods. Further reply to Mr. Bradley's
somewhat lofty and contemptuous remarks upon the tendency

of what he calls 'popular Ethics[1]' must be left to the further course of our argument. The objections apply to every system of Ethics which has attempted to give any intelligible account of 'the good'—that is to say, to almost every system of Ethics except perhaps Mr. Bradley's own. They all represent the good life as an ideal in which many distinguishable elements are harmonized and combined[2]. From such a view Mr. Bradley is estopped by his doctrine of an essential and unavoidable contradiction in the deliverances of the moral consciousness—a doctrine which will be dealt with in another chapter. Meanwhile, it may be observed in passing that Mr. Bradley's own objection can be retorted with some effect upon his system, in which 'self-assertion' and 'self-sacrifice' are pronounced equally good in complete isolation from each other without any attempt being made to build up a coherent and harmonious ideal of life in which each shall find its proper place. If the moral consciousness were incapable of making such an attempt, Mr. Bradley could not be blamed for leaving the matter there: it will hereafter be contended that the moral consciousness lies under no such incapacity, however difficult in detail may be the problems to which this collision gives rise[3].

---

[1] No writer is really so much open to the objection just mentioned as Kant himself, whom even Mr. Bradley will hardly treat as a representative of 'popular Ethics.'

[2] Dorner is right in protesting that 'das Sittliche eine Totalität, eine Einheit ist, die nicht mosaikartig sich zusammensetzen lässt' (*Das menschliche Handeln*, 1895, p. 53).

[3] Book II, chap. iii.

CHAPTER VIII

JUSTICE

I

WE have so far been engaged in considering the nature of the various goods, or elements in *the* good, which it is the individual's duty to realize for human society. But to say that it is our duty to produce the greatest possible good is a principle which cannot by itself determine the right course of action in any single instance. There remains the question, ' Whose good is to be promoted ? ' We want a principle to guide us as to the distribution of good among the various persons capable of enjoying it : and we have so far been content to take as our guide Bentham's principle ' Every one to count for one and nobody for more than one,' though we have already given to this maxim the somewhat different form ' Everybody's good to be treated as of equal value with *the like good* of every one else.' This modification must now be further explained and justified. I have already said as much as seemed necessary about Justice in the popular sense of the term, the relative or conventional Justice which prescribes equal treatment of different individuals upon the basis of some established and accepted social order or con- stitution or system of understandings. We have here to deal with the absolute Justice by whose precepts the morality of the very social order or constitution or system of understandings must itself be determined. If in this chapter I shall seem to be straying into subjects which belong more properly to Political Philosophy or even to Political Economy than to Ethics, I may plead that any treatment of Ethics which does not touch upon such questions must necessarily be theoretically barren and practically unprofitable. Man is a social being, and it is impos- sible to determine his duties, or even to examine into the abstract nature of duty, without dealing to some extent with his relations to the social environment in which he finds himself.

Now, when we ask ' What is Justice ? ', we are at once met by two conflicting ideals, each of which on the face of it seems entitled to respect. In the first place the principle that every human being is of equal intrinsic value, and is therefore entitled to equal respect, is one which commends itself to common sense, a principle which may naturally claim to be the exacter expression of the Christian ideal of Brotherhood. On the other hand the principle that the good ought to be preferred to the bad, that men ought to be rewarded according to their goodness or according to their work, is one which no less commends itself to the unsophisticated moral consciousness. We shall perhaps best arrive at some true idea of the nature of Justice by examining the claims of these two rival and *prima facie* inconsistent ideals— the ideal of equality, considered in the sense of equality of consideration, and the ideal of just recompense or reward—and we shall perhaps do well to start with the suspicion that there will be a considerable presumption against any solution of the problem which does not recognize some meaning or element of truth in each of them.

II

In examining the doctrine of ' every one to count for one and nobody for more than one ' in its Benthamite form, it is essential to bear in mind the context in which it stands. It was put forward by Bentham (not, of course, for the first time) as a canon for the distribution of happiness. He saw clearly enough that his ' greatest happiness ' principle, or the principle of greatest good (however good be interpreted), stands in need of this or some other supplementary canon before it can be available for practical application. It is obvious that in a community of a hundred persons we might produce the greatest possible happiness or good in a variety of ways. It would be quite legitimate, so far as the greatest happiness principle is concerned, to give the whole of our disposable good to twenty-five out of the hundred, and to ignore the other seventy-five, provided that by so doing we could make each of these twenty-five four times as happy as we should make each of the hundred by an equal distribution; and, if by an unequal distribution we could make twenty-five people five times as happy, or give them five times as much good (whatever the true good be) as we could procure for each of the hundred by an equal distribution, we should be absolutely bound by our 'greatest good' principle (taken by itself) to ignore the seventy-five, and distribute our good exclusively among the five-and-twenty. The principle which Bentham adopted as a solution of such problems is the maxim ' Every one to count for one and nobody for more than one.' He failed to see how impossible it is to establish such a principle by experience or to rest it upon anything but an *a priori* judgement. Only a grammatical ellipse dispensed him from the necessity of expanding it into the ' Every man ought to count for one, &c.,' and so introducing an ' ought '—that mystical, meaningless word of which he is said to have pronounced that, if it is to be used at all, it ought to be banished from the Dictionary.

The maxim then does not assert that every one ought to receive an equal share of wealth, or of political power, or of social consideration, but simply equal consideration in the distribution of ultimate good. Bentham was no Socialist; at heart he was not much of a democrat. Equality of political power, when in later years he advocated it, was for him merely a means to secure that legislation should aim at giving every one, as far as possible, an equal share of whatever 'good' legislation is capable of securing. The value of the maxim is not much affected by the fact that Bentham himself recognized no good but pleasure.

Now so long as the amount of good would be neither increased nor diminished by an equal distribution, the justice of such a rule will hardly be disputed. Understood in this abstract sense, the rule merely asserts that, if you have a certain quantity of good to divide between A and B, you ought to give half to A and half to B, so long as all you know about them is that one is A and the other B, or 'other things being equal,' or ' so long as there is no reason for preferring A to B.' How far the axiom ought to be modified in its practical application by the fact that

A never does differ from *B* solely in being a different individual, and what kind of inequality between *A* and *B* supplies reasonable ground for an inequality in the shares assigned to them, are questions which have yet to be considered. But it can hardly be denied that equality is the right rule for distributive Justice in the absence of any special reason for inequality.

Our first difficulty arises in the case where an equal distribution of good necessarily diminishes the amount of good to be distributed. It is clear that this is often the case. It is easy to imagine cases where the difficulty occurs in connexion with an actual distribution of a definite material good thing to a definite and assignable number of persons. In a beleaguered garrison nobody would question the justice of an equal distribution of rations; but supposing it were known that relief could not arrive for a month, and that the provisions available could keep half of them alive, while an equal distribution would ensure the slow starvation of the whole, there would be something to be said for casting lots as to which half should be fed and which should starve. I do not maintain that the conditions indicated could ever be exactly forthcoming, or even that the course suggested would be actually the right one to take if they were. But, if that course would not be right in the case supposed, it must be for some other reason than its injustice. No one would be bold enough to propose that the whole garrison should starve simply to ensure an ideal equality between all the individuals concerned. The kind of Socialism that insists that all should be miserable rather than that any one should be made a little happier than anybody else has been justly described as 'Individualism run mad.' In a less extreme form the difficulty I have indicated is of constant occurrence. The Schoolmaster, for instance, has to face the problem how far a whole class is to be kept back that the ultra-stupid minority may learn something. And when we turn from detailed questions of individual conduct to large problems of social and political action, the case supposed is not the exception but the rule. Nobody will deny that the present distribution of good things is excessively and arbitrarily unequal. The most satisfied champion of the existing social order will not deny that many people are badly clothed,

16 *

badly fed, overworked, and otherwise miserable through no fault of their own. And yet the most extreme advocate of social reconstruction, who is at once sane and well informed, will hardly deny that any attempt to produce an immediate equality of possessions, or of happiness, or of opportunity (whichever it be), would only cure these inequalities by producing, in no long period, a general dead-level of misery and want, or (to put it at the lowest) by seriously diminishing the ultimate Well-being of the country or the race. Here, then, an unequal distribution has to be adopted in order that there may be something to distribute. Either we may say (from a rough, practical point of view) that equality is a good but is not the good, and that we must in practice balance the principle of greatest good against the principle of equality, or (with more scientific precision) we may assert that in such cases there is no real sacrifice of equality. The law is fulfilled even in the case where its practical operation seems to involve the height of inequality, just as the laws of motion are fulfilled when two opposite forces neutralize each other and produce rest. For what the individual is entitled to is simply equality of consideration. The individual has had his rights even when the equal rights of others demand that in practice he should receive no good at all, but even a considerable allowance of evil. It would be the height of injustice, indeed, that the good of ninety among a hundred people should be considered, and the Well-being of the remaining ten wholly ignored. The ninety and the ten are entitled to consideration precisely in the ratio of ninety to ten. The rights of the ten would be grossly violated, if the ninety were to do what would be best for themselves were the remaining ten out of the way; as, for instance, by dividing among themselves all the available provisions, and giving none to the excluded ten. On the other hand there are cases where it would not only be expedient, but just, that ten men should die that the remaining ninety might live, e.g. in war, where an indefensible position has to be defended merely to delay an enemy's advance. In such cases the minority gets its rights as fully as the majority, provided its proportionate claim to consideration has been duly satisfied before it was determined that the measure proposed was on the whole for the general good.   David would have been guilty of no injustice had his choice of Uriah the Hittite for the post of danger been determined by purely military and impersonal considerations.

Not only does the principle of equal consideration not necessarily prescribe any actual equality of Well-being or of the material conditions of Well-being: when properly understood, it does not favour the attempt to draw up *a priori* any detailed list of the 'rights of man.'   It is impossible to discover any tangible concrete thing, or even any specific 'liberty of action or acquisition,' to which it can be contended that every individual human being has a right under all circumstances.   There are circumstances under which the satisfaction of any and every such right is a physical impossibility.   And if every assertion of right is to be conditioned by the clause 'if it be possible,' we might as well boldly say that every man, woman, and child on the earth's surface has a right to £1000 a year.   There is every bit as much reason for such an assertion as for maintaining that every one has a right to the means of subsistence, or to three acres and a cow, or to life, or to liberty, or to the Parliamentary franchise, or to propagate his species, or the like.   There are conditions under which none of these rights can be given to one man without prejudice to the equal rights of others.   There seems, then, to be no 'right of man' which is unconditional, except the right to consideration—that is to say, the right to have his true Well-being (whatever that true Well-being be) regarded as of equal importance in all social arrangements with the Well-being of everybody else.   Elaborate expositions of the rights of man are, at best, attempts to formulate the most important actual or legal rights which an application of the principle of equality would require to be conceded to the generality of men at a particular stage of social development.   They are all ultimately resolvable into the one supreme and unconditional right—*the right to consideration*; and all particular applications of that principle must be dependent upon circumstances of time and place.   What particular legal rights will, in certain conditions of time and place, best conduce to each man being equally considered in the distribution of Well-being, must be ascertained by experience.

In practice most of the crude or dangerous misapplications of the doctrine of equality spring from the attempt to translate an abstract equality of consideration into an immediate equality of concrete possessions, or personal liberties, or political power, or what not. Most of the objections to the doctrine may (I think) be met by bearing in mind the distinction on which I have been dwelling. Thus it might be objected to the principle of equality that an attempt to realize the immediate equality of property, or of some particular kind of property, might be good for the present generation, though it would lead to ultimate anarchy. The objection is met if it be remembered that future generations have rights as well as the present. Generations yet unborn may have the right to consideration; though that is obviously the only right that they are at present capable of enjoying[1].

Then, again, most of the cruder and more direct applications of the equality principle involve the tacit assumption that the legislator has at his command a definite quantity of happiness or other good which he can distribute at his pleasure. A moment's reflection shows that it is never 'good' itself, but simply the conditions of good, that are capable of being 'distributed,' either by the State or by a private individual. This is not (as has sometimes been thought) an objection to Bentham's principle properly understood. It is always possible to aim at an equal distribution of good, to attach equal value to each man's good, to consider each equally, in so far as his Well-being is capable of being affected by our action; but it is not always possible actually to secure this equal distribution of Well-being. Nothing that can possibly be distributed is a good under all circumstances or to all persons. There is no paradise that some people would not contrive to turn into a hell even for themselves. It is obvious that equal conditions of Well-being will not produce equal amounts of actual Well-being to persons of differing mental and bodily constitution. The devotee of equality as a practical watchword will probably say, 'Let the conditions be equally distributed; for the rest, the individual must take

---

[1] If this mode of statement be thought paradoxical, it may be put in another way—that it is a duty now to respect the rights which future generations will have when they are born.

care of himself.' But such a rule of conduct would actually violate the principle of equal consideration. For the end to be aimed at is not equality of conditions, but equal Well-being, or rather (as already explained) so much equality as is consistent with there being as large as possible an amount of good to distribute. But actual equality in the distribution of any concrete thing might not only diminish the amount to be distributed, but might actually widen the inequalities in the resulting enjoyment. A distribution of food, for instance, which took no account of the varying appetites and needs of different individuals might produce a lower average of actual health and enjoyment than an unequal distribution. To insist on according the same measure of personal liberty to children and to adults, to uncivilized men and to civilized, to the insane or half-witted and to the sane, might actually result in lowering the real Well-being which each and every one might enjoy under an unequal distribution: the amount of liberty might be too great for the Well-being of one class, and too small for that of the other. When we come to the higher sources of human pleasure or to those higher kinds of human good which cannot be expressed in terms of pleasure, it is still more glaringly evident that men's capacities for such goods vary enormously, and that an equal distribution of their material conditions would not result in an actual equality of enjoyment and would therefore be opposed to the principle of equal consideration. We assuredly should not effect an equal distribution of aesthetic enjoyment by subjecting every citizen to a uniform course of artistic education. The variety of men's capacity for different kinds of good constitutes by itself a sufficient condemnation of any attempt to equalize conditions irrespectively of the varying capacity to utilize the conditions and to turn them (so to speak) into actual Well-being. Any social arrangements which should wholly ignore differences of character and ability in the distribution of material goods would not only infallibly diminish the amount of good on the whole, but might even militate against the equal consideration of each individual in the distribution of it. It has often been objected to the Benthamite rule that it would require society to treat the drunken idler as well as it treats the industrious and capable workman. Such an objection implies a total misunderstanding of the principle. To treat the drunkard in a way which would encourage him in his drunkenness and his idleness—to give him the wages and the liberty which do conduce to Well-being in the sober and industrious—would not really be to consider his good as much as theirs. It would really not be considering his true good at all, to say nothing of the violation of other men's rights involved in placing the man who makes no contribution to the general good in the same position as those who do. To reward the idler as much as the industrious (even if we supposed that the reward would really be for his good) would be to make him count not for one but for several; since his support would impose additional labour on the industrious members of the community. To examine what social arrangements are best fitted to secure a really equal consideration of each man's good is no part of my present undertaking; but it may safely be said that no social arrangements will have that effect which do not in some way secure that men's material conditions shall have some proportion to their varying powers of utilizing them for their own Well-being and that of the whole society.

Many people will be disposed to meet these difficulties by suggesting that the true idea of social justice is 'equality of opportunity.' I should be far from denying the great practical value, within certain limits, of this ideal; though it would be easy to show the impracticability of a literal realization of it: to give everybody really equal opportunities the State would have to supply every child with an equally good mother [1]. But from a theoretical point of view, the ideal itself is open to exactly the same objections as the ideal of equal distribution when applied to so gross and concrete a matter as food. The English navvy would not be given an equal opportunity of making the most of his life by an allowance of food which would seem wanton superfluity to a Japanese soldier [2]. Equally far removed from the ideal of just distribution would it be to furnish equal

---

[1] Cf. Leslie Stephen's essay on 'Social Equality' in *Social Rights and Duties*, vol. i.

[2] The varying capacity for work is not *here* to the point.

educational opportunities to the dunce and the genius. Here it would, indeed, be difficult to say on which side the inequality would lie. The dunce might want three times the attention that the genius would require in learning to read : while the genius will require for the realization of his capacities a higher education which the dunce is quite incapable of utilizing. It will perhaps be contended that the man who is not capable of profiting by it may be said to 'enjoy' the opportunity as much as the man who is. But this is clearly a mere *façon de parler*. The opportunity is no more a good to the man to whom Nature has denied the capacity for using it than a pair of spectacles is a good to a blind man. But, if by 'equality of opportunity' is to be meant a simple equalization of external conditions irrespective of the individual's power of using it, if we are to eliminate from the inequalities which we are to aim at equalizing all those which are due to the inequality of Nature's bounty, such a principle will lead to some strange results. In that case we shall have satisfied our duty to the idiot by giving him every advantage that we offer to the sane man, while we shall refuse to violate our ideal of equal opportunity by providing him with asylums and keepers, which the sane man does not want. The distinction between men of different race, between the sexes, between the sick and the whole, will have to be equally ignored [1]. In whichever way equality of opportunity is understood, it leads to results which would strike every one as absurd and unjust. 'Equality of opportunity,' however valuable as a rough practical application within certain limits of some deeper principle, cannot be pushed to its logical consequences without absurdity. It leads to such absurdity because it is opposed to the principle of equal con-

---

[1] Another more formidable difficulty arises if we extend our view to inequalities not of physical constitution, but of physical circumstance. If every member of society or of every local community is to have the full benefit of superior soil, climate, &c., we have Capitalism at once, though the Capitalist is a group instead of an individual. On the other hand, we might ask the Socialist who aims at equality whether he is really prepared to give to the Laplander as much extra advantage as would compensate him for not living in the Riviera, or to penalize the inhabitant of Johannesburg to an extent which would put him on a level even with the Londoner.

sideration which commends itself to us as just, while it cannot always be assumed that it will accord with the principle of maximum good which is no less self-evidently reasonable. Equality of opportunity is only a rational maxim in so far as it leads to greater good on the whole and to a more equal distribution of that good. And it is always possible that some measure of inequality of opportunity may lead both to the existence of more good on the whole, and to a more equal distribution of that good. The institution of the family necessarily involves great inequality of opportunity, and yet it is possible that the system under which each child is looked after by its own mother leads to each getting a higher average of attention than would be secured under a system of State crèches and boarding-schools, which after all would not eliminate the necessary inequality of opportunity arising from the varying capacity of different educators. While there can be little doubt that a much greater measure of 'equality of opportunity' is socially desirable, it is not to be assumed that the total extinction of more or less hereditary classes enjoying a certain superiority of wealth, of culture, and consequently of opportunity, is necessarily conducive to the public interest; though the progressive diminution of such differences is undoubtedly involved in every attempt to raise the material, intellectual, and moral level of the least favoured classes. So far as superior opportunity secures on the whole superior efficiency in certain kinds of work by which all benefit, the superior opportunity will receive a social justification, and so be not unjust.

How far the principle of equal consideration requires or would be promoted by an unequal distribution of actual goods is a practical question which I do not desire here to discuss. Any distribution of good things which the world has actually seen is, of course, just as far removed from an equal distribution of actual good as it is from an equal distribution of the conditions or opportunities of Well-being. Whether, on the principle of equal consideration, a particular step towards greater equality ought to be promoted or resisted, will depend upon the question whether, under existing conditions—things being what they are, human nature being what it is, and so on—the change will be in the interest of all, the interest of each being regarded as of exactly equal importance. That equality of consideration would be violated by immediate attempts at forcible and sudden social reconstruction will be generally admitted. But that is not all. A certain liberty of action is, and always will be, a condition of Well-being; and liberty of action implies inequality. It implies *some* power of appropriating to one's self the results of one's own activity, or of disposing of them to others. Granted that necessary *work* might be parcelled out by the State, it is difficult to see how rational beings could occupy their leisure, either in a way agreeable to themselves or in' a way favourable to the development of intelligence and character, without a power of voluntarily disposing of their activities in such a way as to constitute an inequality of enjoyment, either for themselves or for persons immediately dependent upon them or favoured by them. And it is impossible that those inequalities should not be the parent of other inequalities. The man who has been benefited by association with a man of exceptional talent, or learning, or skill, will pass on his exceptional advantages to others. A town which has been blessed with inhabitants of exceptional energy and character will enjoy advantages which the State could not possibly transfer to others, though it might make it its business artificially to destroy them. A remorseless application of the principle of equality would not only be fatal to the family but would involve the enforcement of the unnatural maxim of clerical seminaries, ' pas d'amitiés particulières.'

At what point the attempt to realize equality ceases to be on the whole productive of a greater probability of good for each, is a practical question which experience only will enable us to decide. I merely want to point out (1) that some inequality is a condition of Well-being; (2) that there is only one sort of equality that is always practicable and always right, and that is equality of consideration, since we can always (ideally) give each individual equal consideration in making up our minds whether this or that will be on the whole for the general good; and (3) that, while it is certainly a duty to aim at a social constitution which shall bring about more actual equality of good, it must not be assumed *a priori* that such equality will always

be secured by increased equality of wealth or political power
or by any other kind of external equality whatever. The
principle of equal consideration certainly requires us to aim at
greater equality of actual Well-being, but only on condition that
the greater equality will not violate the equal right of each to
enjoy as much good as it is possible for him to enjoy.

So far I have been able to contend that obvious objections to
the principle of equality properly understood do not really form
an objection to the principle of equal consideration—to the doctrine that each man is entitled to an equal consideration at the
hands of the community; though the result of such equal
consideration, under given conditions, may be an exceedingly
unequal distribution of actual goods. But now I have to meet
a difficulty which is less easy of even theoretical solution.

III

It has already been indicated incidentally that it is not only
the less than normal capacity, but also the more than normal
capacity of exceptional persons, that may impose upon the
community unequal sacrifices to enable them to attain an equal
level of Well-being. Let us look at the difficulty in its least
serious form. The number of persons capable of the highest
intellectual cultivation and of enjoying the good incidental
to such high cultivation is unquestionably a small minority. If
such goods are to be enjoyed at all, they can only be enjoyed by
the few; and yet to give these few the opportunity of such
cultivation imposes upon the community sacrifices of inferior
good (such good as can be enjoyed by all) quite out of proportion
to the number of those for whom the sacrifice is made. It may
be contended, of course, that the extra value of the services
of such persons to the community is well worth the social cost
involved in their long years of unproductive education or
preparation, the number of persons and (it may be) the expenditure of material employed in giving that education, the waste
which (on any conceivable system of selection) will be incurred
by the education of persons who eventually turn out to be
unfitted for the highest work, and so on. So long as that is the
case, we do no doubt escape the difficulty by our formula of

equal consideration.   These favoured persons may be allowed advantages which the many do not enjoy; but it is good for each member of the community that they should enjoy them. Once again, equality of consideration itself demands a departure from concrete equality.   In this way our difficulty is fairly met, so long as we confine our attention to such higher kinds of culture and resulting Well-being as are of obvious social utility. But when we come to what (though the word has somewhat priggish associations) must, I suppose, be called 'the higher culture,' the case is different.   It is greatly to be feared that the cost of higher culture to the community must always be considerable.   It may be doubted whether there is not a kind of culture which demands for its vitality the existence of a class invested with something more than an equal share of all that makes life pleasant and attractive, that relieves from sordid cares and gives room for the free expansion of individuality—a class with a good deal of leisure (at least in youth), a good deal of freedom, an education of the kind that can only be kept alive as an hereditary tradition [1].   But of course such a class can only be maintained by enormous waste.   The leisure will be wasted in a large proportion of cases; the liberty will be abused; the freedom to do with one's life what one pleases without justifying it to the rest of the community, will, in a majority of cases, be used to do with one's life what cannot be justified.   Only a small proportion of these favoured individuals will do enough fully to justify their superior advantages.   It may be said, indeed, that a socialistic or communistic community might devise means for keeping alive such a class if its social value be adequate to the

[1] This view is unaffected by the fact that, where this class exists, individual members of it (often the highest intellects) may come from the classes outside it. They enter into and appropriate the tradition which is kept alive by the favoured families. And it is, of course, superfluous to remark that by the favoured class I do not merely or primarily mean what is called in the conventional sense the Aristocracy or the Plutocracy (neither of which, as a class, cares much for 'higher culture' or contributes much to it), but a class enjoying as an hereditary possession a more than average measure of wealth or opportunity, and the existence of which is often no doubt more or less dependent upon the richest class either by being recruited from it or by supplying its needs.

cost it involves. But, granting for the present this social value, what is the probability of a whole community, organized on principles of pure equality and accustomed to exact in all departments implicit obedience to its collective will, recognizing the value of such culture [1]? That, of course, is a practical question which does not necessarily touch our theory. If such a community would not recognize the value of a class which is essential to the highest social Well-being, then to that extent all attempts at greater equality of social conditions should stop at the point at which the existence of this class begins to be endangered, on the principle of equal consideration itself. But all this is assuming the social value of the class. And yet may there not be a point at which the benefits of 'culture' cease to be capable of very wide diffusion? Is it possible to prove, either *a priori* or *a posteriori*, that there may not be a final irreconcilability between the higher Well-being of the few and the lower Well-being of the many [2]?

Many will be disposed to brush aside the objection somewhat contemptuously. They will be disposed to say, 'Yes, there is a certain exquisite polish of life which probably is not capable of wide diffusion, which demands the existence of a few favoured families with estates, and dividends, and large houses. It is possible that, if an omnipotent Social Democracy were established to-morrow, it would seriously diminish the present expenditure upon professors and libraries in the German Empire. There would be less "research" on matters but remotely connected with life. Fewer monographs would be published. Emendations would not flourish. Latin verse-making would lose the high market value which it still commands in this country. There would even be

---

[1] I need hardly say that many things which are now impossible might become possible with the gradual education of the community.

[2] I mean merely that something must be taken off from the lower Well-being of the many, not that the condition of the many must be made an absolutely undesirable one. It might be, of course, contended that it was actually good that men of lower capacities should enjoy less than the largest possible amount of the lower goods (eating, drinking, &c.). On this view the difficulty will disappear, but this position postulates that all who are capable of it have the opportunity of entering the favoured class. And this is just what no artificial arrangement seems capable of securing.

a general lowering of the standard of Greek and Latin scholarship. Those who would still study Greek and Latin would have to be content with knowing those languages, say, rather better than even learned men are now content to know French and German. And there would be fewer people to take an interest in Aldine editions or old china. But all this is of very little weight—of very little weight even for the serious intellectual interests of humanity at large. To urge such matters as a grave objection to any policy which would bring us even a step nearer the social millennium, is like justifying Egyptian bondage, because without it, in all probability, the modern globe-trotter would have had to eliminate the Pyramids from his programme.'

Personally, I should have a good deal of sympathy with such a reply, though I might feel less confident than our sanguine Socialist that the vulgarizing rust, which might be the price of a real advance towards social equality, would stop at the mere polished surface of our intellectual life. But so far we are contemplating comparatively trifling differences of intellectual level—say the difference between the intellectual level of Berlin and that of a South American University. Let us now suppose it were possible by some scheme of social reconstruction to win for the great mass of European society the social and economic conditions which may be attained by some communistic brotherhood in the United States, but at the cost of extinguishing all Science, all Literature, all Art, all intellectual activity which rises above the highest level known in such communities. That might possibly represent, even on the intellectual side taken by itself, a higher kind of life than is now lived by the vast majority even of European humanity. The extinction of the 'higher culture' could not, therefore, be resisted on the ground of the diffused influence upon the community of the small cultivated class. If asked whether we should as a fact resist such a social revolution as I have contemplated in the interests of the higher culture, many of us would be disposed to answer, 'If the programme included the bringing of human society at large up to the moral level of a Moravian mission settlement, opposition to it would be hard to justify.' If we confine our attention

1 7

merely to the general diffusion of a low material comfort, a dull
contentment, and an education ranging between that of the
Sunday School and that of the Mechanics' Institute, we might
well be in great doubt and perplexity. I for one should certainly
doubt whether, if I had the power, I could doom the world to
a continuance of our present social horrors, although their removal might lead to the evanescence of research and speculation,
'sweetness and light,' full and varied exercises of the faculties,
and all the rest of it. Of course I do not assert for one moment
that such an alternative is now, or ever will be, in its naked
simplicity, presented to the social reformer. In the long run
(putting aside the influence of exceptional outbursts of religious
excitement) it is probable that moral and intellectual progress
are intimately connected. In the long run the diffusion of some
culture among the many is only obtainable by the maintenance
of a much higher culture among the few. But after all it is
easy enough to conceive circumstances in which we might have
to choose between the wide diffusion of a lower kind of Well-
being and a much narrower diffusion of a higher kind of life.
In the intellectual sphere, at all events, there is a higher life
which, if it exists at all, can only exist for the comparatively
few; and, in certain circumstances, it is at least a speculative
possibility that the existence of such a life for the few should
only be purchasable by sacrifices on the part of the many
which are not compensated by any appreciable advantage to
that many. If under such conditions we pronounce that the
higher life ought not to be extinguished, then we do at least
depart from the principle of equal consideration, understood as
we have hitherto understood it.

In the cases already contemplated, some will perhaps doubt
whether the principle should be sacrificed or not. I will now
mention a case in which probably no one will hesitate. It is
becoming tolerably obvious at the present day that all improvement in the social condition of the higher races of mankind
postulates the exclusion of competition with the lower races.
That means that, sooner or later, the lower Well-being—it may
be ultimately the very existence—of countless Chinamen or
negroes must be sacrificed that a higher life may be possible

for a much smaller number of white men [1]. It is impossible to
defend the morality of such a policy upon the principle of equal
consideration taken by itself and in the most obvious sense of
the words. If we do defend it, we distinctly adopt the principle
that higher life is intrinsically, in and for itself, more valuable
than lower life, though it may only be attainable by fewer
persons, and may not contribute to the greater good of those
who do not share it.

I will add a case which calls still more indisputably for the
application of the same principle. When we say, 'Every one to
count for one,' we are no doubt thinking merely of human beings;
but why are the lower animals to be excluded from consideration?
I should be prepared to say that in point of fact they ought not
to be wholly ignored. Their pain is certainly an evil, possibly
as great an evil, as *equal* pain in human beings apart from the
question of the activities with which the pain may interfere:
their comfort or pleasure has a value to which every humane
person will make *some* sacrifices. But few people would be disposed to spend money in bringing the lives of fairly-kept London
cab-horses up to the standard of comfort represented by a sleek
brewer's dray-horse in preference to spending it on the improvement of the higher life in human beings. The lives of animals
cannot be thus lightly treated except upon a principle which
involves the admission that the life of one sentient being may be
more valuable than the life of another, on account of its greater
potentialities—apart altogether from the social utilities which
may be involved in their realization. However inconsiderable
the differences of capacity among human races or individuals
may be when compared with the differences between the lowest
man and the highest beast, the distinction that we make between
them implies the principle that capacity does matter. The claim
of the individual does after all depend upon his capacity for an
intrinsically valuable kind of life; we cannot talk of the value of
an 'individual' apart altogether from the question what sort
of individual it is, and only the Hedonist will seek to judge of

[1] The exclusion is far more difficult to justify in the case of people like
the Japanese, who are equally civilized but have fewer wants than the
Western.

that value solely by the individual's capacity for pleasure. No
positive proof can, as it appears to me, be given that the higher
good of few and the lower good of many may not come into
collision. And when they do come into collision, there are some
cases in which we should, I think, prefer the higher good of the few.

How far then does this admission modify our acceptance of
the Benthamite principle of equal consideration ? Only to this
extent—that, if we still adhere to the formula ' every one to
count for one and nobody for more than one,' we must reduce it
to a still more abstract form. We may still say that every one
is to count for one so long as all we know about him is that he
is one [1]. We may still say, ' *Caeteris paribus*, every one is to
count for one.' But then, this will only amount to the assertion,
' Every one is to count equally, so long as he is equal ; but the
capacity for a higher life may be a ground for treating men
unequally.' Or more simply we may say ' Every man's good to
count as equal to the *like good* of every other man.'

While it is impossible to show that the claims of the few
possessing higher capacities for good will never come into
collision with the claims of the many to such good as they
are capable of, there are some considerations which will, I think,
very largely prevent the necessity of choosing between the rival
claims in practical life. While we cannot theoretically demonstrate that the best sort of life (in the intellectual region) will
always diffuse its benefits over the whole social organism, we
may in general find an ample justification for promoting the
higher culture of the few in the *ultimate* results of such higher
culture to the community generally. The principle of Election
has a place in Ethics and Politics as well as in Theology. It is
often right for governments and for individuals to bestow much
more than their fair share of attention upon the few on account
of the ultimate value to society of there being such a higher
class. We are, in fact, applying once more the principle that, in
the equal distribution of good, future generations have their

---

[1] Or, as it is well put by von Hartmann, ' If Equity demands a distribution,
without respect of persons, that means only : all peculiarities of the person
which are irrelevant (*unwesentlich*) for the purpose of the distribution must
be put aside ' (*Das sittl. Bewusstsein*, p. 438).

share as well as the present. It is sometimes suggested that, in the then condition of the world, Athenian culture and Athenian democracy were impossible without slavery [1]. It would perhaps be hard to show that the actual slaves of the time were much better off for the intellectual and the political life in which they had no share; but it would not be too much to say that in the forces which have ultimately banished slavery from Europe and America, in the forces to which the modern democratic movement owes its existence, that Hellenic city-life of which slavery was the foundation is no unimportant factor. In so far as that was so, slavery might claim a temporary and relative justification. On the same principle, we might justify our comparative indifference to the welfare of the black races, when it collides with the higher Well-being of a much smaller European population, by the consideration that if the higher life is ever to become possible on any large scale for black men it can only be through the maintenance and progress of a higher race. Still more are such considerations applicable to the maintenance of a culture or a civilization within a community from the benefit of which large classes within it are at present excluded, though of course the effort to extend the class that benefits by it should go hand in hand with the effort that maintains and improves the culture of the few. Such considerations will, it may be, practically prevent the necessity of our actually claiming for a smaller class any social expenditure (so to speak) but what can ultimately be repaid to the society (though not always to the actual persons) which makes that Well-being possible. Since, however, the repayment is made to future generations, it supplies no ground for assuming that a communistic or ultra-socialistic community would be sure to recognize the importance of such an expenditure.

It may be well, perhaps, to summarize the conclusions which I have endeavoured to establish.

(1) It is a self-evident truth that in the distribution of ultimate good every one should count for one, and nobody for more than

---

[1] That Aristotle would have thought so there can be no doubt. But it should not be assumed that had men arisen capable of appreciating the essential injustice and the economic defects of slavery, Greek civilization and Greek culture would have been the worse for an Abolitionist campaign.

one, so long as all that we know about the persons in question is that they are individual members of human society. This is the ideal of Justice.

(2) The equal distribution of concrete good things would often produce unequal amounts of actual Well-being, and would therefore be inconsistent with the principle of equal consideration. Strict equality of opportunity equally fails to satisfy the requirements of ideal Justice.

(3) The equal distribution even of actual Well-being would often produce a low total amount of good to be distributed, and would consequently violate the equal right of each to have as large a share of good as it is possible for him to have consistently with respect for the like right in others. Practically this consideration must involve much inequality in actual distribution. The only equality that it is reasonable to aim at is equality of consideration.

(4) All men are not capable of the same kind or amount of good. While the enjoyment by some of such good as, from the nature of the case, cannot be enjoyed by all is usually for the good of all, and hence justified by the principle of equal consideration, it is impossible to show that this will be invariably the case. Individuals, or races, with higher capacities (i. e. capacities for a higher sort of Well-being) have a right to more than merely equal consideration as compared with those of lower capacities. Hence the formula, ' Every one to count for one, nobody for more than one,' must be interpreted to mean ' every one's good to count for as much as the like good of any one else.'

(5) In practice it may, however, usually be assumed that the realization of such superior capacities by those who possess them is for the ultimate good of the human race.

We have, so far, left out of account altogether all strictly moral differences between man and man. We have left out of account the question whether the share of good to be allotted to each man, or rather (as we have seen) his share of consideration in the distribution of good, ought ever to be more than another's on account either (from one point of view) of his greater contribution to the common good, or (from another) his greater virtue or merit. An answer to this question will practically amount to a discussion of the second of the formulae which purport to be an adequate expression of social justice—the formula, ' To every one according to his merits,' the theory of just recompense or reward.

IV

I shall now proceed to examine this second formula which, on the face of it, presents itself to many people as self-evidently just and reasonable—the theory of reward or just recompense. This doctrine is apt to express itself in two forms. Sometimes it is said that every one ought to be rewarded in proportion to his merit; at other times we are told that every one should be rewarded according to the amount of his work or service to society. Sometimes the maxim is ' to every man according to his merit'; at other times ' to every man according to his work [1].'

Although, on a superficial view, these two formulae might be accepted as practically identical, there is really a fundamental difference between them. We may no doubt reduce both of them to the form 'everybody is to be rewarded according to his merit.' But in the first case merit is understood in a moral, in the second in an economic, sense. A moment's consideration will show that the two interpretations would lead to essentially different results. A picture painted with the toes by a handless man may show much more zeal, industry, perseverance, and the like, as well as more skill and ability, than one painted in the usual way. If the two pictures were of equal artistic worth, the painters ought, according to the second formula, to be rewarded equally; while, according to the first, the toe-painter should receive, it may be, ten or twenty times the reward of the hand-painter. And this is by no means an extreme

---

[1] I am here treating the formula in the sense in which it is usually put forward—as a rule for the actual distribution of concrete goods. If it is put forward as a formula for the distribution of actual Well-being, its application would have to be further modified by the principle which has been already dwelt upon in connexion with the formula of equal consideration—the principle that an equal wage will not secure equal Well-being.

illustration of the divergent consequences of the two methods :
for it is not easy to exaggerate the difference between the
maximum and the minimum of human talent, skill, strength,
or other capacities which determine the quantity and value
of the results produced by a given amount of labour.   Let us,
then, examine the economic interpretation of our thesis first.

The theory that ideal Justice means paying each man in proportion to the value of his work to the community looks plausible only
so long as we forget that economic value is essentially relative,
and not absolute.   What we me ı by the value of a given thing
is the amount of other things which will actually be given for
it under certain social conditions.   But, when we are assuming
that the very constitution of society has been, so to speak, put
into the melting-pot—when we are given carte blanche to
reconstruct human society in accordance with ideal Justice,
all the usual means of ascertaining value disappear.   Our
ordinary ideas of value postulate that wealth is divided among
a number of individuals who, under whatever restrictions, are
free to barter one form of it for another.   The value—let us
say—of medical attendance depends upon the amount of other
good things which people are prepared to give up in exchange
for medical attendance, under such conditions as the following :
(1) that the numbers of the medical profession depend upon the
number of persons who are induced to enter it by the advantages
which it holds out, as compared with other professions open to
the same class of persons ; (2) that the profession requires
a certain expenditure upon education ; and (3) that this expenditure is only within the reach of a limited number of
persons who have—themselves or their parents—accumulated
a certain amount of wealth, and become, to a limited extent,
capitalists ; and so on.   I need not take further pains to show
that values, no less than prices, are fixed by competition [1].   The

---

[1] All the conceptions employed by Economists, such as ' marginal utility,'
' marginal demand,' ' consumer's rent,' and the like, seem to be in the same
case. It may be observed that even if some means could be discovered,
in the absence of competition, for measuring the extent to which different
commodities could satisfy the actual desires of men, this would be no criterion of their true ethical value for those who hold that good does not mean
what men actually desire. The ethical disquisitions of some Economists

very instance which I have chosen is, indeed, one of those in which prices are not *wholly* fixed by competition ; and, just at the point at which they cease to be fixed by competition (between different classes of workers, if not between individual workmen), we cease to be able to express the value of the article supplied. It is customary with general practitioners to regulate their fees by the wealth of the patient, of which the probable rental of his house is taken as a rough indication. Now, if patient A pays 10s., patient B pays 7s. 6d., and patient C 5s., for a precisely similar visit, which fee represents the true value of the commodity supplied? This is a question which it is obviously impossible to answer. Now, in a community organized throughout upon a non-competitive basis, it would be as impossible to express in general terms the value of medical attendance as compared with other things that have value, as it is to express the true value of those particular visits which are remunerated according to the wealth of the patient. Value is ascertained by competition. It implies that there is a limited supply of the commodities in question, or at least a limited supply of commodities in general, and that if you have one, you can't have another. Now, medical attendance is precisely a commodity for which there is a by no means unlimited demand. A socialistic State which should determine the vocation of all its members, and provide their whole education, might very conceivably secure medical attendance free for all its citizens. If everybody could have as much medical attendance as he required without giving up his share of any other commodity, it would be clearly impossible to ascertain the economic value of medical attendance to the community.

It may be said that these considerations would cease to be applicable when we think not of the demand for this or that commodity (which is always limited) but of the demand for commodities in general which is practically unlimited. The

(even when they repudiate the hedonistic Psychology) seem to me to be seriously vitiated by the assumption that such is the case. One of the great objections to schemes for the immediate realization of the socialistic ideal is that they would certainly involve an attempt to fix remuneration (including hours of work) by reference to the wants at present felt, and the ideal of ' happiness ' at present entertained, by the average worker.

case would not, indeed, be altered supposing the State undertook to determine how much of each commodity the worker should receive, and exchange were made as criminal as accumulation. But what if the worker were paid by tickets on the stores, and each worker were allowed to take his day's allowance in whatever form he pleased? Two cases are then supposable. The State would have to fix the amount of one commodity which should be exchangeable for another. If it undertook to estimate the value of the article by reference to the amount of skill, knowledge, training, &c., which it took to produce it, we must suppose the problem which we are discussing already solved; since what we are in search of is precisely some common denominator by means of which to compare the value of watch-making and the value of turnip-cultivation. If, on the other hand (to avoid involving ourselves in a logical circle), we assume that the *quality* of the labour is to be neglected, the only criteria by which it is possible to ascertain how much of one commodity ought to be served out as the equivalent of so much of another will be (1) the amount of labour expended on its production, (2) the amount of land or its products and capital required for its production, capital being resolvable into the results of past labour, and of the 'abstinence' or waiting which has saved it from immediate consumption[1]. On the principle now contemplated, the worker who was allowed to take his pay in beef or in bread would, of course, have to choose between several pounds of bread and one of beef, because it takes more land to grow a pound of ox-flesh than to grow a pound of flour. But this element in the relative value of different commodities has, of course, nothing to do with the value of the workman's work *qua* work[2]. Hence, the only

[1] It seems unnecessary for our present purpose to discuss the economic question how far land should be regarded as capital.

[2] It may be urged that the worker whose work has involved expenditure of capital, i.e. 'abstinence' or 'waiting,' should be remunerated for that expenditure. But under such an ideal system as is here contemplated the work which produced the capital would have been adequately rewarded at the time; and, when we presuppose an ideal distribution, there would be no occasion for capital to be accumulated by the voluntary saving of individuals, as the State would have provided all that was required out of the

way in which we can compare the value of two pieces of work (on any hypothesis) is by their respective amounts.

Even then our difficulties are not at an end. What is *amount* of work? Clearly not the time spent on it; for some kinds of work are harder than others. But hardness is not by itself a reason for additional remuneration, except in so far as harder work is more disagreeable than lighter work. Some very light kinds of work may become disagreeable by reason of their extreme monotony; while severe bodily exercise is to some people a positive delight. Hard work may likewise become disagreeable when pursued for such a length of time as would not be disagreeable in the case of lighter work. But all that the hard-worker can claim is that, in so far as his work is more disagreeable than other work, he shall be compensated for its disagreeableness, either by liberty to work for fewer hours, or by other advantages—such as more food, tickets on stores, &c. It is possible that some system might be devised for comparing the relative disagreeableness of work by ascertaining the amounts of each which the average man would be willing to do for the same remuneration, including under that term all the advantages —whether in leisure or food or other conveniences—by which a community might endeavour to equalize the conditions of workers in different occupations. In that way it might be possible to ascertain the quantity of work which different commodities or services to the community cost. And quantity of labour, in the sense explained, is the only criterion by which we could measure the relative value of different kinds of work.

Although this reasoning seems to me to be unanswerable, it is probable that to some minds it will be found too abstract to be satisfying. 'What!' they will exclaim; 'do you mean to say that the Physician does not perform a greater service to society than the ploughman? Is he not therefore to receive a proportionate reward? Granted that the destruction of competition would prevent your measuring this relative value in terms of £ s. d., the general sense of the community is surely equal to the task of appreciating the relative importance of different

common funds. In speaking of 'capital' throughout this chapter I of course mean 'productive' and not 'consumptive' capital.

services, and will act according to its innate sense of what is just or appropriate.' I answer: Is it so clear that the service of the Physician is so much more important than that of the ploughman? At present we measure their relative importance by the comparative difficulty of getting them. But with carte blanche to postulate any form of society that he chooses, the legislator would have no difficulty in making it quite as easy to get medical attendance as to get bread. A sufficient number of people will be educated as Physicians to secure that medical attendance shall be forthcoming for every man who wants it, and sufficient ploughmen will be provided to supply everybody with as much bread as he can eat. And, when these two conditions are secured, no further production either of bread or of medical attendance will be of the slightest value to the community [1]. If you can have enough of both, it is impossible to say which is the more valuable. If you ask which is the more valuable when you cannot have enough of both, it must be admitted that the ploughman performs the more indispensable service. Some of us would die or suffer without the Physician : but we should all die without the ploughman or some equivalent food-producer. If, then, this is the sense which you put upon the principle 'To every man according to his work,' it would seem that the ploughman should be paid more than the Physician. But it is impossible to admit the justice of the principle thus interpreted. The Physician would naturally say to the State, ' If I had known that I was to be served like that, I should have wanted to be a ploughman too. And if you, for your greater convenience, insisted that I should be a Physician, why should I suffer on that account? You say, " Bread is more necessary than medical attendance "; but if you did not want to have both, you should not have insisted on my being a Physician.'

It is evident that the real consequences of following out this maxim, ' Every man according to his work,' would be very different from those usually intended by at least one class of its advocates. When they do not mean that equal work should

---

[1] Foreign trade being, for greater simplicity, ignored. If corn is exported, it is, of course, not serviceable to the community *as bread*.

be recompensed by equal advantages, they usually assume that what is commonly considered the higher work, that which employs the highest faculties, intellectual work, artistic work, spiritual work, &c., should be remunerated more highly than the lower, more mechanical, more animal work. Now, this contention may be based on one of two grounds: either (1) on the ground that by such work a higher service is performed to the community, or (2) that the higher faculty should receive higher remuneration simply because it is higher. In the first case, I am unable to see the justice of the demand. The man who prints Bibles no doubt renders a higher service to the community than the man who prints 'penny dreadfuls.' But, assuming that both minister to legitimate social needs, nobody would propose that the former should receive higher remuneration than the latter. So long as the different values spring from some difference in the mere objective results of work, nobody will contend that the more important or 'higher' consequences should form a ground for unequal reward of exactly the same work. If you say, 'The work itself is different, not merely its external consequences,' I cannot see how there can be a difference in kind between one work and another when abstracted both (1) from the results to the community and (2) from the faculties employed by the worker. If you mean to insist upon the last, then you adopt the second of our two original alternatives, which we have yet to examine.

Is the superior dignity—the moral or aesthetic or intellectual superiority—of the activities employed any ground for additional remuneration? Of course, if intellectual work is considered more disagreeable than unintellectual, then the work ought to receive compensating advantages. But it is not the common opinion that *to intellectual persons* intellectual work is less agreeable than manual labour or mechanical drudgery. Most people would probably say, '*Caeteris paribus*, the intellectual work is infinitely the more pleasant.' Even if we suppose the social estimation and other conditions of intellectual and manual labour equalized, there would probably be more persons anxious to undertake intellectual instead of manual work than the community could provide with adequate employment. For our present purpose, however, it is enough to negative any claim for additional remuneration on the ground of additional disagreeableness. If, however, the intellectual work is supposed to imply a sort of *merit* on the part of the worker, and to claim remuneration on that score, one must ask, ' To what does the intellectual worker owe the opportunity of doing this higher work?' The answer will be, (1) partly to superior education and opportunities, (2) partly, in the case of the higher kinds of intellectual work, to the possession of natural capacities which are confined to a more or less small proportion of the human race. Now, in so far as the position of the brain-worker is due to education, it is clearly not his merit but the organization of society which has put him in this position. Under present conditions, it is generally the command of capital that secures education; and, the capital expended upon education being nearly always accumulated by others than the person whom it benefits, it will hardly be pretended that an accident of this kind can claim remuneration on grounds of abstract Justice, however expedient it may be as a means to the general good under certain conditions that such remuneration should be given. And under altered social arrangements the community could, of course, easily secure that the requisite educational advantages should be given to as many persons as its social needs might demand. In either case, there is no question of superior merit in the intellectual worker.

But how does the matter stand with regard to those capacities for higher work which are due to Nature? Nature has given to many Englishmen intellectual powers possessed by very few negroes. Among Englishmen she has made, perhaps, from two to five per cent. capable[1], with the requisite education, opportunity and application, of obtaining a first-class in *literae humaniores* at Oxford—to take the distribution of one particular kind of intellectual capacity as a sample of the comparative rarity of high intellectual powers. And when we come to the highest kind of intellectual capacity, she gives high originality to one man in a thousand, genius to half a dozen in a generation, and so on. But should the possession of capacities for

[1] I need hardly say that this estimate is little better than guesswork.

doing the precise kind of work which only a certain number
of his fellow countrymen can do—should even the power to do
(a power which is implied, of course, by even the most modest kind
of *originality*) the particular thing which no one else living can
do, constitute ground for superior remuneration? So long as
the question is considered merely as one of 'reward'—of some
additional gratification, not implying or essential to the exercise
of his superior faculty—I must say that I cannot see the justice
of this extra remuneration. Everybody would admit that the
mere rarity of a capacity would be no ground for exceptional
treatment; though, of course, the most mechanical and accidental
kind of superiority (e. g. delicacy of touch enabling a man to
test grain better than anybody else) may, under a competitive
régime, enable a man to appropriate an enormous share of the
world's wealth. Under a competitive régime giants and dwarfs
can make considerable money by exhibiting themselves; but
on principles of ideal Justice is there any reason why they
should be paid more for their day's labour than an ordinary
sandwich-man? Is the case altered when the qualification is
not merely rare but intellectually or artistically or even (in so
far as moral qualities are not under the immediate control
of the will) morally admirable? Should strength of brain or
steadiness of nerve or a natural love of work entitle a man to
a superior share of the good things of life, any more than
strength of arm? If a man has a body of extraordinary size
or strength, it is right that I should look upon him—not, indeed,
with the feeling of awe or respect which is often in fact inspired
by the knowledge that in certain circumstances such a man might
assault us with impunity, but with the feelings of wonder and
interest which are inspired by an elephant or a fossil mammoth.
If he has extraordinary skill and agility of body, it is fitting
that I should look upon him with the half-aesthetic, half-
sympathetic feeling that is inspired by the sight of a gazelle
or a greyhound. If he has exceptional brain-power, the imagination of a poet or the penetration of a philosopher, it is right that
I should treat him with respect, i. e. the intellectual respect that
his qualities merit. If he has moral or spiritual capacities above
those of common men, then it is right that I should treat him

with moral and spiritual respect. But I see no reason why, on account of either the intellectual or the spiritual superiority, I should offer him a bottle of champagne while for my less gifted guest I only provide small beer. Neither intellectual nor spiritual superiority seems to constitute an intelligible ground for assigning to a man a larger share of carnal delights than his neighbour. The opportunity of freely exercising his superior faculty and the power or authority which his particular gift fits him to wield, these strike us as the fitting rewards, and the only fitting rewards, for superiority of this kind. To the man who is capable of a higher kind of happiness than others because of his higher gifts, that higher happiness itself surely is the due reward—not a larger meed than others of those lower kinds of pleasure of which alone his inferior may be capable. If any difference were to be made between the two, it might be plausibly argued that the superior man should receive less of those lower pleasures which he ought better to be able to do without, than the man who is capable of nothing else. Of course it may be suggested that the superior man may be expected to 'make a good use' of his superior wealth, i. e. to use it in the public interest. But if so, the wealth is not really 'distributed;' the distribution is merely postponed. The real problem is, 'what is it just that the superior man should enjoy?'

To translate this somewhat abstract language into terms of actual social arrangements, Justice does not seem to me to require that because Nature has given a man capacities which fit him for superior usefulness to the community, his work per hour should—on any abstract principle and apart from considerations of social utility—be paid at a higher rate than the equally exhausting or disagreeable work of common men [1]. When I say 'paid at a higher rate,' I mean that there is no reason why he should be better fed, clothed, or housed;

---

[1] The fatigue of work demands remuneration only in so far as it (1) makes it disagreeable, which it does not always do, or (2) makes the worker capable of doing less of it. If, on account of the value of his work, it is socially desirable that he should do a longer day's work than others, then no doubt the absence of recreation should be made up to him in other ways.

that he should be indulged in more or more expensive amusements, or allowed longer holidays.

No doubt it is quite true that the man of higher faculty requires for the exercise of those faculties certain external conditions of an exceptional character. And some of these conditions may consist in a larger supply of those conveniences and indulgences which ordinary men are quite capable of appreciating. Nay, the higher faculty may sometimes be a source, not of greater happiness, but of greater misery, unless these conditions are forthcoming. The musical genius, for instance, might be driven distracted by being compelled to live amid the noise and bustle, the barrel-organs and the hurdy-gurdies, which would be Paradise to many an East-end factory-girl. And of intellectual workers in general it may be said that they do require for the favourable exercise of their faculties a larger share of certain comforts and conveniences than would be likely to fall to the lot of the average workman under a régime of absolute equality. It is doubtful whether the luxurious table of a successful barrister is any more conducive to his activity than the humbler fare of the solicitor's managing clerk, who may sometimes do quite as large an allowance of brain-work; but it is probably true that the brain-worker wants more and better food than is absolutely necessary for the less exhausting kinds of mechanical work. Still, if everybody had his fill of plain and wholesome diet, I don't know that the brain-worker could on grounds of abstract Justice claim anything more [1]. Nor is there any reason in the nature of things—existing social conventionalities apart—why the brain-worker should be clad in broad-cloth, and the hand-worker in corduroy. But it is otherwise when we come to less material conveniences. It is probably desirable in the interests of his efficiency that the higher-class brain-worker should be set free from petty worries and anxieties. Under existing conditions, that would mean that he ought to be allowed servants to do for him things which other people have to do for themselves; under any arrange-

[1] It is possible no doubt that a certain amount of luxury, even in matters of eating and drinking, may sometimes be conducive to efficiency, but, if the luxuries were given on this ground, they would not be given by way of 'reward.'

18

ments he would want a larger amount of *service*. It is desirable
that he should have more house-room than the most ideal
Socialism would probably assign to ordinary hand-workers.
The doctor's carriage is none the less a personal luxury because
it is also necessary to his business. The author will want
a study, the artist a studio, the student books and room to
stow them. If his wife is to be capable of sharing his life, and
not to be a mere housekeeper, she must also be secured more
than the normal exemption from household drudgery by nurses
and other servants. And if family life is to be maintained, it is
practically inevitable that some of these advantages should be
extended to his children, who may nevertheless be very far from
inheriting his mental superiority. Then, too, it is probable that,
if the lives of highly cultivated people are to be made as agreeable to them as *their* lives are to people of less cultivation, they
will want amusements or interests that will impose upon the
community a heavier tax than the amusements of the less
cultivated. We can hardly conceive of the most absolutely
socialistic State allowing very extensive opportunities of foreign
travel to every one; and yet it is clearly desirable that they
should be within the reach of some. Moreover, for the exercise
of certain mental gifts, considerable leisure and some liberty of
action may be essential—including the liberty at times to be
unproductive. Literary production of a certain kind has, indeed,
often been stimulated by the most abject bodily want; but it is
certain that the higher kinds of intellectual labour could never
be made into a daily task, to be exacted under penalty of imprisonment or short commons by a socialistic taskmaster. In
ways like these it is probably right that the more gifted man—
or even the more educated man when once the community has
allowed him a higher education than the common—should have
exceptional treatment. But it is rather because these things
are necessary or desirable for the full development and enjoyment of a faculty which ought to be developed, than as 'reward'
for being differently constituted from ordinary men, that he
may rightfully claim from the community the use—in certain
directions—of more wealth than would fall to his lot under
a perfectly equal distribution.

Our examination of the dictum, 'To every man according to his work,' has, so far, tended to this result—that we can accept it only in the sense, 'The development of higher capacity is of more worth than the development of lower capacity, and consequently ought to be provided with all the conditions necessary to its exercise.' And this was, it will be remembered, the one reservation which our examination of the other maxim, 'Everybody to count for one, and nobody for more than one,' compelled us to adopt before we could admit its universal applicability in any sense other than the purely abstract one, 'Caeteris paribus, everybody to count for one,' or 'One man's good to count for as much as the like good of any other if all we know about him is that he is a man.' We came to the conclusion that the higher good was worth more than the lower, and that consequently the man who has more capacity for higher good should count for more than the man who has less.

So far, however, we have confined our attention to those differences in capacity for work which are due solely to differences of natural endowment. But now, what of the differences which are due to will? What of the strictly moral differences? Ought the virtuous to be rewarded? What, in ultimate analysis, are we to make of the popular notion of 'merit'? Here it is necessary to put aside two philosophical problems with which a discussion of this question is usually involved.

(1) I put aside for the present the question of Free-will. The facts of heredity, the phenomena of mental pathology, and the constancy of statistics make it plain that Free-will (in the popular 'indeterminist' sense of the word) is on any view not the *only* cause of some men's goodness and other men's badness. And it is obviously impossible to discriminate in our treatment of other people between the part which undetermined choice (if such a thing there be) may play in the formation of actual good volitions, and the factors in their causation which are due to other influences. Hence it is clear that, if we are in any sense to reward men for their goodness, we must look only to the actual quality of their volitions. We must reward them for being good without raising the question how they came to be so.

(2) The question involves an answer to the theory of punish-

ment. If punishment is retrospective and retributive, then it may be inferred that reward must also rest upon an *a priori* basis, and not be a means to anything beyond itself. That is a question which I reserve for separate treatment in the next chapter: but, even if we deny that the bad man ought to suffer pain as an end-in-itself, independently of the moral effect to be produced upon him and others, it does not follow that we must, on that account, decline to say that happiness ought to be distributed in proportion to goodness. It is one thing to cause a man pain, another to refuse to make him happier than some-body else. When it is a question of inflicting pain, the *onus probandi*, so to speak, would seem to rest with the inflicter; when it is a question of distributing happiness, it may be considered to lie with the claimants. If I hang, or assault, or imprison a man, he naturally demands my authority for doing so; but it might easily be maintained that I do no wrong to *A* by giving a certain lot of happiness to *B*. The question is, there-fore, not settled by the view we take of the theory of punishment, unless, indeed, we look upon punishment in a merely negative aspect as the withholding of some good [1]. We must therefore still ask, 'Is it reasonable that an individual or a community, having the conditions of happiness or Well-being [2] at his or its disposal, should distribute them to all equally, or should dis-tribute them in proportion to the moral worth of the individuals concerned?'

To this question the obvious practical answer will be that we shall distribute in accordance with merit because we want to make as many people good as possible, and that experience shows that the best way of effecting that object is to contrive that, so far as possible, goodness shall lead to happiness, and badness to misery [3]. The question whether, apart from such tendency,

---

[1] See below, p. 294 *note*.

[2] The idea of distribution according to merit is generally understood to refer to the distribution of happiness, since the higher elements of Well-being constitute the merit which is to be rewarded, and cannot therefore be themselves distributed by way of reward.

[3] If we hold (with Aristotle) that Virtue necessarily or intrinsically leads to happiness (given the favourable external conditions or an 'unimpeded exer-cise' of virtuous activities), the question ceases to have any meaning except

Justice would require an unequal distribution of external goods is an extremely abstract question which it can never be necessary to answer for the solution of any practical problem. But, if the question must be answered, I should be disposed to say: If the matter be treated as an abstract question of merit and reward, I can see no reason at all why superior moral goodness should be assigned a superior quantity of external goods, that is to say, the means of indulging desires which have no connexion with this superior goodness. So far as the word 'merit' means anything more than 'intrinsic worth' or 'value,' it must be treated as one possessing no intelligible meaning. Goodness does not merit material reward, as though goodness were a loss to the possessor which can only be rationalized if he be paid for it. But if the question be asked whether the good man ought not to be made happy, I should answer, 'Yes, certainly he ought to be made happy, because the kind of happiness of which the good man is capable possesses so much higher a value than the happiness of the less virtuous character. Just because Virtue is not by itself the only good for man, though it is his highest good and an essential condition of *the* good, the man who has it should be given all that is necessary to complete his true Well-being. Pleasure taken by itself in abstraction from all other elements of consciousness may have a very small value: pleasure taken in connexion with elements of consciousness that are bad—such pleasure in a word as a bad man is capable of—may have still smaller or perhaps a negative value; but such pleasure as accompanies the exercise of the higher faculties under favourable circumstances possesses a very high value indeed.' But if this be the ground on which we pronounce that goodness should be rewarded, it is clear that it is not any and every kind, nor every amount of pleasure or material source of pleasure, that should be the ideal reward of the good man. The fitting reward of the

in relation to God, who may no doubt be conceived of as creating human nature in such a way as to make goodness constitute or contribute to the happiness of the creature. Goodness can hardly be thought to be a good at all without being supposed to be a source of happiness: the question remains whether, in so far as happiness is dependent on external circumstances, the other conditions of happiness ought to be made to follow upon goodness.

18 ★

good man (if we still talk of reward at all) is the opportunity for the freest and most fruitful exercise of his highest capacities—their exercise in such a way as shall be most favourable both to the goodness itself and to the pleasure which, under favourable circumstances, goodness brings with it. It is (as Aristotle puts it) the 'appropriate' or 'cognate' pleasure that is the fitting reward of the activity, together with such other pleasures as are conducive or not unfavourable to the continued exercise of virtuous activities. And to that end the man ought clearly to be assigned not the amount of external goods which he has 'earned,' for moral goodness cannot be expressed in terms of external goods, or of such happiness as external goods can secure, but the quantity of external goods which will be most calculated to secure that ideal of life which includes goodness and culture and happiness [1]. And if it be asked what is to be done when the claims of the good man come into collision with those of less good or bad men, I answer in accordance with the principle which we have already adopted: 'the higher kind of life is worth more than the lower: consequently the man with the higher capacities [2] must be treated as of more value than the

---

[1] This of course represents the Aristotelian idea of the proper relation of external goods to εὐδαιμονία, an idea which Aristotle entirely forgets in his somewhat crude account of distributive Justice. It is perhaps a somewhat paradoxical result of our principle (one which Aristotle would have been little disposed to admit) that the less completely virtuous man might sometimes have to be assigned more material reward than the more virtuous. The average man, even the average good man, certainly does want, to make him really happy, many external goods which would not have increased the happiness of St. Francis of Assisi, or even of an ideal man of less one-sided development than St. Francis.

[2] The higher capacities, not the higher performance. Logically we should have to admit that, if the bad man could be rendered capable of the higher life by expending upon him what it would be prepared to spend upon the better man, the expenditure would be equally justified. And there are cases where that principle may really be acted on. We are justified in spending money to bring one sinner to repentance which might otherwise have been spent in adding to the comforts of ninety-and-nine just persons who need no repentance. How to compare the claims of the sinner and the just might often be a difficult problem but for the fortunate fact that the conversion of the most obviously anti-social sinners involves the saving of considerable expense to the just persons.

man of less capacity :—of how much more value is a problem which the practical Reason must solve when occasion arises for it.'

It should be observed, indeed, that the grounds on which we do, in a sense, admit the good to be entitled to reward will by themselves set a limit to the amount of this reward, in so far as it consists in the means of gratifying the lower or more animal desires. It will be generally admitted that the possession, or at least the consumption, of much wealth in such ways is not favourable to—may even be inconsistent with—the highest moral Well-being. And when the existing inequalities are justified as a means to the encouragement of 'merit,' it is often forgotten that the influence of excessive wealth upon the moral Well-being of its possessors may be as injurious as its influence in decreasing the moral and physical Well-being of the poor. If the question be raised, whether the system of rewarding Virtue is not itself injurious to Virtue, I should be quite prepared to admit that the reward of Virtue might very easily be carried to this point, though in the interests of society we often have to encourage social service even to the injury of the highest character. And this is one of the difficulties that I should feel in admitting, even as an abstract and theoretical proposition, that the good man ought, as a matter of *a priori* Justice, to be rewarded *in proportion to* his merit. For that would mean, if we use words in their ordinary sense, that every increase of Virtue should, on principles of ideal Justice, bring with it a larger house, more servants, better dinners, more expensive pleasures, more splendid equipages, and more costly horseflesh. And these things would possibly not be good for the good man. The House of Lords may be a useful institution under existing social conditions, but it can hardly be said to 'encourage' the highest Virtue in Peers or their eldest sons.

But how far is this principle, that the good ought to be rewarded, available as a canon of distributive Justice in actual life ? For practical purposes hardly at all. We must, no doubt, in criticizing or seeking to alter existing social arrangements bear in mind the necessity of securing conditions favourable to the highest type of life. But in its ordinary economic arrangements the only kind of goodness which society at large has it in its power to reward is positive contribution to social good, and for the most part such contribution to social good as admits of being not altogether inadequately expressed in terms of £ s. d. The only kind of reward, in short, of which it is possible to take much practical account is the economic reward for work done. For how is it possible to discriminate between the portion of the work produced which is due to superior goodwill, to industry, perseverance, integrity, and that which is due to superior capacity? It is obvious that one workman can do in an hour twice as much work as another working equally hard. But how can we test the intensity of a man's application? It is practically impossible to reward industry without rewarding cleverness also. And yet we have seen that the ideal of just reward is not satisfied by paying a man according to the actual quantity of work done irrespective of the qualities which he shows in doing it. It follows then that, if there is to be any diversity of reward at all, it cannot be based upon the principle of ideal Justice, but must be regulated by social expediency. If anybody thinks that men in general could be induced to put forth their maximum activity in the service of the community without the prospect of reward, for themselves and those nearly connected with them, he is a person with whom it is useless to argue. Rewards there must be; and yet rewards cannot be directly justified by considerations of ideal Justice, but only indirectly by their tendency to bring about in the long run equality of consideration in the distribution of good.

And lest I should be accused of taking a low view of human nature or inadequately recognizing its future improvability, let me add two practical considerations which must be borne in mind before our conclusions are used as a justification of the social *status quo*, or as an argument against any suggested modification of society in a socialistic direction. In the first place, it must be remembered that a very small reward is quite sufficient to call forth men's utmost energies when no other is obtainable. A free labourer would laugh in your face if you proposed to allure him to greater industry by the offer of an additional two ounces of bread *per diem*, but such an offer is found a very effective stimulus among the inmates of His Majesty's gaols. German judges probably work as hard as English ones, though they do not receive such large salaries. After a certain point small incomes stimulate activity as much as larger ones when no larger ones are to be had. The other consideration is that even in the existing state of society the rewards for which men work (in so far as they do work for reward) are very largely honorary—rewards which take the form of social consideration or of interesting employment for their higher faculties. The pecuniary gains even of the most remunerative professions are small compared with those of commerce, but they are more attractive to educated men because even at the present day an eminent Physician or Lawyer enjoys more consideration and has a more interesting life than a successful clothier or brewer with a much larger income. And the Civil Service can secure the highest ability at a still lower rate. Even wealth itself is largely valued as the concrete embodiment of success and the source of social consideration. In the society of the future these principles might be carried much further. Rewards will always be necessary, but rewards may be increasingly small in their cost to the community, and increasingly non-material in character; and, though reward must always in the nature of things consist in some sort of differential advantage, the advantage may be increasingly consistent with and conducive to the highest development of the less favoured individuals. Reward must always, under any possible conditions of human life, mean the getting something which somebody else has not got: it need not always mean the gain of one at the expense of the whole. Both the lower kind of non-material rewards (stars, ribbons, titles, newspaper notoriety, conventional social position) and the higher (more responsible and more intellectual work, power, influence, interesting society, the esteem of the best) must always from the nature of the case belong to the few, but they need not involve a burden on the many. And if the enjoyment of the best things in life does involve, and always must to some extent involve, exceptional material advantages, the material side of the reward may still be treated as a condition of that better life which ideal Justice would award to the exceptionally gifted, and not as its essence.

While the principles of ideal Justice can hardly be made into a rule capable of actual application to the actual payment of each individual citizen even in a socialistic Utopia, the principle that the higher life possesses superior value has a most important bearing upon questions of social organization and social policy. It emphasizes the fact that we must not push the search for equality of conditions, or even the pursuit of maximum Well-being for all, to the point which might be fatal to progress and so extinguish the higher kinds of human existence altogether. From the point of view of reward, if that principle is to be admitted at all, it would be only moral effort that could be supposed to carry with it a title to superior remuneration: and the difficulty of distinguishing superior effort from superior ability was, we saw, insuperable. But, if we claim for higher capacity the conditions of its exercise on the ground simply of the higher worth of the life which such capacity makes possible, it will become unnecessary to draw a sharp line between moral and intellectual capacity, between superior exertion and superior success. All kinds of higher life—moral, intellectual, and aesthetic—will be treated as more valuable than lower life. In the distribution of good things—or, to speak more practically, in the criticism and modification of social institutions—each element in life should receive the weight that is due to its intrinsic quality, and not merely to its amount measured by a hedonistic or any other merely quantitative standard. Such is the ultimate meaning of that idea of distributive Justice or just recompense which protests against the Benthamite idea of equal consideration, pure and simple, and seeks to mend it by the Aristotelian formula, 'equal things to equal persons.'

V

The general result of our enquiry has been, I apprehend, to show that each of these competing ideals of Justice is only reasonable in the sense in which it becomes equivalent to the other. We saw that Equality was only reasonable in a sense which implied, not equality in the possession or enjoyment of any concrete good, but only equality of consideration—equality in the degree of importance which is attached to each man's individual Well-being in the distribution of ultimate good so far as such distribution is capable of being effected by human action. And even so, the formula 'every one to count for one and nobody for more than one' requires to be interpreted as meaning 'every one's good to be considered as of equal value with *the like good* of every other individual'. It is not really individuals considered simply as individuals but individuals considered as capable of a certain kind of good that are intrinsically valuable, and entitled to consideration equal in so far as their capacities are equal, unequal in proportion as their capacities are unequal. And when we turned to the other ideal of recompense or reward, we found it to be childishly unreasonable in so far as it meant that every individual should be assigned sugar-plums in proportion to his moral or other 'merit,' but entirely reasonable in so far as it meant that superior capacity constitutes a superior title not only to the conditions for the realization of such capacities, but to those other good things of human life which are necessary to complete that ideal of a desirable life of which virtuous activity is not the whole. These two ideals come to the same thing ; both prescribe equality of treatment when capacities are equal, treatment in proportion to the intrinsic worth of the capacity when they are unequal. And the worth of a capacity is really, as we have pointed out, the worth of that kind of good life which the capacity enables the individual to realize. As the formula of reward according to merit seems too hopelessly charged with misleading suggestions to be adopted by a rational system of Ethics, I prefer to retain the Benthamite maxim with the explanation that it is each man's good that is as good as the like good of another, not the individual abstracted from all those capacities the possession of which can give him worth or entitle him to 'consideration' at the hands of his fellows [1].

[1] If we grant that superior capacity should receive the superior consideration, the question may still be raised whether, if and in so far as the persons enjoying superior culture are not and cannot always be those intrinsically most fit to receive it, the existence of a favoured class enjoying such culture can be justified. To a large extent this state of things actually exists: to a certain extent it must probably always be so if the higher culture is to subsist at all. I should reply: I have already urged that the existence of this class *is* socially useful, if 'useful' be only understood in

The superior man's good is worth more than the inferior man's (whatever the nature of his superiority)—how much more must be decided by our judgement of value in each particular case of moral choice. The superior man's good has more value than that of the inferior man, simply because it is a greater good.

VI

From this point of view it might almost appear as if we had succeeded in reducing our two maxims of Justice and Benevolence to one and the same all-embracing precept—that of promoting a maximum of good on the whole.

But our difficulties are not yet at an end. It may still be asked, ' What are we to do when we can only satisfy equal claims to good by diminishing the total amount of good to be enjoyed ? ' Even the abstract and theoretical solution of this problem is, it must be confessed, a matter of extreme difficulty, to say nothing of practical applications. It may, indeed, be maintained that our theory of equal consideration for good of equal worth will still prove equal to the strain. We have already seen how frequently inequality in actual distribution is demanded by the

a non-hedonistic sense. If it could be shown that its existence could not be justified on social grounds, I should still maintain that a society with a cultivated class would be better than a society without one ; the inequality would be justified by the superior value of higher good. But it would still remain a duty to *aim* at making the favoured class consist of the persons most capable of the higher life. So far as that cannot be done, it is still better that the higher life should be led by some, even though that life be not so good a thing as it might be if the opportunity of it were reserved for the most capable persons. Von Hartmann's tirades against the ' social-eudaemonistic Moral principle ' and the associated ideal of equality (he entirely 'fails to distinguish between the different possible senses of the word) are to a large extent answered by his own convincing, if exaggerated, demonstrations of the necessity for social inequality (*Das sittliche Bewusstsein*, pp. 503-508, &c.). When he seems positively to contend for the maximizing of inequality, his argument turns partly upon an over-estimate of the necessity for competition, so that the fittest (in an intellectual and ethical sense) may be selected, while he forgets that the higher stages of animal and human evolution have been attended by a progressive *diminution* of waste ; and partly upon his pessimistic exaggeration of the incompatibility between progressive culture and happiness whether in the individual or the society.

maxim of equal consideration itself. But are we to assume that this must always be so—that, no matter how great an inequality is required to effect it, the promotion of maximum good on the whole will always be right, because the hardship to the individual or the minority sacrificed will always be no more than is warranted, on the principle of equal consideration, either by the inferior numbers of the minority or by their inferior capacities for good [1]? It is clear that if the sacrifice of good on the whole to fairness of distribution were carried beyond a certain point, we should be violating the principle that one man's good is of the same value as the like good of another. If we were to impose great hardships upon a whole community in order that the life or health of one man might be spared, that would be to treat that man's life as more valuable than the life of many. But what if a very slight increase of good on the whole could be secured by a very gross inequality in its distribution? Ought we never to sacrifice something in the total amount of good that there may be a greater fairness—a greater approach to equality for equal capacities—in its enjoyment? I think it is clear that, if a very small sacrifice of good on the whole could secure much greater equality in its distribution, we should say that the sacrifice ought to be made. Whether the structure of human society is such that we could ever produce mo.. good on the whole by distributing unequally, is a problem which we hardly possess the data for determining [2]. But we may perhaps be tolerably certain that a rigid carrying out of the principle that no sacrifice of individuals is to be condemned which is balanced by an equivalent increase of good on the

[1] It is clear that in this last case Justice, in the sense which we have given to it, might prescribe the sacrifice of the majority to a minority, but it will simplify the discussion to assume that the superior numbers and the superior capacity are on the same side.

[2] That a fairer distribution of material wealth would be worth purchasing at the cost of diminished production on the whole, few would dispute. But then it cannot be assumed that the additional production would really be additional *good*. In all probability it would not be so. A lesser amount more fairly distributed would produce greater good on the whole. Here a law of diminishing returns comes into play. £100 added to a rich man's income would not perceptibly add to his enjoyment; divided among ten poor men it might produce a great deal.

whole would lead to a sacrifice of unfortunate minorities—the
weak in mind or body, the sick, the halt, the maimed—such
as common humanity would condemn [1]. At all events we are
not entitled to exclude the speculative possibility of such a state
of things, and consequently must not assume an invariable
harmony between the ultimate results of our two maxims of
Benevolence and of Justice or Equity.

How then are we to co-ordinate the two principles of action?
One way of doing so is tempting on account of its simplicity.
We might say that equality of distribution is itself a good, and
so that it will always be right to promote the greatest good
on the whole, after giving due weight to the good involved
in equality. The question how much gain in fairness of distribution is to be treated as equivalent in worth to a given
amount of other goods will then be simply an ordinary case
of comparison of values—a very difficult one in practice, but
offering no particular difficulty in theory. But objection may
be taken to regarding as 'a good' so abstract a thing as a
distribution—something which cannot be regarded as the good
of any one of the persons affected nor of all of them collectively,
since we have admitted the possibility of a diminution of good
on the whole in consequence of such an ideal distribution. Such
an objection is no doubt a reasonable one: and it might lead us
to give up the attempt to reduce our axiom of Benevolence and
our axiom of Equity to a single principle. From a practical
point of view it might be enough to say that there are simply
two sides of a single ideal of life, and the practical Reason must
decide in each case which is more important—Justice or good on
the whole. But it seems hardly consistent with the very meaning of 'good' to suggest that it may sometimes be a duty to
promote something which is not the good. If we are to attempt
to defend these maxims of Justice and Benevolence as valid and
self-consistent judgements of the practical Reason, it is a matter
of life and death to our position to find either a common denominator, in terms of which both principles could be expressed,

---

[1] As already suggested (above, p. 163), this consequence might be avoided
by assigning a sufficiently high value to sympathetic feelings—a solution
which is practically much the same as we arrive at below.

or at least some third principle which should govern us in
deciding between their respective claims—in deciding when
to sacrifice quantity of good in favour of just distribution, and
when to sacrifice justice of distribution in order that there may
be more good to distribute. The difficulty may, I think, be escaped
by remembering that, according to the view of the end here
adopted, it is not only the pleasure or other non-moral good which
is promoted by right actions which constitutes the supreme ethical
end, but the qualities of character which these acts express.
And not only Benevolence but Justice also is part of the ideal
life for the society at large and for each individual member
of it. And this inclusion of Justice or Equity in our ideal of life
sets limits to the extent to which we can allow individuals or
societies to promote a maximum of other good at the expense
of great inequality in its enjoyment, just as the inclusion of
culture among our ends or elements in *the* end sets limits to the
amount and kind of pleasure which we can regard as elements in
the good. In insisting therefore that an individual or a society
ought sometimes (if such a collision should in practice occur) to
sacrifice something in amount of good in order to effect its more
just distribution, we are not enjoining any one to subordinate the
pursuit of good to something which is not a good at all, but
simply insisting on one particular case of that subordination
of lower goods to higher which every non-hedonistic system
of Ethics must admit at every turn. An abstract ' distribution '
cannot be a good, but a disposition and a will to distribute justly
may be. A society which for the sake of increasing the pleasure
or even the culture of some should be content to condemn a
minority of its members to extreme hardships would be thinking
too much of its pleasure or its culture and too little of its own
Justice. If an individual or a minority, on the other hand, were
to demand of the majority that this sacrifice should be carried
beyond a certain point, it would be thinking too much of its own
claims or (to put it in another way) too much of the encouragement
of sympathy and mercy to individuals and too little, it may be,
of culture or pleasure in society at large. There is a proper
degree of subordination of the individual to society, and a subordination which goes beyond that degree. Both of these

principles of conduct may be expressed as ultimately qualities of human character. When a Quaker or a disciple of Tolstoi refuses to kill a man in a just war because that particular man has committed no crime, he is, according to common opinion, wrong because his ideal attaches too much importance to kindness and goodwill for individuals and too little to the common interests of human society at large and that system of rights by which those interests are promoted. Were a society to refuse to do anything for its submerged tenth or twentieth—to do more for them than their strict numerical proportion might demand— in the interest of its own comfort or even of its own culture, that would be attributing too much importance to comfort and culture and too little to the moral quality (whether you call it Justice or Benevolence) which revolts against allowing individuals to suffer the worst horrors of poverty because they are only a minority. What is the exact degree of importance which should be attached to each of these elements of character—solicitude for individual interests and the care for other forms of social good—is, just like any other question as to the relative value of goods, a problem upon which the practical Reason must pronounce in each particular case, and which does not admit of being solved by any exact or universal formula.

The principle which I have been contending for may be briefly expressed thus. The claims of social good are paramount. It is always a duty to promote maximum social good. Both the rule of Justice and the rule of Benevolence ultimately turn on the value of certain kinds of consciousness. Benevolence asserts the value of good. Justice asserts the value of persons. There is no real and final collision between these aspects of the ideal end, for good is ultimately the good of definite individuals. Justice and Benevolence are thus the correlatives of one another. Good has no worth—it has indeed no existence—apart from persons : persons have no value apart from the good which they are capable of enjoying. But it is true that the good of some may have ultimately to be secured at the cost of a diminished enjoyment of good by the whole society. And Justice does prescribe that we should aim at bestowing equal good on equal capacity. Some sacrifice of individuals to the whole is, indeed, prescribed by the just claims of the majority. Too great a sacrifice of the individuals does present itself to us as unjust even when it might be prescribed by the principle of maximum good. But when this is the case, it is because consideration for the claims of individuals no less than consideration for the whole forms part of that ideal character which is itself the highest element in the good. When Justice itself is given its due place as part of the true good for society and each individual in it, we may say that it is always a duty to promote the greatest good on the whole.

VII

To apply these highly abstract considerations to practice—to enquire to what conclusions they point in the region of social and political conduct—forms no part of my present undertaking. Every political question is, of course, in the last resort an ethical question. But in so far as the duty of the individual turns upon questions as to the ultimately best form of human society or the means of promoting it by social and political action, the discussion passes into the region of social and political rather than of purely ethical Philosophy. The considerations on which I have insisted will, I trust, have shown the impossibility of any individual immediately effecting by his own unassisted efforts an ideally just distribution, the impossibility even for society of realizing it immediately, the unreasonableness even under any conceivable social order of basing the distribution of good merely upon a principle of ideal Justice to each particular individual without reference to that other side or aspect of Morality which enjoins the promotion of the greatest good on the whole. The enjoyment by each individual of as much good as he is entitled to by his capacities (relatively to the capacities of others) must be looked upon therefore as an ideal—a far-off ideal, to which only more or less distant approaches are possible even in the region of self-consistent Utopias. This would, perhaps, be admitted by many zealous advocates of Equality. But I hope I have further indicated the necessity of not making any actual equality of good, even as a distant ideal, our primary object, but rather general Well-being; and I trust I have shown

1 9

further that such a course is imperatively required by ideal Justice itself, since the only equality that is capable of immediate realization is equality of consideration, and to produce equality of distribution at the cost of lowering the average amount distributed would be a violation of that one essential equality. If in the course of my argument I have incidentally replied to some of the arguments by which the extremer kinds of Socialism [1] are sometimes advocated, I trust it has become no less evident that any attempt to justify the *status quo*—the taking of interest, the system of inheritance, the fixing of wages and prices by competition and the like—as an even approximate realization of Justice is a still more indefensible thesis. This present state of affairs may be for the moment—with the exception of this or that immediately possible reform—a less violation of justice than any other *possible* system; and so long the maintenance of the existing order of society *minus* the possible reforms will be demanded by Justice itself: Justice can never require us to make matters worse. None the less, the discrepancy between the present distribution of wealth and any that could *a priori* be justified in the interests of general Wellbeing emphasizes the fact that one large element of private duty which Justice prescribes for the individual must be the striving after a more socially beneficial system. But we shall be prepared to find that even in the remote future no system of distribution that is at once possible and socially expedient will realize the dream of any other equality than equality of consideration.

The ideal Justice which I have attempted to adumbrate is not capable of immediate political realization. It would open up a large question were I to ask how far it is capable of immediate application in the domain of private Ethics—I mean, how far it is possible for each individual to act upon principles of ideal Justice, in so far as it rests with himself to determine how much

---

[1] In strictness Socialism does not necessarily imply an *equal* distribution of material things, but the more thoroughgoing advocates of the doctrine that the State should be the sole owner of the instruments of production and the sole employer of labour often adopt that programme only as a means to an ultimate equality of wealth or enjoyment.

of that portion of the world's wealth over which he has legal control he shall allocate to himself, and how much to the service of other individuals or of the community. I cannot attempt now to discuss that question adequately; I am at present concerned with a purely theoretical and not with a practical question. And yet it is desirable sometimes, even in the interests of pure theory, to point out some of the practical bearings of speculative ethical controversies. And therefore I do not hesitate to suggest the urgent need of bringing our highest ideal of Justice to bear upon the details of private life and especially of personal expenditure. It is obvious that it is not possible for most people in an un-ideal state to act in accordance with what would be the right in an ideal state of things. For each man to allot to himself no more of the good things of this life than might be his under a régime of ideal Justice would demand a heroism which such equality would not involve under such a régime, and at times would be injurious to others, and even to society at large. In some directions it would be inexpedient for any one; in many directions it would be inexpedient for every one. Such an attempt would not really conduce to Justice itself; for under existing conditions the professional man, compelled to live like an artisan, would suffer much more than the artisan suffers. For the present we must to some extent acquiesce in the idea of a standard of comfort for each class. The maintenance of such a standard is up to a certain point required by the different demands for efficiency in different callings, in part by the necessity for keeping up that stimulus to superior industry, skill, inventiveness and the like, which we have seen to be essential to social Well-being even where it would otherwise be difficult to reconcile with the requirements of ideal Justice. But where different standards of comfort exist, some measure of conformity to the customs of one's class or position, in such matters as eating and drinking, housing, service, dress, entertainment, amusement and the like, is demanded under penalty of hardship and isolation such as would not be endured by any one, were such matters arranged for us on principles of ideal Justice in a socialistic State. If the system is good on the whole, it cannot always be wrong for the individual to fall in with it: the individual cannot be required to act in a way which, if generally imitated, would be socially injurious, and the attempt to do away with all expenditure which exceeds what would be possible if wealth were equally distributed would, we have some reason to believe, be socially injurious. Still, it is a clear duty on the part of every one who is convinced that the share of good things enjoyed by the few is disproportionate and intrinsically unjust, to seek to limit his own personal expenditure wherever he can do so without a less efficient discharge of his own social function or other social inconvenience. It would be a step to the creation of a new morality upon such subjects, if we were to cultivate the habit of compelling ourselves to give some kind of reason for our indulgence in any kind of expenditure over and above what would be allotted under a régime of pure equality, whether the justification be found in our particular social function, in the conditions necessary for the exercise of our own particular capacities, natural or acquired, in the superior intellectual or aesthetic value of our pleasures and their indirect social effects, in the necessity of inequality and competition as a stimulus to industry, or only in the necessities and conventionalities of the existing social code, which sometimes render intrinsically unnecessary expenditure the smaller of two evils. If it is probable that the principle of a class standard of comfort will always be inevitable and even in a measure socially useful, we must at least recognize the duty of trying to reduce the present enormous differences between the highest and the lowest standard; and, in the case of those whose class standard is high, of aiming for themselves at the lower rather than the higher limit allowed by that standard, except when some higher good to the consumer himself or some social advantage to others would seem to result from the higher expenditure. It may safely be said that the scale of expenditure prevalent among the richest classes is as little conducive to their highest Well-being as to that of the poorest. If under existing conditions the existence of such expenditure is necessary as a stimulus to the *entrepreneur* or the captain of industry, the fact that it should be necessary is a moral evil for the gradual removal of which it is a duty to strive.

A word must be added to bring these general considerations to bear upon the duty of the individual. The duty of Justice in the individual seems to consist in (1) seeking to bring about by political or other means such an improvement in political and social organization as will realize a more complete equality of consideration than is possible in his existing environment; (2) observing this principle of equal consideration in his relations to his fellow men in so far as is possible under existing conditions; (3) respecting all those political and social arrangements, however much at variance with the ultimate ideal, as are enforced by the existing social order, in so far as that order cannot immediately be improved upon by the individual's voluntary action under existing conditions. It is to the duties of Justice and Benevolence taken together that we should ultimately refer the duty of Loyalty to existing social institutions and particularly to the State; the duty of Honesty, which means respect for the existing laws of property so long as they are not capable of immediate improvement by the individual's own action; and the observance of such other rules, whether enforced by law or otherwise, as are found conducive to social Well-being. In a sense, as I have endeavoured to show, all duties are social, since it is never either right or possible to aim at one's own individual good without regard to the good of others. In a sense no duty is purely social in the sense of the Hedonist, since every duty is more or less liable to modification by the consideration that the true good alike for individuals and for societies is something more than pleasure. In the highest sense Benevolence and Justice (if we include in it Prudence or due regard for self) may be so understood as to include all other virtues: true Justice and true Benevolence represent two sides, each of them unintelligible or, at least, certain to be misunderstood if taken apart from the other—of the single all-inclusive duty of promoting the different kinds of good in proportion to their true intrinsic worth or place as elements in the good. It is because this good does include various elements that Virtue in general is divided into the many virtues with which we have already attempted to deal in the preceding chapter. To insist on the fact that all virtues can be reduced to the single virtue of

just Benevolence is desirable because it emphasizes the truth
that there is a single all-inclusive ideal of life in reference
to which alone separate 'virtues' become intelligible; over-
emphasis in ethical teaching upon the 'unity of Virtue' and
neglect of particular 'virtues' practically tends either to a
vagueness which may degenerate into Antinomianism, or (if
the consequential test of virtuous conduct in detail is much
insisted upon) to a too hedonistic interpretation of the ultimate
good. Insistence upon Benevolence as the sole ultimate duty
can only be safe when it is duly interpreted as a Benevolence
which is inclusive of Justice, and which has due regard to all
those non-hedonistic elements in the good which are promoted
by and consist of the special virtues to which particular names
have been assigned. In all that has been said about social duty,
it is assumed that the individual's own good is to be given due
consideration, and, when this good is non-hedonistically interpreted, it will include many forms of 'self-regarding' duty
besides Prudence in the sense of due regard for one's own
'interest' in the hedonistic sense.

VIII

Before leaving the subject of Justice some addition seems to
be called for to what has been said about the institution of
property. If the principles which have been laid down in this
chapter are right, the duty of respecting that institution is
simply a particular part of the duty of obeying the State—
a duty which is itself a part of the more general obligation to
respect the conditions of social Well-being. A more detailed
discussion of property seems to belong rather to political than
to ethical Philosophy in its narrower sense. It may be well,
however, briefly to point out in what sense we can, and in what
sense we cannot, regard the duty of respecting property as one
of essential and permanent obligation. It is a duty to respect
the existing laws of property because some system of distributing material wealth or its enjoyment is essential to social
Well-being, and the existing system is the best that has
hitherto been devised ; at all events individual acts of rebellion
against it retard rather than accelerate the working out of

a better system. The same regard for social Well-being and the best possible distribution of it which prescribes obedience to the existing law sanctions any improvement of it that may be possible, the moment that it does become possible. Property is the creation of Law, and what Law has created, Law may modify in the future as it has modified it in the past. *A priori* it might seem that some form of collective ownership in the instruments of production would be more likely to harmonize the conflicting claims of different individuals than any possible system of private Capitalism. This is not the place to enquire, how far the enormous practical difficulties of bringing about such a system without introducing other and worse evils are difficulties inherent in the nature of things, and how far they are difficulties which it may ultimately be found possible to overcome. Whether ownership should be individual or collective is simply a detailed question of the means to social Well-being. But it may be pointed out that there is one limit which is set to the attempt to substitute collective for individual ownership by the nature of the end itself. The end, as we have seen, is, or rather includes, a certain type of character or (more properly) a certain kind of life led by men of a certain character. The end is the perfection of individual lives. The perfect life for the individual is not an isolated or solitary life : it is eminently social, a life whose good consists in activities which minister to the good of others as well as to his own. But still it must be a life in which there is room for the individual to act, to pursue his own ideals, to choose the means to them, to direct his own activities, to reap the fruit of those activities, to experience the consequences both of success and of failure. There can be no true human good life which does not include all this, and it is difficult to see how any system of distribution can minister to this end which does not allow some appropriation of material wealth more individual and permanent than any which is consistent with a thorough-going Collectivism— Collectivism of the kind which aims at securing an absolute equality of distribution or, at least, some close approximation to it. Wealth cannot be made subservient to a truly moral life without some measure of liberty in its use, and consequently even in its abuse. The right use of wealth cannot be secured by the most magnificent system of public maintenance. Just as children brought up in large public institutions are often more deficient in character, initiative, and intelligence than children educated in very unsatisfactory homes, so an institution-bred population could not realize a high ideal of human life. Men and women might be lodged in the most luxurious of workhouses, fed sumptuously every day at the public expense, driven daily from the most moderate of State-regulated tasks to the most refined of State-regulated amusements. They might be dosed periodically with the most carefully considered doses of State-regulated education, culture, and even religion. But all these things could not avail to produce an ideal human life. Character cannot be developed when the will is passive, nor intelligence when there is little demand or opportunity for its exercise. There must be room for initiation, for selection, for choosing what to do or not to do, for laying out plans not from day to day but for a long future. And this there cannot be without not merely some appropriation of material wealth for immediate needs but some power of disposing of it with a view to the deliberately chosen purposes of a man's whole life, and to the good of others in whom he is interested. This line of thought has been well developed by Prof. Bosanquet. 'Is it not enough, we may be asked, to know that one can have what is necessary and reasonable? No; that makes one a child. A man must know what he can count on, and judge what to do with it. It is a question of initiation, plan, design, not of a more or less in enjoyment [1].'

It is possible that all that Prof. Bosanquet contends for, and all that can reasonably be contended for as a matter of principle, might be combined with a much greater extension of collective ownership than he himself would be disposed to contemplate. Socialism does not object to private property, but only to private capital. It is only upon the questionable assumption that private property necessarily carries with it the institutions of unlimited private bequest and private Capitalism that Prof.

[1] Essay on 'The Principle of Private Property,' in *Aspects of the Social Problem* (1895), p. 313.

Bosanquet's demand for a sphere in which individual choice and individual responsibility shall have free play can be considered fatal to the more moderate socialistic schemes. Socialism allows the possession of private property in the only sense in which nine-tenths of the community now possess private property. Private property may perhaps come hereafter to mean something seriously different from what it means now ; but Prof. Bosanquet's general principle ought to be fully accepted. It is the supreme condition of a truly moral system of property-distribution that it shall be the one most favourable to the cultivation and development of the highest individual characters. If in some form the institution of private property must be regarded as permanently necessary for the development of individual personality, we need not dwell upon the extent to which that institution as it now exists—the system of unlimited competition, unlimited accumulation, unlimited inheritance—will have to be modified before it can be regarded as the system best calculated to develope in the individual a moral ideal which includes in itself Benevolence and Justice.

IX

The whole of my treatment of Justice in this chapter will (like the Benthamite formulae which I have accepted in a modified shape) be met in some quarters by the objection that it is inconsistent with an adequate recognition of the ' organic character of human society.' Here again it would lead me too far into the political region to discuss the truth and meaning of the undoubtably important but much-abused formula that ' society is an organism.' What is meant by the objection is, I take it, practically [1] something of this kind. It has hitherto been assumed that man's duty consists in contributing to a certain general welfare of society, as though he could allot a certain amount of good to himself and other lots of good to other individuals: whereas, as a matter of fact, we cannot distinguish between the good that a man does to himself and

[1] I do not here discuss the metaphysical or logical question how far the abstract category of Organism is applicable to Society, and confine myself to the ethical side or application of the doctrine.

the good that he bestows on another. True human good consists largely in activities which are at once my good and the good of others [1]. And further a man's duty does not consist in a general contribution to a lump of good : it consists in performing some special function marked out for him by his position in the social organism. Neither a man's contribution to the general good, nor the quantity or quality of it which he enjoys, can be exactly the same as every other man's. No improved social arrangements can secure that the tailor shall enjoy exactly the same good as the scholar. The tailor's function, his activity, and therefore a large part of his true good, consists in doing his tailor's work and finding his own good in it, and the scholar's good consists in leading the scholar's life. You cannot 'distribute' to the tailor the scholar's good, which consists mainly in leading the scholar's life. All social progress, all culture, all civilization involves a constantly increasing 'differentiation.' It is only in an extremely simple state of society that the lives of different people can exactly resemble one another, a society in which only very simple needs are felt, and in which each family or household supplies practically all its own needs. And the increasing differentiation necessarily carries with it not only unlikeness but inequality. The different kinds of life are not, and cannot conceivably be, all equally pleasant, or equally valuable from any other point of view than that of the goodwill which may be exhibited in all of them. The differentiation involves exceptional sacrifices for some, exceptional advantages and enjoyment for others. To aim at the equalization of individual Well-being is therefore inconsistent with the welfare of society at large. And that is not all. The true good of every individual, even apart from his occupation or sphere of social service, is necessarily unlike that of every other : every individual is more or less unlike every other and therefore to some extent wants a different kind of life to satisfy him. And these differences become greater, the higher the state of social development, the higher the capacities, and the higher the development of the individual concerned. A dead level of individual Well-being could only be secured by cutting

[1] Qualifications of this principle are discussed below, Bk. II. chap. iii.

down all individual eminences, and that would mean the extinction of all the higher kinds of Well-being altogether : for these are essentially dependent upon the multiplication and differentiation of wants on the one hand, and of individual capacities on the other. The formula of equal consideration, even in the modified form which we have given to it, is therefore, it may be urged, no less objectionable from the point of view of a true individualism than it is from that of the 'social organism[1].'

There can be no doubt as to the extreme importance of these considerations from a practical point of view. They do constitute an enormous objection and difficulty in the way of all collectivist schemes. They are absolutely fatal to any crude attempt at an immediate realization of the collectivist ideal. An immediate Collectivism would certainly mean the lowering not merely of material conditions but of modes and ideals of life to the level which the many are immediately capable of appreciating. And they will always be fatal to schemes of Socialism which aim at an absolutely dead level of material conditions, at an extinction of all differences in education, in culture, in modes of life, in quantity and quality of work. The Socialism which proposes to impose six hours' manual work a day on every one—on Physicians and Scholars and inventors for instance—would mean a return to Barbarism. But these consequences are, I should contend, sufficiently guarded against by the interpreta-

---

[1] This principle has been urged with much force, but with some exaggeration, by Simmel (*Einleitung* I, p. 360, *et passim*), though he is not one of those who insist much on the idea of a social organism. On this basis a running fire is kept up against Socialism all through his powerful writings. By way of criticism I will only add to what I have said in the text the following remarks : (1) The only sort of Socialism which he seems to contemplate is one which aims at absolute equality of conditions ; (2) his ultimate good is not either pleasure or Well-being, but a 'maximum of energy,' which is best secured by maximum ups and downs of pleasure and pain : the struggle for existence becomes with him not a means but an end (see further below, Bk. II. chap. iii, *ad fin.*) ; and for this a larger measure of 'differentiation' is naturally required than is wanted on a more commonplace interpretation of ideal Well-being. That a high development of individual capacity requires some liberty, and that all liberty involves *some* inequality and some pain, is no doubt true : but Simmel's view seems to involve a positive apotheosis of Unrest.

tion which I have placed upon the Benthamite formula. What I have contended for is simply equality of consideration; and an absolute equality of conditions would involve a diminution of general welfare which would be inconsistent with the good of all members of the society or the great majority of them, and would therefore be condemned by the formula itself. Moreover, I have admitted the superior rights of the superior kind of Well-being, and therefore of the superior man who is capable of enjoying it. I have only insisted that even the claims of the superior man must be estimated with due regard to the claims, be they small or great, of other people. If any one likes to regard the highest development of a few superior beings as an object compared with which immense masses, so to speak, of commonplace virtue and happiness may be treated as a negligible quantity, such a view would to my mind misrepresent the actual verdict of the healthy moral consciousness, but it would be quite consistent with the formula of equal consideration if we assume that he was right in his judgements of comparative value[1]. But if (to return to the social side of the objection) by the allegation that my view is inconsistent with the organic character of human society it is implied that human society has a good which is distinct from the good of the individual persons composing it, if this ' good ' or 'development' of society is made a sort of fetish to which whole hecatombs of individual lives are to be ruthlessly sacrificed, I can only reply that such a view seems to me a pure superstition—a widely prevalent superstition which is responsible for much of the stupidity and mismanagement with which the world's affairs are often conducted. With the Philosopher the mistake may sometimes be an honest blunder: translated into practical politics this vague talk about the ' interests of the social organism ' generally carries with it the assumption that society is to be organized in such a way as to secure a maximum advantage to the limited class which is actually in possession of the lion's share of good things, and that those who threaten

---

[1] Simmel has suggested that in some cases a man might justifiably treat himself as a person of this importance, like Nietzsche's *Übermensch*. So anti-social an attitude would, in my view, involve the sacrifice of the higher to the lower even in the individual's own life.

to disturb this arrangement are to be shot down forthwith. In practice it means *Beati possidentes*: the existing Prussian constitution in Church and State is the final and highest development of 'the Idea.'

There is no good that is not the good of some individual or individuals, though unquestionably that good is the good of social beings interested in the welfare of their fellows, and occupying definite positions in the social system. It is a clear deliverance of the reflective moral consciousness that we should endeavour to secure as much as possible of this good life for as many individuals as possible. It is true no doubt that, when we come to ask in detail *how* the good life is to be enjoyed by as many individuals as possible, we must remember all those characteristics of human society which are emphasized by the formula 'society is an organism'—that one man's good is not *necessarily* another's loss, that it is in discharging his social function that the individual attains his truest good, that social functions vary, that a man's good must be relative to his function, that increasing differentiation in many respects is a note and condition of social progress, that the life of society is a continuous growth and can only be gradually modified, that some liberty is a condition of all higher Well-being and that all liberty carries inequality with it, and finally that the maxim represents an ideal which it is a duty to aim at but which can never be fully realized. These considerations will be further developed in the chapter on 'Vocation.' But all this does not seem to require any modification of our doctrine that Justice does consist in the apportionment to each individual of his due share of good, in so far as that good can be secured or modified by human agency. Questions of Justice cannot be thought out without assuming that good is a thing which we can distribute. This assumption involves, like all speculative theories, a good deal of abstraction. But it in no way implies that we really suppose that human 'Well-being' or 'good' is a tangible lump of plum-cake which we can serve out in slices according to a tariff prescribed by the intuitive moral consciousness. It merely asserts that the social Organism is not an end in itself but a means to the good of individual human beings, each of whom should be treated (as far as possible) according to his own individual worth [1].

To complete our treatment of Justice one more question must be faced—the question of Punishment. We have seen in what sense it is a duty for the individual, both in his private relations and as a member of a community, acting in concert with others, to aim at rewarding Virtue. It remains for us to inquire 'In what sense, and on what grounds, is it a duty to punish Vice?'

NOTE ON RENOUVIER'S IDEA OF JUSTICE.

An attempt has been made by M. Renouvier in his *Science de la morale* [2]— one of the most serious and earnest efforts to grapple with the real problems of Ethics which has been made in recent times—to resolve all Virtue or at least all moral obligation (in the strict sense) into Justice. Taking his stand on the Kantian principle that Justice represents the conditions upon which the liberty of one (i.e. his opportunities of obtaining his true end) is compatible with the like liberty of all, he attempts to deduce therefrom all the 'strict' duties which man owes to man. But it is admitted that such duties can only be fully discharged in an ideal state of society (the *état de paix*). They postulate a state of things in which every one else is equally willing to perform *his* duty towards the agent and towards all others. Where others ignore their obligations, the right of defence justifies encroachments upon the liberty of others (including all State coercion) which go beyond strict Justice, while scope is afforded for a Benevolence equally going beyond those limits; but such Benevolence can only be considered a duty in so far as it springs out of one's duty to oneself—the duty of developing oneself morally and cultivating one's generous emotions. Hence a code of Ethics suitable to the existing *état de guerre* is not (like the duties of Justice) capable of strict scientific formulation. I admit that it is possible to give a tolerably accurate analysis of our actual moral ideas on this basis. M. Renouvier's work seems to me quite the ablest attempt to develope the Kantian formalism into something like a reasonable and self-consistent system. But it seems to be open to the following objections; (1) The duty of respecting others' liberty is not an ultimate and independent duty, but is derivable from the value of others' good; a certain kind of liberty is an

---

[1] 'The whole developed apparatus of constitution and government would have absolutely no end or meaning if their activities did not ultimately result in the good of individuals' (Sigwart, *Vorfragen der Ethik*, p. 17). It might seem unnecessary to quote so obvious a remark, except as a proof that sanity in talking about the social organism is not quite unknown among philosophers of acknowledged distinction.

[2] Published in 1869.

essential condition of Well-being, but it is not Well-being itself.   To aim at liberty rather than Well-being seems to me irrational.   (2) This being so, it is arbitrary to set the limits which Renouvier sets to the assistance which one man owes to another—to say that he must abstain from interference, but is under no obligation to help others to realize their true good.   (3) We can form so inadequate a picture of a perfect humanity and a morally perfect society that it is hardly worth while to attempt to draw out in detail the duties which in such a state man would owe to man : any value which such an attempt might possibly have would seem to be rather for Law than for Morality.   (4) When the author comes to the critical question of property, he is obliged to admit that the *a priori* rights of property (substantially Locke's divine right of the first grabber) which he claims as necessary to the liberty of each are *in the nature of things* (and not only in consequence of other men's injustice) unfairly restrictive of the liberty of others, so that his *a priori* Morality is not even fit for an ideal society or consistent with itself.   (5) Hence it is practically much more convenient to reduce both the Justice appropriate to the *état de paix* and the restrictions imposed by the *état de guerre* to a general duty of promoting *as far as possible under actual circumstances* the good of each in proportion to its intrinsic value.   This is, I believe at bottom, what all this elaborate apparatus comes to, when its arbitrary and dogmatic accidents have been removed. For a discussion of the idea of ' works of supererogation,' necessitated in a peculiarly harsh and rigorous form by M. Renouvier's system, the reader may be referred to the chapter on ' Vocation' in our second Book.

CHAPTER IX

PUNISHMENT AND FORGIVENESS

I

THERE was a time when the notion that blood demands blood was held so firmly and so crudely that little distinction was made between intentional and unintentional acts of homicide. Ancient law abounds in traces of this inveterate instinct of primitive humanity. We see the legislator of the Pentateuch endeavouring to limit its operation by the institution of cities of refuge, whose walls protected the unintentional homicide against further pursuit by the avenger of blood. We find the same inability to distinguish between voluntary and involuntary homicide in the curious notions of the Canon Law (still, perhaps, theoretically in force among us) about the 'irregularity' contracted by consecrated persons and consecrated places through the most unwitting bloodshed, and not contracted by the most atrocious violence involving no physical effusion of blood. We see the same curious but once useful superstition in the old law of Deodand, which required the forfeiture of the inanimate object or the irrational animal which had, in the most accidental way, been the instrument of man's death. Thus even the horse from which a fatal fall had been sustained, or the boat from which a man had drowned himself, were made the subjects of this peculiar application of retributive justice. At the present day the cruder forms of this old-world cry of blood for blood are no longer heard; but what is, perhaps, after all only a more refined form of the same fundamental notion lingers in the theory which makes the primary object of punishment to be retribution. A man has done wrong, therefore for that reason and for no other, it is said, let him be punished. Punishment, we are told, is an end in itself,—not a means to any end beyond itself. Punishment looks to the past, not to the future. The guilt of the offence must be, in some mysterious way, wiped out by the suffering of the offender; and that obliteration or cancelling of the guilt-stained record, be it noticed, is conceived of as quite independent of any effect to be produced upon the sufferer by his bodily or mental pain. For, the moment we insist upon the effect produced upon the sufferer's soul by his punishment, the retributive theory is deserted for the reformatory or the deterrent. Here is the famous passage of Kant:—

'Juridical punishment can never be administered merely as a means for promoting another good, either with regard to the criminal himself or to civil society, but must in all cases be imposed only because the individual on whom it is inflicted *has committed a crime.* . . . The penal law is a Categorical Imperative; and woe to him who creeps through the serpent-windings of Utilitarianism to discover some advantage that may discharge him from the justice of punishment, or even from the due measure of it[1]!' He goes on to defend the *lex talionis* as the only just principle for the allotment of penalty to crime, and to make the famous declaration that, 'if a civil society resolved to dissolve itself with the consent of all its members' [so that punishment would be no longer required for deterrent purposes], '. . . the last murderer lying in the prison ought to be executed before the resolution was carried out[2].'

There we have the retributive theory propounded by the greatest of modern philosophers; and it is still defended by philosophers and philosophic jurists in Germany, England, and America[3]. For most modern men, whether or not they have consciously abandoned the theory, this view exercises but little influence over their ideas of *human* justice, though it is to be feared that it still casts a black shadow over popular conceptions of the punishment in store for sin in another world.

---

[1] Kant's *Philosophy of Law*, E. T. by Hastie, 1887, p. 195.

[2] Ib. p. 198.

[3] Hegel has usually been understood to maintain the retributive theory. Dr. McTaggart (Hegel's 'Theory of Punishment' in *International Journal of Ethics*, vol. VI, July, 1896) has endeavoured to show that this is a mis-understanding. Dr. McTaggart's own view, whether really 'Hegelian' or not, is in the main that for which I contend.

2 ɔ

It is difficult to argue against a theory whose truth or false-hood must be decided for each of us by an appeal to his own moral consciousness,—by the answer which he gives to the simple question whether he does or does not in his best moments feel this mysterious demand that moral guilt should be atoned by physical pain. That the sight of wrong-doing—particularly when it takes the form of cruelty—does inspire a sentiment of indignant resentment in healthy minds, and that it is right and reasonable that in all legal ways that sentiment should be gratified, no sensible person will deny. But that is only because experience shows that the infliction of pain upon offenders is one of the most effectual ways-—and in some cases the only effectual way—of producing amendment. The question is whether, *apart* from its effects, there would be any moral pro-priety in the mere infliction of pain for pain's sake. A wrong has been done—say, a crime of brutal violence ; by that act a double evil has been introduced into the world. There has been so much physical pain for the victim, and so much moral evil has polluted the offender's soul. Is the case made any better by the addition of a third evil,—the pain of the punished offender, which *ex hypothesi* is to do him no moral good what-ever ? If, as enlightened philanthropists sometimes seem to imagine, the direct effect of all punishment that really is punish-ment were to inspire the offender and others with a passionate de-sire to repeat the offence,—if in our prisons a liberal diet, genial society, free communication with the outside world, artistic cells, abundant leisure and varied amusement were found in practice to be more deterrent and more reformatory than solitude and plank bed, skilly and the narrow exercising yard, how many disciples of Kant would be Kantian enough to forbid the institu-tion of a code of graduated rewards for our present system of pain-giving punishments ?

Perhaps the simplest way of satisfying ourselves that it is impossible to reconcile the retributive theory of punishment, either with the actual practice of our courts or with any practicable system of judicial administration, will be to notice the modi-fication which is presented by Mr. Bradley. Mr. Bradley seems to be so much struck with the obvious disproportion between the moral and the legal aspect of various offences, that he actually gives up the doctrine that the *amount* of punishment should correspond with the amount of the offence, while still maintaining that punishment in general is justified only by the past sin, not by the future advantage.

'We pay the penalty, because we owe it, and for no other reason; and if punishment is inflicted for any other reason whatever, than because it is merited by wrong, it is a gross immorality, a crying injustice, an abominable crime, and not what it pretends to be. We may have regard for whatever considerations we please—our own convenience, the good of society, the benefit of the offender; we are fools, and worse, if we fail to do so. Having once the right to punish, we may modify the punishment according to the useful and the pleasant, but these are external to the matter; they can not give us a right to punish, and nothing can do that but criminal desert. . . . Yes, in spite of sophistry, and in the face of sentimentalism, with well-nigh the whole body of our self-styled enlightenment against them, our people believe to this day that *punishment is inflicted for the sake of punishment*,' &c. [1]

[1] *Ethical Studies*, 1876, pp. 25, 26. In a note which appeared in the *International Journal of Ethics* ('Some Remarks on Punishment,' vol. IV, Ap., 1894, p. 284), Mr. Bradley protests against being supposed to hold that punishment is inflicted for the sake of pain. Alluding to an article in the same Journal, which is substantially reproduced in the present chapter, Mr. Bradley remarks: 'Mr. Rashdall appears to me to misunderstand the view which he attacks. He takes me to hold an "intuitive theory of punishment," by which (so far as I can judge) he means a view based on some isolated abstraction. I find this strange, and what is perhaps stranger is that he treats me as teaching that punishment consists in the infliction of pain for pain's sake. At least I am unable otherwise to interpret his language. Now, I certainly said that punishment is the suppression of guilt, and so of the guilty person. But I pointed out that negation is not a good, except in so far as it belongs to and is the other side of positive moral assertion (*Ethical Studies*, p. 25). Pain, of course, usually does go with the negative side of punishment, just as some pleasure, I presume, attends usually the positive side. Pain is, in brief, an accident of retribution, but certainly I never made it more, and I am not aware that I made it even an inseparable accident. If a criminal defying the law is shot through the brain, are we, if there is no pain, to hold that there is no retribution? My critic seems, if I may say so, to hold an "intuitive theory" of my views.'

Upon this explanation I should like to make the following remarks:—

(1) I admit that for 'pain' I ought to have said 'or other evil, loss of

Now, in the first place, is this consistent? If punishment
is 'modified' for utilitarian reasons, does not that mean that
it is inflicted partly for retribution and partly for some other
reason? If so, we do not pay the penalty because we owe it,
and for no other reason. And, secondly, is it logical? If sin
by itself confers the right and imposes the duty of punishment,
there must be a right to inflict either a definite amount of
punishment or an infinite amount. If the latter, it is obvious
that the State will always have the right to inflict any quantity
of punishment it pleases upon any of its citizens at any time,
since all have sinned and incurred thereby unlimited liability to

something good being treated as an evil.' If it were not thought an evil to
be shot through the brain, the shooting would certainly not be a punishment. What retribution would be in which there was no such evil, I am
wholly at a loss to understand.

(2) I am quite willing to admit that Mr. Bradley recognizes a positive
side as well as a negative side to punishment, but I have entirely failed to
discover what this positive side is. Mr. Bradley goes on to say that punishment is 'the reaction of a moral organism, and this organism has a particular concrete character.' I don't deny that in punishment the organism
reacts against the criminal; and very often the criminal reacts against the
organism. But what I want to know is 'why ought it so to react?' If it
has a purpose in doing so, let that purpose be expressed. If the purpose be
to produce any effect upon society, it seems to be totally misleading to
say that 'punishment is inflicted for the sake of punishment' or for 'retribution' and so on. If that purpose be anything else besides the production
of good effects on conscious beings, it seems to me wholly immoral and
irrational. I cannot look upon an abstraction like 'moral assertion' as an
end-in-itself.

(3) In spite of Mr. Bradley's explanations, I cannot admit that the views
he maintains in the above-mentioned Article are reconcilable with the
chapter in *Ethical Studies.* Mr. Bradley formerly maintained that it was
immoral to punish except for retribution: now he defends 'social Surgery'
(i. e. wholesale Infanticide) for the reduction of population. Any infliction
of pain, loss, or death is justified, it appears, for an adequate social end
provided we do not call it punishment. Surely it is a mere sophism to
suppose that the 'gross immorality,' the 'crying injustice,' the 'abominable
crime' of unmerited punishment can be escaped by the mere trick of calling
it 'social Surgery' instead of 'punishment.' It is fair to add that Mr. Bradley
adds: 'I should have little to correct in the old statement of my view except
a certain number of one-sided and exaggerated expressions.' To me, if I may
say so with profound respect for his later writings, the chapter in *Ethical
Studies* to which he alludes seems to consist in little else but one-sided and
exaggerated expressions.

punishment. 'Use every man after his desert, and who should 'scape whipping?' Such a contention would render the whole theory nugatory. If, on the other hand, wrong-doing confers a right to inflict a merely limited amount of punishment, Mr. Bradley is open to the following objections :—

(1) How can this amount be fixed? How can moral guilt be expressed in terms of physical pain? To any one who believes that punishment is justified by its effects, the right or just amount of punishment is that which will best serve the ends for which punishment exists—i. e. deterrence and reformation. But how, apart from its end, can the amount of punishment due to each offence be fixed? I find in my own mind no intuitions on the subject, and believe that if we were all to sit down and attempt to write out lists of crimes, with the number of lashes of the cat or months of imprisonment which they intrinsically merit, we should find the task an extremely difficult one, and should arrive at very discordant results. At all events, such a task would be hopelessly out of harmony with the actual practice of the most enlightened tribunals. It is obvious that drunkenness in a 'gentleman' will often be, morally speaking, as culpable as burglary in an hereditary criminal. But it is not so much the practical as the theoretical impossibility of the task that I wish to emphasize. The idea of expressing moral guilt in the terms of cat or birch-rod, gallows or pillory, hard labour or penal servitude, seems to be essentially and intrinsically unmeaning. There is absolutely no commensurability between the two things.

(2) Assuming this difficulty removed, it is clear that when the proper amount of punishment has been inflicted, the right to punish has been exhausted. If any further punishment is inflicted for utilitarian reasons, it will be simply, on Mr. Bradley's premisses, so much unjustifiable cruelty. If forty stripes save one is the proper punishment for any offence, the fortieth will be simply a common assault, no matter whether it is inflicted by the private individual or by the public executioner.

(3) The only way of escape open to Mr. Bradley would be to contend that though the State may not for utilitarian reasons increase, it may for utilitarian reasons reduce the ideally just

punishment. The position is on the face of it a somewhat arbitrary one, and it is open to this objection : it involves the admission that in all cases wrong-doing confers a right, but does not impose a duty of punishment. Can it be moral that society, if it might, without failure in duty, remit punishment, should punish just because it pleases so to do? This would be to admit that whether we shall punish or not is to be determined by mere caprice. So, if you say that it is a duty to punish, except where utilitarian considerations demand that less than the ideal amount should be inflicted, you practically admit that whether any punishment should be inflicted at all, and how much, must be determined by teleological considerations. The theory of an intuitive command to punish will have reduced itself to the somewhat barren assertion that you have no right to punish except where there has been wrong-doing. This is a proposition which it is hard to dispute, since, as a general rule, no public purpose is served by hanging the wrong man. There are, however, cases where it must be admitted that suffering may lawfully be inflicted on innocent persons—e. g. where a barony or a hundred is made to pay compensation to persons injured in a riot, or where a savage village that has sheltered a murderer is burnt by a European man-of-war. There are, too, exceptional crises in which it is necessary, in the interests of society, to be less exacting in the matter of evidence than a civilized state ought to be in quiet times.

We are here, however, straying into difficult and disputable questions of details, and it is best to be content with simply pointing out that, when we have applied to the theory the qualifications which are demanded by the obvious facts, it is reduced to very modest limits. It amounts simply to the assertion that punishment should be inflicted only on the guilty ; it admits that in its infliction the legislator should be governed by utilitarian considerations, that is, by the end which punishment actually serves.

From the point of view which we have hitherto been taking, the retributive theory will appear to many a mere survival of bygone modes of thought. Yet, as is usually the case with theories which exhibit so much persistence as the one before us,

the retributive theory of punishment contains a good deal of
truth at the bottom of it,—deeper truth perhaps than the Benthamite view, which has taken its place in popular thought.
There are, I think, three elements of truth which the retributive
view of punishment recognizes, and which the ordinary utilitarian
view often ignores.

(1) Firstly, it possesses psychological or historical truth. It
is correct as an explanation of the origin of punishment. That
punishment originates in the instinct of vengeance is a commonplace of Anthropology. Criminal law was in its origin a substitute for private vengeance. The fact is illustrated by the
Jewish law of homicide, by the Saxon system of Wergilt, and by
the Roman law which punished the thief caught red-handed
twice as severely as the thief convicted afterwards by evidence
taken in cold blood. The theory was that the owner would
naturally be twice as angry in the first case as in the second,
though, of course, the injury done either to himself or the community would be precisely the same. And this connexion between
punishment and vengeance is not simply a matter of history. It
is still (as Sir Henry Maine has insisted [1]) one of the purposes of
punishment to serve as an outlet, a kind of safety-valve, for the
indignation of the community. All laws ultimately depend for
their enforcement upon the public sentiment in their favour;
hence the legislator cannot afford to take no account of popular
sentiment in their administration. There are many features
of the modern criminal law which can only be defended on
account of the desirability of keeping up a certain proportion
between the measure of public indignation and the measure
of legal penalty—for instance, the distinction made between
accomplished crimes and attempts at crimes which have failed
through causes independent of the offender's volition. Public
opinion will sanction capital punishment when the blood of
a brother man seems to cry for vengeance from the ground;
it would not tolerate an execution for an attempted murder
which has failed through a pistol missing fire. It may be doubted
whether this irrational mode of estimating punishment by the
actual, and not by the intended, effects of an act is not sometimes

[1] *Ancient Law*, 4th ed., 1870, p. 389.

carried unnecessarily far, as when, for instance, a Magistrate remands a prisoner to see how his victim's wounds progress. Whence it would seem to follow that, since a total abstainer's wounds heal sooner than a drunkard's, a man is to be punished more severely for stabbing a drunkard than for stabbing a total abstainer. In ways like this, deference to popular sentiment may be carried too far, but there can be no doubt of the soundness of the principle that the criminal law, while it seeks to guide, must not go too far ahead of popular sentiment, nor yet (as American lynch law occasionally reminds us) lag too far behind it.

(2) The second half-truth held in solution by the retributive theory is the fact that punishment is reformatory as well as merely deterrent. Very often, indeed, it will be found on examination that those who most loudly clamour for reformatory punishments do not really believe in the reformatory effect of punishment at all. Punishment is necessarily painful (positively or negatively), or it ceases to be punishment. Those people who denounce any particular punishment on the ground that it is painful, really mean that you ought to reform criminals *instead of* punishing them. Now, of course, it is the duty of the State to endeavour to reform criminals *as well as* to punish them. But when a man is induced to abstain from crime by the possibility of a better life being brought home to him through the ministrations of a prison Chaplain [1], through education, through a book from the prison library, or the efforts of a Discharged Prisoners' Aid Society, he is not reformed *by punishment* at all. No doubt there are reformatory agencies much more powerful than punishment; and without the cooperation of such agencies it is rarely that punishment makes the criminal into a better man. But it is none the less true that punishment does help to make men better, and not simply to induce them to abstain from punishable acts for fear of the consequences. At first sight this may seem to be a paradox; but it seems so only when we forget that every man has in him a better self, as well as a lower self. And if the lower self

---

[1] Or (according to a system which is, I believe, adopted in some American prisons) by the lectures of the Moral Philosopher attached to the prison.

is kept down by the terror of punishment, higher motives are able to assert themselves. Fear of punishment protects a man against himself. If in the punishment of criminals we have practically to think much more of its effects upon others than of its effects upon the men themselves, it is otherwise in education. Fear of punishment by itself will seldom turn an idle boy into a diligent one ; but there are few boys who could be trusted to work their best at all times, if in their weaker moments they were not kept to their duty by a modicum of fear ; and there are few of us, perhaps, whose conduct would not fall still further behind our own ideal than it actually does, if our better selves were not sometimes reinforced by fear of punishment,—at least in the form of social disapprobation or loss of reputation. And in the case of actual crime, that conviction of the external strength of the Moral Law which punishment brings with it is usually at least the *condition* of moral improvement; though that conviction will not make a man morally better, unless the external judgement is ratified and confirmed by the appellate tribunal of his own Conscience. Nevertheless, this external respect for the Moral Law is the first step to the recognition of its internal, its intrinsic authority.

Plausible as it looks to deny *a priori* that mere pain can produce moral effects, the extravagance of the contention becomes evident when it is seen that it involves the assertion that no external conditions have any effect whatever upon character. It is matter of common experience that men's characters are powerfully affected by misfortune, bereavement, poverty, disgrace. Adversity is not, of course, uniformly and necessarily productive of moral improvement. But no one will deny that under certain circumstances, and with men of certain temperaments, great moral changes are often produced by calamity of one kind or another. In some cases the effect is direct and immediate ; in other cases the effect is produced indirectly through the awakening of religious emotion. In either case, of course, all that the misfortune does is to create conditions of mind favourable to the action of higher motives and considerations, or to remove conditions unfavourable to their action. Punishment, on its reformatory side, may be said to be an artificial creation of conditions favourable to moral improvement. The artificial creation of such conditions has, of course, this advantage over ordinary misfortune, that it is seen to be the direct consequence of the wrong-doing, which is not necessarily the case with other alterations of circumstances.

In view of these considerations, we may, perhaps, go one step further and maintain that even in cases where punishment will not have a reformatory effect, where the tendencies to evil are too strong to be kept in check by fear, even then punishment may be, in a sense, for the moral good of the offender. Wickedness humbled and subdued, though it be only by external force, is a healthier moral condition than wickedness successful and triumphant. That is the extremest point to which we can go with the advocates of the vindictive theory. This is, I suppose, the truth which underlies the hackneyed expressions about avenging the insult offered to the Moral Law, vindicating the Moral Law, asserting its majesty, and so on. We recognize that punishment may sometimes be right, in the interests of the offender himself, even when it fails to deter. The pleasures of successful wickedness may be treated as bad pleasures which are of less than no value, and even pleasures not in themselves connected with the successful wickedness may, when enjoyed by a bad man, be regarded as of very small intrinsic value. But still, it is always a certain effect on consciousness and character that constitutes its justification, not merely the satisfaction of an impersonal and irrational law [1].

---

[1] I should be prepared to recognize a larger amount of truth in the *a priori* view of punishment, if the idea of punishment were to be confined simply to the withholding of good things, to what theologians have called a *poena damni*. Whether it would be right to make the bad happy if the absence of happiness would have no effect on their badness—not even that of making them feel that goodness is stronger than evil—is almost too abstract a question to admit of an answer; but that in a sense it is true that goodness and happiness ought to go together has already been admitted in the last chapter. I could accept Mr. Moore's view that 'the infliction of pain on a person whose state of mind is bad may, if the pain be not too intense, create a state of things that is better *on the whole* than if the evil state of mind had existed unpunished,' with the reservation 'whether such a state of things can ever constitute a *positive* good, is another question' (*Principia Ethica*, p. 214). Only I should submit that the ground of our

(3) A word will suffice to indicate the third and the highest truth which the vindictive theory of punishment caricatures. It is the truth—the great Aristotelian truth—that the State has a spiritual end.

We all know that experience sets tolerably strict limits to the extent to which it is desirable that the State should interfere with personal liberty and private life in the pursuit of moral and spiritual ends. There are many grave moral offences which the State may reasonably refuse to punish for quite other reasons than indifference to moral Well-being. The offence may be incapable of exact definition. It might require for its detection a police-force which would be a public burden, or involve an inquisitorial procedure, or give rise to blackmailing and false accusation to an extent which would constitute a greater evil than the offence itself. The experience of the ecclesiastical courts, which continued in full operation in this country down to 1642 [1], or of the clerical government prevalent in Rome under the Papacy, would afford plenty of illustrations of the evils incident to such attempts to extend police supervision to the details of private life. Very often, no doubt, the difficulty arises largely from the fact that the attempt puts too great a strain upon the Conscience of the community. Many offences may be, on the whole, condemned by public opinion which are not condemned with sufficient earnestness to secure the enforcement of the criminal law against them. With all these admissions, it must still be contended that the State is perfectly entitled to repress immorality. If an act is not inconsistent with the *true* Well-being either of the individual or of society, it is not immoral; and, even if it were admitted that the State should not interfere with conduct affecting only the Well-being of the individual, it is impossible that any act which affects the Well-

approval is not the mere fact 'that the combined existence of two evils may yet constitute a less evil than would be constituted by the existence of either singly' (ib., p. 215), but the tendency of the pain to make the state of mind less opposed to our ideal of what it ought to be.

[1] Their jurisdiction over laymen was of course occasionally exercised to a much later date. Since the penances imposed by the ecclesiastical courts were (and theoretically *are*) enforceable by imprisonment, no distinction in principle could be drawn between their action and that of the State.

being of an individual should be without consequences for others also. The distinction between crimes and sins can be found only in considerations of social utility. A crime is simply a sin which it is expedient to repress by penal enactment [1]. Every civilized state punishes some offences which cannot be said to be injurious to the 'public good,' unless moral Well-being is considered to be part of the public good.

It must be remembered that it is not merely by actual and direct intimidation that the State can promote Morality. The criminal law has an important work to do in giving expression to the moral sense of the community. Popular ideas as to the moral gravity of many offences depend largely upon the punishment which is awarded to them by the criminal courts. There are probably thousands who have hardly any distinct ideas about sin except those which are inculcated at Assizes and Petty Sessions. It is no uncommon experience for a clergyman to be told by a dying man—notorious, it may be, for fornication or drunkenness or hard selfishness—that he has nothing to reproach himself with, his Conscience is quite clear, he has never done anything wrong that he knows of, he has no reason to be afraid to meet his God, and so on. Then upon enquiry it turns out that what the man really means is that he has done nothing for which he could have been sent to prison.

There are many offences which the State can do little to check by the directly deterrent efforts of punishment, but which it can do much to prevent by simply making them punishable. Since a few persons with good coats have actually been sent to prison for bribery at elections, the respectable public has really begun to suspect that there may be something wrong in the practice. A very little reflection upon the different estimates which are formed of these forms of immorality or of dishonesty for which people go to prison, and of those for which they do not go to prison, will show at once the enormous importance of the criminal law in promoting the moral education of the public mind. While, therefore, there are some kinds of

---

[1] In practice, of course, this term is usually reserved for the graver kinds of offences against the law. We do not talk about the *crime* of having one's chimney on fire.

wrong-doing which, either from their essential natures or from collateral considerations, cannot be wisely dealt with by the criminal law, we may expect that with the necessary moralization of a community, the sphere of criminal law ought gradually to extend. In the growing disposition to enact and enforce laws against gambling, to assist, if not to enforce, temperance by Act of Parliament, and to protect by the criminal law the chastity of young girls, we may recognize an instalment of moral progress. The doctrine that you cannot make men moral by Act of Parliament is about as true as the doctrine that you cannot make men abstain from crime by Act of Parliament. In spite of all the efforts of the Legislature, the practice of stealing has not been entirely stamped out. The fact that no legislation has succeeded in producing a perfectly moral community does not show that the State cannot do much to make a community more moral than it would otherwise be.

II

It will be urged by some that the enforcement of Morality tends to deprive that Morality of the freedom which is one of its essential conditions. The ideal life that we want to promote is not a society in which certain things are done, but a state of society in which certain things are done from the right motives —by persons 'in a certain state of mind' and 'doing them for their own sake' ($\pi\hat{\omega}s$ $\check{\epsilon}\chi o\nu\tau\epsilon s$ and $a\mathring{v}\tau\hat{\omega}\nu$ $\check{\epsilon}\nu\epsilon\kappa a$ $\tau\hat{\omega}\nu$ $\pi\rho a\tau\tau o\mu\acute{\epsilon}\nu\omega\nu$), as Aristotle would put it. The aim of society, and of the State, is to promote the growth of characters of a certain type.   Too great social pressure, still more decidedly too much State coercion, is destructive of the spontaneity, the individuality, the variety without which the highest types of character will not grow. We do not wish to turn people out exactly in the same mould. That is so partly because the mould which any existing society would be apt to impose is not an ideally perfect one, and we want to have room for further growth in our ideal: partly because (within certain limits) there is room for considerable variety not merely in the type of external conduct, but in actual character. Different types of character are mutually complementary and combine to form an ideal society. But even the character which we do

want to be universal—that devotion to the general good, that
compliance with the primary conditions of social Well-being,
which must be an element in all intrinsically valuable characters
—would lose much of its value if enforced beyond a certain
point. The failure of Monasticism has been largely due to its
attempt to enforce too much. Not only does the prescribed
routine of life destroy individuality and originality, but even
the Morality which is actually secured ceases to be the result of
moral effort. A life in which there are no temptations—or
rather in which the place of natural temptations is taken by
artificial ones manufactured by unnatural conditions of life [1]—
and no room for spontaneous effort is not conducive to moral
growth. There is much in the history of monastic institutions
which goes to show that such a minute regulation of life by
unbending rule encourages a certain childishness of character, to
say nothing of graver anti-social tendencies. That is so even
if the hold which the rule has on the man depends entirely (as
it does in modern times) on his voluntary consent [2]. Still graver
would be the deterioration of character under a system wherein
all life should be regulated by police discipline. Character is
formed by acts of choice; consequently character cannot be
developed when there is no occasion for the individual to choose
at all.

These considerations have been much insisted upon by the
late Professor T. H. Green, and (as it seems to me with considerable exaggeration) by Prof. Bosanquet. To say that 'the
promotion of morality by force . . . is an absolute self-contradiction'[3] is to take a very superficial view of the matter. Such
a dictum assumes that, when an act is enforced, it must be done
merely because it is enforced. It cannot be doubted that dis-

---

[1] With all its beauties, it is impossible to read many pages of the *Imitatio
Christi* without feeling that the writer is incessantly occupied with temptations of this kind.

[2] This, of course, was not the case in the Middle Ages, when the secular
arm returned the 'apostate' monk to his convent; and even now the penni-
less condition of the renegade monk often has the same effect.

[3] Bosanquet, *Philosophical Theory of the State*, 1899, p. 192. The statement
is, indeed, modified by the preceding sentence: 'Whatever acts are enforced
are, so far as the force operates, withdrawn from the higher life.'

honesty would become rampant in a country wherein stealing should be unpunished. And yet it would be the veriest cynicism to assert that the majority of our fellow countrymen keep their hands out of other people's pockets *only* because they are afraid of going to prison if they don't. The existence of punishment for an offence may create a state of feeling in which the act is looked upon as wrong in itself. The individual who begins with abstaining from fear of punishment may end by regarding the act with hearty and spontaneous dislike: and the individual born into a society already permeated with this feeling may simply not be aware that the existence of punishment for the offence has anything to do with his own dislike of it. There may be no great objection to the formula that the State ought rather to create the conditions of Morality than to enforce it, but it is impossible to draw a sharp line of distinction between the two things. One of the conditions for the growth of a 'free Morality' may be the existence of laws which have comparatively rarely to be enforced. There is hardly any kind of legislation in favour of Morality advocated by any sensible person which might not be brought within the formula understood in a liberal sense: understood strictly, it would exclude kinds of legislation to which few sensible persons object. To seek to enforce all Morality would indeed be fatal to the higher growth of character: but it is ridiculous to contend that no room would be left for the spontaneous exercise of Virtue because certain elementary requirements of Morality are enforced by law. Liberty to get drunk is surely no more essential to character than liberty to steal.

When all these admissions have been made, it may still be maintained that there is no fundamental distinction in principle between the offences which the State will do well to punish and those which it will do well to let alone. There is no civilized State which does not in practice punish many offences for no other reason than that there is a strong moral feeling against them. If there is to be moral progress in the future, we may expect the area of conduct dealt with by the criminal law to widen. And it involves no cynicism to predict that there will be little progress unless it does. Bad conduct which people feel

really strongly about they will always want to repress. And
the punishment of the grosser kinds of misconduct, so far from
diminishing people's sensitiveness about the unpunished misconduct, tends greatly to increase it. Conscience is aroused by
the reflection that much misconduct which goes unpunished differs
only in degree from that which conducts men to prison. When
we wish to make people feel strongly the wrongness of idleness
or certain kinds of 'company-promoting,' we point out that it is
really the same thing as stealing. When we attain to a social
condition in which it shall be possible to punish the worst kinds
of company-promoting, perhaps even the worst kinds of idleness,
we shall perhaps feel more sensitive about that excessive pursuit
of self-interest or amusement which at present counts almost as
a virtue.

III

There is another aspect of the retributive theory of Punishment
on which I should like briefly to insist. If the theory of the
moral criterion which has been defended in previous chapters be
a true one, it must be true in every case and without any
exception. The idea that punishment can be an end in itself
apart from the effects which it is to produce is wholly inconsistent with that principle of teleological Morality which (in
every other connexion) would be accepted by most of those who,
in servile adherence to an unintelligent philosophical tradition,
still maintain the retributive theory of punishment [1]. The

---

[1] The influence of mere tradition in this matter is curiously illustrated in
the case of Prof. Bosanquet, who still considers it necessary to speak of
punishment as retributive, while the explanation of punishment which he
gives, though to my mind evasive and unsatisfactory, has really nothing
'retributive' about it except the name. He sums up: 'In short, then,
compulsion through punishment and the fear of it, though primarily acting
on the lower self, does tend, where the conditions of true punishment exist
(i. e. the reaction of a system of rights violated by one who shares in it), to
a recognition of the end by the person punished, and may so far be regarded
as his own will, implied in the maintenance of a system to which he is a
party, returning upon himself in the form of pain. And this is the theory
of punishment as retributive' (*The Philosophical Theory of the State*, p. 227).
Verily one would not have thought so if Prof. Bosanquet had not told us so !
The fact is that Prof. Bosanquet so completely rejects the retributive theory

essence of the moral judgement is, as is scarcely denied by the
modern adherents of the Kantian tradition, a judgement of
value. Nothing can be right except as a means to something
which has value in itself; nothing surely can be an end in itself
except some state of a conscious being, and to say that a state of
conscious being is an end in itself is to say that it is good. The
essence of punishment is the endurance of pain or some other
evil. In spite of the high authorities that may be quoted for
the contrary view, I venture, under the aegis of Plato and the
many Christian thinkers who have found his ideas on this
subject in essential harmony with the Christian temper, to
maintain that an evil cannot under any circumstances become
a good except relatively—either positively, as a means to
some morally good state of consciousness, or medicinally (ἐν
φαρμάκου εἴδει), by way of remedy against some worse evil. If
it be urged that punishment is a good as a means to the vindication or the assertion or the avenging of the Moral Law, I should
venture to ask how an abstract 'vindication' or 'assertion' can
be a good—how a mere event or occurrence in nature can be
a good except in so far as it is the expression of some spiritual
state or a means of producing such a state. Even the Moral
Law itself is not an end in itself, but only souls or wills
recognizing and regulating their action by the Moral Law. If
it be urged that the avenging of the Moral Law is right because
it is the expression of the avenger's indignation, that is an
intelligible answer; and I have already admitted that the
expression and cultivation of indignation is one of the purposes
of punishment, though this can be hardly regarded as an ultimate end, but rather a means to a further end—the spiritual
good of the man himself and of society at large. But, if punishment is to be justified on account of the good it does to the
punisher, we have already gone some way towards the abandon-

of punishment that he really cannot believe that it has actually been held
by any one else. And yet I am free to admit that there is much in all this
talk about involuntary and impenitent submission to an unreformatory
punishment being really the act of the person's own will, which is quite as
unintelligible and ethically objectionable as the crudest form of the retributive theory, as implied for instance in the many popular views of the Christian
doctrine of Atonement.

ment of the retributory theory in its ordinary form; and further
a question arises as to the punisher's right to inflict evil on
another in order to secure a good for himself. He—the punisher
—is no doubt an end in himself, and is justified in seeking his
own good; but what right has he to ignore another's good
except as a means to some greater good of his own or of the
society in which he lives? It will hardly be seriously contended
that such and such a sentence of five years' penal servitude is to
be justified because the pain involved is outweighed by the
spiritual good which Mr. Justice So-and-so may have secured to
himself by passing it. It may be suggested that it is justified
because it is the expression of the indignation of society; that
the sentence tends to promote in society a reverence for the law
which the criminal has broken, or, again, that the punishment
produces moral good in the offender. In that case we have
frankly abandoned the idea that punishment is an end in itself,
and have adopted the view that it is a means to some good in
society at large or in the criminal himself. It is true that the
word 'deterrence' hardly expresses adequately the fact that
the good which punishment confers upon society is in part a
spiritual good; that it tends not merely to deter men from
committing crime, but to impress upon their minds the idea that
crime is wrong—something to be avoided and hated for its own
sake. The word 'reformation,' again, hardly does justice to the
idea that it is good for the criminal to feel the indignation of
society, to feel the external effects of his wrong-doing: that it is
a good in itself, one which it might be worth while (if we are to
raise so abstract and unpractical a question) to promote, even if
we knew that in this particular case it would not lead to that
which is the ultimate object of all punishment (so far as the
criminal himself is concerned), the alteration of his will, the
change of his character. That mere consciousness on the part of
the criminal may even be regarded as in its way a good. The
endurance of evil cannot be itself a good: the utmost length
that we can go is to say that it may be a necessary condition or
element in a state of mind which we can recognize as relatively
good—as better than that of successful and unresisted evil-
doing. Both the 'deterrent theory' and the 'reformatory

theory' are no doubt inadequate to express the whole truth about punishment. There is a side of punishment which might perhaps be best expressed by the term 'educative theory'; or, perhaps, we may simply say that the end of punishment is partly deterrent or utilitarian, and partly *ethical*. Both sides of punishment would be summed up in the assertion that our view of punishment must be a teleological one.

It is sometimes supposed that the utilitarian view of punishment is inconsistent with a proper respect for human personality : it involves, we are told, the treatment of humanity as a means and not as an end. If by the ' utilitarian' theory is meant a view resting upon a hedonistic theory of Ethics, I have nothing to say in its favour; if by 'utilitarian' is meant simply a view which treats punishment as a means to some good, spiritual or otherwise, of some conscious being, I should entirely deny the justice of the criticism. In the first place I should contend that in a sense it is quite right and inevitable that we should treat humanity as a means. When a servant is called upon to black the boots of his master, or a soldier to face death or disease in the service of his country, society is certainly treating humanity as a means: the men do these things not for their own sakes, but for the sake of other people. Kant himself never uttered anything so foolish as the maxim which indiscreet admirers are constantly putting into his mouth, that we should never treat humanity as a means: what he did say was that we should never treat humanity *only* as a means, but always *also* as an end. When a man is punished in the interest of society, he is indeed treated as a means, but his right to be treated as an end is not thereby violated, if his good is treated as of equal importance with the end of other human beings. Social life would not be possible without the constant subordination of the claims of individuals to the like claims of a greater number of individuals ; and there may be occasions when in punishing a criminal we have to think more of the good of society generally than of the individual who is punished. No doubt it is a duty to think also of the good of the individual so far as that can be done consistently with justice to other individuals: it is obviously the duty of the State to endeavour to make its punishments as far as

2 1 ★

possible reformatory as well as deterrent and educational to others. And how the reformatory view of punishment can be accused of disrespect for human personality, because forsooth it uses a man's animal organism or his lower psychical nature as a means to the good of his higher self, I cannot profess to understand. The retributive view of punishment justifies the infliction of evil upon a living soul, even though it will do neither him nor any one else any good whatever. If it is to do anybody any good, punishment is not inflicted for the sake of retribution. It is the retributive theory which shows a disrespect for human personality by proposing to sacrifice human life and human Well-being to a lifeless fetich styled the Moral Law, which apparently, though unconscious, has a sense of dignity and demands the immolation of victims to avenge its injured *amour propre*.

The real basis and stronghold of the theory which I am investigating is to be found in the undoubted psychological fact that the sense of indignation or resentment at wrong arises naturally and spontaneously in the human mind[1] without any calculation of the personal or social benefits to be derived from gratifying it, and in the profound ethical conviction that for societies—though not always for individuals—it is morally good and healthy that this indignation should be encouraged and expressed. 'Revenge, my friends,' says Carlyle, 'revenge and the natural hatred of scoundrels, and the ineradicable tendency to *revancher* oneself upon them, and pay them what they have merited; this is for evermore intrinsically a correct, and even a divine feeling in the mind of every man.' Such language I could cordially adopt[2], though with the proviso (of which more hereafter) that this feeling is not *so* divine as the love which the best men do succeed in feeling towards the worst, and that it must not be allowed to extinguish that higher feeling. The feeling of indignation is a natural and healthy one,—natural

[1] Psychologically, no doubt, this tendency can in a sense be explained by evolutionary causes.

[2] Except in so far as the word 'revenge' may imply the theory which I am disclaiming. I make this quotation (and the following from Stephen) from a second-hand source, and it seems hardly necessary to spend further time in searching for the passages.

and healthy, we may add, in partial correction of Carlyle, in proportion to its disinterestedness. It is one great purpose of Criminal Law to give expression to this natural indignation against wrong. But Law, in the discharge of its ideal function as Reason without Passion (νοῦς ἄνευ πάθους), seeks not merely to express but to regulate, and to regulate with a view to an end. In the words of Sir James Stephen, ' the criminal law regulates, sanctions, and provides a legitimate satisfaction for the passion of revenge ; the criminal law stands to the passion of revenge in much the same relation as marriage to the sexual appetite.' And in both cases the ultimate end of the regulation is to be found in a certain ideal of social Well-being.

The error of the upholders of the retributive theory lies, as it seems to me, in mistaking a mere emotion or feeling— an emotion or feeling which in itself is a good and important element in every well-balanced character—for a judgement of the Practical Reason. The Practical Reason may often judge that the emotion should be freely indulged, though at other times it will no less emphatically pronounce that the most elementary requirements of social order demand its partial or entire restraint. The real question is whether it is right to punish simply because we feel inclined to do so, to gratify a natural passion simply because it is there, or whether in this, as in the case of other spontaneous emotions or desires (including the spontaneous impulses of Affection and Benevolence), we ought to regulate passion by Reason, to act for an end, i. e. for the promotion in ourselves and others of whatever we take to be the ideal kind of human life. How the existence of an instinctive resentment against personal wrong, or in good men against wrong to others or moral depravity, can suspend the one all-comprehensive duty of love to all men (including, of course, ourselves) is a question which will, perhaps, offer no difficulties to those philosophical Moralists whose ethical system seems to consist in the mixture of a little truculent Theology borrowed from primitive Judaism with a good deal of pure paganism ; but which must, I think, be an embarrassing one to those Retributionists who profess any sympathy with Christian standards of Ethics. The most Christian of mediaeval thinkers (e. g. Dante or Wycliffe [1]) always maintained that God's punishments were, and man's should be, the expression of love. And this remark suggests another of the difficulties involved in the retributive theory—the difficulty of reconciling it with that side of the moral ideal which is expressed by the word Mercy or Forgiveness.

IV

It is one of the great embarrassments of the retributive theory that it is unable to give any consistent account of the duty of forgiveness and its relations to the duty of punishment. It is seldom that one finds anybody so logical as to maintain that it is always a duty to punish, and never right to forgive, at least till the wrong-doing has been expiated by punishment,—a theory which runs counter to a strongly felt and widely diffused ethical sentiment and which makes the Berenger law or our own First Offenders' Act a piece of immoral legislation. Others seem to have no answer to the difficulty but the admission: ' Here are two inconsistent moral precepts: it is a duty to punish and a duty to forgive: it is impossible to lay down any general principle in the matter: you must do whatever strikes you as best in each case as it arises.' Such an answer may satisfy those who think that Morality consists simply in a collection of isolated impulses, intuitions, or particular judgements, which Reason is incapable of reducing to any consistent or intelligible whole. It will hardly satisfy those who believe that our ethical judgements can be reduced to a system, and that the emergence of apparent ethical antinomies simply shows that we have not yet succeeded in getting to a really fundamental ethical principle. The absence of internal contradiction, though by itself it will supply no adequate content for the Moral Law, we may surely venture (with Kant) to regard as a necessary condition of any law which can really claim to be moral. If the duty of punishment is to rest upon an *a priori* deliverance of the moral consciousness which pronounces that, be the consequences what they may, sin must be punished, it is difficult to see how forgiveness can ever be lawful. If punishment is sometimes right and sometimes wrong, on what principle are we to distinguish between

[1] Dante in the *Purgatorio*: Wycliffe even as regards Hell.

the two classes of cases? That is the problem to which, as it appears to me, no intelligible answer can be given on the retributive theory, but which is not insusceptible of a solution on the basis of the teleological or educative view.

Among the very few moral philosophers who have bestowed any serious attention upon this question of forgiveness is Bishop Butler. By him the duty of forgiveness is resolved into the duty of being 'affected towards the injurious person in the same way in which any good men, uninterested in the case, would be; if they had the same just sense, which we have supposed the injured person to have, of the fault: after which there will yet remain real good-will towards the offender[1].' The duty amounts to this: 'that we should suppress that partial, that false self-love, which is the weakness of our nature; that uneasiness and misery should not be produced, without any good purpose to be served by it: and that we should not be affected towards persons differently from what their nature and character require.' 'Resentment,' he says again, 'is not inconsistent with good-will; for we often see both together in very high degrees; not only in parents towards their children, but in cases of friendship and dependance, where there is no natural relation. These contrary passions, though they may lessen, do not necessarily destroy each other.'

The duty of resentment and the duty of forgiveness are thus reduced to particular applications of the general law of promoting social Well-being. It is our duty to make our own personal resentment subordinate to the general good of society, just as it is a duty to subordinate goodwill towards individuals to the interests of other individuals. In determining whether we should resent or punish an injury (to ourselves or to others) or whether we should forgive, we should simply consider what is best for the interests alike of the individual himself and of society at large, the offender's good and the injured person's interest alike being assigned its due, and no more than its due, importance. The distribution (so to speak) of punishment and of forgiveness will alike be guided by the general principle of Benevolence or goodwill to society in general, the duty of promoting the

[1] Sermon IX.

greatest good on the whole,—guided and controlled by the principle of ' Equity,' in the sense which has already been defined.

It may also be observed incidentally that on this view of the
duty of forgiveness as simply a particular manifestation of
the general duty of love, we are able to clear up an ambiguity
about the meaning of forgiveness which often occasions some
difficulty in discussions of this kind. We are often told that
forgiveness is not inconsistent with punishment ; that we may
punish first and forgive afterwards, at least where punishment
is a duty arising out of some public function or parental relation
and not a mere gratification by legal or extra-legal means of
resentment against private wrong.   And this is quite true as far
as it goes ; forgiveness may mean simply the cessation of personal
resentment after the exaction of whatever penalty may be
demanded by considerations of social Well-being and public duty.
But, although in practice the adoption of this attitude may no
doubt be easier in the public official than in the private person,
it is impossible to draw a hard and fast line between punishment
inflicted by the official in the discharge of public duty and the
resentment exhibited by the private person, or between the
vengeance which takes the form of legal prosecution and that
which shows itself in private remonstrance or the refusal of
social intercourse. Even legal punishment generally requires
private initiation, and the same considerations of social Well-
being which require legal punishment in some cases require private
resentment in others. It would be to the last degree disastrous
to the Well-being of any society whatever if individuals altogether
ceased to show anger or to express resentment at personal rude-
ness or personal liberties or general want of respect for one
another's personalities ; and from the nature of the case it is
usually the injured party who must take the initiative in such
resentment, though it may be that the ideal society would save
him such a necessity by anticipating the resentment,—an ideal
which is already approximately realized in groups of people
among whom good breeding is combined with that real good
feeling of which good breeding is at its best the expression and
at its worst the caricature.

All this shows that we cannot attain to the ideal combination of punishment with forgiveness by merely laying it down that the magistrate must punish while the man must forgive. Nor, again, can we merely say that the duty of forgiveness begins when the due punishment has been exacted. For what will forgiveness mean in this case? Are we to say that when the formal sentence has been served, it is the duty of the judge or of society generally to treat the criminal with the same cordiality with which we should have received him had he never offended? Undoubtedly society does not give its repentant criminals the fair chance that they may reasonably claim, but to say that we must treat them as though they had never done wrong, or that former convictions should not aggravate the sentence, is surely to demand what is impracticable and pernicious. Nor in private relations can we always be called upon to treat the man who has betrayed our trust—even after repentance or apology—as though he had not betrayed it; nor can a friend, after a quarrel which has revealed in him a character which we had not suspected, ever again be a friend in the same sense or degree as before, even after the most ample repentance or apology. Without, therefore, denying that there is a sense in which forgiveness may be combined with punishment, it is impossible to find for that forgiveness which is compatible with punishment a meaning more definite than this—that punishment should not exclude whatever kind of goodwill can in the circumstances be properly combined with punishment. And that surely is something far too indefinite to satisfy the idea of forgiveness in its full and ordinary sense. It is impossible, in short, to get rid of the popular association of the idea of forgiveness with remission of penalty.

There is, then, a sense in which forgiveness is opposed to punishment. On the view that I have taken it will sometimes be a duty to punish and sometimes to forgive. In determining which we shall do in each particular case, the good man—whether the private individual or the public official, who is after all only the representative of a society of individuals as much bound by the law of love in their corporate as in their individual capacity—will consider which, having regard to all the circumstances of the case, will best serve those social ends to which punishment and forgiveness alike are means. The ideal punishment would no doubt be one which was the best alike in the interests of society and of the individual. Under our present system of legal punishment it is to be feared that this is an ideal not very often attained. A man has often to be punished in the interest of society whose own Well-being would be best promoted by forgiveness. In such a case we have to balance the interest of society against the interest of the individual, or rather perhaps what the society gains by the moral improvement of the particular individual against what it gains from the deterrent and educative effect of the punishment upon other individuals.

And upon this view of the relation of punishment to forgiveness, there is no absolute antagonism between that sense of forgiveness in which it is opposed to punishment and that sense in which it is compatible with punishment. Just the same considerations which impose the duty of punishment will limit the measure of it; just those same considerations which allow of the total remission of penalty in some cases will allow of some mitigation of it in other cases, and will impose in all cases the duty of showing whatever Benevolence and goodwill towards the offender is compatible with that measure of punishment which social duty demands. Punishment and forgiveness, when they are what they ought to be, being alike the expression of love, the mode and degree of their combination will likewise be only the application of the general precept of love to the circumstances of the particular case.

In the main, then, we may accept Bishop Butler's interpretation of the proper relation between punishment and forgiveness, and yet we cannot but feel that something is missed in this cool and calculating utilitarian analysis. We feel that there must be something more in forgiveness than the mere limitation of vengeance by the demands of public welfare. Seeley, in one of the best chapters of *Ecce Homo*, helps us to supply the deficiency[1]. It is true that in its essence the duty of forgiveness is the duty of laying aside *private* or

---

[1] *Ecce Homo*, chap. xxii. Von Hartmann has also recognized this justification of forgiveness (*Das sittl. Bewusstsein*, p. 178).

personal resentment,—of resenting the wrong because it is a wrong and not because I am the victim of it. But what Bishop Butler has missed is the fact that vengeance often loses its moral effect just because the avenger of the wrong is its victim, while forgiveness often touches the heart just because the forgiver is the man who suffered by the wrong,—and therefore the man in whom it is hardest to forgive. The wronged man's forgiveness will often have a moral effect, awaken a gratitude and a penitence, which the forgiveness of the disinterested spectator or the remotely interested 'society' would not secure. It is perfectly true, as Butler taught, that forgiveness is only a particular case of love; but he forgot that to a human being who has wronged his fellow, forgiveness is an infinitely more convincing proof of love than punishment can ever be, and may, therefore, touch the heart as punishment will seldom touch it. In the light of this principle nothing that has been said as to the duty of balancing the good effects of forgiveness against the good effects of punishment need be recalled; only, in choosing between them, this peculiar magic of the wronged person's forgiveness must needs be duly remembered.

In conclusion, I may remark that all these considerations are as much applicable to any punishments which Theists may expect as the consequence of sin in another world as to the clumsy attempts at ideal Justice with which we are obliged to be satisfied in the school or the criminal court. Now as in the days of Plato it is a paramount duty of Moral Philosophy to lay down Canons for Theology (τύπους περὶ θεολογίας). It need hardly be pointed out that the acceptance of our principles about Punishment will involve a considerable amendment of popular ideas about what we shall still do well to think of as divine punishment, while we recognize the inadequacy of such a metaphor or symbol of God's dealing with human souls. Few Theologians of the present day will be bold enough to follow Abelard in defence of everlasting punishment as being justified by the example and warning which the fate of the wicked supplies to the rest of humanity. And the acceptance of the principles here laid down about forgiveness may involve a no less complete reconstitution of many popular schemes concerning divine forgiveness and atonement. The idea of vicarious suffering has nothing immoral about it ; under the conditions of human life love can hardly be manifested in its highest degree without it. It is otherwise with the idea of vicarious punishment. Even on the retributive view of punishment, the idea of substituted vicarious punishment would never for a moment be defended by a modern Christian except with a view to bolster up an obsolete theological tradition—still less so on the view of punishment adopted in these pages. On the other hand the idea that the nature of God has received its fullest revelation in a self-sacrificing life and death is one against which the Moralist can have nothing to say.

THE THEORY

OF GOOD AND EVIL

A TREATISE ON MORAL PHILOSOPHY

BY

HASTINGS RASHDALL

D.LITT. (OXFORD), HON. D.C.L. (DURHAM)
FELLOW AND TUTOR OF NEW COLLEGE, OXFORD

SECOND EDITION

VOLUME II

OXFORD UNIVERSITY PRESS
LONDON : GEOFFREY CUMBERLEGE

FIRST EDITION 1907

Second edition produced photographically
by the MUSTON COMPANY in 1924
from corrected sheets of the first edition

Reprinted 1938, 1948, photographically
by LOWE & BRYDONE, PRINTERS, LTD., LONDON

PRINTED IN GREAT BRITAIN

ANALYTICAL TABLE OF CONTENTS

VOLUME II

BOOK II. THE INDIVIDUAL AND THE SOCIETY

CHAPTER I. THE HEDONISTIC CALCULUS

2 ★

CHAPTER IV.   VOCATION

CHAPTER V. MORAL AUTHORITY AND MORAL AUTONOMY

BOOK III.   MAN AND THE UNIVERSE

CHAPTER I.   METAPHYSIC AND MORALITY

I. Metaphysic and Moral Philosophy are connected because (1) a true account of Morality involves metaphysical postulates, (2) some of the conclusions of Metaphysic are of importance for Morality, (3) Moral Philosophy supplies *data* to Metaphysic   .   .   .   189

Up to a certain point ethical questions may be discussed without

CHAPTER II. RELIGION AND MORALITY

CHAPTER IV. MORALITY AND EVOLUTION

THE THEORY OF GOOD AND EVIL

BOOK II
THE INDIVIDUAL AND THE SOCIETY

CHAPTER I
THE HEDONISTIC CALCULUS

I

HAVING now sketched the outlines of a system of Ethics, I propose in the present book to examine some of the objections which have been or may be made to the positions heretofore taken up, and to consider some points of view more or less opposed to my own. In replying to the objections I hope I may be able to elucidate and develope, perhaps in some ways to qualify and to correct, the conclusions at which we have hitherto arrived.

The first of the objections with which I shall have to deal concerns what has often been called the hedonistic calculus.

It has been maintained in these pages that the criterion of an action—what constitutes it right or wrong—is its tendency to promote for all mankind a greatest quantity of good on the whole. This implies that 'good' admits of being measured, and that particular elements in that good are likewise capable of being measured, and of being compared with one another in respect of their ultimate value. This assumption involves the assertion (1) that each one of the various goods in which the ideal human life consists—Virtue, Knowledge, pleasure, &c.— is capable of quantity, so that I can prefer one course of action to another because it will promote more Virtue or more pleasure than another; and (2) that a given quantity of one kind of good can be quantitatively compared with another, at least to this extent, that there is a meaning in asserting that a given quantity of Virtue is worth more or less than a given quantity of pleasure. Both of these assumptions have been denied.

I shall deal first with the denial that even goods of the same kind are capable of quantitative measurement. I hardly know whether the question has ever been explicitly raised as to the higher goods—Morality, Culture and the like—but the possibility of quantitative measurement has certainly been explicitly denied with regard to pleasure. That is the first question therefore with which we shall have to deal.

The doctrine that pleasures cannot be summed, that there is no meaning in the idea of a sum of pleasures and that consequently the 'hedonistic calculus' is impossible and unintelligible, has long been maintained by a certain section of anti-utilitarian writers, among whom it will be enough to mention the late Prof. T. H. Green and Mr. Bradley. It must be confessed, however, that it is not very easy to extract from either of these writers the exact grounds or even the precise meaning of their contention. Prof. Mackenzie in his *Manual of Ethics* and his *Introduction to Social Philosophy* has performed a real service by putting the doctrine into a form in which it is more easy to subject it to examination and criticism. In the present chapter, however, I shall not confine myself to what Prof. Mackenzie has advanced, as what appear to me the misconceptions which underlie his reasoning are widely diffused, and seem often to be assumed in the language of writers who have been less lucid and less explicit. My object is rather to get to the bottom of the misunderstanding than to criticize any particular writer; I do not therefore wish to be understood to hold Prof. Mackenzie responsible for every argument that I may criticize except where I expressly quote him.

At this stage of our discussion I need hardly repeat that I am not in the least interested in the defence either of the hedonistic Psychology or of hedonistic Utilitarianism, both of which I entirely reject on much the same grounds as those which would be assigned by the writers I am criticizing—writers with some of whom I should largely agree in their general view of Ethics. This is particularly the case with regard to Prof. Mackenzie, who is quite free from that sectarian prejudice against Casuistry and that dislike to the scientific treatment of practical problems which are characteristic of several writers by whom the incommensurability of pleasures has been maintained. I agree with him in holding that pleasure is part of the good, though not the whole of it, as *a* good but not *the* good. It would seem *prima facie* to follow that *ceteris paribus* the course of action which promises more pleasure must be preferred to one that promises less; and that, to ascertain whether an action should be done, I must ideally add together the pleasures or amounts of pleasure likely to be attained by it, and compare them with the pleasure promised by the alternative course. But here we are met by a denial that it is possible to sum pleasures at all.

It will be well to quote in full a few attempts to state the ground of this doctrine.

(1) We will begin with a passage from Green's *Prolegomena to Ethics*: 'A "Summum Bonum" consisting of a greatest possible sum of pleasures is supposed to be definite and intelligible, because every one knows what pleasure is. But in what sense does every one know it ? If only in the sense that every one can imagine the renewal of some pleasure which he has enjoyed, it may be pointed out that pleasures, not being enjoyable in a sum —to say nothing of a greatest possible sum—cannot be imagined in a sum either [1]. Though this remark, however, might be to the purpose against a Hedonist who held that desire could only be excited by imagined pleasure, and yet that a greatest sum of pleasure was an object of desire, it is not to the purpose against those who merely look on the greatest sum of pleasures as the true criterion, without holding that desire is only excited by imagination of pleasure. They will reply that, though we may not be able, strictly speaking, to imagine a sum of pleasures, every one knows what it is. Every one knows the difference between enjoying a longer succession of pleasures and a shorter one, a succession of more intense and a succession of less intense

---

[1] It is difficult to reconcile this statement with the admission ' that there may be in fact such a thing as desire for a sum or contemplated series of pleasures' (*Prolegomena to Ethics*, § 222). All that Green seems anxious to establish in this section is that without a permanent self there would be no such desire.

pleasures, a succession of pleasures less interrupted by pain and one more interrupted. In this sense every one knows the difference between enjoying a larger sum of pleasures and enjoying a smaller sum. He knows the difference also between a larger number of persons or sentient beings and a smaller one. He attaches therefore a definite meaning to the enjoyment of a greater nett amount of pleasure by a greater number of beings, and has a definite criterion for distinguishing a better action from a worse, in the tendency of the one, as compared with the other, to produce a greater amount of pleasure to a greater number of persons.

'The ability, however, to compare a larger sum of pleasure with a smaller in the sense explained—as we might compare a longer time with a shorter—is quite a different thing from ability to conceive a greatest possible sum of pleasures, or to attach any meaning to that phrase. It seems, indeed, to be intrinsically as unmeaning as it would be to speak of a greatest possible quantity of time or space. The sum of pleasures plainly admits of indefinite increase, with the continued existence of sentient beings capable of pleasure. It is greater to-day than it was yesterday, and, unless it has suddenly come to pass that experiences of pain outnumber experiences of pleasure, it will be greater to-morrow than it is to-day; but it will never be complete while sentient beings exist. To say that ultimate good is a greatest possible sum of pleasures, strictly taken, is to say that it is an end which for ever recedes; which is not only unattainable but from the nature of the case can never be more nearly approached; and such an end clearly cannot serve the purpose of a criterion, by enabling us to distinguish actions which bring men nearer to it from those that do not. Are we then, since the notion of a greatest possible sum of pleasures is thus unavailable, to understand that in applying the Utilitarian criterion we merely approve one action in comparison with another, as tending to yield more pleasure to more beings capable of pleasure, without reference to a "Summum Bonum" or ideal of a perfect state of existence at all? But without such reference is there any meaning in approval or disapproval at all? It is intelligible that without such reference the larger sum of pleasures should be desired as against the less; on supposition of benevolent impulses, it is intelligible that the larger sum should be desired by a man for others as well as for himself. But the desire is one thing; the approval of it—the judgement "in a calm hour " that the desire or the action prompted by it is reasonable--is quite another thing. Without some ideal—however indeterminate—of a best state of existence, with the attainment of which the approved motive or action may be deemed compatible, the approval of it would seem impossible. Utilitarians have therefore to consider whether they can employ a criterion of action, as they do employ it, without some idea of ultimate good ; and, since a greatest possible sum of pleasures is a phrase to which no idea really corresponds, what is the idea which really actuates them in the employment of their criterion [1].'

It will be observed that Green's objection is chiefly (1) to the idea of a *greatest possible* sum of pleasure and to the theory which finds in such a sum its ideal of human good.   He does not deny that pleasures are capable of being summed, and that it is possible to compare the amount of pleasure on the whole which an action will bring with the probable results of another.   Green, therefore, is in no way responsible for the view of his disciple, that even such a calculation is impossible.   Of this view we may take Prof. Mackenzie as the representative.

(2) Prof. Mackenzie writes : ' *Pleasures cannot be Summed.* It follows from this that there cannot be any *calculus* of pleasures— i. e. that the values of pleasures cannot be quantitatively estimated.   For there can be no quantitative estimate of things that are not homogeneous.   But, indeed, even apart from this consideration, there seems to be a certain confusion in the Hedonistic idea that we ought to aim at a greatest sum of pleasures.   If pleasure is the one thing that is desirable, it is clear that a sum of pleasures cannot be desirable ; for a sum of pleasures is not pleasure.   We are apt to think that a sum of pleasures is pleasure, just as a sum of numbers is a number.   But this is evidently not the case.   A sum of pleasures is not pleasure, any more than a sum of men is a man.   For pleasures, like men,

[1] *Prolegomena to Ethics,* §§ 358, 359.

cannot be added to one another. Consequently, if pleasure is the only thing that is desirable, a sum of pleasures cannot possibly be desirable. If the Hedonistic view were to be adopted, we ought always to desire the greatest pleasure—i. e. we ought to aim at producing the most intense feeling of pleasure that it is possible to reach in some one's consciousness. This would be the highest aim. A sum of smaller pleasures in a number of different people's consciousnesses, could not be preferable to this because a sum of pleasures is not pleasure at all. The reason why this does not appear to be the case, is that we habitually think of the desirable thing for man not as a feeling of pleasure but as a continuous state of happiness. But a continuous state of happiness is not a mere feeling of pleasure. It has a certain objective content. Now if we regard this content as the desirable thing, we do not regard the feeling of pleasure as the one thing that is desirable; i. e. we abandon Hedonism [1].'

For purposes of criticism it will be convenient to break up the position of my opponents into three assertions, all of which seem to be implied by Prof. Mackenzie but of which the last might possibly be maintained without the second, or the last two without the first. I shall begin, that is to say, with the more extreme position, and then go on to the more moderate forms of the doctrine which I am criticizing. I may say at once that it is the first two which I am chiefly concerned to deny: the third seems to me to raise a more subtle and debatable question, and (while I am prepared to defend my thesis on this point) I attach little importance to it, and would particularly insist that failure to establish my position thereon should not be held in any way to invalidate my argument in relation to the other two. The three positions which I dispute are these:—

(1) That a sum of pleasures is not a possible object of desire.

(2) That while the proposition *this pleasure is greater or more pleasant than that* has a meaning, the judgement is not quantitative.

(3) That even if one pleasure or sum of pleasures can be said to be greater in amount than another, numerical values cannot,

---

[1] *Manual of Ethics*, 4th ed., pp. 229, 230. Cf. the same writer's *Introduction to Social Philosophy*, 2nd ed., pp. 222-228.

with any meaning, be assigned to two pleasures or sums of pleasure ; so that there can never be any meaning in the assertion 'this pleasure is twice as great as that.'

I may add that for the present I am dealing with the comparison of pleasures of the same kind or quality. Afterwards I shall have something to say as to the comparison of pleasures which 'differ in kind.' Meanwhile, the fact that I am confining myself to pleasures of the same kind may perhaps be my excuse if I take my illustrations for the most part from pleasures of a low type, such as those of eating and drinking. I do so simply because what I contend for is most clearly seen in the case of such pleasures. I make this remark to deprecate the wrath of critics who, while apparently not averse to a good dinner, seem to wish it to be understood that the pleasantness of the meal is to them a contemptible—not to say regrettable—accident involved in the pursuit of some higher end, the nature of which they never seem able to indicate with any precision. I need hardly say that I have no desire to emphasize the importance of the element contributed to human Well-being by those pleasures of eating and drinking to which the actual conventions of the most refined societies give a greater prominence than it is easy to justify. But however low we place them, and however strictly we think they ought to be limited, it seems impossible to justify any indulgence whatever in such things which goes beyond the imperative requirements of health and efficiency, unless we treat pleasure—even such pleasure—as a good.

II

Firstly, then, it is asserted that a sum of pleasures is not a possible object of desire.

This position would appear to be maintained upon one of two possible grounds :—

(a) It may be regarded as a corollary of the still more paradoxical doctrine that we never desire pleasure at all. This may mean that we never desire a pleasure, or that we never desire pleasure in general but always a particular pleasure.

Some writers would seem to deny the possibility of desiring either *a* pleasure or pleasure in general.

What lies at the bottom of these assertions seems to be the undeniable fact that it is impossible to *enjoy* pleasure in general or pleasure taken apart from everything else. What we enjoy is always a particular content—a pleasant sound, a pleasant sensation, a pleasant activity, a pleasant idea. A man whose consciousness was at any single minute full of nothing but pleasure would be an impossible variety of lunatic : for he would have to admit that he was pleased at just nothing at all. Pleasure apart from the pleasant something is of course a pure abstraction. When a man is said to desire pleasure, it is meant undoubtedly that he desires pleasant things, and further that he desires them simply because they are pleasant. Is not this a possible state of mind? It would seem that there are those who would be prepared to deny even this—who would say that even a particular pleasure, i. e. (of course) a particular pleasant content, is not a possible object of desire. Such a doctrine claims the high authority of Dr. Caird :—

‘ Further, *when* the desire of pleasure thus arises, it is in us combined with a consciousness for which pleasure *cannot* be the sole or the ultimate end, a consciousness to which, as universal, pleasure is not an adequate end. This may be shown in various ways, the most obvious of which is to point out that pleasure must be had in some object, for which there is a desire independently of the pleasure it brings [1].’

Now I have already contended that many—probably most— of our desires are not desires for pleasure but ‘ disinterested desires ’ or ‘ desires for objects,’ and that in all such cases the satisfaction of the desire gives pleasure because the object has been desired ; it is not desired, or at all events it is not desired solely, because it is calculated that the attainment of the given object will bring with it pleasure, and more pleasure than

---

[1] Caird, *The Critical Philosophy of Kant*, II, p. 229. Prof. Taylor defends the to me still stranger idea that, though pleasure need not arise from the fulfilment of desire, ‘ neither worth nor goodness can properly be ascribed to it unless it is felt to be the realisation, in however unexpected a way, of some previously formed idea, the satisfaction of some previously experienced craving ’ (*The Problem of Conduct*, p. 327).

could be attained by the pursuit of any other object then within reach. As to what is commonly known as the 'hysteron-proteron of the hedonistic psychology' I have already insisted as strongly on it as I know how to do. But the question before us is not whether other things can be desired besides pleasures, but whether pleasures are or are not capable of being desired at all. Certainly I do not believe that an angry man desires vengeance because he has calculated—from his own experience or the recorded experience of others—that the pleasures of vengeance are the sweetest. Certainly there are cases where a man gratifies his anger or his desire of vengeance with the certain knowledge that his act will entail pains which no impartial calculation of pleasures could possibly conclude to be outweighed by the pleasure of satisfied anger or revenge. (We are obliged to use the language of common life, though of course upon the assumptions of the hedonistic psychology there could not really be such a thing as anger or passion of any kind.) Unquestionably there are cases where the uplifted arm would not be stayed by the most demonstrated certainty of the greatest sum of pleasures that earth has to offer. But is all this equally true of cases where a man desires to eat or drink something which experience has shown to be pleasant? The contention we are examining would seem to involve the assertion that, when a man who is not thirsty or in quest of health drinks port, he is impelled by a desire of port—port as such, port for port's sake. The niceness of the port is, it would seem to be hinted, a quite irrelevant circumstance. What he wants is port because it is port, not port because it is nice. If that were so, it would seem that the uplifted glass would not be put down even if some fellow-reveller warned the drinker, 'Don't drink this, it is beastly.' If the desire for port were based upon some antecedent desire other than desire for the pleasure of port-drinking, it would seem that the warning must necessarily pass unheeded. It may possibly be urged that what the man wants is both port and nice port: but that of course is to admit the opponent's case ; the desire for pleasant sensation is one of his desires : he does desire pleasant sensation just because it is pleasant, whatever he desires or does not desire besides.

There can be no doubt that many even of what are called our sensual pleasures are conditioned by the presence of some desire which cannot be described as a desire for pleasure, or by some want or appetite of a kind which it is better perhaps to distinguish from the more rational class of ' disinterested desires.'   There is a pleasure in getting warm when I am cold, in eating when I am hungry, and so on.   But are all pleasures of sense of this kind ? Such a contention seems to be opposed to the most familiar experience.   I certainly often rise from my chair and stand before the fire, though I am not in the least cold, simply because experience has shown me that the practice is attended with pleasure.   The continental stove may more than satisfy our desire of warmth, but Englishmen persist nevertheless in preferring their uneconomical open fires.   The medical profession would be ruined if there were no pleasure in eating after hunger is satisfied, or if such pleasure could not become the object of desire.   Moreover, the pleasure is in many cases quite independent of any previous desire at all—whether for that pleasure or for anything else.   Where the pleasure arises from the satisfaction of desire, the pleasure cannot be felt when the desire is absent.   If knowledge is forced on those who have no desire for knowledge, its attainment is often found by no means conducive to pleasure. But the teetotaler's appreciation of rum and milk might be by no means lessened by the fact that the rum had been surreptitiously introduced into the innocent beverage for which his soul had craved.   That the pleasures of smell and sight and hearing are independent of previous desire attracted the especial notice of Plato.   And while this independence of previous desire is characteristic of certain kinds of mere sensation, it is not limited to sensual pleasures.   It is especially, I think, characteristic of the aesthetic pleasures.   My appreciation of a landscape or a picture is in no way diminished because it comes in my way at a moment when I am thinking of something quite different. And if it be said that it appeals to me only because it satisfies a permanent desire for the beautiful which is capable of being aroused by the presentation of that which will satisfy it, one may ask, ' How in the first instance is the desire of beauty aroused ? '   Is it normally the case that people are led to the

search for beauty by a craving for what they have never experienced—as many both of the highest desires and of the lowest
appetites do undoubtedly exist before they have received any
satisfaction at all ?   Is it not rather some new, some unsought
for, some wholly unanticipated experience of the pleasantness
of beholding beautiful things which first rouses the desire to see
more beautiful things ?

I cannot but think that few even of those who deny the
possibility of a 'sum of pleasures' will agree with Dr. Caird
in holding that even particular pleasures cannot be the object
of desire.   But then it may be said : 'Yes, *a* pleasure may be
desired, but not pleasure—a particular pleasure but not pleasure
in general.'   I have already admitted that we can never desire
to enjoy pleasure alone; the pleasure must always come from
some feeling, thought, or volition.   So obvious a truism has
so far as I am aware, never been denied.   But need we always
set our heart upon the enjoyment of some particular pleasant
thing?   There is something in common between all the things
which give us pleasure : and that something is surely capable of
being made the object of pursuit.   When a boy begins to smoke,
he is certainly not influenced by the desire of the characteristic
smoker's pleasure, which he has never enjoyed and will not enjoy,
very probably, for some time to come.   There can be no image
before his mind of a definite pleasant content; he does not know
what the smoker's pleasure is, but he knows what pleasure in
general is, and knows that he likes all kinds of pleasure.   His
notion of pleasure is made up by abstraction from all the
pleasures he has ever enjoyed; there is no image of any
particular pleasure before his mind.   And, when he has gathered
from the relation of credible witnesses that smoking is a source
of pleasure, that is enough to set him in pursuit of it.   If
a booth were set up in a fair with the announcement 'Pleasure
here 6*d*.,' it is possible that it would not attract a large number
of sixpences because there might be doubts as to the probabilities
of the promised article being really supplied; but it does seem
to me a strange position to deny the psychological possibility
of some one individual paying his sixpence, not (as it is very
likely some would do) for the pleasure of satisfying curiosity

but with the definite expectation of getting a fair sixpennyworth
of enjoyment, and a broad-minded indifference as to the particular species supplied—so long of course as it was a pleasure
to him.

I feel some diffidence in attempting a solemn argument in
defence of a thesis which (with all respect for the eminent
persons who deny it) seems to me so obviously true ; and I
confess I find it difficult to understand what exactly it is that
is really meant to be denied when it is said that pleasure
cannot be an object of desire. Is it the obvious fact that what
we each care about is not all pleasure equally, but the particular
pleasures which appeal to us ? That is quite true, but then
of course that which gives *me* no pleasure will not satisfy *my*
desire of pleasure ; nor shall I be much influenced by a desire for
the pleasures which, though they are pleasant, I care little about,
or which cannot be attained without sacrificing objects about
which I care more than for such pleasures—perhaps more than
for any pleasure small or great. Or is it implied that, though
I do desire all pleasant things which really are pleasant to me,
I do not desire them in proportion to their pleasantness ? I
agree, but that is only to say that I desire other things besides
pleasure, and moreover that (speaking generally) the pleasures
best worth having spring from the satisfaction of desires other
than the desire for pleasure. All that has been admitted. What
I contend for is that it is possible for a man to desire—and that
all or almost all men do desire—pleasant things simply because
they are pleasant, and that, *ceteris paribus* (where no difference
of quality enters into the consideration and where no other desire
would be thwarted), they desire the pleasanter things more than
those that are less pleasant. That is what I understand to
be meant by the assertion that pleasure (and not merely particular pleasures) is a possible object of desire

There is one more line of argument which I would briefly
suggest. Will those who deny that we desire pleasure, maintain
that we have no aversion to pain ? Here it can hardly be
contended that it is merely certain particular psychical states—
which merely happen to be painful—which inspire aversion,
or that it is not the pain as such that we try to avoid, but

merely the frustration of some other desire, of which pain is
a mere accidental accompaniment. It is, of course, often the
case that pain is the symptom of something organically wrong,
and again that mental pains do largely result from the frustration of some desire. But there are many conditions of body
to which we should have no objection for any other reason
than that they happen to be painful. Who would care about
being told by a Physiologist that certain thrills are coursing
down his nerves, if they did not reveal themselves in painful
sensation : or that there was caries in his tooth, if he could
be sure that the tooth would never become either painful or
less useful ? If you will insist on abstracting the content of
pain from the pain itself, it is surely the pain that we avoid,
not the content. We avoid pains, the content of which we know
nothing about. We do not think it necessary to try new pains
which we cannot without experience even picture to the imagination, under the expectation that, though other pains are
to be avoided, it might turn out that this pain was rather
desirable than otherwise. If we know that the psychical state
produced by such and such a bodily affection is painful, that
is quite enough for us. Unless they suppose the pain to be
a means to something other than itself or an inseparable element
in some other good, all rational men avoid it : and it will hardly
be denied that they avoid the severer pains more than the less
severe. All pains are to them objects of aversion, and objects
of aversion in proportion to their painfulness. That is what
is meant by saying that pain as such is an object of aversion.
I do not know that any one who admits that pain is an object
of aversion but still denies that pleasure is a possible object
of desire can be convicted of any actual logical inconsistency :
but the position is, to say the least of it, a singular one.

(b) But, as I have already indicated, there are writers whose
denial that pleasures can be summed or that a sum of pleasures
can be desired does not carry with it the assertion either that
pleasures are not possible objects of desire or even that pleasure in
general may not become the object of pursuit. Their objection to
a summation of pleasures rests upon other grounds ; and seems
for the most part (so far as I can gather) to be based upon the

very simple fact that we cannot enjoy a sum of pleasures all at once—that a sum of pleasures is not capable of existing altogether at a given moment of time. Perhaps the best way of dealing with this objection will be to point out that the contention is as fatal to the existence of a desire for pleasure, or even for one single definite pleasure, as to the desire for a sum of pleasures. The briefest pleasure occupies a sensible time : and there is no time that cannot conceivably be subdivided into two halves. If, therefore, I cannot desire anything which I cannot have all at once, I could not desire either pleasant consciousness in general or any particular state of consciousness which is pleasant. The argument in fact goes further than this : it would prove not merely that pleasure cannot be desired, but that there can be no such thing as pleasure, since an indivisible point of pleasure could not be felt at all and therefore would not be pleasure. If so, of course, *cadit quaestio*. But I must ask to be excused from attempting the task of proving to the sceptic that the word pleasure signifies something which has actual existence [1]. Assuming that there is such a thing as pleasure it must (at least for human beings here and now) be in time : and the time or the temporal state that is incapable of division is not time or in time at all. We have heard, of course, of the timeless self and its aspirations after a good which, though it is not in time, is, it seems, to have a beginning, and to be capable of being brought about by human acts which take place within the time-series : but I am not aware that the supporters of the timeless self have usually assigned to it a timeless pleasure [2]. At all events, if any such thing there be, it must be something quite different from what I—and, I am persuaded, the majority of my readers—understand by the word. As I understand a sum of pleasures, every pleasure is really a sum of pleasures :

---

[1] The reader may possibly demand at this point a definition. Something will be said on this subject at the end of the next chapter. Here I will only remark that most of the attempts at definition fail so grotesquely that I feel little inclination to add to the number.

[2] It is true that Dr. McTaggart has suggested the possibility for beings in another state of a 'timeless pleasure,' but he does not regard such a pleasure as possible in our present condition. As far as this life is concerned, he admits the possibility of a 'sum of pleasures.'

it is impossible to desire pleasure at all without desiring a sum of pleasures. What I understand by the assertion that I desire a sum of pleasures is that I desire to enjoy pleasure as intense as possible and for as long as possible—that I desire two minutes' pleasure more than I desire one minute of the same pleasure, and further that I regard the intensity of one pleasant moment as something which can be equated with the duration of another pleasant state; so that, on comparing the duration and intensity of pleasure which will be secured by one course of conduct with the duration and intensity of pleasure which I may win by another, I can pronounce which on the whole appears to me to possess the greatest pleasure-value, and can (in so far as I am in pursuit of pleasure to the disregard of other considerations) determine my action by that judgement.

Professor Green's argument against the idea that something which cannot be enjoyed all at once can be the *summum bonum* does not directly concern us here, but it seems to me open to much the same objections as have been urged against the denial that a sum of pleasures is a possible object of desire. His argument seems to amount to the assertion that a sum of pleasures cannot be made the object of pursuit because you can never reach it, while a greatest possible sum of pleasures is a contradiction in terms, since when you have enjoyed any given amount of pleasure, it is always still possible to desire more. I should myself be prepared to contend that any other view of the ethical end is liable to the same objection, since any good for man must be in time, and can never be seized once for all as a κτῆμα ἐς ἀεί; I am not, however, arguing that a sum of pleasures is the true ethical end, but only that it is an intelligible object of pursuit. To aim at a greatest possible sum of pleasures means to endeavour that as much pleasure should be got into a given time as possible and that the time in which we are enjoying pleasure should be as long as possible. Nobody, I take it, has ever maintained the possibility of arriving at a sum of pleasures in any other sense. The greater durability of some sources of satisfaction as compared with others is no doubt an important reason for the higher value we attribute to them, but the consciousness which enjoys even the most spiritual good must be in time; the enjoyment of it can never be so far exhausted that we can say that an addition to it would be no addition to the good hitherto enjoyed.   To argue that a sum of pleasures cannot be the good because they cannot be enjoyed all at once is about as reasonable as to argue that the virtues cannot be the good because they cannot all be practised in an 'atomic now' or even during the same five minutes [1].

III

(2) It is asserted that whereas the proposition 'this pleasure is greater than that' has a meaning, the judgement is not quantitative.

The idea that degree involves quantity has been pronounced by Prof. Mackenzie a crude notion [2]; but it is a crude notion which has commended itself (unless I greatly misunderstand them) to Kant, to Prof. Bosanquet [3], and on the whole to Mr. Bradley. I do not propose to discuss the matter more in detail as a matter of pure Logic, but will simply refer to Mr. Bradley's very subtle paper on the question: 'What do we mean by the intensity of psychical states?' [4] I do not underrate the difficulty, insisted upon by Mr. Bradley with his usual penetration, of saying exactly what it is that there is more of in one psychical state— a state of pleasure or a state of heat—than in another.   But Mr. Bradley, though his discussion is aporetic, seems to be indisposed to deny that, however this question be answered,

---

[1] 'So long as we exist in time, the supreme good, whatever it is—perfection, self-realisation, the good will—will have to manifest itself in a series of states of consciousness' (McTaggart, *Studies in Hegelian Cosmology*, p. 109). 'It will, I believe, be found . . . that, reasonably or unreasonably, we are continually making calculations of pleasures and pains, that they have an indispensable place in every system of morality, and that any system which substitutes perfection for pleasure as a criterion of moral action also involves the addition and subtraction of other intensive quantities. If such a process is unjustifiable, it is not hedonism only, but all ethics, which will become unmeaning' (ib., p. 111).

[2] *Social Philosophy*, 2nd ed., p. 230.

[3] 'A quality that changes, and yet remains the same quality, has passed into quantity' (*Principles of Logic*, I, p. 118).

[4] *Mind*, N. S., Vol. IV (1895).   Cf. *Ethical Studies*, p. 107.

the judgement is quantitative. And I find it difficult to treat seriously the assertion to the contrary. We certainly say: 'This is *more* pleasant than that [1].' The position that the word *more* does not involve the idea of quantity is so startling that I must excuse myself from further discussion of it until it be developed in more detail than has yet been the case. It is true that 'intensive quantity' is not the same thing as 'extensive quantity'; but if 'intensive quantity' has nothing in common with 'extensive quantity' why do Philosophy and Common Sense alike call each of them 'quantity'?

Whatever be thought of the logical doctrine that degree does not involve quantity, it is enough for my present purpose if it be admitted that one whole state of consciousness of a certain character is pronounced more pleasant than another, provided it be conceded also: (a) that the total pleasure in each case is made up of a number of successive moments; (b) that a certain degree of intensity is actually judged to be the equivalent of—and may influence desire and volition as the equivalent of—a certain degree of duration: in other words, that a man in pursuit of pleasure may choose, and may judge it reasonable to choose, a less pleasure for a longer time rather than an intenser pleasure for a shorter time; (c) that a whole pleasant state may be analysed into various distinguishable elements.

The first two of these propositions can hardly, as it seems to me, be denied without going the length of saying that the duration of a pleasure, if it only be intense enough, is a matter of absolute indifference to us. And it has been contended by

[1] That Mr. Bradley believes it possible to sum pleasures may, I think, be inferred from his elaborate discussions as to whether, in the Absolute, there is or is not a 'balance of pleasure.' Such passages as the following could have no meaning if it were not possible to add pleasure and pain together, arrive at their sum and subtract the pleasure from the pain or the pain from the pleasure: 'We found that there is a balance of pleasure over and above pain, and we know from experience that in a mixed state such a balance may be pleasant. And we are sure that the Absolute possesses and enjoys somehow this balance of pleasure. But to go further seems impossible. Pleasure may conceivably be so supplemented and modified by addition, that it does not remain precisely that which we call pleasure' (*Appearance and Reality*, p. 534).

Prof. Mackenzie that those who maintain the possibility of adopting the hedonistic calculus as a guide in conduct are involved in some such absurdity.

But, it may be said, we can surely estimate pleasures at least with reference to their duration. I may be aware that at each of two successive moments I have a pleasure of approximately the same degree; and I may thus be entitled to say that the pleasures of these two moments taken together are twice as great as the pleasure of one of them alone would have been. Surely $1 + 1 = 2$. Now, to this the obvious answer is that it is indeed true that $1 + 1 = 2$, but it is also true that $1 + 1 - 1 = 1$. When the second pleasure is added the first is taken away, and there is only one left. If I have only one pleasure now, I am none the richer for the fact that I had another before. It is true that I may survey my life as a whole, and perceive that I was pleased at so many different moments; and it might be an amiable hobby on my part to try to make the number of pleasant moments as large as possible. But I should not be any the better off for such an effort. At the present moment I am just as happy as I am, and no happier: I am not also as happy as I was, or as happy as I shall be. In the past, on the other hand, I was as happy as I was; and in the future I shall be as happy as I shall be. Every moment stands on its own basis; and the number of moments makes no difference to the happiness of life as a whole, because, according to such a view, life is *not* a whole. "A short life and a merry one" is as happy as a long one. A moment of blessedness' [upon the hypothesis that pleasures can be summed] 'would be as good as an eternity, because the eternity would only go on repeating the blessedness and not increasing it [1].'

I can only say that most of us would attach considerable value to what Prof. Mackenzie dismisses with a contemptuous 'only.' If we could attain this moment of blessedness, that is exactly what we should want—that it should be repeated as often as possible. There is no arguing about these matters of psychological experience and ethical judgement. I can only say that as a matter of fact I would not take the trouble to walk

[1] *Social Philosophy*, pp. 231, 232.

across the street to get a moment of blessedness if I were assured that the blessedness would occupy my consciousness only for $\frac{1}{100}$ of a second [1]. I will add once more a reminder —too often forgotten in the polemics of anti-hedonists—of the parallel case of pain. Prof. James has somewhere remarked that the utmost degree of torture of which human consciousness is capable would be a matter of supreme indifference to him if he could be assured that it would last only some infinitesimal time. Would Prof. Mackenzie be prepared to say that, if condemned to such a torture, it would be a matter of indifference to him how long it went on?

Now it is true that Prof. Mackenzie is here indulging in what appears to him a *reductio ad absurdum* of the hedonistic view of Ethics. But I fail to see how he can himself escape adopting such a consequence as his own except by insisting that the good, which is the true end of human life, is something out of time altogether, a view which, however unintelligible, is open to writers like Green who did not regard pleasure as a good at all, but does not seem to be open to those who, like Prof. Mackenzie, do regard pleasure as *a* good and part of *the* good. There is just the same logical difficulty about any view which admits pleasure to be a good at all. A pleasure, however brief, can be enjoyed only while it is there: it can be enjoyed afterwards only in so far as the recollection of the past pleasure is itself a fresh pleasure. It is true that the possibility of such recollection implies the belief in a continuous or permanent self which is denied by such writers as Hume; but Hume's view of the self is not involved in the recognition of the hedonistic calculus as a possible and (as far as it goes) a rational proceeding. If pleasure be of any importance at all, it must follow, it seems to me, that *ceteris paribus* its importance must be proportional to its duration. And, as I have already sug-

---

[1] If what is wanted is a timeless 'blessedness,' though personally I attach no meaning to such an expression, we may usefully remember Dr. McTaggart's distinction: 'Absolute perfection—the supreme good—is not quantitative. But we shall not reach absolute perfection by any action which we shall have a chance of taking to-day or to-morrow. And of the degrees of perfection it is impossible to speak except quantitatively' (*Studies in Hegelian Cosmology*, p. 113).

gested, exactly the same line of objection may be taken to regarding as the good any possible state of a conscious being which is in time. If it may be argued that, supposing pleasure to be the good, a moment of it ought to be as good as an eternity, then why not a moment of holiness or a moment of 'Self-realization'? If the 'self-realization' which Prof. Mackenzie wants is not in time at all, how can it be an object of human effort? If it is in time, would he not think a longer duration of it better than a shorter?

If then duration of pleasure is desired as well as intensity of pleasure, will it be denied that, in choosing between two pleasures (i. e. between the psychical consequences of alternative acts of choice), we do balance duration against intensity, and choose that which promises most pleasure on the whole—the discomforts of a four hours' passage on a good boat against the horrors of two hours on a bad one, or (if income be severely limited) the three hours of fierce delight (*plus* a certain amount of retrospective pleasure afterwards) which five shillings will buy at a theatre against the calmer but more prolonged enjoyment of a five-shilling book? This is all at bottom that is meant by the much-decried idea of a hedonistic calculus—all perhaps that it is absolutely necessary to contend for. But there is, as I have suggested, one point more—not perhaps absolutely essential to the idea, but usually implied in it, and it is this probably which is most apt to be denied by the more moderate of those who object to the expression ' sum of pleasures '— and that is the notion that the total whole of pleasant consciousness is made up of distinguishable elements. I say distinguishable, i. e. logically distinguishable, not capable of actual separation. My consciousness at any given moment is no doubt a whole which cannot be separated into parts like a material object, but it is possible to distinguish in the total ' psychosis ' many different elements. Sometimes the elements are capable of being distinguished even to the extent of retaining approximately when in combination the pleasurableness or painfulness which they have when separate. Thus I may be conscious at one and the same time of a pain in my toe, another in my head, and a pleasant interest in the story that

I am reading. At other times, and this is generally the case, no doubt, where no definitely localized pain enters into consciousness, the elements seem so far fused together that it is only by a considerable effort of reflection (aided by memories which enable me to apply the method of difference or of concomitant variations) that I can distinguish how much of my total pleasant state is due to the different elements. That is the case, for instance, when I ask myself how much of the general sense of exhilaration which I have experienced at a pleasant party was due to the dinner, how much to the champagne, how much to the company; or when I attempt to say how much of my depression is due to biliousness and how much to the disappointment or annoyance on which at such seasons I may be apt to brood.

And yet, in spite of all the difficulties of such discrimination, we do make such distinctions in reflecting upon past pleasures, and we use the result of such experiences in guiding our choice for the future. We have two invitations for the same night. We might say to ourselves: 'True, *A*'s dinner will be more sumptuous than *B*'s, but I like *B*'s superior wine better than *A*'s superior cookery, and the conversation will be much better. Therefore to *B*'s I will go, and *A*'s invitation I will decline.' It is true of course—and this seems to be the only serious difficulty in treating such cases as a summation of pleasures—that the hedonistic value of a pleasure in combination with others may be something quite different from its value when taken by itself, or rather (since we never do enjoy an assignable pleasure absolutely 'by itself') when experienced in a different psychical setting or context. The dinner which helps us to enjoy the evening in pleasant company would simply bore the man who is not a gourmand, if consumed in solitude or in the company of dull persons. The values that we sum are altered by the summing or rather by the combination. And this objection may be treated as fatal to the whole idea of a 'sum of pleasures.' But after all it is not the values that they have in separation but the values that they have as elements in the whole that we are summing; though our experience of them in separation or in other surroundings may be more or less of a help in estimating how much they will contribute to our enjoyment of the total consciousness into which they enter. It is true that my enjoyment of a certain man's company may be either greater or less when I meet him in a Swiss hotel than when I meet him in a College common-room: but that does not prevent my experience of his society in Oxford leading me to think that his presence will be a material addition to my enjoyment at such and such a Swiss hotel and determining me to go there in preference to one which I should otherwise have decidedly preferred. It is then undeniable (as it seems to me) that we can distinguish elements in a whole of pleasant consciousness. The society of my friend and the enjoyment of Alpine scenery may give me a total of pleasure both greater and different in kind than I should derive from the two taken separately. But that does not prevent my putting together in my mind the probable enjoyment which I shall derive from the scenery and the probable enjoyment which I shall derive from the company of my friend, and recognizing that the two elements go to form a whole of pleasure which is greater than either. If on comparing any two whole psychoses I find that one would be preferable to the other but would become less desirable when a certain assignable element is taken away, there is surely a real meaning in saying that such a whole of pleasure is a sum of pleasures. No doubt, as the Logicians remind us, the whole is something more than the sum of its parts; but the expressions 'whole' and 'part' have a real meaning for all that: the whole *is* the sum of its parts, though it is something more. Or to take a more concrete and material parallel, I may judge how many pailfuls of water it will take to fill a cistern by adding together the capacity of each pail, though I must not forget to allow for the considerable quantity which will be lost in the process of adding them together, or the quantity that will be added if it is raining.

IV

(3) There remains for discussion our third and last thesis: that, though one pleasure may be greater than another, it can never be described as twice as great—that degrees of pleasure cannot be numerically expressed.

The question raised by this assertion is to my mind much more difficult and debatable than any that we have so far discussed, and the assertion that pleasures do admit of arithmetical measurement is in no way necessary to justify us in talking about a sum of pleasure or a hedonistic calculus. I hasten to add that as a general rule our judgements about pleasure are expressed in the form of ' more ' or ' less,' not of so many times more or less. It is only in the simplest cases that we can attempt to compare pleasures with so much nicety ; and, as such judgements are of no practical use, we do not commonly make them. Still, I am prepared to maintain that the judgement ' this pleasure is twice as great as that ' is not absolutely without meaning. In the first place, it appears to me self-evident that the value of a pleasure is dependent upon its duration, and that two minutes of a given pleasure may be fairly said to be twice as pleasant as one minute of it—if it is really the same pleasure and is not diminished by satiety. Further, if it be admitted that we are in the habit of equating the intensity of pleasure with a certain duration of it, it would seem possible to indicate our sense of the comparative intensity of two pleasures by expressing them (so to speak) in terms of duration. If it is a matter of indifference to me whether I enjoy one minute of one pleasure or two minutes of another, I may reasonably be said to regard the one pleasure as twice as pleasant as the other [1]. Even in far more complicated cases—even in estimating the extent to which various elements contribute to a total state of continuous pleasure—it does not seem to be meaningless to express one's sense of the comparative value of the different elements by assigning to them numerical values. In comparing one friend's dinners with another's there would be nothing unmeaning—though for many practical reasons we rather avoid such exact mensuration of pleasures—in assigning so many marks to the dinner, so many to the wine, so many to the conversation with (if you like) a few plus or minus marks for the arrangement of the table, the post-prandial music and

---

[1] ' I feel no hesitation in affirming that the pleasure I get from a plate of turtle-soup is more than twice the pleasure I get from a plate of pea-soup ' (McTaggart, l. c., p. 117).

so on. We might express our sense of the comparative enjoyment afforded by the two entertainments and the extent to
which each element contributes to the total, by assigning marks
to each such element and then adding them together. I admit
that such numerical expressions would in general be wholly
useless, but it would correctly express the sort of way in which
we do make up our minds between alternative courses by a
mental or ideal summation of the pleasure which we expect
to derive from them. When we have decided on which side the
balance lies, we usually stop, because when we have determined
that we are going to prefer A's entertainment to B's, no purpose
is served by attempting to estimate or to express the degree
of our preference. As a general rule there would be no use
in such an attempt, but it is possible with a little ingenuity
to imagine circumstances in which it *would* be of use. If
a prize were offered to the host who would give us most pleasure
in the course of six entertainments with or without a certain
limit to the expense, the judges in such a competition would,
I imagine, have to record their impressions of each entertainment
in some such way—very much as a man who is judging prize
poems might quite intelligibly (though I do not recommend the
method) arrive at his decision by assigning so many marks for
language, so many for ideas, so many for rhythm, and so on.
To avoid an irrelevant objection I admit at once that it is very
rarely—only, perhaps, in regard to the choice of mere amusements,
and not always then—that we do make our conduct depend
upon such purely hedonistic calculations, unmodified by other
considerations. But, if there seems to be something rather
tasteless and repellent about the analysis of these hedonistic
calculations for ourselves, we have constantly to make them for
others. A man who has determined to provide a school treat
for a number of children, and to devote thereto a definite sum of
money, aims, I suppose, at producing a maximum of pleasure;
though I have heard a Moral Philosopher of some distinction
gravely express a doubt as to whether the good will could ever
express itself by giving pleasure to others. The giver of such a
treat knows that, if he provides fireworks, he must cut down the
prizes for races, that if he gives the children a better class

of cake he will not be able to give them sweets too, and so on.
If it helped him (and it is quite possible that it would help
an old Schoolmaster) to express the value of the pleasure which
each shilling expended in different ways would buy by assigning
marks to each item and then totting them up, I do not see that
there would be anything essentially unmeaning or irrational
about his procedure.   No doubt in such cases our estimates are
exceedingly rough, but that does not make it actually impossible
to express our judgement in numbers.   It is far easier to say
that one flock of sheep is bigger than another than to say by
how many it is bigger, but that does not alter the fact that
if one flock is bigger than another, it is because it contains more
sheep.   Our estimate is none the less quantitative because it
is vague [1].

But I have not yet done justice to Prof. Mackenzie's strongest
argument.   He tells us that the proposition 'this is twice as
pleasant as that,' is as unmeaning as the judgement 'this is
twice as hot as that.'   Now it is to my mind undeniable that in
the case of sensible heat or of any other sensations which admit
of being arranged in a scale, quantitative measurement is essentially impossible.   But I contend that pleasure does not belong
to this category at all, and I will try to show why.   The reason
why it is impossible to express degrees of sensible heat quantitatively is that there is no equivalence between the difference between any two degrees of sensible heat and the difference between
any two other degrees [2].   Let the line $A\ Z$ represent the various
possible degrees of sensible heat ranging from a coldest A to
a hottest Z (of course I do not attempt to answer the physiological question whether there is a minimum or maximum of
possible sensible heat).

$A\ B\ C\ D\ E\ F\ .\ \ .\ \ .\ \ .\ \ .\ \ .\ \ .\ \ .\ \ .\ \ .\ \ .\ \ .\ \ .\ \ .\ \ Z.$

The reason why I cannot mark off this line into degrees to which
I might assign numbers like the numbers which express the de-

---

[1] Attempts have been made to show that such judgement *may* be only
qualitative (e. g. the unreflecting and unanalysed judgements of savages);
but they are not convincing.

[2] It may be that for many practical purposes it may conveniently be
assumed that the degree of sensible heat will correspond to the degree of
the physical stimulus.

grees of physical heat on a thermometer is that I cannot say that D is as much hotter than C as Y is hotter than X [1]. But in comparing pleasures I have no difficulty in doing this [2]. If I would as

---

[1] This position is admirably defended by M. Bergson in his *Essai sur les données immédiates de la Conscience* (4me éd., 1904), pp. 42 seq. I cannot, however, follow him in his attempt to show that there is no meaning even in saying that one psychical state is *more* intense than another—that psychical states differ *only* qualitatively, and that there is no such thing as intensive quantity. Is it possible to deny that we can arrange feelings of heat or sensations of blue in a scale entirely apart from the association of these sensations with their physical causes? M. Bergson demands what it is of which there is more in one such state than another. No doubt this 'something more' is something which cannot be isolated and experienced by itself: we do not, in experiencing a sensation of dark blue, experience a sensation of light blue + another distinct sensation. That would no doubt involve the fallacy of 'mental chemistry.' But in denying that a sensation of light blue has in it something in common with a sensation of dark blue, he seems to fall into the fallacy of psychological Atomism. He does well to insist on the uniqueness of all psychical experience. It is true that our concept of blue is not any particular sensation with all its particularity, and that each degree of a sensation has a quality of its own which cannot be expressed quantitatively: but, unless conceptual thought could detect something *common* in various experiences of oneself or others, it would not only be an inadequate representation of reality, but would have no resemblance or correspondence to it whatever: it would be a mere delusion to suppose that one mind could know anything whatever of another's mental state, or even of its own past states. Surely psychical states may resemble each other, and resemble in different degrees: M. Bergson would find it hard to refute Mr. Bradley's doctrine that resemblance = identity + difference. Still more unsuccessful does M. Bergson seem to me in his attempt to show that there is no quantity even in real 'duration' (duration as it is actually experienced). He is highly instructive in pointing out many mistakes which have originated in the transference to Time of the characteristics of Space: he is less convincing when he contends that Time and Space have nothing whatever in common: and that the application of the idea of Quantity to mental states arises not merely from a transference, but from an illegitimate transference of spatial ideas to the case of time. But this question is too large a one to be discussed here: suffice it to say that I admit it is only because we estimate a certain duration of a pleasure to be of equal value to a certain increase of intensity that we can intelligibly think of the interval between a degree of pleasure A and a degree B as being *as great as* that between B and C, and so speak of a greater or less sum of pleasure. Those who deny this ought to follow M. Bergson in denying that we can measure even the duration of pleasures.

[2] Of course from the merely hedonistic point of view.

soon have pleasure X raised to Y as pleasure C (lower down on the scale) raised to D, then I can intelligibly say that the difference between X and Y is equivalent to the difference between C and D. To take a concrete case : if a bank clerk is offered an addition of £50 a year to his salary or a diminution of his day's work by half an hour, and were, after consideration, conducted wholly on hedonistic grounds, to say ' I really don't care,' we should be entitled to say that the pleasure which he would obtain by the expenditure of £50—made up of course by an addition of the pleasure derived from so much better eating and drinking, so many more nights at the theatre, or from so many more books and a more enjoyable summer holiday—was the equivalent of the enjoyment which he would derive from 280 half-hours' leisure. It may be said that after all we have here only quantitative equality, not numerically defined inequality. But then it might be argued that the enjoyment of say 280 half-hours' leisure is made up of the pleasure derivable from the repetition 280 times of the enjoyment derivable from one half-hour's leisure. The amount of pleasure derived from an extra half-hour would of course in fact vary on different days ; but he would expect a certain average of enjoyment on each day : and it would therefore be quite intelligible to say that the pleasure derived from £50 of additional income would be exactly 280 times the pleasure derivable on an average from half an hour's additional leisure. Once again it must be admitted there seems something rather childish in such calculations which are never made in practice—any more than we attempt to say by how many grains one heap of sand is bigger than another. Nevertheless, I maintain that in such cases the judgement is quantitative and might (so long as we confine ourselves to quite simple cases) intelligibly be reduced to numbers [1]. The fact that we can have a very decided and well-grounded opinion that one total is larger than the other total, while any attempt to express

---

[1] It may be suggested that in such calculations our thought becomes more and more abstract, and so leaves out elements of which in the concrete we really take account. This to a certain extent I admit ; but then it must be remembered that all thought is abstract, and so leaves out elements of our actual perceptive experience.

our comparative estimate by numbers would be the wildest and most unprofitable guess-work, does not affect the question. The difficulties in the way of any exact mensuration of pleasures seem to me to be practical rather than theoretical. Some of these difficulties are too obvious to mention, but there is one which it may be well to notice, because it is, I believe, at the bottom of many people's objection to the whole idea of a sum of pleasures.

V

It is sometimes assumed that we cannot sum pleasure unless we suppose pleasure to be made up of a number of isolated pleasures, as though quantity were necessarily discrete. But space and time and everything that occupies space and everything that occupies time possess quantity, and yet space is not made up of points or time of moments. Pleasure, like time and space, is a continuum. In measuring things in space and time we have recourse to arbitrarily chosen units. And, in so far as we are taking account of the duration of pleasures merely, the units of time are applicable also to the case of pleasures ; there is nothing essentially unmeaning in applying these units to the measurement of pleasures, and saying that a pleasure that lasts an hour is four times as great as one that lasts only for fifteen minutes. But such calculations are of little use to us, because as a rule we cannot assume that the same feelings, emotions, occupations or what not will continue to produce pleasure at the same rate for long periods which they produce for short periods. What interests us for five minutes would bore us in an hour ; and conversely things which would interest us if we had an hour to give to them would awaken no interest in five minutes. There are books which we do not care to read for less than an hour and others which we should not care to read for so long. Duration, therefore, though an important element in the mensuration of pleasures, does not often practically help us much to an accurate measurement, even where we are dealing with the same external source of enjoyment: and, when we turn to the intensity of pleasures, the want of any satisfactory unit of pleasure is still more obvious. But the difficulty of saying how many units of pleasure there are in a given lot or sum of pleasure does not prevent our arriving at a mental estimate of its quantity and comparing it with the quantity of other pleasures—just as an ignorant savage engaging to carry burdens across the Sahara may have very clear ideas of magnitude and weight without any knowledge of inches or pounds.

That we make such comparisons and pronounce which of two stretches of consciousness is the more pleasant on the whole, seems to be admitted by some who still object to the term 'sum of pleasures.' Such persons seem to mean that our estimate of the total pleasure that we shall get from one course of action as compared with what we shall get from another is arrived at without any previous mental addition or summing of pleasures. That we do not, as a rule, consciously divide up our prospective pleasure into units, and then do a sum in arithmetic, I have already admitted. But how we can arrive at an estimate of the amount of a whole without putting together a number of parts is to me unintelligible. When we are deciding in which of two ways we shall spend a day or a month devoted to recreation, do we not go over in imagination the various hours of the day or the probable occupations of the various days in a month, as it will be spent in each way, and make a rapid estimate (picturable in imagination, though not actually reduced to terms of any pleasure-unit) of the amount of pleasure which we shall get into each portion of it (though no doubt the portions are not necessarily marked off from each other by exact time-measurements), and then think which total is the largest? If any one tells me he is not conscious of doing so, I should be quite prepared to admit that he really makes such calculations in a less conscious and deliberate way than I am at times conscious of doing myself. Indeed, I believe that the disputes which have arisen on this subject are very largely traceable to differences between the mental habits of individuals; but the idea of a quantity—a quantity occupying time—which does not consist of parts, and is not made up of the addition of parts, will remain to most minds an unintelligible paradox. If it consists of parts, the parts must surely all be looked at before we can pronounce upon the

pleasurableness of the whole. Whether we can take in the
whole quantity of pleasure by (as it were) a single mental
glance, or whether we mentally run over the parts in succession,
is a mere accidental difference of psychological habit. I am no
less summing the number of sheep in a flock when (as may be
done by an experienced shepherd) I pronounce how many they
are by a look at the whole flock together than when I have
laboriously to count them. Further, I am directly conscious
that in estimating the total of pleasure I take into account the
intensity of successive time-reaches as well as their duration ;
and this process can hardly be performed without thinking
of the successive portions of time. If the whole time is likely
to be equally pleasant, I may no doubt proceed at once to
multiply (so to speak) intensity by duration : if the successive
portions are likely to be very variable, I must surely think how
much pleasure or pain there will be in each before I can say
how much there will be in the whole. If such a process of
estimating a total quantity after estimating the constituent
quantities is not to be called addition and subtraction, I should
be grateful to any Logician who will tell me more precisely
what mental operation it is. At all events that is what I mean
by summing pleasures. If anybody means the same thing but
objects to the word, I can only say that I see no objection to
it except the fact that it has been used by Hedonists, and that
some people consider it necessary to object to everything which
has been said by Hedonists : but the question of the word is
of comparatively small importance. And if in the view of some
of my readers I have not succeeded in hitting the exact point of
their objection to the idea of a ' sum of pleasures,' I may be
allowed to add that I have never yet met two persons who
are exactly agreed as to the grounds of their anathema. And
with some Philosophers, as with some Theologians, the anathema
is the great thing : the grounds of it matter less.

One more of these objections may, however, demand a
moment's notice. For some minds the objection to the notion
of a sum of pleasures seems based upon the alleged impossibility
of adding one man's pleasure to another's. It appears to be
denied that two people's pleasure is *more* than the like pleasure

of one person. Of course it may be possible to find senses in which this might be the case. In the mind of those who make the objection, the summing of the pleasure of different persons seems to carry with it some suggestion that pleasure is a thing that can be actually separated from the consciousness of the person enjoying it, divided into lots, and handed about from one person to another. If any one has fallen into such a confusion, I venture to submit that it is the people who object to the mental addition of different people's pleasure, and not the people who contend for its possibility. The objection seems, in fact, to be little more than a question of words. The question whether two people's pleasure is not twice the like pleasure in one person's consciousness must depend on the purpose for which the addition is to be used. The meaning which I attach to the assertion is that I regard a certain amount of pleasure in two persons as twice as important as the same amount in one ; and *ceteris paribus* I regard it as a duty to promote more pleasure rather than less pleasure. If this last proposition is to be denied, we have arrived at an ultimate difference of ethical ideal : if it be admitted, I do not see how duty is to be fulfilled without mentally multiplying the amount of pleasure by the number of persons enjoying that pleasure or (to avoid cavil) enjoying a like amount of pleasure. If this is admitted, where is the objection to the convenient phrase 'a sum of pleasure'?

VI

So far I have been dealing with the comparison of pleasures which are the same in kind—that is, as I understand it, in which the greater or less pleasurableness of the two pleasures is the only ground upon which we base our judgement as to their comparative preferability. Is the case altered when one pleasure is higher than another? It is impossible to answer the question without attempting to define what we mean by saying that one pleasure is higher than another. I have already endeavoured to show that, when we pronounce one pleasure higher than another, we mean that, though both of them are pleasant—it may be equally pleasant—the one is more valuable than the other for some other reason than its pleasantness. What I prefer is really

the superior moral or intellectual quality of the pleasant psychical
state, not its superior pleasantness. If I compare them simply
as pleasures, I make abstraction of all qualities in them except
their pleasantness. And pleasure in the strict sense of the
word—the abstract quality of pleasantness—can differ from
pleasure only in quantity, extensive or intensive. Hence it
appears that, strictly speaking, there is no difference in quality
between pleasures considered simply as such, though there may
be between pleasures in the popular sense of the word, i. e. there
may be difference in intrinsic value between two states of consciousness equally pleasant. The distinction would be conveniently expressed by saying: 'Pleasure can be estimated only
quantitatively, but pleasures may differ in kind'; or, 'Pleasures
differ in kind, but not *qua* pleasures.' Some Philosophers who
are not Hedonists may be prepared to deny that any distinction
can be made between the value which things have as pleasure
and the value which they have on other grounds, and to contend
that our ethical judgement always refers simply to the ultimate
value of a certain state of consciousness. Such a contention
(to which I shall revert hereafter) would seem either (1) to bring
back Hedonism under another name, or (2) to get rid of the idea
of pleasure altogether. I am quite clear that in my own mind
I make a distinction between the pleasantness of things and their
value. As I understand the word 'pleasure,' the less pleasant of
two states of consciousness sometimes presents itself to me as the
more valuable [1].

When it is said (as it is by some, though I cannot point to
any published expression of that view) that pleasures differ
in kind *qua* pleasures, I do not know what can be meant by the
doctrine unless it be the undoubted and important fact that
the pleasurableness of a total state of mind is inseparably bound
up with the value that it has on other grounds. It is not a mere
accident that various states of mind to which we attribute higher
value than other states of mind on account of their intrinsic
worth do happen to be also pleasant. When I say that the contemplation of beauty seems to be good as well as pleasant, while
the sensation derived from eating turtle-soup seems to me

[1] See below, p. 50 seq.

pleasant but to possess a very low degree of goodness or ultimate
value, I do not first form an estimate of the value which looking
at the beautiful picture would have if it were not pleasant, and
then add to it the additional value which it derives from being
also pleasant. The pleasantness of the aesthetic gratification
is an essential part of my conception of it. I do not know what
beauty would be like if it were not a source of pleasure, or
whether I should attribute any value to it at all if it were not
essentially pleasant ; and yet I am conscious that the pleasantness
is not the sole source or measure of the value that I attach to it.
All this seems to me perfectly true ; and it goes to show that comparison between very heterogeneous pleasures simply in respect
of their pleasantness is a very difficult and delicate proceeding.
Fortunately it is for the most part useless and unnecessary, but
not wholly so. It is often exceedingly difficult to say how much
of the value we attribute to some occupation springs from its
pleasantness, and how much from our sense of the value which
it has on other grounds ; and yet that is what we must do when
we compare a higher and a lower pleasure simply as pleasures.
And such comparisons, though difficult, can be made. I may
say to myself in a certain mood : 'I should get more pleasure
from going to this farce than I should from going to that
tragedy'; and yet I may say to myself : 'The tragedy is the
nobler and higher pleasure ; therefore to the tragedy I will go.'
On the other hand, if I were thinking only of amusement, and
felt that in the circumstances it was right that I should think of
pure amusement rather than of culture and aesthetic gratification,
I might say : 'Though it is the lower pleasure, I will choose
it.' I do not think it can be denied that we do not unfrequently
go through such a process—sometimes for ourselves, more often
in choosing pleasures for others. We should prefer to take
a child to this elevating and aesthetic performance rather than to
that somewhat vulgar pantomime, provided he will get a fair
amount, though it may be a less amount, of pure amusement out
of the former. But will he ? We want to satisfy ourselves of
this before we decide against the pantomime. Life is full of such
problems, and however much we may insist on the difficulties of
such comparisons, they have to be made and are made.

2

It is thus possible, though it is difficult, to compare heterogeneous pleasures simply in point of pleasantness. It is unnecessary to insist further on the difficulty or to analyse its causes more elaborately. But one very important practical consideration may be pointed out. It is difficult and frequently undesirable to compare very heterogeneous alternative pleasures simply from the point of view of their quantitative intensity, because to do so is to put oneself into a state of mind unfavourable to a due appreciation of the higher kind of pleasure even as pleasure. I may enjoy (say) a sermon by a great preacher and a light but amusing novel. The pleasures are very different pleasures; but, as both are pleasures, it must, I should contend, be possible to say which is the greater pleasure when there is any very considerable difference in the pleasantness. I am certainly conscious that I have derived more pleasure from some sermons than from some novels, and equally so that I have derived more pleasure from some novelists than from some preachers. But, if I propose to make the question whether I will go to church and hear the preacher or stay at home and read such and such a novel turn wholly on the question which will be most pleasant, if I deliberately put out of sight all the considerations other than love of pleasure which may draw me to the preacher's feet, I should be putting myself into a state of mind in which I should be very likely greatly to underestimate the amount of pleasure which I really should get, were I to throw aside the book and go to church. Nay, more, supposing me to decide for church on these grounds, and supposing this voluntarily adopted mood to continue, I should be very likely to miss the pleasure; for the pleasure in this case arises largely from the gratification of other desires than the desire for pleasure or for such kinds of pleasure as are common to the preacher and the novelist. These desires will *ex. hypothesi* be in a state of repression, whereas I shall have stimulated my appetite for those pleasures which the novel would supply in greater abundance than the sermon. Considerations like these may show the inadvisability of frequently permitting ourselves to make these purely hedonistic comparisons between very heterogeneous sources of enjoyment, but they do not disprove the fact that the comparison can be, and in some cases must be, made.

The higher pleasure is, I have suggested, a pleasure to which we attribute value on other grounds than its mere pleasantness. The problem of the commensurability of pleasures has led us up to the more difficult and, ethically speaking, more important problem of the commensurability of goods. I have tried to show that it is possible to compare pleasures—no matter how heterogeneous—and to say which is pleasantest. But is it possible to compare heterogeneous *goods*—say, Virtue, Culture, and pleasure —and say which is *best*. It is possible, though it is not always right, to aim at a greatest attainable quantum of pleasure : is it possible to aim at the production of a greatest quantum of good? That such is a possible aim certainly seems to be implied by those who make the greatest good of society the criterion of conduct (and there are few Moralists of any school who have not used some such language), and yet refuse to interpret 'good' in the hedonistic sense. With this larger problem we shall be occupied in the following chapter.

But there is one last objection to the idea of a 'sum of pleasures' with which I will briefly deal before dismissing the subject. It is admitted by some (though once more I have to deal with a class of opponents whose modesty prevents them putting their views into a form in which they can be criticized) that we do 'prefer one lot of pleasures to another'; but it is said that we are not summing pleasures because the statement 'this amount of pleasure is greater than that' is merely a statement of our preference. We do not prefer the one alternative to the other because it contains more pleasure ; it may be said to give more pleasure simply because we prefer it.

I reply : (1) My preference is not the same thing as my judgement that I shall get or have got more pleasure out of one set of experiences than out of another ; for, though the expectation of pleasure may be the ground of my preference, I may make my preference turn on other grounds and prefer one course of action to another in spite of a clear judgement that it will yield less pleasure.

(2) My preference lies in the present, whereas the pleasure

lies in the past or the future. The present judgement is determined
by the past or the anticipated experience, not *vice versa*. My
preference for course *A* is based on my judgement that I shall
get more pleasure from it, but it is not the same thing as that
judgement. For I may prefer course *A* under the expectation
that I shall get more pleasure from it than from course *B*, and
find by bitter experience that I do not get the pleasure. The
amount of pleasure which I shall actually get from an act of
choice is not created by the act of choice, and is quite independent
of my volition. It seems strange to find anti-hedonist and
anti-sensationalist Philosophers confusing the act of choice with
the judgement that the object chosen will be pleasant. If it be
admitted that the future pleasure in any case or to any degree
influences our choice, we must make such judgements before we
choose ; and since any duration of pleasure is made up of
successive smaller durations, it is impossible to deny that the
judgement as to its pleasurableness, and *pro tanto* its preferability,
must depend upon our judgement as to the pleasurableness of
these separate durations. How it is possible to be influenced by
these many distinct judgements without putting them together,
and how it is possible to put quantities together without a
' calculus,' the writers whom I have criticized have never
succeeded in explaining.

CHAPTER II

THE COMMENSURABILITY OF ALL VALUES

I

In the last chapter I have endeavoured to defend the possibility of a hedonistic calculus. I maintained that it is psychologically possible to compare different lots of pleasure and to say which, on the whole, duration and intensity being both taken into account, is the greatest. If that be admitted, the fashioning of life in such a way as to attain either for oneself or for Society a greatest quantum of pleasure becomes a possible and intelligible ideal. It is possible to aim consistently at doing what will promote the greatest pleasure on the whole. But we have already seen reason to reject such a conception of the ethical end. The argument against Hedonism need not be repeated. Suffice it once more to remind the reader that, while I do regard pleasure as *a* good, I do not regard it as *the* good. It seems to me perfectly clear that the moral consciousness does pronounce some goods to be higher, or intrinsically more valuable than others; and that at the head of these goods comes Virtue, while many other things — intellectual cultivation and intellectual activity, aesthetic cultivation, emotion of various kinds — are also good and of more intrinsic value than mere pleasure. It is true that pleasure is an element in every state of consciousness to which we can assign ultimate value. I can attach no meaning whatever to the proposition, 'I find this picture supremely beautiful, and yet it gives me no pleasure to look at it.' Even with regard to Virtue, it is difficult to answer the question whether I should judge Virtue to possess value, if it gave me no sort of pleasure or satisfaction. The belief in *a priori* judgements of value must not be interpreted to mean that we can see what in detail is good for human beings apart from the actual psychical and emotional constitution of human nature. If a being could exist (the very supposition doubtless involves an absurd abstraction) capable of appreciating the idea of duty, capable of willing that duty, and yet for ever by the very constitution of his nature incapable of deriving the smallest amount of pleasure or satisfaction from the performance of duty by himself or another, I do not know that I should attach any meaning to the assertion ' Virtue to such a being or in such a being is a good.'   Another person might no doubt regard such a being's Virtue as a good, but then he would judge also that the other person ought to derive pleasure or satisfaction from his goodness : he would hold that it was a good inasmuch as it ought to exist, but he would hardly think that the man himself had attained even that good which consists in being truly virtuous.   Pleasure is an element in everything to which we attach value : and yet we do not attach value to consciousness *in proportion to* its pleasantness : pleasures differ in kind or quality.   And as I endeavoured to show in the last chapter, this amounts to the assertion that something else in consciousness possesses value besides its pleasantness : there are other goods besides pleasure.   On what principle then are we to choose between these different kinds of good ?   It is to my mind a perfectly clear deliverance of the moral consciousness, that no action can be right except in so far as it tends to produce a good, and that, when we have to choose between goods, it is always right to choose the greater good.   Such a doctrine implies that goods of all kinds can be compared, that we can place goods of all kinds on a single scale, and assign to each its value relatively to the rest.   The defence of this assumption is the object of the present chapter.

In the first place I must begin by distinguishing between two different senses in which it may be asserted that goods of different kinds are commensurable.   It may mean that a certain amount of one good can be regarded as a sufficient and satisfactory substitute for the other, so that, however much superior Virtue may be to Culture, a sufficient amount of Culture could be regarded as an entirely satisfactory compensation for the absence of all Virtue : that, given enough sensual pleasure, the absence of either Virtue or Culture would cease to be an object of regret. If this were the only possible meaning of the commensurability of heterogeneous goods, I should fully sympathize with the assertion that the value of the higher goods (particularly of Virtue) is incommensurable with that of anything else. But that is not the only possible meaning of our assertion. It may mean only that, when we have to choose between a higher and a lower good—*when we cannot have both*—we can compare them, and pronounce that one possesses more value than the other.

And this is the only possible interpretation of the formula which is open to those who hold that no one of the competing goods, not even Virtue, is by itself *the* good. The true good of a human life does not consist either in Virtue only, or in knowledge only, or in pleasure only. I altogether decline to pronounce εὐδαίμων, or in the highest possible degree 'blessed,' a man who has enjoyed twenty years of unbroken Virtue in a loathsome dungeon, cut off from books or human society, and afflicted by perpetual toothache or a succession of other tortures. Such a man has not attained the true end of his being. He may be much more blessed than the successful sinner, but his lot cannot be pronounced a wholly desirable one; he is blessed for his goodness, but he is not altogether blessed. Equally little would any abundance and variety of sensual pleasures make me attach high value to the life of a stupid sensualist; nor will any amount of refinement or intellectual enjoyment induce me to regard as supremely desirable the life of a Borgia or even a Goethe. No amount of one kind of good can compensate for the absence or deficiency of the other. But when circumstances make it impossible for me to secure for myself or for others all these kinds of good, then I can and must decide which of them I regard as best worth having; and that implies that *for the purpose of choosing between them* they are commensurable.

It is quite true, as will be indignantly protested in some quarters, that each of these 'goods' taken by itself is an abstraction. No one of them can exist wholly without the other, or at least without the opposite of the other. Pleasure cannot exist—at least for a human being—without some kind or measure of knowledge or intellectual activity. Knowledge can hardly be supposed ever to be accompanied by no kind or sort of pleasure, though the pleasure may in some cases be greatly outweighed by attendant pains.

And, if you stripped off from a human being all activity of thought (even that implied in the most mechanical occupation or the most humdrum routine of duty), and all feeling of satisfaction in one thing rather than another, it would be difficult to see wherein the Virtue of such a being could consist. It is not upon each one of these things taken by itself that we pronounce our judgements of value, but upon each of them taken as an element in a whole [1]. Our ideal of human life is not a certain amount of the higher goods mechanically added on to a certain amount of lower goods, but a connected whole in which each is made different by its connexion with the others. It is not Virtue + knowledge + pleasure that we desire for a man—a waking day, for instance, in which seven hours are devoted to Virtue, six to knowledge, and four to pleasure—but that he may be virtuous and find pleasure in his virtuous activities; that he may study and derive pleasure from his studies; that he may enjoy the pleasures of eating and drinking, but enjoy them in such a manner and degree as may be conducive to the development of his higher nature, and consistent with the highest good of his fellows. But, when through unfavourable circumstances this ideal is not realizable, we can surely distinguish between the various elements in a human life and form a judgement as to which of them seems to be more important—a large amount of this, or a small amount of that. If we were not thus

---

[1] It is equally true that we could not pronounce on their value as elements in a whole unless we found a value at least in some one of them taken separately, just as we could not find a picture beautiful unless blue, red, and green were found beautiful in themselves, though the aesthetic value of the colours may be enormously enhanced or (in the case of unpleasing contrast) diminished by the combination. Just so pleasure is a good taken by itself, but it may cease to be so if by its excess it spoils the true proportion of higher and lower goods in our life. Mr. Moore's remark that the value of two goods in combination may be very different from the combined value of each taken separately (*Principia Ethica*, p. 214) is a new and striking way of stating a very old truth.

capable of distinguishing between various elements in human life [1], all thinking or talking about the moral ideal, or indeed about practical aims or objects of any kind, would be estopped. And if, when we have distinguished them, we are not to say which of them is best and to act upon our answer, there is an end to the possibility of any ethical system which admits that the morality of an action depends upon its consequences. The latter admission is now generally made by the most anti-hedonistic writers. There is a general consensus that Ethics must be ' teleological,' though not hedonistic. And this admission seems inevitably to carry with it the further concession that all values must be, in the sense defined, commensurable. If the morality of an act depends upon the value of all its consequences taken together, we must be able to say which of two sets of consequences possesses the more value; and, if different kinds of consequence are to have any weight assigned to them, we must be able to attribute more or less weight to each of them. To deny this seems to amount to the denial that there is any one fixed and consistent meaning in the word ' value ' or ' worth ' or ' good,' and to make impossible any system of Ethics which is based upon this conception.

II

The only way of escaping the admission that different kinds of good are commensurable would be to assert that it is always right to choose the highest. Now (if we assume that Virtue is the highest of goods) this contention involves all the difficulties of the formalistic Ethics (to use Prof. Paulsen's term) of Kant and his stricter disciples. If nothing in the world possesses value except the good will, we cut ourselves off from the possibility of assigning a rational ground for regarding one volition as better than another. To repeat once more the stock criticism,

---

[1] It is true, of course, as has been admitted above, that we never get one element *wholly* apart from the other. The greediest *bon-vivant*, with his attention wholly concentrated on his food, is thinking of something, and the student absorbed in his books may be enjoying the carnal pleasure of sitting in a comfortable chair, but we may make abstraction of these things sufficiently to ask ' Which is best-- eating or study ? '

a will that wills nothing but itself has no content. The term 'right' is meaningless except in reference to the good. The good will may possess infinitely more value than any consequence that it wills; but, unless that consequence be good, the will cannot be good either. Charity is no doubt better than the eating of food by hungry persons, but unless that eating be good, there is no reason for applying the word 'right' or 'good' to the charitable act. To deny that anything possesses value but a good will (which Kant after all did not do) is to deny that such a thing as a good will is possible. The attempt may, indeed, be made to escape the force of this criticism by pleading that it is only where some lower good is incompatible with the higher that it must be treated as possessing no value at all. But, in the first place, it seems difficult to escape the admission that, even when we assign some value to the lower and a value to the higher which always overweighs any conceivable amount of the former, we are in a sense treating them as commensurable: we do in a sense measure the value of the one against the other, even when we pronounce that their values are related as finite quantities are related to infinity. But the question arises whether we do always pronounce that the smallest quantity of the higher is worth more than the largest quantity of the lower. And here of course the appeal can only be to the actual moral judgements of mankind.

So long as I confine myself to my own Virtue, it seems clear that it can never be right for me to prefer any quantity of a lower good to the doing of my own duty. And if goodness, Morality, a rightly directed will, be the thing of highest value in the world, I shall always be choosing the greatest good for myself by doing my duty. If in any case it is right or reasonable for me to choose a lower good rather than a higher one, then *eo ipso* I shall not be violating my duty by pursuing it, and therefore I shall not be postponing my own Morality to anything which is not Morality. The principle that all values are commensurable can never in practice bring the morality of any individual into competition with any other good, so long as his own voluntary acts alone are concerned. It can never compel us to say, 'For an adequate quantity of some other good it is reasonable for me to commit a sin.' So much results from a mere analysis of the idea of duty.

But can we say that there are no cases in which we have, in judging of the effect of our conduct upon others, to institute comparisons between the intrinsic worth of goodness and the intrinsic worth of other and lower goods—knowledge, culture, bodily pleasure, immunity from pain? Can we say that it is always right to regard the very smallest amount of moral good— in that sense of moral good in which one man's goodness may be increased and diminished by the act of another—as preferable to the utmost conceivable quantity of any lower good? It seems to me that to maintain that such is always our duty would involve an austerity or rigorism by which few would even pretend to guide their judgements of conduct outside the pages of an ethical treatise. Take the case contemplated by Cardinal Newman. Cardinal Newman, in defending himself against the charge of depreciating Veracity because lying is only, according to Roman Catholic Moral Theology, a venial sin, has laid it down that it would be better for millions of the human race to expire in extremest agony than for a single human soul to be guilty of the slightest venial sin. Mr. Lecky has declined to endorse this tremendous judgement [1]. And, I believe, few who in the least realize the meaning of the words which they are using would do so either. And what does this mean but that we judge that a little Morality (so far as Morality may be the result of another's conduct) possesses less value than an immense quantity of pleasure or the prevention of a vast amount of pain—that it is from the point of view of Reason more important that so many thousand people should not suffer torments than that one man should not commit a small sin?

It will perhaps be objected that such an alternative could never be presented; but such a contention would, it seems to me, betray an extraordinary blindness to some of the most difficult practical problems with which we are confronted every day of our lives. I have a limited sum of money to spend on charity. I believe that spiritual good can be promoted by efficient Curates, that intellectual good can be promoted by education, and that

[1] *Hist. of European Morals* (1877), I, p. 111.

pain can be saved by hospitals. Shall I give it to an Additional Curates Society, or to education, or to a hospital? I have a son who wishes to enter the Civil Service of India. Shall I send him to a 'crammer's,' which (in his particular case) may give him the best chance of getting in, or to a Public School and University, which will be best for his moral and intellectual well-being? A problem more exactly resembling the hypothetical case propounded by Newman arises when some great material benefit can only be obtained by the bribery of an official. Few people would hesitate to bribe a Chinese Mandarin to be unfaithful to his superiors, a traitor to his country, disloyal very possibly to his own highest ideal (which may enjoin relentless hostility to foreigners) in order to set free a score or so of Europeans who would otherwise be exposed to torture and death. By such an act a man would distinctly be causing a small amount of moral evil in order to produce a large amount of hedonistic good.

Such an admission could only be escaped if we were to adopt the extravagant position sometimes taken up by extreme Libertarians—the position that the virtue of one man can never be increased or diminished by the action of another. The admission that in some cases it is right to prefer a larger amount of lower good to a smaller amount of a higher in no way involves, be it observed, the principle 'to do a great right do a little wrong.' The individual must himself always do right : the moral evil that he causes is not even a little wrong in him, if (as the view I am defending maintains) it is right for him to cause in another that little moral evil rather than be the cause of an immense amount of undeserved physical suffering. And I fail to see how moral judgements which would in practice be assented to and acted upon by the holiest of mankind can be explained or justified upon any other view.

There are, I must freely admit, very many more cases in which I am certain that the accepted morality of our time and country implies such a preference of much lower to a little higher good than there are cases in which I am certain that such a preference is really justifiable. We compel large masses of young men to remain unmarried, well knowing the moral consequences which are likely to ensue from such a state of things, because we hold that the country must be defended and that it would be too expensive to allow all soldiers to marry. We allow the children of the working classes to be withdrawn from school at the age of twelve or thirteen, though no one doubts that they would benefit morally and intellectually by staying till sixteen, because we think it would be too great a strain upon the resources of the country and of the individual parents—here, now, for the moment, under existing social and economic conditions—to compel them to keep their children at school any longer. In other words, we hold the enjoyment of luxuries by rich taxpayers, of Culture by the educated, of comforts by poor taxpayers, of the necessaries of life by poor parents to be of more intrinsic importance than the higher moral and intellectual advancement of the children. I need not pursue such illustrations further. There is, in fact, no single expenditure of money—public or private—upon material enjoyment which goes beyond the bare necessaries of life which can justify itself upon the theory that it is never right to promote lower good when we could promote ever so little of some higher good [1].

It is quite true, and it is important to remember, that the opposition between higher and lower good is seldom so absolute as has been here assumed. It is seldom, in such practical problems, that all the higher good is on one side and all the lower good on the other. When we insist that, given certain circumstances, the claims of national defence must take precedence of education, and even of certain branches of personal Morality (in so far as Morality can be promoted or hindered by external influences), we may plead that we attach importance to national defence, not only in the interests of commerce and material well-being, but in the interests of national independence, national character, and international Morality. When we refuse

---

[1] 'If we ask whether I ought always to choose to slightly elevate another person's ideals, at the cost of great suffering to him, or if I ought always to choose to slightly elevate my own ideals, at the cost of great suffering to some one else, it becomes clear that happiness and development are ethically commensurable, and that we have no right to treat a loss of either as ethically indifferent' (McTaggart, *Studies in Hegelian Cosmology*, p. 122). It will be seen from what follows (p. 47) that it is only in a very restricted sense that I should admit that the second possibility can ever arise.

to burden poor parents beyond a certain point for the education of their children, it may be suggested that further pressure would involve the semi-starvation of the children, which would not be ultimately in the interests of their moral and intellectual Well-being. And, more generally, we may contend that a certain indulgence of the lower appetites and desires of human nature—an indulgence going considerably beyond the paramount requirements of health—is in average men more conducive to moral Well-being than a semi-compulsory asceticism with the inevitable reaction which such asceticism is apt to provoke. All this is very true; but still we cannot, as it seems to me, avoid the admission that in some cases the balance of moral good is on one side, and that of lower good on the other. Give that bribe, and the moral character of your Mandarin will have taken a downward turn: withhold it and twenty European men, women, and children will die in torture and dishonour. It is only a fanatic to whom the small deterioration of one Mandarin, *ex hypothesi* not a character of the highest order, will seem a more valuable end than the saving of twenty European lives with all their possibilities of happiness. It may be said that there are possibilities of goodness also. Then let us suppose that death is unavoidable, and that it is only a question of torture. No doubt the prevention of injustice may have good moral effects. But all these are vague possibilities as contrasted with the certain moral evil of corrupting the Mandarin with all the incidental moral effects which that corruption may carry with it. Our moral judgement is not really determined by these speculative possibilities. We really think it more important to spare so much suffering than to avoid the slight deterioration of one Mandarin's character.

For the agent himself it can never, we have admitted, be right to prefer his own lower to his own higher good, for the simple reason that to do right is always his own highest good. And yet, even in considering one's own moral good, there may be cases in which it may be right, just in order to do one's duty, to adopt a course of action which may be likely on the whole to have an injurious effect on one's own character, in that sense of character in which a man is made better or worse by influences not under the immediate control of his own will. It may sometimes be right for a man to adopt a profession which in the long run may have a lowering effect upon his ideals and upon his conduct, in preference to one which would be likely to have a more elevating influence; or in innumerable other ways to face temptations which he does not know that he will always be able to resist rather than to purchase his own moral purity at the cost of other people's Well-being. Our own future Well-being, in so far as it lies beyond our own immediate control, is in the same position as other people's moral Well-being—to be weighed against the other kinds of good, and assigned a value which, though enormously transcending that of lower goods, cannot be held to be absolutely incommensurable with them. But still, this admission does not involve any abandonment of our previous contention—that it can never be right for a man to do an immediately wrong act for the sake of any other advantage to himself or others. By choosing the greater good, he has done his duty (even in choosing a course which may in the long run react in some ways unfavourably upon his own character), and by doing his duty he has chosen the greatest good for himself. He would have become a worse man by taking the opposite course. Paradox as it may seem, he would have become a less moral man on the whole by attaching too high a value to his own Morality. In reality he is only preferring one element in his own moral good to another—a higher element to a lower—since the preference of the greatest good is itself the highest Morality.

III

So far, we have been comparing the value of Morality or character with that of all other goods. When we come to the weighing of higher goods other than the highest—of intellectual and aesthetic goods for instance—against the lower, there will be perhaps less objection to admit that a small amount of the higher may sometimes have to give way to a large amount of the lower. At all events the task of showing that this is the principle upon which ordinary good men act is here an easy one. Some of the instances already given will serve to illustrate this

case also—the sacrifice of education to health and comfort, the
spending of national money upon armies and guns instead of
Universities, libraries, and scientific expeditions, the cutting
down of the British Museum grant in the interest of the South
African War.   However much we may regret and condemn the
indifference which our own Parliaments and Governments (more
than any other Parliaments and Governments in the civilized
world) show to such intellectual objects, few of us would be
prepared to push the expenditure of public moneys upon them
to a point which would on the material side lower the general
standard of comfort to the level of bare health and subsistence.
And here there will be little scruple in admitting that it is not
merely in conduct affecting others but in conduct affecting
primarily only ourselves that we act, and feel that we do right
in acting, upon the principle that the quantity as well as the
quality of various heterogeneous goods must be taken into
account in choosing between them.   We feel that Art is higher
than comfort and good eating, but we do not feel bound to
lower our standard of comfort below a certain point in order to
buy books and pictures.   We recognize that study is intrinsically more valuable than ordinary conversation, but we feel
justified in spending on the enjoyment of society a considerable
amount of time which might be spent upon study.   We acknowledge the claim of Culture, but we do not feel bound to pursue
Culture when it would interfere beyond a certain point with
health and comfort and the ordinary enjoyment of life—an
enjoyment consisting in the following out of natural tastes and
inclinations which, however harmless, we cannot upon reflection
pronounce to have a very high intrinsic value.   We may admit
on reflection that we do not care for and pursue our own
intellectual improvement as much as we ought to do; but in our
most serious moments of self-examination we hold that it is
sometimes lawful to spend half an hour upon some lower amusement without proving that the giving up of that amusement
would injuriously affect our health or cause some other evil
than the mere loss of the amusement.   In such cases there is,
indeed, no great disproportion between the amount of the higher
and of the lower goods.   If we think of cases where the dis-

proportion would be very great, the verdict of the practical Reason will be still more unhesitating.   If we had to weigh the sufferings of some thousand tortured rabbits against the purely intellectual gain of some theoretically unimportant and practically unfruitful piece of scientific knowledge[1], or a woman's heart broken and her life wrecked against the scientific or aesthetic advantage to a Philosopher or a Novelist in being enabled the better to analyse the passion of love—in cases like these there will be little doubt what the verdict will be on the part of any person of common humanity not sophisticated by the gospel of Self-realization.

All these judgements then imply that we do actually weigh very heterogeneous goods against one another, and decide which possesses most value, and in making that estimate we do take into consideration the amount of the two kinds of good as well as the quality.   We do hold that a little of some higher good is too dearly bought by a great sacrifice of some lower good, and, on the other hand, that a very small quantity of one good is sometimes worth a great deal of another.   If a facetious opponent forthwith challenges us to produce a graduated table of goods, a tariff by reference to which we may at once say how much headache ought to outweigh the Culture implied in the reading of a Shakespearean play or the like, the answer is the one which the opponent will probably urge against the whole scheme— that there are no means of measuring with exactitude such things as Culture or Charity, and, again, that the value of a 'good' is relative to many circumstances.   The reading of a play of Shakespeare may be an intellectual revolution—the beginning of a new intellectual and (it may be) moral life to one man, while to another it will be of less value than the same number of pages of Miss Marie Corelli.   But, as I have so often had occasion to point out, the impossibility of reducing to numerical precision judgements of this kind does not imply that the judgements are not made, or that they are not quantitative.   It is only in quite recent times that mechanical methods have been invented for instituting exact comparisons between lights of

---

[1] I have nothing to say against Vivisection duly regulated in the interests of Humanity.

2 6

different strength[1]: yet, long before such methods were invented, men judged that one light was stronger — much stronger, moderately stronger, or a little stronger—than another light, and acted on their judgements. A little ingenuity might perhaps find cases in which we could with some meaning say that one higher good possessed twice the intrinsic value possessed by another. But I have admitted that even in comparing pleasures, and pleasures of the same order, such exact measurements are rarely possible and never of use. It is a characteristic of these higher goods that their value, or rather the value of goods springing from the same objective source, varies with circumstances more even than is the case with simple physical pleasures and pains. And therefore here the attempt to find cases in which such a mensuration might have a meaning is too far removed from anything which actually takes place in our practical life to be worth attempting, even by way of playfully illustrating the quantitative character of these judgements.

IV

There is one really formidable objection to the position taken up in this and the last chapter which I must attempt briefly to meet. Among those who strongly hold that all goods can be compared, that 'value' must always have the same meaning, and that the true way of deciding between two alternative courses of action is to ask, 'By doing which shall I produce good of most value?' there are some who will object to the distinction which has here been drawn between pleasure-value and value of a higher kind. It has been assumed that we sometimes say, 'This course will produce the most pleasure, but the pleasure is not sufficient to outweigh the evil of another kind which is involved in it: the course which produces least pleasure will produce most good.' But it may be urged that if we are really to be faithful to our doctrine that all values are comparable, we must refuse to recognize more than one kind of value: and that if we reject the doctrine that pleasure is the only thing that has value, we cannot really compare states of con-

---

[1] Even here the comparison is only made by the aid of an assumption which perhaps cannot be strictly defended. Cf. above, p. 25.

sciousness as pleasures, and then override that judgement by a second valuation of them as goods. 'The ideal or rational standard of comparison,' it may be urged, ' is the only one.   Whether it is pleasure or Culture or Morality that we are comparing, all that we can do is to say which appears to us to be worth most.' I have some sympathy with the spirit in which this objection is made.   For I freely confess that I find it impossible either to get hold of a satisfactory definition of pleasure or to distinguish in any sharp or scientific way between pleasure-value and that higher kind of value which, though doubtless normally accompanied by more or less pleasure, is not (for the developed moral consciousness) measured in terms of pleasure.   It would be easy to show how wildly wide of the mark are most of the definitions of pleasure which have been put forth by eminent authorities. After each of them one exclaims, ' Well, whatever I mean by pleasure, it is certainly not that.'   And yet I cannot readily bring myself to believe that pleasure is simply a *vox nihili*; for nothing less than that would be the logical consequence of saying, ' Pleasure is neither identical with value nor one of the things which possess value : we can compare values, but we cannot compare pleasures.'   It might be possible for an ascetic to say, ' I know what pleasure is, but it has no value' : but those who hold the view which I am criticizing are not ascetics.   They do attribute value to pleasant things.   The value of some things is not measured by their pleasantness, but the value of other things surely does cease to exist when they cease to be pleasant. We must, therefore, be able to estimate their pleasantness before we can pronounce upon their value, and compare that value with the value of things which do not owe their value entirely to their pleasantness.   It has been fully and frankly admitted that pleasure is an abstraction, that it is one particular aspect of consciousness ; but it is not the only one.   Now I do not think it possible to define what this aspect is sufficiently to mark it off with absolute precision from those other aspects which we have in view in pronouncing upon the absolute or ultimate value of some state of consciousness.   And yet it is certain that it does represent one of the aspects under which we are practically in the habit of considering and valuing such states.

I tremble at the thought of putting forth a new definition of pleasure, and protest that what follows is not intended as such : but I venture to suggest that, when we try to estimate the value of a state of consciousness as pleasure, we are thinking of its value simply as immediate feeling, abstracting as much as possible from all reference to the other parts of our nature. Our appreciation of the value of duty does not depend *merely* upon the immediate feeling that accompanies the doing of duty : to hold that is the ' moral sense ' view of the matter which (as Hume has shown once for all), when fully thought out, ends in Hedonism. It depends upon our appreciation of the relation between this present consciousness of ours and our own past and future, upon our consciousness of our relation as persons to other persons, upon the presence of all sorts of desires and aspirations which go beyond the moment—beyond even our own consciousness at all. The same may be applied in a modified degree to the value which we find in intellectual or aesthetic cultivation. All these things are put aside when we estimate our consciousness simply as present feeling. This is most clearly seen in the case of those conscious states which have no value except what they possess simply as so much pleasant feeling. If we found that the drinking of a certain liquid not required for purposes of health was not satisfactory simply in and for itself, we should pronounce it to have no value at all. It would be easy and tempting to essay a definition of pleasure by making it consist in the satisfaction of our lower as distinct from the satisfaction of our higher desires. But this will not express what we really mean by pleasure. For pleasure is clearly something which the lower sources of satisfaction have in common with the higher. When we compare the glow of satisfaction which *sometimes* attends a conquest over temptation, we feel at once that the resulting feeling has something in common with the state of mind into which we are put on other occasions by a cup of tea.

It is this something which we seek to indicate by the term pleasure. And yet I do not feel that the value of that good will of ours is wholly dependent upon the satisfactoriness of the present feeling, or of any future succession of such feelings. Apart from that, we judge that the good will has value ; and,

indeed, it is this recognition of its value which is the cause, or at
least one condition of the pleasure—quite otherwise than in the
case of the tea; *there* we cannot say what value it has till we
try it, and, if we do not like the feeling, it has no value at
all.   To the man who desires goodness, or cares about doing his
duty, the doing of it must bring some pleasure, for there is
pleasure in the satisfaction of all desire; and it would be (as
I have admitted) meaningless to ask whether we should attach
value to Morality for a being who was for ever incapable of
feeling, or being brought to feel, any such satisfaction in good
conduct.   But we can equally little assert that the value of the
good act depends upon the amount of the resulting pleasure.
For, while a good act must bring pleasure to him who has any
sense of its value, the amount of the pleasure is dependent upon
very many other things than the amount of the good will—upon
health, temperament, spirits, surrounding circumstances of all
kinds.   But these variations in the actual pleasantness of the
good will exercise no influence upon our estimate of the higher
value which goodness possesses as compared with the drinking
of good wine.   And we judge that those who do not experience
this pleasantness at all, whatever other pleasures they enjoy, are
in a state of mind which we cannot wholly approve.   They
ought to feel this pleasure.   We hold that goodness has a
pleasure-value which may be compared with the pleasure-value
of champagne, which may sometimes exceed and sometimes fall
short of that value, but that it possesses besides a value of its
own which it does not share with the champagne.   We are
brought back at last to the simple fact of consciousness.   The
only way of defending the possibility of a judgement, or the
existence of a category, is to show that we do actually think in
that way; and it is clear to me that each of the three attempts—
(1) to analyse all value into pleasure-value, or (2) to merge
pleasure-value into value in general, or (3) to deny that sometimes we are driven to compare pleasure-value with some higher
kind of value—fails to represent the actual verdict of our moral
consciousness.

If the view which we have taken of the relation in which the
idea of pleasure stands to the idea of value be well founded, it

will be obvious why, from the nature of the case, no very sharp distinction can be drawn between them. Among the things to which we attach value, some appeal so entirely to the higher or rational part of our nature that, except for the bare fact that they do satisfy desire, they seem to have nothing in common with the lower. When a man does his duty at the cost of toil and suffering, it is so exclusively the higher part of his nature that impels him to the sacrifice that we should feel it unnatural to say that it is the pleasure to which he attaches so high a value. This higher nature of his is, indeed, so closely connected with his lower that it is impossible that the satisfaction of that higher impulse can fail to excite some pleasant feeling, but it is not valued simply as feeling. On the other hand, the mere 'prick of sense' ceases to have value when it ceases to give pleasure. The vast majority of those states of consciousness to which we attach value are intermediate between the two cases. They appeal to our higher and to our lower nature at the same time. The performance of duty, even at the sacrifice of much that under other circumstances would be valued, the activity of our intellect in an interesting profession or an interesting study, social intercourse with those whom we really care for—all these under favourable circumstances are accompanied by feeling of a kind which has much in common with the feeling that one gets from bathing or basking in the sunshine. They appeal to the higher and to the lower part of our nature at one and the same time. It would be ridiculous to talk as if we valued them simply as pleasures; for, when, through unfavourable circumstances or interfering unpleasantness, they practically cease to appeal to the lower nature at all, we value them still. It would be equally impossible to pronounce that our judgement of their value is wholly independent of that which they have in common with the merely animal satisfactions. In these cases it is practically impossible to say how much of the value is due to one source and how much to the other. If we supposed the lower side of this satisfactoriness progressively diminished, it would be virtually impossible to say exactly when we had reached the point at which we had ceased to prefer them as pleasant states of mind, and begun to prefer them only as states of mind which we value apart from their pleasurableness. It is only when we attempt by a deliberate effort of abstraction to compare the higher and the lower from the same point of view —the point of view of immediate feeling—that we do actually distinguish between the value of our mental condition on the whole and its value as pleasure. And such efforts, being seldom useful, are seldom made. It is only when the higher and the lower elements of interest get violently separated—when the value which some object of desire has for us as rational and reflecting beings gets very far removed from the value which it has for us as sensitive beings[1], that it becomes natural to say, 'We prefer this to that, but we do not prefer it simply as pleasure.'

It is probable that in practice different people use this term 'pleasure' with considerable differences of meaning. Some people, even among Philosophers, seem to be unable to dissociate the term pleasure from bodily indulgences : while the existence of high-minded Hedonists seems to show that others really use it almost or entirely in the sense of 'intrinsically valuable consciousness.'

On the whole, then, it is clear to me that we cannot do without this distinction between value and pleasure. To merge the idea of value in that of pleasure practically involves all the fallacies of Hedonism ; to merge the idea of pleasure in that of value involves the refusal to distinguish different elements in the supremely valuable kind of conscious life which the moral consciousness undoubtedly does distinguish. Practically we cannot get on without both the idea of value and that of pleasure. Yet it may be admitted that the idea of value belongs to the language of strict philosophical thought, the idea of pleasure rather to the region of those popular conceptions which the Philosopher must take account of, which he is bound to use but which are from their very nature incapable of exact definition, and which, therefore, must necessarily be used without exact scientific precision. We want a term to express the something which is common to the higher and the lower of those states of consciousness in which we recognize value : but, just because higher and lower shade off into one another, pleasure

[1] Of course we are never in reality *merely* sensitive.

must needs shade off into something that is not pleasure, or at all events not mere pleasure. We may speak of pleasure as the value which feeling possesses simply as feeling; yet, just because feeling does not exist apart from the other elements in consciousness, but is one aspect of an indivisible reality—the thinking, feeling, willing self—it is impossible sharply to distinguish the value which we attach to consciousness simply as feeling from the value which we attach to it because it satisfies our rational nature: for the lower kind of satisfaction often depends upon and arises from our consciousness of the highest kind of value. Enthusiasm for an idea—religious or other —may produce some of the emotional, even some of the physical, effects of the keenest sensuous enjoyment. It will no doubt be urged that Philosophy has nothing to do with such a vague and indefinable conception; but a Philosophy which fails to take account of the vague and inadequate language in which alone it is possible to express our moral experience must be a Philosophy which deliberately refuses to deal with one side—and that the most important and fundamental side— of that spiritual experience in which Reality consists. It is all very well to protest against abstractions, but without abstractions there is no thought. A Philosophy that would avoid abstractions must be speechless : and the Moral Philosophy of some of my friends would seem to be practically speechless, except in so far as it indulges in splenetic outbursts of abuse or contempt against those who humbly endeavour to put their ethical views into intelligible words. It is right no doubt to protest against ' one-sided abstractions '; but every abstraction must be one-sided while it is actually being made. The only way to neutralize the abstraction involved in looking at one side of a thing apart from the other side is to look at the other side also at another time. I trust that in contending for the indispensability of the distinction between the pleasure-aspect and other aspects of consciousness, and in contending that both have value, though one has a higher value than the other, I have not violated this doubtless important principle. The ideal end of life does not consist in a mere aggregate of goods piled together without mutual influence or interaction upon one another. No one of them indeed can be enjoyed or can exist in absolute isolation from the other.   And yet the nature of this ideal can only be indicated for thought and for language by describing it as a whole made up of distinguishable elements—a good made up of an hierarchy [1] or ascending scale of goods.

V

There is another concept which seems to demand a brief treatment in this connexion—that of happiness. If we repudiate the hedonistic identification of pleasure and happiness, what account, it may be asked, are we to give of the latter? If we regard pleasure as part, though not the whole, of the life that has supreme value, is not this last, it may be suggested, very much what we mean by happiness? If we attempt (apart altogether from theory) to analyse what as a matter of fact we commonly mean when we talk of happiness, the answer will, I think, be something of this kind. Happiness represents satisfaction with one's existence as a whole—with the past and the future as well as with the immediate present. Happiness certainly cannot be identified with pleasure, not even with the higher or more refined kinds of pleasure. It is possible to get an enormous amount of pleasure into one's life—of pleasures that are recognized as having a value and even a high value—and yet to be on the whole unhappy through the presence of desires which are unsatisfied, dissatisfaction with the past [2], anxiety as to the future, unfulfilled aspirations, baffled hopes and the like [3]. It

---

[1] Cf. the great Theologian Albrecht Ritschl's conception of the Kingdom of God : 'The task of the Kingdom of God . . . includes likewise all labour in which our lordship over nature is exercised for the maintenance, ordering, and furtherance even of the bodily side of human life.   For unless activities such as these are ultimately to end in anti-social egoism, or in a materialistic overestimate of their immediate results, they must be judged in the light of those ends which, in ascending series, represent the social, spiritual, and moral ideal of man' (*The Christian Doctrine of Justification and Reconciliation*, Eng. Trans., 1900, p. 612).

[2] Thus St. Augustine holds that ' perfecta beatitudo ' is impossible in this life on account of the moral failures of the past and the present.

[3] This distinction between happiness and pleasure is no doubt present to the minds of those who make the end of life to be satisfaction of a 'timeless

is possible to endure a considerable amount of hardship, of positive pain both bodily and mental, and yet to be on the whole happy; though we should certainly say that the removal or mitigation of those pains would add to the happiness even of those who are most 'self-sufficient for happiness.'

There is therefore a difference between happiness and pleasure. And yet it is impossible without paradox to dissociate the idea of happiness altogether from that of pleasure. A happy life must include some pleasure: all happiness is pleasurable, though not all pleasure is happiness. The pleasure which is an essential part of happiness is no doubt pleasure of the kind which is most dependent upon the man himself and least dependent upon circumstances—the kind of pleasure which, as Aristotle contended, the higher activities necessarily bring with them. But happiness is by no means altogether independent of external circumstances : there must, as Aristotle puts it, be that unimpeded exercise of the higher faculties which is very much dependent upon circumstances. Happiness depends largely upon health, upon suitable work, upon a congenial marriage : and these are emphatically things which are not in our own power. It is true that some kinds of ill health or of uncongenial environment are in some men compatible with a considerable measure of happiness; and the people who are most capable of such happiness are, no doubt, on the whole the best men. But nobody would

self.' But, apart from other objections, happiness, though it is distinguished from pleasure (a) by being commonly attributed only to some considerable period of a man's life and (b) by involving the satisfaction of desires which 'look before and after,' the satisfaction of the more permanent and dominant aims and desires of a man's life, is still emphatically something in time. Some people, it is probable, would say that parts of their life have been happy, other parts unhappy, and most people that some parts have been more happy or less unhappy than others. The objections which I make below to regarding even a sublimated happiness as *the* end may be urged also to the attempt to make the end consist in satisfaction of any kind. It is true no doubt that any experience which we pronounce valuable must give satisfaction, but to make satisfaction the end almost inevitably suggests that things are valuable in proportion as they satisfy this or that individual's actual desires, irrespective of their nature, whereas in fact we feel that it is better to be 'a human being dissatisfied than a pig satisfied; better to be Socrates dissatisfied, than a fool satisfied' (Mill, *Utilitarianism*, p. 14).

contend, 'except when defending a thesis,' that those complaints which bring extreme depression with them as a mere physiological consequence are compatible with any high degree of happiness. And there are 'blows'—public or private calamities, failures, bereavements—which make the recovery of happiness impossible to most men; nor can it be laid down as a general proposition that all good men are happy. To say how far a bad man can be happy would involve pushing the definition of an essentially vague conception further than it is commonly pushed. We should have to talk of different kinds or different senses of happiness. The bad man is no doubt generally unhappy because any better desires that he has are unsatisfied, and because very often his desires and inclinations are of a kind that are incompatible with one another, so that one part or aspect of his nature is always unsatisfied: his life has no wholeness or unity. But this is not perhaps always the case: the bad man no doubt cannot get the same happiness as the good man, but he may get what he wants, and so may attain a kind of happiness. At all events we may say that, though, on the whole, goodness tends to make people happy (far more generally than it tends to increase the sum of their pleasures), men are not happy in proportion to their goodness. We cannot, therefore, without using words in unusual and unnatural senses, so far sublimate the idea of happiness as to identify it with the end of life in general, with consciousness that has value, with Well-being. It is a most important element no doubt in true Well-being— a far more important one than pleasure; or (if we say that happiness is a particular kind of pleasure) it is a far more valuable kind of pleasure than any other, and far more inseparable than most other pleasures from the goods to which we ascribe the very highest value. And yet it is not by itself *the* good. We cannot say that it actually includes all forms of pleasure that are valuable, high intellectual or aesthetic development or even goodness, though the most complete kind of happiness may presuppose the last. Still less, when the good is unattainable, can we say that, among goods or elements of the good, happiness is always the one that possesses the most value, or is the one to which all others should be sacrificed. The noblest kinds of self-devotion do involve a real sacrifice not merely of pleasure but of happiness.

Happiness has this much in common with the good—that for most of us it represents an ideal which we can hardly say that we have ever enjoyed in the undiluted and unruffled fullness which we picture to ourselves as possible and desirable ; that we can only form an ideal conception of it by putting together, amplifying, idealizing moments or periods or elements of our actual experience, supposing them continuously prolonged, and leaving out all that disturbed or qualified the joyous moments while they were actually there. Perfect happiness is no doubt an ideal, but it is a different ideal from that of perfect Well-being. It is an ideal which, at least for people who have in their way higher desires and aspirations, is closely connected with the highest elements in life, but still it cannot safely be made the sole and direct object of pursuit by each individual for himself. Perfect Well-being would doubtless include perfect happiness, but it would include much more than we ordinarily mean by happiness. The idea of happiness can no more be dispensed with in any concrete account of the ideal life than the idea of pleasure, and can equally little be identified with that of value. It is not the whole of the ideal life, but an element or an aspect of it. , The ideal life or the good is an ultimate conception which does not admit of further definition, and the content of which we can only express by enumerating the various elements or aspects of it, and then explaining in what way they are to be combined. Among these elements happiness and pleasure are both included, but they are not the whole ; though no doubt the kind of happiness and the kind of pleasure which do enter into the ideal life are inseparable from those other elements of it which we call goodness or the good will, knowledge, thought, the contemplation of beauty, love of other persons and of what is best in them.

CHAPTER III

SELF-REALIZATION AND SELF-SACRIFICE

I

AT this point it seems desirable to define further the attitude towards two opposite views with regard to the end of human life which is implied in the preceding chapters, although the question has not yet been raised in its conventional form. On the one hand we are met by a doctrine very fashionable in philosophical circles which finds the key to all ethical problems in that comfortable word 'self-realization'; on the other hand we have a doctrine, hardly ever expressly adopted in modern Europe as the basis of a Moral Philosophy, but prominent in much of the popular religious teaching, and some of the highest religious teaching, of our age—the doctrine which resolves all Morality into self-sacrifice.

With the psychological doctrine that some form of personal good is the object of every desire (though that good need not be pleasure) I have already dealt. It seems to be open to exactly the same objections as those urged by its supporters against psychological Hedonism, into a refined form of which the doctrine of self-realization shows a strong tendency to degenerate. I shall here therefore confine myself to the purely ethical aspect of this fascinating formula—'Self-realization is the end of life.'

In order to subject the doctrine to any profitable criticism, it seems necessary to attempt the by no means easy task of distinguishing the various possible senses in which this watchword seems to be used by its devotees. The formula would probably have proved less attractive, had these various senses been distinguished by those to whom it presents itself as a 'short and easy way' out of all ethical perplexities.

(1) Firstly, then, we may suppose that the upholder of self-realization means exactly what he says. If he does, it seems easy to show that what he is committing himself to is mere self-contradictory nonsense. To realize means to make real. You cannot make real what is real already, and the self must certainly be regarded as real before we are invited to set about realizing it [1]. Nor is the task to which we are invited rendered easier when we are assured that the self, which is to become something that it was not, is out of time, and consequently (one might have supposed) insusceptible of change.

(2) But of course it will be said that what is actually meant by self-realization is the realization of some potentiality or capacity of the self which is at present unrealized. In this sense no doubt it is true enough that Morality must consist in some kind of self-realization. But to say so is to say something 'generally admitted indeed but obscure' (ὁμολογούμενόν τι ἀλλ' ἀσαφές), as Aristotle would have put it. In this sense the formula gives us just no information at all. For whatever you do or abstain from doing, if you only sit still or go to sleep, you must still be realizing some one of your capacities: since nobody can by any possibility do anything which he was not first capable of doing. Morality is self-realization beyond a doubt, but then so is immorality. The precious formula leaves out the whole differentia of Morality; and it is a differentia presumably which we are in search of when we ask, 'What is Morality?' and are solemnly told, 'It is doing or being something which you are capable of doing or being [2].'

(3) It may be maintained that Morality is the realization of *all* the capacities of human nature. But this is impossible, since one capacity can only be realized by the non-realization or sacrifice of some other capacity. There can be no self-realization

---

[1] It is of course possible to hold that the self is not real in an ultimate metaphysical sense, but in that sense it is hard to see how it can be made more real than it is, unless 'real' is used as a mere synonym of 'good.'

[2] '"Self-realisation" has always impressed me as a conundrum rather than as its solution' (Adamson, *Development of Modern Philosophy*, II, p. 109).

without self-sacrifice. The good man and the bad alike realize one element or capacity of their nature, and sacrifice another. The whole question is which capacity is to be realized and which is to be sacrificed. And as to this our formula gives us just no information.

(4) Or more vaguely self-realization may be interpreted to mean an equal, all-round development of one's whole nature— physical, intellectual, emotional. To such a view I should object that, interpreted strictly and literally, it is just as impracticable as the last. It is impossible for the most gifted person to become a first-rate Musician without much less completely realizing any capacity he has of becoming a first-rate Painter. It is impossible to become really learned in one subject without remaining ignorant of many others : impossible to develope one's athletic capacities to the full without starving and stunting the intellect, impossible (as a simple matter of Physiology) to carry to its highest point the cultivation of one's intellectual faculties without some sacrifice of physical efficiency. There is a similar collision between the demands of intellectual cultivation and those of practical work. Up to a certain point it is extremely desirable no doubt that every man should seek to improve his mind, and also to engage in some sort of practical, social activity. There is no practical work, except that which is purely mechanical, which will not be the better done for a little study of some kind or other : and, even where a man's ordinary work in life is most purely practical, he has, or ought to have, a life of practical citizenship outside his daily task which will be enriched and enlarged by some kind of intellectual cultivation. It is scarcely possible to exaggerate the extent for instance to which the efficiency of the clerical or of the scholastic profession would be increased if every clergyman and every schoolmaster, however much absorbed in the work of his profession, were to devote a few hours a week to serious study. And equally valuable to the intellectual man is a certain measure of practical experience—equally valuable, at least in many cases, even in the interests of his purely intellectual work. Familiar illustrations are to be found in the value to Hume of his diplomatic appointment, the value to Macaulay and Grote (as is acknowledged by

the critics of a nation which has little experience in free political life) of their parliamentary careers, the value to Gibbon even of a few months' home service in the Hampshire militia. And, even in spheres of intellectual labour less connected with practice than the writing of History, a literary life may gain something from more active occupations. Up to a certain point it is no doubt desirable that a man should endeavour to develope different sides of his nature : but that point is soon reached. Beyond that point there must come the inevitable sacrifice—of body to mind or of mind to body, of learning or speculative insight to practical efficiency or of practical efficiency to learning or insight.

It is the same within the intellectual sphere itself. There too the law of sacrifice prevails. Up to a certain point no doubt the man who is a mere specialist will be a bad specialist, but that point is soon reached. Charles Darwin found that the cultivation of reasoning power and observation had extinguished his once keen imagination and aesthetic sensibility. And yet who would wish—whether in the interests of the world or in the interests of what was best worthy of development in Charles Darwin's own nature—that his work should have been spoiled in order that one of the three hours which was the maximum working day his health allowed should have been absorbed by politics or philanthropy? Who would decide that the origin of species should have been undiscovered, in order that the man who might have discovered it should retain the power of enjoying Wordsworth? This notion of an equal, all-round, ' harmonious ' development is thus a sheer impossibility, excluded by the very constitution of human nature, and incompatible with the welfare of human society. And, in so far as some approximation to such an ideal of life is possible, it involves a very apotheosis of mediocrity, ineffectiveness, dilettantism.

And there is a more formidable objection to come. If the ideal of self-realization is to be logically carried out, it must involve the cultivation of a man's capacity for what vulgar prejudice calls Immorality as well as of his capacity for Morality. It is quite arbitrary to exclude certain kinds of activity as ' bad,' because what we are in search of was some definition of the good in conduct, and we were told that it was the development of all his capacities.   Mr. Bradley would really appear not to shrink from the full acceptance of this corollary :

'This double effort of the mind to enlarge by all means its domain, to widen in every way both the world of knowledge and the realm of practice, shows us merely two sides of that single impulse to self-realization, which most of us are agreed to find so mystical.   But, mystical or intelligible, we must bow to its sway, for escape is impossible [1].'

'To widen in every direction the sphere of knowledge.'   That may, in the abstract, be accepted.   It would perhaps be hypercritical to suggest that there are some things not worth knowing, that it would be an unprofitable employment to count the grains of sand upon the sea-shore, and that even the pursuit of knowledge must be governed and controlled by a certain selection based upon an ideal comparison of values, which is the work of the practical Reason.   And again it might be well to remember that there are things of which (with Mill) we may say that 'it is necessary to be aware of them ; but to live in their contemplation makes it scarcely possible to keep up in oneself a high tone of mind.   The imagination and feelings become tuned to a lower pitch ; degrading instead of elevating associations become connected with the daily objects and incidents of life, and give their colour to the thoughts, just as associations of sensuality do in those who indulge freely in that sort of contemplations [2]'—a reminder which, in view of Mr. Bradley's plea for the apparently unlimited 'freedom of Art,' might seem to be not wholly irrelevant.   But to 'widen in every direction the sphere of practice'!   In the name of common sense, would not an occasional incursion into the higher branches of crime vary the sameness of Virtue and the dull monotony of Goodness ?   Is not a life compounded of good and evil 'wider' than an experience which includes only good ?   Could the attempt to widen 'in every direction' the sphere of practice end otherwise than in a prison or a lunatic asylum—if not in both ?   A German thinker has urged that the failure of most Moral

---

[1] *The Principles of Logic*, p. 452.
[2] *Three Essays on Religion.* p. 248.

Philosophers may be set down to the fact that as a class, they have been rather exceptionally respectable men : the Moral Philosopher should have experience both of Virtue and of vice [1]. If 'wideness' is to be sole criterion of practice, one does not see why this catholicity of experience should be confined to professional Moral Philosophers [2].

(5) One possible interpretation of our formula remains. Self-realization may mean the realization of a man's highest capacities by the sacrifice of the lower. No doubt, in a sense every school of Moral Philosophy which allows of the distinction between a 'higher' and a 'lower' at all would admit that Morality does mean the sacrifice of the lower to the higher—though it might be objected that this ideal, taken literally, is too ascetic : the lower capacities of human nature have a certain value : they ought to be realized to a certain extent—to be subordinated, not 'sacrificed,' except in so far as their realization is inconsistent with that of the higher. But then there is nothing of all this in the word 'self-realization.' And even with the gloss that 'self-realization' means realization of the 'true' or 'higher' self, it tells us just nothing at all about the question what this true

[1] See Simmel's article on 'Moral Deficiencies as determining Intellectual Functions' in the *International Journal of Ethics*, Vol. III, July, 1893, p. 490. Of course I do not profess here to do full justice to the distinguished writer's argument.

[2] 'The sinner realises capabilities—in this broad sense—as much as the saint. I lay stress on this, because it is important to recognise that one of the subtlest and deepest of the impulses that prompt intellectual natures to vice is the desire for full and varied realisation of capabilities, for richness of experience, for fulness of life' (Sidgwick, *Ethics of Green, Spencer and Martineau*, p. 64).

In a recent article on 'Truth and Practice' (*Mind*, N. S. no. 51, 1904, p 322) Mr. Bradley writes, 'I have of course not forgotten that there are "developments" of human nature which are undesirable and vicious. Why these are undesirable is a question which I cannot discuss here. The answer in general is that such things not only are contrary to the interest of our whole nature, but also are hostile to the realisation of that very side of it to which they belong.' If Mr. Bradley had always remembered this and some other things which he says in this article, the above criticism would have been unnecessary. A thinker who is so ready to find contradictions or absurdities in other people should surely be a little more precise in his own use of language.

self-realization is.   In fact the formula which is presented to us
as the key to the ethical problem of the end of life, turns out
on examination to mean merely 'The end of life is the end of
life.'   No doubt it has been said that every attempt to define
Morality must have the appearance of moving in a circle.   In
a sense that may be the case.   The moral cannot be defined
in terms of the non-moral.   But then that is just what
our formula attempts to do, and that is just the source of its
futility.   Moreover, when the word 'self-realization' is presented
to us, not merely as an account of the end, but also as the
immediate criterion for the individual's conduct, it is open to
the objection that it says exactly nothing about the fundamental
question of Ethics—the question of the relation of my end to
that of others.

(6) This last difficulty would be removed if, with Mr. Bradley
in one of his phases (a phase difficult to reconcile with the
definition given above), we contend that the self which is
realized in Morality, actually includes in itself all the selves in
whom I feel an interest:

'If my self which I aim at is the realization in me of a moral
world which is a system of selves, an organism in which I am a
member, and in whose life I live—then I cannot aim at my own
well-being without aiming at that of others.   The others are
not mere means to me, but are involved in my essence [1].'

Now to the adoption of self-realization in this sense as an
answer to the ethical problem I should object (a) that the interpretation is not the one which is naturally suggested by that
term.   If the end of life is (in part or in whole) to attain the
ends of others besides myself, that is a most important truth
which should surely be emphasized in any answer, however
summary, to the question, 'What is the end of life?'; and not
left to be understood in a formula which takes no explicit account
of it.   (b) We are as far off as ever from knowing what the
'realization' of the other selves, which is included in the realization of mine, really is.   (c) The proposition that I cannot attain
my end without promoting the end of others is at all events

---

[1] *Ethical Studies*, p. 105.

an intelligible proposition. Not so, I respectfully submit, the proposition that 'others are involved in my essence [1].' Such an assertion seems to me to ignore the very essence of self-hood, which excludes an absorption or inclusion in other selves, however closely related to us. Of course, Mr. Bradley will reply that we cannot distinguish a thing from its relations. And yet Mr. Bradley has himself taught us—no one more effectively—that there cannot be relations without something to relate. No doubt a *thing*, which does not exist for itself, but only in and for a mind, cannot even in thought be abstracted from its relations : the thing is made what it is by its intelligible relations, if we include in its relations the content which it has for a mind other than itself. But this is not so with a self. Unquestionably there can be no subject without an object : the very nature of a subject is constituted by its knowledge of such and such objects. The objects that it knows are part of the self : in the view of a thorough-going Idealism, indeed, the subject and its experiences make up one spiritual being. But, all the same, of such a spiritual being it is not true that it is made what it is by its relation to other spiritual beings in the same way as a mere thing, which exists for others and not for itself, is made what it is by its relations. The *thing* has no *esse* except to be felt, thought, experienced ; the way it enters into the experience of minds is the only sort of being it possesses. On the other hand, the ' esse ' of the soul is to think, to feel, to experience. This thinking, feeling, experiencing does undoubtedly include relations to other selves ; but such relations are not the whole of its being. The experiences of a soul may be *like* those of another soul : they may be caused by and dependent upon the experiences of another soul. But the experiences of one soul cannot be or become identical with the experience of another soul : the content of two consciousnesses may be the same—the universal abstracted from the particular, but not the reality [2] : neither, therefore, can the good of one soul or self be the good of another, or be included in or be part of the good of another. Hence, if we are to avoid

---

[1] A position further developed in the Chapter on 'Good' in *Appearance and Reality*.

[2] I have further discussed this matter below in Bk. III, chap. i.

a mysticism which frankly takes leave of intelligibility, we cannot include any realization of the capacities of others in our conception of self-realization, however essential to such realization the good of others may be. If all that is meant is that other selves may be ends to me, not mere means, that is precisely the point which is usually disguised, if it is not denied, by those who employ the formula 'self-realization.' The tendency of the phrase is to represent all moral conduct as motived by a desire for my own good, into which consideration of others can only enter as means to the realization of my end. Even if there be a more ultimate metaphysical sense in which my self and others are really the same self, that is not in the sense with which we have to do with selves in Ethics : in Ethics at least we are concerned with the relations between a plurality of selves [1].

Further defence of this last objection would carry us more deeply into the metaphysical region than it would be in place to go at present. But I trust that what has been said will be enough to suggest that there is nothing to be gained by the use of this ambiguous, mysterious term. It tells us nothing important, nothing that could not be better expressed in some other way. It is an attempt to evade the real problems of Morality instead of answering them. That is sufficiently indicated by the fact that it is equally popular with writers whose real ethical ideals are as wide apart as the poles—with the school of the late Professor Green and with the school of Mr. Bradley, with those whose ideal is austere to the point of Asceticism and with those by whom a large part of what the plain man calls Morality is regarded as an exploded superstition. For some people it has the attraction of a vague, imposing technicality, acting like 'that comfortable word Mesopotamia' upon the mind of the pious old woman. With others it is a mere cover for a more or less refined Hedonism [2]. What they really mean is 'the end of life

---

[1] 'From "self-seeking" to disinterested benevolence there is no road, and the apparent subsumption of both under a common name by the theory of self-realisation, turns out at closer inspection to be little more than a piece of verbal legerdemain' (Taylor, *The Problem of Conduct*, p. 193).

[2] I do not say that this is so with any English Philosopher of repute, but the possibility of thus understanding the phrase accounts for the enthusiasm of some of its younger votaries.

2 7 ⋆

is to have a good time,' but they do not quite like to say so because there is a vulgar prejudice against that view; and besides, in academic circles there is a general consensus that Hedonism is unphilosophical. To minds of a higher order no doubt the term appeals simply because it is a protest against the practical exaggerations and the logical difficulties of the attempt to exalt 'self-sacrifice' into an all-sufficing expression of the moral ideal. The best way, therefore, of bringing out the truth expressed—as it seems to me, badly and cumbrously expressed— by the use of the term 'self-realization' will be to examine the claims of the counter-ideal of self-sacrifice to sum up in itself the essence of all Morality.

II

Why cannot the ideal of self-sacrifice be accepted as the last word in Ethics?

(1) For the same reason that we saw to be fatal to the antagonistic formula of 'self-realization.' Just as there can be no self-realization or (to use a term less open to objection) 'self-development' without self-sacrifice, so there can be no self-sacrifice without self-realization. In denying or sacrificing one part or element or capacity of the self, a man is necessarily asserting or developing another. Complete or absolute self-sacrifice is possible only in the form of suicide, if even so; for after all suicide is always a kind of self-assertion, and often a kind of selfishness. What of course is meant by those who use the term is that the highest self is to be asserted or developed, and that the individual attains his true end by the sacrifice of his lower inclinations or desires for the sake of other people. To gain the lower life is to lose the higher: to lose the lower is to gain the true life. That is the very essence of the highest moral teaching that the world has known. But then the formula 'self-sacrifice' only expresses one half of that doctrine; and the one-sided formula often leads to much one-sidedness and exaggeration in ethical thought and even in practical Morality.

(2) It needs little reflection to show that self-sacrifice for its own sake is always irrational and immoral. It is the object for which the sacrifice is made that gives it its moral value. It is

always some good of another or some higher good of the individual that is the object of legitimate self-sacrifice. On reflection this would probably be admitted by the austerest of ascetics. The flesh is to be subdued to the spirit—that is the theory of Asceticism. And to a large extent the fallacy of Asceticism in its ordinary sense consists in a sheer psychological mistake about the tendency of bodily austerities or privations to promote a higher and more spiritual life. That long-continued hunger will eventually lead men to see visions and dream dreams which, in minds educated in a certain way, will assume a religious form, is no doubt a psychological fact, which is of great importance historically as supplying at least a partial explanation of the practice of fasting as a religious rite. But (waiving the question of the religious value of such psychical states or of the less vivid ecstasies which may sometimes be produced by fasting of a less extreme character) it is the testimony of countless ascetics in all ages [1] that the more they scourged and tormented themselves, stood up to their chins in swamps or rolled themselves among thorns, the more gross became their sensual imaginings. the more clamorous and insistent their passions. In less extreme cases it is probable that there has been an enormous exaggeration of the spiritual value, for the great majority at least, of solitude, hardship, and privation. The tendency of such self-conscious effort to crush the appetites is simply to concentrate attention upon them. In general, a man's mind is not raised above the level of the lower desires and animal inclinations by austerity, but by healthy preoccupation with social or intellectual activity. Of course there may be room for Asceticism by way of discipline. We may deny ourselves in things that do not matter in order to strengthen the will in resistance to inclination where it does matter. But it may be doubted whether the self-consciousness attendant upon such self-inflicted disciplinary privations—at least in communities where they are not recognized by social custom—is not a grave objection to them. The real needs of our fellow men afford the completest scope

[1] Even to the attenuated fasts of modern times these remarks are not wholly inapplicable. There is a sermon of Cardinal Newman on ' Fasting a Source of Trial.' Ought temptations to be artificially multiplied ?

for rational curtailment of the lower kinds of self-indulgence, whether this takes the form of periodical abstinence, of habitual moderation, or of self-denial in other things besides eating and drinking.

But, whatever may be thought about the kind and degree of self-denial which really promote the higher life, there will be little quarrel with the general principle—that self-sacrifice is not the end, but a means to the good of others or to the higher good of the man himself: and perhaps it will even be admitted that self-denial for our own spiritual good is more likely to attain its end, the more directly the indulgence which is surrendered stands in the way of something higher—for instance, by wasting time or money which might be employed upon self-improvement or social service. This will generally be conceded: and yet there can be no doubt that in practice the preaching of Asceticism has a tendency to degenerate into the idea that self-inflicted pain has in it something intrinsically virtuous or meritorious and is therefore well-pleasing to God, even when God is conceived of as a righteous and loving Father. And at one point such a notion may find formal defenders among Christian Theologians. There has been in various ages, if there does not now survive, a widespread belief in the expiatory value of suffering. Such a notion seems to be implied in the retributive theory of punishment which has already been examined and rejected. If punishment really does wipe out guilt or assert the Moral Law or what not, there seems no reason why it should be confined to the case of legal offences or why it should not be self-inflicted: and it might even be contended plausibly enough that its expiatory value need not be diminished when the penalty is paid by some one other than the sinner [1]. As I have already discussed

---

[1] It is a deeply significant fact that, according to some authorities, the original idea of ritual sacrifice was not expiation, but communion with the Deity through participation in the common meal—originally the blood of the Totem-animal. The idea of expiation only came in because the natural way of renewing the tie between the tribe and the god when it had been weakened through an offence seemed to be a special repetition of the act by which the blood-bond had been created and kept alive. Thus the idea of expiation as the dominant idea in sacrifice represents a degradation of the original conception. (See Robertson Smith's Chapter on 'Sacrifice' in his

what is virtually the same question in connexion with the theory of punishment, I need only add that I can see no meaning in expiation except the tendency of suffering (under certain conditions) to make the sufferer morally better. Even within the limits of severely orthodox Theology much support might be found for the proposition that the remission of sins necessarily follows upon repentance, and that repentance ultimately means change of will or character.

(3) Not only does a one-sided doctrine of self-sacrifice exaggerate the value of thwarting lower desires as a means to the gratification of the higher, but it errs by denying all value to those lower goods the surrender of which it advocates. In the first place it fails to appreciate the fact that desires other than the pure impulse to do one's duty for its own sake have a value of their own, and may become, when duly regulated, the basis of the highest virtues: and that is the case not merely with such purely intellectual impulses as the love of knowledge, but with many which, in themselves and apart from their subordination to a higher purpose, are purely animal, and may degenerate into the inspiring motives of crime and vice. The raw material, so to speak, of Virtue and Vice is the same —i. e. desires which in themselves, abstracted from their relation to the higher self, are not either moral or immoral but simply non-moral [1]. Anger in some forms is the most anti-social of all passions: while indignation against vice is an essential element in the ideal character. To hate the right things, to hate that in persons which is worthy of hatred, is as essential an object of all moral education as to love the right things, and to love those possibilities of higher things which exist in the vilest. An animal impulse is to many men the basis of the most powerful temptation and of the highest affection that they ever know.

Religion of the Semites, p. 213 *sq.*, and Jevons, *History of Religion*, p. 144 *sq.*) Whatever may be thought of the chronological order of the ideas, the corruption and degradation of Religion at every stage of its development is closely connected with the prominence of the idea of expiation as compared with that of communion or fellowship between the Deity and his worshippers.

[1] Ἐκ τῶν αὐτῶν καὶ διὰ τῶν αὐτῶν καὶ γίνεται πᾶσα ἀρετὴ καὶ φθείρεται. Aristotle. *Eth. Nic.* II. i. (p. 1103 *b*).

The gregarious instinct that prompts us to seek the society and approval of our fellow-men is the most fruitful source of moral failure when it attaches itself to narrow social circles and low social ideals: duly developed in a certain direction and cultivated in a certain way it blossoms into the 'enthusiasm of humanity.' The denial of this truth forms the great fallacy into which the ascetics of all ages have fallen. The principle was inadequately grasped by Plato, who, while recognizing the moral usefulness of the combative instinct (τὸ θυμοειδές) as the ally of Reason against the lower passions, did not see that these too were capable of being, and ought to be in various degrees, educated and guided by Reason, instead of being merely crushed and suppressed. It was ignored by Kant when he thought that every wise man would fain be wholly free from desire. It was ignored by the Stoics when they recommended the suppression of emotion. It is the great glory of Aristotle, and of his disciples the mediaeval Schoolmen, to have grasped firmly the idea that Reason should control, discipline, regulate the desires instead of extinguishing them, and that rightly regulated desire is as essential an element of the ideal character as the paramount supremacy of Reason or Conscience [1].

(4) In certain directions and to a certain extent, then, all natural impulses are susceptible of being taken up into, and actually transformed into, those more social tendencies of the self the predominance of which is ordinarily spoken of as self-sacrifice. But, even where this is not the case, moral Reason does not seem to sanction the idea that these lower desires, or the goods which are the objects of them, possess no intrinsic value at all. The ideal human life does demand a certain amount of these

---

[1] This constitutes the real meaning and importance of the doctrine that Virtue is a mean περὶ πάθη καὶ πράξεις, a mean between the excess and defect of each kind of feeling or acting, however inadequate such a doctrine may be as a moral criterion. Aristotle's mistake was to give an exaggerated prominence to one of the most important ways in which Reason regulates the πάθη and πράξεις, that of quantity; this made it necessary to find two vices between which to place each virtue. This can generally be done, but not always. The inadequacy and unsatisfactoriness of Aristotle's list of virtues arises largely from the necessity of excluding all virtues which cannot conveniently be squeezed into the form of a mean between two vices.

lower goods. The ideal human life is not a life of pain and want and discomfort. The ascetic seldom suggests that we should promote such a life for others. To be virtuous on the rack is better than to be vicious off it; but there is one thing that is better than being virtuous on the rack, and that is to be virtuous off it. 'It is better' (according to the admission of J. S. Mill) 'to be Socrates dissatisfied than to be a fool satisfied:' but there is one thing that is better than either—to be Socrates satisfied. What is the relation of the higher and the lower goods, what amount or degree of the lower is consistent with or most conducive to the due predominance of the higher in human lives, is a question about which men may reasonably differ, but it must not be assumed that it is always the irreducible *minimum*. And the true answer will of course be different for different men. The great practical mistake of the more moderate ascetic teaching has been to lay upon average men burdens too great *for them*, to require a repression of natural instincts and desires which *in them* (whatever be the case with exceptional natures) does not promote the healthy development of character and the efficient conduct of life. The necessity of exercise, amusement, society, even in the interests of moral Well-being, is recognized by the best religious Ethics of the present day as it has hardly been recognized by the religious teaching of the past. This of course, it may be said, implies merely the treatment of those lower goods as means to a higher end: but it would be perhaps hard to defend the place which the best men of our day would assign to them in the life which they want to promote for the mass of men without admitting that there are elements in the ideal life —elements possessing an independent, though subordinate, worth of their own—other than the cultivation of the good will, other than socially useful activity or high intellectual cultivation. And even for the best men it is hardly felt that it is wrong to eat or drink more than is absolutely essential to health, to spend time in conversation or light reading that might without mental breakdown be devoted to work. Or, if for exceptional persons it is felt that this indulgence of lower goods ought to be cut down to the minimum point that is compatible with the maximum of social efficiency, we should probably on reflection justify this course, partly on the ground that such men will attain the greatest good for them in exertions which go beyond the powers of most; and partly on the principle that, if for some persons it is a duty to sacrifice much that is not normally inconsistent with the predominance of the highest interests, the sacrifice is demanded by the value of the other lives which are helped by their exertions, without any disparagement or contempt for the ordinary sources of healthy human enjoyment. The ascetic life which is devoted to the procuring of an enjoyable life for others, for the sake of that life, is no longer ascetic in principle.

(5) And that brings us to a last necessary qualification of the one-sided ideal of self-sacrifice. Normally and in the abstract, Reason does not demand that a man should give up any good of his own except for the greater good of some one else. And, in estimating the greatness of the good, we must of course not include the good implied by the sacrifice itself. The test would become nugatory if we held that the man who sacrifices himself always gets the greater good, just because his act is one of self-sacrifice. Speaking broadly and generally, Reason does not (as it appears to me) hold that it is good to promote (say) the comfort and convenience of another person by the sacrifice of a much greater comfort and convenience of one's own. Of course the stronger altruistic impulses will tend to overleap this restriction, to

> reject the lore
> Of nicely calculated less or more.

And there may be times and circumstances in which the calmest reflection may discern such a beauty and propriety in the sacrifice that it will pronounce 'good on the whole' to result from it, as when a mother, not grudgingly or of necessity but willingly and spontaneously, gives up much more for her child than he will gain by the sacrifice: but normally and apart from any special circumstances or relations of the persons, I do not think it can be said that we do on calm reflection approve the sacrifice of more for less. If Sir Walter Raleigh's act in spreading his cloak in the mud to make a dry place for Queen Elizabeth to walk on be approved in spite of the fact that the gain to the Queen was probably smaller than the damage to Sir Walter's cloak, it must be on account of the special relation in which a Queen stands to her subject.

(6) The requirement of unlimited Altruism would involve self-contradiction. If I judge that another's pleasure is a good thing for me to promote I cannot logically deny that my own pleasure is a good too—a good intrinsically worthy of being promoted. It cannot be right for me to spend my labour in producing that which it is wrong for another to receive—in growing fruit, for instance, which it would be wicked for another to eat. At some point or other enjoyment must begin : the end of life cannot be a continual passing on of something to another. It may be urged that the ideal is that I should be producing something for another, and find my good in doing so : while he is working in turn for my good, and finds his good in doing so. That is no doubt the true ideal—a life in which work for lower needs is elevated by becoming social or reciprocal. enjoyment of lower goods consecrated by being shared. But common sense will clearly set some limit to this exchange of services : some things each of us does better for himself than another can do them for him. The greater part of most ordinarily good men's lives resists this sharp distinction into an egoistic and an altruistic part : it is egoistic and altruistic at the same time. But this very interchange of services, which is at the basis of all social life, would be impossible if men would not consent to be served as well as to serve. We may share enjoyment with another, but not the enjoyment of the very same thing : two people cannot possibly eat the same apple. If the apple is ever to be eaten instead of being passed on, that implies a limit to Altruism [1]. If it were never right for me to eat it, it would not be right for me to encourage the egoism of my neighbour by inviting him to do so.

So long as we confine ourselves to the higher goods, the limitation of altruistic self-sacrifice in the interests of personal

---

[1] I am here thinking of the normal or average man. What is said about limitations to self-sacrifice (and to Asceticism in so far as self-sacrifice involves Asceticism) must be qualified by what is said below in the chapter on 'Vocation.' In particular cases much sacrifice may be right which would become irrational if imposed upon all.

culture will readily be admitted. It will be conceded that the whole energy of a community ought not to be absorbed in the production of material goods ; nor can it well be conceived of as being entirely absorbed in the work of mutual edification, in the direct improvement of each other's characters. What is to be done then with the rest of it ? Various forms of intellectual or aesthetic self-development and enjoyment seem to remain as the only possible objects of rational pursuit. No doubt most intellectual activities are capable of assuming a social direction. I can write books or compose poetry or research or play the piano for the benefit of others, and not merely for my own enjoyment. But then it cannot be right for me to play or compose music which it would be sinful waste of time for another to listen to. It is clear, therefore, that some portion of an individual's time and energy may rightly be given to the enjoyment of higher goods for their own sake without any further social object.

With regard to lower goods, more scruple may be felt at the employment of this argument. It may be said that there is really no inconsistency in holding that it is always better to surrender to another any lower object of enjoyment which is not positively demanded by my own efficiency, and therefore, ultimately, the good of others : for it is not because it is good for another to enjoy himself that I think it right to make the sacrifice, but because it is a charitable act and beneficial to my character to give him that pleasure. But, once again, if pleasure is not to be thought of as a good, how can it be morally good to spend time and labour in producing it ? And, if it is good for another, it must be good—up to whatever point, within whatever limits—for me also. The ideal of unlimited self-sacrifice involves obvious and inevitable self-contradiction.

III

Considerations like these may easily be pushed to the point of representing that the idea of self-sacrifice forms no essential part of the true moral ideal. That ideal, it may be urged, is always the subordination of the lower to the higher—the development of the different parts of the man's nature—not, indeed, in all directions equally, but in the true order of their relative worth or importance. And in this subordination there need be nothing which can be properly called sacrifice at all —no sense of pain or contraction, no struggle or resistance to inclination. For the good man will recognize in social service the opportunity of developing his truest self. It will cost him no pain to be temperate, to control his appetites, to be (within reasonable limits) unselfish and hard-working: for he sees that these things are for his own good. All his desires are so completely dominated and directed by Reason that he has no desire for indulgences which would interfere with perfect intellectual clearness and perfect control of appetite: he loves work, occupation in the service of the community, or some intellectual pursuit for its own sake. This perfect 'harmony' between the various elements of a man's nature, it may be urged, is the true ideal. Self-sacrifice must be at most an incident of imperfect 'adjustment' between the individual and his environment. The requirement of it must belong to the imperfect Morality of youth; to the youth of the race, or at most to the defective organization of human society. This line of thought is in various forms so prevalent that, at the risk of some repetition, it may be worth while to consider what amount of truth we can recognize in it. Briefly I should reply that the kind of harmony which such speculations bid us seek is rendered for ever impossible (1) by the nature of man, (2) by the nature of things, (3) by the nature of human society.

(1) The extinction of self-sacrifice, felt as such, is inconsistent with the attainment of the highest character owing to the constitution of human nature.

That Virtue cannot be attained without a struggle was admitted even by Aristotle. But then to Aristotle the man was not good until the virtuous 'habit' was fully formed. He assumed that the imperfectly virtuous acts by which the habit of virtuous action was formed would be done from some non-moral motive. How the repetition of a series of acts influenced by *wholly* non-moral motives would result in a habit of acting from moral motives, of doing the virtuous act for its own sake, is never satisfactorily explained; that is the great hiatus of

Aristotle's ethical system. So far is it from being true that there is no moral value in the struggle against temptation so long as the pleasantness of the pleasure renounced is felt, that moral value seems to the modern mind to be at its maximum in such struggles[1]. The amount of struggle which goes to the formation of a virtuous character is no doubt very various. To some men goodness seems more or less to come naturally; to others only after long and strenuous conflict. That natural tendency to evil which Theologians have called 'original sin' seems to be very unequally distributed; and very unequal in different men is the strength of those purely animal impulses which, though in themselves not evil, do not at once submit to rational control. The needful struggle is doubtless proportionately unequal. But it is difficult to see how without some struggle a virtuous character can be formed at all. Certainly, in the absence of temptation the character cannot be tested; and until the character has been tested, there would seem to be rather the potentiality of Virtue or character than the actuality of it. The struggle need not be always kept up, but it must have been gone through. Perhaps we may have in this consideration some glimpse cf a clue to the real meaning of evil in a rationally governed Universe. But at all events, confining ourselves to human life as we know it, we may say that it is in and through the struggle that the good will most emphatically asserts itself. In this sense at all events Morality can never lose the aspect of self-sacrifice.

But is this all? When is this education of the character to stop? Even Aristotle admitted that for the mass of men the necessity of moral discipline, in the shape of Law, was not confined to youth; and that implies that for them at least the desirable harmony could not be practically attained in absolute perfection. It was probably the extreme moderation of the demands which, under ordinary circumstances, Aristotle's

---

[1] It is curious to find a writer so little prone to any form of Rigorism as Simmel exaggerating this aspect of Morality so far as to maintain that there is no merit except where the virtuous impulse has had to struggle against another, and that the merit is proportionate to the effort (*Einleitung*, I, p. 264 *sq.*).

ethical code imposed upon the inclinations of a cultivated Greek gentleman that prevented his recognizing that that desirable condition in which nothing that was wrong would ever present itself as pleasant was practically not attainable in this life even by the best of men. This consideration will at least suggest the practical danger of making 'harmony' the primary aim of moral effort : the feeling of 'harmony' in the self-satisfied man of culture, like the 'peace' of conventional religionism, is quite as likely in practice to be the outcome of a low ideal as of a perfected 'habit' of Virtue. Still, it may be urged, however far off and difficult of attainment it may be, 'harmony' is the ideal : the feeling of struggle is always a note of imperfection. But is this always and necessarily so ?

Aristotle's account of the formation of the virtuous 'habit' with the consequent disappearance of struggle is no doubt a fairly accurate description of the inner life of the good man *under favourable circumstances*, so long as we confine ourselves to the very limited range of moral experience which was probably present to Aristotle's mind. We should not think highly of a man who continued to feel very painfully throughout life the struggle to prevent the more violent explosions of temper or to avoid grossly over-eating and over-drinking himself. No doubt the effort to overcome the more vulgar or animal temptations does normally become indefinitely easier after a certain period of resistance. But does it always do so ? And is not the extent to which it does so quite as much dependent upon physiological constitution as upon character ? Can we say that a man's character is defective because a healthy appetite would always prompt him to eat somewhat more than a sedentary life or a weak digestion or a slender purse or the claims of others may make it his duty to take ? Is a man intemperate because he could always enjoy one more glass of wine or a better wine than it is right habitually to indulge in ? No doubt in normal cases, where the mind is duly occupied with higher interests, and where outward circumstances are favourable, the struggle does become something which it sounds a little ridiculous to call pain or sacrifice. But, however small, the struggle is sufficient to prevent our talking of perfect harmony. It must be remembered, however, that there are other passions against which in some men the struggle is longer and fiercer; and then again we cannot limit our attention to these grosser temptations. There are temptations which are closely connected with the development of the higher part of a man's nature. Every moral conquest brings subtler temptations with it—spiritual pride, love of power, love of everything good (other than the supreme good) above its true value, at the wrong time, in the wrong place. It would not be a note of perfection but of imperfection not to feel temptations such ,as these. However attenuated in the higher characters the struggle may become (though I am not sure that it is in the highest characters that the struggle is mildest), still the mere feeling that something which is not right would be in itself very nice is enough to preclude the possibility of absolutely unruffled 'harmony,' and to compel us to regard self-sacrifice as a necessary element in all Morality as it exists under present human conditions. And that brings me to my second point.

(2) The extinction of self-sacrifice is inconsistent with the nature of things—with the actual conditions of life on this planet.

Even Aristotle admitted that it was only under perfectly favourable circumstances that the exercise of Virtue brought with it complete and perfect εὐδαιμονία. 'External supplies to a greater or a lesser extent' were necessary—freedom from pain and grave misfortune; free scope for the energies and activities, moral and intellectual, in the exercise of which true happiness was to be found. And this was not all. There was at least one virtue whose exercise was normally painful. The courageous man would no doubt feel the joy of battle; he would feel pleasure at the accomplishment of his desire to do brave deeds: but toil and wounds and death were not less painful to him than to other men—nay, more so, inasmuch as it is to the best men that life is most desirable [1]. Now the

---

[1] Aristotle, *Eth. Nic.* III. 9 (p. 1117 *b*). The passage concludes: οὐ δὴ ἐν ἁπάσαις ταῖς ἀρεταῖς τὸ ἡδέως ἐνεργεῖν ὑπάρχει, πλὴν ἐφ' ὅσον τοῦ τέλους ἐφάπτεται. The last words contain the truth which the psychological Hedonists and the 'self-realizers' exaggerate. They forget that this pleasure is often, as Aristotle points out, very small in comparison with the surrounding pain.

absence of favourable circumstances, which from the point of
view of the affluent Greek gentleman might be fairly treated
as exceptional, is in truth with the mass of human beings
the normal state of things. What presented itself to Aristotle
as a somewhat anomalous characteristic of a particular virtue
is, to an age which recognizes social obligations in excess of
Aristotle's standard, the normal accompaniment at least of
the higher kinds of moral effort. The virtue no doubt brings
pleasure, but the circumstances of the struggle are painful.
Opposition, unpopularity, failure, ill health, boredom, monotony—
these at the lowest (to say nothing of the graver ills of more
strenuous and heroic lives) good men must normally be prepared
to face in greater or less degree, and the acceptance of such
evils—often the direct consequence of their goodness—constitutes self-sacrifice. The amount of such things which the good
man has to face varies no doubt enormously. A man is not
necessarily to be thought less good because the circumstances
of his life make the exercise of his capacities pleasant and
interesting to himself: but still in a rough way it is true
that what are in our view the noblest qualities of human
character—less so no doubt in Aristotle's view, still less so
in that of modern paganizing Moralists—have normally to
be exhibited in ways which involve a good deal that is unpleasant. And in the most fortunate lives the mere necessity
of working when one is tired would be enough to prevent
our taking the pleasantness of our activity as an all-sufficient
index of the degree to which a virtuous 'habit' has been
formed. Aristotle, it is probable, would hardly have recognized
under normal circumstances the necessity of a man working
when he would rather rest. It is doubtful whether even a
leading statesman in ancient Athens was required to pass many
more hours in an office than was agreeable and hygienic: and
as to theoretic activities, why should a Greek gentleman of
independent means (and no one else could be truly virtuous),
who studied, and researched, and talked for his own pleasure
and not for the sake of others, go on thinking or reading or
writing when he was tired ? In Aristotle's view working when
one was tired might be left to slaves. By any one who is

not prepared to admit either that it is always right to stop work when one is tired, or that physical weariness is a sign of moral imperfection, the idea of the complete correspondence between duty and inclination, even in the best men, must be given up. And if so, we must look upon self-sacrifice as no mere accidental, temporary, or occasional accompaniment of Morality, but as a very important element in the normal virtuous life. Inasmuch as it asserts this fact, the popular tendency to identify Morality with self-sacrifice possesses far more and far deeper truth than the 'self-realization' doctrine of our ethical exquisites.

(3) The attempt to banish self-sacrifice from the virtuous life is inconsistent with the structure of human society.

The nature of man and of his material environment is such, we have seen, that even the effort to develope his own highest capacities cannot always, even in the best men, be altogether free from painful struggle. Still more obvious and still more serious is the collision between the claims of the individual and the claims of his fellows. The fullest development of what might (apart from such social considerations) be regarded as the highest capacities of the individual is, not exceptionally but normally, inconsistent with the development of those same capacities in others. Both the material and the higher interests of mankind constantly demand of the individual the sacrifice of his personal culture and self-development—physical, emotional, and (in a sense) even moral, i. e. many sides of character which it would in the abstract be good to cultivate. The fullest development of the individual must be sacrificed in order that there may be some development of other individuals. Or, if we say that the social self which is cultivated by the sacrifice of intellectual growth and emotional culture is after all the highest self, still the sacrifice of lower capacities to capacities in themselves good and noble must be made long before the point at which it could be said that they positively interfere with the higher, except in so far as their further cultivation is incompatible with the highest principle of all— the principle of submission to that moral Reason which dictates the subordination of the individual's good to the requirements

of social Well-being. If that 'harmony' or wholeness in the
moral life on which it is the fashion to insist means the
subordination of all other impulses to this, then indeed the
harmony is possible. If it is this self that is to be 'realized,'
then indeed self-realization is possible, but such a self-realization
is necessarily also a limitation : it involves, that is to say, much
of what ordinary men call self-sacrifice—sacrifice not merely of
the bad self but of much that is intrinsically good and noble [1].
There is no realization of the 'self' as a whole, or even of
the 'higher self' as a whole : and, if that is so, it were best
surely to avoid putting forward the catch-word 'self-realization'
as the essential feature of the moral life.

IV

And yet, as I have already endeavoured to show, the ideal of
self-sacrifice, though it undoubtedly insists on what is from a
practical point of view a more important aspect of the moral
life than 'self-realization,' is no less one-sided. It fails to express the fact that Morality is the individual's highest good
and is therefore not altogether sacrifice : and it fails to express
the truth that the ideal life does include other elements besides
self-sacrificing social service—some of them elements of high
intrinsic worth. How then are we to reconcile these two principles ? The general line of the reconciliation cannot be doubtful
if there be any truth in the conclusions which we have tried to
establish. Reason clearly pronounces that even what would otherwise be the highest good of the individual ought to give way to the
like good of others. If so, it is clear that individual self-development [2] ought to bow to the claims of the like self-development
in others ; and from that it follows that the individual must find
his own highest good in the cultivation of such capacities as can

---

[1] 'The hardest choice which Christian self-denial imposes is the preference of the work apparently most socially useful to the work apparently
most conducive to the agent's own scientific and aesthetic development'
(Sidgwick, *Ethics of Green,* p. 70).

[2] In future I shall use this word alone, as it seems to me to express all
that there is of real meaning in 'self-realization,' while free from some of
the objections that have been urged against that term, even as expressing a
one-sided aspect of Morality.

be subordinated to the supreme requirements of social Well-being. The kind and the limits of this self-development and the self-sacrifice which this principle will demand of the individual will depend on the nature of his vocation. But, in view of the prominent place which this question has assumed in recent ethical speculation, it will be well to develope a little further our attitude towards it. Mr. Bradley has made the alleged inconsistency between the claims of self-development or (as he sometimes prefers to call it) self-assertion and self-sacrifice into a ground for preferring an accusation of hopeless and irresolvable internal contradiction or ' dualism ' in the deliverances of the practical Reason. Our moral ideas are therefore doomed to go the way of the rest of human knowledge, and are pronounced to belong to the region of mere 'Appearance,' not of true knowledge—the knowledge of ' Reality.' A brief examination of this thesis may serve to elucidate what has already been said on this subject.

Here are Mr. Bradley's words :—

'I am far from suggesting that in morality we are forced throughout to make a choice between such incompatible ideals. For this is not the case, and, if it were so, life could hardly be lived. To a very large extent by taking no thought about his individual perfection, and by aiming at that which seems to promise no personal advantage, a man secures his private welfare. We may, perhaps, even say that in the main there is no collision between self-sacrifice and self-assertion, and that on the whole neither of these, in the proper sense, exists for morality. But, while admitting or asserting to the full the general identity of these aspects, I am here insisting on the fact of their partial divergence. And that, at least in some respects and with some persons, these two ideals seem hostile no sane observer can deny.

' In other words we must admit that two great divergent forms of moral goodness exist. In order to realize the idea of a perfect self a man may have to choose between two partially conflicting methods. Morality, in short, may dictate either self-sacrifice or self-assertion, and it is important to clear our ideas as to the meaning of each. A common mistake is to identify the first with the living for others, and the second with living

for oneself. Virtue upon this view is social, either directly or
indirectly, either visibly or invisibly. The development of the
individual, that is, unless it reacts to increase the welfare of
society, can certainly not be moral. This doctrine I am still
forced to consider as a truth which has been exaggerated and
perverted into error. There are intellectual and other accom-
plishments, to which I at least cannot refuse the title of virtue.
But I cannot assume that, without exception, these must all
somehow add to what is called social welfare; nor, again, do
I see how to make a social organism the subject which directly
possesses them. But, if so, it is impossible for me to admit that
all virtue is essentially or primarily social. On the contrary, the
neglect of social good, for the sake of pursuing other ends, may
not only be moral self-assertion, but again, equally under other
conditions, it *may* be moral self-sacrifice. We can even say that
the living "for others," rather than living "for myself," *may* be
immoral and selfish.'

*   *   *   *   *

' The ends sought by self-assertion and self-sacrifice are, each
alike, unattainable. The individual never can in himself become
an harmonious system. And in the wider ideal to which he
devotes himself, no matter how thoroughly, he never can find
complete self-realization. For, even if we take that ideal to be
perfect and to be somehow completely fulfilled, yet, after all, he
himself is not totally absorbed in it. If his discordant element
is for faith swallowed up, yet faith, no less, means that a jarring
appearance remains. And, in the complete gift and dissipation
of his personality, *he*, as such, must vanish ; and, with that, the
good is, as such, transcended and submerged. This result is but
the conclusion with which our chapter began. Goodness is an
appearance, it is phenomenal, and therefore self-contradictory.
And therefore, as was the case with degrees of truth and reality,
it shows two forms of one standard which will not wholly
coincide. In the end, where every discord is brought to harmony,
every idea is also realized. But there, where nothing can be
lost, everything, by addition and by rearrangement, more or
less changes its character. And most emphatically no self-

assertion nor any self-sacrifice, nor any goodness or morality, has, as such, any reality in the Absolute. Goodness is a subordinate and, therefore, a self-contradictory aspect of the universe[1].'

I must not now attempt to discuss as a whole the metaphysical position of the most brilliant and original thinker of our time. I venture only to make a few remarks exclusively upon the ethical side of the difficulty here presented:

(1) I trust it will not be thought in any way disrespectful to Mr. Bradley if I say that the whole of this charge of ' inconsistency ' in the deliverances of the Practical Reason seems to me to turn upon a confusion between the idea of good and the idea of right. Mr. Bradley's doctrine is not merely that each of these modes of action is good, but that they are *equally* virtuous and right[2]. If Practical Reason really said that two inconsistent courses of action were both right, its ' dualism ' would no doubt be hopeless enough. .But there is no inconsistency in saying that two things are both good, though (where you cannot have both) it is right to choose that which is best. And Practical Reason, as I hold, does not pronounce that self-development and self-sacrifice are both right in all circumstances. It pronounces—to my mind unequivocally—that it is always right to choose that which is from the universal point of view the greatest of goods : and, though to determine what is the greatest of goods constitutes the gravest of practical difficulties, Reason is not essentially incapable of this task of distinguishing the value of goods, and so of pronouncing which of two courses is for a given individual under given circumstances the one and only right course of action.

Therefore, if the question be put nakedly, ' Which is to give way — self-assertion to self-sacrifice or self-sacrifice to self-assertion—when there is a collision between a smaller good of mine and a larger good of my neighbours ? ' I have no hesitation in saying that it is I and not Society that should be sacrificed. Or, if it be said that this is begging the question whether my intellectual cultivation may not be sometimes the greater good of the two, I should contend that no self-development of mine can

[1] *Appearance and Reality*, Ed. ii, pp. 415–420.
[2] Ib., p. 418.

ever be so great a good as to justify me in pursuing it to the total neglect of all social considerations. It has, indeed, to be admitted that men's capacities are not equal; and that unequal capacity does, in the abstract, constitute unequal value. One person may be entitled to more consideration than another; and it may be urged, as a speculative possibility, that there might be a person of such exalted capacities that his intellectual well-being might be held to justify an exclusive devotion to his own improvement; but then I should hold (*a*) that even then the subordination of his own self-development to that of his fellows would always be demanded in the interest of his own highest Well-being, for the man's capacity for love and social service is higher than any intellectual capacity however exalted; and (*b*) that practically there are no such monsters of intellectual superiority. Even if it were suggested that the majority of his countrymen were so much inferior to him that the claim of their development could not practically count in comparison with his own, yet there must be at least a minority whose capacities must be such as to enter into some sort of comparison with his own. These at least must be considered, nor should I for one admit that any human beings were so low in the scale of creation as to be of no importance at all, though undoubtedly they may be of smaller importance than others. Practical Reason demands some measure of self-sacrifice of the highest towards the lowest. To hold otherwise would be to hold that they might lawfully be treated as mere ὄργανα—instruments of the higher culture of their betters—in other words, be made their slaves [1]. Possibly, some of the apostles of self-realization might not shrink from the conclusion that this is (in principle) the true function of 'the lower classes' in a modern society. At all events there is a very observable tendency for a hyper-intellectual ideal in Ethics to associate itself with anti-popular or reactionary political views.

(2) If as a matter of fact Society were so constituted that

---

[1] This has been practically maintained by Nietzsche, who often says straight out what some of our English self-realizers only hint. He carries his principle out to its logical consequence, and appears to hold that the true ultimate end is the enslavement of the whole world to a single purely egoistic 'Übermensch.' Any one who is inclined to take Nietzsche seriously should read the scathing criticism by Hartmann in *Ethische Studien*, pp. 34-69.

the cultivation of the higher intellectual or artistic capacities really had no tendency to promote the good of any one but the possessor of them, the position would be an awkward one. So far as one can answer hypothetical and abstract questions which postulate a human nature different from any we know, I should be prepared to say, ' In that case, to the extent of the incompatibility between social and private good, the higher faculties must remain uncultivated.' On that supposition intellectual cultivation must simply be treated as we treat those lower goods the enjoyment of which by one is normally inconsistent with their enjoyment by another : each must take his just share and no more. The share may vary with the individual's capacity, but in no case can we rationally allow one man to be treated as an end only, while another is treated merely as a means to his enjoyment. Even on this supposition, there would be no formal ' dualism ' in the moral judgement : the ethical problem would still be answered. But we should in that case have to admit that some of the highest desires and impulses of our nature would be divided against themselves ; that some of the highest capacities in the race (and not only in the individual). would have to go unrealized ; that some of the highest values in human life would be known only, from the point of view of Ethics, as values condemned on account of their conflict with yet higher values. But, as a matter of fact, the true Well-being of human society does not demand this vast sacrifice of intellectual goods. In a number of distinct ways the highest intellectual goods do conduce to social Well-being, and so are not incompatible with the attainment by the individual of that other and higher good which lies in the subordination of self to others.

It will be unnecessary to dwell at length upon the high intellectual qualities which are cultivated and exercised by callings useful in the most commonplace sense of the word—in political life, in administration, in literature, in Physical Science and its more advanced applications, in the professions, in the mere giving of amusement. But it must not be forgotten that in our view the true good of human society does not consist either in mere ' edification ' or in the enjoyment of material good things. The cultivation of the intellectual and artistic faculties is itself part of the social end.   Consequently, the man who in any way communicates the results of his intellectual activity to the world is thereby performing his share of social service, and the subordination of his own ends to those of others involved in such communication will effect that reconciliation between 'self-assertion [1]' and self-sacrifice which his own moral life demands.   And fortunately things are so constituted that the development of the intellectual and aesthetic nature in the many to that moderate pitch which seems alone to be practicable in their case imperatively demands a much higher cultivation of them in the few.   The pleasure and the culture which the average man derives from an occasional visit to a picture gallery, and from the constant contemplation of good copies or less valuable originals on private walls, is only possible if the Artist is allowed to devote a laborious lifetime to the study and practice of Art: The comparatively uneducated can only find intellectual enjoyment if there is a leisured literary class to produce books for them to read; and the leisured literary class that produces the books which such men actually read, if they are good of their kind, is one which could not itself exist unless there were a small class in which a still higher, or at least a less popular and more specialized, culture or learning prevailed.   The teacher must know more than those whom he teaches; the writer must know more of his particular subject than the average reader; the man of letters utilizes and absorbs the labours of numerous specialists.   The maintenance, in short, of a highly cultivated class is an absolutely essential condition of healthy cultivated life in the nation at large.   And the study of History would further seem to suggest that the connexion between intellectual health on the one hand and social and moral Well-being on the other is much closer than is sometimes supposed.   The attempt to substitute an ideal of pure Morality for an ideal of wider human good, the attempt to confine culture within the limit wherein it directly subserves personal goodness, is always suicidal.   The 'dark age' was an age of moral anarchy and wickedness.   The moral and religious progress of the twelfth

[1] Mr. Bradley more often uses the word 'self-assertion' than 'self-realization,' but he does not appear to attach importance to the distinction.

and thirteenth centuries was intimately connected with a great
intellectual revival. Moral progress is largely dependent on
intellectual progress, and it is impossible to determine in advance
what kinds of intellectual advance will react on ethical ideals
and ethical practice. But nothing can be further from my
intention than to rest the defence of intellectual pursuits upon
their moral influence in the narrow sense, i. e. their tendency to
promote for Society some good other than themselves. The
different elements in human Well-being can undoubtedly exist
to some extent apart. Intellectual development is none the less
a part of the true ideal for society or individual because it is
not the whole good or the highest good of human life. The
ideal which would pronounce moral a life of absolutely self-
centred culture or study is to my mind an irrational and immoral
one [1]. But the student even of the most 'useless' branches of
knowledge can socialize and moralize his life by communicating
his discoveries or stimulating other students, even though the
gain to the world may be a purely intellectual gain, and though
the persons capable of directly and immediately benefiting by
his work may be counted on the fingers of one hand. It is no
paradox to say that there is nothing more useful to the world
than 'useless' knowledge.

In no case, then, can it be right for a man to disregard social
Well-being. In many cases a man's social duty may consist, so
far as is compatible with the ordinary duties of the man and the
citizen (themselves involving, of course, some measure of self-
sacrifice), for the most part in the highest intellectual self-development. Even the man of genius must renounce that exceptional
license to be immoral which the ideal of self-realization sometimes
seems disposed to concede to him. And generally of course the
communication to the world of the results of his studies on which
I have insisted will take off something from the absolutely possible maximum of intellectual development – something varying

---

[1] Here for once (which is very rarely the case) I prefer Mr. Bradley's
earlier to his later self: 'It is quite clear that if anybody wants to realize
himself as a perfect man without trying to be a perfect member of his
country and all his smaller communities, he makes what all sane persons
would admit to be a great mistake' (*Ethical Studies*, p. 182).

from an occasional week spent in the sort of literary composition or proof-reading which does not promote intellectual advancement to the self-sacrifice of the man who deliberately accepts a far lower position than he might have achieved as a scholar or a thinker to make himself an effective teacher or the apostle of some unpopular cause. It is unnecessary to dwell on the compensating gain which human interest and practical sympathies bring to the student even within the intellectual sphere itself. It is perhaps only in the region of the most purely physical sciences that there is no such compensation, and in the pursuit of these sciences complete detachment from all human interests is for the most part avoided by the enormous possibilities of conquest over Nature which they bring to the life of man, and by the much greater opportunities of really adding to the intellectual wealth of the world which are in this region open to the most commonplace student than is the case in the 'humaner' studies. The student of many other subjects may be, weighed down by the consciousness that the world really wants no more books of the kind that he can write; but the world can never know too many facts of physical Science or despise the attempts at scientific explanation which lie within the reach of every competent investigator.

Thus, when we turn from the individual to the society, there is no ultimate collision between intellectual self-development and that positive moral goodness of which self-sacrifice is the negative side. For the individual there is no doubt a collision : but the problem which the collision raises is one which Reason is not incompetent to solve. Reason recognizes that the direction and the degree of each individual's capacities must be, if he wants to be moral, limited by the equal value of the like capacity in others. And, that being so, it follows that the highest life for the individual is only attainable by that subordination of self to Society which constitutes self-sacrifice. The measure and degree of that sacrifice must itself be determined by the requirements of social Well-being. Each individual must develope the capacities which will realize on the whole the good of greatest intrinsic worth [1], having

---

[1] To avoid repetition I ignore the question of distribution of good which has already been dealt with in Book I, chap. viii.

regard to the fact that social good is best realized on the whole by some specialization of social function. If there be any truth in the theory of Vocation, Reason is not incompetent to determine what, under a given set of circumstances, is the vocation of the individual. The course dictated by that principle, the particular balance between self-development and self-assertion which in each case social Well-being demands, is the one and only course which for that individual is *right*.

So far I have felt bound to deal with Mr. Bradley's indictment against the Practical Reason. I have tried to show that Practical Reason is never reduced to saying, 'Two inconsistent plans of life are good, and I cannot decide which of them is the right one for any individual at any one time to adopt.' If that be established, that is as far as it is necessary to carry the discussion in any ethical interest. Into the wider metaphysical implications of the controversy it is not necessary to go at the present moment. I need only remark that if the ethical question is not beyond the capacities of the Practical Reason, any metaphysical conclusions which may be based upon the assumption of its irreconcilable dualism must so far be unfounded. If the position which I have taken up be accepted, the allegation of self-contradiction in the moral consciousness can only come to this—that there are many things which would be good if the nature of things had only not made their enjoyment incompatible with the enjoyment of still better things. Under these circumstances the question may be raised, 'Are they really good?' How that question may be answered is a matter of no directly ethical importance. The only metaphysical consequence which might result from the admission that one good is sometimes incompatible with another would be the admission that it is possible to conceive of a better world than actually exists. This is a position which it is no doubt highly unphilosophical to adopt at a period when a 'cheap and easy optimism' is regarded in many quarters as almost essential to the philosophical character. But it is a position with which few will quarrel except professed Philosophers. But, once more, any ethical difficulties that may remain about this collision between self-realization and self-assertion, when once we have got rid of the confusion already pointed out, are difficulties created for Ethics by Mr. Bradley's particular system of Metaphysic—not difficulties created for Metaphysic by Ethics. From the ethical point of view there is no difficulty about the admission that goods are sometimes inconsistent with one another. So long as it is admitted that it is possible to choose the greatest good, and that such a choice—and this only—is always right, there is no latent contradiction in our ethical judgements: and, if that be admitted, one at least of the counts in Mr. Bradley's indictment against Reason is pronounced bad.

V

Since the greater part of this chapter was written Mr. Bradley's thesis has received an elaborate development at the hands of Professor A. E. Taylor. My reply to Professor Taylor's argument is substantially the same as that which I should make to Mr. Bradley, with this addition, that in Professor Taylor's case it is much more easy than in Mr. Bradley's to reply to him out of his own mouth. Mr. Bradley evidently does believe in the 'duality' or internal contradiction of the Practical Reason, and he does not believe in either of his fundamentally opposed ethical creeds overmuch. I do not mean, of course, that he is practically indifferent to ordinary moral interests, but he is not one of those thinkers in whose speculative outlook confidence in the dictates of the Practical Reason occupies a paramount position. In Professor Taylor, however, the divorce between the man and the philosopher is carried much further than with Mr. Bradley. Professor Taylor as a man is evidently inclined to an enthusiastic belief in the Practical Reason. So long as he confines himself to the ethical point of view, he demonstrates with admirable effect the unreality of the alleged ethical antinomy. He shows— nobody more conclusively—that neither the ideal of self-realiza- tion nor the ideal of absolute and exclusive self-sacrifice is Morality as we know it. He is never tired of exhibiting the fact that each of these ideals pushed to its logical extreme would land us in what every unsophisticated Conscience would pronounce to be hopelessly and irredeemably irrational and immoral. The true moral ideal includes both elements: a truly moral man will choose now one, now the other, whenever (which, after all, is the exception rather than the rule)[1] there is a real necessity of choosing between them. If Professor Taylor has not done much to analyse the principles upon which the moral consciousness chooses between the two, he constantly assumes that it is possible to choose, and that there is a right and a wrong answer to the question. Some of the alleged contradictions find admirable solutions in Professor Taylor's own pages. It is only in exceptional cases that he even alleges that there is any real difficulty in making a right choice; and the existence of such difficult cases is no argument against the inherent capacity of the moral consciousness or the validity of its decisions, any more than the difficulty of discovering the laws of Nature, or the existence of different opinions on historical problems, is an argument against the validity of physical law or the existence of objective historical truth. Sometimes, indeed, it seems difficult to acquit Professor Taylor of failing to see (or perhaps of finding it convenient to ignore) the difference between the claim of validity for the moral judgement as such and the claim for personal infallibility or omniscience on the part of the individual Conscience. At all events it is only on the basis of such a confusion that the existence of difficult questions of Casuistry on which no wise or charitable man will care to pronounce with much confidence—still less to judge severely those who pronounce otherwise—can be regarded as the smallest argument for an inherent and irremovable internal contradiction in the moral consciousness itself.

VI

There is one other view connected with the collision between self-development and self-sacrifice about which I should like to add a word. It is sometimes assumed as a sort of postulate that the good must be good not only for one but for all—that there can be no real discord between my good and another's. We have already adopted many positions which preclude us from

---

[1] 'There is probably no single virtue of all those recognised by popular nomenclature which can be satisfactorily accounted for by either the requirements of full self-development or of social justice considered by themselves' (*The Problem of Conduct*, p. 218).

sharing that assumption. It is one which is hardly intelligible except upon the assumption that the good will is the only true good. If things like pleasure and Culture are admitted to be good, the assertion that one man's pleasure or culture cannot be inconsistent with another's is clearly opposed to experience. To say that, when the enjoyment of such things by the individual is inconsistent with the good of another, it is not really good for the former, implies that confusion between the idea of good and the idea of right which lies at the root of so much chaos in more than one system of Moral Philosophy. If the distinction between good and right is to be kept up, it is clear that it is often right for the individual to make a sacrifice which is not for his good *in all respects*. Inasmuch as the doing right is for him the highest good, he does promote his own highest good by the sacrifice : but to say that it is not a sacrifice of good is to deny that the conception of good is logically prior to that of right. I fail to see how any clear ethical thinking is possible except upon the assumption that many things are good which nevertheless the actual conditions of life prevent our attaining, and that therefore the only possible object of moral effort is to attain the greatest possible good—not all conceivable good. It may no doubt for some extra-ethical reason be held that there is a sense in which, when the right course has been chosen, we must assume not merely that the adoption of that course is the greatest good attainable by the individual in the given circumstances, but that all its consequences and concomitants—as well those in spite of which it is chosen as those for which it is chosen—are wholly good, and involve no evil at all to any one. But that is a metaphysical theory with which we are not now concerned : and it is so far from being a necessary postulate for Ethics that it may rather be pronounced to be unethical or anti-ethical. There are many bad things in the world besides bad voluntary actions ; some of the consequences of the best actions are consequences which our judgements of value undoubtedly pronounce to be bad. If any one pronounces that they are nevertheless very good, that is an assertion which cannot be made on ethical grounds ; it must be maintained on the basis of some Metaphysic (like that of Mr. Bradley) which denies the ultimate validity of our moral judgements, not from the point of view of those who believe in the validity of our practical judgements. To this subject I hope to return in the chapter on 'Metaphysic and Morals.' Meanwhile, a word must be said about a form of this denial of all collision between my good and another's which does rest apparently upon purely ethical grounds [1].

The assumption that what is good for one man must be good for all has found its most explicit expression in that theory of the 'common good' which plays so large a part in the ethical teaching of Green and his followers. The phrase 'common good' is so loosely used by Green himself that it is sometimes doubtful whether to him it always meant anything more than 'the general good [2]'; but, in other passages and still more as used by the disciples who have turned Green's vague but stimulating Mysticism into hard and rigid dogmas, it is quite clear that the idea of the common good means something which is equally my good and that of every one else. Nothing, it is assumed, can be moral which produces any evil

[1] To meet an objection which would, I think, here be irrelevant, I may say that I fully recognize that in strictness nothing can be good for one person which is not a good absolutely, since the term 'good' always implies objectivity; but, since nothing can (as it seems to me) be good but a state of some consciousness, I think it would be pedantic to object to calling a good state of a certain person's consciousness 'his good' or a 'good for him,' even where that good involves a greater evil in some other consciousness.

[2] Sidgwick points out how far Green is from consistently maintaining this idea of a 'common good.' After quoting Green's account of the just man as one who 'will not promote his own wellbeing or that of one whom he loves and likes . . . at the cost of impeding in any way the wellbeing of one who is nothing to him but a man, or whom he involuntarily dislikes,' he remarks, 'How, after writing this description of an ideally just man, Green could possibly go on to say (§ 232), that "the distinction of good for self and good for others has never entered into that idea of a true good on which moral judgments are founded," I cannot imagine' (*Ethics of Green*, p. 67). If Green were prepared to stick to the position that there is no good but a good will, the contention that one man's good can never be incompatible with that of another might be plausibly (only plausibly) made, but the extravagance of the position becomes glaring when (as he often does) Green includes Art and Science in his conception of the end in spite of his declaration that 'the only good which is really common to all who may pursue it, is that which consists in the universal will to be good' (*Prolegomena*, § 244).

at all for any living soul [1]. Now I readily admit—and of
course from a practical point of view it is most important to
insist—that it is a characteristic of the higher goods that they
are capable of being enjoyed by a larger number of persons
than the lower. In promoting knowledge I am not promoting
something which is necessarily my gain and another's loss.
I am exercising my faculties, attaining my good, getting my
enjoyment (or, as our friends will have it, 'realizing' my
higher self) by the very same acts which are also adding to
the common intellectual wealth of the world. Knowledge is
not a thing which, like champagne or plum-pudding, becomes
less by being shared. My enjoyment of Shakespeare does not
diminish the amount of Shakespeare which there is to be enjoyed by others: rather it has a tendency, so far as my
conduct has any effect on others, to stimulate, encourage, and
facilitate in them the reading and appreciation of Shakespeare.
No less clearly is that the case with a charitable action which
'blesseth him that gives and him that takes.' This very simple
fact is, I take it, the real basis of the assumption that what
is good for me to do cannot be bad for another. But I would
observe that this is not universally the case even with the higher
goods. A picture can, it is true, be looked at by several people at
the same time, and by several hundred people one after the other,
in the course of a day. Practically, a Londoner can get a sight of
any particular picture in the National Gallery as often as he
wants to see it. But, if the passion for Art were equally distributed throughout the inhabitants of the Metropolis, if every
Londoner wanted to refresh his soul by gazing on a particular
Turner once a week, the crowding around that picture would
become highly inconvenient : the enjoyment of this privilege by
one certainly would be incompatible with its equal enjoyment

---

[1] The assumption reminds me of the much-ridiculed doctrine of Mr. Herbert
Spencer that 'conduct which has any concomitant of pain, or any painful
consequence, is partially wrong' (*Data of Ethics*, p. 261). The extravagance is not really diminished when a similar assertion is made by those who
exclude pleasure from their idea of good. Many right acts—the preaching
of really good sermons, for instance—often do some moral harm to persons
to whom they do not happen to appeal.

by others. Even as matters actually stand, it is not the case that the accumulation of pictures in Trafalgar Square is a 'common good' to the world in general. What is London's gain is certainly Italy's loss, and cannot, except in a very restricted sense, be set down as Cornwall's gain. Still more easy is it to show that the enjoyment of higher goods by one involves a loss of lower goods by others. The Artists and the Connoisseurs eat and drink a good deal, and the necessity of supporting them adds to the toil and diminishes the profits or enjoyments of many thousand working men. Doubtless the encouragement of Art is good on the whole for the world, but it is not all gain. Moreover, it is important to remark that even in the typical case of the charitable act which 'blesses him who gives and him who takes,' the good of him who gives is not the same as that of him who takes. The good Samaritan gets exercise for his Benevolence, the man fallen among thieves gets the healing of wounds. The Surgeon exercises his intellectual faculties and professional skill; his patients benefit by that skill, but what they get is quite another good from his. This seems to make the term 'common good' unsuitable. The end of Morality is a just distribution of goods, not the simultaneous enjoyment by all of one and the same good.

In the case of those lower goods which nevertheless we have agreed to call good, it is clear that the enjoyment of a good by one is, not exceptionally but normally, incompatible with its enjoyment by another. Two men cannot eat the same cake. We all live at the expense of some one else's labour. No doubt it is true that if we look at the whole effect upon Society—at the whole social system or reciprocal exchange of services which Morality enjoins—we may say that when two men treat each other justly, the one gains as much in one way as he loses in another. The ideal of human society is precisely a state of things in which each contributes to the good of Society in one way as much as he gets from Society in another, and so helps to set up that 'kingdom of ends' in which we have already discovered the sanest and most workable of the Kantian formulae. And it is naturally an element of this ideal that, as far as possible, each should find his own pleasure in something

which is as good for others as for himself.   But this is only an
ideal, and the conditions of human life permit but a distant
approximation to it.   The harmonizing of one man's interest
with that of another must to a very great extent be effected
simply by the choice of the least evil—an evil which really is
evil to some, though good for the whole.

I am not quite clear, however, whether in these somewhat
obvious reflections I am not really expressing what is meant by
many of those who profess the philosophy of the 'common
good.'   If I am doing so, I can only submit that the phrase
'common good' is badly chosen to express their meaning; and
as used by some it certainly suggests the ideas which I have com-
bated.   The doctrine of the 'common good,' strictly interpreted,
really implies Green's doctrine that nothing but the good will is
good at all (for only so can it soberly be asserted that goods
never collide with one another)—a doctrine in which many of
those who inherit his phraseology decline to follow him.   And
the position of Green on this matter is really open to the very
objection which he himself urged with so much force against
Kant—the objection that it leaves the good will without content.
This position is merely disguised by talking about 'character'
or 'perfection' as the end instead of 'the good will.'   If nothing
but the good will is good, there is no reason why one act of will
should be considered as better than another.   And the good will
is the only good of one man which can never be actually inconsistent with the like good in another; though after all it may be
doubted whether one man's good will is actually in itself the
good of another, and it is quite easy to imagine cases in which
one man's moral good could only be promoted by the neglect of
another's.

In some of the writers with whom the 'common good' theory
is popular, it is connected with a further metaphysical theory—
the theory that not only the good but the self which is to be
realized is a common self—common to each individual and to 'the
Absolute'—so that in promoting his own true good the individual
is necessarily promoting the good of every other individual.
And it is further suggested at times that it is only upon this
assumption that there can be any logical basis for obedience to

the moral law. Altruism can only be justified by showing that it is really Egoism [1].

I have already touched on the metaphysical aspect of the theory, and shall return to it hereafter. But even if there be a sense in which we may treat individual men and women as being 'manifestations' or 'appearances' of an all-embracing Absolute, Ethics surely has to do with the 'manifestations' or 'appearances,' and not with the Unity. Ethics is concerned with the relations of these apparently different and mutually exclusive 'appearances': and it is impossible to give any meaning to the simplest ethical conceptions except upon the assumption that I and my neighbour are (for ethical purposes) different persons, and that my good is distinguishable from his good. I am told to promote my neighbour's good because, since I and my neighbour are really the same being, his good is really my good. But I may quite reasonably reply that upon that supposition I have only to promote my own good, and need not trouble about my neighbour's, for in promoting my own good I must necessarily be promoting his also. The theory can be used as a defence of Egoism quite as reasonably as against it. Nor does the consideration that I and my neighbour equally derive our being from the same Absolute seem to me to constitute any ground or basis for moral obligation which would not exist apart from that supposition. If all that is meant by the theory is that when the

---

[1] I have noticed above Mr. Bradley's use of this doctrine (Vol. I, p. 67), but the most explicit formulation of the assumption which I have met with is to be found in Bishop d'Arcy's *Short Study of Ethics* (pp. 102, 120 *et passim*). 'Why,' he says (p. 143), 'should a man sacrifice his desires for the sake of a common good ? The religious view of morality answers the question at once : Because all are one in God, and the common good is the true good of every individual.' I should not deny the truth of the last proposition in a certain sense, because my moral consciousness does judge that action for the general good possesses value, but if my moral consciousness did not so judge, Bishop d'Arcy's Metaphysic certainly would not convince me of the duty. Would the Bishop (with Schopenhauer) hold that I must also impute to myself (and to the Absolute) my neighbour's sins ? The last contention would seem to be quite as reasonable as the former. Dr. d'Arcy, being a Bishop, shrinks from pronouncing the absolute identity of every individual (good or bad) with his neighbour and with God (and uses the vague phrase 'one in God'), but his Logic requires the omission of the 'one in.'

idea of objectivity inherent in the very nature of all moral
obligation is thought out to its logical consequences, it implies
Theism, that is a doctrine with which I fully sympathize, and
on which I hope hereafter to insist. But the idea of moral
obligation is no deduction from the idea of God, whether conceived of in a purely theistic or in a more or less pantheistic
sense. Rather it is one of those immediate data of consciousness
from which the idea of God may be inferred. If the notion of
obligation or intrinsic validity or objectivity were not inherent
in the immediate affirmation of the moral consciousness, no
demonstration of the metaphysical unity of God and man or self
and neighbour could possibly put it there. If the practical
Reason did not recognize an intrinsic value in my neighbour's
personality, no demonstration as to the common metaphysical
origin and the actual identity of the two selves could possibly
convince me of such value. Ethical truths may, and, I believe,
do, contain metaphysical implications; but no ethical truth can
possibly be deduced from or proved by any metaphysical considerations which are not ethical. Ethical truth can rest upon
nothing whatever but the actual deliverances of the moral consciousness. And the moral consciousness certainly knows nothing
of any metaphysical identity between myself and my neighbour.
On the contrary it assumes that we are two and not one. If in
any sense it is to be shown that we are one, that is a position
which must be established on grounds independent of Ethics.

VII

There is another conception of the ethical end which has
many analogies with the ideal of 'self-realization.' Professor
Simmel, the most brilliant of recent ethical writers, has attempted
to find an ethical criterion in the idea of a 'maximum of Energy'
(*Thätigkeit*)[1]. It is not merely pleasure which gives life its
value; a life in which there is much pain and much pleasure
would be positively better than one in which there is only

---

[1] *Einleitung*, I, p. 371 *sq.* He wholly fails to show that in any natural sense
there is a greater 'Quantum von Zwecksetzung' (II, p. 359), or a 'Willens-
maximum' in good rather than in bad conduct.

pleasure. The most desirable kind of life is one in which there are many ups and downs, plenty of excitement, many a 'crowded hour of glorious life,' a maximum 'swing' or oscillation between the heights of exaltation and the depths of depression [1]. Now in some ways it may be freely admitted that Simmel's ideal is a great improvement upon the ideal of 'self-realization.' His formula is far less of a mere form; it is to some extent a concrete ideal. And it emphasizes many points which we may recognize as important aspects of a high ethical ideal. Unlike the 'self-realization' ideal, it is not purely self-regarding: it is not only for himself that the good man will promote a 'maximum of activity,' but also for others; and there is no confusion between one's own good and that of others. Simmel's ideal man will promote the kind of life that has most value on the whole, though in particular cases he may judge that an exciting career for himself is really so good a thing that he may sacrifice to it large masses (as it were) of inferior life. Moreover, the doctrine exhibits impressively some of the differences which would exist in detail between a hedonistic standard of Ethics resolutely applied and one which recognizes other elements of value in human life besides pleasure. As against the ideal of 'harmonious development,' it insists that what is best in human life as we know it is often a state of violent internal discord, of struggle and unquiet, rather than of smug and contented spiritual self-complacency. And again it is valuable as a reminder that we cannot in the region of Ethics maintain a sharp and rigid distinction between ends and means; the means are part of the end. All ethical thought becomes, indeed, impossible, unless we do recognize a distinction between ends and means: it is because the end has value that the means to it are justified. But Moralists who have thoroughly grasped this doctrine are beset by the temptation to suppose that the character of the means is unimportant, and may be ignored in estimating the rightness or wrongness of the act. All human activity does, indeed, consist in the pursuit of ends, but the end is often in itself far less valuable than the pursuit. Human life consists chiefly in the

---

[1] '... die Schwingungsweite zwischen der Lust und dem Schmerz eines Lebens der Grösse seiner Thätigkeit proportional ist.' *Einleitung*, I, p. 388.

doing of things which are means to ends: the end must have
value, but whether it is worth pursuing or not must depend
very often upon the character of the activities which will lead
to that end.   From one point of view such activities must be
looked upon as means; from another they are part of the end.

   That is obviously the case even from the hedonistic point of
view, as is seen most conspicuously in the case of games. 'Sport'
has been well defined as the overcoming of difficulties simply for
the sake of overcoming them: and from a non-hedonistic point
of view it must be still more emphatically recognized that the
activity which is involved in the pursuit of an end is often
something much higher and more valuable than the end that it
attains, as that end would be apart from the activity.   Man does
not live by bread alone.   His energies are largely absorbed in
the pursuit of bread, but the bread-winning is often a higher
and nobler thing than the bread.   The true good of human life
(as we know it) does not consist in the pursuit of some end
which we first pursue and then enjoy at leisure, but in activities
which are constantly seeking to satisfy needs which, even if
satisfied, are only supplanted by fresh needs.   Both the enjoyment and the nobleness of life often lie in the pursuit.   When
people have no unsatisfied needs, they can only give a value to
life by more or less successful efforts to invent new ones.
Simmel's theory brings out, too, the fact that in detail the
duty of one man—even, it may be said, the concrete ideal which
it is right for one man to pursue—is not the same as that
of another.   It insists on the need for varieties of individual
development and practical activity.   All these elements of truth
we may freely recognize in Simmel's formula, but when it is put
forward as an exclusive and adequate ideal, it is too hopelessly
vague to be worth serious examination.   How can 'amount of
activity' be measured?   I can, indeed, compare the value of the
very dissimilar activities;   I can even by a considerable effort of
abstraction estimate the amount of pleasure which there is in
each.   But how am I to say whether there is a greater quantity
of activity in the most exciting kind of historical research or in
a steeplechase, in Philosophy or in football?   So far as quantities of activity can be estimated, no one probably ever crowded

more of it into his own life or caused more of it in others than Napoleon Buonaparte, but no one who attaches any meaning to the idea of Morality can well recognize in Napoleon his highest ethical ideal. Simmel's doctrine is one of those which spring from the desire to invent new theses, without which it is impossible to write sensational works on Moral Philosophy. The airing of new ideas is often, no doubt, more exciting, more full of activity (of *Thätigkeit*) than the elucidation, correction, and harmonization of older and truer ones. Acts can only be considered right or wrong relatively to some end other than the acts themselves, however true it may be that the will which wills that good is a greater good than the good which it wills. Neither 'duty for duty's sake' nor 'activity for activity's sake' is a rational ethical watchword, unless each is supplemented by the doctrine that the end which duty aims at promoting must be a good one, and that the 'activity' which is a good must be either part of the end which we pronounce good or a means to it. Such formulae as 'activity for the sake of activity' or 'self-realization' spring from an unwillingness to admit the simple, ultimate, and unanalysable character of the idea of good, without the admission of which there can be no such thing as Morality. The contents of our moral consciousness cannot be translated or paraphrased into any language which does not contain the word 'good' or its synonym.

Both the difficulties which have been raised as a ground for accusing Morality of internal contradiction, and some of those which lie at the root of Simmel's exaggerated theory of maximum activity, are, we have seen reason to believe, met by the due recognition of the fact that though duty is incumbent upon every one, though the good of society is the end for all, that good demands and includes a great variety of individual goods, and that not all these goods can either be promoted or enjoyed within the compass of a single life. This represents a side of ethical truth which is generally expressed by the doctrine that different men have different vocations—a doctrine which will be further examined and developed in the next chapter.

CHAPTER IV

VOCATION

I

I HAVE tried to establish the position that acts are virtuous in so far as they tend to promote and to distribute justly a Well-being which consists in various elements possessing very different degrees of intrinsic value. The ideal life would be a life into which the different elements of 'good' should enter in the degree appropriate to their intrinsic worth; in which, roughly speaking, intellectual should be subordinated to moral well-being, while lower desires are indulged in such a way and to such an extent as are most conducive to the due predominance of the higher; or, more simply, in which every desire, every element in consciousness is accorded the place which is due to its own intrinsic worth. It might seem to follow that the ideal of Morality in its narrower sense, the ideal aim of the virtuous will, must be to realize these various 'goods' in proportion to their relative importance for each and every human being. But such an account of human duty takes no account of the fact that for Society in general the highest amount of good cannot be realized by each individual endeavouring to secure for himself and to promote for every other all sorts of good. In no one life is the gratification, in any high degree, of all even among the better desires possible; while the very attempt to gratify all equally makes impossible the attainment of any one of the best kinds of life. And, again, from the point of view of Society, a certain specialization of function, or what, looked at from the economic point of view is known as division of labour, is equally imperative. Not only is it practically impossible for the same individual in every case to devote his time and energy to the promotion of highest and higher and lowest goods in the proportion of their intrinsic worth, but even among goods of the particular rank which it is his social function to promote, he must devote himself to the promotion of some one particular good, if a maximum return, so to speak, is to be produced. The labourer must devote the bulk of his time not merely to producing food but to producing a particular kind of food. And the conditions of human life are, unfortunately, such that a very much larger proportion of the energies of most men have to be devoted to producing the lower kind of goods than to the production of the higher.

Moreover, this specialization of the good-producing energies of each individual carries with it a further specialization of the good which he must himself enjoy. For, though the abstraction is useful and legitimate for some purposes, we cannot treat the production of good as though it were really a totally distinct thing from the enjoyment of good; as though a man simply produced by his social activity one sort of good, while the good that he himself enjoys is something wholly distinct and separable from it, something produced by other people for him, and given to him in exchange for his services by the other members of his society, just as the wages received by a husbandman are something quite distinct from the corn which he produces. We have seen that a large part of the good which can be enjoyed in human life consists precisely in these socially directed activities. Both moral and intellectual goods are attained by contributing in some special way to the good of Society. And, consequently, if a man concentrates his energies on the production of some one kind of good, that will largely determine the nature of the good which he will enjoy, when good life comes to be looked at as the individual's share in a social Well-being. The nature of his contribution to social good must largely determine, so to speak, the nature of his dividend. If a man's social function is to plough the fields, that energy of ploughing will not be so much energy taken off from the production of higher good and concentrated on the production of lower, but it will determine to a large extent the nature of the Well-being that will fall to his share; for it is in and through this social function of ploughing that he will attain that highest good which consists in the direction of his will towards good, or, more simply, in the performance of his duty. And, though in the particular case of ploughing, the limitations which it sets to intellectual activity are more conspicuous than the scope which it affords, it is none the less true that even mechanical occupations involve some intellectual activity. The ploughman, even when ploughing, is at least doing something that cannot be done by a beast. He will attain his highest good in ministering to the bodily wants of others; while, though it is obviously desirable that the ploughman should enjoy some of those higher goods of life which have no special relation to his function, the kind and amount of other goods—higher and lower alike—which will fall to his lot must be largely such as are incidental to or compatible with the occupation of ploughing. As compared with the town workman in a factory for instance, the country labourer enjoys a more varied and interesting occupation, an occupation which brings with it a greater variety of mental activities and a greater development of individual initiative, the pleasures and the health that come from life in the open air, the use of a less crowded house and a garden of his own; he cannot enjoy the social and political life, the social interests (outside his work) and the exciting amusements which partially atone to the townsman for the squalor and discomfort of his surroundings. Of course some of these limitations in either case are due to defective and improvable social arrangements; but it is clear that in any society different individuals must enjoy, as they promote, different kinds of good. Hence a large part of human duty consists in acts which are not the duty of all men. A large part of human duty consists in the duties of one's 'Vocation.'

It is not only in the discharge of his formal social function, the function which constitutes (as we say) his business or profession or 'state of life,' that there must be some specialization. Even in the kinds of good that it is not the business of any recognized profession to promote, it is clearly desirable and necessary that different men should contribute to social good in different ways. In philanthropy, in social service, in the choice between different modes of life, there is room for different vocations. An exhaustive treatise on Casuistry would have to deal not merely with the duties of different vocations, but also with the question, on what principles a man should determine what is his social function, whether in the way of formal or official calling or in the direction of his own voluntary energies within the limits allowed by universally binding moral obligations and by those which are incident to his profession or occupation. Moreover, in resolving duty into an obligation to contribute to general Well-being, it is not merely the kind but the amount of such contribution that is undetermined. Here there is another group of questions upon which Moral Philosophy ought to have something to say, if it is to aim at a complete analysis of the contents of the moral consciousness. It must give some answer to the question, 'What are to be the limits of the individual's self-sacrifice?' And if there are limits which a man is not bound to pass, the question may further be raised whether he is at liberty, if he pleases, to do more? If not, must we admit that it is possible for a man to do more than his duty? Can there be works of Supererogation?

II

There is yet another reason for devoting some special consideration to this question of Vocation. In the question 'How am I to know and recognize my Vocation?' we have a peculiarly good illustration of the inadequacy of Intuitionism in any of its various forms to formulate the procedure by which reasonable men really do determine, and feel that they ought to determine, their duty under particular circumstances. This difficulty is well illustrated by the treatment of the subject by James Martineau, a writer whose Intuitionism takes the form of a theory that a man's duty is always that course of action to which he is prompted by the highest motive, a motive which is recognized as such by the immediate affirmation of Conscience. Let us see how such a test would work as applied to this very important duty—that of choosing one's Vocation rightly.

Martineau's ethical criterion is thus formulated: 'Every action is RIGHT which, in presence of a lower principle, follows a higher: every action is WRONG which, in presence of a higher principle, follows a lower [1].'   The moral order of precedence among the possible principles or 'springs' of action is elaborately determined by that writer, while immediately after the table in which he sums up the results of this enquiry there follows a section on the question, 'How far a Life must be chosen among these.'   Martineau here distinctly faces the objection that it rests in great measure on our own action which motives shall be presented to the mind and which shall not. Unless the higher motive be actually present to the mind, the action motived by the lower 'spring' cannot, according to him, be wrong.   'Ought we to content ourselves,' he asks, 'with treating the springs of action as *our data*, with which we have nothing to do but to wait till they are flung upon us by circumstance, and then to follow the best that turns up?' [2]   The objection could not be more aptly stated.   Martineau meets it by admitting that 'if there be at the command of our will, not only the selection of the better side of an alternative, but also a predetermination of what kind the alternative shall be, the range of our duty will undoubtedly be extended to the creation of a higher plane of circumstance, in addition to the higher preference within it.'   But on what principle is a man to make his choice between the higher and the lower 'plane of circumstance'?   How is he to recognize the higher plane?   From Martineau's fundamental principle it would seem to follow that a man is always bound to choose that 'plane of circumstance' on which he will be likely to find the higher motives streaming into his consciousness in the richest abundance and with the greatest force.   Martineau himself raises the question : 'If compassion is always of higher obligation than the *love of gain* or *family affection*, how can a man ever be justified in quitting his charities for his business or his home?'   But to this question he has supplied no adequate answer.   The only way in which he strives to beat down the difficulty which he has himself so forcibly raised is by the contention that 'the limits . . . within which the higher moral altitudes can be secured by voluntary command of favouring circumstances are extremely narrow.'

[1] *Types of Ethical Theory*, 3rd ed., II, p. 270.
[2] Ib., p. 267.

This view he supports by insisting upon the undoubted fact that a man cannot entirely alter his nature by artificial change of environment, upon the moral advantage of the 'various clashing of the involuntary and the voluntary,' upon the moral ill effects of setting aside 'relations human and divine' by the choice of an apparently higher walk of life. Now, in the first place, I remark that, in so far as a man deliberately turns a deaf ear to the solicitation of a higher motive from regard to the considerations insisted upon by Martineau, he is deserting the fundamental principle of the system. In urging a man to repress his benevolent aspirations for fear of the moral effects (social and personal) of the neglect of family relations and the like, Martineau is distinctly transferring the object of moral discrimination from the motives to the consequences of the alternative courses of action. He is deserting the Highest-motive criterion for the principle (to use terms invented by Sidgwick) of individualistic or of universalistic Perfectionism. He bids the seeker after moral truth in certain particular cases act upon the lower in preference to the higher motive; [1] and yet no adequate rules are given for the discrimination of these exceptional cases. If in one particular instance a man is permitted to disobey Martineau's fundamental canon from fear of the moral ill consequences which might subsequently ensue, how can he obey it in any case in which he foresees that the net moral results of acting on the higher motive will be less satisfactory than those which result from choosing the lower motive? The method of Ethics to which such a principle would lead would be a very different one from the method of introspection into motives.

But we must return to Martineau's contention 'that the limits within which the higher moral altitudes can be secured by a voluntary command of favouring circumstances are extremely narrow' Here I venture very decidedly to join issue. It is all very well to point to the moral failure of monastic systems, and the danger of neglecting natural 'relations, human and

---

[1] *Types*, II. p. 270. It might, indeed, be pleaded that the desire of doing right as such is higher than the benevolent desire; but Martineau does not admit the existence of a desire to do the right thing in general, as distinct from an impulse to satisfy some particular good desire.

divine'. But what relations does Martineau mean? It may be
true that a man cannot desert ' his business or his home for his
charities ' without neglecting ' relations human and divine,'
when once he has got a business or a home. But it rested with
himself to create or not to create the business or the home in
the first instance. And on what principles is he to decide
whether to create them or not? Practically, Martineau's advice
to any one in doubt as to the choice of an employment or
profession seems to be, ' Don't choose one at all.' ' Let him
accept his lot,' he tells us, ' and work its resources with willing
conscience, and he will emerge with no half-formed and crippled
character [1].' This might be good advice to one born heir to an
estate or a great business; it would be intelligible advice—
though there are cases in which its morality would be questionable—to a son brought up by an arbitrary father for a particular
profession; but to the man who is really free to choose between
half a dozen different ' lots,' and in anxious doubt which of them
to adopt, the precept ' Accept your lot ' will seem but a mocking
echo of the problem that distracts him. If ' one's lot ' means
one's actual profession, the advice is meaningless to the boy or
the man who has not entered upon any ; if ' one's lot ' means the
lot to which one is called, the precise difficulty lies in knowing
what that lot is. The maxim ' Perform the duties of your
vocation ' is of no use to a man grappling with the tremendous
problem—to many a man the most difficult practical problem
which he ever has to face—of finding out what his true vocation is.

The duty of choosing a profession has been well called—I
think by Sir John Seeley—the most important of all duties, and
the same writer very reasonably complains of the almost total
neglect of this department of Ethics by Moralists. And the
neglect is not the least conspicuous in the writers who most
tend to limit the whole duty of man to the ' duties of one's
station.' ' My Station and its Duties ' is the title of the only
chapter of *Ethical Studies* in which Mr. Bradley faces the
question of the moral criterion. ' My station and duties ' is
the formula by which he seeks to answer that question ; and yet

[1] *Types*, II, p. 270.

in the whole chapter there is not a word as to the principles
upon which a man's station must be chosen except what is
contained in the lines :—

> One place performs like any other place
> The proper service every place on earth
> Was framed to furnish man with [1].

It should be observed that this question of choosing a profession is precisely one to which the ordinary objections to the
systematic treatment of questions of Casuistry do not apply at
all. Against such a treatment it may plausibly be urged in
ordinary cases that the decision, when the difficulty actually
arises, has to be taken without prolonged and self-conscious
deliberation ; that to deliberate in the face of an apparent duty
generally means to seek an excuse for evading it ; that there is
something morally unwholesome in elaborate introspection and
self-analysis, and still more in the anticipation of abnormal moral
perplexities, or even in dwelling upon them when they arise ;
and, finally, that the details of Morality as opposed to its general
principles do not admit of scientific adjustment : ' the particulars
are matters of immediate perception,' as Aristotle puts it [2].   But
the choice of a profession is precisely a question which from the
nature of the case *must* be deliberated on, and about which, in
numerous instances, conscientious men do deliberate long and
anxiously.   Here, if anywhere, it would appear reasonable to
expect that a system of Moral Philosophy might have some
guidance to offer to anxious seekers after Right.   Even if the
scientific discussion of such a subject were of little direct use to
the doubting Conscience of the individual (as no doubt must
generally be the case with theoretical determinations of practical
questions), it might at least be expected to be of some value in
determining the advice which should be given to others upon
a subject upon which more than on any other moral question
men are wont at times to seek for counsel and advice.   The
Moral Philosopher as such is no more capable of answering such
a question than any one else ; but he ought surely to be able to
point out the considerations upon which its solution turns, and
so to state the question in a manner in which it admits of an

[1] *Ethical Studies*, p. 183.   [2] αἰσθητὰ γὰρ τὰ καθ' ἕκαστα.

answer. I need hardly say that in the present chapter I make
no pretension to contribute to the discussion of the subject anything which would be likely to be of much value either to
enquirer or adviser in such cases. I merely wish to point out
that the question of choosing a profession is a peculiarly good
test of any philosophical criterion of Morality, and to show that
Martineau's criterion is one which could not practically be
applied to its determination, or at least that the results of its
adoption would be such as would not commend themselves
to the practical moral judgement of thoughtful and reasonable
men.

It will be well perhaps, at this stage of my argument, to call
attention to the psychological grounds upon which Martineau
bases what I must respectfully call his evasion of this problem :

'The limits, however, within which the higher moral altitudes
can be secured by voluntary command of favouring circumstance
are extremely narrow. Go where we may, we carry the most
considerable portion of our environment with us in our own
constitution ; from whose propensions, passions, affections, it is
a vain attempt to fly. The attempt to wither them up and
suppress them by contradiction has ever been disastrous : they
can be counteracted and disarmed and taught obedience only by
preoccupation of mind and heart in other directions. Nothing
but the enthusiasm of a new affection can silence the clamours of
one already there [1].'

Martineau's treatment of the whole subject seems to have been
warped by the assumption that the only way in which a man
can attempt to raise himself to 'the higher moral altitudes by
the voluntary command of favouring circumstance ' is by ' going
out of the world ' in the monastic sense. He insists with much
force upon the folly of attempting to suppress the lower ' propensions, passions, and affections ' by one tremendous sacrifice
of the external goods or surroundings which seem most obviously
to call them into activity. It is quite true that ' it is a vain
attempt to fly ' from one's natural ' propensions, passions, and
affections,' by change of external environment ; but it is entirely
possible to give a wholly new direction to them by such a change.

[1] *Types*, II, p. 268.

I 2

It is precisely because 'the affections can be counteracted and disarmed and taught obedience only by preoccupation of mind and heart in other directions' that the influence of environment upon character is of such decisive importance. It is just because 'nothing but the enthusiasm of a new affection can silence the clamours of one already there,' and because some occupations are so much more favourable than others to the growth of 'new affections' of the right kind, that a man's character is so largely determined by himself—determined by himself, but determined in ordinary cases once for all—by the choice of his walk in life.

Without denying to every honourable and worthy calling either its characteristic virtues or its characteristic vices, it is surely undeniable that some professions are as a rule more favourable to the development of character than others. It is not to the purpose to allege that all callings are compatible with the highest Morality. Exceptional men may lead exceptional lives in any walk of life; the very obstacles to Virtue which some careers present will become so many occasions for moral achievement to those who are capable of triumphing over them. But we are not dealing with exceptional men, but with ordinary men, though (since *ex hypothesi* they are desirous of regulating their choice on the highest principles) with ordinary good men. And the characters of ordinary men are enormously moulded by their environment—by the nature of their work, by the people with whom it will bring them into contact, and by the nature of that contact. To such men when hesitating as to the choice of a profession such alternatives as these are constantly presenting themselves. A man hesitates between the profession of a physician and that of an officer, more or less clearly foreseeing that if he becomes an officer there lies before him (in time of peace) a life of idleness just disguised and sweetened by a moderate quantity of routine work, a life of comfort and pleasure, if not of luxury and self-indulgence, to say nothing of the actual temptations naturally associated with such a life. Against this there may seem to him (rightly or wrongly) little to be set except the rare opportunities of heroism and patriotic service which may from time to time present themselves in war. As a doctor there lies before him a life of hard work and great usefulness—a life in which there will be daily and hourly calls for the exercise of sympathy, self-denial, and devotion. Or again, take the case of a man hesitating between the life of a parish clergyman and some commercial occupation. Of course the temptations of the highest callings—the degradation of the man who cannot in some measure rise to the moral level which they demand—are great in proportion to the opportunities which they offer. But it will hardly be denied that most men who have adopted the profession of a parochial clergyman from not wholly unworthy motives —sometimes even that exception might be omitted—are made better by the demand which such work incessantly creates for sympathy, for self-judgement, for moral effort, for charity in the highest sense of the word. How constantly does one find the highest qualities developed by a few years of serious clerical work among the poor in a man who certainly showed no signs of their possession as an undergraduate [1]? Can it be doubted that those virtues might very probably have remained, to say the least of it, equally dormant and unobtrusive had he gone into business? It is not, however, necessary for my argument to show that the actual moral performance of one profession is on an average superior to that of another, though I should myself have little doubt of the fact. The question is, whether some professions do or do not make greater and more frequent demands than others upon the higher 'springs of action' and so create a 'higher plane of circumstance.' Here I should have thought there could not be room for the smallest doubt. Professions which bring a man into contact with human suffering must surely more frequently suggest benevolent impulses than those whose work is done in the study or the office, whatever be the response which is actually made to such higher suggestions. Professions which offer opportunies for work not wholly dictated by personal interest call for these higher motives more frequently than work

---

[1] Of course, to other men the opposite choice might be morally the more successful. I am assuming the case of the man who possesses in some measure the particular capacities which clerical work might call out. It must be remembered that I am myself contending that the character of the 'springs of action' to which the work appeals is not the right principle on which to base the choice of a profession.

in which there is comparatively little room for any honesty
except the narrow honesty which is the best policy. Professions
which necessarily involve an attitude of antagonism to moral
evil must clearly be more likely to excite those sentiments of
compassion and reverence which Martineau places at the head
of his table of 'springs of action' than professions in which the
existence of evil is either kept out of sight or has for the most
part to be accepted as a datum instead of being grappled with.
If that be so, I cannot see how, on his principle, a man to whom
the profession which will secure the presence of these higher
motives has once suggested itself, could ever be justified in adopting one which will place him on a lower 'plane of circumstance.'
Whether he possesses the capacity or taste for the work, whether
it is probable that he will succeed in making as frequent response
to these higher springs as he might make to the good but inferior
springs of action suggested by work of a less morally exacting
kind, whether he will be more useful to Society by adopting the
calling which makes the greater demand upon the higher springs
—all these are, as it seems to me, utilitarian considerations with
which the Intuitionist of the 'highest motive' school cannot
logically concern himself. Whether the moral value of the
motives immediately prompting a man to choose the one calling
or the other be considered, or whether we have recourse to
Martineau's supplementary rule of choosing the 'higher plane of
circumstance,' nothing could, as it seems to me, justify a man in
choosing what we may for the sake of convenience call the lower
profession in preference to the higher, but the fact that the
desire of adopting the latter had never occurred to him, or that
he had never had one moment's experience of those higher
desires which would be gratified by the adoption of the higher
profession. Exactly the same difficulties would arise if we
assigned a higher value than Dr. Martineau to the intellectual
and aesthetic impulses, and attempted to base the choice of a
profession upon the extent to which it would promote the man's
own self-development.

It must be remembered that the collision of motives respectively impelling a man to the choice of two alternative walks of
life is not commonly limited to the collision between one higher

motive and one good but somewhat lower motive. Martineau, indeed, shows a disposition to deny the possibility of action impelled by a mixture of motives; but whatever be the case with actions actually performed, there can surely be no doubt that, so long as alternative courses are still in contemplation, it seldom happens that the man is impelled to the one or other course by one motive alone. This is eminently the case with the choice of a profession. Sometimes, indeed, some of the lowest inducements will persist in arraying themselves on the side of the highest of all. What more common in religious men than a coincidence between the 'love of power or ambition' (placed seventh on Dr. Martineau's list), or even 'love of gain,' and the promptings of 'compassion' or 'reverence'? So again in the familiar struggle between intellectual and philanthropic impulses, the lowest desires of all will commonly take the side of the former. 'Love of ease and sensual pleasure' will ally itself with 'love of culture' in deterring a man from those active professions to which he is prompted by 'generosity' and 'compassion' in the present, and in which those motives of action are likely to be most frequently called into activity in the future. It must be remembered that where a higher desire and the wish to provide for a future supply of such desires point one way, and the lower desires the other, the higher desire is by no means always a predominant, habitual, or overmastering desire. Where that is the case, it may be a man's duty to adopt it irrespectively of inclination. The thought of the higher vocation may, indeed, be a mere transient, intermittent aspiration. The man may shrink from the higher vocation (though willing to accept it if proved to be his duty) with an aversion in which dislike of its hardships, felt incapacity for its duties, and the overmastering attraction of some less exalted though not unworthy passion or ambition will mingle almost inextricably. Yet, if it be once admitted that the moral value of the impelling motives must determine the choice, it must follow that no man attracted to the army by 'love of power or ambition' could ever conscientiously devote himself to that profession if a 'love of culture' had once suggested to him the thought of being an artist; that no man who had ever felt

sincere compassion for the sorrows of the poor, and recognized
the supreme nobleness of philanthropic work, could ever devote
himself conscientiously to the cause of Science or learning; that
no woman who had ever aspired after the usefulness of a hospital
nurse or a schoolmistress could ever conscientiously consent to
marry a squire or a man of business[1].

In fact, since the profession to which a man is most strongly
attracted commonly presents itself to him in an agreeable light—
i. e. as likely to satisfy some of his lower desires as well as one
or more of the higher ones—it would scarcely be an exaggeration to say that on Martineau's principles it will generally be a
man's duty, when hesitating between two or more professions, to
choose that which he dislikes most[2]. Such a preposterous conclusion would, of course, have been rejected by Martineau as
emphatically as it would by any other sensible man. Yet from
the perplexities and paradoxes which we have been considering
there seems to be no way of escape so long as we confine
ourselves to a purely subjective criterion, and refuse to consider
the consequences of our action upon social Well-being.

It is true, indeed, that Martineau might point to not a few
passages of his book where the calculation of consequences is
admitted to have a place in morals; but the relation of the

[1] The following words from a letter of Ruskin may illustrate the situation
I am contemplating: 'I am . . . tormented between the longing for rest and
lovely life and the sense of this terrific call of human crime for resistance
and human misery for help' (Collingwood, *Life and Work of John Ruskin*,
1893, II, p. 7). And yet it may be safely asserted that, even if we measured
its value solely by its effects upon the condition of the poor, Ruskin's
actual career accomplished far more than he would have done had he
turned his back upon Literature and Art and devoted his life to some
directly philanthropic cause: but such indirect social effects could not of
course be expected in all cases.

[2] It is difficult to bring within Martineau's table some of the motives
which frequently have most weight in disposing a man to one or other
profession. Perhaps the strongest likings or dislikings for particular
callings commonly rest upon a love of society or of society of a particular
kind, or upon dislike of a particular kind of society. (By society I mean all
kinds of intercourse with one's fellow men.) It is hard to explain such
likings or dislikings by any of Martineau's 'springs,' whether taken singly
or in combination. The only love of pleasure which he recognizes is 'love
of *sensual* pleasure.'

'canon of consequences' to the canon of motives is nowhere adequately explained. In one passage [1], indeed, it is admitted that such a 'computation is already more or less involved in the preference of this or that spring of action; for, in proportion as the springs of action are self-conscious, they contemplate their own effects, and judgement upon them is included in our judgement of the disposition.' If this admission be pressed, it seems to me to amount to the practical adoption of a consequential or teleological criterion of the morality of at least all deliberate actions. All action must affect some one, and if a man is reflecting upon the course of conduct which it is right for him to pursue, it must surely occur to him that the consequences of one course of action will be more socially beneficial than those of another. How, then, can he fail to be moved to the adoption of that alternative by 'Compassion'? And Compassion [2] in the table before us takes precedence of all other springs of action except 'reverence.' Except, therefore, in so far as its dictates may be modified by those of reverence, compassion seems to be practically erected into the ethical criterion. This, however, is not explicitly admitted by the framer of that table, and we are obliged to assume that comparison of motives is meant to be his working criterion.

III.

It may be urged that, however unsatisfactory Martineau's criterion for the determination of cases of Conscience such as these may be, no more satisfactory guidance is to be obtained from any other. If we adopt tendency to promote social good (however understood) as our test, is not the difficulty, it may be asked, quite as great? If a man's duty is to adopt the course of conduct which produces the greatest amount of good on the whole, how is it possible to set limits to the self-denial, the asceticism, which such a principle of conduct seems to demand? How is it possible, except by a cynical or pessimistic disbelief in the usefulness of all social or philanthropic effort, to justify the

---

[1] *Types*, II, p. 255.

[2] This is not a suitable word to denote the impulse to promote all kinds of social good, but Martineau's list of motives supplies no other.

adoption of a less useful in preference to an intrinsically more useful or laborious profession—the expenditure of time upon abstract thought or study which might be spent in teaching the ignorant and brightening the lives of the wretched, the expenditure of money upon the conventional comforts of a middle-class home (to say nothing of the luxuries of 'the rich') when it might be spent upon hospitals and young men's clubs?

I do not pretend to offer a complete solution of this most difficult problem of practical Morality. I only wish to point out that, on the theory which makes universal Well-being the supreme end, it is not incapable of a solution which may commend itself to 'common sense' without in any way repressing the highest moral aspirations. I propose to notice a few of the more prominent of the considerations which must be taken into account in a solution of this question, whether in its application to the choice of a career or the choice of a mode of life in so far as such a choice remains open to those who have already adopted some recognized profession. However obvious they may seem (as most of them certainly are), an attempt to enumerate them will be the best way of illustrating the practical adaptability to such cases of our method of ideal Utilitarianism.

(1) In the first place, there are those considerations of what I have called 'moral prudence,' on which Dr. Martineau has—as I venture to think quite inconsistently with his main principle—sufficiently insisted. Before embarking under the influence of some higher motive upon a course of action not required by strict duty, which will require for its maintenance the continued presence of such higher motives, a man should have a reasonable prospect that the necessary inspiration will hereafter be forthcoming; otherwise the adoption of the higher course of life will lead to a moral fall rather than to a moral advance. In such cases the surrender to the 'higher motive' will not be conducive to the man's own moral Well-being on the whole, and therefore not conducive to the good of Society. Of course this principle will not hold where for some reason or other the course of action to which man is called is one of plain duty. But if the true canon of duty be, 'Act always on the highest motive,' it is difficult to see how any aspiration after some more heroic or

more saintly walk could ever be rightly repressed from a fear of
its possible moral consequences. In that case the answer to
such fears would be, 'Better do right now, even if you will not
be able to live up to the level of your present enthusiasm hereafter.' If, on the other hand, it be the duty of the individual
to realize the highest attainable moral and other good for
himself and others, he will recognize that, though the career of
a philanthropist may be higher than that (say) of an honest
lawyer, he will himself attain a higher moral level as a lawyer
than by the more imperfect fulfilment of a higher ideal.

(2) These considerations naturally lead us to the observation
that certain social functions require for their adequate fulfilment
that they should be done in a certain spirit. Such functions
demand the possession of certain qualities of mind or heart or
character which cannot be summoned up at the command of the
will, and cannot be satisfactorily performed merely as a matter
of duty. Common sense agrees with Roman Catholic Moral
Theology in recognizing that it would be positively wrong for
any one to enter upon certain careers which make great demands
upon the moral nature, merely from a strong sense of duty,
when they have no 'internal vocation' for them. The principle,
no doubt, requires to be extended to many careers beyond those
afforded by the priesthood and the religious orders, or the
modern equivalents of such orders; and the true ultimate ground
of such a distinction must, from our point of view, be found in
the social advantages (moral and hedonistic) which flow from its
observance, and the social disadvantages which would be entailed
by its neglect. The average sister of mercy is, no doubt, a more
valuable member of Society than a Belgravian lady who is
somewhat above the average; but a sister of mercy with no
natural love or instinct for her work, with no natural love for
the poor or the sick or the young to whom she ministered,
would be far less useful to Society than the Belgravian lady who
performs respectably the recognized duties of her station, even
though she may devote what must in the abstract be considered
a somewhat excessive amount of time to domestic trivialities
and social dissipation.

(3) While the principle just laid down applies pre-eminently

to certain special callings—such as those of the artist, the scholar,
the man of letters, the clergyman, the teacher—it applies in
a certain measure to all work which is capable of being liked at
all, or for which any special aptitude is possible. It is for the
general good that every man should do the work for which he is
most fitted ; and, as a general rule, a natural liking for the work
or kind of life adopted is one of the most important qualifications for it. There are, of course, obvious limitations to the
principle thus laid down. The highest tasks are necessarily
repulsive to the lower part of a man's nature. A due distinction
must be drawn between the kind of dislike which there is
a reasonable prospect of overcoming and the dislike which is
insurmountable ; and, again, between the dislike which interferes
with the due performance of the work and the dislike which
does not interfere with it. A surgeon who could not overcome
a physical squeamishness at the sight of blood would be more
useful to Society as a billiard-marker. On the other hand,
absolute callousness to human suffering, though it might increase
his love of his profession, would scarcely, I presume, be a qualification for its duties.

(4) Regard must be paid not only to the effects of the individual's conduct, but to the effect of the general adoption of
a like course of conduct on the part of others. Thus it would
not be socially desirable to encourage all high-minded men to
forsake the careers which seem from some points of view to
stand upon the lowest moral level. A life of money-making
(abstracted from the use which is to be made of the money
when accumulated) may from some points of view seem one to
which nobody could lawfully devote himself who had ever felt
an aspiration after some higher kind of work ; for, however
necessary to society may be the work of merchants and stock-
brokers, there would always (under existing conditions) be
forthcoming a sufficient supply of duly qualified persons who
would be attracted into these professions from purely mercenary
motives. Against this, however, must be set the demoralization
which would result to such classes or professions, and the consequent injury to Society, if all men of high character were led to
avoid them. It may be questioned whether, upon this principle,

it may not sometimes be a positive duty on the part of some good people to continue in, if not to adopt, professions which may be in various degrees unfavourable to the improvement of their own personal character, or which at least involve much that is disagreeable to what we may call their moral taste, provided that they minister to legitimate social needs. The most extreme ill effects of the adoption of a contrary principle were experienced in the Middle Ages. The 'religious' life being assumed to be the highest of all careers, every man or woman anxious about his or her soul was driven into a religious house, unless, indeed, they were wealthy enough to found one. The consequence was an appalling relaxation of the standard of ordinary 'secular' morality—a complete de-spiritualization of all 'secular' life, including that of the secular priest. Even the work of the pastor had to be abandoned to worldly men, because it was not disagreeable enough to satisfy the religious man's hankering after self-mortification.

(5) Similar considerations are applicable to the innumerable difficulties which beset the Conscience of every man possessed with something of the 'enthusiasm of humanity' in the matter of personal expenditure, conventional luxury, and so on. In the first place, he will apply the principle of 'moral prudence' to the effects of his conduct upon himself and his capacity for work. He will make recreation subordinate to work, social pleasures to social usefulness, and so on. There is, however, room for as many different vocations, so to speak, in respect of the use that may be made of leisure hours as there is in the choice of a life-work : and some of them are higher than others. It is no doubt a morally higher thing to spend one's evenings in teaching a night school than to spend them in amusement or light reading. But if a man to whom some higher motive suggests the idea of taking up with the former occupation feels that the work would be excessively distasteful, and that as a consequence he would be less capable of efficiently discharging his duties in the day, and probably become irritable, discontented, and dyspeptic, he will do much better to play whist of an evening instead, even in the interests of his own moral Well-being. Still more evidently will such a course be recommended when we

extend our view first to the direct effects of the two alternatives on the happiness of others, and then to the effects which would follow an extensive imitation of a conscientious but uncheerful philanthropy. On Dr. Martineau's principle, it is difficult to see how it is possible to justify a rich man under any circumstances living the life of a country gentleman, even as such a life might be lived under the inspiration of a ' social Conscience ' far above the average, when once it has been suggested to him that he might spend his fortune on some great work of social usefulness. He would certainly be prompted to the last course by ' compassion' and deterred from it (among however many other and better motives) by 'love of ease and sensual pleasure.' On the other hand, when once the appeal is made to social Wellbeing, a number of other important considerations suggest themselves which may well justify a man who does not feel strongly moved to make such a sacrifice in accepting the more agreeable alternative. He will reflect that the habits of a class cannot be suddenly changed, but that they may be gradually modified. He will remember that certain kinds of work can only be done in connexion with certain social positions : a hardworking professional man may do much more work than a resident squire, but he cannot do precisely the same work that a good squire may do. He might therefore do more good by setting an example of liberality, care for dependents, devotion to public duties, and moderation in amusement and personal expenditure, than by letting his country house and giving the proceeds to public works or well-administered charities. He will reflect that some forms of luxury have good social effects,— such as the encouragement of art and superior workmanship,— which ultimately benefit the community at large. He may feel that it is better to indulge to some extent in forms of luxury demanded by the customs of his class, but difficult to reconcile with abstract ideas of Justice, such as good dinners, expensive wines, a large house and numerous servants, rather than abandon great opportunities of social or political influence and usefulness.

It is not my intention here to discuss from a practical point of view the extent to which this principle should be carried. It is probable that, while the existence of different standards of class expenditure and of considerable inequalities in the expenditure of individuals is socially beneficial, a vast amount of the conventional expenditure of the rich and well-to-do classes, in view of the surrounding sordid misery, is wholly unjustifiable; and that a still larger amount is only provisionally and relatively justifiable, because under existing conditions the non-conformity with established usage would on the whole, for such and such persons and in such and such circumstances, be the greater of two evils. But it is clear that very different standards of expenditure must be admitted, unless we are to pronounce many occupations or professions absolutely barred to persons whose social Conscience has once been aroused. If a man cannot justify to his Conscience the provision of champagne for his guests, it is clear that diplomacy is an impossible profession for him. If he cannot make up his mind to mess and contribute to regimental amusements as other officers do, he cannot enter the army; and in many other positions in life it is impossible to escape the choice between total isolation—with much loss not only of pleasure but of influence and professional effectiveness— and acquiescence in some kinds of expenditure which we may feel to involve a very unjust and socially inexpedient distribution of external goods. No doubt these 'necessities of one's position' should be duly weighed before the position which necessitates them is accepted. In many cases they might constitute a good reason for refusing to accept that position, and, when it is accepted, the duty remains of reducing them within reasonable limits; but I do not believe that it would be for the general good, and therefore I do not believe that the moral consciousness allows us to lay it down, that all positions involving a high standard of personal expenditure should be closed to any one whose eyes had once been opened to the responsibilities of wealth.

I need hardly add that the other side of the matter—the enormous need for men who will adopt exceptional modes of life, and devote themselves to public or philanthropic work in ways which do demand exceptional self-sacrifice—is an equally important one, and that for men who feel that need strongly and their capacity for meeting it, the exceptional sacrifice may become the most imperative of duties. On this side of the matter I shall have more to say hereafter.

(6) Another consideration which must be borne in mind is that, if Well-being or Good in general be the supreme end, my good is a part of that end: and my happiness is a part of my good, though not the whole of it. It ought not, therefore, to be sacrificed to promote a less amount of it in others. And up to a certain point the general Well-being is best promoted by the principle that within the limitations demanded by strict duty every one shall exercise a reasonable care for his own happiness, and shall not make such complete sacrifices of material goods or advantages as will (he being what he is) involve the destruction of his tranquillity and contentment, although such sacrifices might be compatible with happiness in better men. This principle may be admitted even for the guidance of the individual Conscience—and still more when there is a question of inculcating such sacrifices on people in general—without going the length of saying, with the late Mr. Justice Stephen, that 'human nature is so constituted that nearly all our conduct, immensely the greater part of it, is and ought to be regulated much more by a regard to ourselves and to our own interests than by a regard to other people and their interests [1].' It is obvious that the extent to which this principle can be admitted will be very considerably narrowed by the acceptance of a non-hedonistic interpretation of Good. As soon as Morality is recognized as an end in itself and an essential part of true Well-being, it becomes impossible to admit that a pursuit of his own happiness, unmixed with and unregulated by a desire for other people's, could ever be the vocation of any man, even if in his particular case such a course of conduct should chance to be coincident with that dictated by the public Well-being. The individual should pursue his own Well-being as part of the general Well-being, but he will recognize that his moral Well-being demands a measure of self-sacrifice.

(7) The principle that the rationality of self-sacrifice logically implies a limitation to self-sacrifice, may be used to justify not

---

[1] In the *Nineteenth Century*, No. 118. p. 783.

merely some enjoyment on the part of every individual, but even a very unequal enjoyment on the part of some individuals. In proportion as we hold that competition, the struggle to raise the personal or family standard of comfort, the indulgence and development of individual tastes and inclinations in ways which involve considerable expenditure of wealth, the increase of differentiation in modes of life, and the like are good for Society, the individual must in some cases be justified in allowing himself an amount of luxury and enjoyment which would not be possible for all under the most ideal socialistic régime. It is possible to admit that civilization and progress demand considerable inequalities without accepting von Hartmann's doctrine that to promote maximum inequality is necessarily and under all circumstances to promote true social progress. The principle must be balanced by the complementary principle that such inequalities of enjoyment have a tendency to increase beyond the point which is socially expedient. To what extent this principle will justify the individual in choosing the easier and more enjoyable careers, and enjoying an exceptionally favourable social position or exceptional good fortune, will depend partly upon the answer he gives to a number of social and economic questions, and partly upon his personal circumstances and disposition. It is unnecessary to repeat once more that this consideration cannot possibly justify any individual under any circumstances in being merely an enjoyer of other men's labours. It may be good for Society that the wages of different classes and individuals should vary, even to a very large extent: it cannot possibly be to the advantage of Society or to the moral advantage of any individual that his wages should be wholly unearned.

(8) And, lastly, there is the fact that some kinds of work which do not call into activity the very highest 'springs of action' are as useful as, perhaps more useful than, those that do: and that in reference to some of these kinds of work it is even truer than of more distinctly spiritual kinds of work that 'the harvest truly is great, but the labourers are few.' In England at least this is notably the case with all the higher kinds of intellectual labour. I for one cannot assent to that beatification of intellectual pursuits—and even of the most

3 1

selfish forms of intellectual sybaritism—which is not unknown among persons of literary and speculative tastes, but a demonstration of the supreme social value of such work—when it really is *work*—will be superfluous in the eyes of any one who is at all likely to read this book. All history is against the attempt to encourage intellectual Obscurantism in the interests of a narrow moral or material Utilitarianism. All history testifies to the intimate connexion, in the long run and within certain limits, between moral and intellectual vitality. The darkness of the dark ages was not merely intellectual darkness; the stagnation of China is not merely intellectual stagnation. And if an appeal may plausibly be made to a few brilliant periods, such as the Renaissance, as an exhibition of the possibility of high intellectual development in combination with a low *morale*, it must be remembered that the early phases of the Renaissance were periods of high moral as well as intellectual enthusiasm, and that the intellectual decay which set in so soon in those countries where the Renaissance was not also a period of moral and religious progress may be distinctly traced to the moral corruption. High excellence in Art involves such a long period of technical training that the greatest technical perfection of an Art movement often comes long after the decline of the moral and intellectual forces which produced it.

It is obvious that these reflections might be spun out indefinitely. Enough, it is hoped, has been said to illustrate the kind of guidance which may be afforded in the solution of such problems of vocation by the adoption of a consequential but non-hedonistic criterion of Morality.

IV

It will by this time have become evident that the course of our argument has led us from the discussion of a particular duty, that of choosing an occupation, into the discussion of a much larger and more fundamental question of ethics—the distinction between Duty and the morally good, between what are sometimes called duties of 'perfect' and those of 'imperfect obligation,' the question whether there are or are not such things as 'works of supererogation.' I have already contended that there are

cases where it is good for a man to contribute in certain ways to
the general good, though it would not be wrong for him to
refuse to contribute to it in those ways—that there are cases
where a man may rightfully decline to perform socially beneficial actions for the reason (among others) that he does not feel
a natural inclination or strong desire to perform them. On the
other hand, it has been assumed (as it must be assumed by every
system which recognizes moral obligation at all) that in some
cases no amount of disinclination, no consideration of the sacrifice involved, will justify a refusal to adopt the course of action
which will make the largest contribution to social good. But
how, it may be asked, can such a distinction be admitted without
involving ourselves in the *prima facie* immoral corollary that
a man can do more than his duty? I believe that we have
already by implication arrived at something like an answer to
the question. One course, and one only, can ever be a man's
duty; but duty itself requires *in certain cases* that regard shall
be paid to the inner dispositions and inclinations of the individual. It is always a man's duty to do what conduces most to
the general good; but the general good itself demands that,
whereas some contributions to social good shall be required of
all men placed under the same external circumstances, in other
cases contributions differing both in kind and in amount shall
be demanded of different men. It will be well, however, to
dwell a little more at length upon the difficulty and importance
of the problem under discussion.

The case for and against works of supererogation shall be
stated by two modern French philosophers of the last generation, Émile Beaussire and Paul Janet. The contrast between
their views on this point is the more striking on account of
their general agreement in philosophic tendency. In the former
writer's works we find such utterances as these:—

'Merit and virtue arise from accomplished duty, but in their
highest degrees they tend to pass the limits of duty: they rise
to the point of devotion. . . . To surrender one's children to the
service of one's country, when she claims them in the name of the
law, is a duty of obligation (*devoir de droit*). To offer them for
it, when the law allows one to keep them, is a duty of virtue, or

rather an act of devotion which goes beyond duty. To withdraw them from the legal obligation of a public education where one sees a danger for their faith or for their morality, is perhaps the most imperious of duties [1].'

On the other hand, Janet, a typical representative of the ' spiritualistic ' Philosophy once dominant in France, writes as follows :—

' The distinction of two domains, the domain of good and that of duty, would conduct us to the inadmissible supposition, that between two actions, of which one would be manifestly better than the other, the individual is at liberty to choose the less good. From what source could this privilege be derived? Is it not under another form that opinion of the Casuists so severely condemned by Pascal and by Bossuet, the opinion, that is to say, that between two probable opinions one is allowed to choose the less probable? [2] '

The writer then proceeds to explain the apparent collision between the verdict of reflection and the verdict of what Sidgwick would call ' common sense ' on this head by the following considerations :—

(a) The degree of self-sacrifice demanded for the performance of a man's duty depends upon his circumstances, especially upon his ' rôle ' in society. When it is demanded either by that ' rôle ' or by the exceptional circumstances under which any man may find himself placed, ' devotion ' becomes in the strictest sense a duty. This is the principle on which I have myself insisted. What I desiderate in Janet's admirable treatment of this subject is some discussion of the principles by which a man is to determine his ' rôle ' in society. A theory of duty requires a theory of Vocation as its necessary complement.

(b) The highest degrees of moral perfection are not attainable by all men. It is a duty to strive after the highest degree of moral perfection that circumstances permit. ' No one is bound to do what is impossible : all are bound to do what is possible.'

(c) The popular distinction between duties and acts which it is good to do but not wrong to omit, depends mainly upon a particular characteristic of the subject-matter or content of certain duties, i. e. their indeterminateness.

[1] *Les Principes de la Morale*, pp. 169, 241.   [2] *La Morale*, p. 227.

(d) The development of the moral consciousness in different men being unequal, the same actions do not always suggest themselves to all men; acts of extraordinary heroism, ideals of extraordinary self-devotion, present themselves only to rare and exceptionally endowed natures.

'Further, in so far as the idea of an action has not presented itself to our minds, it is evident that it cannot be obligatory on us; that ceases to be the case as soon as this idea has been conceived by our consciousness. The action, once represented in thought, presents itself to us with all the characteristics of duty; and we cannot refuse it without remorse [1].'

Thus the popular distinction between duties and acts which it is good to do is to a certain extent justified, while the immoral deduction that it is possible to do more than one's duty, and sometimes right to do less, is avoided. With this position I should in the main agree. At the same time, I do not think that Janet has quite got to the bottom of the difficulty. He is no doubt right in holding that it is a duty to aim at doing the utmost amount of good that lies in one's power: and therefore it is not possible for a man to do more than his duty. Moreover, it is an essential characteristic of the moral law that it should be (in the Kantian phrase) 'fit to serve for law universal,' i. e. that what is right for one must be right for every one else in the same circumstances—when they are really the same. But it is perfectly consistent with this principle to include a man's character, moral, emotional, and intellectual, among the 'circumstances' or conditions upon which his duty in the particular case depends. The neglect of this distinction between external and what I may venture to call 'internal' circumstances or conditions, has been the main source of the vagueness and uncertainty which has generally characterized the treatment of the distinction between duties, and actions that it is good to do but not wrong to omit. By Janet the principle of internal or subjective conditions is to a certain extent recognized; but the interpretation which (here approximating to the position of Martineau) he would give to the principle seems to me at once too wide and too narrow. The only subjective circumstance, according to

3

---

[1] *La Morale*, p. 232.

Janet, which could ever justify a man in omitting a good action which it would have been good for another to perform seems to be the circumstance that the good action did not happen to occur to him. Similarly, according to Martineau, an act done from the highest motive actually present to the agent is always right; an act is never wrong unless a higher motive than that which prompted his actual choice was present to the agent's consciousness. Now, it seems to me that the practical maxims of such a system would under certain circumstances fall very much below, at other times rise too far above, what would generally be recognized as the requirements of duty properly understood. A crowd stands by while a child is drowned in three feet of artificial water in a London park. Would it altogether remove the moral disapprobation with which we regard the act of one of the individuals concerned if he pleaded that it never occurred to him to jump in and save the child? It seems to me that it is quite conceivable that to many persons in that crowd the thought did not occur. But it surely shocks all common sense to say that in that case they did not fail in their duty. There are surely many cases in which a man is ignorant of his duty, but in which we cannot deny that such and such a course was his duty, whether he knew it or not. From Martineau's point of view, indeed, such a statement would be an absurdity : since his criterion of duty is wholly subjective, it is impossible for a man to be ignorant of his duty. There is, according to his view, no objective right or wrong in actions; only a higher and a lower. But Janet insists strongly on the necessity of an objective criterion of Morality. It would seem, therefore, that we must exclude from the internal conditions that may vary the duty of two men placed in similar external circumstances the want of knowledge of what the duty is as well as the want of will to perform it, however much ignorance may in some cases mitigate the culpability. In asking under what subjective conditions A may be right in omitting an act which it would have been right for B in like external circumstances to perform, we must exclude the absence of sufficient devotion to duty on the part of A, or sufficient care to find out what his duty is : when we ask what is A's duty, we assume that he is anxious to find out his duty and willing to do it when found.   But we may include in the internal conditions that vary duty the presence or absence of all moral qualities which are not under the immediate control of the will—which may be more or less cultivated, but which are not producible to order.   Now, there are some good actions which do and there are others which do not require for their fulfilment moral qualities of this kind. A man's duty under all circumstances is to do what is most conducive to the general good : but, while the general good demands that certain good things shall be done by all men irrespective of their natural disposition and the degree of moral perfection which they have attained, there are other good things which the general good only demands that persons of a certain disposition and moral character should perform.   Thus the social value of truth-speaking is not dependent upon the strength of the agent's natural love of truth, or the degree of moral advancement which he has attained in other respects.   However reluctantly he speak the truth, Society gets the same advantage ; if he lies, the injury to Society is the same.   The public Well-being demands that *all* shall speak the truth.   A man cannot therefore plead that he has no vocation for contributing to social good in that particular way : the general good demands that to this rule of conduct there shall be no exceptions [1].   Indeed, the more exceptional be the lie, the more harm it is likely to do.   On the other hand it is good for a rich man (with no obvious private claims upon his purse) to sell all that he has, and to give the whole of his time and money (in ways consistent with sound economical principles) to the service of the poor.   But this only becomes a *duty* in persons endowed with a sufficient love of the poor to do this not grudgingly or of necessity, and placed in certain perhaps rather exceptional external circumstances.   In that sense it might even be called a work of supererogation, though the term is on the whole an objectionable one : not only is it not an action demanded by social Well-being of all men placed in similar circumstances, but this is one of those cases in

---

[1] I mean of course exceptions in favour of particular persons ; I recognize the existence of exceptional cases when it is the duty of all not to speak the truth.

which (as Janet says of the voluntary adoption of celibacy from the highest motives) ' it is even evident that this state cannot be chosen by some, except on condition of its not being chosen by all [1].' The good of Society demands that there should be different vocations, some of them morally higher than others. A man can never do more than his duty, or without sin do less when once he knows what his duty is. But it is sometimes right, because desirable in the highest interests of Society, that a man should choose what must still be recognized as being from many points of view the lower vocation. It is morally as well as socially desirable that there should be a great liberty of choice as to the particular way and as to the extent to which he will contribute to social good ; but that liberty of choice is conditioned by the duty—and that the most imperative of all duties—of adopting the vocation to which upon a fair review of all circumstances, internal and external, a man believes himself to be called. It is conditioned also, I may add—and this is a consideration which would demand much fuller treatment were I writing primarily with a practical object—by the duty of moral progress; that is to say, of gradually fitting himself (so far as the external conditions of his life allow) for a higher degree of devotion to social good than any to which, being what he is, he could at present wisely aspire.

The general tendency of non-utilitarian Philosophy has been either to assume that there is in all cases some one course of action which all moral men placed under the same external circumstances would recognize as their ' bounden duty,' or to find in the mere definiteness or indefiniteness of the received rules of conduct a sharp and fundamental distinction between ' duties ' and acts which it is good to perform if one likes—between the terms ' right ' and ' good ' in their application to actions. On the other hand, it has been the tendency of Utilitarian Philosophy to reduce all duties to a general obligation to or encouragement of a philanthropy the extent and limitations of which are usually left undefined. By means of the principle of Vocation it is possible to justify the popular distinction between duties and charitable actions, without detracting either from the imperative-

[1] *La Morale*, p. 229.

ness of duty or from the claims of a more abounding charity, and to find the basis of that distinction in the requirements of social Well-being itself.

The positions at which I have arrived in the foregoing pages may be summarized by the following definitions :—

(1) It is always a man's *duty* to adopt the course of action most.conducive to the general Well-being. A man can never do more than his duty, nor can he ever (when he knows his duty) without sin do less.

(2) The name of *absolute duties* may be given to those rules of conduct which the general Well-being requires to be observed by all men under given external circumstances, irrespectively of the subjective condition or character of the agent.

(3) Acts or omissions which the general good only requires under certain *internal* circumstances or subjective conditions may be termed *duties of Vocation.*

The question has been one of the traditional subjects of debate between Protestant and Roman Catholic Theologians. Catholicism has formally asserted, Protestantism has formally denied,.the possibility of 'works of Supererogation.' If we look to the practical effects of the two one-sided doctrines, it would seem that Protestantism has in its periods of austerity and enthusiasm imposed upon all men a standard too rigid, too restrictive of natural and innocent pleasure, to be attainable or morally wholesome for the majority of men ; while in its periods of dullness and spiritual lethargy it has reduced its moral ideal for all men to one of mere respectability, and tended to discourage acts or careers of exceptional self-denial and devotion. Catholicism, on the other hand, has at no period of its history failed to give all due encouragement to exceptional missions and high religious or social enthusiasms[1]; while it has at times relaxed the minimum standard of Morality required as 'necessary to salvation' to a dangerous and deplorable degree. A true and

---

[1] It has of course too often sought to bring the ideals and the practice of exceptional men into conformity with a single too narrow ecclesiastical type. The result has been either rebellion and schism, or (as with St. Francis) that the enthusiast's work was largely spoiled by the transformation which ecclesiastical authority imposed upon it.

healthy view of the matter will combine the two one-sided doctrines. With the Protestant it will insist on the necessity of a high standard of social duty for all; with the Catholic it will encourage and find room for any amount of self-devotion— of self-devotion of a kind which really conduces to social Well-being—in those who find within themselves the capacity and the call for such sacrifices.

V

The theory that there exists a certain sphere for the indulgence of the individual's spontaneous impulses and aspirations seems to me the germ of truth involved in the principle which in the hands of Prof. Höffding has been developed into a system which may be called one of 'Optional Morality [1].' He has rightly insisted on the fact that duties in detail may be different for different persons, and that the difference depends upon natural character and not merely upon external position, but he leaves out what appear to me to be the necessary qualifications of the doctrine. Upon his view, it would appear that the requirements of sexual Morality will be just what any one likes to make them. Prof. Taylor has also rightly insisted upon the idea of Vocation, but he seems to me to go much too far when he says that such a problem as that of Isabella in *Measure for Measure*, called upon to choose between her chastity and her brother's life, is 'altogether a problem for the agent herself to decide, and to decide by reference to her own personal feelings [2].' It may be quite true that 'what might in one woman be an act of heroic self-sacrifice might in another be a cowardly desertion of duty';

[1] See his interesting and instructive article ('The Law of Relativity in Ethics') in the *International Journal of Ethics*, Vol. I (Oct., 1890).

Prof. Simmel has also insisted much on the fact that the 'ought' (*sollen*) for one individual is quite different from what it is for another, a principle which he pushes almost to the point of allowing the superior individual to disregard the conditions of social Well-being, but at the same time he very strongly insists that there can be only one duty for a given individual at a given time and in given circumstances (*Einleitung*, II, p. 39, &c.). All the writers mentioned (Höffding, Simmel, Taylor) seem to me to ignore the limitations which must be put to the application of a principle very sound in itself.

[2] *The Problem of Conduct*, p. 43.

but that would be in all probability because of the partial
knowledge which each would possess of the circumstances and
consequences of her act, and of like acts, upon general Well-being;
or because, though the ideal of each might have much in it that
is valuable, one or both of them may have been more or less
imperfect and one-sided. The case seems to be by no means
a good example of a matter in which duty is really dependent
upon subjective inclination. I see no reason to doubt that the
ideal woman ideally informed of the situation would know
what to do under the circumstances; though, when considerations are so evenly balanced, the external critic would do well
to respect, or at least to shrink from severely condemning, either
choice conscientiously made. But, though the instance seems to
be an unfortunate one, there can be no doubt that there are
other cases where the duty really is different for different people.
The best that is in one man is different from the best that is in
another, and in order that the best in each should be developed,
it is desirable not only that there should be limits to the extent
to which uniform rules of conduct should be externally imposed
by law or social pressure, but that, even from the point of view
of the highest Morality, it should be recognized that the duty
of the individual depends within certain limits upon his individual
tastes, inclinations, aspirations. The same considerations of
social Well-being which prescribe this liberty will prescribe also
its limits.

We have so far discussed the subject without reference to
those religious considerations which actually underlie the use
of the word Vocation to indicate those particular spheres of
social activity which are different for different individuals.
A fuller discussion of the relations between Religion and Morality
must for the present be postponed. Here it may be enough to
remark that the religious or teleological view of the world,
insisting on the idea that every human being is intended to
realize some end, and an end in some measure perhaps different
from that of every other individual, encourages the view that
the individual is within certain limits allowed a choice between
different kinds and different degrees of self-sacrifice; but it will
emphasize also the fact that there is some one course of action,

if only he can find it out, which is the individual's duty; and it will encourage also the disposition to assume that a strong prompting towards or aspiration after a particular kind of social service constitutes a presumption that that particular kind of social service is one to which the individual is really called by God.

VI

This chapter may conclude with a brief reference to a rather curious thesis of Professor Simmel [1]—the doctrine that a man ought to choose his social function in such a way as to utilize his moral deficiencies in the public interest. I should quite admit the principle as far as it goes. A man with a love of arbitrary power might be well advised in making himself an Indian civilian or a schoolmaster; a man in whom the passion of curiosity is strongly developed, a detective; a man with a great distaste for regular work might justify his existence as an explorer; and so on. On the other hand, a man exceptionally sensitive to other people's sufferings would be disqualified for the profession of a soldier or criminal judge, while he might make a good clergyman. What I should not admit is that the deficiencies would actually make him better in the work of his profession, if they are really moral deficiencies and not merely intellectual or emotional capacities which have a value in some men but which it might not be desirable for every one to possess in the same degree. The soldier will not be the worse soldier for being tender-hearted if he has also a strong sense of duty and a strong will, though a hard-hearted soldier will not be so useless or pernicious as a hard-hearted doctor or clergyman. The clergyman will be less valuable even as a clergyman if his philanthropy overpowers zeal for righteousness or his sense of Justice. What makes the man socially useful is not really the absence of certain good qualities but the presence of certain good qualities in spite of the absence of certain others. A merely one-sided emotional development may from a rough practical point of view seem a positive help to a man's usefulness

[1] 'Moral Deficiencies as determining Intellectual Functions,' in *International Journal of Ethics*, Vol. III, 1892-3, p. 490 sq.

in a particular position, because human nature is so constituted that extreme and yet valuable developments of this kind are frequently found in persons who lack the complementary qualities (which may be relatively unimportant for that particular place in life); but still the man would be nearer the ideal if he did combine both sides of character.

It might be possible, indeed, to contend that even the ideal man's character (and not merely his conduct) must be to some extent relative to his vocation. There is a sense, no doubt, in which this is true. We might perhaps adequately recognize this truth by saying that in the ideal man the qualities less required by his special vocation would be there potentially, if not to any great extent actually. The student cannot be so often under the influence of strong social or humanitarian emotion as the preacher of social reform or the worker in slums, but he *may* be (though unfortunately he *tends* not to be) equally capable of such emotions upon occasion, and just as ready to perform such social or humanitarian duties as are actually duties for him. And so he will not be the better student on account of any defect which can strictly be called a moral defect. A strictly moral defect would be, in fact, by definition, the absence of a quality which ought to be present in some measure in all men.

The question how far there is any single ideal of human character is one which deserves a little further consideration[1]. If by 'character' we mean actual, developed tendencies to feel and act in a certain way, it may be freely admitted not merely that there is an ideal character appropriate to each particular vocation or position in life, but that even within the ranks of the same occupation, or in matters which have no special relation to any particular mode of life, there is room for considerable variety of character. The perfection of human society demands the interaction of many different types of human excellence, moral as well as intellectual. Some kinds of conduct are good only in so far as they are exceptional, and would become socially pernicious if they were practised too frequently or too exclu-

[1] That there is such a single ideal has been denied by von Hartmann, *D. sittl. Bewusstsein*, p. 131.

sively; and there are, as we have seen, certain departments of conduct in which a certain type of conduct only becomes right, as it is practically only possible, for persons of a certain temperament. There are duties peculiar to particular vocations—that is to say, not merely duties connected with particular offices or professions or classes, but duties incumbent on individuals of a certain temperament or certain capacities without being incumbent on all— ; and there are divergent types of intellectual and emotional constitution which qualify a man for one occupation or mode of life rather than for another, and make it his duty to adopt one rather than another. Within a certain range, Society wants for its perfection men of very divergent qualities and tendencies. Society requires born Radicals and born Conservatives. That everybody should exhibit the ideal mean between the two would not answer its purposes so well as a division of labour between men of different temperaments. The ideal 'moderate' in a state of society ripe for revolution would be too moderate for a revolutionary, and too progressive for a functionary. The moderate Liberal may have his place and his work, but he cannot perform the function either of the revolutionary or of the good Conservative who makes the best of a bad system, or tries to mend it by unheroic improvements. Both social functions are useful, but they cannot both be performed by the same person ; the fact that a man performs one makes it impossible that he should perform the other. A man cannot be a religious or political reformer of the more thoroughgoing kind and at the same time a guide of timid consciences and a gradual improver of existing institutions. There is room for a Luther, and there is room for an Erasmus ; but the same person cannot undertake both rôles. No doubt a man more reasonable than Luther and less timid than Erasmus might conceivably have taken either line, though it would have been, doubtless, the same with a difference ; but sooner or later there must have come the alternative—to break with the Roman Church or not to break with it. Good might have been done by either course, but not the same good ; and, though it is possible to think of an ideal man who might have done more good than either a Luther or an Erasmus, it is possible, also, that one task was best done by a man of a vehement or violent temperament and the other by a man of somewhat timid character.

All this may be fully and freely admitted [1]; but there remains a sense in which we may nevertheless speak of a single ideal of human character, and cannot refuse to do so without contradicting the most essential deliverances of the moral consciousness. In no individual whatever, no matter how circumstanced, can there be too great a devotion to duty or to the good, though that devotion will show itself in different ways, varying not merely with outward circumstances but with intellectual and emotional constitution.   Moreover, among the emotions, desires, or tendencies to action which inspire men to promote the good, or which are recognized by the moral consciousness as having an intrinsic value of their own, there are some which, we feel, ought to exist in all men, and without which no man can attain the ideal in any position of life, though within certain limits the relative prominence or strength of them may sometimes vary without making one a better man than the other.   But there are other desires, emotions, and inclinations which may be pronounced good, though in this or that individual they may be almost entirely absent or undeveloped without his being on that account placed on a lower level than those who have them.   Under this head will fall not merely purely intellectual or aesthetic tendencies, but also many qualities which do in a sense belong to character, though they are practically inseparable from certain intellectual or aesthetic capacities.   The capacity to produce or to 'understand' music is an intellectual gift which possesses value, but the love of music is in a sense a quality of character.   Still, it is a quality of character which we do not recognize it as a duty for all individuals in all circumstances to possess or to acquire, since in some cases it either could not be acquired at all, or could only

[1] To a large extent of course the one-sided man is only made more effective by the moral and intellectual defects of other people; in a more perfect society there might be no need for such men.   But I do not think we could suppose the need for such one-sidedness altogether eliminated in a society which should still be human.   I am here speaking in a merely popular way, and do not profess to draw a sharp distinction between a difference of qualities or 'characteristics' and different degrees of development of one and the same characteristic.

be acquired at the cost of certain other qualities of equal or greater value both intrinsically and on account of their social effects. In such cases we do not regard the man who possesses these qualities as necessarily a better man than the man who lacks them.

With regard to those qualities which are more closely connected with the state of the will, and have a bearing upon the performance of duties which are duties for every man, we recognize a certain ideal scale of values. We pronounce that such and such qualities are morally higher and better than certain others; but inasmuch as these qualities are not always under the immediate control of the will, we do not say that a man has necessarily failed in his duty because in his character this ideal scale of relative prominence has not been reached. But still, I think, we should recognize that, so long as we confine ourselves to these more general and universal ingredients, so to speak, of human character, there is an ideal balance of these qualities which a man cannot fall short of without being a less ideal man than he who exhibits it, though in one position the higher qualities may be less frequently called into activity than in others. For the man of higher nature it might be wrong to accept positions in which these higher qualities would have small opportunities for their due development and influence upon Society. But the ideal man would not be actually disqualified by the possession of these qualities for any position in life whatever; though, no doubt, in point of fact their presence is often found to be accompanied by other qualities or defects of quality which might make him less efficient in some positions than a less good man. Not only could no man have too much devotion to the good in general, but such qualities as love, truthfulness, purity, courage, and the like are qualities which no man in any position could have too much of, or be deficient in without falling proportionately below the true human ideal. Without some measure of those qualities he could not have that devotion to duty without which he could not be a good man at all. And even with regard to their relative prominence there is to some extent an ideal, and a man cannot fall short of the ideal without being a man of lower character than the man who approximates to it more nearly, though he may succeed in doing his duty just because for a man of lower type duty may be something different than for the man of higher type. Of these universal qualities there can be no excess. A man could not be too brave, so long as bravery means simply a willingness to face danger when duty calls. On the other hand, there is a kind of intrepidity, of positive delight in danger, which the ideal scholar might well be without, but which might be an excellent quality in a soldier. Nobody can be too charitable, i.e. too desirous to do good to his fellows ; but the positive longing for disagreeable kinds of service exhibited by a man of the St. Francis type, though an excellent and beautiful thing, is not a necessary part of the ideal character. It is a quality which makes an excellent Friar, but would be a disqualification for the career of a statesman or a scholar. We should wish all men to have as much goodwill for their fellows as St. Francis of Assisi ; we should not wish them all to have the same liking for disagreeable duties or the same dislike of learning. All good men must have some love of humanity, but a special liking for the young or for the old, a desire to save one's country collectively or to save individual souls, a special zeal for Temperance or for Justice or for the relief of suffering—these are qualities which may be present in a high or a low degree without the man being any better or worse than other men somewhat differently constituted. A certain respect for knowledge or beauty is a characteristic of the ideal good man, as also is a disposition to subordinate them to the more imperative claims of Justice and Humanity. In so far as men of the philanthropic type altogether lack such respect, it must be pronounced a moral defect, though not a breach of duty or a sin ; in so far as its relative non-development is merely incidental to the strength of the humanitarian impulse and the demands of a particular occupation, the man with this defect is not morally worse than the man who is without it. Indifference to human suffering in an Artist is a defect of character ; the ideal Artist would possess the potentiality of caring for human suffering, which on proper occasions would be called into activity. But an Artist might be habitually occupied with the pursuit of his Art, his mind might be habitually

32

occupied with dreams of beauty and his will absorbed in realizing them, while he was comparatively seldom occupied with reflecting on human suffering or with efforts to relieve it, without being in any wise a worse man, or even representing a lower type of humanity, than the ideal Philanthropist.

We may thus recognize three meanings in the term character when used in this connexion : (1) Character in the narrower sense means the degree of a man's devotion to the good in general. In this sense the ideal is the same for all. To be less devoted to the good must always mean to be a lower man, while to fall below that measure of devotion to good which is necessary to the performance of the man's particular vocation is to fail in duty. (2) By character may be meant the possession of those emotions, desires, tendencies to action, likings and dislikings which we always recognize as good (irrespectively of any particular occupation or course of life), a measure of which is demanded by the true moral ideal for all men, but which may be present in very different proportions without occasioning failure in duty, and sometimes even without placing the man on a higher or lower moral level. (3) Character may be held to include those qualities, desires, inclinations, likings and dislikings, or more specialized applications and developments of the more universal qualities, which, though they may be good in themselves, are incompatible with others equally good, and which, therefore, we do not recognize it as good for all men to possess in all circumstances. Here even the total absence of some qualities which we cannot deny to possess high value may be compatible with the highest moral excellence in the ordinary sense of the word : that is to say, we recognize that the defect has nothing to do with the will, though for particular persons it may, of course, be a duty to seek to overcome the defect.

That these three kinds of excellence run into one another, that a high development of each of them presupposes some development of the others, and so on, I not only do not want to deny but should strongly assert. Any more exact account of them would involve elaborate psychological analysis for which this is not the place. The sole purpose of this enumeration is to draw a distinction between a sense in which there is only one moral ideal and a sense in which there are many, all of them excellent but to a greater or less degree incompatible with one another. That devotion to the good or to duty which is the crowning excellence of all is one and the same, however diverse are the particular forms in which it manifests itself; and some other qualities and characters are so closely connected with this devotion to the good in all its forms that no one could be altogether without them, or could depart from a certain ideal balance or proportion between them, without falling below the highest ideal of humanity, though it is possible to fall below the highest ideal of humanity without actual sin or failure in duty. As the qualities assume more and more specialized forms, have less and less connexion with that devotion to the good in general which is incumbent upon all, become more and more dependent upon intellectual and purely emotional (as distinct from moral) characteristics, have more and more special reference to particular circumstances of life and the specialized activities which correspond with them, absolute or relative failure in some of them becomes more and more compatible with high excellence of the man on the whole. In the human ideal there are universal elements and particular elements ; the ideal man must be a good man in general, but on the other hand there is no such thing as goodness in general which does not express itself in one or more alternative types or specialized kinds of good activity. In each of these types some common characteristics can be discovered, but also some elements peculiar to itself. Nay more, since both the natural endowments and the external circumstances of each man are in some degree unlike those of any other man, there is even, we may say, an ideal for each particular individual.

To deny either of these sides of the truth leads to exaggeration and one-sidedness. To make the degree of a man's devotion to the good in general the only thing that is excellent in human character is to set up an empty abstraction—a universal with no particulars, to make into our ideal a universal man who is not and cannot be a real man at all, to forget that devotion to good in general can only be realized by devotion to some particular kind of good in detail. Or at best it is to substitute an abstract sense of duty for the human affections and emotions which are really better motives of conduct than a sense of duty which is without love. On the other hand to deny absolutely that there is any such thing as a single ideal for Humanity is virtually to deny the objectivity of our moral judgements, or at the very least to deny the unique value of Morality in the stricter sense—the supreme value of the rightly directed will, and of those more universal qualities of character without which there cannot be a rightly directed will in any man or in any circumstances. Since Morality means contribution to the true good of Society, a defective devotion to that good, and the absence of qualities which impel to the promotion of it, could not be positively demanded in the interests of true Well-being, and therefore could not in any individual, however circumstanced, constitute no moral defect.

Plato seems to have hit the essential truth in this matter when he demanded Justice of all, and a certain measure of the other Virtues, while he insisted that the same measure or development of them was not demanded of all men. This principle of the specialization of character corresponding to a specialization of social function must be carried much further than he carried it— so far indeed that we may perhaps regard it as p obable that for each man there is an ideal which is not exactly the same as any other man's ideal ; and for Justice, as the one indispensable and dominant Virtue for all, we should perhaps substitute a love which may assume very varied forms, but which will always be a love of Humanity which is also love of all that is good as such.

CHAPTER V

MORAL AUTHORITY AND MORAL AUTONOMY.

WE have hitherto conducted our enquiry as though each man actually arrived at his moral judgements by the independent workings of his own moral consciousness, thinking out each problem as it arises *de novo* in complete independence of his fellows and their moral judgements. Now it is obvious that this representation entirely fails to correspond with the facts. Every individual finds himself from the earliest dawn of moral consciousness a member of a society in which there are established rules of conduct, standards of praise and blame, social institutions, accepted models, recognized ideals. And the morality of the society has been most emphatically enforced upon the individual by all kinds of social pressure, ranging from actual or threatened punishment down to the most faintly indicated 'disapproval' or the mere withholding of positive commendation.

The beginning of the process by which the individual becomes indoctrinated with the ideals of his society is of course to be found in the earliest education of children. The Intuitionism which supposed that the young child finds written upon his consciousness a ready-made code of right and wrong,—the whole content of the Ten Commandments or of the Ethics of Aristotle or of the Sermon on the Mount,—is an Intuitionism which, in so far as it ever existed outside the imagination of utilitarian critics, is a thing of the past. Without entering upon the difficult question how far moral ideals or predispositions towards them are matters of actual inheritance, it may confidently be denied that a child deserted in the woods and suckled by wolves would have any moral ideas at all, or that an English child brought up by savages would, on attaining the age of twenty-one, find himself in possession of the same moral ideas as his father and mother. Nobody attains to his moral ideas without moral education, and this education is more or less continued through-

out life.   The difference between an Englishman's moral ideas
and a Chinaman's is enormous.   There is a difference even between
the moral ideas of European nations on much the same plane of
civilization.   There are very few Englishmen, even among the
highly educated (on whom the pressure of the immediate environment is weakened by familiarity with a wider range of moral
ideas through literature, itself of course a kind of social influence),
who can suppose that their moral ideas on all points would be
exactly what they are, had they lived entirely among French-
men from their earliest years.   And with the great majority of
men the influence of the immediate environment is paramount.
Their dominant or operative ideal (though there may be some
higher _view of life which shares the secret homage of their
hearts) is to a greater or less extent the morality of their school,
their class, their social circle, their profession, their neighbour-
hood.

Now in the admission that people come by their moral ideals
through education there is nothing whatever to encourage moral
scepticism, to encourage the doubt whether Morality is after all
anything more than what other people *de facto* think about our
conduct, the doubt whether there is such a thing as an absolute
Morality discernible by Reason.   The discovery that men's
moral ideas are in a sense the result of education is often in
actual fact a very fruitful source of moral scepticism, both in
theory and in practice, but some moral scepticism is a necessary
condition of moral progress.   It was the discovery of the fact
that the morality of the Persians was not quite the same as that
of the Greeks, nor the ideal of Sparta precisely that of Athens,
which originated the crude scepticism of certain Sophists, and
the theory that Justice was a matter of convention, not of Nature
(νόμῳ, not φύσει), with which Plato does battle in the *Republic*.
But after all the necessity of moral education supplies no more
reason for thinking that Morality is purely arbitrary than the
fact that Mathematics have to be taught is any reason for doubting the truth of that Science.   I do not, of course, suggest that
the influence of education upon moral ideas is precisely the
same in kind or in degree as the influence of education upon the
development of mathematical capacity.   The Science of Mathe-

matics was, indeed, slowly developed, and that not by experience
in the ordinary sense of the word, but by mere thinking out of
the consequences of very simple, self-evident truths; but it has to
be laboriously communicated to each individual who wishes to
become a Mathematician. So far the parallel is complete. But,
although people do not become Mathematicians without teaching,
they do all ultimately come to have the same mathematical ideas
if they have any mathematical ideas at all. Some men are
incapable of coming to see mathematical truths, but they seldom
attempt (though I should imagine that such cases might be
found [1]) deliberately and consciously to deny what have become
accepted truths of Mathematics. Yet, even in Mathematics, it is
the consensus of practically all persons endowed with adequate
mathematical capacity who have seriously applied their minds to
the subject, that causes that Science to be accepted as the type of
scientific certainty—an explanation which, however, is not complete without the addition that the tests of adequate capacity
and adequate study are here simple and unmistakable. But the
moment we leave pure Mathematics and the physical Sciences
which have reached a mathematical form, this consensus of the
competent begins to disappear. Even in the less advanced
branches of physical Science, and in the higher reaches even of
the most advanced, there is room for wide difference of opinion;
and be it observed, this difference is partly due to purely
intellectual causes, to the different degrees of intellectual insight,
lucidity of mind, logical power, observation and judgement
possessed by different men, but only partly. Even here—in a
region comparatively remote from the great practical interests
which inspire passion and distort judgement—every one knows
to what an enormous extent men's opinions are liable to be
swayed by such influences as personal loyalty, personal antagonism, fashion, party spirit, caprice, carelessness, laziness,
ambition, conceit. Still more obviously do those influences—the

[1] As for instance when Hobbes, finding ' almost all geometers ' against him
in his controversy with Wallis, declared that ' either I alone am mad, or I
alone am not mad ; other alternative there is none, unless, perchance, some
one may say that we are all mad together ' (quoted by G. Croom Robertson
in *Hobbes, Phil. Classics for Eng. Readers*, p. 183).

influence of the environment on the one hand and the ' personal
equation ' on the other—mould men's views upon such matters as
speculative Philosophy, History, Social Science, Politics.   And
yet, in these departments of knowledge nobody seriously doubts
that there is a truth to be found, and that it is discoverable by
a proper use of the intellectual faculties which we possess, or
supposes that there is any remedy for these defects of our
thinking, any infallible criterion by which to distinguish truth
from prejudice, except a further, more thorough, more conscientious use of the very faculties whose limitations we acknowledge.

In so far as the differences of ethical opinion turn upon the
question of the right means to be adopted with a view to a given
end, this difference is of exactly the same kind as differences of
opinion on any matter of common life.   The fact that people
at one time did not see the wrongness of indiscriminate charity
could hardly be supposed to weaken our confidence in the validity
of moral judgements, any more than the Science of Heat is discredited by the fact that the steam engine is a modern invention.
But when we turn to the question of ends, there are special
reasons why in this matter, more than in many others, differences
of opinion should be peculiarly frequent and why one man's
opinion should be emphatically not as good as another's.
Although the power of judging of moral value is, I believe,
essentially an intellectual faculty, it is a highly special intellectual faculty.   Sensitiveness to the moral ugliness of drunkenness or impurity or appreciation of the moral beauty of unselfishness are qualities which vary in different individuals to
an enormous extent.   And these differences of moral insight, like
the differences of aesthetic appreciation, by no means correspond
with differences of general intellectual capacity.   Like the power
of musical appreciation, they appear to be almost wanting in some
individuals not destitute of high intellectual powers.   Moreover,
intellectual as it is, its actual exercise is, as I have endeavoured
to show [1], largely conditioned by the emotional capacity and the
emotional development of the individual.   The judgement
' Suffering ought to be relieved ' might indeed be made on purely
intellectual grounds by one who had little or no sympathy with

[1] Cf. above, Bk. I, ch. vi, p. 154 sq.

suffering. But in practice the clearness with which this truth has been seen, and the intensity of conviction with which it has been accepted, depend at least as much upon the emotional as upon the intellectual endowments of the race or the generation or the individual. Moreover, to a great extent, our moral judgements are judgements upon the intrinsic value of certain kinds of feeling, and in these cases the judgement of value cannot be made unless the feeling is actually felt, except so far as a man may (on account of some inferred analogy with what he has felt) judge that a certain feeling in another deserves respect, even though he may not chance to experience it himself, or may condemn it on account of its incompatibility with a feeling which he has felt and values. Here again differences between the emotional capacity of different individuals affect the value of their ethical judgement. Not only do the individual's powers of correct ethical judgement vary, but, except in those in whom this power is strong and in the particular directions in which it is strong, these judgements of value (like aesthetic judgements) are peculiarly liable to be swayed by the judgements of others, and by the influence of those emotions and associations through which the judgements of others appeal to us. It should be observed that *some* moral or aesthetic capacity is actually presupposed in this sympathetic influence, and there are limits to the extent of such influence. A man who really does not know what Beauty is, will probably not be induced by the *ipse dixit* of the connoisseur to grow enthusiastic, unless it be as a piece of conscious hypocrisy, over the work of some fashionable school. It is the man of dim, confused, undeveloped aesthetic perceptions, who will grow into an admiration for what he is told to admire. He may be induced to admire what is less worthy of admiration, and to depreciate what is more worthy; but he could not be induced to admire that which possesses no merit or beauty whatever. He would be imposed upon by a fairly good copy of an Old Master, but not by an execrably bad one. It is just the same in the moral sphere: only here the modifying influence of environment is multiplied a thousand-fold by all the influences, the emotions (some of them of high moral worth), even the moral principles which link us to our fellow men.

There is another important difference between moral and other judgements. Not only is the power of judging rightly as to ultimate moral values dependent upon a faculty distinguishable from a man's general intellectual capacity, but it is to a large extent dependent upon the degree in which his will responds to those judgements. That moral discernment is the outcome of a habit of moral action was the theory of Aristotle. No doubt it is much more possible than Aristotle supposed to judge well, not merely about means but about moral ends or ideals, and to act badly; but it remains true that to a large extent the power of moral intuition may be improved or impaired by our voluntary conduct, and therefore the truth of men's moral judgements depends not merely upon insight, but upon character. Here we have an additional source of inequality in men's powers of discerning between right and wrong.

In view of all these facts, it must appear that the attempt on the part of the individual to think out his moral code *a priori*, in entire independence of his environment, is an impracticable one, and one which would be disastrous, if it were practicable [1]. That this is so with the great mass of men is sufficiently obvious. They have not the knowledge, the experience, the leisure to trace out all the advantages and disadvantages of conflicting courses of action, whether in detailed circumstances or with regard to general principles of conduct. They could not have become moral beings at all without moral education; and yet that moral education has been gradually unfitting them for the impartial exercise either of their ordinary understanding in dealing with means or of their moral Reason in choosing ends. They can only have learned to approve and disapprove by actually approving or disapproving particular things, and such approval or disapproval has been making it more and more difficult for them to approve

[1] Dr. McTaggart writes: 'Nothing can be more important to me, in respect of any branch of knowledge, than my own immediate certainties about it. Nothing can be less important than the immediate certainties of other people' (*Studies in Hegelian Cosmology*, p. 72). But surely even in other branches of knowledge than Ethics a man may have to rely on other people's immediate certainties – e.g. a dyer or a Physicist investigating the cause of colour might well consult an Artist who would see shades of difference in colour which he could not perceive himself.

or disapprove something markedly different. Other men's moral judgements, sympathetically appropriated by them, have given a bias to their emotions, and the emotions have reacted upon their judgement. It may be suggested that, on attaining years of discretion, the individual would do well to emancipate himself from the distorting influence of his social environment, and school himself into thinking entirely for himself on moral questions. And to some extent this is no doubt desirable; but, if it were done completely, the individual would be thereby withdrawing himself from the school in which alone Virtue is teachable. Once more the aesthetic analogy may help us. It is only by studying great Masters that a man can himself become an Artist; and that study implies that he is submitting himself to influences which are moulding his taste and judgement, which are every moment limiting in certain directions his power of impartially and independently judging between their ideals and other ideals. And yet without such education he would never acquire any power of independent judgement at all [1].

[1] Von Hartmann, with his accustomed ethical insight, recognizes that the ordinary Morality of the average man is not and cannot be ' reine Autonomie noch reine Heteronomie' but 'eine Konkurrenz beider,' and that in the average individual intrinsic moral activity must necessarily present itself in the form of an external rule which represents an autonomous Morality in the community to which he belongs: such Morality is ' nur für das Individuum als solches eine Heteronomie, aber für das ganze Volk als Individuum höherer Ordnung betrachtet ist sie Autonomie, nämlich ein Integral aus allen auto- nomsittlichen Individualwillensakten' (*Ethische Studien*, pp. 110, 114). At the same time he strongly insists upon Autonomy as the ideal. In much that is said in some quarters about Heteronomy and Autonomy there seems to be a certain confusion between two senses of the word. A man's *will* may be autonomous enough to satisfy Kant himself, although in some of the details of Morality he defers to the judgement of others. Nobody but a lunatic refuses to accept the judgement of others in matters of which he knows nothing: and nobody can have an independent judgement in every depart- ment of conduct. It is only when we come to the most general principles of Morality that lack of Autonomy necessarily implies a low level of personal Morality. A man is not the less moral because he allows Church or State to decide for him the morality of marrying his deceased wife's sister; though he would be an undeveloped moral being if his respect for unselfishness were wholly based upon authority. If this be denied, it can only be in the sense that absolutely ideal Morality would imply an ideally complete intellectual development.

Are we then to condemn the attempt to think for oneself in moral matters? Are we to say that a man must simply submit himself wholly and unreservedly to the maxims, the traditions, the ideals of the society in which he finds himself? A moment's reflection is enough to negative the suggestion A principal object of moral education is to form the habit of judging for oneself. The ancient philosopher who most emphasized the necessity of moral education by habituation insisted no less strongly that the moral education was not complete until the man had come to see and appreciate for himself the reason, the ground, the principle of the maxims which he at first accepted on authority[1]. And if the man's moral education has been a success, if he really has been taught to use his moral Reason, it cannot invariably stop in its exercise at the exact point which would prevent the deliverances of his own moral consciousness coming into collision with those of his moral instructors. The majority of men, of course, are not likely to rise on the whole far above the moral ideal of their society; but, if we do not confound Morality with the mere observance of a few traditional, and for the most part negative, maxims of conduct, it is clear that very ordinary men must have some moral originality or individuality. A man who thought and felt with the majority on every detail of life and conduct would be, as nearly as it is possible to be, a man without a character. And it is precisely to the men in whom moral education has been most successful, who have absorbed most completely all that was best in the teaching and example by which they were educated, that there are most certain to come moments at which they are impelled to question the teaching they have received; and to apply the principles which they have imbibed to the criticism of those principles themselves, or to carry them out into applications not dreamed of by those from whom they learned them. Moral innovations of this sort may of course take a great variety of forms. Sometimes there will be a violent reaction against morals that have been taught; and yet the greatest of moral revolutionaries have owed not less to their environment than the most rigid traditionalists. The environment of Athens produced Socrates as much as it

---

[1] Aristotle, *Ethic. Nicomach.*, VI. 12 (p. 1144 *a*).

produced the Sophists. Ruskin appeared to his average contemporaries from one point of view as a dangerous reactionary,
from another as a dangerous revolutionary. And yet Ruskin
owed as much to early nineteenth-century Evangelical education as Macaulay. The most violent reaction often owes much
to the ideas against which it reacts, and the reaction in turn
often contains within itself the germs of the most startling
revolutions. And in more ordinary cases moral improvement
takes place through the expansion, the development, the intensifi-
cation, the fresh application of principles already acknowledged,
the clearer vision of truths of which there have been already
at least many glimpses.

It is not necessary for our present purpose to analyse further
the nature of these new stages in moral progress. Sometimes
the innovation is a purely intellectual discovery, a recognition
that such and such a principle must necessarily lead to such
and such a consequence, or that such and such an end could
be best attained by some hitherto undreamed-of means; sometimes it is an emendation of the fundamental axioms (so to
speak) of moral thought, as when the civic morality of the
Hellene or the tribal morality of the Jew is supplanted by
a comprehensive principle of universal Benevolence; sometimes
it is some signal increase of the emotional intensity with which
a quite accepted principle is realized; sometimes it is the revision
of the values recognized in ultimate ends or elements of Well-
being, as when it is seen that a stricter restraint of appetite
than pagan Ethics required is better worth having than its
indulgence, or that Christian Humility (properly understood) is
more beautiful than the self-assertion of Aristotle's μεγαλόψυχος.
To tie the individual down to absolute acquiescence in the judgements of his predecessors or his contemporaries would be to put
a stop to the possibility of moral progress. To tell the man of
the least gifted moral nature that he is never to think for
himself about what he ought to do would be to doom him to
moral stagnation or sterility. Mr. Bradley (who seems rarely
to touch upon practical matters without violent and obvious
exaggeration) has laid it down that for a man 'to wish to be
better than the world is to be already on the threshold of

immorality [1].' It would be truer to say that the man who is content to be as moral as his neighbours has already passed considerably beyond that threshold. Would not any one who really supposed that at all times ' wisdom and virtue consist in living agreeably to the Ethos of one's country ' inevitably have voted for the condemnation of Socrates, and have joined the crowd which shouted ' Crucify him, crucify him ' ?

II

How, then, are we to adjust these two principles—the principle of moral authority and the principle of private judgement, both in their way essential to a sound Morality in society and in individuals? At the earlier stages of moral development the question can never arise; for to a large extent the influence of the Authority is unconscious : to question it already implies the first stage of emancipation. Authority achieves its most complete success when it is no more felt as Authority than we are directly aware of the pressure which the atmosphere is at every moment exercising upon our bodies. But if we suppose a child or a man who has arrived at the stage of intellectual and moral development at which he is capable of asking, ' How far should I obey Authority in Ethics ? ' we should have to say to him just what we should have to say to a man who asked, ' How far am I to rely upon Authority in matters of historical criticism or of aesthetic judgement ? ' In the latter case, for instance, we should tell him, ' You must begin by accepting provisionally the judgement of the best guide you can find. If you begin to paint Nature without the assistance of those who have studied Nature before you, it is unlikely that you will ever paint better than some crude predecessor of Cimabue. On the other hand, if you try to form your taste by studying all the pictures that you

---

[1] *Ethical Studies*, p. 180. Elsewhere Mr. Bradley quotes with approval Hegel's commendation of a purely particularistic morality (ib. p. 169): ' Hence the wisest men of antiquity have given judgement that wisdom and virtue consist in living agreeably to the Ethos of one's people.' This nearly approaches the doctrine of Kirchmann (' Jedes Volk muss sein Sittliches für ein Unbedingtes und Unveränderliches halten '), against whom von Hartmann polemizes as the typical representative of the ' moral principle of Heteronomy ' (*Das sittliche Bewusstsein*, p. 63).

come across without allowing your judgement to be warped by the suggestion that you will probably find the best pictures in the National Gallery, you would be in great danger of never finding your way to Trafalgar Square at all. And even at Trafalgar Square it is not every boy or man who would learn to think the Old Masters better than an average English Academician if he had never been told that they were generally so considered. But it is in vain to suppose that in following this course you will not have contracted a bias. The greatest of the great Masters show the influence of their teachers. But in course of time you will learn from your chosen guides themselves, in proportion as you have chosen them well and in proportion as you are capable of learning it, how gradually to correct that bias, and to judge for yourself what is beautiful. You will give up your reliance upon Authority just where and in so far as you see reason to suspect that your chosen guides were wrong, and that you are more likely to be right.'

There are, indeed, differences between Morality and other matters which tend to increase the necessity of caution in attempting to strike out a new line in practical Ethics. I have already emphasized the much greater liability of moral as compared with other judgements to be distorted by our private passions and wishes; and this is a consideration which may recommend Green's useful maxim that, while a man may not go far wrong in imposing on himself some new restraint which is not generally recognized by his contemporaries, he ought to hesitate very much longer before he allows himself any indulgence which the accepted Morality condemns. We must likewise bear in mind the very much greater importance of such innovations in Morality as compared with judgements on mere matters of opinion. The publication of a new theory may aid the progress of Science even when it is ultimately refuted; the harm which may be done by a word lightly spoken against accepted moral standards may be great, even when the particular scruple which is derided may chance to be a baseless one; though we have also to remember the tendency which un-necessary restrictions have to weaken men's respect for those which are necessary, particularly when the unnecessary restraint is no longer really approved by the consciences of those on whom it is imposed. It is not every occasion on which we fail to see the reason of some established rule, or even every occasion on which we think we see a reason against it, that calls upon us to break the commandment and teach men so [1]. Just the same considerations which make it a duty in ninety-nine cases out of a hundred to obey a law even if we think it pernicious may often make it a duty to fall in with some social convention which we think irrational. There are many matters in which it is of more importance that there should be a rule universally accepted and obeyed than that the rule should be the best possible. This is, of course, the case with the great mass of petty matters regulated by the etiquette of Society, or the custom of nation or class, or, again, with matters so fundamental that they can only be altered by a legal or social revolution. Sometimes, even when we think the rule pernicious, there may be many circumstances in which the evil consequences of compliance are less than those of non-compliance. We are bound, again, to take account of established moralities, even when we ourselves feel it a duty to protest against them. We may feel that the evil of gambling makes it desirable that even moderate playing for money should be banished from respectable society; but, till the rule is established, we are not justified in treating a man who breaks it as an offender against acknowledged Morality or good manners. It is impossible to define the degrees of clearness and conviction on our part which will make it a duty to violate some established rule of our society. It is only important to insist that the *ultimate* standard of right and wrong should be the individual's own, and that he should exercise his own moral judgement even when he ultimately decides that respect for some authority compels him

---

[1] Simmel, a by no means conservative Moralist, has pointed out how, through association with acts really immoral, the doing of acts merely conventionally wrong may produce upon the consciousness of the agent all the effects of real wrongdoing and so lead to real moral deterioration (*Einleitung*, II, p. 406 sq.). The fact may be used on both sides—as a warning both against lightly disturbing accepted rules of conduct, and against binding unnecessary burdens upon Consciences which do not really acknowledge their obligation, though they may not be sufficiently clear-sighted deliberately to repudiate them.

to act otherwise than he would do if he had no such authority before his eyes. And that brings me to a consideration which has hitherto been left out of account—a consideration of vital importance, which is, however, too generally neglected in discussions as to the relation between the society and the individual in the sphere of Ethics.

III

I have hitherto written as though each individual found himself a member of a single homogeneous 'society' confronted with some one clearly defined, universally accepted moral code or ideal, professed and more or less practised by every member of that society (subject to modification only by his own personal and individual aberrations), commended to his acceptance equally in all its parts by the united weight of that society's authority, and enforced upon him by its 'social sanctions.' In practice we know that this is very partially the case. In a very primitive tribe, or within the limits of an Indian caste, there may be some approach to such a concentration of social Authority; in such societies there may be found a single standard of conduct, unanimously accepted, and in its more important articles enforced with such uniformity that transgression of established custom is almost unknown. But such is not the case at any more advanced stage of moral development. Least of all does this representation correspond with the circumstances of any modern man in any civilized modern community; in any such society there is not one moral ideal but many ideals, more or less exalted, more or less conflicting. It is not merely that different individuals have different ideals; there is in truth no such single 'society' as is contemplated by the conventional way of speaking. The individual is not a member of one 'society,' but of a network of (if we may so say) interlacing 'societies,' each of which has its more or less clearly defined and more or less peremptorily enforced ideal. The schoolboy is a member of one society called his family; the adult outside world is for him largely represented by his Schoolmaster; through literature he is brought into connexion not with one but with a number of more or less harmonious, more or less discordant moral worlds;

while he is also the member of a society with a quite distinct
ideal of its own, an ideal forced upon his attention with far
more peremptory insistence than either of the former—i. e. the
society of his schoolfellows; and even here there may be
a collision between the ideals of many conflicting sets or strata
of school society.   These considerations are of importance for
our subject in several ways.   On the one hand, it should be
observed that the environment which exercises the maximum of
social pressure upon the individual is generally the immediate
environment.   Now the moral level of this environment may be
considerably below that of the surrounding society, and yet its
'sanctions' are enormously more powerful.   The only public
opinion that matters much to an unmarried officer is that of
his mess, and there is no guarantee that the public opinion of
a mess will be up to the level even of that entirely vague
and indefinite 'public opinion' which is supposed to exist in
Society at large.   Moreover, in certain particular points and
respects the public opinion of a man's immediate society is
nearly always—paradoxical as it may appear—below the level
of that of the surrounding society.   For the public opinion of
each of the particular groups of which Society is composed is
likely to be weakest precisely on those points on which for that
particular group the temptation is strongest.   The opinion of
the 'general public' on the subject of adulteration and tricks
of trade is sound enough; but what practically presents itself
as public opinion to the average grocer is the public opinion of
grocers, or at most of tradesmen at large.   The general public
condemns in the clergy the practice of preaching sermons stolen
wholesale without acknowledgement, and taking credit for their
originality; it is among the clergy that the condemnation of it,
though not non-existent, is least strong.   In many cases the
public opinion of a man's own particular group is absolutely
opposed to the interests and to the public opinion of the wider
society around.   It is probable, of course, that every member of
this smaller group is more or less aware of the wider opinion;
and this wider public opinion will often present itself as an ideal
which his own higher self respects, however little he may seek
to live up to it.   But still it is the lower and narrower ideal

that is most conspicuously illustrated by the conduct of a man's 'neighbours,' and to which the 'sanctions' of public opinion are for the most part attached. It is this fact which renders so futile the Utilitarian attempt to find in public opinion a 'sanction' which will identify the interest of the individual with the interest of the whole, and which renders so deeply immoral (if it is to be taken seriously) the teaching of 'ideal Morality' when it bids a man take as his ultimate moral criterion the average practice of his neighbours—not (be it observed) the ideal of his neighbours, but their actual practice.

The truth is that Philosophers like Mr. Bradley habitually write about Ethics as though the average man were perfectly moral, that is to say the average man of the 'respectable' classes, for they seem usually to leave out of account the most numerous class of their fellow citizens. It is the man who reads the *Times* or the respectable shopkeeper who always does duty for 'the plain man' in practical matters, though (in Mr. Bradley's own case) this apotheosis of middle-class respectability jostles oddly enough with pleas for very startling innovations or revisions in certain departments of Morality. Now this way of representing the moral life is not merely defective; it betrays a want of sympathy with all efforts after anything higher than the conventional ideal, with all forms of moral enthusiasm, with all intenser forms of moral life in every age—with the more enthusiastic Christianity of past or present, with the heroism of Russian revolutionaries, with what is best in socialistic or labour movements nearer home. It misrepresents and caricatures that moral life of the average man which it affects to find so satisfactory. For that average man is deeply conscious for the most part of a higher ideal than that which is realized in his habitual conduct. His conduct would fall below the level which it actually attains if it were not for the partial and occasional influence of the ideal with which his higher self identifies itself: and yet it is not the strivings of the higher self so much as its defeats which most obviously force themselves upon the notice of any one who is prepared to take average practice as representative of the average man's ideal and therefore of his own. The public opinion of our neighbours is not the source of what is best in the lives of most men: for those who are really struggling towards the light ' the world ' often becomes synonymous with all that is evil. It is the public opinion of the immediate environment which is practically most important to a man, and that public opinion often assumes the form of persecution in its dealings with the individual who aims at an ideal higher than its own, all the more because it is secretly conscious that it is higher and truer than its own [1].

The average man is thus normally more or less conscious of, and more or less influenced by, an ideal or ideals higher than that of ' his neighbour's ' average performance. But it is none the less important to remember that this ideal is as much a social ideal as the other. The Conscience that accepts it, with whatever degree of clearness and consistency—whether as the deliberately chosen rule of life, or with distant homage as an ideal almost too high for daily practice, or with confused and intermittent allegiance—is not indeed the passive reflection of other people's opinions which it is represented to be by those who insist most upon the social origin of our moral ideals; for (as we have seen) it is only a consciousness that has in it some power of recognizing right and wrong for itself that is capable of education by Society. But still it is a Conscience moulded and educated by Society. Its ideal is for the most part—though not without more or less of modification through the independent exercise of the individual's trained faculty of moral judgement—an ideal built up for it by a society, and received from a social environment. But it is an ideal deliberately chosen and selected by the individual from a number of competing social ideals. Take any person whose actual conduct is in some particular markedly above the level professed and the practice of his immediate surroundings— the schoolboy who stands out against the all but universal bad custom sanctioned by the school opinion, the trader who is impoverished by his honesty, the member of a worldly family

---

[1] 'Each little society, distinguished from the background of universal humanity by reason of certain ideas and endeavours that are common to its members, represents a social will, which has all the characteristics of an independent reality, in that it operates as a self-active force both on the individuals comprising it and on the regions of life above it' (Wundt, *Ethics*, E. T., III, p. 36).

who gives himself or herself to good works.   In most cases you could definitely tell where this apparently isolated individual has got his ideal from.   No doubt in many cases he has, in a sense, got it from the very persons who commended it so little by their habitual maxims or their usual practice.   For mere ordinary common sense may be sufficient to detect the inconsistency of the schoolboy who is indignant enough against other kinds of falsehood or deceit but introduces an illogical exception in favour of 'cribbing': the dishonest trader has himself denounced the corruption of government officials: the worldly mother may herself have taught her children that it is good to be charitable to the poor.   But if there is really nothing in the immediate environment to suggest the higher ideal, the social source of the ideal could still in general be traced in the wider environment.   In most cases it could be discovered in an actual personal or social influence—a teacher, a friend, a social group, or a 'movement' with which the person has been in some kind of contact, a book, a preacher, or the higher ideal to which the dullest, the deadest, the most conventional worship bears witness. Even where the individual seems most completely cut off from the society in which the highest ideal is formally professed or actively lived out, there is still through education or literature some contact with a wider environment.   The most 'secular' education can hardly keep the pupil in entire ignorance of a literature that is steeped in Christian ideas: the most mundane circles read newspapers which communicate a knowledge of the existence of human suffering and of active efforts to relieve it.

The individual Conscience, however active, still almost invariably finds its highest ideal, or at least the suggestion of its highest ideal, not in any actually new creation of its own, but in an ideal already active in some other soul, more or less realized in other lives, more or less accepted by some actual society of human beings.   If any doubt remain on this matter, one may point to the fact that the most original moral teachers nevertheless generally betray the source of their moral inspiration.   No doubt the very existence of an absolute moral truth which human Reason has the faculty (more or less of it in different individuals) of discerning for itself implies that those in whom the faculty is most active should exhibit some tendency towards an approximation in quite independent moral judgements. Nothing is more childish than to assume that every coincidence between the teaching of early Christianity and some other literature shows that one borrowed from the other. But still in the emphasis which is laid on this or that aspect of Morality, in the form which is given to their moral theory, in the more subtle and delicate tones of character, the men of highest moral genius and strongest moral faculty will always show the influence of the social ideal by which their own moral capacity has been evoked. To say nothing of the broad contrast between Hellenic and modern civilization, the best men even within the pale of civilized Christendom rarely fail to show where they got their ideals. The ideals of the best Roman Catholics and of the best Protestants approximate to each other much more closely than those of the worst in each faith, but they are never the same. The difference remains even where the strictly theological side of Christianity has been abandoned. Comte's ideal was Catholicism without Christianity : Carlyle's was Puritanism without its Theology. The difference remains even in the most powerful, the most individual, the most erratic of moral natures. The ideals of Count Tolstoi are steeped in a Christianity which is palpably Eastern, ascetic, half Manichean.

IV

And yet all this talk about the social character of our moral ideas and the social education of the moral consciousness must not blind us to the fact that after all the sole ultimate source of moral truth is the immediate affirmation of the individual moral consciousness. No matter how widely diffused a moral idea may have now become, it was once probably the judgement of an individual at variance with the whole of his environment. No doubt when an idea is ' in the air ' as we say, it seems to have occurred to a great many minds at once without any one of them owing it to the others ; and, when that is so, each of those minds must have been itself working (to whatever extent it went beyond the accepted standard or the new suggestion received from outside) independently of any other mind.

But quite as often the individual was at first a *vox clamantis in deserto* to the people immediately around him, though other scattered individuals were at the same moment thinking much the same thoughts.   Minds may react on one another, but there must be action first or there can be no reaction.   No doubt some great steps of moral progress do take place in a spontaneous, collective way in which it is scarcely possible to trace the contributions of individual minds.   This is usually the case with the later phases of great movements.   But the greatest of all moral revolutions have definitely originated with the conscious work of an individual mind [1], and at all events they originate with the few, not with the many.   It is of fundamental importance to recognize the unequal distribution of moral capacity.   The men of moral genius are few, and yet it is to them that we owe what now passes for the accepted moral code or ideal of Society.   The power of recognizing a moral truth when it is once pointed out is much more widely diffused than the power of independently discovering it, just as the power of recognizing and appreciating good music is more widely diffused than the power of composing it. And yet even this power of recognizing and appropriating moral truth is by no means uniformly diffused.   Some measure of it is probably possessed by nearly every human being, though there may conceivably be such a thing as actual moral insanity even where there is no general insanity; and there probably exist large

[1] Wundt is one of the few formal writers on Ethics who, in talking about 'society,' do not forget the 'enormous importance of leading minds,' in the formation of the moral code.   'In the totality of psychical development all individual wills have not the same importance.... Hence a theory like Hegel's historical philosophy, which regards the social will as the sole objective ethical force, and holds that the function of the individual will is merely an unconscious partaking in and fulfilment of the social will, is an exceedingly partial view of the truth.   Such a theory is a complete antithesis to the equally one-sided individualism of the preceding centuries' (*Ethics*, E. T., III, pp. 34–5).   So again : 'the majority of individual wills represent the passive and receptive element ; the real force that occasions every alteration and transformation [of social institutions] being exerted by the leading minds.   The original, creative intellectual power is thus always the individual will' (ib., p. 36).   All this is the more significant inasmuch as Wundt goes to the verge of mysticism in recognizing the 'reality' of the social will.

numbers of people in whom the capacity, though existing, has never actually been awakened [1]. But the higher degrees of moral susceptibility are the possession of the few. When an ideal or a moral rule is said to be accepted by a society (in so far as any beyond the most negative and elementary conditions of social life ever are accepted by so heterogeneous a society as a modern nation), it is accepted with infinitely various degrees of independence and of intensity. It is often only the few whose moral consciousness actually sees the truth of the ideal for itself; the many accept it on authority from the many, and this acceptance may vary from a clear and whole-hearted recognition to a mere reluctant acquiescence which commands obedience only in so far as the rule or ideal is enforced by an adequate sanction.

This unequal distribution of moral faculty prevails as regards all the various elements of which the moral faculty (in its wider sense) is composed—the purely intellectual power of applying means to ends or of applying a principle to the particular case, the power of discerning and realizing universal moral truths, the capacity for pronouncing the judgement of comparative value in the concrete case, the capacity for those various kinds of emotion which are the condition of our passing those judgements. But it is especially and pre-eminently in the power of comparing the moral value of the various elements of our Well-being, and most of all in duly appreciating the higher of those elements, that this inequality is at its greatest. It is here that the acquiescence of the many in the accepted moral standards is most obviously due to the influence of Authority. The great majority of men in a modern community really do believe—not very consciously or analytically, nor with very profound depth of conviction or emotional fervour—but still do see for themselves that it is good to promote the Well-being of Society, or at all events to avoid what is grievously detrimental to it; and they have no difficulty in recognizing that Well-being includes health and food, clothing, shelter and the like. But when we come to the intrinsic value of intellectual goods, how far can this be said to be actively recognized by the majority

---

[1] Aristotle recognized the existence of men πεπηρωμένοι πρὸς ἀρετήν (*Eth. Nic.* I. 9, p. 1099 b).

even of fairly educated persons? There is a more or less distinct feeling that the more intellectual kinds of amusement are better than the coarser or more sensual—perhaps not much more. Certainly the idea of serious study (except when directly 'useful') is a common subject of open derision in much society which is supposed to consist of educated men. Many of our professional teachers are constantly enforcing the unimportance of intellectual culture in comparison with athletic exercises and a certain boyishness of demeanour which they call manliness. The judgement that study is good is one which is not actually made except by a small number of intellectual persons, and not by all of them. The influence of the minority which believes in such things is (in many circles) only just sufficient to prevent a life devoted to such pursuits (at least when unpaid) being treated as positively immoral—and this, perhaps, only because 'public opinion' has hardly yet risen to the point of treating any form of idle life as immoral. By the narrower religionists a life of study is often explicitly condemned. When we come to the intuitive judgements on which the duties of Purity and strict Temperance are based, who shall say what proportion of men really see for themselves the moral value of the good implied, the moral worthlessness of the pleasures condemned? And what proportion of those who acknowledge and who practise these virtues would judge the same apart from the influence of the authority by which they were commended? In the vast majority of cases in which these virtues are practised there is, no doubt, a consciousness of the moral obligation which goes far beyond mere submission to an externally imposed rule; in the vast majority of those who do not even aim at practising these duties, and who would loudly protest to themselves and to others that they 'see no harm' in disobedience, there is probably an uneasiness of Conscience which is much more than a mere consciousness that their conduct would be condemned by their stricter contemporaries. But it is probable, also, that in these cases the dimmer intuitions of the many are in a peculiar degree dependent for their own existence, and for the influence which they exert upon conduct, upon the clearer and more powerful intuitions of the few.

V

That the more obvious moral problems are already settled for the individual by the accepted rules of his country, or class, or profession, and that it is, as a rule, not wise for the average man to transgress these universally accepted rules, will be generally admitted by all but the very fanatics of moral 'Autonomy.' But it is often forgotten that it is only in the region of the most elementary Morality that there is this universal consensus. It is agreed that a man should earn his living if he has no 'private means'; that he should support his wife and children, and not ill-treat them; that he should pay his debts, with a possible exception in favour of persons of very exalted social rank; that he should keep the letter of the seventh commandment (sometimes with a similar reservation); that he should not tell any lies or practise any dishonesties except those sanctioned by the customs of his class or profession. That is almost as far as this accepted morality of the community will carry him. But when he gets beyond this, it is often assumed (so far as it is admitted that any further morality is desirable, or even allowable) that the individual who is anxious to do his duty should fall back upon the unassisted deliverances of his own moral consciousness. It is forgotten that, just as it is only by the ordinary discipline of social life that the Conscience of the individual is educated up to the low minimum standard which receives a pretty general recognition, so it is only by a higher social education—by contact with characters, ideals, socially accepted standards of a higher type—that he can hope to carry his own moral education further. The mere preaching of the rule 'Obey your Conscience,' as the whole duty of man, tends to make men satisfied with their actual performance, and to obscure the duty of educating the Conscience. It is often forgotten, even by· people who are conscious of the existence of a higher standard of conduct than their average performance, and are not without desire to rise above it, that they are only likely to come nearer to their own ideal by seeking to elevate the ideal itself. For practical purposes, the process of educating the will to more faithful obedience to Conscience, and that of increasing the sensitiveness of Conscience itself, are, if not actually identical, at least very closely connected. More than this I must not say as to the practical importance of a due recognition of the necessity of what we may call the higher education of Conscience. I must be content with pointing out certain corollaries in the region of strict ethical theory which flow from what has been said as to the influence of Authority on ethical ideals and ethical practice :—

(1) There is a whole group of duties which hardly find a place in most recognized classifications, the duties which may be comprehensively included under the duty of moral self-culture. This will include the duty of doing all the things which the individual has reason to believe (from his own experience or his knowledge of other people's experience) will tend to elevate his moral ideals, enlighten and strengthen his moral judgement, cultivate and discipline the emotions in the way most favourable to the growth of high ideals of his duty, and to the influence of those ideals upon his will. For the believer in any form of Religion, this duty will include worship of the kind dictated by that faith, and all religious practices which really tend in the direction indicated; for the non-believer it will include whatever forms of self-examination, meditation or reflection, instruction or association with persons influenced by the same ideas and pursuing the same ideals as himself may have been found morally beneficial by such persons. Some of the forms of Comte's ritual may fairly excite a smile; but he ought not to be ridiculed for recognizing that disbelief in Theology (whether well founded or otherwise) does not dispense with the necessity of moral culture, and that such moral culture must be essentially social. But I would not be supposed to be merely pleading here for a recognition of the duty of going to Church. The forms and instruments of moral self-culture must vary enormously with time, place, circumstance, and individual disposition, and in no case can the duty be considered to have been exhaustively discharged by simply 'going to Church,' valuable and important as that undoubtedly is to those who share the beliefs which make it possible. The duty is only a particular application of the principle that a man has not

performed his duty until he has considered and adopted the best means of knowing his duty better, and of caring more intensely to do it.

(2) In considering any question of duty on which doubt may have arisen, a man should give due weight to Authority; but the authority to which he should attach weight will not be the authority of the majority, of 'public opinion' (e. g. the *Times* newspaper), or of his neighbours (i. e. the little circle of persons by whom he happens to be surrounded), but the authority of the best men and of the best circles, of the rules and maxims which they have prescribed, of the ideals which have commanded and still command the greatest weight and have inspired the noblest action in such persons and circles. Aristotle was not wrong in the weight which he attributed to the judgements of the Wise; he did not adequately emphasize the fact that when a man's own moral judgement is clear and strong enough he ought to defy the judgement even of the Wise, after he has duly endeavoured to educate and instruct himself in their school.

(3) Of course in the majority of cases—at least where the doubt relates to some question of moral principle as distinct from a mere doubt about the wisdom, say, of some political measure, or some technical matter on which he may avail himself blindly of expert advice—the individual, after availing himself of the instruction and advice of his authority, will come to see for himself the truth of the rule or principle which comes to him commended by the greater weight of moral Authority, though he may not always be sure that he would have found it out for himself, or have assented to it if it had been propounded to him by an authority for which he felt no reverence. But there are cases where it may be right for a man to bow to moral Authority when he finds no clear answer to problems in his own moral consciousness, or even when he feels that his own judgement (in so far as he can isolate it from the influence of his authority) would have been the other way. Whether a man should act on his own view of right and wrong against a consensus of the best men whom he knows will of course depend (a) upon the clearness and strength of his own con-

viction, (b) upon the nature of the alternative before him. It might often be right for a man to forgo an indulgence in which he sees himself 'no harm' in deference to Authority, where it would not be right to take upon himself the responsibility of what presents itself to his own mind as an act of injustice. The logical basis of this submission to Authority in the more strictly moral sphere is exactly the same as that upon which it is reasonable to rely in any sphere of life upon the authority of others, and it is needless to observe that nine-tenths of our actions are in practice based upon knowledge which we accept upon authority without being able to explain the grounds upon which it rests. We act upon the judgement of the man who seems to us most likely to know; and, when we are unable directly to test the fact of a man's possessing the knowledge he claims, we assume that the man who is most often right where we can test his judgement will be right in similar questions which our own insight or experience is insufficient to decide. We have found that the judgement of the artistic expert has proved right so far as we have been able to follow him; we think he is likely to be right even when we have not succeeded in admiring what he admires. We know by the way he sings and plays that another man's musical powers are much in advance of ours; we infer that he is likely to be right when he tells us that we are singing out of tune, though we are unable ourselves to perceive the fact. And so in the ethical sphere it would be quite right for a man who saw no harm in occasional drunkenness to defer to the consensus of persons whom he recognizes in other ways as men of more delicate moral perceptions than himself [1].

It can hardly be seriously doubted that most good acts of most good men are done without deliberate and self-conscious reflection on the reason why they are good. In most cases their belief is really (as the outside observer can see) dictated by Authority; in some cases the agents are themselves well aware

---

[1] A friend suggests that it is a mistake to assume that the 'most delicate' conscience is always most likely to be right. I certainly do not mean that the person who has most scruples is the most likely to be right: I should myself regard the ultra-scrupulous person as one of the worst possible advisers in some kinds of moral difficulty.

of the fact. They could give no reason why this or that act is wrong except that it had always been thought so. As a rule, of course, the same tradition, or habit, or example, or association which psychologically explains their conduct causes them also to think that their dislike of such and such an act is the result of their own judgement. The more completely their moral consciousness is moulded into accord with the ideal of their authority, the less are they aware of its influence. But sometimes, in moments of reflection, a man must say to himself, ' I do not know any reason why this is wrong except that it is forbidden by an authority which is likely to know better than I do.' In some cases the considerations which make a particular act detrimental to the general good are too complicated to be intelligible to the unreflecting or uneducated. A great many honest men, for instance, could give no adequate or coherent answer to the question why it is wrong to steal. They would entirely fail if they attempted to construct a clear and consistent theory of Property. In other cases, where the question relates to the goodness of the end, the individual must often either lack the experience necessary to pronounce upon the matter, or be unable to appreciate that the end is good, even when he knows what it is. It is only by submission to Authority that a very ignorant person can recognize that it is not a waste of time to spend many hours a day in study ; and there are probably many people besides children who would frankly confess that they could not, if it were not forbidden by the Bible, or the Church, or general opinion, ' see the harm ' of polygamy. Without some measure of submission to Authority in moral matters Society could not be kept together.

VI

I know that there are many persons to whom the very suggestion that anybody is ever in his moral action to defer to any external authority whatever will present itself as positively immoral ; and who will be quite unable to dissociate the contrary thesis from the idea of ' Priestcraft ' or ' State Socialism ' (according as the Authority is ecclesiastical or secular), tyranny over Consciences, ' spiritual bondage ' and the like. With a view to meet such objections it may be desirable to make a few additional explanations and reservations :

(1) It is a curious fact that the people who assert with peculiar, if not exaggerated, emphasis the social origin of the individual Conscience are often the people who most strongly repudiate the idea of Authority in Ethics. Yet if a man is never to trust any other moral consciousness than his own, he ought to distrust even his own Conscience, which has been moulded by the moral consciousness of other men. It is admitted that at least in the period of early education a man must accept the undemonstrated assertions of the wise—the *ipse dixit* of parent or teacher. But can it be said that a man's moral education is always complete because he has attained the age of legal manhood ? Are not many people, in the moral sphere, children throughout life, and are not the great majority of us children in such matters in comparison with the Saint or the Sage ?

(2) Even if it were admitted that the act done in obedience to Authority has no moral value in itself, it has consequences; and the good man will wish to avoid the bad consequences to others of his wrong acts, even if his own unassisted judgement would have failed to anticipate them. Everybody admits that it is right to obey the Physician though we cannot understand the reasons for his advice; and it is surely not merely in technical matters that one man's opinion is likely to be better than another's.

(3) But it is not true that there is no value in an act done from respect for Authority. There will be a moral value in an act motived by a desire to do the best, even though a man may come to the conclusion that such and such an act is the best merely because some one else thinks so. If this were not so, we should have to deny all moral value to the acts of whole generations whose morality has been to an enormous extent based upon obedience to a book or other authority believed to be infallible [1].

(4) It must be remembered that the man has already performed an act of independent moral judgement in choosing his authority, in so far as he has chosen it on truly ethical grounds.

---

[1] Of course the submission, even when nominally absolute, has always in practice had limits.

It was because such and such a man's character or the known rules and actual practice of such and such a society or of such and such a Religion appealed to himself as the noblest that was within his ken that he placed himself under their guidance, even when in detail he could not feel confident that they were right. To choose one's moral authority wisely is at least the beginning of wisdom in the moral sphere. Acceptance of an authority vaguely discerned (or at first merely suspected) to be the highest—this in ultimate analysis would be found to be the real source of a large part of the best conduct that the world has known, and must still be more or less the case, though the guidance by Authority naturally and rightly tends to diminish with the maturity of individuals, classes, and races.

(5) The respect which the judgement of any ethical authority ought to command must depend upon the extent to which it rests upon really ethical grounds. If another man's advice to me is itself dependent upon an authority which I do not respect, the value of that advice disappears, however much better or wiser I may know a particular adviser to be than myself. For instance, the authority of a good man who may recommend such and such a practice or rule of action is seriously weakened for me if I discover that his judgement is so far enslaved to an ecclesiastical system, accepted on non-ethical grounds, that a doubt arises whether he recommends it as the result of his own moral judgement or moral experience, or merely because he finds it prescribed by the Fathers and Canons of the Church, which a theory of the Church's infallibility compels him to accept: while equally good men who have been brought up in a different ecclesiastical tradition seem blind to the moral advantages of the practice or the obligation of the rule.

(6) It is assumed throughout that our acceptance of Authority does not, and never can, imply a total abdication of individual judgement. Not even the most mechanical moral code could possibly be lived out without the constant exercise of such judgement, and a true moral ideal will emphatically condemn the incessant dependence either upon some traditional body of Authority or upon a living 'director.' Moreover in the last resort, if only the 'voice within' is clear and decided enough, it

is a duty to hearken to it, no matter what the weight of contrary Authority. It is only asserted that it is often right for a man to act upon the intuitions of others when he has none of his own, and sometimes even where his own contrary intuitions are weak and confused. The extent to which confidence in one's own ethical judgement should overrule any weight of antagonistic authority is of course as little capable of exact definition as any other ethical question which assumes the form of a ' how much ' or a ' how far.'

VII

The aspects of ethical truth which we have been dwelling on are, as it appears to me, of great importance in dealing with the relation between Morality and Religion. That subject must hereafter be considered more at length. But the view which we have taken will help us to appreciate certain aspects of that relation as it has actually existed in History. It will enable us to appreciate and to justify, at least on their purely ethical side, two important elements in all the historical religions, and especially in Christianity—(1) the authority of exceptional personalities ; (2) the authority of the religious community. It is largely because these influences are so completely ignored in the treatment of Morality by professed Philosophers that their accounts of the moral life are often so widely removed from the facts which History reveals.

If the moral consciousness is formed and moralized by the social environment and particularly the influence of the persons in whom the moral capacity of the human soul has reached its highest development, if it is right that in all moral judgements great weight should be accorded to the authority of the best men, sometimes even in preference to the man's own spontaneous ideas of right and wrong, when he finds them confused or defective, then we are able to justify the reverence with which the highest ethical religions of the world have regarded the teaching of their founders, and particularly the altogether unique authority which Christian Theology has ascribed to the life, teaching, and character of Jesus Christ, an authority which is often recognized in practice by many who would refuse to accept

any theological formulation of it.   There is no supersession or
surrender of a man's own moral judgement in ascribing this
position to Christ, if it is by the individual's own moral judgement (seconded and confirmed by that of others in whose
moral insight he believes) that the moral value of the authority
is discerned.

But while the principles which have already been laid down
will fully justify such a submission to the authority of the moral
consciousness at its highest, it will also suggest the limits of such
submission.   Even in respect of this highest kind of moral
Authority it is important to bear in mind the limitations within
which alone it can be morally healthful for individuals or for
communities to acquiesce in obedience to an external authority
in conduct.   It is clear that such submission can only be morally
healthful when the authority is accepted, at least in part, upon
ethical grounds.   When a certain stage of intellectual or moral
development has been reached, it may even be said that the
acceptance ought to be based solely upon an independent acceptance of the ethical ideal set up by the authority.   For the
individual it may, indeed, be quite reasonable that, when a certain
moral Authority is once accepted on ethical grounds, respect
should be paid to it even in details which may not actually
commend themselves to the private judgement of the individual.
But this cannot well be permanently the case for the community,
or for that inner circle of ethical intelligence from which the
community really derives its highest ethical ideas.   By the
community at large a moral authority can only be healthily
recognized because and in so far as the social consciousness
accepts and ratifies the ideal set before it by the authority.
To accept it beyond this point would put a stop to that independent working of the moral consciousness upon which all ethical
progress is dependent.   And that comes to very much the same
thing as saying that it is only in respect of the widest and most
fundamental ethical ideas that we can expect the judgements
of any ethical teacher permanently to commend themselves to
the world.   Even for the individual the acceptance of moral
ideas or rules on authority must not and cannot preclude some
independent exercise of his own moral intelligence.   For even

the most precise moral rules cannot be applied without such an exercise of the independent value-judging faculty. A moral rule may say ' be kind,' but a person whose reverence for kindness was wholly based upon authority would be quite unable to recognize what particular actions were kind. The result of attempting to treat the *ipse dixit* of some moral code—no matter how true and venerable—as a mere external authority to be applied to the particular case after the manner of a parliamentary Statute has been summed up in the adage that the devil can quote Scripture to his purpose. But still more in the case of the community it is clear that changing circumstances and events are continually bringing about the need for fresh applications and developments of existing moral rules, for the revision of old applications of such rules, and for passing judgements upon wholly new questions of Ethics upon which no rules at present exist.

The idea of a unique crisis or turning-point in the moral history of mankind has nothing in it in the slightest degree inconsistent with a due recognition of the principle of development, or even with the idea of perpetual progress in any sense in which it is rational to cherish the hope of such progress. It will be unnecessary to dwell upon the existence of certain unique crises in the evolutionary history of the Universe. Such crises are constituted by the beginning of organized life, still more emphatically by the beginnings of consciousness, and (though here the crisis must be assigned to a definite era of considerable duration rather than to a definite moment of time) by the first beginnings of the moral life. It will perhaps be more to the purpose if we point to analogous crises in the growth of the Sciences. It is quite misleading to treat scientific progress as if it consisted in the perpetual revision of traditional views, in the constant giving up of old theories, and the acceptance of new ones. There are discoveries in the Sciences which constitute epochs, and which are practically final. That these discoveries should always be open to criticism and be held liable to revision, should any need for it present itself, goes without saying, but in many cases there is no reason to apprehend that any such necessity will occur : nor is it even considered desirable to encourage the expectation that it will.

Copernicus, Newton, Darwin are the names which most conspicuously associate themselves with such epochs. After such
an epoch there is no going back. Mistakes in detail such heroes
of scientific achievement have made, but their main ideas have
not been revised ; there is no reason whatever for thinking that
they ever will be. Not only so, but such discoveries gradually
narrow the ground of possible fresh discovery. It may safely be
said that in the realm of Physics, for instance, there is no room for
any new discovery of the same magnitude with the discovery of
the Newtonian Laws. For all time Physics must be based on
the discovery for which Copernicus prepared the way, and which
Newton actually made. Equally little room is there, I imagine,
in Biology for a new idea which can be so new or revolutionary
as the idea of Darwin in its most general form, apart from the
details of his theory which are and may long be matter of dispute. Such parallels may suggest the kind and measure of the
finality which may reasonably be expected in Ethics. That such
a crisis in the spiritual history of mankind occurred in connexion
with the rise of the Christian Religion, is almost universally
admitted ; and it is the general verdict of sober criticism that,
when all due allowance is made for the long evolution of ideas
which prepared the way for that crisis and for the existence of
a certain amount of development even in the earliest records of
its Founder's life, that crisis was chiefly due to the personality
of that Founder. Considering the enormous place in the entire
moral life of the world that is occupied by the idea of the
paramount authority of the teaching of Christ, it will not,
I trust, be thought an irrelevant digression in an ethical treatise
definitely to raise the question whether there is anything
opposed to a due recognition of the ideal of ethical Autonomy
in the recognition of a certain finality and completeness in the
' Christian ideal.'

VIII

It is clear that in many senses of the word there can be no
finality in Ethics. The details of right conduct are obviously
relative to changing circumstances of time and place. So long
as we confine ourselves to means, every new piece of knowledge

in the world alters the details of many duties. It became wrong for a busy man to travel from London to Oxford by coach as soon as a quicker way of reaching his destination was invented. And discoveries as to the relation of means to ends—discoveries in Physiology, in Psychology, in Economics—are continually revolutionizing whole regions of duty. It is needless to give illustrations of the way in which increased knowledge of physical and social laws has modified our conception of our duty to the poor, to the sick, to the insane, to children and the like. And it is not only in respect of the means, but also in respect of the end, that we must expect indefinite change and development. If the view taken in these pages be well founded, duty consists in promoting the true good of all human beings in proportion to their intrinsic worth or capacity. But wherein does that true good consist? At any given moment in the history of the world the individual (in so far as he relies upon his own judgement) must fix for himself the content of that good by his own judgements of value. But, even if his intuitions of value were incapable of improvement, his power of passing such judgements would still be relative to his experience. He can only estimate rightly the value of such things as he knows. But human experience is constantly growing. In all departments of human activity we are continually hearing of the new this or the new that—the new humour, the new Trade Unionism, the new Art, the music of the future, and so on. Each of these new ideas introduces fresh moral problems, which cannot possibly be settled in detail by appealing to any existing canons, any more than it would be possible to apply the old rules of tactics to the altered conditions of modern warfare. It is not that any old rule or principle has necessarily been found to be wrong, but there is no rule at all which is applicable to the new case. The most gifted moral nature cannot possibly say whether the listening to Wagner's music forms an element in true human good till he has heard at least a little of it. The question must be settled by a fresh exercise of the value-judging faculty. In this way and in this sense our ideal of human life is constantly growing and expanding in its actual content. The proposition that it is good to be charitable remains as true as it ever was;

but Charity must now mean promoting for our neighbours a very different kind of life than any that could have been lived in the Palestine of the Christian era.

Now, in view of these considerations, it is clear that it is only in respect of the most general ethical principles that any finality can be claimed for the Christian ideal. The law of Brotherhood—the supreme duty of promoting the true good for every human being—may, indeed, be treated as occupying in Ethics very much the position which the law of universal gravitation occupies in Physics.[1] The law must be accepted simply in the last resort because it appeals to our Moral Reason, and only so long as it does appeal to the Moral Reason of successive ages. But it is as gratuitous to contemplate the coming of a time when it shall be superseded as it would be to expect the advent of a second Newton who will overthrow and supersede the discoveries of the first. And yet, as we have seen, this law would mean comparatively little for us apart from some idea of what the good is. It would mean little to assert the finality of the Christian ideal if we did not include in our conception of that ideal some conception of what the good is that is to be promoted for each individual soul. And for the central elements of Christ's estimate of goods—the supreme value of love, the superiority of the spiritual to the sensual, the value of personal purity, the subordination of sensuous gratification to higher things without any ascetic condemnation of natural and healthy pleasure—there is every reason to expect as much permanence as for the law of Brotherhood itself. But from the nature of the case it is impossible to define more exactly the line which separates the essential from the unessential, the permanent from the temporary, the germ from the full-grown organism. Within the limits thus indicated there is room for a very large development in the moral ideal. The attitude of Christians towards intellectual and aesthetic culture has, for instance, varied considerably

---

[1] How far this idea can be found in other ethical systems earlier than, or independent of Christianity, it is not necessary for us here to consider. Broadly speaking, I believe the answer to be that it is to be found in other ethical systems, but side by side with a great many ethical ideas which are quite inconsistent with it.

at different times in the history of the Church. That development has taken place in the past is a matter of history. That it will take place, and ought to take place, in the future results from all that has been said about the impossibility of detailed finality in any ideal, the necessity for the constant exercise of the value-judging consciousness, and the consequent need for development in the ethical code. Only in so far·as it is supplemented by this principle of development can we regard the association of a moral ideal with a certain epoch and a single great historical Personality in the past as morally healthful and intellectually defensible. That Christianity accepts, and always has accepted, this principle of development through its doctrine of the Holy Spirit would be a leading topic in any reasoned apologetic for Christianity as the absolute Religion.

The dominant school of liberal Christian Theology in Germany—the school which takes its name from Lotze's great disciple and colleague, Ritschl—rightly bases the claim of Christ and of Christianity upon the permanent truth and unique value of the ideal taught by Christ in work, act, and character[1], as recognized by the value-judgements of the individual moral consciousness. That school, rightly to my mind, regards Christian dogma as the progressive effort of the Christian consciousness to express in the philosophical language of the time its sense of the supreme and unique value to humanity of the moral and religious consciousness of Christ, and makes its fidelity to that idea the ultimate test of dogmatic truth. · But unfortunately the Ritschlians have exaggerated this ' Christo-centric ' tendency in a way which is as inconsistent with historical facts as it is with sound ethical theory. Their tendency to disparage Metaphysic, whether in the form of modern Philosophy or of ancient dogma ; their suicidal attempt to rest the truth not merely of Christianity but of Theism wholly and solely upon the emotional experience of the individual Christian soul ; their depreciation of all knowledge of God such as is derivable from philosophical reflection or is contained in other historical Religions, it would be irrelevant

---

[1] Including of course his religious consciousness, his sense of union with the Father and his teaching about Him, of which it would here be out of place to speak more in detail.

here to criticize in detail. What it does concern us here to insist upon is that an Ethic is fundamentally erroneous which refuses to recognize the necessary and healthful interaction between the moral consciousness of the individual and that of the community, the need for constant development in the ethical ideal, the impossibility of a final or supreme ethical revelation which is not also a continuous and progressive revelation. On ethical grounds alone we may say that the doctrine of the Son requires, as its indispensable complement, a doctrine of the Holy Ghost.

It must not be supposed that in asserting that the true ground for the acceptance of the Christian ideal is the fact that it commends itself to the moral consciousness we are in any way disparaging the importance of the life and teaching of Christ in the moral evolution of mankind, or the value of a knowledge of that life and teaching to individuals and communities at the present day. The Conscience of the average man is quite capable of accepting ideals which he could never have thought out for himself. The moral level once attained by a community can only be kept up by the continued operation of the influences which raised it to that level. It is true that ideas may sometimes live when their origin is forgotten. But even in the region of Physical Science education consists largely in the history of past discovery. And there is this difference between scientific ideas and moral ones, that moral ideas and ideals are far less separable from the personality of those who have taught them. The strongest ethical influences are personal influences. To say that the truth of the moral ideal presented by the teaching of Christ must rest upon the appeal that it makes to the moral consciousness of mankind is a very different thing from saying that the influence which that ideal has exercised and still exercises over the world has been or ever can be separated from the influence exercised by the character and personality of Jesus. It is as well established a fact of history and of sober criticism that the Christian ideal, in the form in which it would be recognized by any modern Christian, even if he be a Ritschlian Theologian, does represent much ethical teaching not explicitly to be found in the teaching of Christ, as that the development has flowed from that moral new birth of the world which is to be associated with his work. It is childish to dispute whether the fountain-head or the stream be the more important to the thirsty traveller; nor need a due recognition of the fact that the main stream of Christian ethical thought can be traced back directly to the historical Christ prevent us from recognizing that it has received not unimportant accessions by the way. The very capacity for absorbing into itself what is most valuable in ethical teaching outside itself constitutes one of the chief qualifications of the Christian 'deposit' of ethical truth to be the basis of a universal Ethic and a universal Religion.

IX

From the point of view here suggested, the notion of an authority residing in the Christian community, so far from being regarded as part of that 'Aberglaube' which it is the business of an emancipated Theology to sweep away, will present itself as a vital condition of our being able to recognize in any historical Religion a claim to finality and to universality. The authority of the Church in ethical as in religious matters means the authority of the Christian consciousness—the growing and expanding moral consciousness of those who in the full and deliberate exercise of their own faculty of moral discernment have recognized in the fundamental Christian ideas the highest moral truth which the Spirit of God has revealed to the world. What from the point of view of the individual is Authority becomes, as I have already insisted, when looked upon from the social point of view, liberty or Autonomy. The ideal purpose of the visible Christian society is to serve as the organ of this consciousness. The Church in its ultimate idea is a society for the promotion of the highest ideal of life, under the guidance of a true theory of the relation of man to God. All that has been said about the existence of many conflicting social ideals, representing a variety of distinguishable though mutually interacting 'societies,' within each geographical or political 'society' tends to emphasize the necessity for a society specially concerned with the promotion of the highest life. That each and every one of the societies commonly known as Churches have fallen very far short of being adequate organs for this purpose is too obvious a proposition to need historical justification. They have all been more or less imperfect realizations of a high ideal. In dealing with the State we have long found it possible to believe in the divine right of Government without believing in the divine right of any particular ruler or any particular constitution. We have found it possible to recognize side by side a divine right of Government and a divine right of Rebellion—to recognize the duty of the individual to submit himself to the society, and to recognize none the less that that submission has limits. It is high time that a similar mode of thinking were applied to the relations between the individual and Society in all its forms and all its organs—and not least in that most important organ of all (according to the true ideal of it) which we call the Church or the Churches.

All that has hitherto been said as to the limit of the authority which the society can claim over the individual needs to be remembered and emphasized with peculiar distinctness in regard to the religious society. A prejudice against the very word Authority has sprung in part from its confusion, both by friend and foe, with the totally different idea of Infallibility. All that has been said about the right and the duty of individual judgement and of self-assertion in individuals and in societies, about the necessity for progress, about the process by which the moral discoveries of the individual spirit are appropriated and enforced by the community, constitutes a protest against that confusion. Sometimes the social consciousness itself is misrepresented by the official organization whose function it is to serve as its expression: sometimes it is the right and duty of the individual to rebel against what really is for the moment the dominant ideal of his society. But, all the same, we must recognize the idea of an ethical authority residing in the society, and the need of a definite organ or organs for the expression of that authority, as a counterpoise and complement to the authority which is rightly ascribed to the highest embodiments of the moral consciousness in the past. For Christians the authority of the Church is required as the necessary complement and development of the unique and paramount authority which with ample justification they have ascribed to its Founder.

The true ideal of human nature is undoubtedly the ideal which has been expressed by the word Autonomy. The ideal is that each individual should do what in the exercise of his own consciousness he sees to be right. But the education of the moral consciousness up to this level is only possible through the action of a strong social Conscience, and the recognition of its authority by the individual, up to the point at which his present knowledge, experience, and ethical insight require its support. It is only through the principle of Authority that the individual enters into the accumulated ethical inheritance bequeathed to him by the past. Apart from social education, each individual would have to start at the level of the savage, and by his own unassisted efforts he could scarcely avoid sinking even below that level. It is the object of social education to quicken and develope the individual's power of independent ethical thought and feeling to an extent which shall make him not so much independent of Authority as unconscious of its influence except in so far as he sees the necessity for going beyond it. If in a sense the individual in the course of his moral growth becomes less and less dependent upon social Authority, in a sense he becomes more and more identified with it. The commands to which he once submitted as mere external commands now become to him the commands of his own higher self: he who was the subject over against an actual legislator now becomes himself the legislator as well as the subject—legislator for himself and, as a member of the society, legislator for others. But this very growth of independent ethical power will have fitted him and compelled him to develope existing ideals further than they have been developed, and even to correct and contradict them when necessary. Even to the last this ideal of Autonomy is one which no individual can fully reach: in a sense it is one which he ought not to reach. The limitations of his knowledge and experience, sheer want of time for enquiry and reflection, the impossibility of becoming an expert in a hundred different directions, must compel him to take on trust the judgements of others as to means, and to a large extent even as regards elements in a true ideal of the good. He must continue, he ought to continue, sensitive to the ethical ideas of the people about him, of the

society as a whole, and, above all, of the best people in it ; but he
ought also to criticize them and to react upon them. The attempt
to deny or ignore the principles of Authority in Ethics altogether
would mean moral anarchy : to prohibit the individual from
going beyond, and, if need be, rebelling against the accepted
moral standard, would mean ethical stagnation and abject
' heteronomy.'   In truth the ideal of Authority and the ideal of
Autonomy both become absurd and self-contradictory if either
is pushed to the point of excluding the other. Reliance on
Authority can only justify itself by the assumption that there
exist individuals or societies which are ethically autonomous,
and there could be no Autonomy in the society if there were no
relatively autonomous individuals, or if they exercised no
authority over their fellows.

BOOK III
MAN AND THE UNIVERSE

CHAPTER I

METAPHYSIC AND MORALITY

I

THE relations of Moral Philosophy to Metaphysic may be conveniently treated under three heads: the two subjects are connected:

(1) Because any true and adequate account of the nature of Morality must involve certain metaphysical postulates or presuppositions.

(2) Because some of the conclusions of Metaphysic, even though Morality might in a sense exist if they were not true, are of high importance to Morality and seriously affect our attitude towards it; so that, if not postulates of any Morality whatever, they are postulates of a rational and coherent ethical system.

(3) Because Moral Philosophy involves certain metaphysical consequences, or supplies some of the data which it is the business of Metaphysic to interpret.

Like every other branch of knowledge Moral Philosophy implies or assumes certain ultimate conceptions which it is the business of the Metaphysician to examine. But we do not usually consider it necessary to begin the study of a Science by an enquiry into its ultimate metaphysical implications. Mathematical Science assumes that there are such things as space and quantity, and that our ideas about their nature constitute in some sense knowledge of Reality. Physics assume the existence of matter and force: Psychology assumes the existence of mind or consciousness. The ultimate meaning of all these conceptions is matter of grave metaphysical controversy; and yet the

Physicist at least, if not to the same extent the Psychologist, is content to leave metaphysical controversy severely alone. In the same way the ultimate nature of Morality and its relation to other kinds or elements or aspects of Reality are questions which open up the most momentous metaphysical issues. It is no doubt possible simply to assume the existence of the moral consciousness, and to analyse its contents. That is the task with which for the most part we have so far been concerned, though at times (as for instance in the chapter on Reason and Feeling) it has been impossible altogether to maintain the attitude of indifference to metaphysical problems. And that task represents, I believe, the primary aim of Moral Philosophy. That it is a possible task, the object of a possible Science, is proved by the existence of many books on the subject in which there is hardly any explicit metaphysical discussion: while, even in those writers who are most in the habit of insisting upon the intimate relation between Moral Philosophy and Metaphysic, we do not find as a rule that their arguments turn on any metaphysical considerations so long as they are engaged on the questions which have so far occupied our attention. Let the question be 'What is the moral criterion?', 'Is pleasure the chief good?', 'Is Casuistry possible?', 'Why is it a duty to speak the truth?', or the like—so long as they are discussing matters like these, we do not find that their arguments turn upon any explicit metaphysical assumption: they are arguments of precisely the same kind as those which are employed by writers combining the same ethical views with a different metaphysical basis or by their opponents in support of opposite ethical theories. Metaphysic does not contain in itself the solution of any of these questions; and it requires no metaphysical knowledge to follow the arguments commonly employed in discussing them. It is no doubt true that the views of such writers as Kant or Green upon such questions imply certain metaphysical presuppositions; but only in the sense in which every Science assumes metaphysical postulates. Morality, as understood by them, would have no reality or validity if certain metaphysical theories inconsistent with their own could be regarded as true. But then speculatively these writers would also hold that the same or certain other metaphysical positions are inconsistent with the ascription of any objective significance to the truths of Mathematics or Physical Science. In so far as such writers have used metaphysical propositions for the determination of purely ethical questions, their Metaphysic has often proved a source of error and confusion rather than of enlightenment, as for instance when Green argues that pleasure being in time cannot satisfy a self which is out of time. So long as the Moral Philosopher confines himself to this analysis of the moral consciousness, he is only forced to make metaphysical assumptions in the sense in which the Mathematician makes metaphysical assumptions in asserting that we know certain things about space and quantity and number.

Are we then to say that the real connexion between Moral Philosophy and Metaphysic is no more intimate than the connexion between Metaphysic and any of the so-called 'positive' Sciences? If such an assertion were well founded, it would certainly imply that the majority of Moral Philosophers have been the victims of some strange illusion or some extraordinary accident. There are not unimportant Moral Philosophers who have written practically nothing on Metaphysic, but theirs are hardly the greatest names in the history of Moral Philosophy : and there are few Metaphysicians who have not dealt with Ethics in however incidental a fashion. The reason of this is not far to seek. Speculatively, indeed, it is impossible to deny a very close connexion between sound ideas on the subject-matter of Metaphysics and sound ideas about the subject-matter of Mathematics. Sensationalism, and perhaps some other forms of Empiricism, deny all meaning or objective validity to those necessities of thought with which Mathematics are concerned. But practically we find that a man's views as a Metaphysician exercise no influence upon his treatment of Mathematics. Mathematicians of the most opposite views, or of no views at all, about the ultimate nature of space and time are content to assume the truth of the same axioms ; and the different sense in which (if they are Metaphysicians at all) they interpret these ultimate assumptions exercises no practical effect upon the conclusions which they reach as Mathematicians. It is the same with the Physicist, and possibly even with the Biologist [1], so long as they really confine themselves to the subject-matter of their respective Sciences. It ought theoretically to be the same with the Psychologist, though in his case the isolation of the psychological problem from the metaphysical involves a degree of abstraction which in practice only a trained Metaphysician, if any one, can keep up [2], and which it is perhaps not very desirable to keep up. Nobody in practice doubts that it is shorter to go across the grass in a quadrangle than to walk round two sides of it, no matter how sceptical or sensationalistic may be his theory of space. No physical law is ever in practice questioned on the ground of some idealistic or sceptical theory about matter [3]; nor does the most materialistic of psychologists who has passed beyond the stage of elementary confusion ever ignore in practice the difference between a wave of ether and a perception of blue. In Ethics it is far otherwise. Particular theories about the nature of knowledge, or of matter, or of mind are constantly made into grounds for the denial of the Moralist's primary assumption,—the existence of the moral consciousness and the validity of its dictates; or at least for admitting them only in a sense which revolutionizes the meaning of every proposition included in the Science itself. So long as he is content to assume the reality and authority of the moral consciousness, the Moral Philosopher can ignore Metaphysic; but, if the reality

---

[1] Here, indeed, at a certain point metaphysical differences (conscious or unconscious) about the nature of Causality are likely to emerge, but they need not emerge till an advanced stage has been reached in the study of the subject.

[2] The same remark may certainly be made with regard to some of the more speculative questions to which the higher Physics lead up, but the ideal of the two Sciences is that they should be as distinct as possible. The uncertainty of division only exists when the Physicist's conclusions are speculative. So long as that is the case, the Physicist is always liable to become, or to be accused by the Metaphysician of having become, a Metaphysician without knowing it. Physical facts, when once established, have simply to be accepted by the Metaphysician. To interpret them in their relation to other aspects of Reality is his business, and not that of the Physicist.

[3] The tendency of Physicists to deny the possibility of an *actio in distans* may perhaps be accounted for by the unrecognized influence of metaphysical assumptions.

of Morals or the validity of ethical truth be once brought into question, the attack can only be met by a thorough-going enquiry into the nature of Knowledge and of Reality ; we have to clear up the relation between the particular sort or aspect of Reality with which the Moralist deals and all Reality, between ethical truth and truth in general.   In practice it is hardly possible to write many lines about some very fundamental questions of Ethics from which some people would not dissent on metaphysical grounds.

Each of the special Sciences deals with some particular aspect of Reality taken in abstraction from the rest.   In Moral Philosophy, in so far as we are considering the nature of the moral consciousness apart from other aspects of Being, we are still in a sense abstract ; we are dealing with a departmental Science ; but the discussion cannot practically proceed far without touching upon the most ultimate of all questions.   We are dealing with such a large and fundamental aspect of ultimate Reality that it is practically impossible to deal with it thoroughly without taking a very important step towards the determination of our attitude towards Reality as a whole.   It is impossible that our views on the ultimate problems of Ethics should not be influenced by our attitude towards Reality as a whole, or that our view of Reality as a whole should not be influenced by our attitude towards Morality.   It is not from any doubt about the importance to Ethics of certain metaphysical ideas that the treatment of our subject was not preceded by an exhaustive enquiry into the nature of Knowledge and Reality ; but rather because it would have been extremely difficult to draw the line between the specially ethical side of Metaphysics and the whole of that Science.   The metaphysical ' prolegomena to Ethics' tend to become identical with the Science of Metaphysic itself, or at least with the main outlines of it.   All that can be attempted here, consistently with the plan of this work, is to indicate, without fully justifying, the metaphysical positions which in my view are necessary either as presuppositions or as corollaries of a reasonable system of Ethics.

II

The first point of contact between Ethics and Metaphysics lies, as we have seen, in the fact that the former Science involves certain metaphysical presuppositions. There are two directions in which ethical conclusions such as those at which we have arrived might be directly [1] impugned on metaphysical grounds. The attack might be based upon a theory of the nature of knowledge or upon a theory as to the nature of that self with which in Morality we are concerned. It need hardly be said that the two lines of objection are very closely connected. We will look at the matter first from the epistemological point of view.

The tendency of all theories which make experience the sole source of knowledge is to undermine belief in that element of our moral ideas which most obviously cannot be derived from experience : and that is, if we are right, precisely the element which constitutes the essence of Morality. By the doctrine that all knowledge comes from experience is very likely to be meant the doctrine that all that we really know about things is the feelings that they give us : Empiricism does not perhaps in every sense of the word necessarily involve Sensationalism, but the historical 'school of Experience,' in proportion to its thoroughness and self-consistency, has tended to identify experience with mere sensation. Now if we know ultimately nothing but feeling, the knowledge of right and wrong, so far as it is knowledge of anything real, must also be based upon a kind of feeling, or rather, it (like every other kind of knowledge) must be, at bottom, nothing but a mode of feeling. The attempt may, indeed, be made to show that moral approbation represents a specific feeling different in kind from all other feelings : but the up-holders of a 'Moral Sense' wholly fail to show why this feeling, however distinct, however much *sui generis*, should have any better claim to be attended to than any other feelings. Of course the constructive Moralist of the Moral Sense school really takes his subjective feeling of 'approbation' to be an

---

[1] Later in the chapter I shall deal with the metaphysical or theological questions which have an indirect bearing on their validity.

index of some objective reality, but this is just what he has no right to do so long as he attempts to analyse all knowledge into mere feeling.   Mere feeling can testify to nothing beyond itself.   Feeling again can appeal only to him who feels it: the Sensationalist cannot logically recognize any ideal of what men ought to feel, whether this or that man actually feels it or not. As long as feeling is treated simply as feeling, it is arbitrary to assign to one feeling a higher value than another for any other reason than its actual intensity or the actual strength of the impulse which it excites: all distinctions of quality between feelings[1] imply a reference to an ideal or rational standard which mere feeling can neither set up nor acknowledge.   The logical Sensationalist must also be a Hedonist, and an egoistic Hedonist[2]. He may (with Hume) recognize as a psychological fact that in persons of a certain mental constitution the pleasures and pains of others have a tendency to cause pleasure and pain by sympathy: but this (as it is Hume's great merit to have recognized) constitutes no reason for attending to these sympathetic pleasures or pains, or allowing oneself to be influenced by them beyond the point to which one is inclined to go by one's natural taste for this particular source of pleasurable feeling. The consistent Sensationalist can know nothing of an absolute or objective Morality, of intrinsic value, of moral obligation[3].

Even if Empiricism does not take the form of pure Sensationalism—even when it recognizes (that is to say) that knowledge is something more than subjective feeling—it still puts great difficulties in the way of a constructive system of Ethics.   So long as Reality is supposed to reside in 'things'—conceived

[1] If quality means anything more than difference in the actual content of the feeling.

[2] It is, indeed, possible for the merely 'naturalistic' Moralist to avoid Hedonism by defining the good as that which we actually desire, and measuring the amount of the good by the strength of the desire, without assuming that that something is always pleasure, but the distinction between desire and feeling is a difficult one for the Sensationalist.

[3] Strictly speaking, of course, even the calculating pursuit of a maximum pleasure would be impossible if knowledge were mere sensation.   I am assuming that the Sensationalist does not see that his position is destructive to the possibility of any knowledge whatever, even of what is necessary in order to aim at a maximum of pleasure on the whole.

of as having their nature altogether independently of our minds or of any mind (even though it may be recognized that the knowing mind must possess powers other than a mere capacity for feeling), it remains difficult to recognize truth or validity in a kind of knowledge for which obviously no such basis can, he found in 'external' Nature. It may no doubt be contended that the Empiricist is not necessarily a Materialist. He may acknowledge the existence of mind and of mental states in himself and others; these are facts of experience no less than outward 'things.' But if nothing is supposed to be knowable about mind except 'mental states' known by immediate experience and abstracted from all reference to any Reality beyond themselves, there is no possibility of comparing these 'states' with any ideal standard not given in experience, and the 'states of mind' tend to be valued merely in proportion to their experienced intensity, and that is very much the same thing as valuing them merely as sources of pleasure or pain: and, so far as this is the case, the Empiricist's position in regard to Morality becomes identical with that of the Sensationalist. Indeed, strictly speaking, so long as he really confines himself to experience, the question of value cannot arise at all. The Empiricist can know by experience whether things are pleasant: he cannot attach any meaning to the assertion that pleasure is a good unless he understands it to mean that people actually do pursue pleasure. We have already seen that no accumulation of experiences of pleasure and pain can give us the ultimate major premiss which is implied by all Morality; from 'is' to 'ought,' from existence to value, from the actual to the good, there is no way by the road of experience. No doubt it is possible to take up the position that this one particular kind of knowledge has a different origin from that of any other knowledge: that other knowledge does, indeed, come only from experience of external and material 'things,' but that in this one function the human soul is in contact with a Reality which is not material. And, in so far as the Empiricist passes into the dualistic Realist—in so far, that is, as he recognizes the activity of the mind in knowledge and the reality of mind side by side with that of matter—the resulting Metaphysic ceases to

have any direct or immediate tendency to undermine the reality
and authority of a non-empirical [1] moral law, except in so far
as its inherent unsoundness may end in its own collapse, and so
in the collapse of any ethical superstructure which may be built
upon it. All that we can say is that the more moral judgements
are treated as a solitary exception to the rest of our knowledge,
the more difficulty there is in explaining their character and
justifying their validity ; and the more is suspicion apt to be
excited that, in assigning them an origin so different from that
of all other recognized knowledge, we are seeking to bolster
up a mysterious, 'mystical,' or unintelligible theory in some
practical interest.

The more fully it is recognized that in all knowledge—even in
knowledge of the most ordinary matter of fact—mind is active
or creative or constitutive of Reality and not merely a passive
recipient of impressions from the outside, the more fully it is
recognized that in knowledge the mind is building up or contributing an essential factor to Reality, and not merely recognizing
a Reality which is what it is quite independently of itself or of any
other subject, so much the more intelligible does it become that
there should be a truth which has no external ' thing-in-itself '
corresponding to it, a knowledge which is not derived from mere
' sensible experience,' a Reality or aspect of Reality which cannot
be expressed in the language of merely physical Science or
of mere psychological experience. The bare supposition that
there is an ' external ' and independent thing behind our ideas
about the thing, that the 'active powers' of the mind merely
recognize what is already there ' in the thing,' independently of
such recognition by itself or any other mind, has no doubt by itself
nothing in it to provoke distrust of the conclusions to which the
Moralist may be led by an examination of the moral consciousness. At the same time a position much more favourable to
a cordial acceptance of moral objectivity is reached when from
admitting the activity of mind in the recognition of the objects

---

[1] Of course I do not mean to deny that all moral ideas, like all other
ideas, are derived from human 'experience' if that word is used in a sufficiently wide sense – to include the power of building up knowledge and
ideals which are something other than immediate presentation.

of our knowledge we pass on to the view that these objects exist only for mind, and have no reality of their own apart from mind. Hence the imperishable value of the Kantian analysis of our knowledge, which shows that those special properties which the plain man regards as constituting the very essence of the 'thing' as it is apart from mind are really a creation of mind and unintelligible apart from it—that the 'oneness,' the 'substantiality,' the 'causality,' the 'actuality,' the 'quantity,' which to common-sense seem wholly independent of mind, turn out on reflection to be mental relations unintelligible and inconceivable except in reference to a knowing mind, so that the things that we know have no independent existence apart from our own or some other experience of them. It is true that Kant acknowledged, like all Idealists, the necessity of sensible experience for the constitution of this phenomenal world : though, unlike most of his successors, he assumed that the sensations which (with the relations) go to constitute the world as we know it are derived from an unknown and unknowable world of things in themselves. But these spaceless and timeless 'things-in-themselves' of Kant have so little in common with the ordinary man's idea of 'matter'[1] that the practical effect of this modified or 'critical' Idealism is for Morality much the same as that of the more thorough-going Idealism which absolutely denies the existence of 'things' which are not either mind or essentially relative to mind. And when it is recognized that the very 'things' which the plain man is apt to take as the absolute antithesis of thought, the very 'matter' beside which all mere creations of the mind are apt to appear unreal and phantasmal, are nevertheless in a true sense the 'work of the mind,' the difficulty disappears of realizing that moral judgements may be none the less true and trustworthy, because they are not 'inductions from experience,' or of discerning in the Moral Law a reality or validity which is none the less real because it is ideal. Idealism in Metaphysics, though not logically necessary to Idealism in Ethics, is its natural support and ally. Such a Metaphysic is, as leading up to the recognition of the activity of mind in

[1] At certain moments Kant himself is disposed to identify the 'thing-in-itself' with God, or the world as it is for God.

knowledge, the natural groundwork and basis of a Moral Philosophy which is to be proof against sceptical objections. In
Ethics, as in many other branches of knowledge, the plain man
who is content to know particular things without knowing the
ultimate meaning and basis of knowledge itself, can get along
without any Metaphysic at all; but when we are confronted
by difficulties or objections based upon a bad Metaphysic, the
only solution of them must be found in a better one. And,
when once the common-sense knowledge of Morality begins
to pass into a systematic study of Ethics, these objections are
likely to meet us very early and very persistently. There may
be a practical Morality, or even a more or less scientific attempt
to analyse and formulate practical Ethics, without Metaphysic,
but a purely ethical Science which attempts to avoid Metaphysic
must correspond very imperfectly with our idea of Philosophy.
A sound theory of Morality implies a sound theory of knowledge.

III

From another point of view our metaphysical difficulties may
take the form of doubts about the reality of that self which
is presupposed by every constructive Morality. And the answer to
those doubts must be the same which has to be made to empirical
theories of knowledge. To show that in talking about a self we
are talking about something real, we must begin by proving that
the existence of a continuous self is implied in all knowledge.
Knowledge comes to us piece by piece; and, if we cannot treat
the successive moments of our conscious life as successive moments
of a continuously existing self, these successive experiences can
never be built up into a single world. Deny the reality of the
self, and you have no ground for believing in the existence of
a world which is only known on the assumption of that reality.
Or, from a slightly different point of view, we may urge that
objects are known to us only as the correlative of a subject; at
least therefore we may contend that the subject is as real as the
object, even if we do not (with the thorough-going Idealist)
go on to infer that the object exists only in relation to, or
as the 'other' of, a subject. Given the existence of a self which

cannot be broken up into a succession of isolated feelings or
ideas or psychical atoms of any kind, and which cannot be
treated as the *mere* attribute or accident of a material organism,
Morality becomes possible. The actions of the individual can be
treated as the work of a single self which has a definite character
of its own, a spiritual character which expresses itself in those
actions, and which is susceptible of spiritual changes and
amenable to spiritual influences.

And something more must be implied than simply the
existence of the self and its activity in knowledge. It is a presupposition of all Morality that the self is the cause of its own
actions. In what sense precisely this must be asserted we shall
have to consider further in our chapter on Free-will. Meanwhile
I need only notice in passing that this postulate of Ethics is
implicitly or explicitly denied by two schools—by the school
which regards the self as a mere accident or attribute or bye-
product of material processes (a view which cannot be further
discussed in this place), and by the school which so completely
merges Will in Reason and the individual Reason in the universal Reason that there ceases to be any difference between the
acts of the man and those events in Nature or those actions of
other men [1] for which no one dreams of holding the individual
himself to be in any sense 'responsible.' All alike—natural
events, the actions popularly spoken of as those of other men,

---

[1] This objection is not removed by the simple admission that the mind that
makes Reality is Will. Schopenhauer, while he avoids the mistake of identifying the Absolute with Reason, destroys the ethical value of his position by
so completely identifying the individual with the universal ,Will that he
regards the individual's sufferings as a just punishment for the original sin
committed by the universal unconscious Will in giving birth to consciousness
and so to the world, before he, the individual sufferer, was born—a position
to which orthodox Theologians have sometimes approximated in their desperate attempts to justify immoral theories of Atonement. Schopenhauer
quotes with approbation Calderon's saying, that 'the greatest crime of
man is that he ever was born' (*The World as Will and Idea*, trans. by Haldane
and Kemp, I, pp. 328, 458). Where a man is made in some transcendental
sense responsible for the sins which he did not commit, the practical effect
is to relieve him from responsibility for those which he did commit. Von
Hartmann has pointed out that Schopenhauer's acceptance of Kant's
'noumenal freedom' in Ethics implies the existence of an individual self
which is not recognized by his general Metaphysic.

and his own individual actions—become according to this view mere happenings of which he is conscious but of which he is not the cause, or of which he is only the cause in the sense in which he may equally be called the cause of all other happenings in Nature. By this school the most splendid compliments are indeed paid to 'the Ego.' The Ego makes 'Nature,' but only in the sense that it knows Nature—in the sense, that is, that apart from knowledge there would be no Nature. The self makes Nature not because it determines of what sort Nature shall be, but just because it cannot help Nature being what it is. The very identity of principle between God or the 'Universal Self-consciousness' and the individual self is made the ground for despoiling the latter of any responsibility for its own actions which it does not possess for the events of the world in general. Nor can an illusory share in the responsibility for the Universe and its history be regarded as any satisfactory equivalent for the loss of any individual causality; for, when we turn to the relation between God and the world, we discover that that relation too is resolved into a relation between the knowing subject and the things which it knows. No Causality is recognized in the Universe except the necessary connexion of thought between phenomenal antecedent and phenomenal consequent. Between the events of the world and the subject without which it would not be, there is no relation of Causality at all. God is the universal Thinker (if indeed He is not resolved into Thought without a Thinker), but He is not a Universal Willer. In the same way the actions which the individual self knows are not in any case whatever the events which it causes, but just the events which it cannot help. If Causality is recognized at all in regard to human actions, it is recognized only in the same sense in which Causality is recognized between one natural event and another. The fact that the antecedents of human action are facts of consciousness makes no difference to their essential character. We have a 'psychological mechanism' instead of a physical mechanism; that is the only difference. It is not the self (individual or universal) that is the cause of the action, but an event in consciousness which is the cause of other events in consciousness. The self does not cause these events, but simply looks on while they happen. Actions are regarded as causing one another in just as mechanical a way as that in which the movements of a billiard ball are determined by antecedent movements. If the series of events which make up the conscious life of the individual may in a sense be spoken of as a kind of self, this is merely the so-called 'phenomenal self¹'; quite a different self from the self to which the categories of knowledge, and consequently in some sense the existence of Nature itself. are attributed. This phenomenal or empirical self is persistently degraded to the level of a merely animal sensibility; it is the tendency of the school in question hardly to distinguish between the individual's voluntary actions and events in unconscious nature. No doubt the presentation to the self of the successive events which we call human actions is necessary to their happening, but this self is not individual but Universal, and the presence of this world-making Self is only necessary to human actions in the same sense in which it is necessary to other events in the world's history. It causes neither the one nor the other.

How fatal are these ideas to the conception of duty, of moral responsibility or imputability, of an objective moral law to which the individual self is subject, need hardly be pointed out; nor will it have escaped the reader how nearly we have arrived by a different route at the same position as that which is involved in the theory of a purely materialistic Automatism according to which spirits and spiritual or psychical states are never causes but always effects—the accidental bye-products or 'epiphenomena' of physical changes which determine one another (and their psychical concomitants) in a purely mechanical manner. Both theories refuse to attribute human actions to a self; both attribute them to the Absolute or ultimate Reality. That Reality may be differently conceived of by the two theories; the one may conceive of it materialistically, and the other spiritualistically; but in either case we have no room for attributing the causality of any human action to a real human self. And this is exactly what the ethical point of view involves. In what

¹ For the school in question tends to abolish the individual 'noumenal self' of Kant. It recognizes no 'noumenal' self but the Universal Self-consciousness.

relation the individual life and its activities may stand to the Universal Will and its volitions, in what sense all the events of Nature may be attributed to the Universal Self, what is the relation between the Reason and the Will in the Universal Self —these are no doubt matters about which many questions may be asked. But that in some intelligible sense, primarily and immediately, actions may be attributed to the individual self as their cause and are good or bad according as the self is good or bad—that is the starting-point and primary postulate of Ethics. Wherein and in what sense this ethical point of view may be regarded as ultimate, whether it is the truth and the whole truth, or merely a truth which holds at a 'certain level of thought,' are questions of which something will be said hereafter. But that these propositions possess objective truth, and are not as a mere seeming which adequate philosophic insight can reduce to a delusion, must be declared to be a primary and absolutely essential presupposition of every system of Ethics which can attribute any meaning to the word 'ought.' And the very fact that this assumption is a postulate of Ethics is by itself a sufficient reason for declaring that it possesses metaphysical truth. It is implied in the idea of Morality, and the idea of Morality is a datum of the moral consciousness; and the data of consciousness are the only ground which we have for believing anything at all. No doubt this, like all other immediate data of consciousness, has to be harmonized and recon ciled with other data of consciousness, if it can be shown that there is any *prima facie* collision or irreconcilability between them, but there is, to say the least of it, an enormous presumption against any 'harmonization' or 'conciliation' which turns such an ultimate datum of consciousness into a mere illusion. To this subject we shall return hereafter: meanwhile I shall merely insist that the existence of our moral ideas has as good a right to be taken into consideration in the construction of our ultimate theory of Universe as any other kind of fact. We must not reject the deliverances of the moral Consciousness merely because they are inconsistent with some metaphysical theory which has been arrived at without taking those deliverances into consideration.

It may be asked against precisely what school or what individual writers these criticisms are directed. I will not attempt to discuss how far they are justly attributed to Hegel[1]. I will only say that it is a point of view which is implied in at least one interpretation of Hegel; and that interpretation of Hegel is precisely the one which has most powerfully influenced, to say the least of it, those through whom Hegelian ways of thinking have become common among English students of Ethics. To say without qualification or reserve that the mode of thought above indicated was that of Thomas Hill Green would be unfair and one-sided. As a Moralist, no one recognized more earnestly than Green the facts of moral responsibility and imputability; but that there is a logical hiatus between Green's ethical system and the metaphysical system with which he sought to connect it is coming to be very generally recognized both among those who sympathize with, and by those who dissent from, Green's practical attitude towards Morality[2]. If no individual self is recognized except a merely phenomenal or psychological self, if the self which is active in Morality is identical with the 'spiritual principle not in time' implied by all our knowledge, if this ' principle not in time ' is further identified with a Universal Self-consciousness which is regarded as Reason and is denied Causality or volition, it is difficult to see how Green can escape the consequences which I have suggested. No doubt much is to be found in Green's writings which is inconsistent with such a view. We read much of the strivings of the self (presumably of the individual self) after ' self-satisfaction,' of the self imputing to itself its own actions, of God as a Mind which, though He does not act or will or feel or love, has some vague and undefined connexion with the moral law. But how a timeless self can find a satis-

---

[1] If we substitute for a 'Universal Self-consciousness' the idea of God considered under the attribute of Thought, and recognize that (in his view) the Thought manifests itself only in individual selves, it may be said fairly to represent (as far as it goes) Spinoza's attitude toward Ethics. Here, as in other matters, Spinoza held, with full and explicit consciousness, the view of the world to which Hegelianism tends, but which the practical aims of its exponents have often prevented their explicitly recognizing.

[2] Green's ethical views are most fully expounded in his *Prolegomena to Ethics*, 1883.

faction, not previously experienced, in human actions which have a beginning in time; how a self which is not differentiated (except perhaps on the side of the animal organism) from the Universal Self-consciousness can impute to itself its good or bad acts without imputing them in exactly the same sense and degree to the Universal Self-consciousness; how any events at all can be 'imputed' to a self which thinks all things but originates nothing—these are questions which it would be difficult to answer in a satisfactory manner without glossing the text of Green's writings altogether past recognition.

Many minds will no doubt regard a system of Moral Philosophy as very incomplete which does not set out with a much more detailed and elaborate analysis of the self than is to be found in these pages. No doubt a Moral Philosopher may, if he chooses, properly devote much more time than I have done either to the metaphysical, or again to the psychological, treatment of the self. I am far from depreciating the importance of either sort of enquiry. I can only repeat that I have not gone into greater detail (a) because it seemed to me that an elaborate and detailed investigation of the nature of the self from a moral point of view cannot easily be separated from the whole body of metaphysical and psychological questions which can be raised about the self; and (b) because I should contend that in the whole of the preceding pages I have really been engaged in examining the nature of the self, in so far as that nature is a matter of directly ethical import. The conclusions to which we have come have most important metaphysical consequences—consequences which it belongs to Metaphysic proper to develope and trace out. But I do not consider that these conclusions are *prima facie* inconsistent with any metaphysical theory about the self which recognizes (a) that the self is a permanent reality; (b) that that reality is spiritual, in so far as it has a permanent life of its own not identical with the changes of the material organism with which it is (in whatever way) connected; (c) that the acts of the man really proceed from and express the nature or character of the self[1]. I call the existence of such a self a primary postulate of Ethics, because without it we can recognize no meaning

---

[1] This point will be dealt with more at length in the chapter on Free-will.

in the language which we are compelled at every moment to use in all ethical discussion. It is the postulate without which we cannot even set out on our ethical journey. Whether there are any other postulates of Ethics; whether, as we proceed with our attempt to understand and systematize the facts of our moral life and to co-ordinate them with other facts, we are not irresistibly led on to make further metaphysical demands; whether there are not in this secondary sense some further 'postulates of Ethics,' we must now proceed to enquire.

IV

We have seen that certain metaphysical presuppositions as to the nature of knowledge and the nature of the self are necessary to the very existence of an ethical system which can be regarded as representing and justifying the deliverances of the moral consciousness. When we have admitted that knowledge is not mere subjective feeling or passive experience, that the self is as real as or more real than any 'thing' of which Physical Science can tell us, and that the self causes certain events which are commonly spoken of as its actions, then we are able to recognize the reality of duty, of ideals, of a good which includes right conduct. And *prima facie* it might appear that the truth and validity of these ideals are independent of any particular conclusions as to the ultimate nature of things which go beyond these simple presuppositions. The man who wishes to see any meaning in the deliverances of his own moral consciousness and to represent to himself the attempt to live up to the ideal which they set before him as an intelligible and rational aim, must assume this much about knowledge and about the self; but it may possibly be contended that he need assume nothing further about the ultimate nature of things, except that it is a Universe, part of whose nature is to produce this moral consciousness of his. And it is no doubt true that the Agnostic (in Metaphysic or Theology) cannot be convicted of any positive inconsistency, if he simply accepts the dictates of his moral consciousness as final, and says: 'I know nothing as to the ultimate source of these moral ideas, except that they come to me in the same way as the rest of my knowledge, or anything as to the ultimate outcome of this moral life which I feel to be incumbent upon me. I simply know the meaning of the good, and that it is right for me to aim at it, and that I can, to some extent, bring it into existence by my voluntary action.' Psychologically this attitude is a possible one. The term ' good ' or ' right ' does not contain any *explicit* reference to any theological or metaphysical theory of the Universe. The proposition that some things are right, others wrong, is not in any sense an inference or deduction from any such theory ; it is an immediate datum or deliverance of consciousness. The truth is assented to, and acted upon, by men of all religions or of none, by persons who hold most dissimilar views as to the ultimate nature of the Universe, and by men who profess to have no theory of the Universe at all. And it is impossible to say that the words ' good ' and ' right ' have no meaning for such persons or an entirely different meaning from what they have for the Metaphysician who refuses to acquiesce in Agnosticism. In this sense it is of the highest possible importance to recognize what is sometimes spoken of as the ' independence of Morality.' But it remains a further question whether the true meaning of Morality is capable of being made explicit, and of being reconciled or harmonized with other facts of our knowledge or experience without necessitating the adoption of certain views concerning the ultimate nature of things and the rejection of certain other views. If this should turn out to be the case, Morality will be in exactly the same position as any other part of our knowledge. So long as we refuse to bring any piece of our knowledge or experience into connexion with any other part of it, the particular piece of knowledge cannot be shown to be either consistent or inconsistent with such other parts of our knowledge. So long as that is the case, it may no doubt from a high metaphysical attitude be maintained that this knowledge may not be altogether true, since it may require to be corrected and limited in order to bring it into harmony with other parts of our knowledge : for the only test that we have of the validity of any part of our knowledge is its capacity for being harmonized or co-ordinated with the rest of it. But, from a rough practical point of view, it is possible to be certain of the truth of Science without holding any meta-

physical position at all : and in that sense it is equally possible
to combine a strong conviction of the reality or objective validity
of moral distinctions with complete Agnosticism as to the general
nature of the Universe, though in practice Agnosticism is very
apt to involve negative assumptions the irreconcilability of which
with what is implied in the idea of moral obligation, can with difficulty remain unrecognized.   But after all the question remains
whether this refusal to bring one part of our knowledge into connexion with the rest is a reasonable attitude of mind.   It is always
easy to escape inconsistency by resolutely shutting our eyes to a
portion of the facts, by refusing to think or by arbitrarily stopping
the process of thought at some particular point [1].   When we ask
whether a certain intellectual attitude is ultimately reasonable,
we presuppose that we are making up our minds to look at the
whole of the facts.   Agnosticism is not a reasonable attitude
of mind when it is possible to know.   And the question arises
whether, when the attempt to harmonize and so to justify our
beliefs is honestly made, the man who wishes to defend and
rationalize his practical recognition of moral obligation may not
be forced into the alternative of giving up his ethical creed or of
giving up certain views of the Universe which reflection has
shown to be inconsistent with that creed.

Are there then any metaphysical positions about the ultimate
nature of things which logically exclude the idea of an objective
Moral Law ?   Let us suppose, for instance, that, without giving
up that bare minimum of metaphysical belief about the self
which we have found to be absolutely presupposed in the very
idea of Morality, a man has nevertheless adopted a materialistic

---

[1] The strongest assertion of the validity of the idea of duty that has ever
been made from an agnostic point of view is perhaps to be found in Huxley's
brilliant Romanes Lecture on *Evolution and Ethics* (Collected Essays, Vol. IX).
It is interesting to see how near the contention that Natural and Moral Law
have equal validity brings him to the admission that they have ultimately
a common source.   What Huxley refuses to ask is whether the validity of
the Moral Law does not throw some light upon the nature of that Reality
which is revealed both by Physical Law and by Moral Law—whether the
belief that we ought to resist the ' cosmic process' and the impulse to act
upon that belief are not as much a product of the Cosmos, and a revelation
of its ultimate nature, as those physical and psychological tendencies which
Morality bids us resist.

or naturalistic view of the world to this extent—that he believes that the origin of the self, and of the knowledge which resides in the self, may actually be traced to certain material processes of a Reality in which previously no mind resided except as a 'promise and potency' of the future. Such a man is not, indeed, technically in the most thorough-going sense of the word a Materialist if he admits that after all a true view of the Universe must include a recognition of the spiritual nature which the Universe has ultimately, by whatever process, evolved. And it is quite right to emphasize the difference between a position of this kind and the old confused puzzle-headed Materialism which was inclined to look on matter and motion as real things and on thought, feeling (with perhaps some not very logical exception in favour of pleasure and pain), emotion, aspiration, ideals as mere arbitrary inventions or hallucinations. But, putting aside for the present the purely metaphysical difficulties of such a position, we have to ask how it must affect our attitude towards Morality.

So long as the ultimate reality of things is regarded as purely material, so long as material process is regarded as the sole cause or source or ground of mind and all its contents, there is always the possibility of scepticism as to the knowledge of which this material world has somehow delivered itself. Our knowledge may be conceived of as representing, not the real truth of things, but the way in which it is most conducive to the survival of the race that we should think of them. Error and delusion may be valuable elements in Evolution ; to a certain extent it is un- deniable, from any metaphysical standpoint, that they have actually been so. But on the naturalistic view of things the doubt arises not merely whether this or that particular belief of ours is a delusion, but whether human thought in general may not wholly fail to correspond with Reality, whether thought *qua* thought may not be a delusion, whether (to put it still more paradoxically) the more rational a man's thought becomes, the more faithfully the individual adheres to the canons of human Reason, the wider may be the gulf between his thinking and the facts. Arguments might no doubt be found for putting away such an 'unmotived' doubt as to the trustworthiness of our knowledge about ordinary matters of fact—its self-con-

3 6.

sistency, the constant correspondence of the predictions which it makes with subsequent experience, the practical serviceableness for the purposes of life of its assumed validity, and the uselessness of entertaining doubts as to the trustworthiness of our faculties which from the nature of the case can be neither confirmed nor refuted; though after all such arguments at bottom assume the validity of thought. But these considerations do not apply in the same degree to moral knowledge. It is often possible to explain in a sense this or that particular ethical belief by the history of the race, the environment of the individual, and the like. Such considerations do not shake belief in the ultimate validity of moral distinctions for an Idealist who believes that the Universe owes its very existence to the Mind which assures him of these distinctions (though he is aware that the evolution of his individual mind has been conditioned by physical processes and social environment); but they wear a totally different aspect for one who has no general *a priori* reason for assuming a correspondence of thought with things [1]. The Idealist has every reason for believing the ultimate moral ideas to be true that he has for believing any other ideas to be true, though he realizes that he does not know the whole truth, and that his knowledge of this or ignorance of that element in the moral ideal (like his knowledge or ignorance of ordinary scientific truth) is in part explicable by the accident of antecedents or environment. But to the man who regards all spiritual life as a mere inexplicable incident in the career of a world which is essentially material (were it not for the human and animal minds which it is known to have produced) and as a whole essentially purposeless, there is no conclusive reason why all moral ideas—the very conception of ' value,' the very notion that one thing is intrinsically better than another, the very conviction that there is something which a man ought to do—may not be merely some strange illusion due

---

[1] I am quite alive to the difficulties involved in the 'correspondence theory' as to the nature of Truth, which have been brilliantly developed by Mr. Joachim in his recent Essay on *The Nature of Truth*, and it is one which no Idealist can well regard as the final and ultimate account of the matter, but any discussion of such a question would be quite out of place in an ethical treatise. Mr. Joachim would no doubt admit that we cannot help employing such language in such a connexion as the present.

to the unaccountable freaks of a mindless process or to the exigencies of natural selection. It cannot be said that a man who allowed such doubts to shake or modify his allegiance to the dictates of Morality, where they do not happen to coincide with his actual desires or inclinations, would be doing anything essentially unreasonable. Reasonable conduct would for him mean merely 'conduct conformable to his own private reason': intrinsically or absolutely reasonable or unreasonable conduct could not exist in a world which was not itself the product of Reason or governed by its dictates.

Another way of putting much the same difficulty is this. We say that the Moral Law has a real existence, that there is such a thing as an absolute Morality, that there is something absolutely true or false in ethical judgements, whether we or any number of human beings at any given time actually think so or not. Such a belief is distinctly implied in what we mean by Morality. The idea of such an unconditional, objectively valid, Moral Law or ideal undoubtedly exists as a psychological fact. The question before us is whether it is capable of theoretical justification. We must then face the question *where* such an ideal exists, and what manner of existence we are to attribute to it. Certainly it is to be found, wholly and completely, in no individual human consciousness. Men actually think differently about moral questions, and there is no empirical reason for supposing that they will ever do otherwise. Where then and how does the moral ideal really exist ? As regards matters of fact or physical law, we have no difficulty in satisfying ourselves that there is an objective reality which is what it is irrespectively of our beliefs or disbeliefs about it. For the man who supposes that objective reality resides in the things themselves, our ideas about them are objectively true or false so far as they correspond or fail to correspond with this real and independent archetype, though he might be puzzled to give a metaphysical account of the nature of this 'correspondence' between experience and a Reality whose *esse* is something other than to be experienced. In the physical region the existence of divergent ideas does not throw doubt upon the existence of a reality independent of our ideas. But in the case of moral ideals it is otherwise. On materialistic or naturalistic assumptions the moral ideal can hardly be regarded as a real thing. Nor could it well be regarded as a property of any real thing : it can be no more than an aspiration, a product of the imagination, which may be useful to stimulate effort in directions in which we happen to want to move, but which cannot compel respect when we feel no desire to act in conformity with it. An absolute Moral Law or moral ideal cannot exist *in* material things. And it does not (we have seen) exist in the mind of this or that individual. Only if we believe in the existence of a Mind for which the true moral ideal is already in some sense real, a Mind which is the source of whatever is true in our own moral judgements, can we rationally think of the moral ideal as no less real than the world itself. Only so can we believe in an absolute standard of right and wrong, which is as independent of this or that man's actual ideas and actual desires as the facts of material nature. The belief in God, though not (like the belief in a real and an active self) a postulate of there being any such thing as Morality at all, is the logical presupposition of an ' objective ' or absolute Morality. A moral ideal can exist nowhere and nohow but in a mind ; an absolute moral ideal can exist only in a Mind from which all Reality is derived [1]. Our moral ideal can only claim objective validity in so far as it can rationally be regarded as the revelation of a moral ideal eternally existing in the mind of God.

We may be able, perhaps, to give some meaning to Morality without the postulate of God, but not its true or full meaning. If the existence of God is not a postulate of all Morality, it is a postulate of a sound Morality ; for it is essential to that belief which vaguely and implicitly underlies all moral beliefs, and which forms the very heart of Morality in its highest, more developed, more explicit forms. The truth that the moral ideal is what it is whether we like it or not is the most essential element in what the popular consciousness understands by ' moral obligation.' Moral obligation means moral objectivity. That *at least* seems to be implied in any legitimate use of the term : at least it im-

---

[1] Or at least a mind by which all Reality is controlled. Want of space forbids my discussing the ethical aspect of Pluralism or of a theory which regards spirits other than God as having no beginning.

plies the existence of an absolute, objective moral ideal. And
such a belief we have seen imperatively to demand an explanation of the Universe which shall be idealistic or at least spiritualistic, which shall recognize the existence of a Mind whose
thoughts are the standard of truth and falsehood alike in
Morality and in respect of all other existence. In other words,
objective Morality implies the belief in God. The belief in God,
if not so obviously and primarily a postulate of Morality as the
belief in a permanent spiritual and active self, is still a postulate
of a Morality which shall be able fully to satisfy the demands
of the moral consciousness. It may conveniently be called the
secondary postulate of Morality.

V

That belief in God involves something more than the belief
that there is a universal Mind for which and in which the moral
ideal exists. There can be no meaning in the idea of Morality for
a Being who is mere Thought and not Will. If human Morality is
a revelation, however imperfect, of the ultimate nature of Reality,
it must represent, not merely an ideal existing in and for the
Mind which is the ultimate source or ground of Reality, but also
the nature of the end towards which that Reality is moving.
The very idea of Morality implies action directed towards an
end which has value. If the value of 'good' has its counter-
part in the divine Mind, the course of events is itself governed
by the same Mind which is the source of our moral ideas, and
must be ultimately directed towards the end which the true moral
ideal, disclosed however imperfectly in the moral consciousness
of man, sets us up as the goal and canon of human conduct.
The Universe itself must have a purpose or rational end, a purpose which commends itself as reasonable to the Mind which
wills it: and the nature of that end must be at least in part
disclosed by our moral judgements. What valid human judgements pronounce to be good must be part of the divine end, and
the rest of that end must be such as could, consistently with the
principles governing these human judgements of value, be pronounced good.

That an objectively valid Morality implies belief in the fundamental rationality of the Universe will no doubt be admitted by some thinkers whose belief about its ultimate nature falls more or less short of what is commonly understood by Theism, who do not believe that Nature is (as a genuine Theist, like Lotze, holds) an effect whose cause is God, or at least who decline to think of that God as 'personal.' Intense belief in a rational principle behind nature combined with much vagueness about the personal, or even the self-conscious nature, of that principle meets us already in the writings of Plato. And a similar vagueness, which might have been supposed to belong to a stage of human thought in which the distinction between subject and object, mind and matter, thought and will, was still imperfectly grasped, has beset the path of philosophic thought in later times. I have not space to defend the position here taken up, or to meet the objections which will at once be raised in many quarters; but I will simply state that to my own mind the only form in which belief in the rationality of the Universe is intelligible is the form which ascribes the events of its history to a self-conscious rational Will directing itself towards an end which presents itself to Him as absolutely good [1]. However inadequate our conceptions of 'Will,' 'Mind,' 'Purpose,' 'Reason,' Personality,' may be to express the nature of such a Being, they are the best we have. Thought does not become more adequate by becoming vaguer. It is not the limitations inherent in human personality that we imply when we ascribe personality to God; but all the positive attributes that constitute man's superiority to the beasts carried to a much higher level and freed from the limitations by which they are in us conditioned [2]. Applied to God, all such

---

[1] Creation in time, though possibly involving no greater difficulties than any other solution of the Antinomy which arises from the attempt to think of the beginning or non-beginning of the existing world (an Antinomy which has never been satisfactorily 'transcended.'), is not necessarily implied by this belief. All that I mean is that the events (whether the series be endless or not) are caused by the Will of God. I quite recognize the difficulty of thinking of the divine Will as antecedent to the series or as a cause which is not antecedent to its effect. This consideration forms one of the difficulties. The impossibility of solving the Antinomy rests upon our ignorance of the true relation of Reality to Time, as to which see below, p. 245 sq.

[2] It may be asked why Morality itself should not be one of the limitations

terms must be understood (as the Schoolmen said) 'sensu emi-
nentiori.' And if the end imperfectly revealed in Morality be
the end of the Universe or the end of God, it must, it would
seem, be fulfilled. In what sense and to what extent it must
be fulfilled, is a question on which much might be said, and I
shall return to that question hereafter[1]. But at least it would
seem that the end which presents itself to the divine consciousness as good must be so far fulfilled as to make the being of the
world better than its not-being: otherwise, we have no explana
tion as to why it should be willed at all[2]. But can any one
seriously maintain that the world as it is—human life as it is
—is so good as to account for its having been willed by a perfectly good and perfectly rational Being, except as a means to an
end beyond itself? Is human life, whether we look at its moral
side or its hedonistic side, so good as to seem an adequate end
for such a Being to have willed? If it be admitted that human
life, as it is, is not adequate to the justification of the Universe,
it may perhaps be suggested that in the future it is going to be
so. But apart from the difficulty of regarding as reasonable an
arrangement by which countless generations of human beings
have been called into existence *merely* as a means to the Well-
being of other generations, there is as little empirical justification
for an optimistic view of the future of humanity as for an
optimistic view of its past or its present. Only if we suppose
that the present life of human beings has an end which lies in
part beyond the limits of the present natural order, in so far as
that order is accessible to present human observation, can we

incident to human personality. I should answer, 'Because the other limitations—such as partial knowledge, intermittent consciousness, liability to be
thwarted by other persons over whom one has no control, the distinction
between present feeling and the thought of an absent feeling, and so on—
we can ourselves see to be connected with limitations which cannot apply
to God. There is no reason for supposing this to be the case with ultimate
moral principles any more than for supposing that $2 + 2 = 4$ is only true
from a human point of view.'

[1] Below, chap. iii.

[2] It has been suggested that the not-willing of any world at all may be
one of the inherent impossibilities or limitations in God. I should reply
that a Being obliged to cause what seemed to Him bad could not be said in
any intelligible sense to will at all.

find a rational meaning and explanation for human life as we
see it; and by far the most natural and intelligible form of such
a world-end is the belief in Immortality [1] for the individual
souls which have lived here. If human life be a training-
ground and discipline for souls wherein they are being fitted
and prepared for a life better alike in a moral and a hedonistic
sense than the present, then at last we do find an adequate explanation of the willing of such a world by a Being whose character
the moral consciousness at its highest presents to us as Love.

And it is not only the actual amount of moral badness and the
actual amount of pain in the world that make it so desperate
an attempt to claim rationality for the Universe on the assumption that the life of the individual ends with death. It is the
distribution of good and evil—the relation in which goodness
and happiness, badness and misery, stand to each other—which
it is so difficult to reconcile with that postulate of a rational
Universe which is implicitly contained in the claim of the moral
consciousness to objective validity. We have, indeed, examined
and rejected the idea that Virtue carries with it an intrinsic
title to reward, or that vice demands punishment for punishment's
sake, but we have discovered in the popular belief about reward
and punishment a crude testimony to the rationality of an order
of things in which goodness and happiness should go together.
The real meaning of the belief that Virtue should be rewarded
is that Virtue is not by itself the whole of human good; the real
meaning of the theory that vice should be punished, not merely
as a measure of social protection but as a demand of absolute
Justice, is that happiness without goodness is not the true good.
The good, we have seen, is neither goodness nor happiness, but
both together [2]. If the Universe does not tend to promote the
good, it cannot be rational. And another element in rationality
is the Justice which prescribes that, as far as possible, beings of
equal capacity shall be equally treated in the distribution of good.
A coincidence between goodness and happiness is, according to

[1] As to the reasons for preferring 'Immortality' to a simple 'future life,'
see below.

[2] For the sake of brevity we may for the moment ignore all the other
elements in the Universe of Good.

the deep-seated popular conviction, a necessary characteristic of a rational world-order; and that conviction is one which, subject to the explanations already given, justifies itself to philosophical reflection. In present human life nothing but the roughest and most general tendency to such a coincidence, if even that, can possibly be discerned. *The* good—the ideal life of our highest ideals—is unknown to human experience. Goodness as we know it, if it brings with it some internal sources of happiness, brings with it also (in its own nature and apart from external circumstances) much internal pain—the pain of sympathy, the anxiety of the scrupulous Conscience, the pain of failure to attain its ends: in fact, in so far as happiness is regarded as including pleasure and the absence of pain, there is hardly any connexion between the possession of it and the moral character of the possessors. Christendom has found its highest moral ideal in one who was a man of sorrows. Whatever be the explanation of such an order of things as a temporary or partial phase or aspect of the world's life, the deeper our conviction of the rationality of the Universe, the stronger becomes our unwillingness to believe that such an order can be final and permanent. Hence it is that a sincere Theism has nearly always carried with it a belief in Immortality. The belief in Immortality has not been due merely to a defective appreciation of the intrinsic goodness of Virtue or of the intrinsic badness of vice; on the contrary it is a belief which is usually held with an intensity proportional to that appreciation. It is a necessary corollary of the rationality of the Universe that its course should be so directed as to bring about an ultimate coincidence between the higher and the lower kinds of good, which are both alike essential to the full and true Well-being of a human soul. So long as it was possible to believe that happiness and misery, prosperity and failure, were distributed in this life on principles of absolute Justice, belief in the rationality of things did not necessarily carry with it belief in Immortality. The Jews were at one time behind other nations in the distinctness of their belief in personal Immortality, just because (it would seem) of the intensity with which they believed that obedience to Jehovah's laws would be rewarded by national victory and agricultural prosperity—a belief ultimately shattered by the experiences of the Exile[1]. A further knowledge of History and of Physical Science has taught us that, however much we may recognize a general tendency to make man under ordinary circumstances happier with goodness than without it, no complete or even general coincidence between the higher and the lower kinds of good can be traced in the actual course of human affairs. When this fact is clearly recognized, belief in Immortality becomes a postulate of the belief in a rational world-order or (what is for most minds the same thing) of belief in God. And therefore belief in Immortality comes to be (for those who share that view of the empirical facts) a postulate of Ethics in the same sense as the belief in God.

I may sum up the position at which we have arrived by saying that a certain belief about the self and its relation to human action may be described as the primary postulate of Ethics, since the incompatibility between its negation and a real belief in an objective or absolute Ethic is obvious on the face of it, obvious at the level of common-sense thought. The belief in God may be described as a secondary postulate of Ethics, since, though no explicit reference to it is contained in the ethical judgement itself, its implication in that judgement discloses itself as soon as the attempt is made to develope what is contained in the actual moral consciousness and to harmonize it with other parts of our experience. And finally belief in Immortality may be described as in a tertiary sense a postulate of Ethics, inasmuch as it is a postulate of belief in God for all minds to whom the actual constitution of things without that hypothesis presents itself as one which could not possibly be willed by a Being whose nature, character, and purposes are of the kind implied by the ideals revealed to us in our own moral consciousness.

[1] It must be remembered that the Jewish Theology only reached the level of pure Monotheism a very little before a developed belief in Immortality (as distinct from a mere survival which could hardly be called life in a shadowy Sheol) began to appear. And if Theism be held to include belief in a God who is just and impartially benevolent to all mankind, it was certainly not attained by the Jews before the Exile, even if it was ever reached by pre-Christian Judaism at all.

The course of events must itself be governed by the same Mind which is the source of our moral ideas, and be ultimately directed towards the ends which the moral ideal, disclosed, however imperfectly, in the moral consciousness of man, sets up as the goal and canon of human conduct. The Universe itself must have a purpose or rational end, a purpose which a perfect Reason would pronounce to be good. The end which our Reason sets before us as the true end of conduct must be the end likewise of the Mind from which that Reason is derived. This seems speculatively necessary if Morality is to be regarded as ultimately and in the fullest sense rational—rational not merely from the point of view of this or that actual intelligence, or even from the point of view of all human intelligences, but from the point of view of all Reason whatever, universally, absolutely. And, as it is speculatively necessary, so it is, if not practically necessary in every individual case, at least highly conducive to Morality in practice that it should be believed that the ends which Morality sets before itself are destined to be realized. Unless the Universe be rational, no course of conduct can be said to be wholly and absolutely rational; we could only say ' I am so constituted ' or at the very most ' *we* are so constituted that this or that seems rational to me or to us.' And the Universe is not rational because there is a rational intelligence *for* whom it exists; if it is to be in the true sense rational, it must be directed towards ends which a rational intelligence would pronounce good [1]. I do not say that without this belief Morality would become irrational; moral conduct would still be as rational as anything could be in

[1] Much confusion has been caused by the ambiguity of the word ' rational.' It may mean ' intelligible ' or ' reducible to a coherent system such that one part of it could (with adequate insight) be inferred from another.' In this sense the Universe might be rational if it were a sort of infernal machine. Or it may mean (and that is the only sense in which we ought to talk about a reality which includes events as ' rational') realizing an end which is absolutely good. It has been part of the legerdemain of a certain school to prove that the Universe is rational in the first sense, and then to assume that it must be rational in the second, and therefore, it is urged, anything in it which strikes us as bad must be mere appearance. In this way a Universe in which Sin and Misery habitually triumph over goodness is represented to us as eminently ' rational ' and therefore as a satisfying object of moral and aesthetic contemplation, if not of religious Worship.

an irrational Universe, i. e. it would seem rational to some
persons who think that they see clearly.   And a man to whom
it appeared good to diminish human suffering, and who desired
that which he saw to be good, would still allow himself to be
influenced by the desire, even though he thought or suspected
that the Universe was very bad—though of course if his view of
the ultimate badness of things reached a certain intensity, the
encouragement of universal suicide might present itself to him
as the only way to attain his end[1].   But a belief of this kind
is obviously one not calculated to encourage or stimulate what
is ordinarily called Morality.   To some minds no doubt the impulse to fight against the evil in a world in which evil was the
stronger power would always seem good and noble.   But Pessimism is not the belief about the Universe which is best calculated to call forth the highest energies even of the noblest souls.
Still less is it calculated to foster the ethical education of those
(and they are the vast majority, especially as regards the earlier
stages of the individual's moral life) who recognize the intrinsic
goodness of the Moral Law, but whose desire to fulfil it is faintly
and fitfully struggling against a host of conflicting impulses.
The belief that the Universe has a rational end is speculatively
a postulate of an absolute or unconditional Morality : and the
speculative necessity is one which is evident enough to minds of
by no means a highly speculative cast.   A Morality which is
not absolute or unconditional is not Morality as it presents
itself to the developed moral consciousness.

VI

We have been investigating the metaphysical postulates of
Morality.   There remains the question ' how far can such postu-
lates be reasonably granted ? ' We have seen that a system of
Ethics such as is here defended assumes a certain metaphysical

---

[1] Pessimists like Schopenhauer and Von Hartmann only escape this consequence by the assumptions (a) that such a universal extinction of consciousness is impossible, because the Absolute would create fresh individuals to
prevent it, (b) that there is such a complete identity between all individual
manifestations of the Absolute that there would not be really less suffering
even if the number of sufferers were greatly reduced.

position : there remains the question ' Is that metaphysical
position a true one ? ' To answer that question in full is the
business of Metaphysic itself, and it is a task which cannot here be
attempted. But there is one aspect of it which must be touched
on in even the most meagre sketch of the relations between
Ethics and Metaphysics. We saw that Ethics were related to
Metaphysics not merely because certain metaphysical positions
are essential to Ethics, but also because some of the conclusions
of Ethics are of importance for Metaphysic. We have dealt with
the debt of Ethics to Metaphysic : we must go on to ask what is
the debt of Metaphysic to Ethics. And in answering that question, we shall be to some small extent contributing towards
a solution of the question how far the metaphysical view of the
Universe which we have seen to be essential to our ethical
position is on its own merits a true and reasonable theory of the
Universe. For the bare fact that the moral consciousness requires certain metaphysical postulates—that without them we
cannot explain and justify an important part of our actual
thought—supplies by itself a strong ground for inferring that
those postulates are true, and for accepting a theory of the
Universe which admits their truth. Cardinal Newman has made
the assertion that the bare existence of Conscience is by itself
a sufficient reason for believing in the existence of God.[1] It
would be hard to say how much we should be entitled to infer
as to the ultimate constitution of the Universe from the existence
of Conscience taken entirely by itself. For the very idea of
Conscience, or of the Morality which Conscience proclaims, is
unintelligible in complete isolation from other elements in our

---

[1] Compare Von Hartmann's statement : 'The bare fact that we possess
moral instincts is, even taken by itself, the refutation of all anti-teleological
views of the Universe' (D. sittl. Bewusstsein, p. 465). Most of those who
accept Von Hartmann's convincing demonstration of the teleological character
of the Universe will fail to find a sufficient explanation of the facts in an
Unconscious Absolute who, however, becomes conscious in the act of Creation
and, though declared to be identical with individual selves, has apparently a
pain which is not merely the pain of any particular individuals, since sympathy with the sufferings of the Absolute is appealed to as a powerful motive
for Morality, not only in this or that individual, but in humanity collectively.
Humanity is invited to bear its own sufferings patiently because they are so
much less than those of the Absolute !

knowledge both of ourselves and of the world. The idea of
Morality implies a good deal of other knowledge. It implies
the existence of a self which knows and feels and wills, of other
selves which know and feel and will, of a world which we are
capable of modifying to some extent but only to some extent.
And, even if this much non-ethical knowledge be admitted,
it would be too much to say that the existence of God was
sufficiently established if, though apparently demanded as the
presupposition of one part of our experience, it should turn out
not to be required by, or even to be inconsistent with, other
parts of it. If the last were the final verdict which Metaphysic
found it necessary to pronounce, we should be confronted with a
hopeless antagonism between our practical and our scientific
beliefs. If we thought that Morality pointed to a God and
Nature did not, we might be obliged (with Kant in his more
sceptical moments [1]) to declare that such a belief is indeed
a postulate of Ethics, but does not justify our turning this postulate into a piece of speculative knowledge. And even this
position, full of difficulties both practical and speculative as it is
generally admitted to be, is only open to us so long as we assume
that there is at least no positive inconsistency between the view
of the Universe to which we are led by our examination of other
aspects of our experience and that which seems to be presupposed by our moral consciousness. If the apparent postulates
of our ethical nature should prove positively inconsistent with
the view of things to which the rest of our experience conducts
us, we might be placed under the necessity of admitting that the
interpretation of our ethical experience which involved such
postulates must be a mistaken one. This is exactly what
actually happens with those Philosophers whose Metaphysic
does not allow them to concede the postulates to which the

---

[1] At other times Kant admits that the postulate does give us even
theoretical knowledge *that* God exists, though it does not enable us to know
speculatively *what* He is. How we can know that anything is without *some*,
however imperfect, knowledge of what it is, is a question the bare statement of which is now generally felt to be fatal to the Kantian position. We
must either go forward to a more constructive, speculative Theology, or give
up an ethical position which compels us to assume speculative positions
which we are forbidden to assert to be objectively true.

admitted contents of their moral consciousness would naturally
point. Recent writers who tend towards a purely psychological
or naturalistic view of Ethics—writers like Simmel, Höffding,
and Prof. Taylor [1]—have corrected the crude Psychology of
their predecessors so far as to admit as a psychological fact the
idea of an absolute 'ought': but they see also that from the
standpoint of Naturalism this 'ought' can have but a purely
subjective validity—in other words, that it is, from the point
of view of the person who has discovered its purely subjective
character, no 'ought' at all. Undeniably the conclusions to
which the examination of some one part of our nature or our experience might seem to point have constantly to be corrected
in the light which is supplied by other parts of our experience.
And therefore I can neither (with the believers in 'ethical
culture' as a substitute for Religion) pronounce a complete
divorce between Metaphysic and Ethics, and declare that
Ethics have no need of any metaphysical background or presupposition whatever; nor (with Kant or Newman) attempt
to erect a Theology on an exclusively ethical basis [2]. Our belief
about the ultimate nature of things must be founded upon an
examination of our experience as a whole—not upon any one
part of it. It is of the utmost importance to insist that the
facts of the moral consciousness shall be duly taken into consideration by any one who attempts to frame a theory of the
Universe as a whole: but we cannot exclude the possibility that
our examination of the universe as a whole might forbid us
to accept the view of things to which Morality, when looked
at by itself, might seem to point. We are therefore obliged
to ask whether the presuppositions which our Moral Philosophy
requires are such as a sound Metaphysic can concede.

[1] Prof. A. E. Taylor has adopted a purely psychological view of Ethics,
though it would be unfair to describe his attitude towards the Universe in
general as purely 'naturalistic.' He is very decidedly an Idealist.

[2] This attitude of the mind is sometimes described as a recognition of the
'primacy of the Practical Reason.' I should myself be quite prepared to
accept the phrase so long as it is dissociated from Scepticism or Agnosticism
as to the powers of human thought in general, and is held to imply merely
the idea that Practical Reason makes the largest contribution to our knowledge of the ultimate meaning of the world.

A full answer to this question is one which cannot be given in a mere appendix to a treatise on Ethics. I can only direct the reader to the line of thought which he will find developed elsewhere in formal treatises on Metaphysic or the Philosophy of Religion. Amid much disagreement there is a general tendency among those who have really faced the metaphysical problem to recognize the inherent contradictions and unthinkability of matter without mind. An analysis of our knowledge reveals the fact that all that we know is essentially relative to mind. Feeling cannot be except for a consciousness that feels; equally little can an abstract 'idea' or 'content' derived from feeling have any meaning except in reference to a consciousness which at some time or other actually feels. Whatever in the content of our consciousness[1] is not feeling, or a content ultimately derived from feeling[2], is found to consist in relations which are only intelligible to a consciousness which can grasp those relations. The so-called primary qualities of matter—form, magnitude, solidity, and the like—are (as Berkeley was the first to see) just as essentially related to consciousness and unintelligible without it as those 'secondary qualities'—colour, sound, and the like—which the most superficial reflection shows to reside in our mind and not in any supposed thing-in-itself, though Berkeley was doubtless wrong in failing to recognize the importance of the distinction between feeling and thought. The Idealism which begins with Kant has shown that the relations, for instance, which constitute space cannot be analysed into a mere subjective feeling of the individual. It is of the very essence of space that all its parts should be thought of as co-existing and having a relation to each other, whereas our feelings of touch and sight (considered merely as feelings) follow one another in time, and cease to be as soon as they cease to be felt. In the Kantian

[1] Except what is Volition. I put aside, as unimportant for the present purpose, our knowledge of other minds and of what they experience.

[2] e.g. the thought of a blueness which is not at the time being perceived. It is quite true that this general idea, which is neither light blue nor dark blue, but inclusive of both, is something which the eye of man has never seen and never can see, but the judgement that this or that is blue would have no meaning, except as a symbol or representative of the blue sensations which have been or under certain conditions might be actually perceived.

analysis of our knowledge the relational character of space points to its essentially subjective character, in the sense that it exists for mind only, while it is essentially objective in so far as it is not mere feeling but a system of relations and a system of relations valid for all minds whatever [1]. Relations cannot exist in things as they are apart from thought, but only in things as they are for thought; and often the relations are relations between what exists only in or relatively to experience. And the subjective character of space, its essential relativity to consciousness, carries with it the subjective character (in that sense) of all that is in space—in other words, of what is commonly meant by 'the material world.' Moreover, the whole tendency of post-Kantian thought is to show the impossibility of stopping exactly where Kant stopped on the path which leads to pure Idealism. If the world that we know is essentially relative to mind, the suggestion that there may be another world that we do not know and which is not relative to mind becomes as meaningless as the doubt whether after all we know the real nature of this mind which all our experience implies and of that world which we have shown to be essentially the experience of that mind. And yet it is quite clear that the world itself cannot be supposed to exist merely in the individual mind. Thought itself necessarily leads the individual up to the idea of a world which is not merely his world, of a world which exists independently of him, of a world which is common to all minds, but which no human mind knows all at once and in all its completeness. Things exist only for mind, and yet the things that the individual knows he does not create but only discovers. He discovers that they existed before he knew them, before he was born, before (so far as he knows) any mind like his existed upon this or any other planet. And yet, if matter can exist only for mind, there must be some mind *for* which all that is exists : and if the world is one, that mind must

---

[1] Kant—arbitrarily, as later Idealists hold—practically limited this objectivity to all human minds : for, though he always held that the Categories were valid for all intelligences, he held that we are only capable of applying them to matter given under the forms of time and space, which are the forms of human perception only.

3 7

be one Mind.   That the world implies a Mind to think it is the conclusion to which almost all Idealists [1] feel driven by an imperious
necessity of thought.   That that necessity has not always led to
an unequivocal acceptance of that view of the Universe which is
usually called Theism has been due largely to the one-sidedness
with which idealistic thought has fastened upon the cognitive
side of our conscious being to the exclusion of that side of it
which·is revealed in our voluntary action.   Recent Psychology
and recent Metaphysic have alike directed attention to the will
as a no less essential element in our consciousness than thought
and feeling.   If we are justified in inferring a universal Thinker
from the analogy of our own thought, we are surely justified in
inferring a universal Will from the analogy of our own wills,
however fully we may recognize the inadequacy of such terms to
express the different sides or aspects of the One Spirit [2] in which

---

[1] There are a few thinkers (Prof. Bosanquet is perhaps one of them) who seem
to find it possible to accept the idealistic view of things, and yet to suppose
that the only thoughts for which the world exists are the limited minds which
began to be so long after the world began.   Such writers never seem to me to
have made even a serious attempt to meet the difficulties which such a view
involves.   In the system of Dr. McTaggart, with whom the Absolute is simply
the sum of individual minds, its difficulty is to some extent lessened by the
assumption that individual minds are pre-existent as well as immortal, but
still I fail to find in *Studies in the Hegelian Cosmology*, or in anything which
Dr. McTaggart has written, a real answer to the question *for what mind* the
world (which as Idealists we must admit to exist only for some mind)
really exists.   To insist on the timelessness of the Absolute does not help
us, since (according to him) the Absolute as such is not self-conscious, but
only the individual minds which are differentiations of the Absolute, and
such individual minds, each or any of them or all of them together, cannot
reasonably be regarded as omniscient.   The idea of a Mind which is simultaneously omniscient in its timeless or universal aspect and limited in
the knowledge possessed by its differentiations in time is one which I cannot
grasp or think it reasonable to postulate.   In his more recent *Some Dogmas
of Religion* Dr. McTaggart has attempted to meet my difficulty in a somewhat different way.   I may refer to my review of this work in *Mind* (N. S.,
Vol. XV, No. 60) as an apology for not having dealt in this place with a system
which, though to my mind involving far more difficulties and improbabilities
than Theism, seems to me the only non-theistic system which it is difficult
to meet with an absolutely conclusive metaphysical refutation.

[2] I should equally strongly assert the necessity for admitting the existence
in God of feeling, without which, indeed, the idea of Will is unintelligible,
but the argument does not require that I should here insist upon this

we must recognize the ultimate cause or ground of the world's existence and of all the other spirits which (with Him) form the totality of real Being in the Universe.

And this line of thought is supported by another to which I can now only barely allude—the argument which (accepting from Hume the position that we can discern no such thing as Causality in external nature) refuses to accept the denial that in our own minds we are immediately conscious of exercising Causality, and sees in will the only actual realization of that causal idea which is as essential a category of our thought as the idea of Substance or the idea of Quantity. It is a self-evident axiom of our thought that everything which begins to be must have a cause. The only cause that we immediately know of is the self. If the events of the Universe are not caused by myself or by any human or other self of similarly limited capacity, it is reasonable to infer that they are caused by some other spiritual being or beings, and the order and consistency which we discover in Nature is a reason for supposing that the cause of natural events is not many such beings but one Being. The idealistic argument and the argument from Causality thus support one another: both lead to the conclusion that the natural Universe exists only in and for a mind which is both Thought and Will [1].

This bare sketch of the argument on which theistic Metaphysicians rely for the proof of their idea of God will not of course be sufficient to explain it to those to whom it has pre-

point. I may add that I quite recognize the impossibility of supposing that Thought, Feeling, and Will stand side by side with one another and occupy exactly the same relation to one another in God as they do in us, but each of these aspects of Experience—which even presuppose one another—has as good a right as the others to be taken as revealing aspects of the Divine experience.

[1] I have explained and defended the idealistic Theism here assumed in a volume of Essays ('by six Oxford Tutors') entitled *Contentio Veritatis* (1902) and in an Essay on the 'Personality of God' in *Personal Idealism* (edited by Mr. H. Sturt, 1902), but I am, of course, aware that these two Essays taken together form a very inadequate sketch of a religious Philosophy. I may refer to Prof. James Ward's *Naturalism and Agnosticism* and Prof. Pfleiderer's *Philosophy of Religion* for a fuller development of the line of thought here suggested.

viously been unfamiliar. Still less will it remove the objections of
those by whom it has been considered and rejected. These, few
sentences must be regarded merely as a personal confession
of faith—as a bare statement of the grounds by which the
present writer is led to the belief that the view of the Universe
which our moral consciousness demands is also the view to which
we are led by an examination of all other parts of our experience—in short, that the postulates of Ethics are identical with
the conclusions of Metaphysic. The fact that our moral consciousness demands the idea of God as the source of our own
moral ideas and the justification of their objective validity lends
additional and independent support to these conclusions.

VII

Though our idea of God cannot be built up on the basis of the
moral consciousness taken by itself, the moral consciousness does
contribute one most important element to that idea. That the
Universe has its ultimate ground in a Spirit who must be thought
of as Will, Reason, and Feeling[1], is a view which a rational
Ethic presupposes, but which it cannot by itself be held to
establish. It is established, I believe, by metaphysical considerations. But a purely metaphysical analysis (so long as it excludes
from its purview the data supplied by the moral consciousness)
can tell us nothing further about the nature or purposes of that
Spirit. That the Universe has a purpose is, indeed, implied in
the assertion that it is the work of Reason. The mere analysis
of the causal idea may lead us to the belief that it must have an end.
No conception of Causality will satisfy that demand for a cause
or 'sufficient reason' set up by Reason, in its attempt to explain the
world, which does not include final Causality. Even in setting up
the bare, abstract idea of a final cause Reason has already, indeed,

---

[1] To discuss in what way these three activities are related to each other
in God is no part of my present task, though after all little could be said
except that we do not and cannot know. I fully accept Mr. Bradley's
demonstration that we cannot think of God's thought as consisting in the
clumsy processes of abstraction and inference from immediate feeling which
are involved in human knowledge. But the divine experience must include
elements analogous to those which present themselves in our experience in
these three distinguishable ways.

gone beyond the region of merely speculative activity, and borrowed a concept from the moral consciousness—an important warning against the attempt to erect sharp barriers between the speculative and the ethical activity of the one spiritual self. For the idea of a final cause implies the distinction between ends and means, and that distinction—the distinction between that which is brought into being for the sake of something else and that which we value and seek to produce for its own sake—is entirely unintelligible apart from that idea of Value or Worth which we have seen to be the root-idea of the moral consciousness. The distinction between means and end lies not in the fact that the former precede the latter, but in the fact that the former are valued for the sake of the latter. Even therefore the proposition that the world has a purpose is one at which the purely speculative reason is incompetent to arrive in entire abstraction from the Practical Reason. It is one for which Logic or Metaphysic must be held indebted to Moral Philosophy, or rather it can only be arrived at by that wider Metaphysic which includes the study of the moral nature of man in its due relation to the other sides of the one Reality. But if, in the ordinary sense of the words, the considerations which lead us to the idea that the world has an end are rather logical and metaphysical than ethical, it is certain that, apart from the facts of the moral consciousness, it could say nothing whatever as to the nature of that end, or as to the character of the Being whose end it is. Hence speculative · Reason, if it attempts to answer that problem at all, must borrow not merely from the form but from the content of the moral consciousness.

Is such a borrowing justifiable ? It has been assumed throughout this chapter that it is, and we have already added on the strength of it the postulate of Immortality to those of self and God. But it is of great importance to define the exact sense in which we are prepared to say, not only that the world has a purpose, but that we know what that purpose is. It is right to insist (as has been done by Von Hartmann) that the mere idea that the world has a purpose is of infinite value for Ethics, even if we did not regard our moral ideal as disclosing the nature of that purpose. For, if the world has a purpose at all, the ideal which presents itself to us as a necessity of thought must be in some way included in the purpose. The realization of our ideals may not be the ultimate end of the Universe, but it must at least be a means to that end, and it would be difficult to suppose that it was *merely* a means, and not one of those means which (like most of the means which we employ in human life) are also a part of the end. And this would be enough to give an objective significance and validity to our judgements of value which they could not possess upon a non-teleological view of the Universe. But the suggestion that what presents itself as a necessity of ethical thought may nevertheless turn out to contain no revelation as to the ultimate nature of things seems to me to be as entirely gratuitous and unreasonable as any other kind of ultimate scepticism. To infer from the existence of our own moral consciousness the existence of a good-in-itself or good from the point of view of the Universe, and then to say that our ideas of good tell us nothing about that good-in-itself, seems just as unreasonable as it would be to declare that the laws of Mathematics are valid only relatively to us, that they convey to us a mere knowledge of phenomena which may turn out to be a mere self-consistent system of error containing no information as to the real nature of the Universe or 'things-in-themselves.' It is suggested in many quarters[1] that, while the category of good is one which is valid for God as well as for man, the whole content of that category as it works in us might turn out to be a complete illusion, and that consequently no one of our moral judgements, even the most fundamental, can be supposed to be valid for all intelligences and therefore for God. That seems to be very like arguing that the category of Causality or of Quantity may, indeed, be regarded as unconditionally valid for all intelligences, but that no single concrete conclusion of Mathematics or Physical Science can reasonably be supposed to represent anything but a way of thinking which is imposed upon ourselves by the constitution of human nature, but which contains no information at all as to the real nature of things or the real content of the Mind which expresses itself in Nature.

[1] A more detailed criticism of the writers in question will be found in the next chapter.

The ethical scepticism of the present day seems to be repeating all the mistakes of the Kantian ' Phenomenalism '—the very side of the Kantian Philosophy which, in other departments of thought, modern Metaphysicians are most generally agreed to give up. We have every bit as much right to assume that the conclusions to which we are led by the proper use of our ethical faculty are valid for God and for all intelligences as we have for assuming that the laws of pure Mathematics and the calculations which are based upon those laws must be no mere local prejudice of a particular race of human beings who have flourished during a ' brief and transitory episode in the life of one of the meanest of the planets [1],' but part of the eternal nature of things. Our Moral Reason is the same Reason as that which gives us the laws of thought, and the concrete results which flow from them, though a different side or aspect of that Reason. And we have every right to say that the judgements derived from both sides or activities of our Reason must be equally a revelation of that objective truth which is ultimately the thought of God.

Of course there is all the difference in the world between the assertion that in principle our moral faculty is an organ of truth and contains a revelation of Reality and the assertion that infallibility may be claimed for any particular moral judgement of any particular person. We may make mistakes in Morality just as we may make mistakes in Science or even in pure Mathematics. I trust I have already insisted sufficiently upon this distinction. In so constantly comparing the judgement of Morality to those of Mathematics, I do not mean to imply that the possibilities of error are in practice as small in the one case as in the other. It may be admitted at once that these possibilities are very much greater in the case of Ethics.

I will not ask at the present moment in what amount of uncertainty or inadequacy the truths of Physical Science may be involved by the speculative principle that to know anything thoroughly you must know all its relations and therefore must know the Universe as a whole. Mathematical truth is of so abstract a character, the abstraction so complete, and the limitation which that abstraction places to the application of its

---

[1] Balfour, *The Foundations of Belief*, ed. ii, p. 33.

results so clearly discernible that there seems no reason for supposing that the fullest knowledge would ever reveal any actual error in conclusions arrived at by what human Reason recognizes as the valid use of the Categories and self-evident principles of Mathematics. They avowedly express only one particular aspect or side of Reality ; but there is no reason to suspect that this one-sidedness involves positive error. They are one-sided, but the one-sidedness does not involve actual falsity just because the limits within which the truth holds good are so well understood. In Physics the liability to error is greater, both because of the imperfection of the experience on which the conclusions rest, and because by the mind of a particular enquirer at a certain stage or level of scientific development the one-sidedness and abstractness of the particular department of truth with which each special Science is concerned are not so sure to be remembered, allowed for, and corrected. But even here the errors arising from incomplete knowledge are errors which in the progress of knowledge human thought may hope to correct. The admission of these possibilities of error does not involve an indictment against human Reason as such, still less Mr. Bradley's paradox that all thought, just because it is thought, is necessarily false to an unknown and unknowable extent [1].

Absolute certainty and completeness of knowledge is, no doubt, when you have got beyond the most abstract truths of Mathematics, unattainable enough ; but it is a goal to which we are continually approximating, and to which we may hope to approximate more and more nearly as we reach conclusions of the most general character, and conclusions which rest upon the largest mass of experience. The possibility of inadequacy, and such error as may be involved in inadequacy, does not justify the position that Science itself possesses a merely relative or subjective or human or phenomenal validity. Now, when we turn to Morality, we must acknowledge this peculiarity of ethical truth, that in an exceptional degree ignorance of the whole may involve mistake in any particular judgement. To

---

[1] Of course I am omitting here the explanations and reservations by which the paradox is qualified.

claim absolute certainty and absolute adequacy for a judgement
as to what a man ought to do in any given collocation of
circumstances, it would be necessary for the individual to have
a complete knowledge of all that is contained in the moral ideal
as well as a complete knowledge of all those facts and laws
which may possibly affect the suitability of the means adopted
to promote that ideal on any particular occasion. He would
have to know that the particular end which he is now aiming
at is a part or element of the ideal end, that it is a more
important part or element or representative of the ideal end
than any other particular object at which in the given circumstance he might aim, and also that the particular means that
he adopts are the best adapted to attain that end. I need
not insist on the impossibility of attaining in practice any such
certainty. Our judgement as to the relation of means to ends
may always be mistaken; our judgements as to the value of any
particular element in that end, and still more as to its relative
value as compared with other elements, may be erroneous and
one-sided.

And there are many other circumstances which tend to make
impossible in Ethics the kind of certainty and adequacy which
is practically attainable in the region of pure Mathematics or
even of the concrete Physical Sciences — the dependence of moral
judgement upon the emotional, aesthetic, and other capacities
of the individual pronouncing them; the difficulty of explaining
and communicating to others the results of any one individual's
moral experience; the difficulty of distinguishing between real
judgements of our Reason and the dictates of passion or impulse;
the absence (when we go beyond certain very broad generalities)
of even an approximate consensus, and the like. But all these
admissions throw no doubt upon the validity of our moral
thought as such, and supply no ground for the suggestion
that from the point of view of God or the Universe our existing
moral code might turn out to be precisely the contradictory of
the true. It is impossible to define the limits of the possible
discrepancy between our moral judgements and the perfect
moral ideal as it exists in the mind of God. We can only
say that in proportion as ethical truth becomes more and more

general, more and more universally admitted by developed minds, more and more internally consistent and coherent, we approach the same kind of practical certainty which we justifiably claim for the main conclusions of Science or History. The judgement that there is a good is a necessity of thought as much as the principle that for whatever happens in the Universe there must be a cause, though there are individuals who have denied both truths. That this good is the ultimate aim of the Universe is a proposition which rests upon the same kind of evidence as the belief that the world and our knowledge of it can only be explained by the existence of a universal Spirit in whom are united Thought, Will, and Feeling. When we come to the detailed filling up of this formal idea of Good, and still more to the question of the means to be taken to realize that good, there is room for much difference in the degree of certainty and adequacy which we ascribe to our judgements. When I pronounce that the choice of a particular candidate at an election will promote the true, ultimate end of the Universe, I may myself see many grounds for doubt and hesitation even at the moment that I make up my mind that it is my duty to vote for him. And I know that many sensible and virtuous persons will vote for his opponent. It is extremely probable therefore that I may be mistaken. That my judgement as to the exact degree of relative importance which we should in our own lives or in that of the community assign to the promotion of Art and to the prevention of physical suffering corresponds exactly with the degree of relative importance which a perfect moral intelligence would assign to them is no doubt extremely improbable, though I may hope that the limits of probable error may be relatively small. But when we come to such extremely general propositions as that pleasures, or some pleasures, are better than pain, or that love is better than hatred, then we may claim for such judgements exactly the same practical certainty as we do for the law of gravitation or for the proposition that an event called the Norman Conquest actually occurred. There may no doubt be a sense in which all scientific knowledge may be regarded as abstract, and therefore inadequate to the reality; in that sense moral ideals may be imperfect and 'abstract,' but to say that in the Absolute our judgement that cruelty and pain are bad must be turned into the judgement that they are very good would be like saying that in or for the Absolute the denial of universal gravitation is as true as its affirmation.

Doubtless the judgements of a particular individual as to a particular moral question may be mistaken and his whole ideal narrow and one-sided. Doubtless the highest ideal that is at this moment entertained by the most perfect ethical intelligence living on this planet represents but a part of the whole aim and plan at which the Universe is aiming; but we have every reason for asserting, and no reason at all for doubting, that the moral ideal which is summed up in Humanity's highest ideal of universal Love, and in a certain estimate of the relative values to be assigned to the various goods which this Love will promote, does represent a revelation, ever growing and developing, of the ideal which is present to the mind of God and towards which therefore the Universe is directed.

VIII

To consider all the difficulties, real or imaginary, which may be found in the view of ultimate Reality which is here presupposed, would lead us further into the province of Metaphysic and religious Philosophy than lies within the scope of this work, but there is one difficulty so obvious and so fundamental that it seems scarcely honest to pass it over without indicating the general lines on which in a metaphysical treatise I should attempt to deal with it. If the world is rational, how (it will be asked) can we account for the presence of so much which our moral consciousness pronounces to be evil, and which, if our view of the relation between the human consciousness and the divine be right, we may suppose to be evil also for the mind of God?

To attempt to show empirically the necessity of evil in the world is a task which I for one have not the smallest inclination to attempt. It is true that we can show without difficulty how some of what we call evil in this world, as it is actually constituted, is the condition of the good. We can see that much good implies a struggle against both moral and physical evil; and that that dependence of one individual upon another out of which arise all the higher moral or social qualities of man implies also the possibility of constant injury and injustice, and the like. Goodness is developed by opposition ; happiness, as we know it, depends on the satisfaction of wants which imply imperfection and, in their intenser form, positive pain, and so on. But it is not so much the existence as the nature and quantity and distribution of evil in the world that constitute the difficulty So much evil seems wholly unnecessary : so much smaller a measure of it in quantity and quality would have sufficed, so far as we can see, to satisfy these necessities. A different distribution of it would seem far more conducive to the highest welfare of humanity than the present distribution of it. Even to attempt to show that there is more good than evil in the world—whether the good be understood in some higher ethical or in the purely hedonistic sense—would be a very bold undertaking. If we were to confine ourselves to empirical evidence alone, I confess that I should see very little to lead us to the conclusion that the world was even good ' on the whole,' or that it had any good end or object in the future. From this point of view the complaints of the more moderate Pessimists only seem to me exaggerated. It is not when they insist on the existence of evil in the world or even on its amount, but when they insist on the non-existence of good, the impossibility of happiness even for some, the worthlessness and vanity of the best that this world affords, that their diatribes seem to represent merely the idiosyncrasies or circumstances of the particular writer. It is only the evidence of the moral consciousness, taken in connexion with the idealistic or theistic argument as a whole, that forces us to believe that the world must have an end, that that end is good, and that the good is in principle the same good of which, in the moral judgements of the developed moral nature, we have a doubtless inadequate but not fundamentally misleading revelation. On this supposition whatever evil exists in the world must be supposed to exist because it is a necessary means to the greatest good that the nature of things makes possible.

IX

But, it will be said, in thus talking about the best possible, in justifying the world's existence because it is good on the whole, in speaking of evil as the condition of good, are we not limiting God ?   I answer: 'If Omnipotence is to be understood as ability to do anything that we choose to fancy, I do not assert God's Omnipotence.'   I am content to say with sober divines like Bishop Butler that there may be some things which, with adequate knowledge, we should see to be as impossible as that God should change the past.   And if it be urged that the existence of conditions limiting the possibilities of the divine Will is inconsistent with the idea of a God who is infinite, I answer that neither Religion nor Morality nor, again, reasonable Philosophy has any interest in maintaining the infiniteness of God in the sense in which a certain tradition of the schools is accustomed to assert it [1].   The limitation must not be conceived of as a limitation imposed by the existence of some other 'being'—some other spirit or a 'matter' with definite properties and an intractable nature of its own.   The suggestion that a limit necessarily springs from without is due to that ever-present source of metaphysical error, the abuse of spatial metaphor.   The limitations must be conceived of as part of the ultimate nature of things.   All that really exists must have some limits to its existence ; space and time are unlimited or infinite just because they are not real existences.   And the ultimate nature of things means, for the Idealist, the nature of God.   All that we are concerned with from the ethical point of view is that God should be regarded as willing a Universe that is the best that seems possible to a Mind to whom all the possibilities of

[1] I am pleased to read in a work by a learned Theologian of unimpeachable orthodoxy, the Dean of Christ Church: 'This word [Infinite] is purely negative in its associations ; it means literally nothing but the absence of all limits.   And there is nothing in it to show that it does not include the absence of all positive existence.   Positive existence involves limitations of a certain kind ; it is impossible to imagine a being who has not some definite character, i. e. who is not also necessarily without certain other definite characters, and if all positive characteristics are equally derogatory to an Infinite Being, there is nothing for it but to deny His existence' Strong, *Manual of Theology* (1892), p. 203).

things are known, and who wills the existence of all that is actual because he knows it to be best.

I cannot here discuss all the objections which have been urged against the idea of possibilities which cannot be realized. Putting aside for the moment the question of human Free-will (which I reserve for later treatment), I should admit that this possibility is merely a possibility when looked upon from the point of view of limited, human knowledge. To perfect knowledge nothing could seem possible except that which is or will be actual.

Doubtless a God so conceived is not the traditional Infinite or Absolute of Philosophy. The Absolute is the Being which alone truly is and of which all other beings may be treated as attributes or predicates: our consciousness cannot intelligibly be treated as the mere attribute or predicate of another consciousness. The Infinite is that Being besides which and beyond which no being exists: our consciousness cannot intelligibly be treated as included in or a part of a divine consciousness, though undoubtedly there is a totality of Being in which both are comprehended. Even a single moment of consciousness—whether the most evanescent sensation of an amoeba or a moment of highest insight in the soul of Plato—possesses a certain uniqueness, and is no *mere* predicate or adjective of something else, though it is also an element in, and so far supplies a predicate of, a larger being[1]. Still less can a permanent and conscious self, combining together and relating to one another a succession of such unique experiences, be treated as the same thing as another more comprehensive consciousness, no matter how well the content of the lesser consciousness is known to, or 'penetrated' by, the greater. The notion that God includes in Himself all the individual selves of the Universe seems to have arisen chiefly from a forgetfulness of the essential difference between our knowledge of a thing and our knowledge of other selves. A thing is simply what it is for the mind that knows it; it exists for other, not for itself ; what it is for the experience of a mind is therefore its total being. The essential characteristic of a conscious self is that it exists not for others only, but for

---

[1] That is, in the sense in which we may speak of that which is included in a whole as qualifying that whole.

itself. Its true being is not merely what it is for another mind that knows it, but what it is for itself. Uniqueness belongs to the very essence of consciousness. The 'content' of the consciousness may be shared by another consciousness, may be common to many minds; but this is only because a 'content' consists of abstract universal qualities taken apart from the being whose experience they describe. The content is 'common' to many minds just because in speaking of it we have made abstraction of the uniqueness which belonged to the experience when it was living, present, conscious experience, not yet reduced to abstract universals by the analytic work of thought. Two minds may experience, as we say, the 'same' sensation because, in calling the sensation the same, we have made abstraction of the fact that two people have experienced it. The blueness of which I think is a universal experienced by many minds; blueness as it is actually felt belongs only to the mind that feels it. Even the blueness that I think is the same with what another mind thinks only in respect of its content; the fact remains that my thinking of it and the thinking of it by my neighbour, as pieces of conscious experience, are different. Thoughts as abstract contents are common to many minds; thinking as a psychological phenomenon is always peculiar to one mind. But the Reality of the world is not abstract content, but living experience. Further discussion on this question must be reserved for other occasions. I can only here indicate the view that one mind or conscious experience cannot form a part of another mind.

The Absolute cannot be identified with God, so long as God is thought of as a self-conscious Being. The Absolute must include God and all other consciousnesses, not as isolated and unrelated beings, but as intimately related (in whatever way) to Him and to one another and as forming with Him a system or Unity. And, in so far as God is not any of these spirits (when once they have come into being), however they may be ultimately related to Him, He is not, in the most obvious sense of the word, infinite. We may, if we like, call God infinite in the sense that there is no other Being but what proceeds ultimately from His will and has its source or ground in Him;

and this seems to be all that is meant by many of those who are attached to the term ; but the term 'infinite' would seem more properly to belong to that Absolute which includes God and other spirits. It may even be doubted whether it is well to apply the term infinite to anything but space and time (which are not real beings), and whether it is possible to apply it to anything that has real being without being more or less misled in our interpretation of the term by the analogy of space and time. There must be a definite amount of Being in the world [1]. Whether we say that from some point of view transcending time there is eternally a definite amount which can be neither increased nor diminished, or whether we content ourselves with maintaining that at any one moment there is a definite amount of Being in the world, will depend upon the view we take of that most difficult of all metaphysical problems—the ultimate nature of time [2]. Avoiding any attempt to deal in a summary way with that profound question, I will only say that in my view metaphysical and ethical considerations alike require us to recognize a real distinction between God and the lesser spirits who derive their being from Him, yet remain in intimate relation to and dependence upon Him, and with Him make up the totality of real Being in the world. If we must use a word which might well be dispensed with, God and the spirits are the Absolute— not God alone. Together they form a Unity, but that Unity is not the unity of self-consciousness ; nor can it, without serious danger of misunderstanding, be thought of as even analogous

[1] We might of course say that the Absolute is infinite in so far as time and space form aspects of its being. It will be observed that I do not here assert that God is finite, for experience shows that (in spite of all protests and explanations) it is impossible to use the term without being supposed by careless or prejudiced critics to imply the idea that God is limited by a plurality of independent, unoriginated, and isolated centres of consciousness, and provoking pleasantries about polytheism and the like.

[2] The notion that the total amount of 'Being' in the world cannot be increased seems to arise either (1) from a mere misapplication of the physical doctrine of the indestructibility of *Matter*, or (2) from taking 'Being' to mean not consciousness but the ultimate ground of consciousness. That the amount of 'consciousness' or 'conscious being' in the Universe is increased or diminished at different times is a truth which we prove every time we go to sleep.

to that personal unity which is characteristic of consciousness in the highest form in which we know it.

I cannot but suspect that those who insist that all minds are ultimately one with each other and with the divine mind are partly under the influence of a confusion between 'consciousness' and 'mind' understood in some sense in which it is regarded not as equivalent to consciousness or the conscious, but as the ultimate ground or basis of consciousness. That a certain unity of 'substance' or 'essence' may be ascribed to all minds in the Universe is an intelligible proposition. And there is no harm in such language if we can only keep the idea of Substance free from spacial and naturalistic associations, and also interpret it in such a way as not to exclude the idea of 'activity' or 'power' or 'will.' It is no doubt quite true that every consciousness in the Universe at every moment of its existence, while it may be looked upon as itself power or will, must also be looked upon as an effect or manifestation of the single Will to which all things and all spirits owe their being, though *qua* consciousness it is distinct from that and every other consciousness. From this point of view the 'unity of substance' doctrine expresses only what the old Theology expressed in holding that the world (including souls) was upheld by a continuous act of divine conservation.

The ultimate Being, we may say, is One—a single Power, if we like we may even say a single Being, which is manifested in a plurality of consciousnesses, one consciousness which is omniscient and eternal, and many consciousnesses which are of limited knowledge, which have a beginning and some of which, it is possible or probable, have an end. We may, if we like, regard all the separate 'centres of consciousness' as 'manifestations' of a single Being; but if so, we must distinctly remember, if we are Idealists and refuse to regard as ultimately real any being which is not conscious, that this 'Being' has no existence except in the separate centres. God may be conceived of as the cause or source of all the centres except Himself, and may know them through and through; but to deny that *qua* consciousness He is distinguishable from those other centres of consciousness represents a line of thought which, when

3 8

thoroughly followed out, must end (as historically it always does end) *either* in the denial of all reality, permanence, independence, or personality to the individual souls and the reduction of all individuality to a mere delusive appearance, *or* to a conception of God which no longer includes the idea of self-consciousness at all. And both ideas—God and the self—are necessary to Morality and to any Religion that is to be consistent with the demands of our moral consciousness.

The ethical importance of this view of the relation between God and individual souls, which it is impossible here further to develope or to defend, lies in the following considerations:

(*a*) Only where a real distinction can be recognized between the divine Mind and the individual minds to which it has given being can we attribute good or bad acts to the individual man without attributing them *in the same sense and degree* to God. Whether in any more ultimate sense God may or may not be regarded as the cause of our good and bad actions is a question which I reserve for separate treatment. I only insist here that there must be a real meaning in regarding them as acts of the individual.

(*b*) Only if it is recognized that our moral judgements are expressive of the real nature of things, and that therefore the evil of the world is not evil merely from our point of view, is there an intelligible meaning in ascribing to God the character which our moral consciousness recognizes as good. The ethical necessity of this conception has already been dealt with.

(*c*) Only where it is recognized that God's action, though directed to the best that is possible, is limited by those eternal necessities which are part of his own eternal nature, is it possible to combine the assertion of his moral perfection with the recognition of real objective validity in those judgements of our moral consciousness which pronounce many things in the world to be intrinsically evil, however much they may ultimately be conducive to a higher good. Only when this is admitted, does it become possible to acknowledge that a rightly directed human action is conducive to the true objective good of the Universe. If it be supposed that bad actions, just in proportion as they are actually committed, tend to the good of the Universe as much as good ones, we immediately remove all motive for abstaining from any so-called bad act to which we may be inclined. On such a hypothesis the fact that the bad act occurs is a sufficient proof that a good act in the like place would have retarded the true end of the Universe. On this view there is no answer to the suggestion that it were well to ' continue in sin that grace may abound.' On our view the bad may be the necessary means to a greater good, but it remains bad all the same. The Universe without that act (had its absence been possible or in accordance with the actual nature of the world) would have been better still. The whole value of Metaphysic or Theology to Ethics lies in its allowing us to ascribe an objective significance to the moral law. And this objective significance is destroyed the moment it is admitted that what our moral Reason pronounces, and rightly pronounces, to be bad may nevertheless from the point of view of a higher and completer view be very good. A Metaphysic that is optimistic in this sense is as fruitful a source of acute demoralization as the Theology which makes moral distinctions depend upon the arbitrary will of God[1]. In certain of their manifestations the two forms of thought tend to become absolutely indistinguishable. Once let it be admitted that a bad act can under no conceivable circumstances really take anything away from the true good of the Universe or be really opposed to the ultimate aim of the Spirit to which the Universe owes its being, and Morality, as it presents itself to the unsophisticated moral consciousness, exists no more[2]. Hence to the three postulates

---

[1] I confess I feel strongly tempted to adopt the words of Schopenhauer : ' I cannot here avoid the statement that, to me, *optimism*, when it is not merely the thoughtless talk of such as harbour nothing but words under their low foreheads, appears not merely as an absurd, but also as a really *wicked* way of thinking, as a bitter mockery of the unspeakable suffering of humanity' (*The World as Will and Idea*, Eng. Trans., I. 420). Of course Optimism must here be understood to mean the belief that the world and everything in it are perfectly good—not the creed that the world on the whole is tending towards the good.

[2] The point of view against which I protest is forcibly expressed by Prof. Taylor: ' Hence for Religion the classification of acts and men as "good " and " bad " must appear unsatisfactory and superficial. For, on the one hand, ultimately all acts and all characters are good as fulfilling,

of Ethics which I have already enumerated I propose to add
a fourth—the negation of Optimism, the assertion that not
everything in the Universe is very good, and that the distinction
between good and evil belongs to the real nature of things and
not merely to appearance.

X

I am quite aware how incomplete such a treatment of the
relation between Metaphysics and Ethics as the present must be in
the absence of a complete discussion of those logical and metaphysical questions as to the relation of knowledge to Reality
which lie at the root of the whole matter.   On that momentous
question I will only make one remark.   That all our human knowledge is inadequate to express the true nature of the ultimate
Reality will be universally admitted by Metaphysicians of almost

each in its own place, the perfect world system, and on the other every act
and every character is bad as failing to realise the perfect world-system in
more than an infinitesimal fragment of its concrete fullness.   Religion thus
knows nothing of merit and demerit.   Instead of the customary classification
of men as on the one hand respectable and good, and on the other hand as
disreputable and bad, it substitutes a double estimate according to which, on
the one hand, the outcast and the sinner are already, as members of the
perfect world order, really perfect *if they only had the faith to perceive it*, and
on the other all men alike—the man of rigid virtue and strict habits no less
than the reprobate—are equally condemned and equally guilty before God'
(*The Problem of Conduct*, pp. 473, 474).   But why the qualification I have
italicized?   On the premisses they must be as good whether they have faith
to perceive it or not; and some (perhaps fortunately) have not this faith.
Optimism always breaks down somewhere.   If Professor Taylor means that
the world is equally perfect whether they perceive it or not, he has omitted
to show that they are likely to be the better if they do perceive it, and if he
admits that they are not, he has failed to point out any ultimate justification
for the relative authority (as regards human beings) which he himself claims
for Morality.   If Religion (as Professor Taylor assumes) makes men think
a bad act to be really (if actually committed) equally conducive to the true
end of the Universe with a good one, and so more likely to commit bad acts,
what right have men (on whom human Morality is, by his own admission,
binding) to be religious?

It is instructive to notice that Dr. McTaggart has now retracted his
former view as to the perfection of the Universe.   To any reader who is
unsatisfied by this slight and fragmentary treatment of the question I may
commend Dr. McTaggart's chapter on 'God as Omnipotent' in *Some Dogmas
of Religion*.   As to Professor Taylor's change of view, see below, p. 285.

all schools. The only serious question must be as to the kind and the degree of the inadequacy, and as to the answer that is given to the enquiry how far it is possible to arrive at any clearer and more adequate knowledge of Reality by denying and seeking to 'transcend,' as the phrase is, distinctions which are admittedly inherent in the very nature and constitution of human thought. That question will be further dealt with in the following chapter, but meanwhile there is one particular source of imperfection in our knowledge to which a momentary reference must be made. It will, doubtless, be contended that my argument has assumed the absolute validity of our ideas of Time. Here, too, the real problem is as to the amount and kind of inadequacy which is involved in this particular condition of human thought. What I should contend, if I had the opportunity, would be that our time-distinctions must express, however inadequately, the true nature of Reality, and that the attempt to think of Reality as out of time or timeless is certain to lead us further astray from the truth than the assertion that time-distinctions are valid, though we cannot tell in what way they present themselves to God or how far they express the full truth about Reality as a whole. If the position that Reality is out of time makes it impossible to ascribe objective validity to our judgements of value, compels us to distort and virtually contradict the ethical part of our thought, and forbids us to give its proper weight to that side of our nature in our speculative construction of ultimate Reality, that is one further objection to such theories. The doctrine of a timeless Reality makes the world's history unmeaning and all human effort vain. The Buddhists, whose Creed is often patronized by our modern believers in a timeless Absolute, at least have the merit of admitting that corollary of their system, however much inconsistency and contradiction there may be in the anti-social ascetic's effort to escape from effort. The Western who uses this language about the vanity of all that is temporal neither believes it nor acts as if he believed it. Time and its distinctions, as we know them, may not express the whole truth about the Universe and the ultimate spiritual ground of it, but at least they must express more of it than a to us meaningless negation like timelessness.

If there be any meaning in the idea of transcending time-distinctions, that meaning must be something other than that of merely negating and abolishing them, and it is only on the assumption that from the point of view of absolute knowledge time-distinctions are simply negated and abolished that the temporal character of our moral thinking can be used as an argument for denying its objective validity and refusing to admit the postulates which that objective validity carries with it.

NOTE ON THE 'TIMELESS SELF'

So much prominence has been given to the doctrine of the 'timeless self' in the writings of Green and his disciples that it seems hardly possible to pass over the matter altogether, though a full discussion of it does not enter into the plan of this work.   The doctrine seems to me to be mainly traceable to the following misconceptions and confusions :

(1) The necessity, for knowledge, of a permanent self, persisting through change, is often treated as proving what is quite a different thing – a self which is out of time altogether.

(2) The doctrine is founded upon the fact that for two events, past and present, to enter into and become the basis of knowledge, they must be compared together, and to be compared they must both in a sense be 'present' to the mind which compares them.   But this presence is a presence *in idea*: to make the reality of a *past* event consist in its presence to my mind *now* would involve a worse extravagance than can be attributed to any sort of 'subjective Idealism' that has ever been explicitly maintained.   It is no doubt real as an 'idea in my head,' and considered as an 'idea in my head' it has its own time, the present, which is different from the time in which the event which I think really occurred.   There is, no doubt, in the judgement a reference to reality – to the real event, but the real event is not my judgement about it or any present experience of mine.   From this point of view the doctrine represents a monstrous distortion of the ultimate fact that a being who is now in one time can know events which were in another time.   This may or may not be difficult or unintelligible or mysterious, but it is not made more intelligible by using language which plainly distorts the facts.   I did not exist in the eighteenth century because I can know events which occurred at that period, nor am I now in the nineteenth century because some of my personal experience occurred in that century.

(3) Another way in which the idea of a 'timeless self' seems to be arrived at is by a mistaken inference from the discovery that the relations

between facts are themselves not in time at all. The fact that A occurred after B is not a fact which can be said to be in A's time or B's time or in both together. The relation of posteriority is out of time altogether. But then it is forgotten that this relation of A to B taken apart from A and B themselves is not a reality at all but a mere abstraction. Considered as knowledge it is of course out of time, but all knowledge implies abstraction. Knowledge is not real apart from the thing known on the one hand or the knowing mind on the other. Abstract knowledge is out of time, just because we have made abstraction both of the time in which the knower is and of the time in which the events known occurred, and think of the knowledge apart in abstraction from its presence to any particular knower. 'The system of relations,' the interconnected judgements which make up Science are no doubt out of time when, and in so far as, we make abstraction both of the knower and of the events related. But the abstract system of relations, when taken apart from the events related, is not the actual events, and the events related are in time. This confusion leads up to that view of the Universe which identifies the real world with a 'system of relations,' supposed to be real without anything to relate, with a world timeless, changeless, static, existing for thought only and consisting of nothing but thought—according to some, of thought without even a thinker. Such a mode of thinking seems to culminate in the doctrine that the Universe is nothing but a 'continuous judgement.'

(4) The system of categories which the self, in Kantian language, imposes upon the data of sense, and which are supposed to be derived from the Ego, has been confused—not by Kant but by Green and others—with the self by which these categories are, in the Kantian system, imposed upon the matter of our knowledge. This system of categories, abstracted from the matter which is known by means of them and from the concrete thought in which they are manifested, is no doubt out of relation to time: but then this system of thought-relations is still less capable of identification with Reality than the concrete judgements in which those categories are used. The real self certainly knows abstract *truths* which are abstractions and therefore out of time, and events which are in other times ; but it is itself born at a certain time and may (so far as actual experience goes) be out of existence at another, while every moment of its thought or volition is in some time or other.

(5) If it be said that the 'self' which is present in knowledge is not the individual but the universal self, I should reply (a) that God cannot, any more than the individual self, be identified with a system of abstract categories, and (b) that the self with which we are concerned in Morality must be the individual, and not the universal, self-consciousness. The fact that God is 'out of time,' if it be a fact, cannot be used as an argument against considering pleasure as any part of human good on the ground that it cannot satisfy a 'timeless self.' The self which desires and wills and is satisfied in Morality is assuredly the individual self, and that is a self which has a beginning and which might (so far as any merely metaphysical consideration goes) be supposed to have an end.

The question whether in any sense God is 'out of time' or 'above time' is a far more difficult problem. And, as it is not a matter of any directly ethical import, I do not intend to discuss it here at length. Here we have, it must be confessed, a real difficulty to face – the 'antinomy' involved in the impossibility either of thinking of a first event, a beginning of the world's history, or of supposing an endless succession of events. But this 'antinomy' is not really solved by talking about the whole series being simultaneously or extra-temporally present to a timeless consciousness: for, even if God contemplates the whole series at once, He must contemplate that series as having a beginning and an end or as endless: and we cannot understand how either is possible. The antinomy remains unsolved. The existence of the antinomy does constitute a good ground for saying that we do not fully understand the nature of time, and that God's relation to time must be different from our relation to it. But it does not justify us in talking about God being 'timeless' or 'out of time' as though we really knew what such phrases meant, and could ourselves attain to this extra-temporal view of things; or in talking about time-distinctions as merely 'subjective,' as though the events of the world's history had their real being out of time but only appeared to us to be in time because of the imperfection of our knowledge—as though all difference between past and future were merely apparent, as though the idea that human acts really effect any change in the Universe were a simple delusion, as though the reality of the world were something static and unchangeable, and the like.

All these positions seem to me to involve at bottom (1) a confusion between knowledge and reality, and (2) the idea that the individual self is timeless. From no possible point of view can human experience appear to be out of time, except a point of view which does not look at things as they really are. If we admit that the individual self is not timeless, I can attach no meaning to a point of view from which the experiences of beings in time—whose experience comes to them in time—shall be seen to be really timeless. Any point of view from which God may in any sense be said to transcend time must at least be a point of view which admits of the possibility of his knowing the experience which is in time and of knowing it as in time—that is to say, as it really is, and not as something which it is not. If God supposed that the pain which I suffered in the past really exists in the present or eternally or out of time, He would be thinking of things as they are not.

It is impossible to discuss the question of the relation of God or the Absolute to time more fully, and I am far from thinking that it is one which can be disposed of in a few sentences. To discuss the question at all adequately would involve a whole Metaphysic: all Metaphysical questions are, indeed, apt to run up into this supreme difficulty. It is not necessary here to do more than to justify my refusal to admit the validity of any arguments or theories about Ethics or otherwise which assume that time is 'subjective.' There is, as I have said, no direct connexion between this question and any ethical problem, but indirectly the connexion is considerable. Theories of the merely subjective, apparent, delusive character of time and all that is in time underlie, or have a strong tendency to associate themselves with, the ethical scepticism which declines to recognize the objective validity of our ethical judgements, or to admit that the ethical point of view (admittedly implying the temporal point of view) contains any trustworthy revelation of the ultimate nature and meaning of the Universe. Such theories I have to some extent examined in other chapters, especially Book II, chap. iii, and Book III, chap. ii.

CHAPTER II

RELIGION AND MORALITY

I

In the last chapter I tried to explain the sense and degree in which a sound system of Ethics presupposes certain metaphysical beliefs. It may be well briefly to recapitulate the results. (1) We saw that certain beliefs about the self may be described as postulates of Ethics in the first degree,—that is to say, in the sense that no real meaning whatever can be given to Morality without assuming the truth of those beliefs, though they may not be explicit in every individual consciousness. (2) The belief in God was found to be essential to the logical justification of that idea of objective validity which is implicit in the moral consciousness, at least in the higher stages of its development. The idea of God may, no doubt, in particular persons of strong moral convictions not only not be explicit, but may be formally denied. The tendency, however, of its denial [1] is and must be in the long run (since all men are in some degree rational beings with a desire for rational self-consistency) to weaken or destroy belief in objective Morality and so the influence of all higher Morality in the world. (3) The idea of a future life seemed an equally essential implication of Morality for those who find it impossible without it to reconcile the facts of life with such a conception of God and of the world as is essential for the rational interpretation of the moral consciousness.

It is not pretended that these metaphysical implications of Morality have always been apparent either to systematic thinkers or to all those in whom moral ideas have been operative. To

---

[1] In strictness we should say the denial of God's existence or of some other form of the belief in a rational Universe, such as is involved (however imperfectly and inadequately) in Buddhism. Reasons have been given for regarding the theistic view as the only one which fully and adequately satisfies the implications of an objective Morality.

many individuals these truths, presented in an abstract meta-physical form, have been no more apparent than any other metaphysical truths which are nevertheless no less really implicit in the ordinary thought of ordinary persons. Nevertheless the history of practical Ethics tends to support the belief that there is a real connexion between certain principles of action, and certain metaphysical verities. The way in which meta-physical truths have been held by and have impressed the great mass of men is in the form of what we call Religion. Religion represents an element in the life of all nations which have risen above a very low stage of savagery [1], and the Morality of a people has always been very closely connected with its Religion, though the closeness of the connexion has varied at different stages of moral and religious development. This Religion has not always been Religion of the kind which we have attempted to represent as the logical presupposition of a sound Morality, any more than the Morality connected with it has always been the Morality of civilized man. We are not concerned here with the historical aspect of the connexion between the lower forms of Morality and the lower forms of Religion. But the nature of the connexion between developed Morality and developed Religion is of such great importance, both theoretical and practical, that it will be well to devote a separate chapter to its consideration.

I shall not in this chapter ask what is the ethical value of religious systems other than those which recognize the three fundamental principles which we have already seen reason for regarding as logical postulates of Ethics—belief in God who wills the highest good and in the Immortality of the soul or at least of such souls as are worthy of Immortality. In the present chapter I propose to ask how far such beliefs are practically necessary or useful to Morality, and in what relation Religion and Morality ought to stand to one another in the ideal human life.

[1] Probably even this exception need not be made. Where travellers or Anthropologists have attempted to point out the existence of a people without Religion, the attempt is generally based either upon insufficient information or upon a too narrow conception of what Religion is.

The first of these questions is of course to some extent distinct from the question on which we have been engaged. Religious belief might possess an important and beneficial moral influence without being in any sense speculatively necessary to a complete and self-consistent ethical creed: or again theistic belief might be speculatively necessary, although the absence of it might have no important practical influence upon those who are content to do without speculative justification for their practical beliefs. But though distinct, the two questions are not unconnected. For no absolute line can be drawn between speculative or scientific Metaphysics and popular Theology. Popular religious beliefs, positive or negative, represent an implicit Metaphysic, though often no doubt, for their adherents, resting partly upon grounds which could not in the ordinary sense of the word be described as metaphysical. Metaphysic represents the reflective and articulate form of beliefs which may quite well be held in a more or less chaotic, a more or less unreflective, way by un-metaphysical and even uneducated persons. All Religion is, always has been, and always must be essentially metaphysical. The crudest savage ' Animism ' is a metaphysical theory as much as the most esoteric Brahminism or the most cultured modern Theology. The modern Theologians of the Ritschlian type, who declaim against Metaphysics and propose to reduce Theology to a belief in the Fatherhood of God, are Metaphysicians as much as the most elaborately technical Schoolman or the most speculative Hegelian. The belief in the Fatherhood of God is none the less a metaphysical belief, because it may be shared both by unlearned men who are entirely without metaphysical training and by learned men who are not good Metaphysicians. Metaphysic after all has no data but the facts of outer and inner experience, and no instrument but human Reason ; and all men have some experience, and use their Reason to a greater or less extent in interpreting that experience. The beliefs of those who think for themselves gradually spread, and influence those who think little or not at all. This is particularly the case with the Metaphysic which deals with the facts of the moral conscious-ness, and with matters in which the moral consciousness has an especial interest. And the practical influence of religious belief or its absence upon Morality is due, as I believe, in a large measure to an instinctive consciousness of its necessity as the presupposition of that objective validity in ethical judgements on which I have already dwelt. The 'plain man' finds it difficult or impossible to believe in Morality as anything more than the actual opinion of his neighbours about his conduct, unless he can believe that it is the law of the Universe; and this belief is for him, at least, and I have tried to show that in the main he is right, possible only in the form of a belief that Morality is the will of God: and, if God is just, He must (so he will argue) reward the good and punish the bad. So the plain man argues; and any weakening of this conviction is apt to react upon the intensity, if not upon the detailed content of his ethical creed. Reflection may bring him hereafter to a more refined view of what is crudely represented as 'reward' and 'punishment'; but the heart of his belief is right, and may be expressed more exactly in the form that the Universe is directed towards the working out of an ideal end for individual souls.

II

But here, perhaps, exception may be taken to my seeming to identify Religion with Monotheism, and even with a Monotheism which carries with it the belief in personal Immortality. I have already disclaimed the attempt to give any historical account of the relation between Religion and Morality, which is in many respects a very different relation at different stages of human culture. Historically, of course, the origin of Religion may be said to be almost independent of Morality, except in so far as all primitive Religion was closely connected with that family and tribal sentiment which was the earliest form of Morality. In primitive times Religion and Morality represented two streams of human thought and feeling which were indeed to a large extent parallel and independent, but which were never without frequent points of contact and interaction. Elements in primitive Religion were quite unconnected with Morality; elements in it were contrary to Morality, or at least contrary to what would have been regarded as moral but for the influence of those religious ideas. Still more emphatically elements or aspects of

Morality have at certain periods of History had nothing or very little to do with Religion. This has been the case especially at certain times and places where the ethical development has temporarily gone beyond the religious development.

We are apt to underestimate the closeness of the habitual relations between Morality and Religion through our familiarity with just those periods of ancient civilization in which for a very small class the ethical development was most conspicuously in advance of the religious[1]. But, even for the average pagan outside the small cultivated class, religious duties (in so far as they were recognized as duties) were also moral duties, although the act prescribed might be an act which at other times and places might be regarded as immoral, and necessarily affected (for good or for evil) his general ideas about Morality. Some moral duties at least were at all times specially connected with, and encouraged by, Religion, even when the highest ideals of the community had little connexion with and exercised little influence over its religious ideas except by undermining them. And on the whole the tendency of progress—both moral and religious—has been to bring Religion and Morality ever more and more closely together, until in the ' ethical religions ' there is professedly a complete coincidence between the requirements of Religion and those of Morality; though only in the more spiritual forms of these—completely perhaps only in the purest forms of Christianity—is this coincidence fully, systematically, and consciously realized. These higher Religions may all be fairly described as monotheistic with one exception; and they all teach a future life of the soul. Buddhism in its pure and original form was certainly not theistic; though it probably tends to become so in the popular consciousness[2]. But Buddhism is certainly not an instance of

---

[1] How small this section was we are reminded by Mark Pattison : ' We are apt to speak as if in the Roman world of the first century A.D., pagan worships had died, or were dying out. This is an illusion generated by literature' (*Sermons*, p. 151). Another ' illusion generated by Literature' has restricted our conception of Religion in the ancient world too much to the official State worship ; it takes too little account of the more popular and the more ethically influential cults such as Orphism and Mithraism.

[2] So difficult is the experiment of a non-theistic Religion that Buddhism has had practically to deify its atheistic Founder. An exception ought

a Religion which is independent of metaphysical belief, nor yet of a Religion without the idea of a future life, and its belief about that life is no doubt one great source of the beneficent moral influence which it has exercised. It is true that in its orthodox form Buddhism regards the extinction of consciousness as the ultimate goal of human aspiration ; but even this implies the conception of a future good which depends upon present conduct, though that good is conceived of as a negative good or escape from evil. And for the great mass of Buddhists many lives intervene between the present and the soul's final goal : while the best authorities seem to doubt whether even Nirvana has ever really been regarded, except by a few thinkers in their most speculative moments, as an actual extinction of consciousness. The ethical influence of this non-theistic Religion is undoubted, but it may quite well be contended that its negative Theology is largely responsible for its ethical defects. The comparative history of the two Religions—Christianity and Buddhism—would seem to confirm the suspicion that the ethical results of a Religion which makes death its highest ideal must be inferior on the whole to those of a Religion which finds the end of man in a more abundant and satisfying life.

Comparison of particular Religions is, however, quite beside my present purpose. I am concerned here only with estimating the ethical value and importance of Religion in what I regard as its highest form, the only form (as I believe) in which Religion is fully in harmony with a sound reflective Metaphysic, and at all events the only form in which its influence is practically felt in civilized Western societies. I have added these remarks on account of the wild language in which an eminent thinker has indulged about the unhistorical mistake of those who assume that there can be no Religion without a personal God or personal Immortality. I have not overlooked the possibility of a Religion without either a God or a future life : but it remains a question what would be the ethical results of such a Religion. There

perhaps also to be made of the old Persian Religion, inasmuch as its admission of an independent principle or power of evil is inconsistent with Monotheism : but even there the good Spirit is thought of as more powerful than the evil.

may undoubtedly be such a thing as Religion which is positively unfavourable to the moral life. I am not sure that the Religion which Mr. Bradley has sketched for us is not of that character. The worship of an Absolute which is conceived of as non-moral could hardly be of much positive ethical value. The worship of an Absolute who has a moral character and that the moral character which Mr. Bradley (if he is to be taken seriously [1]) in his more anti-orthodox moods attributes to the object of his esoteric cult might well lead to ethical results not unlike those associated with the worship of the less respectable deities in the pagan Pantheon. Fortunately the experiment of such a Religion has never been tried on any large scale at an advanced stage of civilization.

III

What then are the ethical advantages of Theism? To deal with the subject adequately would really involve an examination of Religion itself, not only in the form of an abstract Philosophy but in its historical manifestations, and particularly in the form which even those who do not regard it as in any sense final will for the most part admit to be the highest which has hitherto exercised any widespread influence on mankind. The following remarks must be regarded as the merest indication of the main heads under which the very manifold and far-reaching influences of Religion upon Morality may be grouped—the main grounds on which I reject the tendency to regard an ethical creed as a satisfactory substitute for a theological creed based upon Morality.

First, however, let me repeat what I have already more than once insisted on, I trust with some emphasis—that the moral consciousness itself contains no explicit or immediate reference to any theological belief whatever. A man's consciousness of

[1] Recent utterances of his, e.g. in an article on 'Truth and Practice' in *Mind*, N. S., Vol. XIII, No. 51 (1904), seem to suggest that the mood in question is passing away. At all events.I find it quite impossible to reconcile the reverent and theistic spirit of those remarks with such a suggestion as that which he makes in *Appearance and Reality*, Ed. ii. p. 194, that human error is justified in the world-plan because of the contribution which it makes to the amusement of the Absolute.

value, and in particular of the supreme value residing in the good will, does not necessarily include, as a matter of simple psychological fact, any recognition of duty as the will of God, or any expectation of happiness or misery in another life as the consequence of duty performed or neglected.. Nor can the consciousness of duty be regarded as in any sense a logical deduction or inference from such beliefs. These beliefs logically presuppose the moral consciousness. It is for the rational interpretation of the moral consciousness that metaphysical or theological beliefs are required; just as they are required for the rational interpretation of Science, though eminent men of Science may be innocent of all conscious metaphysical theory or indulge in metaphysical speculations really fatal to their own Sciences. Where no such interpretation presents itself as reasonable or where it is deliberately rejected, the good man in proportion to his goodness will still no doubt aim at that which seems to him the highest ; and no difficulty which he may experience in metaphysically interpreting his conduct will lead to the cessation of his efforts—if only he is good enough and strong enough. In proportion to his goodness and his strength he will cling to his ethical ideal. The absence or rejection of metaphysical justification seems, however, to have a tendency varying in strength according to circumstances and temperament, a tendency which shows itself in the spiritual life of communities even where it does not immediately tell upon the spiritual life of individuals, to weaken the hold of the belief in Morality itself upon life and conduct. It does not necessarily involve a direct, conscious, immediate alteration of ethical creed. In the majority of cases a man who has given up every form of theological belief will continue to say ' I believe in Morality '; and if you ask him what Morality means he will possibly give much the same account of it as he did before his rejection of the theological belief. He does not, except perhaps as regards certain particular points of Morality which for him may have been specially connected with some organ of religious Authority, reject anything that he believed before : he does not consciously and deliberately make up his mind to aim no more at what he aimed at formerly, or to drown scruples which he once respected. But the intellectual hold of Morality upon his mind is weakened when he can give no account of it except that it is a way of thinking that Evolution has somehow produced in creatures of his species. It ceases to occupy the place that it did in his habitual thoughts about the Universe and his own place in it. For the only form in which the majority of men can grasp tenaciously the idea of an objective Moral Law is by regarding it as the will of a spiritual Being to whom they feel themselves responsible [1]. Even among highly-educated persons it is doubtful whether many find it possible to realize the belief in an abstract Morality, and to make the aspiration after it the dominant aim of their lives with as much intensity as the best of those who have believed in a living God. For after all rationality exercises some influence over human conduct; and a belief which the holder of it is forced to regard as irrational or non-rational will exercise in the long run, in proportion as its non-rational character is realized, less influence on a man's conduct than one which justifies itself to his Reason as well as to his emotions. Nor can it well be denied that most of those who reject the idea of God do advisedly and deliberately reject also as a matter of speculative belief the idea of an absolute or intrinsic moral obligation, though some of them may more or less successfully endeavour to prevent that rejection from having any practical effect upon their conduct. But in the long run speculation does affect conduct. To state the practical connexion between Re-

---

[1] At least this may be said of Western men. If it does not hold of Buddhists, it must be remembered that the Buddhist very distinctly regards the Universe as morally controlled, though by an impersonal law. I should fully admit that such a creed as that of Dr. McTaggart—the belief in Immortality without a belief in God—does supply a metaphysical justification for Morality. Whether it does this so well as Theism, whether the creed is intrinsically as reasonable as Theism, and whether its influence over life and conduct is likely to be as powerful, these are questions which I cannot here explicitly discuss. It seems hardly necessary for a Theist who thinks a belief in Immortality with Theism more reasonable than a belief in Immortality without it to attempt to decide exactly how much of the ethical influence arising from belief in God and Immortality could be secured by belief in Immortality and a morally governed Universe without God. The reader will see that some of the considerations urged in this chapter could be equally urged from Dr. McTaggart's point of view, while others could not.

ligion and Morality at its lowest, the belief in a personal God
represents the form of belief about the Universe in which the
intellectual hold of Morality upon the human mind tends to
attain its maximum intensity. And the firmer or weaker intellectual grasp of a belief reacts upon its emotional influence.

Theism of the Christian type is the creed which secures the
maximum emotional hold of human Morality upon the mind.
Action motived by no other desire than the desire to fulfil the
Moral Law for its own sake, accompanied by no emotion but
what is produced by the direct consciousness of duty, is undoubtedly not impossible. But such a desire is not commonly
the sole or (unless reinforced by other feelings or emotions)
the habitually dominant motive of action even in the best men.
Morality seldom excites the strongest emotion till it is embodied
in a self-conscious Being. Personal influence is the strongest of
all moral motive powers. And yet there is clearly no kind
of personal affection or social emotion except the fear or love
of God which can be trusted to range itself invariably on
the side of the Moral Law. It is not easy to exaggerate the
increase of emotional intensity which the Moral Law acquires
when the reverence for it fuses inextricably with a feeling of
reverence for a Person who is conceived of as essentially and perfectly good. And this reverence is almost independent of the
hope of reward or fear of punishment, except in so far as
a belief in the divine Justice is necessary to the individual's
conception of God as a Person worthy of reverence. This is
a consideration often forgotten when advocates of a purely
'ethical Religion' expatiate on the additional purity which
a non-theistic creed gives to moral aspiration. It is forgotten
that the love of God means simply love for a Person who is the
highest good and the source of all other goodness.

There is, indeed, one sort of emotion and only one which can
be compared in its intensity and its moral efficacy with religious
emotion—and that is Patriotism and other forms of social feeling[1]. John Stuart Mill has declared that, though he enter-

[1] Historically Patriotism, when it has practically acted as a moral motive
power of great intensity, has usually been associated with some form of
religious belief in the moral sense of the word. That is so even with the

tains 'the strongest objections to the system of politics and morals set forth' in Comte's *Système de Politique Positive*, that treatise 'has superabundantly shown the possibility of giving to the service of humanity, even without the aid of belief in a Providence, both the physical power and the social efficacy of a religion [1].' I do not doubt that the love of country or of Humanity is capable of producing in particular natures—even in whole nations—moral results comparable in strength with those which spring from the fear or the love of God. But it must not be forgotten that this social enthusiasm is extremely difficult to cultivate, and that when cultivated it is not always a security for a sound Morality. For the effect of good conduct on social Well-being is often very remote and indirect: affection for individuals or for small groups of men—even for the whole present generation—may inspire conduct which is really anti-social. The strongest temptation to most men lies in the disposition to conform to the moral standard, and to win the applause, of their immediate environment. Moreover, even the philanthropy which is really inspired by a love of Humanity at large may be divorced from the love of moral goodness. What we desire for others may be mere pleasure or contentment, not the highest sort of life. Against these dangers there is no more valuable counteractive than the faith which identifies Morality with the love of a God who wills exclusively the true and highest good of all his creatures. The love of God is at once a stimulant, a complement, and a corrective to the love of man. The true love of Humanity is the love of Humanity at its highest—'the love not of all men nor yet of every man, but of *the man* in every man [2].' And love of the ideal man becomes

---

modern Japanese. Vague as the creed of the average Japanese appears to be, it does eminently tend to produce the conviction that Morality is the law of the Universe, and not simply the public opinion of a particular community. Both Buddhism and Shintoism, in the form in which they are popularly accepted, conduce to that result by producing belief in the future of the soul after death, and in a communion with still living ancestors. The pessimistic, ascetic, and anti-social side of Buddhism appears to have exercised little influence on the Japanese mind.

[1] *Utilitarianism*, p. 49.

[2] Seeley, *Ecce Homo*, ed. xiii, chap. xiii, p. 145.

a stronger force the more the ideal end for man is identified with the end of the Universe. In the Christian or the Theist the love of the ideal man is the love of man as God wills him to be.

IV

The belief in a future life I regard as of the highest value both as a postulate or a corollary of belief in God, and for its own sake. The idea of such a life is simply caricatured when it is spoken of as a mere belief in the distribution of posthumous ' rewards and punishments.' Even in this aspect its educational influence is not to be despised. Theists need not be ashamed to acknowledge that they do regard it as a gain to Morality that that ' education by pleasure and pain ' which thinkers like Plato and Aristotle regarded as the function of the State should be continued in another life; and that men should act habitually with the thought before them of a future in which the principle of ' reaping what they have sown '—to some very imperfect extent the law even of life here—shall be far more fully and adequately realized. It is true that conduct motived *wholly* by fear of punishment or hope of reward has little or no moral value[1], so long at least as the reward and punishment are conceived of in a purely hedonistic sense; and that the ideal is not reached till this motive is supplanted by or merged in other and higher motives. But we do not despise such influences in ordinary moral education. What parent or schoolmaster would say to a young child, ' My good child, enlightened Philosophers are agreed that conduct motived by fear of punishment or hope of reward is worthless; therefore henceforth I shall leave you to be guided by your own innate sense of right and wrong. I will not corrupt the purity of your will by threats or promises. Your virtues shall be their own reward ; your misdeeds shall never interfere with your pleasures or cause the withdrawal of my favour '?   What child would flourish morally under such treatment as this ?   And yet it would be a very cynical view of human nature to suppose that the average schoolboy is actuated

---

[1] And yet after all Prudence does represent a higher motive than mere animal impulse.

by no motive higher than selfish hope or fear. He has higher
motives, but he requires to be aided in his efforts at self-conquest
by lower ones. And after all most of us are a great deal more
like children than it is fashionable among Philosophers to believe—at least in our moments of weakness and strong temptation. How many people could honestly assert that the promptings
of their internal Conscience require or derive no support and
assistance from the ' external Conscience '—their fear of social
disapproval or the disapproval of those whom they most respect ?
How many of us will pretend that it would be morally good for
them to have all such restraints suddenly withdrawn ? And
yet, as we have seen, the ' external Conscience ' does not always
echo the promptings of the inner Conscience. It is just at such
times that the external conscience which is supplied by a belief in
a God who rewards and punishes becomes most valuable. Plenty
of non-religious Moralists will admit that it is wrong to fight
a duel : it may be doubted whether a duel has ever been declined
upon conscientious grounds, where the social sanction insists on
its being fought, except by religious men.

We do not hesitate to appeal even to the coarser physical
pains and pleasures in moral education just so far as this may be
required. If a man does not see that drunkenness is disgusting,
we do not think it degrading to point out to him its physical
ill-effects—still less its ultimate tendency to weaken his will and
paralyse every energy that he possesses. It is difficult to see
how moral education can be conducted in any other way than by
associating pleasure and pain with the right objects, and gradually
appealing to more and more remote and refined pleasures and
pains—pleasures and pains more and more intrinsically connected
with the good or bad conduct itself ; while at the same time, as
moralization advances, we more and more allow the highest motives
—the respect for duty and regard for others—to take their place
or to transform all lower motives. Moral ' Autonomy ' is no doubt
the ideal, but it is only at a very advanced stage of moral and
intellectual growth that pure Autonomy is attainable. At the
lower levels of moral education, there is no objection to insisting
on the mere reward and punishment aspect of the future life, so
long as these are never represented as constituting the true

ground for moral conduct. But even at this stage the value of this idea of a future 'judgement' consists even more in its tendency simply to emphasize the reality of moral obligation, the idea of an objective Moral Law and of personal responsibility, than in the actual influence which the terror of personal ill-consequences exerts over the mind [1]. And, as moral education advances, it will first sink into the background or be evoked only as an aid to resist the force of violent temptations, and then with the highest souls be altogether superseded by a love of God and man of that perfected kind which is said to 'cast out fear.' In its highest form a Morality based on the idea of God is only a personal, and therefore a far more practically influential, form of 'ethical Autonomy.'

In the higher religious life the anticipation of future rewards and punishments passes into the expectation of a better life in which greater perfection of character and greater opportunities of exercising our highest capacities than are attainable in the present stage of existence shall be combined with all the other elements that constitute our highest conception of the good. Belief in another life enhances the value of the life that now is and the importance of the moral struggle of which it is the scene. The conviction that a man's present conduct will influence his future is the very beginning of all Morality: the larger that future, the more influence does that conviction exercise upon conduct. Moreover, it is not only in regard to ourselves but in regard to others that the vision of eternal consequences emphasizes the importance of every act of moral choice. The promotion of human pleasure and the prevention of human misery would not be ignoble things to aim at, even though the days of man were but threescore years and ten ; nor is the value of the higher spiritual life wholly dependent upon its duration.

---

[1] I suspect that, when the fear of Hell plays a prominent part in the more ardent and emotional kind of religious conversion, it does so mainly by breaking down the apathy and the slavery to immediate sensation which has hitherto prevented moral reflection. It awakens reflection : after that, it is rather the sense of the justice of the punishment depicted by authority or imagination than the actual fear of it, which effects the moral regeneration, though the one idea may often be psychologically inseparable from the other.

But it does seem to me the mere obstinacy of philosophical dogmatism to minimize the influence which is likely to flow from the thought of endless consequences not merely for Society at large but for our own individual souls and the soul of each individual whose character is affected by our acts. Is not that reflection eminently calculated to strengthen our sense of the importance of the moral life? And is not the thought that after all in a few years' time it will not matter a straw to myself or to any one else now living whether I have struggled against temptation or yielded to it, a thought eminently calculated to depress the moral energies, and to reinforce every passion or inclination which may suggest that it is our wisdom to live only for the passing hour? 'Let us eat and drink, for to-morrow we die,' was not indeed a necessary or logical deduction from the denial of Immortality, but it is undoubtedly the inference which the natural man is very apt to draw from it.

It is not, be it remembered, the absolute importance of the moral struggle and the spiritual life for ourselves and others so much as its relative importance when compared with all lower enjoyments and interests which may stand in its way that is so enormously enhanced by the conviction that character lasts beyond the grave. In persons not of a highly imaginative or emotional temperament it is perhaps more in this way than in any personal sense of craving either for future happiness or future perfection that the need for a belief in Immortality is most powerfully felt. They quite recognize that their efforts to be useful ought not to be diminished by any loss of faith in Immortality, and yet the feeling of the poverty and unsatisfactoriness of human life, as it is for the great mass of men, will tend to make their philanthropy unhopeful and uncheerful; and still more probably it will tend to lower their ideal of the good which they desire for their fellows. To the non-believer in Immortality the lower goods will seem a more attainable and a more solid aim than that effort to improve character which often produces so little immediate fruit. And after all it is not wholly a question of 'seeming.' For the superiority of the higher goods to the lower does in part depend upon their duration. The superior duration of the higher goods is one of the most familiar topics of the least theological Moralists. In particular when the possibilities of life are narrowing in, a man's estimate of the superior value of higher goods is likely to be vitally affected by his Eschatology. The belief in Immortality ought not to revolutionize our estimate of moral values, but it may rationally enough be held in some cases to alter to an appreciable degree our *comparative* estimate of values. When the hope of Immortality is treated as irrational, it is hard to believe that men will think it worth while to spend time and labour upon the improvement of character in themselves or others at an age when their work in life is done, and when their powers of social influence on other lives may be treated as a negligible quantity. I have already dwelt upon the influence which a thoroughly realized belief in human mortality would be likely to exert, and perhaps ought to exert, upon the general estimate of Suicide and some departments of Ethics connected therewith [1]. There is no need to repeat this here.

There is yet another way in which Morality seems to crave, if it does not logically demand, the belief in Immortality, or rather one other way of re-stating the connexion which we have already been studying. On the supposition of universal mortality the contrast between the capacities of human nature and its actual destiny, between the immensity of the man's outlook and the limitations of his actual horizon, between the splendour of his ideals and the insignificance of his attainment, becomes such as to constitute, in a mind which fairly faces it, a shock to our rational nature sufficient to destroy belief in the rationality of things, and to imperil confidence in the authority of Moral Reason as a guide to human life. To those who have once accepted the rationality of things, and most emphatically to those who have once accepted the faith in a personal God, the improbability that a being of such capacity should have been created to be simply the creature of a day, that 'cometh up, and is cut down, like a flower, and never continueth in one stay,' has almost invariably amounted to an absolute impossibility. It is the favourite argument alike of reasoned Philosophy and of the intensest moral intuition. It is the argument implicit in

[1] See Vol. I, p. 209.

the intuition of Jesus Christ, that beings once admitted to spiritual communion with the Eternal Father, like the traditional fathers of the Jewish race, could not be doomed to extinction after so brief and so imperfect a vision of Him. 'God is not the God of the dead but of the living.' Plato and Cicero are full of the same thought. It is the argument drily and somewhat abstractly expressed by Kant when he made it a postulate of the Moral Law that its commands should be capable of fulfilment, and argued that, as in this life only distant approaches to the true ideal are possible to the best, there must be a hereafter in which a progressively closer approximation to it should be possible. It is at bottom the basis of that faith in Immortality which, in greater or less intensity, is to be found in nearly all modern thinkers in whom ethical convictions have been profound and paramount [1].

And, be it observed, it is not among those whose ideas of Morality are such as to demand a 'Trinkgeld' for Virtue, but precisely among those whose sense of the intrinsic worth of goodness is strongest, and whose appreciation of the higher side' of the present life is keenest, that we find the most passionate conviction that this cannot be all. If this conviction, this necessary inference from the existence of the Moral Law, should be shown to be false, it would tend to throw doubt upon the validity of all their higher thought, upon the worth of all higher ideals, even upon the validity of the moral judgement itself. It can hardly be doubted that psychologically it would have this effect. And, if there be any validity in the argument of the last chapter, that effect would only be the psychological expression of legitimate metaphysical considerations. It is not only the 'sense of obligation' that would disappear, but also the reality of it, that is to say the objectivity which at bottom is the ultimate meaning of moral obligation [2].

---

[1] The natural tendency of such minds, when the drift of their thought takes them away from the belief in God and Immortality, is towards Pessimism. I should certainly include Von Hartmann among the thinkers in whom ethical considerations have been profound and paramount.

[2] Or, at least, the basis of it. In popular thought the idea of 'moral obligation' usually includes not merely the belief in an objective mind or law but the belief that the Universe is ultimately governed in accordance with that law.

Belief in a future life is, I hold, an essential element of Religion in any form which is likely to satisfy a modern Western intelligence whose Ethics are not those of Asceticism, and whose conception of the Universe is not pessimistic. But at the same time I should strongly insist that this belief derives its moral value largely from its close connexion with the highest form of the religious emotion—the love of God. For God to be loved He must be thought of as worthy of love, and it is difficult to believe that He is worthy of love if He wills such a world as ours except as a means to some better one, for those at least of his creatures who are worthy of it. But I would once more emphasize the fact that the religious motive at its highest is the love of God for his own sake, and not merely for any reward that is to be expected from Him, however sublimated be our conception of that reward. In the love of God the two strongest emotional forces which make for Morality in this world find their fullest and most harmonious satisfaction—reverence for the moral ideal and love of Humanity. When God is conceived of as the realization of our highest moral ideals, love of God and love of duty become one and the same thing, with all the additional strength which love of a person can claim over the love of an abstract law. Love of a person includes the desire to promote that person's end: and the end of God, as we have thought of Him, is the highest welfare of his creatures[1]. Devotion to the moral ideal and to the true good of Humanity is, indeed, at bottom identical with the love of God. But it is hardly possible to exaggerate the reinforcement which that devotion receives, both on the rational and the emotional side, when it is identified with the love of a person in whom our highest ideal is realized, and on whose side we are called upon to contend in a real, and not a merely illusory, battle for the realization of that same ideal in others. That the love of God may be implicit in all reverence for the moral ideal and all true love of Humanity, even when the thought of God is not consciously present to the agent's mind, I should be the first to

[1] So far as known to us and so far as it can be promoted by human action. I do not of course deny that this may be in reality but a small part of the ultimate world-end.

assert [1] ; but implicit beliefs are generally not so strong as explicit beliefs. Implicit beliefs tend to wither away when they are never made explicit; still more so, when in their explicit form they are scouted and ridiculed. Belief in the moral ideal attains its maximum momentum when it is identified with the love of a Person.

It would involve an artificial and unreal separation between the spheres of natural and of what is popularly known as 'revealed' Religion were I to abstain from pointing out how Christianity satisfies the demand for a personal object of the highest reverence by concentrating it upon an historical human being who is regarded at once as the supreme and typical revelation of the divine Will and character and as the truest type of the human race. Love of God and love of man meet in the love of Christ. The love of Humanity cannot degenerate into an unethical humanitarian sentiment when Humanity is represented by its worthiest type. Love of God cannot degenerate into an other-worldly or anti-social pietism when God is thought of as represented by Humanity at its highest ; while, according to the Christian view of Ethics, social enthusiasm receives its highest satisfaction in the pursuit of that ideal of a regenerated human society which Jesus bequeathed to the world, and which has taken outward and visible form in the organized communities of his followers.

V

There are some to whom the view which has been taken of the relation between Religion and Morality will seem to concede too little to Religion and too much to Morality. They will contend that the sphere of Morality and the sphere of Religion are

[1] Von Hartmann points out that just as the love of particular animals (e. g. in children) is often an undeveloped love of man, so the love of man is an undeveloped love of God. '... er in seinem Bruder das Ebenbild oder die Inkarnation Gottes sieht. Die Gottesliebe ist die Wahrheit der Nächstenliebe, wie die Nächstenliebe die Wirklichkeit der Gottesliebe ist ' (*Ethische Studien*, p. 207). The writer is here only developing principle implied in Christ's own 'Forasmuch as ye did it unto the least of these my brethren, ye did it unto me,' whether we regard these words as the *ipsissima verba* of Christ, or as representing the working of his spirit in the mind of the early Church.

wholly distinct, the sphere of Religion being the higher of the two. The sphere of Morality is that of human action and of human action alone. Morality cannot reasonably be attributed to God. It implies the coexistence of evil and good. It implies that some things happen which ought not to happen; whereas from the religious point of view nothing can happen but that which God wills, and what God wills is what ought to happen. The good and the bad alike contribute, it will be urged, to the fulfilment of the divine Will. It is merely owing to the limitations of human nature that we present some things to ourselves as bad and others as good. Not only must we suppose, therefore, on speculative grounds that the divine Will is 'super-moral,' and that acts and principles of action which to us seem immoral are in God perfectly good, but it is possible to some extent even for the human mind, in a general way, if not in detail, to see that they are good; and by an effort of not irrational faith to trust that they are so even where it cannot point out how and why they are so. The religious consciousness can rise above the abstract and one-sided point of view to which the mere moral consciousness is confined; it can acquiesce, not only with pious resignation but with joy and exultation, in the perfect order which faith reveals; and pronounce that in this world, wherein there are many things which it is wrong to do and much evil which it is a duty to struggle against, there happens nevertheless ultimately nothing which ought not to happen [1].

Now in this contention it is extremely important to distinguish between two possible senses in which such language may be used. It is one thing to maintain that *our* Morality is defective, and inadequately represents the true and final aim of the Universe: it is another thing to maintain that moral distinctions of any and every kind are transcended in the mind of God, and in the soul of the religious man who has managed to think himself or feel himself out of the moral into the super-moral

---

[1] Indeterminists will of course except what is due to 'free-will'—on any view a very small part of the total evil in the world. This point of view is not usually adopted by Indeterminists, but it is occasionally approximated to by a few Indeterminist Theologians who have picked up a philosophy which does not suit them.

sphere. That our conception of the ethical ideal is a more or less imperfect one will be admitted in some degree by thinkers of every school. The defectiveness of *our* moral notions might be asserted in a very much stronger way than I see any reason for doing without implying that for God there is no Morality [1] or that our moral judgements, not because they are bad and erroneous moral judgements but just because they are, from the ethical point of view, sound and reasonable, are nevertheless from the point of view of the Absolute false or meaningless. To maintain this last position implies the denial of all objectivity to the moral judgement, and reduces all Morality not merely to ' an appearance ' but to a false and delusive appearance. It is of the essence of the moral consciousness, as it actually exists, to *claim* universal validity; if it possesses no such validity, it is not merely particular moral judgements that are false and delusive but the whole idea that there is such a thing as an end which absolutely ought to be promoted, and that we have a power (more or less adequate) of determining what that something is.

Now it seems to me that many of those who indulge in the now fashionable talk about a ' super-moral sphere ' are not clear in their own minds as to the sense in which they maintain it. Mr. Bradley, for instance, has used much language which could only be justified if he meant to uphold the second and more destructive of the two positions above indicated. But, when he pronounces that, though the Absolute is not moral, he or rather ' it ' is nevertheless ' in a sense ' good [2], or that, though both goodness and badness ' are good alike, ... they are not good equally [3],' he is as much implying the validity of that category of good from which Morality derives all its meaning as he would be if he made the less startling assertion that human Morality is an imperfect revelation of the divine. When he pronounces that the Universe as a whole is perfectly good, I may dissent from

---

[1] Of course if by Morality is meant the choice of the good in spite of inclination to the contrary, there is no harm in saying with Kant that God's Will is a ' holy ' and not a moral Will. Kant of course was as far as possible from the point of view which I am attacking. He made a ' holy will ' the ideal goal even of human character-development, and he never hesitates to speak of God as a moral Being.

[2] *Appearance and Reality*, p. 412.   [3] Ib., p. 440.

his Optimism; but he is as much assuming the absolute validity of his own moral judgements, and consequently of that category of good which those judgements involve, as I do when I assert that the whole is not perfectly good, though God's Will is for the best possible. When he supposes that the Absolute may enjoy something much better than Morality in willing not merely particular acts (which in God may be means to a greater good) but *ends* at which it would be cruel and malicious for a man to aim, I may dispute his reasons for making such an assumption; but, if the promotion of divine laughter at human ignorance be really better than love, it would follow not that God was not moral but that our judgements in detail were wrong[1]. There would in this view be such a discrepancy between our actual moral judgements and the true ones that the question might well be raised why we should trust them at all. Nay, if a Philosopher like Mr. Bradley is clever enough to find out that the real end of the Universe is something very different from what kindly and merciful men aim at, I fail to see why we should not, under his tuition, aim at co-operating with the aims of the Absolute, and universalize the maxim that heartless practical joking is better than kindliness and mutual goodwill. Mr. Bradley would doubtless reply that he does not seriously pretend to have discovered what the absolute end is: but, if he does not know what it is, why should he assume that it is so fundamentally different from

[1] See ib., p. 194. I am here using more theistic language than Mr. Bradley would himself use, for I can attach no meaning to the terms 'good' and 'bad' as applied to mere things; but, since he admits that the Absolute is *as much* Will as Reason (without actually being either) I do not think I am seriously misrepresenting him or at least one side of his thought. Mr. Bradley's whole doctrine about the Absolute seems to me to represent an impossible compromise or see-saw between a genuine theistic Idealism (which represents, I believe, his real mind), and a Spinozism into which he is led partly, no doubt, by his imagined discovery of fundamental contradictions in all thought (not merely human thought but all thought as such), but probably much more by his anxiety to differentiate his positions as much as possible from that of all Theologians, orthodox or liberal. There are many less unorthodox thinkers who play with Mr. Bradley's doctrine of a super-moral sphere, while professing to believe in a deity who is not (as with Mr. Bradley) an 'it' (though, it would appear, an 'it' which possesses or is consciousness or 'experience') but a spiritual Being to which some of them do not even hesitate to ascribe personality.

that which we think it to be? I have already attempted to
show that there are no such fundamental contradictions in our
actual moral judgements as to make it inconceivable that they
should in principle be a true revelation of the absolute end [1].

But whatever may be thought about Mr. Bradley's reasons
for doubting the validity in actual content of our moral judgements, he does not at bottom—in such passages as have been
referred to—deny the validity of our moral categories. It is
not a super-moral sphere that he has called into existence so
much as a sphere in which a different Morality holds good—not
a ' non-moral' or ' super-moral ' Absolute so much as an Absolute
with a truer and higher Morality. He who rejects Mr. Bradley's
reasons for assuming this fundamental discrepancy between the
divine end and that approved as good by our moral consciousness,
and who likes Mr. Bradley's own Morality much better than that
which he attributes to his Absolute, has on that Philosopher's
own showing a right not merely to call the Absolute good but to
regard the Morality of the best men as a revelation of his. By
his doctrine that the Absolute is good and cannot be described
as bad, he has precluded himself from saying that the words
good and evil have no meaning in reference to the Absolute.
Morality means aiming at the good; and Mr. Bradley does not
deny that the Absolute aims at the good. Even on his own
view of our actual, partly self-contradictory, Morality, there seems
no reason why he should not admit that Morality has as good
a right to be regarded as a revelation of the Absolute as our
scientific consciousness [2]; and even the doctrine that both are
riddled with contradictions would fail to reveal such a discrepancy between the moral and the religious point of view as
he is anxious to discover. Morality would supply us with the

---

[1] See above, p. 209.

[2] Mr. Bradley goes near to admitting this when he says that 'higher,
truer, more beautiful, better and more real—these, on the whole, count in the
universe as they count for us. And existence, on the whole, must correspond with our ideas ' (ib. p. 550). But why should we be right when we
judge that one thing is lower than another, wrong when we judge that
a thing is ' bad '—something which ought not to exist at all? And how
can an Absolute be perfect which produces something lower instead of
something higher, unless he or it is limited in power?

best and truest way of thinking of the Absolute, though the inadequacy of such a view might be greater according to him than Moralists with a less keen eye for 'contradictions' see any reason for admitting[1].

It will be suggested, no doubt, that I am here overlooking that doctrine of degrees of Truth and Reality by which the doctrine of the non-morality of the Absolute is qualified. Mr. Bradley admits that to say that the Absolute is immoral or bad would be more untrue than to say that he is moral or good. The question which suggests itself is, 'how does Mr. Bradley know even that much, if our moral judgements are untrustworthy?' There are no doubt many strong assertions of the goodness of the Absolute side by side with the denial of his or 'its' morality—many strong assertions of the superiority, even from the point of view of the Universe, of goodness over badness. I ask on what Mr. Bradley's handsome testimonial to the goodness or perfection of the Absolute is supposed to rest, when the verdict of our own moral consciousness is discredited? To say that our moral judgements fail to some extent to correspond with moral judgements as they are in the Absolute[2] is one thing; but to say that we can correct their deficiencies is another. And it is the last that Mr. Bradley attempts to do when he pronounces what we call evil to be really good. To admit the probability that our ideals are defective is one thing: to attempt their correction by directly contradicting them is another. To declare that the judgement 'cruelty is bad' must in

---

[1] When Mr. Bradley in his chapter on 'Ultimate Doubts' (*Appearance and Reality*, chap. xxvii) admits the possibility (though not the probability) of an ultimate element of evil in things, he seems to assume that the evil must be found in the Will which wills the Universe (in so far as Will may be taken as an imperfect and one-sided aspect of the Absolute). It does not seem to occur to him that the evil may be something which, in language as inadequate but no more inadequate than that which he is himself compelled to use, may be described as a lack of Power which may be compatible with a Will for the good—a Will which wills the evil only as a necessary means to the good.

[2] Mr. Bradley, of course, will not admit there are judgements at all in the Absolute. This is too wide a subject to discuss here; but, at all events, he will admit that we cannot think about the Absolute without talking as though there were.

4

the Absolute be transformed into the judgement 'cruelty to the exact extent to which it actually exists is good,' is not merely to pronounce that our moral judgements are inadequate and are ' somehow ' transcended in the Absolute, but dogmatically to say that they are false and that others, which are admitted not to commend themselves to our actual moral consciousness, are true. Any inadequacy, or doubt, or invalidity that may cleave to the former judgement must cleave surely *a fortiori* to the last.

And on what does the supposed intellectual necessity for this reversal of all our canons of value turn ?   Upon an ideal of our thought.   It makes a neater, tidier, more compact and coherent system of the Universe to think of the whole as perfectly good than to think of it as a whole in which, though good predominates, there is some evil.   But why should this intellectual ideal of self-consistency or harmony be regarded as a safer guide to the true nature of things than that ideal of Morality which claims in us to be of absolute and objective validity, and so to represent the true end of a rational will ?   There can be no real ' harmony ' or ' perfection,' or ' coherence,' or absence of contradiction, in any picture or ideal or system of the Universe in which our highest ideals of value are flatly contradicted.

The only way in which, as it seems to me, Mr. Bradley could escape the force of these objections would be by absolutely giving up the use of the terms good and evil in thinking of the Absolute, and cancelling all that he has said about the goodness of the Absolute, and, I must add, all that he has said about the intrinsic reasonableness of the Universe ; for a reasonable Universe means a Universe which realizes ends that are intrinsically good, and it is only from our judgements of value that we know anything about goodness or indeed about ' ends.'   And on one side of his thought Mr. Bradley certainly goes very near to an avowed adoption of this position.   When Mr. Bradley pronounces the Absolute good, we naturally suppose him to mean something by the assertion ; but eventually, in the last paragraph of his book, he comes near to admitting that he means nothing by it.   For there he tells us that ' the Reality is our criterion of worse and better, of ugliness and beauty, of true and false, of real and unreal.   It in brief decides between, and gives

a general meaning to, higher and lower[1].'   If, then, the real is
our sole criterion of worth, if a thing is good in proportion to
the amount of real being in it, the assertion that the Absolute is
good means no more than the assertion that the Absolute is real.
Now for us it is quite certain that the word 'good' does not mean
the same as 'real,' unless Mr. Bradley chooses, by definition, to
make the word 'real' include our idea of good. If it be said that
in the Absolute this difference is to be transcended, at all events
our idea of good must be allowed to represent as important an
aspect of the Absolute as our idea of real. It must not be
simply cancelled, as is done when it is suggested that in or for
the Absolute cruelty is good. The idea of good has as much
right to be taken into consideration in our speculative construction of the ultimate nature of things as our idea of the real.

I will sum up this necessarily brief and inadequate criticism
of Mr. Bradley's position in the form of a dilemma. Either our
moral consciousness is a guide to the ultimate nature of Reality
or it is not. If it is, some things in the Universe—pain and sin
for instance—are bad, and are none the less bad because they
may be means to a greater good. If it is not, Mr. Bradley has no
right to assert that the Absolute is good, for the idea of good is
derived from the moral consciousness and cannot be derived from
any other source. To say that our ideas of 'higher' and
'better' 'count in the Universe as they count in us,' and at the
same time to speak of the 'good' as meaning merely the 'real,' is
(if I may be pardoned for using language which Mr. Bradley
has used in another connexion) 'to trifle indecently with a subject
which deserves some respect.'

VI

The theory of a super-moral sphere assumes another form in
the writings of the great Pessimist, Eduard von Hartmann[2]. And

---

[1] *Appearance and Reality*, p. 552. This passage seems to involve formal
contradiction with the statement that 'that which is highest to us is
also in and to the Universe most real' (p. 560). In the first passage we are
bidden to interpret goodness by Reality, in the latter Reality by our notions
of goodness.

[2] These views are expounded in his best-known work, *The Philosophy of
the Unconscious* (trans. by W. C. Coupland, 1893), and in his elaborate

here the collision between the religious and the moral point of view is avowedly far less complete. Von Hartmann recognizes the existence of three spheres or stages in moral development. There is the sphere of mere Nature, the stage below Morality—that of the beasts and, it may be, of purely 'natural man'; the moral stage; and the super-moral. He contends that everything that happens, what we call moral and what we call immoral, is equally tending to the furtherance of an end—the ultimate end of the Universe—, that is (according to him) the extinction of evil and therefore, since consciousness necessarily brings with it more evil than good, the extinction of consciousness [1]. But the great modern Pessimist recognizes also that each of these views of the Universe, if taken by itself, is one-sided and imperfect; that either the first or the third, taken alone, would lead to immoral consequences in practice, and in theory to the negation of all objective moral obligation, in the existence of which there is no more convinced or more convincing believer than Von Hartmann himself [2]. Animals and infants are furthering the true end of the Universe by yielding to their natural instincts and impulses as each comes uppermost— instincts and impulses which are unerringly guided to an end of which they are themselves entirely unconscious. But a moral being would not be promoting the true end of the Universe by so acting; he can only further that end by being moral. It is true that from the third or super-moral point of view it must appear that the bad man's acts are also furthering the ends of the Absolute Will. But Von Hartmann recognizes that to say this

treatise *Das sittliche Bewusstsein*, but the clearest expression of his views as to the relation between Morality and Religion is to be found in his shorter *Ethische Studien*, 1898.

[1] It is, however, according to Von Hartmann, no use to attempt this extinction by individual or even universal Suicide, because the same Absolute which has produced the existing number of men would immediately [why ?] produce other individuals to take their place (*Das sittl. Bewusstsein*, p. 476). Would he say that when by celibacy or other checks on population the number is restrained, the Absolute must necessarily create a corresponding number in other parts of the Universe? The contention really reminds one of the old scholastic idea that the number of the saved must exactly equal the number of the fallen Angels.

[2] '... Ethik ohne Objectivität keinen Sinn hat ' (*D. sittl. Bewusstsein*, p. 92).

alone would be fatal to the very idea of moral obligation.   He is
not one of those who think it possible for a rational being to go
on acting as a man upon moral principles the vanity of which he
has as a Philosopher himself exposed.   He recognizes that the
end which Morality prescribes to man is not only the true and
valid end for man, but part of the true and absolute end of the
Universe.[1]   When the moral consciousness assures us that
Morality is an end-in-itself, that the diminution of human suffering is better than its promotion and the like, the Absolute is not
playing a trick upon us, or promoting its ends by a delusion of
which all but Philosophers at least are the victims.   The
Absolute is telling us what is strictly and finally true.   But
there is a further truth which the moral man, as such, has not
discovered—that Morality, though an end-in-itself for man, is
also something more.   It is also a means to a further end—the
supreme end of the Universe.

The immoral man is no doubt also promoting that end.   And
the religious man recognizes that fact, and acquiesces in the will
of the Absolute.   But such an admission carries with it no such
destructive moral consequences as it does for the Optimist.   For,
though the general tendency of things is towards the good, it is
not true, according to Von Hartmann, that all things are very
good.   The end which the Absolute is pursuing is only relatively
good ; it tends towards the minimization of a radical evil, due to
the fatal blunder of the Unconscious in giving birth to the
world and with it to consciousness.   And therefore, though in
his way the bad man may possibly be promoting that end, he is
never promoting it as much as the good man.   Von Hartmann's
philosophically enlightened religious man can never be tempted
to do evil that good may come.   He can never avail himself of
the excuse to which no logical Optimist has ever succeeded in
giving a satisfactory reply, ' Why should I not sin, when all will
be the same in the end, since my sin will in the end contribute
to the glory of God or true end of the Universe quite as much
as my victory over temptation ? '[2]   The Hartmannian Pessimist

[1] 'So hat das sittlich Gute seinen Ursprung immer unmittelbar oder
mittelbar in der übersittlichen Sphäre ' (*Ethische Studien*, p. 23).

[2] It has been urged in reply to this line of thought (*a*) that the fact that

must feel that, if he sins, he really does keep back the true end of the Universe ; the true end of the Universe may ultimately be attained, but not so soon, and therefore in a sense not so completely as it would be if he had resisted that temptation instead of yielding to it.

What then, it may be said, does Von Hartmann's doctrine of a super-moral sphere amount to? It seems to involve two positions :

(1) That Morality is a means to a further end beyond itself, and an end in which Morality itself is not included. It is, indeed, relatively an end-in-itself inasmuch as, upon the hypothesis of a radical evil, it is an end-in-itself to minimize it ; but the good to which the Absolute is tending can only be attained by the extinction of consciousness, and therefore also of Morality in the sense in which we know it [1].

the sin if it occurs will make the Universe better supplies no reason why it should occur, and (b) that to the good man vice is distasteful *per se*, and therefore he will avoid it even though its avoidance will not improve the Universe. I should reply (a) that my argument is that, on the optimistic hypothesis, there is no reason against sin *if* a man feels inclined to it, and (b) that the second argument really implies that this distastefulness of vice to the good man is a make-weight, so that the world without the wrong act is better than the world with it. According to the hypothesis, this must be a delusion which a rational man will surely seek to get rid of.

[1] It is true that Von Hartmann sometimes seems to treat even the minimization of evil in the present as having no objective value as an end but only as a means to the further ultimate end (e. g. *Ethische Studien*, p. 156). Elsewhere, however, he recognizes that the minimization of human pain and the promotion of human Culture (which between them represent his view of the end for man) are a part of the absolute end (ib. pp. 182, 183). Here and in *Das sittliche Bewusstsein* he seems to oscillate between making Morality an end which it is moral to promote *merely* as a means and making it intrinsically valuable, though also a means to a further end. The statement that 'der Mensch nicht Selbstzweck ist,' but 'nur ein relativer Mittelzweck im universalen teleologischen Organismus der Welt' (*Das sittliche Bewusstsein*, p. 442) seems to me formally inconsistent with the admission that 'Allerdings ist jedes Individuum selbst ein objectiver Partialzweck im Reiche der Zwecke' (p. 461). His difficulties arise in part from features of his system which it is impossible here to criticize in detail. While, in dealing with human Morality, he insists upon 'autonomy' and self-denial to the point of Rigorism, all this suffering is supposed to be imposed upon man merely as a means to the Well-being of the Absolute, whose end is purely 'eudaemonistic' (i. e. hedonistic or selfish).

(2) It involves the denial of Morality to the Absolute, but then Von Hartmann quite consistently refuses to pronounce that the Absolute, or the world in which the Absolute has revealed his unconscious essence, is perfectly good.   The present course of things is, indeed, directed towards the best possible, since it is doing its best to get rid of the original evil; and so far there seems no reason why the Unconscious should not be looked upon as perfectly moral or good (as we are expressly told that it is perfectly wise), but then after all the Absolute as Will is itself the cause of that original evil of which as Reason the same Absolute is consistently endeavouring to get rid.   Whatever may be thought of this strange cosmogony, which recalls some fantastic gnostic system rather than a sober philosophical thesis, Von Hartmann is not involved in the difficulties of those who believe in a conscious Absolute who is perfectly good, and yet wills things contrary to a Morality which is nevertheless pronounced reasonable.

It is clear that any objection which may be taken to Von Hartmann's position from our point of view turns upon his pessimistic view of the world and not upon his theory of a super-moral Absolute taken by itself.   He has what seems to me fundamentally the right conception of the relation between Morality and Religion, though his Religion is not mine.   Whether an unconscious Will, which by a strange freak of irration-

If there is any real validity in our moral judgements, how can we escape condemning the Absolute for his selfishness?   The only answer which Von Hartmann supplies is (1) that the suffering of the Absolute, if it could not work out its redemption, would be endless, and therefore greatly in excess of those which it imposes upon man as a means to deliverance; and (2) that, in some sense which he wholly fails to explain, the sufferings of the Absolute are also the sufferings of the individual, who is therefore after all only redeeming himself by the sufferings which are (after his own extinction) to work out the redemption of the Absolute.   The fundamental difficulty in Von Hartmann seems to be this: either the Happiness of the Absolute is an end in itself or it is not.   If it is, so in its measure must be the happiness of men.   If human happiness is intrinsically worthless, so must be that of the Absolute.   Moreover, if happiness, though part of the end, is not the whole end for men, it can only be part of the end for the Absolute.   Von Hartmann can only escape this dilemma by treating as a delusion that objectivity of the moral judgement on which his whole system reposes.

ality in the past created the evil against which that same
Unconscious, under the guidance of Unconscious Reason, is in
a state of continual strife, can be an object of religious emotion,
and whether such an emotion as He or it may be capable of
kindling can be a powerful moral lever, we may be allowed to
doubt.   Whether again a creed which holds that the ultimate
end is extinction of consciousness and conscious Morality can
emphasize the value of goodness, and invite to the pursuit of it,
as effectually as one which represents the good of all conscious
beings as the end, and Morality as an element in that end, is
another point on which my view differs fundamentally from
Von Hartmann's.   But at bottom that very acute writer admits
the fundamental postulate of all rational Morality and all ethical
Religion—that the ultimate end of human conduct is (albeit,
according to him, somewhat indirectly) to promote the true end
of the Universe.   And he realizes the futility of attempting to
find an adequate theoretical justification or an adequate motive
in practice for a Morality going beyond compliance with the
conventional requirements of one's immediate circle in any view
of Ethics which does not involve this intimate connexion with
Religion.

<h2 style="text-align:center">VII</h2>

The two eminent thinkers whom we have last examined have
been found to be after all not thorough-going in their doctrine of
a super-moral Absolute; and I have attempted to contend that
this want of thoroughness involves inconsistency.   In the case
of Professor Taylor, however, it is otherwise.   With him the
contradiction between the moral point of view and the 'absolute'
point of view inadequately adumbrated in the religious consciousness is final and irreconcilable, unqualified by the doctrine
of 'degrees of truth and reality,' of which in other connexions
he makes so much [1].   I have already pointed out that Professor
Taylor, in refusing to accept Mr. Bradley's doctrine that the moral
consciousness pronounces all self-sacrifice and all self-realization
to be good and equally good, has really given up the principal
ground on which Mr. Bradley seeks to convict Morality of

[1] *The Problem of Conduct*, chap. viii.

internal contradiction, and therefore refuses to attribute it to the Absolute. Professor Taylor's indictment against Morality seems to me, if I may say so with sincere respect, to turn upon more obvious confusions than those which I have had the temerity to suspect in Mr. Bradley. In the first place, he confuses the practical difficulty which the moral consciousness experiences in deciding questions of Casuistry with the intrinsic impossibility of such a solution. He fails to see that our mistakes and difficulties in this department constitute no more ground for doubting the objective validity of Moral Reason as such than the blunders or perplexities of a schoolboy do for attributing a merely subjective validity to the multiplication table. On this point I have already dwelt. Secondly, Professor Taylor seems to think that the position of those who attribute objectivity to the moral judgement, and consequently moral goodness to God, is sufficiently refuted by pointing to the undoubted fact that the details of human duty depend in part upon the circumstances and physical organization of human nature—that the Seventh Commandment, for instance, would have no meaning in reference to the conduct of sexless beings, and so on. But to maintain that for beings otherwise constituted the details of the Moral Law might be different from what they are for us does not impugn the objective validity of the judgement that for men adultery is wrong. By saying that the judgement is objectively true we mean that every intelligence, divine, angelic, or otherwise, must recognize its truth, or, if it does not recognize it, is in error. And the judgement as to what is right or wrong for man must ultimately be based on judgements of value which ought to govern the volition of all rational beings in all circumstances. The judgement that the mutual love of husband and wife in an ideal marriage is one of the noblest things on this planet is none the less true because the lower animals are incapable of it, or because beings of a higher order may be above it. And the truth of that proposition depends ultimately upon the judgement which asserts the value of Love in general—a judgement which we have every reason for believing to spring from one, and that the most important, element in the character of God.

Against the position taken up by Professor Taylor I can only refer back to those arguments in favour of the objective character of the Moral Law, and against the Moral Sense position of which his ethical system is virtually a revival, which have already been developed in the chapter on 'Reason and Feeling.' If by giving up the attempt to recognize in Morality even an imperfect revelation of ultimate Reality, Professor Taylor has avoided some of the difficulties which beset the position of Mr. Bradley and Von Hartmann, it is hard to see what grounds a writer who takes so thoroughly naturalistic or 'psychological' a view of Ethics can have left for the assumption which is intelligible in ethical Rationalists—that, though God is not moral, the Universe as a whole is good. If our moral judgements are, not merely (as they are to Mr. Bradley) riddled with contradictions, and so very inadequate and untrustworthy presentments of Reality, but purely and unmitigatedly sub-jective, what reason has Professor Taylor for pronouncing that the Universe as a whole is perfectly good? Mr. Bradley has never denied that moral judgements are rational; he has not even denied them a kind of objectivity; Professor Taylor has reduced them to modes of feeling. This seems to follow from the declaration [1] that our moral judgements are simply 'feelings of approval and disapproval,' while it is further admitted that 'to say that I approve such and such an action or quality is, in fact, to say that when I imagine its entrance into the course of my future experience my state of mind is a pleasant one [2].' Yet if the idea of value is not a category of thought, what can be meant by the judgement that the world is perfectly good on the whole? What can 'good' in such a connexion mean? For Professor Taylor it ought only to mean that it excites a particular kind of feeling in the genus *homo* or some of its members. But Professor Taylor admits that it does not excite this feeling in him, for to him as a man sin and pain appear bad. On what ground then can he pronounce that for the Absolute or in the Absolute they appear good? If the judgement of value be merely a feeling, why should we suppose that the Absolute shares the peculiar mode of human feeling which we style moral; or if we do think that the Absolute shares these human emotions, or

[1] *The Problem of Conduct*, p. 104.　　　[2] Ib. p. 124.

something analogous to them, why should we suppose that they are excited in Him by different courses of action from those which excite them in us? To oppose to our deliberate judge ments of value an *a priori* construction about the requirements of absolute harmony and the like in a perfect or absolute or 'pure' experience seems to me to put mere intellectual aspirations in place of the rational interpretation of actual experience.

Professor Taylor does not seem to me to escape the difficulties of his position by the admission that, though the moral judgement does not actually constitute a revelation of pure truth, it does tell us something about the nature of absolute Reality. He pro- nounces not merely (like Mr. Bradley) that from the point of view of the Absolute badness is good, but that it is *as* good as goodness. The paean in praise of wickedness with which Professor Taylor has concluded his book is as eloquent as any that was ever sung in praise of Virtue. Now this seems to imply that Professor Taylor has not made up his mind whether Morality is self-contradictory and one-sided (1) only in the same sense as all the Sciences, or (2) *unlike* ordinary scientific knowledge. The former contention, even if established, would not justify the assertion that the bad man in his place contributes as much to the good of the Universe as the good man, any more than a theoretical admission of abstractness or 'one-sidedness' in scientific knowledge would justify the assertion that the denial of the law of gravitation is as true as the assertion of it. And when Professor Taylor pronounces that the vice which the moral consciousness pronounces bad is as valuable as the virtue which it pronounces good, he is declaring not that our moral judgements are an inadequate expression of the nature of Reality, but that the nature of Reality is the opposite of that which the moral consciousness pronounces it to be. And in so pronouncing he claims (let me urge once more) to possess precisely that know- ledge of absolute truth which his theory disclaims. Once more, to all forms of the assertion that what we call badness is actually good I oppose the verdict of the moral consciousness. If that verdict is to be trusted, the assertion is false: if it is not to be trusted, it is impossible for Mr. Bradley or Professor Taylor to know that badness is good: for it is only by an exercise of the moral consciousness that we can know whether a thing is good or not.

Professor Taylor will no doubt appeal to the testimony of the religious consciousness. It would take too long to examine here all the astounding things which Professor Taylor and other super-Moralists have told us about the religious consciousness. It is true that in flights of religious rhetoric and ecstasies of Mysticism religious minds have sometimes involved themselves in all the difficulties of philosophic Optimism. But, speaking broadly, the religious consciousness has never really 'transcended' the distinction between good and evil in the way in which it is assumed to do by Professor Taylor. It has never declared that the distinction between moral and immoral is already abolished, and has for the religious man no existence [1]. It has always recognized the existence of evil in the present. Its faith has been—not, indeed, that the distinction between moral and immoral is to be done away with—but that, for all or for some, evil is already partially and will hereafter be more completely turned into good. Its faith has been

that good shall fall
At last—far off—at last, to all,
And every winter change to spring.

This has been at bottom—in greater or less degree—the real attitude of the deepest religious thought and feeling towards the evil in the world. And in so far as that faith has been accepted, Religion has, I venture to think, done more for the world than it would have done by persuading it that the difference between virtue and vice is a mere human delusion.

It is difficult to understand how Professor Taylor can believe that the Moral Law can, either from the point of view of reflective Reason or as a matter of psychological fact, retain its full force and validity for minds which have seen through it, and know that from the absolute point of view, and therefore for God, that Law possesses no validity whatever. If the Absolute had kept its own secret, one might understand how the delusion might have done its work in furthering the Absolute's 'super-

[1] Always excepting the Theologians who make Morality dependent upon the arbitrary Will of God.

moral' purposes; but, now that Professor Taylor has found it out, must not people put to themselves the question whether the absolute point of view is not the right point of view, and whether they can be blamed for doing what will promote the absolute end, and ignoring distinctions which for the truly rational consciousness have no existence or meaning whatever? Professor Taylor is not, indeed, very anxious to claim Religion as an ally of Morality : that, he appears to consider, would involve a kind of degradation for Religion. And yet, as he does not disavow a real sympathy not merely with the highly esoteric 'Religion' of our super-moral Philosophers but with the ordinary 'Evangelical Christianity' which is known to history and common life, he would, I presume, regard Religion as not wholly unconnected with, or, at all events, as not antagonistic to, ordinary human Morality. How belief in a deity who, it would appear, delights in wickedness at least as much as he delights in goodness can be in any way favourable to the moral life it is difficult to understand. Some connexion at least between the end for man and the end of the Universe is essential to the recognition of an objective significance in the moral judgement, and without the recognition of such an objective significance, Morality becomes a very different thing from what it is for the developed moral consciousness [1].

[1] In justice to Professor Taylor I ought to say that the attitude which he adopts towards Morality in his later *Elements of Metaphysic* seems to me materially different from that taken up in the *Problem of Conduct*. In the former he is willing even to accept (doubtless with reserves and apologies) the idea that one side of the Absolute's nature may be expressed by the word Love, and generally appears—not merely in his character as a man, but also as a Philosopher—to interpret the nature of the Absolute in terms of our moral ideals. Whether he would attempt to reconcile these assertions with the position taken up in his earlier work I am unable to say. I will only add that the Optimism of the former work seems to be much qualified. It would now appear that Reality is only 'good on the whole,' and that it is not better because that would be impossible. These propositions, with which I for one should not be disposed to quarrel, seem to me quite different from the through and through perfection which, in the *Problem of Conduct*, is ascribed not merely to the world as a whole, but to everything in it. Since writing this note I have seen Professor Taylor's review of Dr. McTaggart's *Some Dogmas of Religion* in the *Philosophical Review* (July, 1906), in which he explicitly gives up the view which I have criticized.

VIII

We have, then, discovered no reason in the arguments of the super-moral Religionists for abandoning the position that the end prescribed to man by his own moral consciousness must be part of the true end of the Universe. That there is one absolute standard of values, which is the same for all rational beings, is just what Morality means. Nothing less than that is implied by the idea of absolute value which underlies the simplest moral judgement, when its implications are analysed and reflected on.

It may, indeed, be suggested that we do possess in human intelligence the form of the Moral Law—the bare idea of an end, the bare notion of something which ought absolutely to be done—without any power of giving a content to that form, of saying what things in particular possess this value, and what things therefore ought actually to be done. But such a view implies a more than Kantian divorce of form from content. The form or category of the Moral Law is only got by abstraction from actual concrete moral judgements. To maintain that we do know that the Universe has an end, though we are wholly without the power of determining what that end is, would be (as I have already suggested) like maintaining that we have indeed a conception of number which is of objective validity, but that we have no reason to believe that the actual contents of the multiplication table belong to any region but that of mere 'appearance.' Neither in the ethical nor in any other department of human thought is it possible to prove that our thought does not deceive us : and in this as in other spheres our thought is doubtless inadequate. The wide differences of opinion which are found even in the developed human intelligence in the matter of Ethics constitute a reason, indeed, for supposing that our conception of the ultimate end—the conception hitherto reached by any actual human being—represents an inadequate view of the truth ; but they supply no reason for assuming a total and fundamental discrepancy between a moral truth, which is merely human, and a metaphysical or religious truth, which is divine. Our ethical, like all our knowledge, is inadequate—more inadequate no doubt than the knowledge already attained in some branches of Physical Science, which is less inexact within its own limits just because it is more abstract and incomplete. It is not enough to say, as Von Hartmann [1] at times seems disposed to say, that moral judgements do represent a particular means to the ultimate end, but that the end itself may be quite different. For the very essence of the moral judgement is that the end towards which we conceive it to be right to direct our actions possesses absolute value. If we are fundamentally deceived as to that, we have no reason to believe that these acts are even a means to the true end [2]. That the ends to which we attribute value may be ends which ought not in particular cases to be attained because their attainment would make impossible the attainment of ends still more valuable, may very well be the case. That in some such direction is to be found the ultimate explanation of the existence of evil has already been asserted, but that evil is a means to the greatest attainable good is a proposition which is only maintainable upon the hypothesis that there is in the ultimate nature of things— that is to say the ultimate nature of God—an inherent reason why greater good should not be attainable. It may be im-possible to prove—even in the sense in which any ultimate meta-physical truth is capable of proof—that that ultimate reason is not to be sought in a defect of goodness in the Being from whom all Reality is derived. But the dilemma forces itself upon us that the explanation must be sought either in such a moral limitation or in some other kind of limitation—a limita-tion which, in the doubtless inadequate and analogical language which we are always compelled to use in speaking of ultimate

[1] I have pointed out above (p. 278) that this is only one aspect of his thought.

[2] This is quite consistent with maintaining that, when there is no consciousness of an end at all, in the lower animals and in men so long and so far as they have impulses which are independent of their rational judgements, such impulses may be directed towards the true end of the Universe. The savage's passion of Revenge tends no doubt in many ways to the true end of the Universe, but, as soon as he is capable of feeling that he ought to restrain it, the restraint must tend to that end more than the unlimited indulgence of it.

Reality, may be best described as a limitation of Power. To adopt the former alternative would involve the strange idea that the Being from whom all our ideas are derived, and who cannot reasonably be thought of as subject to the limitations which are connected with the life of the bodily organism, deliberately acts in a way contrary to the dictates of his own thought, to judgements which present themselves to Him as necessary truths : the latter view has nothing against it but a groundless assumption. To this consideration may be added the extreme improbability (on any theory which represents the Universe as rational) that the derived human consciousness should be superior in reasonableness of insight or in reasonableness of will to its source, or at least under an unavoidable necessity of thinking itself so—a far greater improbability than is involved in supposing that the power of realizing its ideals possessed by the ultimate Will, while enormously transcending that of the derived will, should still fall short of a power to produce good only with no evil at all.

Not only is the hypothesis of pure Optimism not necessary to Morality ; it is positively hostile to it. It is a postulate of Morality that the ends that we feel ourselves bound to work for should be in some measure attainable if we will them, but it is a postulate of Morality also that they should not be completely attainable, if we do not will them. The very essence of the moral judgement is not merely that the right act promotes the end, but that the wrong act retards it. The judgement that the act is really a means to the end may of course be erroneous like any other particular human judgement; but it is the very heart of all our ethical thinking that, if and in so far as the judgement is ethically justified, it is a real means to the absolute end. Even the really bad act may of course be a means to an ultimate good, but it must be a means to a less good than might have been attained if the action ethically right in the circumstances had been done. Had the agent a full knowledge that his act would produce more good than harm, the action would have been a right action. When more good than harm comes·out of an action which it was sinful in the agent to will, that must be because he did not know of the good effects, or because he willed them for some other reason than these good effects. So the moral consciousness pronounces, and its pronouncement can only be a true one if a wrong act really makes the world worse than it would otherwise have been[1]. Only if the Universe is less good than a Universe which we can imagine, can the alternative which is presented to us in every act of moral judgement be, as our moral consciousness assures us that it is, a real alternative. It is not here asserted that in every or any such choice between alternatives the possibility of the alternative actually rejected was, even from the point of view of absolute and complete knowledge, a real possibility [2]: but only that, if the act ethically right had been done instead of the act ethically wrong, the Universe on the whole would have been a better Universe than it actually is. Such is the postulate implied by every moral system which really accepts the idea of an objective Morality reflected, however imperfectly, in our ethical judgements—reflected imperfectly, but reflected less and less imperfectly as those judgements become ethically more advanced and more reasonable. The end of the Universe must be the evolution of souls in which what our moral consciousness pronounces good shall be more and more realized. If less good is at any time realized in preference to more good, that represents one of those inherent limitations without the assumption of which we cannot give any reasonable or intelligible account of the Universe being what it is.

In speaking of the end of the Universe we must not of course assume that the realization of this end lies only in the future, that it is literally a 'far off divine event': whatever has any value in the present forms part of the end. In so far, for instance, as the lower animals enjoy pleasure, that is good— a partial realization of the ultimate end, though it may be also a means to some further and greater good. When an

---

[1] If the 'O felix culpa' of the Roman Liturgy is to be justified, we should have to say that, had Adam known the consequences (according to traditional Theology) of his sin, it would not have been a sin. I do not deny that a particular wrong act, done with bad intentions, might sometimes incidentally leave the world better than it would have been without that particular wrong act, but then a world in which the good effect would have been produced without the sin would have been still better.

[2] I am not here arguing for a 'liberum arbitrium indifferentiae,' as is explained in the next chapter.

animal suffers, that must be a means to a good otherwise unattainable for itself or its fellows or for some higher race yet to be evolved. If the animal is incapable of the higher goods which human beings enjoy, that must be because the inherent limitations of Reality make it impossible that that animal should have been a moral being without a larger loss of good upon the whole. The end which we must suppose to be the end of the Universe must be the greatest good on the whole, the greatest good that is possible; that is to say, the good that necessarily flows from a Will of perfect goodness but limited power. And human duty must consist in co-operation with that Will. Only the Religion which proclaims that identity between the divine end and the end revealed in the moral consciousness at its highest can be regarded as finally and absolutely valuable either as an aid to Morality or as an end in itself, though, of course, Religions which more or less fall short of this ideal may have their relative and temporary justification. And if a Religion is not of use in the interests of Morality—that is to say, of that end which Morality bids us promote—it is of no use at all, upon the assumption which we have throughout made and attempted to justify—the assumption that our moral judgements possess objective validity.

It may be objected that we have no right to oppose the Goodness of God to his Power, as though they were distinct qualities controlling and limiting one another, and to pronounce the one unlimited, and the other limited. I should reply that every distinction of elements or of aspects in the divine nature based upon the analogy of human experience must necessarily be an inadequate representation of the ultimate nature of Reality. We can distinguish between thought and feeling and willing in men: and we cannot think of the divine Mind at all without supposing that in that Mind, too, there is thinking and feeling and willing, or something analogous to each of them. And yet it is impossible that thought and feeling can be related in God as they are related in us—that in God the object of thought should be, as it is in us, something not actually experienced, something merely representative of a reality without being that reality; that God's thought consists in making abstractions which (as Mr. Bradley has taught us) necessarily leave out so much of the actual fact [1], in inferences which imply that something has become known which was previously unknown; or again, that feeling should be in God exactly what it is in beings whose experience is limited and conditioned by a material organism. And yet without these distinctions of thought and feeling we cannot attach any significance to the idea of Mind, and could mean nothing when we say that God is Mind or Spirit. All human thinking implies abstraction—that is to say, the separation in thought of aspects of Reality which in actual fact are not apart but together. When we oppose God's Goodness to his Power, we are using exactly the same kind of abstraction which we use in distinguishing between feeling and thought and will in God. And there is this further justification of our procedure. I can attach a definite meaning to the idea of perfect goodness—as definite as any conception that I can form of a Spirit in which the limitations and imperfections of the spirits actually known to my experience are left out. The idea of 'infinite' or 'unlimited' power is a meaningless expression. It implies an ultimate Reality—a Will which has no definite characteristics or properties at all. And further, such a concept implies a contradiction to what we mean when we say that God is perfectly good. However much good there was in any actual world—even if that good were unqualified by any evil,— we could always ask ' why should there not have been twice that good?' And to that question there could never be an answer as long as we regard God as a Being in whom there are infinite or unlimited potentialities of creation.

IX

To ask what is the truth and value of the various historical Religions in accordance with the standard here set up, is an enquiry which would carry us far beyond the limits of the present work. It cannot be too strongly insisted on that Religion has never exercised any great or widespread moral influence over mankind in a purely abstract or philosophical form.

[1] e.g. the statement 'trees are green,' or even ' this tree is green,' does not tell us anything about the particular kind of green: no tree is green in general, and yet all thought involves the use of Universals.

In their historical form the higher Religions of mankind have always been, and are likely to be for the most part, the creations of great personalities, developed and appropriated by societies. In this social appropriation of Religions which have been founded by a particular Founder or have gradually evolved at a particular epoch in time, the criticism, the interpretations or the corrections supplied by Philosophy, and particularly by ethical Philosophy, have played an important and conspicuous part. But the business of the Philosopher who has any belief in the power and value of Religion is rather to determine the attitude of the reflective mind towards existing Religions and Churches than to substitute some system of his own for them. An examination of the áctual contents of the higher Religions is the business of religious, and not of purely ethical, Philosophy. But a few remarks may be made on the attitude which ought to be adopted towards existing forms of Religion by any one who has so far followed the present writer's argument.

All theistic Religions have more or less consciously and consistently asserted that view of the relation between the absolute end and the moral end which has been set forth in this work. They have all asserted that the Will of God is a Will for the best possible. The religious consciousness has at all times been exposed to the temptation to distort this proposition into the assertion that what God wills is, just because it is actually willed, the ethically best. But, though many historical Religions have tended towards Theism and consequently towards that identification of Religion and Ethics which I have here pleaded, only three great historical Religions have completely and consistently realized that goal: Judaism, the Christianity which has grown out of Judaism, and the Mohammedanism which, if not actually a mere corruption of Judaism and Christianity, would certainly not have been what it is without them. Only perhaps in Christianity, and in Christianity at its best, has that identification of the ethically best with the actual Will of God been fully reali.ed and kept free from degenerating into the immoral proposition that the Will of God, as revealed not in the moral consciousness but in the actual course of events, is the ethically best [1]. The

[1] I do not, of course, deny that at certain periods this idea has appeared

claim of Christianity to be the 'absolute' or 'final' Religion must rest in the long run firstly upon the superior clearness and definiteness with which it proclaims a conception of God based upon the ethical ideal; secondly, upon the fact that its ethical ideal represents the moral ideal at its highest.

It may be asked 'where is this Christian ideal to be found, and how is it known to be the highest?' To the second of these questions I need only answer that the moral consciousness alone can be the final judge of the truth, validity, and sufficiency of a moral ideal. The first is an historical question which I have here no room to answer, except by expressing my belief that the ideal alike of human life and of the divine Nature actually to be found in the critically sifted records of the life and teaching of Jesus Christ is, in its essential principles, the ideal which the moral consciousness of Humanity still accepts and proclaims [1]. At the same time it is only in principle and not in detail (as has been already insisted [2]) that there can be any finality about any moral ideal whatever, and consequently in any Religion which is to include a moral ideal. The idea of a development through the consciousness of the religious community is as essential to a just conception of Christianity as the assertion of the unique importance of the historical Christ. If there were no development of the moral ideal, and of the Theology which is based upon the moral ideal, the inherited and stereotyped ideal of the past would no longer express the living convictions of a world which moves. In proportion as any development should not be in its essence a real development in harmony with the spirit of the historic Christ, that development could not claim to be really Christian, but it is impossible to define *a priori* what degree of development would involve

in Christian Theology, or that it is familiar to individual enlightened adherents of other Religions, particularly to the late Judaism which can hardly have been uninfluenced by Christian ideas.

[1] If I should be wrong in this view, I should have made a mistake as an Historian, and as a Theologian in so far as the content of Theology is necessarily in part derived from History, but the mistake would leave my Moral Philosophy unaffected. I make this remark to avoid a possible misrepresentation of the above pages.

[2] Book II, chap. v.

such a new departure as to render the Religion that admitted it
no longer entitled to the distinctive name of Christianity. That
the ideal which is still approved by the most developed moral
consciousness of the present day is such a legitimate development of the teaching and character of Jesus is a proposition
which could, I believe, be supported by a critical examination of
the historical facts. If the reasons which have been given already[1]
for believing that that ideal in its essence will not be transcended are sound, the Religion of the future will remain Christianity, however much it may hereafter be developed by growing
experience on the one hand and by the development of the moral
consciousness on the other. If the essence of true Religion
be the identification of the Will of God with the highest ethical
ideal, every development of the moral ideal will necessarily
carry with it a corresponding religious development. Both on
the religious and on the ethical side, therefore, Christianity can
only claim to be the final or absolute Religion by showing itself,
at the same time, also a constantly growing and developing
Religion. And the belief in such a development is historically
an essential and characteristic element in the Religion itself.
Belief in the Holy Ghost is as much an article of the Christian
Creed as belief in the historic Son of God.

X

The view that the religious attitude carries us into some
super-moral region and enables us to attain a point of view
from which moral distinctions are 'transcended' has already
been sufficiently dealt with. That such a Religion is possible
may be freely admitted. But such Religion is, as I contend,
a Religion which, even from the point of view of those who
regard Morality as of merely human and subjective validity,
ought not to be encouraged. Such is precisely the kind of
Religion which at every age of the world's history exists in
sufficient abundance to supply no little justification for the
Lucretian verdict upon Religion in general:

Tantum religio potuit suadere malorum.

[1] Above, p. 177 sq.

If the value of everything is determined by the moral judgement, there can be no value in a Religion which is opposed to
Morality.   But even those who believe in a Morality which is in
essential harmony with Religion, and in a Religion which does not
seek to 'transcend' Morality, may possibly object to our limiting
the contents of the religious consciousness entirely to the moral
ideal.   And no doubt a certain amount of explanation or qualification is required to justify the language which I have used.
It has already been pointed out that we cannot isolate the moral
consciousness.   Every moral ideal implies a great deal besides
itself.   If the end which it is a moral duty to pursue includes
the effort to attain a true view of the Cosmos and a true appreciation of everything in it which there is value in knowing
or beauty in contemplating, the assertion that our knowledge of
God is based entirely upon the moral ideal will not necessarily
imply that our idea of God must owe nothing to the development of the scientific or the aesthetic consciousness, or foster
that narrowness and austerity of view which is often associated
with strong assertions of the importance of 'moral,' 'ethical,' or
'practical' interests.   An adequate recognition of the value
which our Moral Reason discovers in Science and in Art, in the
beauty possessed by the worlds of Nature and of imagination,
is part of true Morality, and therefore must contribute its share
to our conception of God and of the divine end.   If God wills
Nature, every part of Nature must tell us something of God.
And every change in our scientific or aesthetic attitude towards
the world must bring with it some change in our attitude or
subjective feeling towards God.   If by Religion we mean a man's
total attitude—intellectual, emotional, and practical—towards
the Universe as a whole, it cannot be denied that intellectual
progress is continually bringing with it changes in Religion,
even apart from the changes which increased knowledge of
Nature necessarily brings with it in the details of human duty.
It is of great importance, no doubt, to recognize that, while the
detailed knowledge of scientific law affects very slightly either
our emotional or our practical attitude towards the Universe as
a whole or the Mind of which that Universe is the expression,
the larger changes in man's attitude towards Nature—know-

ledge of the vastness of the Universe, belief in the universality
of natural law, the substitution of evolution for special creation
and the like—do affect in important ways our attitude towards
God.   But after all it remains true that it is only from the
moral consciousness that we can gather any idea of the character
or final purpose of God.   Nature tells us something about what
God actually wills, but knows nothing of the difference between
ends and means : it tells us nothing about values ; and therefore,
by itself, it tells us nothing about the character of God and the
deeper meaning of the Universe.   For it is not merely because
things *are*, but because they have value, that we believe that they
form part of the end for God.   And our knowledge of the
character or will of God is based upon our conception of his end.
The scientific consciousness may tell us that a law is true ; the
aesthetic consciousness may tell us that the world is beautiful.
But that Truth and Beauty in general, or that particular truths
and particular beauties, have value, is revealed to us only by the
moral or value-judging consciousness.   And it is our ideas of
value that determine our practical attitude towards God and the
world, and that inspire those emotions which are capable of
affecting the will.   It is the attitude of the will, together with
the knowledge and the emotions which affect the will, that we
generally understand by the term Religion.

That mere intellectual knowledge of Nature's laws does not
by itself constitute Religion or even what we call religious
belief, there is a general consensus.   There is perhaps a tendency
in some quarters to give the name of Religion to the emotion
which is inspired by the scientific knowledge and the aesthetic
appreciation of Nature, even when the emotion does not in any
direct and immediate way affect action [1].   Whether such emotion
can be called religious, is a question of words which it is hardly
worth while to discuss.   Knowledge and aesthetic appreciation and
the emotions associated with them are no doubt elements in the
ideal relation towards God, and so far they may be called religious.
But they can only be regarded as constituting a very subordinate
element in Religion for two reasons.   In the first place, religious
belief is, according to the ordinary use of language, belief about

---

[1] e.g. in Seeley's *Natural Religion*.

the ultimate nature of things, not about their detail. In the second place, there is a pretty general disposition to recognize that even belief about the ultimate nature of things is not religious except in so far as it has, directly or indirectly, some bearing upon practice. And, though the pursuit of Truth and Beauty are elements in the practical ideal, they are so only in a very subordinate degree for the great majority of men. Though for artists or scholars the pursuit of these things forms a large part of their duty (just as detailed knowledge of particular Sciences may have an important bearing upon the duties of particular professions), it is only that part of a man's belief and that kind of emotion which have some bearing upon human duty in general which we commonly regard as religious. Knowledge of the Universe in general and the emotions which its Beauty excites do, indeed, contribute something to our knowledge of God, and to the ideal feeling towards Him ; but, since such knowledge and feeling form only in a restricted degree the duty of every one, we shall not be far wrong in saying that the value of right religious belief and religious emotion lies chiefly in their tendency to promote right action. It is only the kind of truth which is capable of affecting practice, and the kind of emotion which conduces to right practice, that we can naturally regard as belonging to Religion. Such an account of the matter is no doubt vague, and anything but a vague definition would necessarily misrepresent the facts : for a man's Religion is not marked off by any sharp dividing line from other aspects of his life. Religious belief is one particular aspect of a man's total belief about the world ; religious emotion is not any one specific emotion, but a particular aspect of his emotional attitude towards the Universe or its ultimate source ; religious conduct is good conduct in general when looked upon as representing a right attitude of the will towards the ultimate source of Reality.

If, therefore, we ask whether we are to regard Religion as *merely* a means to Morality, we shall answer that we shall do so only upon the condition that our idea of Morality is wide enough to include the duty of seeking for Truth, and of aiming at a right state of the emotions, for their own sakes. Truth and ideal emotion no doubt include much that has no direct and immediate bearing upon the duty of the individual man, except his duty towards the true and the beautiful. And, inasmuch as we do not recognize the pursuit of all kinds of truth and the cultivation of every kind of emotion as the duty of every man, we are not accustomed to include detailed knowledge of the world and the cultivation of every kind of emotion in our conception of Religion, though no doubt the cultivation of these things forms the duty of some people. But we do hold that some knowledge about the world in general and some kind of emotion connected with that view are essential to the ideal life of every one: and it is just that knowledge and emotion which we regard as religious. Not every one need be or can be a Philosopher or an Artist, but everybody can be and ought to be religious. The objection to speaking of Religion as a mere means to Morality is that it seems to suggest an ideal of life in which Knowledge and Beauty have no place. On the other hand, the tendency to emphasize the ' religious ' character of mere intellectual insight and ordinary aesthetic emotion tends to an underestimate of the supreme value which the healthy moral consciousness accords to the rightly directed will. By general consent of those who take the religious view of life at all, Religion is the most important thing in the world. Any view of Religion, therefore, which encourages the disposition to give a higher place to any other aspect of life than that which is taken by the moral consciousness must be a false or one-sided view of it on the supposition which has been defended in these pages; namely, that the moral consciousness is the organ of truth, and the chief source—in a sense the sole source—of religious knowledge. Religion can only be the most important thing in life if it includes Morality and the feelings, emotions, desires to which the moral consciousness attributes supreme value, and excludes those which the moral consciousness condemns. We are dealing here with a question of values, and if our moral consciousness does not give us any true information about values, assuredly we can know nothing at all about values: for the moral consciousness means that side of our consciousness which judges of values.

XI

We have been dealing so far with the question of the relation between Religion and Ethics in general. But the subject leads on to the discussion of a particular ethical question—the nature of what are usually called, in a narrower sense, religious duties. Are worship and other religious observances of a similar character ends in themselves, or are they merely means to the performance of duty ? The answer is substantially implied in the view we have already taken of the relation between Religion and Ethics in general. If our conception of God be grounded upon our moral ideal, it is impossible to suppose that He has arbitrarily prescribed duties which have no bearing upon our relation to the highest moral ideal. To fear God, as the perfectly righteous Will, and to keep those commandments which necessarily flow from a perfectly righteous Will, must literally constitute the whole duty of man. We cannot—after the fashion not so much of the older Christian thinkers as of the semi-deistic eighteenth-century divines—speak as though, by a kind of arbitrary appendix to the moral law, a duty of going to Church had been imposed, as a sort of personal compliment to the Almighty, independently of its effects upon the mind and character of the worshipper. There is nothing substantially wrong in saying that the value of all such observances consists solely in their effects upon character and life. Only it must be remembered that the cultivation of right ideas about the world in general and a right emotional response to those ideas is a part of the true ideal of life. The outward acts of worship—the saying or singing of words, the performance of ceremonies, the utterance of prayer or praise, the listening to exhortation or instruction—can only be regarded as valuable because they express and tend to cultivate a right state of the soul, but that right state of the soul is in a sense an end-in-itself. If the Will of God is that we should serve our brethren, the right state of the soul will be one which is dominated by that desire ; but inasmuch as a certain state of intellect and emotion as well as of will forms part of the true end for man, acts of worship which tend to promote true knowledge of God and a sense of the beauty of God's world will have a value

of their own independently of the utility which they possess as
a direct incitement and preparation for action. In the ideal love of
God there are aesthetic and intellectual elements—knowledge of
God's nature, awe and reverence for the wonder of the world,
admiration of its beauty, considered as a revelation of the Mind
which makes it—as well as the distinctly moral element (in the
narrower sense of the word) which consists in reverence for the
character of God. In so far as these things enter into Religion,
there is a meaning in saying that Religion is an end-in-itself,
and an end which does not consist exclusively in practical
Morality ; and, in as far as worship is a means of cultivating
such a religious state of mind, it may be regarded as more than
a means to an end beyond itself. It becomes a kind of spiritual
culture, which, like the more purely intellectual and aesthetic
culture, is both a means and an end—a means to the ideal life of
the soul but also one of those activities in which that life consists. I need not repeat here what has been said about the
duty of subordinating the pursuit of truth and of beauty to the
true love of our fellow-men—that is to say, the desire to promote
for them also a good which includes the love of truth and of
beauty. Only when thus subordinated do they form elements
in the love of God, and become part of the end which worship
promotes, and of which in a sense it forms a part.

Socrates was wont to ask whether Virtue can be taught.
Whatever exact sense be given to the word ' teach,' few reflecting persons would deny that it is possible for people to make
themselves and one another more virtuous by systematic cultivation of the ethical side of their nature. In the history of the
past by far the most successful means of direct moral culture
which the world has succeeded in inventing, among peoples
which have risen to the level of ethical Religion, have been the
societies called Churches and the institution called public Worship in all its forms[1]. It is hardly possible to exaggerate the

---

[1] If we except the influence of Education, which, where it has possessed
sufficient power to be compared in its influence on life with that of ethical
Religion, has seldom been unconnected with a more directly religious
influence. If it be suggested that private devotion is often a still more
powerful influence than that of public Worship, I should admit the fact,

naïveté of the idea that individuals as a rule or societies in any case can give up this means of moral culture, and put nothing in its place, without a more or less serious descent to a lower moral level.   We may smile at some of the Positivist imitations of Catholic worship, but the Positivists are assuredly right in holding that Morality requires the support of instruction and exhortation, of spiritual self-expression and recollection, of social observance and mutual encouragement.   A comparative survey of the moral condition of different civilized countries at the present moment supplies strong empirical evidence in favour of such a view.   Those who believe that the institutions of Church and Worship in their old forms have lost their efficacy, or that they are incapable of a reform which will restore it, are bound to give serious consideration to the question how they can be replaced.   For those who do believe in their efficacy and value, there is no more pressing or more obvious duty than to consider how they may be made more efficient organs for the discharge of their absolutely indispensable social function.

but should add that there is little reason to believe that on any large scale such habits of private devotion have survived, or ever will survive, the entire desuetude of public Worship.   Just as the internal Conscience is only created and educated by a powerful 'external Conscience,' so private Religion is created and educated by the external manifestations, and social organization, of Religion.

CHAPTER III

FREE-WILL

I

In dealing with the metaphysical postulates or presuppositions of Morality, we came to the conclusion that there can be no Morality unless our theory of the Universe is such that the acts of the individual can in some real sense be ascribed to the self. But as to the exact sense in which these acts are to be so ascribed, nothing has yet been determined. A full discussion of the problem usually known as that of Free-will belongs, in my opinion, rather to a general system of Metaphysic than to a treatise on Ethics. Yet the idea of Free-will is, or has been supposed to be, so intimately connected with our ultimate moral ideas that the Moral Philosopher must at least give some account of his own attitude towards it, although it may be an attitude which could only be adequately justified by a complete exposition of his theory of the Universe.

What then is the question of Free-will? There can be no doubt that the plain man, prior to reflection, does habitually assume that his actions are not the necessary results of preceding actions or of anything else in the Universe before those acts took place; that no knowledge of his previous actions, or even of his previous character—at least of his original character before it was gradually moulded by his own acts of voluntary choice—could possibly enable any one else, or even himself, to predict with certainty how he would act in any given complication of circumstances. When he looks back upon past misdoing, he declares that that misdoing is something which need not have occurred. No matter what he was or what he did before that act, no matter what original nature or character he brought with him into the world, all else up to that moment might have been the same, and yet that act might have remained undone. If a small amount of reflection will induce some hesitation as to the unconsidered or impulsive acts which seem traceable to habit—formed, as he may still be disposed to contend, by previous acts of free and undetermined choice—he will at least insist that acts of deliberate and reflective choice between alternatives of real moral significance are strictly undetermined and essentially unpredictable, at all events by any intelligence which can only arrive at a knowledge of the future by inference from the past and the present. This is what the plain man understands by freedom of the will: and there are Philosophers who declare that the plain man is right, and are ready even to follow him into his further assertion that, if Free-will in this sense did not exist, Morality would lose all its value, its meaning, its very existence. On the other hand, it is maintained by the Determinist that actions are the necessary results of the man's original nature or constitution, as modified by the whole series of influences, social and physical, which have acted upon him from the moment of birth up to the moment of action. Actions are the necessary result of original character and environment. Original character and environment being the same, the act could not have been different. Given an adequate knowledge of both, the act could always have been predicted. An easy way of realizing the problem, the nature of which is frequently misconceived, and that by no means only by beginners in Philosophy, is to suppose (*per impossibile* no doubt) two twin brothers endowed originally with absolutely identical natures, and exposed from the moment of birth to exactly the same social and other influences. At the age of twenty, according to the Determinist theory, their characters would be precisely the same, and in any given circumstances they would act in precisely the same way: according to the libertarian view one of them might have become a saint, and the other a scoundrel.

We may assume for the present that the question of Free-will or Determinism turns upon this question of predictability, though hereafter some qualification of this assumption may be required. It must not, indeed, be supposed (as is often done in popular argument on both sides) that the Determinist imagines that an adequate knowledge of psychological or sociological law would enable him to predict a man's future conduct from his past actions. Whatever we understand by character, and however we envisage its relation to brain and nervous system, no man's character is fully expressed by his actual conduct in the past. Character must always include undeveloped possibilities. The response which a character will make to a new stimulus, or even to the repetition of an old stimulus [1], can never be inferred with absolute certainty from the response it has made to previous stimuli. Nor need a sudden alteration in a man's habitual conduct necessarily imply that some fresh and unusual external influence has been brought to bear upon him. For a man's character may be such as to react in one way to a given stimulus ninety-nine times, and in a different way to the hundredth, just because it is the hundredth. A man may be so constituted as to listen unmoved to a thousand sermons, and yet to have his whole life altered by the thousand and first—not essentially different in its general character from the former ; while another, whose outer and even inner life has been to all appearance previously similar, may remain equally inaccessible to any number of such appeals. A more frequent experience is the abandonment of a mode of life simply because a certain experience of it has proved its unsatisfactory character. There is, therefore, no ground for the idea—often suggested both by supporters and opponents—that Determinism is inconsistent with conversion or change of character, or even that such change can only take place in consequence of some palpably new feature in the external environment. Change of character, whether gradual or sudden, is as easily explainable on Determinist grounds as continued identity of character. It is not only the outward behaviour that may change, but the character also—in the sense in which we are accustomed to use that word in ordinary life or ethical discussion—though doubtless some characteristics of the man must remain even after the most startling of such changes if he

---

[1] Of course the repetition is by itself a new feature in the environment. It may very plausibly be suggested that the earlier experiences have already modified the character or (as modern Psychologists say) the ' sub-conscious self,' but these effects may not have risen above the ' threshold of Consciousness.' This principle has been used by Professor James in his *Varieties of Religious Experience* to explain the phenomena of religious conversion.

is to remain the same man. Not only his acts, but his motives, his emotions, his principles of action may become quite different from what they were before the hitherto latent capacity of his nature was called into activity. Of course, if by 'character' we choose to understand the whole of man's capacities for reacting to different stimuli [1], the original man with all his possibilities, then it must be admitted that on Determinist principles character is unchangeable. But this is not what we mean by 'character' in ordinary ethical judgements. To maintain that a man gradually or suddenly 'converted' is still a bad man because, but for some change in his circumstances, he would still have been a bad man, is to confound character with some ultimate psychological or metaphysical ground or basis or source of 'character,' true or false. It would be better to say that the 'self' remains the same—identical through differences, the same and yet not the same—though character may change. From the point of view of Ethics real change of character is undoubtedly a fact of experience—one of the facts which each side in the controversy must take as data for the discussion. It is only a very crude Determinism which denies this, and only a very crude or unfair Indeterminist who can suppose that his opponent is logically bound to deny it.

Another unfair mode of statement often adopted by Determinists is to accuse their opponents of admitting the possibility of 'unmotived willing.' The Indeterminist, if he knows how to do justice to his own case, admits that action is always inspired by motives. But it must be conceded on all hands that the 'motive' cannot be identified with some factor in the external environment taken by itself, or even with some imagined object of desire as it would be apart from the individual's reaction upon it. It is unquestionable, not only that in the same external environment two different men will act very differently, but that the same imagined pleasure or pain [2], the same anticipated

---

[1] The change of stimulus need not always be intellectual, as Schopenhauer assumes when he says 'Repentance never proceeds from a change of the will (which is impossible), but from a change of knowledge' (*The World as Will and Idea*, Eng. Trans., I. p. 382).

[2] It might no doubt be maintained that in strictness it never is the same: it is made different in the two cases by the difference of the psychical context

4 2

personal experience or external event, will·call forth a very
different response in different individuals.   Both sides must
admit that conscious and deliberate action (we may for convenience here ignore all other kinds of human behaviour) is
always instigated by a desire : nor ought there to be any hesitation on either side to admit that it is always the strongest desire
that determines action.   It need not be the desire which seemed
strongest to the man at the moment before he acted; but, when
he has acted, that fact shows that the desire which prevailed was
the strongest.   We have no criterion for estimating the relative
strength of conflicting desires except the influence which they
exercise upon action.   But unquestionably the relative strength
of the desire is not due to anything in the desired object (as it
is when taken apart from the consciousness of the individual),
but to something in the man himself.   The question about which
the Determinist and the Indeterminist are at issue is precisely
this : 'What is it that makes a desired object appeal more
strongly to one man than it does to another?'   The man always
acts in obedience to the strongest motive, but the question remains :
'What is it that determines the greater strength of one desire
as compared with another in different individuals?'   'Clearly
something in the man himself,' both sides will reply.   But to the
Determinist that 'something in the man' must mean 'something
in the man as he was at the moment before the alternative was
presented—something itself the result of his original constitution
(material or spiritual) as he was at the moment of birth together
with the whole environment of his life up to the moment of
action.'   To the Indeterminist it will mean 'something which
came into existence at that instant, which had never been in
existence before, which was not the necessary result of anything
that had been in existence before, which could not be inferred
by any sagacity from anything that was in the world up to that
moment, an absolutely new creation.'   The action on this view is
due to the man certainly, but not simply to the man as he was
born, or even the man as he has made himself by previous acts

in which it stands in the two cases.   This is the same thing as saying that
a particular 'object of desire' has no existence which is independent of the
whole personality of the desiring subject.

of choice, but to the man as he makes himself at that minute.
It is this power of making himself anew by successive acts,
unfettered even by his previous self, which more than aught else
constitutes him (according to the Indeterminist) a moral being.
The acts flow from the self, but the self is a self-creative self.
Whether such a conception is ultimately intelligible, we shall
have hereafter to examine.   But that is the fairest way of
presenting the Indeterminist case.

   The case has so far been stated as though the Libertarian
maintained that every act—at least every act of deliberate and
reflective choice between alternatives morally significant—were
wholly uninfluenced either by original character, by environment, or by previous acts of free choice—that every such act
is undetermined and equally undetermined.   A position so
obviously inconsistent with the most familiar experience has
never perhaps been deliberately maintained by any human
being, but it must be confessed that till very recently advocates
of Indeterminism have taken little pains to protect themselves·
against such a travesty of their position.   A moment's reflection
will be enough to show that such a contention would amount to
the denial that there is such a thing as character, that there is
any permanence or continuity at all about the self to which
action is referred.   All that the Libertarian is bound to maintain
is that these acts of undetermined choice constitute one of the
factors which determine the character of the man's life, a factor
whose moral significance from the Indeterminist point of view
need not be diminished even if it were admitted that—externally
considered—it is the smallest of these factors.   Ninety-nine
hundredths (so to speak) of a man's life might be due to
heredity, education, environment, and original constitution ; but
provided there were a hundredth part referable only to undetermined acts of choice, that would be enough to satisfy the
postulate of Freedom.   On this view it would be *that* hundredth
part—some difference scarcely visible to superficial observation,
a little more or a little less of kindliness or family affection in the
man whom circumstances have turned into an habitual criminal,
a little more or less conscientiousness and self-denial in the
man whom circumstances have made respectable—that stamps

him as morally good or bad in the true ethical sense, or at least
in the truest sense, of those words.   This point of view was once
paradoxically expressed by an able advocate of Indeterminism—
the late Professor Chandler of Oxford—when he said that it
was enough that one act of a man's life should be free.   But in
truth it is not necessary that even an isolated act should be
referable *wholly* to the free will.   It would be enough that it
should enter as a factor into the determination of a man's acts or
some of them, that a man's acts and matured character should
be referable not to two factors but to three—birth-character,
environment, undetermined choice.

Much confusion has been caused in this matter by the use
of the term 'Freedom' in a variety of senses which are not
always clearly distinguished from one another by those who use
them.   In particular the word Freedom has been employed in
the following three sharply distinguishable senses :—

(1) Sometimes it means that an act is one done in obedience to
Reason or to the higher self : because only in such acts is the
agent conscious of no discord between the higher and lower self,
because only then is the man's deliberate conviction of what is
highest and best for him not dominated and controlled by passing
desires, capricious lusts, and fleeting passions.   In this sense it
is clear that good acts alone are free.   The idea that goodness or
the service of God is 'perfect freedom' is from a practical point
of view an extremely valuable and stimulating idea.   But it
obviously involves a metaphor, and its introduction into the
controversy between Determinism and its opposite has led to
endless confusion.   The idea is one which, in works of technical
Ethics at least, had better be expressed in some other way [1].

---

[1] This usage is in modern times due to the example of Kant, who regarded
every good act as motived by respect for the Moral Law and so as determined
by pure Practical Reason; but, since at the same time that act *qua* event
was a link in a series of causally inter-connected phenomena, it was really,
according to him, not the particular act but the whole series that was
determined by a single act of timeless, undetermined choice.   In supposing
that a man determines his own character by an act of timeless choice, Kant
was an Indeterminist.   His followers have mostly followed more or less
closely his use of the term 'free' in the sense of 'rationally determined,'
while dropping the Indeterminist side of his doctrine.   Kant's position

(2) Good and bad acts alike may be regarded as free by all who recognize a difference between mechanical causality and the causality of a permanent spiritual self. In this sense Freedom implies the power of self-determination, but does not necessarily involve the existence of undetermined beginnings in the stream of volitions which make up a man's inner life. That Freedom in this sense is an absolutely essential postulate of Morality, I have already insisted in the chapter on 'Metaphysic and Morality.'

(3) Freedom may be used to imply a power of absolutely undetermined choice in the self—a power of originating acts which have absolutely no connexion with or relation to the self as it was before the act.

It is of extreme importance to distinguish the kind of Determinism which recognizes the existence of a spiritual self and refers human actions to the character of that self from the mechanical Necessarianism which regards actions as caused by one another, or by the physical events of which what we call 'actions' are the psychical concomitants. But the ambiguous use of the terms ' free ' and ' freedom' has been responsible for vast confusion. Many writers have supposed themselves to be defending

involves the difficulty of applying the category of Causality to something which has no beginning. That which has no beginning cannot be caused by itself or anything else : it can only be uncaused. The only intelligible sense which can be given to the idea of ' noumenal freedom ' is to interpret it as meaning that the individual is uncreated, and either 'out of time' or 'pre-existent.' But there seems to be no evidence that that is what Kant intended by it. He probably meant merely that the timeless self is the cause of the series of acts in time. How there can be a timeless individual self which is not also uncreated he did not ask himself. Bad acts were to Kant apparently free in the sense that the rational self could have interfered with the causally determined series of natural events in time, but left them to be determined by motives of pleasure and pain, which Kant always assumed to be the only possible motives of non-moral or immoral acts, and to be of a purely ' natural ' character —just like cases of mechanical or physical causality. But the distinction between the first and second senses of the term 'free' is never clearly stated by Kant or by most of his followers. Leibniz has also added much to the confusion by trying to persuade other people, and perhaps himself, that he was an Indeterminist when most of his arguments only go to establish freedom in the second of the senses distinguished in the text.

Indeterminism when they were really Determinists themselves in
the sense of Self-Determinism. Still more have been so understood by readers not unwilling to be deceived. St. Thomas
Aquinas, and Hegel, and English Idealists like Green have
often been taken for Indeterminists or defenders of Free-will in
the popular sense. The materialistic, hedonistic, and other misleading associations which have gathered around the word
'Necessity' certainly justify the use of the word Freedom for
any doctrine which allows that actions are really determined
by a spiritual self capable of being influenced by ethical, as
opposed to purely hedonistic, motives. Only, those who avail
themselves of this usage should make perfectly plain the sense
in which they do so. I shall myself claim the right of using the
word 'Freedom' to include belief in 'Self-determination' in
a sense which is not inconsistent with one kind of Determinism :
but with a view of avoiding ambiguity I shall usually speak
of the creed which denies Determinism altogether as 'Indeterminism.' The word Libertarianism is also so definitely associated
with Free-will in the indeterministic or popular sense that it had
better be allowed to remain synonymous with Indeterminism,
even by those who give a wider significance to the term
'free.'

II

Having thus tried to make plain the nature of the question,
I shall proceed to glance at the arguments used on both sides.
At different periods in the history of thought different lines
of argument have played the largest part in the controversy.
Putting aside the ancient world, which, even in the Stoic-
epicurean period, was, perhaps, hardly alive to the real difficulties
of the problem, we may say that the controversy has passed
through three stages. In the earlier stage it was primarily
a theological controversy : the difficulty was to reconcile the
Freedom which Morality *prima facie* seemed to require with
the Omnipotence and Omniscience of God : and at this stage
it may be observed that it was generally the more emancipated
or Humanist thinkers who defended the cause of Freedom, while
it was the more enthusiastic representatives of authoritative

Religion who took the deterministic side. The philosophically educated Greek Fathers were on the side of Liberty [1] : the half-cultured Africans and other Westerns on the side of Predestination. St. Thomas in a slightly disguised form, Wycliffe and Huss avowedly, were Determinists of the Self-determinist type : the critical and sceptical Occam was a Libertarian. Luther and the Reformation Theologians were Predestinarians : Erasmus and the champions of Humanism were Indeterminists. In the second stage of the controversy the arena was chiefly metaphysical. The difficulty was to reconcile moral Freedom with the idea of Causality and the universality of Law. From the time of Hobbes it may broadly be said (subject no doubt to many exceptions and reservations) that the sceptical intellect has been on the side of Determinism, while the champions of Religion and Morality have usually been the upholders of Indeterminism. If among the Philosophers as many great names can be claimed for some form of Indeterminism as for Determinism, their advocacy has been for the most part based wholly and avowedly upon ethical grounds. In recent times, while the old difficulties continue to play their part in the controversy, the most powerful impulse towards the deterministic mode of thought has been derived not so much from *a priori* metaphysical difficulties as from empirical considerations—from the discovery of the close connexion between capacity and temperament on the one hand and the structure of brain and nervous system on the other, from the emphasis which modern Evolutionism has given to the always familiar influence of heredity, from the constancy of statistics, and in general the more vivid appreciation of the intimate relation in which individual conduct stands to social environment.

I will postpone for the moment any further exposition of the speculative difficulties (which perhaps after all remain the most formidable), but will add for the benefit of readers who may be very unfamiliar with the controversy a few words as to the way in which these empirical considerations have tended to bring about a state of things in which, if common sense has not given up its

---

[1] Only later Greek Philosophy and Theology invented a word for ' free-will '—an idea which Aristotle never succeeded in expressing—αὐτεξουσία.

instinctive Indeterminism, the prevailing tendency both of Science and Philosophy is towards the deterministic view of the question.

(1) Without exaggerating the extent of our knowledge as to the relation between mind and brain, it is a well-ascertained fact that there is some correspondence between the shape, structure, or quality of the brain and nervous system on the one hand and the character and conduct of the man on the other. With regard to purely intellectual characteristics this will hardly be disputed by any one, and it can hardly be denied that this is to some extent the case with moral characteristics also. Southern Italians and Spaniards are usually more irascible, emotional, and impetuous than Englishmen or Scandinavians, not because they all happen to use their freedom in that way, but because they are born with a different cerebral and nervous constitution. It will be said (and justly), that we have to do here with the emotional or pathological constitution of different individuals, and not with their moral character proper—with the impulses which excite them to good actions or bad and not with their actual conduct. But we observe also that on the average the resulting conduct of the respective races is what might be expected from this difference in their emotional tendencies, and it is easy to infer that further knowledge of such physiological facts might explain the actual volitions as well as the impulses against which the inmost self of each individual reacts—the extent to which he yields to his good or bad impulses as well as the nature of those impulses themselves. As the physical difference between races becomes wider, moral differences widen also. We should be almost as surprised to find the moral qualities of a Kant or a Gladstone as we should be to find the intellectual powers of such men in combination with the physical characteristics of a Toda. And when we turn to the widest moral differences between men of the same race, the same correspondence between character and physique is traceable to a greater or less extent. No one now doubts that insanity is due to a disease or original malformation of the brain and nervous system—a disease sometimes engendered, and to some extent curable, by purely spiritual influences, but nevertheless a physical disease when once produced, and one often traceable to purely physical causes. And insanity reveals itself

in erratic morality as well as in erroneous judgements about matters of fact. The influence of brain upon character is seen most conspicuously in those cases where a physical injury—a blow on the head or a sunstroke—is followed by violent or criminal behaviour in persons of previously irreproachable character. It is probable that Lombroso and his followers have failed to establish their theory of a 'criminal type' of head; there is, at least, much exaggeration about the definiteness and certainty of their results: but it cannot be denied that a majority of criminals—at least, criminals of the kind who usually find their way to penal servitude—are persons of exceedingly low mental calibre with a low facial angle and the cast of features which commonly accompanies very low mental development. In these exceptional and abnormal instances the correspondence between character and constitution becomes so glaring that it is hardly possible to avoid the recognition of some causal connexion in that sense of the word in which we usually speak of causal connexion in the physical Sciences [1]: and it is at least plausible to argue that further knowledge would reveal a like correspondence in the case of those less glaring differences of character and conduct which the Libertarian refers to the free will of the agent. It must be remembered, indeed, that all this evidence is quite inadequate to prove that purely physical characteristics are the *sole* cause of intellectual and moral characteristics, but it tends to show that these physical characteristics must be included among the antecedents of human actions, and to suggest that, if not wholly determined by physical causes, they are at least determined by causes.

(2) There are the familiar facts of heredity, emphasized by modern biological investigation, but not really much better known

[1] We have no experience of brain by itself: it is always brain *plus* something which is not brain with which we have to do, and it must, of course, be remembered that when he treats brain as a cause, the Idealist does so only in a relative and not an ultimate sense, since the brain itself exists only for mind. But the question of the relation between mind and body does not fall within our subject. No view of it is inconsistent with the position taken up in this chapter provided that it admits (1) the real causality of the individual self, (2) the spiritual character of Ultimate Reality.

to us than to those who lived before Darwinism and the ideas associated with it were dreamed of. The hastiest empirical observation taught men that people had a tendency to resemble— not only in their mental but in their moral characteristics—one or both of their parents:

> Fortes creantur fortibus et bonis :
> est in iuvencis, est in equis patrum
> virtus, neque imbellem feroces
> progenerant aquilae columbam[1].

Observation a little more extended and careful taught them that, even when there is a glaring contrast between child and both parents, a resemblance may often be traced between the character of the child and some remoter ancestor or collateral relative. The observation of this familiar fact is by itself fatal to the crude Libertarianism (if such has ever really been maintained) which represents each act of every individual as wholly and equally due to the use which he makes of his free will ; and it is at least plausible here again to use the argument from analogy, and to contend that, had we full and adequate knowledge of the causes which determine the course of embryonic development, we should be able to account for the original constitution with which a man is born into the world in those cases in which the earliest manifestations of character are *prima facie* least like what we should have expected as easily as we do in those cases in which they most obviously recall the parental type. Just as the generalizations which have enabled meteorologists to make rough predictions with regard to the weather have, in spite of many inaccuracies and some total mistakes, convinced the general public that there is such a Science as Meteorology, so it may be contended that a man's birth-character could with adequate knowledge of data and laws be predicted with as much certainty as the weather : and that by the birth-character is explainable everything in the man's conduct that is not due to his social and other environment.

(3) There is the argument from statistics. Though we can seldom obtain sufficient knowledge of the individual's character to enable us to predict with great certainty and accuracy how

---

[1] Horace, *Odes* iv. 4. 29-32.

he will act, we are in many cases able to foretell the action of masses of men not only with certainty but with a high degree of quantitative accuracy. We can be tolerably sure, indeed, that some individuals will be late for dinner, but we cannot say to a minute or two how much, and such calculations are always liable to be upset by disturbing causes: the most unpunctual of men may be in time when his watch goes wrong. But with masses of men it is otherwise; we are able by the examination of the statistics to predict with a very small margin of error how many people in London will commit suicide in a year. If one country shows a higher rate of suicide than another, we seek to account for it by something in its social conditions, as for instance by its Religion being Protestant rather than Roman Catholic, or by the cruelties connected with its system of compulsory military service, or by the prevalence of Landlordism instead of peasant Proprietorship. And fluctuations in the statistics we try to account for in a similar way. Within small areas or periods the fluctuations are of course considerable. They become smaller as we extend our view to larger areas of time and place. Or, if a sudden variation occurs, the instinct of every man—be he Determinist or Libertarian—is to account for it by some change in the environment; and in many cases we can so account for the sudden or gradual variations of statistics of this kind with at least as much success as we meet with in the attempt to account for variations in the statistics of death or disease, which everybody admits to be due to fixed, ascertainable, and calculable causes [1]. If we find a sudden increase in the number of offences punishable on summary conviction at a particular date, we ask ourselves whether any legislative or social change took place at the time, and we find it in the growth of bicycling and the consequent necessity for the prosecution of highly respectable persons for riding upon footpaths. If the statistics of desertion in the English Army show a rapid and startling change in a certain year, we are not satisfied with accounting for it by a freak of Free-will, and find it more satis-

---

[1] Even Insurance statistics involve the assumption that we can to a large extent predict human conduct. An uncaused outbreak of murder on a large scale might involve the winding-up of the safest company in Europe.

factory to connect it with some change in the manner of dealing
with such offences or with the state of the labour market.   Moral
statistics in short—statistics of crime or pauperism for instance—
are almost as constant as vital statistics.   The conduct of men in
masses can be predicted with more certainty than the weather.
How can this fact, it may be asked, be reconciled with the
hypothesis of Indeterminism?   Upon that hypothesis, it may
be urged, we ought to regard it as quite conceivable that in one
year vast numbers should freely will to commit larceny, in the
next year none at all.

It may be suggested that on the doctrine of probabilities the
number of undetermined bad volitions might be supposed, in
the absence of disturbing circumstances, on an average to bear
about the same proportion to the number of undetermined good
ones, though it will always be uncertain upon which particular
persons it falls to keep up the average.   But the doctrine of
probabilities is itself based upon degrees in our knowledge
of causes; and the question arises whether, in regard to any
class of phenomena not governed by causes [1], we should have
any rational ground for expecting such a constancy of averages.
The idea of pure chance, understood as a matter of objective fact,
is open to exactly the same difficulties as the idea of undetermined volition.   To refer the constancy of statistics to the operation of chance is therefore no explanation of their approximate
constancy.   It is quite true that the explanation of moral statistics
by social causes taken in connexion with the original constitution of individuals is not made out with sufficient completeness to constitute positive proof; but it can hardly be denied

---

[1] I do not identify the law of Causality with the law of the Uniformity of
Nature.   But our belief in the universal prevalence of Uniformity within
the mechanical sphere is itself based upon a probable inference as to the
modus operandi of the ultimate Cause which logically presupposes that the
events must have some Cause.   We assume *a priori* that events must have
some cause : we learn by experience that the cause is one which operates
within a certain sphere in accordance with a mechanical 'uniformity of
succession,' and even in the biological sphere with a certain regularity
which, however, cannot be reduced to a mechanical 'uniformity of succession.'   For further explanation of my meaning I may refer to Mr. R. B.
Haldane's *Pathway to Reality*, Vol. I, p. 240 sq., and Dr. J. S. Haldane's two
Guy's Hospital lectures on *Life and Mechanism*.

that the whole of our information points to the conclusion that with complete knowledge we should be able to see an exact correspondence as clearly as we now see a rough correspondence.

In the present state of our knowledge it might safely be affirmed that, while unreflective common sense may retain its instinctive Indeterminism, such a theory would never even occur to a scientifically trained mind acquainted with such facts as I have mentioned and accustomed to deal with social and psychological phenomena, unless it were in the first instance suggested by ethical or religious considerations. The most important question to be discussed is, therefore, the question whether any demand of the moral and religious consciousness really necessitates, or even strongly recommends, the theory of Indeterminism. Our knowledge of the empirical facts is far too small to enable us to say that, if it were so recommended, the hypothesis would be indefensible. If we could not explain or justify the facts of our moral consciousness without this hypothesis, we should have as good a right to assume Indeterminism as we have to accept any other postulate which is required for the rational interpretation of our experience. The facts of our moral consciousness are as certain as any other facts, and logical inferences from or implications of those facts have as good a right to be believed as any isolated fact accessible to immediate experience. There would still remain, indeed, the speculative question which we have hitherto waived—whether the very idea of undetermined choice is really thinkable; but, if we found it impossible to understand or explain an important department of our thought without such an hypothesis, it might well be urged that any logical or metaphysical presuppositions which stand in the way of doing so would stand in need of re-examination and revision. We might even feel driven to acquiesce for the nonce in an unresolvable contradiction between two sides or elements in our knowledge and experience. Such an admission of irresolvable antinomies would be a far more rational proceeding than to dismiss as fictitious the intellectual implications of one part of our experience because we cannot at present reconcile them with those of some other part, even without taking into consideration the greater importance for practical life of the moral as compared with tne scientific side of our conscious life. The question before us is then this—Does Morality postulate Indeterminism ?

III

The best way of raising the question will be, I think, to state as clearly as possible the position of those who assert the necessity of Indeterminism for Morality in the most extreme form. They do not deny that men are born with natural tendencies to good or evil, or that such tendencies are modified by education and environment, physical and social. And these inborn or acquired tendencies exercise an influence upon their actual conduct. But, in pronouncing a man good or bad, we must, it is contended, make abstraction of all that is due either to original endowment or to subsequent environment. It is not these things that make a man good or bad, but only that portion of his actual conduct and character which can be traced to the use that he makes of his own free will. It is only that part of a man's conduct which (his original nature and all surrounding circumstances being the same) might still have been different, that stamps the man as good or bad in the true, moral sense of the word. No doubt a man who is born so that he cannot fail, with such and such a social environment, to turn out what is commonly called a good man, is a more desirable citizen, more useful to his fellows and more at peace with himself, than one so constituted as, under like circumstances, to turn out a ruffian : but, morally speaking, he is not one whit the better man. We may bestow upon him a utilitarian, a social, perhaps a kind of aesthetic approbation : but to strictly moral approbation he is no more entitled than a clock which keeps time or an animal whose physiological constitution forbids it to indulge in aggressive or predatory behaviour. It is not only that the man's actions are materially correct ; they may be done from the right motives —from motives of humanity, of charity, of duty—and yet they are morally worthless, so long as these sentiments are due to his original nature or his fortunate surroundings. It is not only, be it observed, the man of natural good tendencies who is pronounced to be destitute of moral worth if his actions are not free ; every moral system must recognize some difference (what difference will depend upon the system) between the man of natural good qualities and the man who is good on principle— between (for instance) natural good nature and a hot temper duly controlled : and it may conceivably be contended that the latter represents the higher type of character. But this is not all. The extreme Libertarian is prepared to maintain not only that a man's natural sentiments, desires, inclinations may be of the best possible quality, but that his will may be steadily directed, in the presence of the fiercest temptations, towards the good for its own sake ; and yet that, if that will be itself the outcome of birth and education, it possesses no moral value whatever. It earns no merit ; and, according to this School, moral value and merit are synonymous terms. The determined saint is no better than the determined sinner.

Now it will, I think, be easy to show that, stated in this extreme form, the Libertarian position is totally at variance with the deepest moral convictions and the clearest of moral intuitions. Granted, for the moment, that there is such a thing as undetermined choice, and that for certain purposes—in order to pronounce our final judgement upon a man—it may be necessary to take into consideration, not merely the character of his volitions but also the extent to which his will was undetermined ; yet it is certain that we do not attribute *exclusive* moral value to that part of a man's character which would have been the same, no matter what his original character and his subsequent environment. Supposing I meet with a man of whose antecedents I know nothing, but whom I find spending his life in the practice of every virtue under the sun. He not merely does virtuous actions, actions externally in accordance with the Moral Law, but he does them from the highest motives : he is conscientious, charitable, self-denying, free (*quantum humanae potest fragilitati*) from any vices that the most intimate acquaintance can discern. But one day he tells me his history. His father and mother belonged, it appears, to the salt of the earth : he can point back to a long line of equally exemplary ancestors ; no member of his family, for generations back, is known to have been selfish or unconscientious : he has enjoyed the best of educations, and been fortunate in his teachers, his friends, and his professional associates. Now I do not deny that a knowledge of these facts may somewhat weaken my admiration for his character. They may suggest, not only that under less favourable circumstances he might have acted differently, but that his will is really not so strong as it appears to be : that he would not be able to resist stronger temptations than those which have fallen to his lot, and that a less 'sheltered' life might even now produce a serious lowering of his moral level, and reveal the existence of faults hitherto unsuspected by himself or by others. But if I were sure that his will would now be proof against the strongest temptations, the mere knowledge that, without that excellent ancestry and education, his will would have been different would produce surely not the smallest lowering of my moral esteem. A virtuous family commands my respect no less than a virtuous individual. Certainly, the Philosopher who proposes to base his Indeterminism upon the spontaneous deliverances of the unsophisticated moral consciousness will find it difficult to support the contention that in the case contemplated our esteem would be turned into total indifference or contempt. Or take another case—the case of 'conversion.' I have already protested against the notion that Determinism is inconsistent with change of character. As a matter of fact the greatest believers in conversion have been Determinists—St. Augustine, Wycliffe, the Reformers (of every school), the Jansenists, the English Puritans [1]. There may indeed be cases of conversion, as I have already suggested, in which no great visible change of environment accounts for the moral revolution. But that is not the common type. The change usually connects itself either with some striking event in the man's personal history—an escape from great danger, an illness, or a bereavement, or, more commonly still, with the influence of another person brought to bear upon him through a sermon, a book, or private intercourse. Suppose then I meet with another char-

---

[1] The Methodist movement, or rather one half of it—the section which followed Wesley and not Whitefield—was the first great religious revival that was based on a Libertarian Theology. Perhaps we ought to add that the Franciscan Theology, though its origin is later than the great missionary successes of the movement, was Libertarian.

acter such as I have already contemplated, but find on enquiry that in this case the man has not always been so. He used to be a selfish and self-indulgent profligate, and (as he will tell you him-self) would doubtless have continued so but for the fact that on such an occasion he listened to the sermon of such and such a preacher, came into intimate relations with such and such a friend, or chanced to peruse such and such a book. Since then not merely his outward life but the inner life of his soul has been altogether different. Am I then, in estimating his real character, to make abstraction of all that has been due to that externally conditioned crisis in his life, and say that his true moral status is just what it would have been, had some accident stood in the way of his hearing the preacher or falling in with the friend or the book? It is true no doubt that the fact that, when he does hear, he hearkens and heeds—that the seed sown is not carried away by the fowls of the air or withered by the stony ground of his heart or choked by the growth of tares—does show that even before that event he was not altogether the frivolous being that he seemed. There were potentialities of goodness in him already; but there will be an end of all possi-bility (even for the profoundest insight) of classifying men into good and bad, better or worse, if possibilities are to be treated as of the same moral value as actualities. If that were so, what would be the use of preaching or other efforts to make men better? If the possibilities are to be counted for righteousness, why try to develope them into actualities? It may be admitted also, without any undue suspiciousness as to the value of religious conversion, that the tendencies which previous to the moral crisis were dominant and unchecked very often prove to have been less entirely eradicated than the stock phraseology of revivalist movements may sometimes suggest. In the language of a dogmatic formula the old 'infection of nature doth remain, yea, in them that are regenerated,' and its influence may some-times be traced in altered forms throughout the man's subse-quent life. But the position that the true moral status of the man is really what to a discriminating moral vision it would have appeared to be, had his old and bad mode of life continued unaltered, is assuredly not one which can base itself upon the

4 3

ordinary judgements of mankind. The only really logical form
of such extreme Indeterminism would carry with it (as it did
avowedly for Kant) the startling consequence that no man can
really be made better by the influence of another. A mode of
thinking which compels us to deny the sanctity of St. Paul
because it might never have existed but for the influence of
Christ, of St. Augustine because it would not have existed but
for St. Ambrose, of St. Francis because he was once a profligate,
or of his own disciples because without him they would in all
probability never have risen above the low average level of their
contemporaries, is more flatly opposed to the deepest moral convictions of mankind than the crudest and most mechanical
theory of human conduct by which Determinism has ever been
caricatured.

Equally startling deductions might be arrived at if we were
to invert this line of argument, and to trace out the consequences
of treating as really good all the people who under favourable
collocations of circumstances might have become good. At that
rate all the bad men who failed to become good, because the
preacher who might have converted them did not happen to
come their way, would have to be set down as paragons of
Virtue. And on this mode of thinking the question might
be raised where we are to discover men really bad. There are
some personalities of such transcendent spiritual energy that it
seems scarcely possible, given circumstances under which their
influence could have a maximum play, for any human being
altogether to resist that influence—assuming that it was brought
to bear upon them at a sufficiently early age and that there
were no counteracting influences. Granted that there are a small
minority on whom no good influence could have any effect, it
must be remembered that present environment is not the only
factor of which the view under examination would compel us to
make abstraction. The influence of heredity must be eliminated
also. And how many of the actually bad would have been bad
if they had enjoyed the advantage not only of the education best
calculated to develope their possibilities of good but also of the
best possible parents and ancestors for many generations? Even
if there were any meaning in such a question, it is obvious that

the enquiry into any particular person's 'real character' becomes one with which not only the most profound and trained insight of the 'disinterested spectator,' but even the most penetrating self-examination, is quite incapable of grappling. Indeed, if we push the argument far enough, we might even have to go the length of denying that the moral value of a man was greater than that of an animal in so far as his evolution from the animal condition was due to influences independent of his own undetermined choice.

These considerations do not by themselves disprove Indeterminism. But they do show, I submit, that Indeterminism of this extreme type can gain no support from the 'common-sense Morality to which it generally appeals. They do show that the element in a man's character and conduct which is due to undetermined choice (if any such element exists) cannot without paradox be regarded as the only element which possesses not merely value but that particular kind or degree of value which we are in the habit of bestowing upon a good character or a good will. Granted that an inmost kernel of undetermined choice exists, it is something which is wholly inaccessible to human observation. Granted that the significance of this fact be admitted, and the inference drawn that in the last resort we have no materials for a final and adequate pronouncement upon the total character of any man, still that is a very different thing from saying that those elements of character which are accessible to observation have no value at all in so far as they are due to anything else but this hypothetical element of undetermined choice, the existence of which in any particular person we have no data even for conjecturing. Such a contention would carry with it the consequence not only that our estimates of character—our own or other people's—are often erroneous and always inadequate, but that they bear no relation whatever to the realities of the case. In venerating the saint, we may mistakenly be venerating a bad man to whom a good father and favourable circumstances may have given a benevolence and a self-denial which are morally worthless because 'determined.' In morally condemning a Caesar Borgia, we may be condemning actual bad tendencies which are no more deserving of moral censure

than physical disease, while all the time acts of Free-will
sufficient under favourable circumstances to have made a
Socrates or a St. Paul were wholly prevented from taking
actual effect because the poor man chanced to be the illegitimate son of a Renaissance Pope, and to have breathed the most
polluted moral atmosphere that social evolution has ever
generated. If such extravagances are to be avoided, we must
at the least admit that besides this inaccessible kernel of
character the actual character and volitions of human beings,
as they stand revealed directly to introspection or indirectly to
observation, have a real value, and a very different value from
that attributed to the hedonistic or other consequences which
character and volition may produce for the persons themselves
or for others. Granted that the undetermined choice may
possess moral value—it may be supreme and unique moral
value—it is not the only thing which possesses such value. We
can no longer say that in a determined world there would be no
such thing as value or moral value, and consequently no such
thing as Morality. Granted the existence of some higher sphere
of transcendental Morality for which Indeterminism may be
a necessary postulate, we cannot say that without it our ordinary moral judgements would be destitute of all meaning and
significance.

Now, if this much be admitted, it is obvious that the argument
for Indeterminism as a postulate of Morality is at least very
seriously weakened. The strength of the case for Indeterminism
lies in its appeal to common sense: that case is therefore enormously weakened when it is found that its logical consequences
are such as to shock common sense and that, to become capable of
rational defence, it has to assume a form which common sense
would not recognize. We have seen that, unless we are to
substitute for the moral judgements of our ordinary moral
consciousness a kind of moral judgement the very existence of
which has never been suspected except by a few Indeterminist
Philosophers, we cannot say that Morality would be destroyed
by the admission that this element of undetermined choice does
not exist at all. Morality would still remain: our judgements
of value would remain, and there would be no reason for denying

their validity. We should retain our conception of 'the good,' and should still ascribe a peculiar value to acts voluntarily directed towards the good. Morality would not be destroyed; would it in any way be weakened? The suggestion that it would, might mean one of two things : either it might mean that the validity of the Moral Law would be affected for the reflective consciousness, or that in practice a general conviction that Determinism is true would bring with it some weakening of the motives which work for Morality and deter from Immorality.

Let us assume then that we knew for certain Determinism to be true. Ought that logically to make, and would it practically make, any difference to us? First, let us get rid of some misleading associations. In the first place, Determinism does not imply psychological Hedonism, though psychological Hedonism does imply Determinism. The 'motives' which determine conduct may be of the most unhedonistic or rational or spiritual character. It is a mistake to assume (with Kant) that, because a motive is 'pure'—a pure desire to obey the Moral Law—the resulting act can be due to nothing but undetermined choice, or that because the act is determined its motive must be purely 'natural.' The fact that, with sufficient knowledge of a man's character and of the spiritual dynamic possessed by a given sermon, we could predict that he would be converted by it, does not show that the operation of the sermon was due to self-interest. Secondly, Determinism does not imply any particular theory as to the relations between mind and body. There can be no doubt that certain features of physical constitution are among the causes or conditions which determine character and conduct, but these need not be the only ones. *Prima facie*, and without any attempt to offer a complete solution of the problem, the influence of mind upon body is at least as obvious a fact of experience as the influence of body upon mind. A blow on the head may be the new factor which turns a man of given physical and mental constitution into a criminal. But it is equally certain that a thought may cause blushing or death, that cheerful society aids digestion; and that elevating spiritual influences will alter the whole expression of a man's face. It is possible that there may be the same mental interaction or concomitance between the, at present, unconscious soul and physical facts even in embryonic life. But, whatever may be thought of such a suggestion, it is enough here to say that Determinism postulates nothing as to the nature of the 'original constitution' which, in conjunction with environment, determines the bent of a man's character and actions. It merely asserts that, given a certain original constitution of mind and body, whatever is not due to the environment is due to that original constitution. And, thirdly, it must be remembered that in asserting that a man's acts are caused, we do not say that they are caused in the same way and sense in which mechanical events are caused by one another. It is totally misleading to assume that a man's acts in the present are determined by his past acts, just as the motions of a billiard-ball at a given moment are determined by its past movements. It may be true that rough predictions as to a man's future conduct may be made on the basis of past acts, but these past acts never reveal the whole of the man's character. The act is not caused by previous acts, but by the same self which caused the previous acts[1]. And the way in which a self causes is quite different from the way in which mechanical events cause one another. It is possible (and I for one should maintain) that even in mechanical action the real and ultimate cause of the event is not the previous event or any mysterious necessity of thought which requires that like physical antecedents should have like physical consequents, but the Will of God which within the region of Mechanics works invariably (we have every reason to believe) according to this law of uniform succession. But I am not writing a treatise on Causality, and it is enough to say that the causality of motives is in most important respects a very different thing from the causality which in the ordinary language of Physical Science is attributed to events. The self is not an event or a series of events. The desires, emotions, and other

---

[1] That the idea has arisen from a completely unjustified application to the relation between successive acts of the idea of mathematical necessity has been admirably shown by M. Bergson, *Essai sur les données immédiates de la Conscience*, p. 158 sq., though I cannot accept all his views which seem to involve actual Indeterminism.

psychical influences which are said to move the self have no existence of their own apart from the self. The self is present in each of them, and makes them what they are. Moreover, even if we regard the desires or inclinations which successively enter into the consciousness of the self as causes which determine its successive volitions, these are not mere events which act on succeeding events as it were *a tergo*, but presented objects which influence the self after the manner of final causes. In Mechanics the present is determined by the past : in the region of human action it is in a sense the future which determines the present.

It is true that for the future to determine the present, that future must become an idea in the present [1]. But the causality of ideas—ideas inaccessible to psychical observation—is a very different thing from the causality of physical events. And after all the idea does not produce the consequent by itself —in isolation from the whole nature of the self for which it is an idea ; we say, no doubt, that the idea acts upon the will and thereby causes the resulting action, but it would be just as true to say that the will acts upon the idea. The act results not

---

[1] By this I do not mean to deny that in animal or even vegetable organisms, or again in unreflecting human behaviour, final causes may not operate without being present in consciousness. But this implies that there must already be a striving or tendency towards this end, even though it is not a conscious striving. The postulate of the 'Uniformity of Nature,' as we use it in the purely Physical Sciences, is precisely the assumption that we may exclude all conditions except antecedent *physical conditions*. A striving which is not yet revealed either in consciousness or in any physical change is, even more than a fact of consciousness, something very different from the 'conditions' of which Physical Science takes account. I should venture to add further that, though this causality of ends should not be spoken of as something miraculous or outside the laws of nature (as long as we avoid the assumption that mechanical 'uniformity of succession' is the only kind of natural law), the causality of an end not present to the individual consciousness seems to me ultimately intelligible only on the supposition that it is already present to the divine consciousness. The views on Causality with which I am most in sympathy are to be found in Professor James Ward's *Naturalism and Agnosticism*, especially I. p. 108 sq., II. 189 sq. See also Professor Taylor's *Elements of Metaphysics*, Book IV, chap. iv, and the works mentioned above, p. 316, *note*. I have dealt with the subject somewhat more at length in an Address to the Aristotelian Society on 'Causality and the Principles of Historical Evidence' (1906).

merely from the idea which occupied the mind the moment
before, but from the whole state of the man, and the man is not
merely a knowing and feeling but a striving being [1]. Much of
the dislike commonly felt for deterministic modes of thought
arises from the use by Determinists of expressions which suggest
that the man himself is simply the theatre upon which a certain
action and reaction between ideas take place, an action and
reaction of which he—the man himself—is the passive victim.
But Determinism is not at all bound up with the mode of
thought which denies real causality or activity to the self: on the
contrary some Determinists would contend that there is no real
causality in anything but a self or a spirit, and that when we
say that this or that physical or psychical event causes another
such event, we are really describing merely the mode or order in
which some conscious will acts; so that, when such events are not
determined by some human or similarly limited will, they must
be really willed by God. But confining ourselves to the case of
the human will, we may say that the very essence of the Self-
determinist's case is that it is the real nature of the self (as modified
by its environment) which determines of what sort its successive
acts shall be. It is not because I have acted in a certain way in the
past that I am necessitated to act in a certain way in the future, but
because I am at this moment the sort of spiritual being to whom
such and such an enjoyment, such and such a reform in my
society, such and such a moral ideal presents itself as attractive.

Now let us assume that we have accepted Determinism in the
'Self-determinist' sense: what ethical consequences will such an
acceptance involve? It will not destroy the meaning or validity
of my judgements of value: that is a suggestion which we have
already dismissed. Voluntary acts (in any sense of 'voluntary')
are not the only things which possess value. Hurricanes and

---

[1] 'C'est donc une psychologie grossière, dupe du langage, que celle qui
nous montre l'âme déterminée par une sympathie, une aversion ou une
haine, comme par autant de forces qui pèsent sur elle. Ces sentiments,
pourvu qu'ils aient atteint une profondeur suffisante, représentent chacun
l'âme entière, en ce sens que tout le contenu de l'âme se reflète en chacun
d'eux. Dire que l'âme se détermine sous l'influence de l'un quelconque de
ces sentiments, c'est donc reconnaître qu'elle se détermine elle-même.'
Bergson, *lib. cit.*, p. 126.

eruptions are bad—that is to say, the suffering they cause in conscious beings is bad; and it is not the less bad because it is not due to human volition. Knowledge is good and a very much better thing than sensual pleasure, though nobody asserts that stupidity is due to Free-will or denies that ignorance is due to many causes besides lack of goodwill. And as knowledge has a higher value than mere pleasure, so a benevolent act or a benevolent character has a higher value still. That value of act or character is no doubt dependent on the fact that the particular act is willed, and character means the whole sum of psychical forces which produces a tendency to voluntary action of a certain kind : the difference between a crime and a disease is exactly the same for the Determinist as it is for the Indeterminist. The difference lies just in the fact that a better will would have prevented the one, while it could not have prevented the other. We cannot prove of course that there is this superior value in voluntary good conduct. It is an immediate affirmation of the moral consciousness. If the Indeterminist chooses to dispute this, it is he and not his opponent who is indulging in ethical scepticism, and contradicting the verdict of his own moral consciousness. If he likes to say that the same moral consciousness which assures him that his acts have value tells him also that these morally estimable acts are undetermined, the reply is that this apparently immediate affirmation of consciousness generally disappears for those who understand the nature of the question ; and that even Indeterminists fail (as I have endeavoured to show) to carry their theory to its logical consequences, and to withhold all moral approbation from that enormous proportion of human conduct and character which is obviously not due to the alleged undetermined choice of the individual will. At all events, I can only say for myself that, while I am conscious of the immediate judgement or intuition that a charitable act has value and a much greater value than a good dinner, I have no such immediate intuition that the charitable act was an undetermined act, nor can I by any analysis whatever discern the slightest logical or psychological connexion between the two propositions [1]. If judgements of

---

[1] I have against me the high authority of the late Professor Sidgwick, who

value are not to be trusted, then the whole basis of indeterministic Morality disappears as well as that of deterministic Morality. If they are valid, their validity cannot be upset by any theory as to how the moral act or immoral act came to be done. An act inspired by such and such a character is good, no matter what be the historical explanation of the genesis of such a character.

IV

The denial of Indeterminism then does not affect the logical or metaphysical validity of our value-judgements. Neither need it, so far as I can discover, psychologically have any effect in undermining any possible motives that may impel me to perform acts which my moral consciousness recognizes as good or to abstain from the contrary acts. Determinism is not Fatalism. The Fatalist (in so far as so confused a belief admits of analysis) believes that he is preordained to perform certain acts or that certain events are preordained to happen, no matter how much he may struggle against them. The Turk, we are sometimes assured, will sit down and calmly watch his house burn without making any effort to extinguish the fire, because, if it is the will of Allah that it shall be burned down, it is of no use for him to struggle against it; while, if Allah wills that it shall be saved, Allah does not want his assistance. What the rational Determinist tells him is that the question whether the fire is extinguished or not will depend (in part) upon the question whether he brings a hose to bear upon it or not : and that depends upon what sort of man he is. If he is an active and energetic sort of person with a strong desire to save his house, he will certainly make the effort, and the amount of the effort will depend upon the strength of his desire. No doubt it is impossible to deny that mental confusion, such as is implied in Fatalism or misunderstood Determinism, is sometimes a cause of inertia or other moral obliquity. But so may all sorts of true ideas—the goodness of God, the

attributed great weight as an argument for Indeterminism to the 'immediate affirmation of consciousness in the moment of deliberate action' (*Methods of Ethics*, Bk. I, chap. v, § 3). I can only say that I never was strongly conscious of this 'affirmation of consciousness' in my own case, even when I thought that Morality, or at all events Religion, postulated Indeterminism.

possibility of forgiveness, the discovery that there is a 'soul of goodness in things evil'—be abused to justify and encourage indulgence in wrongdoing to which people are already inclined. What is denied is that there is anything logical or rational about such arguments. If I have a real desire to be better, that will and must influence my conduct: how much it will influence it, depends upon the strength of that good desire relatively to other desires and impulses. If on account of my discovery that I owe this good desire to my parents or my education I abandon the effort to be better, that shows that there could never have been any very earnest desire to be better, but only perhaps a desire to escape punishment, or at best some form of self-reproach, which I have persuaded myself would no longer be deserved if my evil tendencies could be shown to be determined. If it be true that the value of good character and conduct is not really affected by the question of its genesis, it is impossible that, except under the influence of intellectual confusion, any doctrine as to that genesis could destroy or weaken any reason for moral effort which I can possibly give to myself or urge upon another.

Not only cannot the theory of Determinism weaken any of the influences which make for Morality in the world : it cannot even affect the character of that Morality. There is, indeed, one particular branch of Morality which may perhaps be supposed to be so influenced. The disappearance of the idea that a man's moral worth is (at least in the highest and fullest sense of the word) dependent upon the use which he makes of his power of undetermined choice may introduce a certain change into our ideas of merit and demerit. But we have already discovered that the amount of a man's action which is really due to this power of undetermined choice cannot be even roughly and approxi-mately ascertained. The man who is the maker of his own virtue (as it were) and the man whose virtue is due to the psycho-physical law which has caused him to reproduce the character of some remote ancestor behave (it may be admitted) exactly alike : their internal impulses, desires, emotions, and so on exhibit even to the closest introspection—still more to another person—not the smallest difference. Hence a standard

of ' merit ' based upon the theory which pronounces the one kind
of Virtue to be of the highest value and the other of no value at
all must be entirely unavailable for the guidance of human
conduct—for the distribution of praise and blame, reward and
punishment, even of self-approval and self-condemnation. How
far the idea of merit and demerit is really (apart from the
question of its practical availability) based upon the theory of
Indeterminism, will depend in part upon the question whether
we were right in the interpretation which we gave to that notion
in our chapters on ' Justice ' and ' The Theory of Punishment.'
The notion of merit in so far as it does not involve the retributive view of punishment in no way presupposes the theory of
Indeterminism.

But the mention of punishment brings me to another form of the
ethical objection to Determinism.   It is said that that doctrine
can give no meaning to the idea of remorse or repentance or
to the idea of responsibility. First, as to the idea of remorse. It
is probable that the acceptance of Indeterminism may introduce
a slight psychological difference into this feeling, or rather into
the way in which the individual articulately formulates the state
of his consciousness in moments of remorse and repentance. It
is probable that the common-sense person who has more or less
consciously and deliberately adopted a theory of philosophical
Indeterminism may sometimes say to himself, ' My Ego was the
sole cause of that wrong action, and my Ego as it was simply at
the moment of action. No matter how I was born, no matter
what my education, no matter how I may have acted previously,
no matter what I was at nine o'clock that morning, the sin that
I committed at ten o'clock might perfectly well not have
occurred.' Such a view of the facts must be admitted to be on
determinist principles a delusion. But it may be doubted what
(apart from such confusions as have already been exposed) is the
real moral value of that conviction. It is not the conviction that
his previous self had nothing to do with the act that inspires
remorse, but the fact that his present self abhors it. The man
who repents of the act is a man in whom *ex hypothesi* good and
bad impulses are struggling for the mastery, or in whom a good
impulse has permanently, or for the moment, got the better of the

bad. If the man had no bad impulses, he would not have done the act; if he had no good impulses, he would never have repented of it [1]. On the deterministic view what the man will say to himself will be something of this kind: 'No doubt it is quite true that, I being what I then was, my antecedents being what they were, circumstances being what they were, it was inevitable enough that I should have acted as I did. The fact that I should be the sort of being that the act showed me to be is precisely what causes me pain when I think of it. In the light of further reflection, in an altered mood, through the " expulsive power of a new affection " or in consequence of some other psychological change, I now loathe that side of my character which was uppermost at that moment. I regard it as bad, and desire to be rid of it.' Could any theory about the genesis of that bad self cause the man now to repent of such a ' godly sorrow,' or weaken the tendency of such sorrow to improve his conduct for the future ? If such a theory did have that effect, this would seem to show that the sorrow was less sorrow for sin than a desire to throw the blame of it upon somebody else—God, or Nature, or ' circumstances,' or the like—or a desire to escape the punishment which he thinks would be no longer due, if it was really his permanent self that was partly bad and not a momentary act of undetermined choice which might reveal nothing as to the character of that self.

But it may be alleged that it is not remorse or repentance in itself that cannot be explained on deterministic principles, but that consciousness of responsibility which is presupposed by that experience. What does responsibility really mean ? Etymologically the word signifies of course the liability to be called upon to answer for an act, with the implication that, if the agent cannot make a satisfactory defence of it, he may justly be punished. A man is said to be responsible for an act for which he might justly be punished. We hold that a sane man is responsible for a crime, because it is just to punish him for it, if he cannot disprove the allegation that he committed it.

[1] I here substitute 'repentance' for 'remorse,' since a mere wish that we had acted otherwise inspired by no moral aversion for the past, and accompanied by no desire to be better, has confessedly no moral value.

We hold that a man is not responsible for a fever not caught through any neglect of duty, because it would be unjust to punish him for it.   The suggestion that Determinism undermines the idea of responsibility means at bottom that on the deterministic view punishment would be unjust.   Whether that is so or not, must depend upon the view we take of the nature of punishment.   And that is a subject which has already really been sufficiently discussed.   If the true object of punishment be retribution, there might be something to be said for the suggestion that Determinism would make it unjust.   It is true that such a connexion between Indeterminism and retributive punishment has not always been recognized : some peculiarly truculent supporters of vindictive punishment are Determinists.   Still it may, perhaps, be admitted that retribution would be slightly more intelligible and less irrational upon an indeterministic than upon a deterministic basis.   But if we were right in rejecting the idea of retribution, the fact that a man ' could not help ' being born as he was, or educated as he was, is no reason why he should not be punished.   If the judgement of value is to be trusted, he is (to the extent of his actual wrongdoing) a bad man ; and (again assuming the validity of our moral judgements) a bad man is a being who ought not to exist or who, if he does exist, ought to be turned into a good one by every means in our power.   The protection of Society is of course another reason why he should be punished, the protection of Society meaning the true good of other individuals, each of whom may be worth as much or more than the offender.   Ideally punishment ought to secure both ends: practically, in the administration of ordinary criminal law, the social object has to be the prominent one.   But, whichever side of punishment we look at, Determinism does nothing to make it unjust or irrational.   To allow the man guilty of a crime freely to prey upon Society, because that crime was in the circumstances the inevitable consequence of a bad character, would be unjust, because it would be treating that individual's freedom from pain as of more value than the Well-being of many thousands, which it is not ; and Justice means treating every one (as far as possible) according to his true worth.   To refuse to make him better because the process of making him so is one which involves

some pain would be to treat freedom from pain as of more importance than moral character, which it is not. No greater kindness can
be shown to a bad man than to make him a better one, though the
process may be a painful one. If punishment be 'social surgery'
or a moral medicine for the individual, the fact that a bad man was
produced by causes is as poor a reason for refusing to apply it
as it would be to condemn a needful operation because the
patient's disease or accident was no fault of his own. In saying
that wrongdoing is a disease, we must always bear in mind the
immense difference between physical disease and spiritual disease,
and the consequent difference in the necessary remedies. It is
not only from the point of view of Society and legal punishment
that Indeterminism is not necessary for responsibility, but from
the point of view of the individual himself. If he is sincerely
penitent, the discovery that he has got a bad self will not make
him ask for the remission, but for the infliction of punishment, if haply by that means the bad self may be turned into
a better one.

Not only is Determinism not inconsistent with responsibility,
but it may even be maintained with much force that it is Indeterminism which really undermines responsibility. A free act
is, according to the Indeterminist, an absolutely new beginning,
not springing from, or having any necessary connexion with, the
past [1]. The question may be raised, What is the meaning of
holding me 'responsible' for some past act of mine if that act
did not really proceed from and reveal the true nature of the
self which I still am? If the act sprang up of itself (so to speak)
without having any root in my previous being, no goodness of
my previous self could possibly have prevented its perpetration.
And, as it revealed nothing of my past self, so it would be
unwarrantable to regard it as reflecting upon my present
character; since the present self is, *in so far as free*, simply the
momentary new beginnings which from time to time intervene
in the series of my actions without springing from those actions,

---

[1] This is sometimes evaded by saying that the act is not *wholly* unconnected
with the past. The answer is that *so far as it is free*, it is so unconnected:
in so far as it is not unconnected with the past, it is not free in the
Indeterminist sense.

or from the permanent self revealed in them. It is proposed, for instance, to punish me for a theft which I committed five years ago. On the determinist hypothesis it is reasonably held that the self which stole is the same self which I now am. It is proposed to punish me either (from the retributive point of view) because the Categorical Imperative says that those who steal shall be punished, or (from the medicinal and curative point of view) because it is presumed that the same thievish tendencies which revealed themselves are still there, and may be removed or counteracted by punishment. But from the indeterminist point of view I might protest: 'It is true that this is the same animal organism in connexion with which five years ago a regrettable incident occurred. But that theft did not spring from the same Ego as that which now directs the movements of these hands. It was not a self with thievish tendencies that stole. Previous to that act I was not thievish. You, my Indeterminist Judge, admit that so far as that act was free, it did not spring from anything in my character, but from some extraneous and incalculable force which had never revealed itself in me till that unfortunate moment. And, as it was not my past self that committed it, so neither was it my present self. You admit that so far as anything in my past may have necessitated or determined what I am now, I am not free; and you say it is only free acts for which people are responsible. But I, the present free-willing self, am quite a different sort of person from the self of five years ago which stole. I now deeply deplore the strange behaviour of the undetermined volition which caused my hands to steal, but you might just as well punish any other person for the act as myself. And, as punishment would be unjust from a retrospective point of view, so it would be useless as regards the future. In so far as my present self determines my future, my acts are not really free, and it is (you say) only free acts that are of any moral value. No efforts on my part, no efforts on the part of my punisher, can possibly prevent an undetermined theft taking place to-morrow in connexion with my organism: but they might equally take place in connexion with yours. What is the use of punishing and reproving me if, in so far as my present self determines my future, my acts are unfree and therefore morally worthless; while, in so far as they are really free, they cannot be influenced by anything that I or you can do now?'

On indeterminist premisses it seems to me that this line of argument is absolutely unanswerable. The Indeterminist will attempt to evade its force by admitting that character does influence, though it does not completely ' determine', our acts; that there is always a possibility of action not in accordance with previous character, a possibility which the gradual formation of character is progressively diminishing and perhaps may ultimately extinguish altogether; while the character and the resulting acts still retain their moral value because they are (in so far as free) the results of the previous undetermined acts. But, when such a plea is urged, it is forgotten that ' chances ' or 'probabilities' are not real things, but merely modes of our judgement based on imperfect knowledge of the causes at work. In so far as we believe in events undetermined by causes, we believe in pure chance ; and in pure chance we have no ground for estimating degrees of probability at all.   Pure chance is as irrational and unthinkable an idea as Fate : and to admit that our acts are—whether wholly or partially—determined by pure chance is surely as fatal to the idea of responsibility as to ascribe them to an external, overruling Fate.   And if there were such things as human acts determined by pure chance, they could not with any reasonableness be regarded as acts for which any particular person is responsible.   We have now come round from the purely ethical to the metaphysical aspect of the question.   Without entering in detail into the idea of Causality, we may say that all accounts of that category agree in this—that everything *which has a beginning* must be accounted for and explained as the necessary outcome of something already in existence before that beginning.   There are such things as new beginnings in the world, but every new beginning has the reason or ground of its occurrence in that which was before.   In that sense the law of universal Causality—quite a different thing from the mechanical uniformity of Nature—does present itself to my mind as an absolute necessity of thought.   An absolutely new beginning, unconnected with the past, is unthinkable.   No

4 4

indeterminist theory has ever been able to get over that difficulty, so far as I (with the strongest predisposition to believe in
a theory so often associated in other people's minds with the
beliefs which I hold most firmly and cherish most reverently)
have ever been able to discover.

Nevertheless, so great are the difficulties of the subject, so
small is our human capacity for adequate and self-consistent
thought when we reach these profound questions as to the ultimate nature of things, that I should be quite willing to acquiesce
in an ultimate antinomy between our speculative and our ethical
thinking, if the idea of Indeterminism presented itself to me as
in any sense a postulate of Ethics.   Antinomies cannot both be
true, but *we* may sometimes be unable to resolve them; though
the belief in unresolvable antinomies or contradictions more
often springs from intellectual laziness or intellectual cowardice
(when they are urged in a conservative interest) or love of
paradox (when used for destructive purposes) than from real
intellectual humility and love of Truth.   Any one to whom the
idea of Indeterminism still seems ethically necessary has the best
of rights to declare his belief in it (for our ethical thinking is as
trustworthy as any other kind of thinking), even though he
should be unable to reconcile it with that idea of Causality
which is the postulate of his scientific thinking.   But for myself
I am unable to discern any ethical objection to Self-determinism,
or any ethical advantage in Indeterminism, which does not spring
from misunderstanding.

V

Indeterminism is then to my mind no postulate of pure
Ethics.   But there is another point of view from which it may
be urged that the idea is essential to the rational interpretation
of the Universe.   It may be regarded as essential to the true
appreciation of the relation between the human will and that
universal Will from which a sound Metaphysic sees reason to
believe that the human will is ultimately derived.   And here let
me admit that, in dealing with this aspect of the matter, I should
wish to speak in a less confident tone.   Here we are approaching
the 'greatest wave' not merely of the Free-will debate but of

all metaphysical controversy. A full discussion of such a question cannot be expected in a purely ethical treatise ; but neither can all reference to it be avoided by a writer who believes that a true theory of Ethics should connect itself with a true theory of the Universe. 'We must do what we can.'

When the theory of Determinism is held in connexion with a philosophy which finds the ultimate ground and source of all being in a rational will, it is impossible to escape the inference that the Will of God ultimately causes everything in the Universe which has a beginning—including therefore souls and their acts, good and bad alike. There is nothing in this admission which can compel us to take back anything that has been said about the idea of self-determination, and the responsibility of the individual soul for its own acts. That we are the cause of our own acts is a matter of immediate experience [1], as well as a necessary implication of our ethical consciousness. And that truth is not in the least affected by the undeniable fact that we did not make ourselves, and consequently are not the sole causes of those acts. Whatever difficulties there may be (especially from an idealistic point of view) in the old distinction between the 'first Cause' and 'second causes' as applied to purely natural events, some distinction of the kind is certainly required in dealing with the causation of human acts. Human acts are not merely acts which succeed one another in a necessary order imposed from without (like events in the world of matter), but events the character of which is really determined by the nature of that soul whose acts they are, a soul which is active, which is ever growing and modifying its own nature by its own self-development. And yet the development is a development of an original nature which the individual did not create for himself, and is dependent for its continuance from moment to moment upon the continued existence of a world which the individual did not create. Theologians usually express this twofold aspect of human acts by speaking of the 'co-operation' of God in every act of human volition. Philosophers may prefer some other mode of expression, but in one way or other we have to recognize

[1] For a defence of this position I may refer to Dr. Stout's chapter on 'the Concept of Mental Activity' in *Analytic Psychology*, Vol. I, Bk. II, chap. i.

that the individual is the real cause of his own acts, and yet that
(on the determinist hypothesis) he is not the sole or only or
ultimate cause of them.   From any philosophical standpoint [1]
the ultimate cause of every particular event is the original
nature of a Whole which has no cause and no beginning.   If
the idealistic Theist is right, the Whole consists of God and the
system of souls, including the world which is their experience :
and, if the souls have a beginning, then (though in some ultimate
metaphysical sense they may conceivably be regarded as part of,
or of one substance with, God) the beginning of their conscious
individual life, as well as all subsequent stages of that life, must
be regarded as ultimately due to the Will of God.   There is
nothing in all this to alter the fact that the individual is the
cause of his own acts : the individual is immediately conscious
of his own activity.   If God causes those acts, He causes them
in quite a different way from that in which He causes other
events—events in the natural world, or even the acts of non-
moral animals.   For purely ethical purposes we need not look
beyond the immediate cause of the acts : the cause why a bad
act is done really is the fact that there is a bad soul in the world.
Nothing can alter that, and that is all that we want from a purely
ethical point of view.   Yet from the metaphysical or theological
point of view we must admit also that the soul is made or caused
by God : and one cannot help asking oneself the question why
God should make bad souls, and so cause bad acts to be done [2].

I have already explained that I find the answer to that question, in so far as any answer to it can be given, in the theory

[1] Except *in a certain sense* that of Pluralism, which I deal with below.
[2] Many Philosophers will attempt to evade the difficulty by merely
protesting against the use of such terms as 'making' or 'creation.' But the
objection, when applied to the beginning of souls, seems based upon some
idea of the eternity of Substance which (if it is to be admitted at all) is
really applicable only to matter.   It is possible to find a meaning for the
idea that souls are all parts or manifestations of a single Substance, but
I can find no meaning for the idea that they are parts of a single consciousness (see above, p. 238).   Any one who admits that the individual
consciousness is not without beginning, and is in time, and is the cause
of acts in time, must admit that God causes that consciousness to begin, and
is so far (if only so far) the cause of each successive event in its subsequent
development.

which—expressed in the inadequate and analogical language which the Philosopher of any school is obliged to use when attempting to explain the ultimate nature of things—must be described as the union in one and the same Being of absolute Goodness with limited Power. Inasmuch as the limitation of Power springs not from outside but from within, we may continue to speak of God as the Infinite, if it makes us any happier to do so ; but, in view of the pantheistic tendency of this mode of speech, when adopted in its strict philosophical sense, it may be well to avoid the term altogether. The point of the theory which I advocate is that God causes bad souls to appear as a means to an ultimate good, a good which is unattainable without them. The bad is willed, or (if we like to use that rather anthropomorphic term) 'permitted,' by God as a means to a greater good, without on that account ceasing to be really bad. A better Universe is imaginable, but a better Universe is not possible, because nothing is *really* possible but what is or will be actual. If we say that God might possibly have created a worse world than that which He has created or does create, we can mean only that, if we looked only to his Power and not to his Goodness, we should see no reason why the world should not be worse than it is ; and, if we say that God might possibly have created a better world than ours, we mean that, if we looked only to his Goodness and not to his Knowledge and his Power, we should see no reason why the world should not be better than it is. It must be admitted that the world is made what it is by a divine volition or series of volitions which is made what it is by the positive and eternal nature of God. That all things flow with rigorous necessity from that nature might truly be said, were it not that the use of the term 'necessity' is generally associated with the denial of just that doctrine which is here asserted—that whatever happens in the world is really willed by a self-conscious Spirit for the attainment of the ends which He knows to be essentially best.

It will be contended by some that we are still making God the author of evil, though He wills it only as a means, and not as an end. But how far, after all, would our theory of the Universe be improved by the admission of undetermined choice, side by

4 4 ★

side with original character and circumstance, as a source of
human conduct with a resulting reaction upon character?
Undoubtedly, if we could bring ourselves to believe in Indeterminism, we could regard the possibility of sin (but not its
actuality) as a necessary condition of real Morality, which is
the highest kind of good. So far the difficulty of accounting for
evil in a God-willed Universe would be diminished. And, if the
difficulty were wholly removed by such a hypothesis, that might
be a sufficient reason for accepting it, while frankly acknow-
ledging our inability to reconcile it with the self-evident law of
Causality. But, unfortunately, the difficulty is not removed,
but only a little attenuated or disguised. Only a small part of
the evil in the Universe can, on any view which does not refuse
to look at the facts, be traced to the abuse of our power of
undetermined choice. The hypothesis will not account for the
sufferings of animals, or for that enormous proportion of human
suffering which does not in any way arise out of moral evil [1]: in
so far as the human suffering is accounted for as necessary for
discipline and formation of character, that explanation is equally
open to those who reject Indeterminism. Nor will it account
even for *all* moral evil. Such an enormous proportion of the
moral evil in the Universe is clearly not due to the abuse of
Freedom that the difficulty is only slightly attenuated by the
introduction of an undetermined factor into the well-springs of
action. It may, indeed, be alleged that much of the evil, which
in the individual is due to inheritance and environment, originally sprang from the acts of undetermined wrongdoing. But
our knowledge of the actual causes of human wrongdoing is
sufficient to make it extremely improbable that, if such an
element of undetermined choice exists in human life, it can
account for any large proportion of the moral evil which in the
individual arises immediately from inheritance and circum-

---

[1] This has been so strongly felt by Renouvier that in *La Nouvelle
Monadologie* he has elaborated a theory of a pre-natal Fall. Renouvier's is
perhaps the ablest modern attempt to think out the Indeterminist position;
but it is unconvincing, and involves much which strikes the unconvinced
reader as pure mythology. That the idea of a possible sinless evolution of
humanity under the actual conditions of this planet is unthinkable, no one
shows more convincingly than the Neo-Leibnizian Philosopher.

stance : certainly it cannot account for all. And we have
already seen that to declare that only the undetermined good
volition is truly and morally good, or the undetermined bad
volition truly evil, contradicts the plainest deliverances of the
unsophisticated moral consciousness.   And if we admit the existence of *any* moral evil whatever which the individual 'cannot
help' (in the sense in which the Indeterminist alleges that
Determinism makes sin something which we cannot help), that
evil is really *for him* determined, and springs in the last resort
from that ultimate constitution of the Universe which to the
Theist is identical with the nature of God.   The Indeterminist
at least cannot blame the objector for following a too anthro-
morphic line of thought, when he urges that God is as much
responsible for evils which He foresees will certainly flow from
the use which some individual will actually make of the freedom
with which He has endowed them, as a human being would be
responsible for the consequences if he placed loaded fire-arms
in the hands of people who would be sure to commit murder
with them.   If it be said that God does not know that the
freedom will be abused, and we frankly give up the idea of
Omniscience [1], it may be asked whether we should consider that
his responsibility was much diminished if a man put the fire-
arms into the hands of children without knowing whether they
would or would not make a proper use of them.   And after
all a doctrine of Free-will which involves a denial of God's

---

[1] As is done by Professor James in *The Will to Believe*, p. 180 sq., where
the attempt is made to reconcile this undetermined element with the
rationality of the Universe by the suggestion that God is like a consummate
chess-player encountering a novice : he does not know what move the novice
will make, but he does know that, whatever move the novice makes, he will
beat him in the end.   This is perhaps the best attempt that has ever been
made to deal with the difficulty, but it does not get over the objection that
these estimates as to what is possible are based upon the assumption of
Causality.   The expert knows all the moves that the laws of nature and the
rules of the game permit the novice to take.   Where there is an absolutely
undetermined element, it is difficult to see on what grounds its limits can be
fixed.   If God cannot foresee what use the creatures will make of their
freedom, how could He foresee that they will not all choose evil, and persistently choose it so far as and so long as they are free ?   And such a choice
would presumably defeat the purpose of God.

Omniscience cannot claim any superiority over such a theistic Determinism as I have defended on the score of avoiding a limitation of the divine Omnipotence. Omniscience need not involve Omnipotence, but Omnipotence (in the popular sense) certainly includes Omniscience. These are old difficulties; but they have never been satisfactorily met either by Philosophers or Theologians, except in so far as they have candidly admitted a limitation of divine power. Indeterminist theories introduce that limitation quite as much as determinist theories. Not to be able to cause good without a possibility of evil is as much a limitation as not to be able to cause good without the certainty of evil. All the Theodicies really admit such a limitation, except those which frankly throw Morality to the winds, and save the divine Omnipotence or the divine 'Infinitude' at the expense of the divine Love. In this case either Morality degenerates into obedience to the arbitrary and capricious commands of a being who pursues ends not intrinsically good (or at all events an end in which Morality finds no place), or the idea of a divine Will disappears altogether and with it all possibility of attributing Love or any other ethical character to God. An unethical Deism and an unethical Pantheism are the Scylla and the Charybdis between which religious thought can only steer its way by admitting that God's ends can only be attained by the adoption of means which, in themselves and abstractedly considered, are bad, and which remain bad from whatever point of view we look at them ; however much they may be justified as involving less evil on the whole than the omission of those means and the non-attainment of the ends to which they are means. In truth the very idea of means to an end is unintelligible when the means are supposed to be adopted by a being who can attain any end whatever without any means at all. The idea of a being who is omnipotent, in the popular sense of the word, is the idea of a being who has no determinate character or nature whatever. A Universe in which everything might happen would be a Universe in which nothing was caused. The idea of a Universe in which there was an 'infinite' amount of good contains a *contradictio in adiecto*. However much good there was in the world, we could still ask,' Why not more good ?'—and so on *ad infinitum*.

Real being must be being of a definite amount.   A God who was unwilling to create more good for any other reason than inability to do so would not be perfectly good.   On the other hand, there is no similar contradiction in the idea of a Will or a Being who is perfectly good inasmuch as He causes all the good that his own nature makes it possible for Him to cause.

We have seen then that the only point at which a difficulty is created either for Morality or for Religion by the acceptance of Determinism lies in its tendency to make God in a sense the 'author of evil'—a sense which in no way excludes the equally true proposition that man is the author of it.   In a sense, indeed, man is the sole author of evil; for man alone wills the evil otherwise than as a means to the true good.   God wills the evil only as a means to the good, and to will evil as a means to the good is not *to be* evil, or to will evil as such, or to exhibit any defect of Goodness.   And we have seen that this is a difficulty which·Indeterminism has equally to admit, since to cause a possibility of evil is equally to be the author of evil, while the plea that the evil is a means to the good is equally open to the Determinist.

After all that can be said on this side I admit frankly that it would be more satisfactory to be able to say that God was in no sense the cause of evil.   That is only to say that I could wish the Universe were better than it is; and, if God be the God who is revealed to us by our moral consciousness, He wishes that too.   All Libertarian Theologies represent God as wishing ends which are not fully attained : and a Self-determinist Theology which is content to maintain that the end is attained sufficiently to justify the means involves no further limitation of the divine power.

VI

The desire to avoid the admission that God originates souls with evil potentialities which must necessarily develope into evil actuality is the inspiring motive of those theories of Pre-existence which, from the days of Plato and of Origen to those of modern 'Pluralism,' seem always to have sprung up wherever men have grappled in earnest with the problem of evil.   According to such theories souls are uncreated; while the world-process is one by which a good but not omnipotent God is getting rid of the evil in those souls, and bringing them to the highest perfection of which they are intrinsically capable [1]. We thus get rid of the necessity of tracing any evil, even indirectly and as a means, to the Will of God. We trace it to the limitation of souls on their ethical side, instead of to the limitations of God on his non-ethical side. We are thus able not only to trace all moral evil to human willing (we can do that without Pre-existence), but to nothing else; the individual soul is not only the cause, but the sole and ultimate cause, of its own sin. In that way we do seem to meet the instinctive demand which has found expression in the popular indeterminist theory. For even Indeterminism has seldom found it necessary to attribute undetermined choice to God. In proportion as Theologians have done so, they have tended towards a non-moral view of God's nature, and have ended by making a non-moral divine caprice the sole standard of right and wrong in human conduct [2]. Ethically minded Theologians have generally found it enough to insist that God's actions are limited by no necessity but what arises from his own goodness, that (in the words of Hooker) 'the being of God is a kind of law to his working [3].' And the theory of eternal Pre-existence ascribes to man as much freedom as it allows to God. This is so far satisfactory. But for one difficulty which the theory of Pre-existence removes it creates a hundred. The connexion between mind and body, between character and organism, between parental or racial character and individual character, is so close, that, if the real inmost core of a man's character be due to an original eternal nature modified by the acts of previous lives,

---

[1] e. g. in Professor Howison's *Limits of Evolution* and Mr. Schiller's *The Riddles of the Sphinx* and other writings. These last writers, however, so far as I understand them, think that Pre-existence is not a sufficient explanation of the origin of Evil without Indeterminism, thereby giving up what would seem to my own mind the chief attraction of the system.

[2] This tendency is exhibited by Duns Scotus, who based the second table of the Decalogue upon the arbitrary Will of God, and by Occam, who subsequently referred both tables to such a Will—a course in which he was followed by many ultra-Calvinistic Divines.

[3] *Ecclesiastical Polity*, Bk. I, chap. 2.

we must suppose that every soul after each successive death is kept waiting in some extra-corporal limbo till Evolution has developed parents to whom it can suitably be assigned, and an organism which will serve as a faithful expression of its present moral status no less than as an adequate discipline for its future moral advancement. The theory is certainly not capable of positive disproof, but it is unsupported by the obvious and *prima facie* evidence of experience; and involves, the more it is worked out, a ramifying network of difficulties only to be disguised by some mythological structure which itself is the greatest difficulty of all. And in the end it seems to give us no ethical advantage which we cannot have without it. If the bad acts of the eternal soul do not spring from its own eternal nature, we have all the difficulties of Indeterminism just as acutely with Pre-existence as without it. If they do spring from that nature, the evil springs from the inherent limitations of a Universe which tends towards the good but has not fully attained it, and so far contains an inherent element of evil. Why should it be more satisfactory to account for this evil as due to the uncaused limitations of the individual, instead of being due to the uncaused limitation of the divine nature on its non-ethical side? Pre-existence limits God, and limits Him from the outside. Determinism without Pre-existence limits Him from the inside only, without limiting the perfection of his moral nature. God is limited, but only by his own nature and by the existence of other beings which owe their existence to that nature, and such a limitation is one which involves no ethical imperfection. On the speculative difficulties—apart from Ethics—which the theory of Pre-existence involves, I forbear to dwell. It is enough to say here that the order of the Universe is more easily accounted for by a Monism which does not deny the reality of individual selfhood than by the Pluralism which recognizes a number of entirely distinct and independent sources of Being.[1]

---

[1] Most of the difficulties urged against pluralistic theories seem to apply equally to Dr. McTaggart's system, according to which the Absolute consists in a society of eternal souls, none of which is sufficiently superior in power to the rest to be exalted to the name of God, or to be invested with the

VII

I believe that at bottom the unwillingness of ethical natures to acquiesce in Determinism of the kind which I have indicated arises from their inability to get rid of the idea of a determination from the outside—a suggestion which is really no doubt involved in the more materialistic varieties of Determinism. They cannot get rid of the suggestion of an external coercion constraining the man to act in a way in which he—the real man, who is (as they rightly hold) no mere product and plaything of purely physical forces—does not wish and desire to act. And that is to confuse the causality of a self-developing self with the causality of mechanical forces which always is determination *ab extra* [1]. Or, if they do realize that it is the nature of the self that determines the particular act, they limit their idea of the self to the self already revealed in present consciousness, and suppose that Determinism negatives the possibility of repentance, improvement, change of character. They forget that the self is a being whose whole nature is at present unrevealed by anything outside itself at present existing in the Universe— unrevealed either to self-observation or to any human observation, though (we may suppose) not unrevealed to the Universal Mind. And this consideration sets strict limits to the possibility

attributes usually associated with the idea of Godhead. The speculative difficulty of Pluralism is, indeed, nominally removed by the declaration that the souls collectively form a ' unity' or 'system', but the difficulty of accounting for the unity and order of a material world which is admitted to exist only in the experience of selves is still greater on this view than it is on the hypothesis of a God ominiscient and enormously superior in power to other spirits, but not limited by their independent existence. According to Dr. McTaggart the spirits simply happen to find their experience partially identical and capable of being reduced to an intelligible system, though it never actually exists as a system in any one mind, does not completely exist (so far as we know) even in all of them taken together, and is (except as regards the infinitesimally small portion of the Universe known to consist in the voluntary acts of human or similar spirits) not willed by any or all of them. These difficulties will be felt with peculiar force by those who (like the present writer) regard the causality of Will as the only true causality.

[1] Except in so far as the successive changes of the material Universe are regarded as ultimately willed by God, and are so due to the successive volitions which are the unfolding of his eternal Nature.

of that prediction of future conduct which is instinctively resented by minds for which ethical considerations are predominant [1]. The possibilities of gradual improvement, or, occasionally, of apparently sudden new departures which look as if they were unconnected with everything in the previous life, can never be estimated with certainty by any knowledge of the character as it has already unfolded itself in the man's actual consciousness. Experience does no doubt show us that the question whether and how far those possibilities shall unfold themselves is largely determined by the nature of the environment, and there is no ethical advantage in denying that

[1] This possibility is further limited by the consideration that our psychical states differ qualitatively, and that what we call the same psychical event (emotion, feeling, desire, &c.) in two different persons, or at two different times in the same person, is not really the same. There is a certain uniqueness about each person, and even about each mental state of each person. Hence it may safely be said that we shall never succeed in framing 'laws' from which all human actions could be predicted: the principle that the same cause will always produce the same effect will not help us in the psychical sphere, for the same cause can never recur. All this has been admirably pointed out by M. Bergson (*Sur les données imméd. de la Conscience,* passim). But (1) that writer seems to ignore, and even to deny, the fact that there is something alike in psychical states as well as something different : we can therefore to a certain extent discover laws or uniformities, both in the connexion of the psychical states *inter se* and in their relations to physical events, though the laws will express tendencies which are always liable to be modified within certain limits by the unique peculiarities of individual persons. (2) M. Bergson hardly seems to recognize that there may be causal connexion even when there is uniqueness. It is true that no knowledge of the 'laws of character' would enable us completely to say how a given individual (in so far as he differs from all other individuals) is going to act without a knowledge of the fact that he will actually act in a certain way, but that does not prevent us from regarding the act as the necessary result of what he originally was: to an intelligence that knew him through and through the future act would be seen, as it were, latent in the character, though such a knowledge is absolutely inconceivable for an intelligence such as ours. M. Bergson's own position, which he regards as the opposite of Determinism, is one which seems to be fairly describable by the word 'Self-determinism.' I know of no better definition of Freedom (in the true sense) than his 'nous sommes libres quand nos actes émanent de notre personalité entière' (p. 131), but it is desirable for the sake of clearness to admit that this is not the liberty which the Indeterminists want, and I am not sure that this would be admitted by M. Bergson himself.

determination. From this point of view Determinism is far more encouraging and stimulating to moral effort than a logically thought-out Indeterminism. Even if we do not push the demand for Freedom to the point of denying that a man can ever be made really better by another's efforts, the prospect of ridding the world of at least its worst evils must be small indeed, if no spiritual influence from outside, no response to that influence from within, no continuance in well-doing, no education of character can ever exclude an unmeasurable possibility that sudden and undetermined moral evil may break out afresh in the apparently purified will, and be followed by all the determined moral and other evil which such an outbreak must necessarily bring with it for other beings.

The deep-seated moral repulsion against Determinism which used at one time to characterize the most zealous champions of the rights of Conscience was, I believe, largely due to the association of Determinism with a gloomy and unethical Theology, and in particular with the idea of everlasting punishment. The attempt to vindicate the ways of God to man on the assumption that He makes bad men only in order that they may be tortured everlastingly, and that not as a means to the moral improvement or future Well-being of themselves or others, was indeed a desperate task [1]. Even now Indeterminism is often maintained by conservative Theologians because it seems to make the doctrine of everlasting torment a trifle less repulsive to the moral consciousness. When we once get rid of such baseless figments, the idea that God creates men with some bad elements in their characters, and societies containing some men on the whole bad, in order that in the end a good greatly over-balancing that evil should be realized, is one which has nothing in it offensive to the religious consciousness or depressing to the moral energies. Indeterminist Theologies and determinist Theologies alike represent the history of the world as a divine education of souls. According to indeterminist systems that

---

[1] It is rarely that the idea of everlasting punishment has been defended, as it was by Abelard, on Utilitarian grounds—as an example to the rest so valuable as to make the everlasting punishment of a certain number of sinners productive of a maximum of good as the whole.

education may, and (some would add) must, fail in a certain number of cases: the older Theologians did not hesitate to say the vast majority [1]. To admit that, is to admit a limitation of the divine power: God, it is represented, wishes that all should be saved, but some are not saved. Their explanation is the intrinsic impossibility of the greatest good without this possibility of evil—a possibility which we know, and which God foreknew [2], to be actual. And that constitutes a limitation.

VIII

When once we admit any kind or sort of inherent limitation to the possibilities of divine action, it becomes impossible, no doubt, dogmatically to determine the extent to which the ends desired by the eternally loving consciousness will actually be realized. To declare that every soul will, immediately on death, or even eventually, attain the same kind or the same level of moral, intellectual, and aesthetic excellence would be a very foolish assertion, completely opposed to all the analogies of our present experience. Souls are not the same, and it does not look as if they ever would be. To say that every soul will reach some particular level of happiness or moral perfection which we may choose to understand by the term 'salvation' would be going beyond what we have a right to affirm, though perhaps, in so far as we can distinguish between positive moral evil and a limitation of moral goodness, the ultimate extinction of the former is not beyond what we may hope. What we have a right to affirm is that the Universe must be moving to an end which is good on the whole in the sense that its existence is better than its non-existence, a good which is worth the evil that it costs. That there is at no point a final sacrifice of the part to the whole is more than we can positively affirm; but the more profoundly we believe in the ultimate rationality of things, the more strongly we shall be disposed to believe that for each

[1] It was not only Calvinists who took this view. See Newman's appalling sermon 'Many called, few chosen.'

[2] From the point of view of Orthodoxy. Few modern Libertarian Theologians are bold enough to admit that Indeterminism is incompatible with complete foreknowledge: if foreknowledge is denied, we have limitation again.

soul once born with the consciousness of a moral ideal an end is
realized which will on the whole make it good for that soul to
have lived. We must not push such a reasonable hope beyond
the limits prescribed by the actual and undeniable facts ; but,
within those limits, the more completely any theory of the
Universe allows for such a final triumph of good, the more
probable will it become for a mind which has once taken the
initial step of recognizing in the objectivity of the moral consciousness a revelation of the ultimate meaning and nature of
the Universe.

How far this principle will allow us to believe in the
immortality of animals we have no adequate data for determining. In the case of the lowest animals the continuity of their
existence is so small that it becomes difficult to suppose that
any future destiny of theirs would intelligibly allow us to
regard their existence as ' good on the whole ' in the case of
those (we may hope, the comparatively few) who have failed in
their present existence to attain an overplus of good (such good
as they are capable of) on the whole. If we suppose a creature of
a very low type rewarded hereafter by elevation to a higher kind
of existence, such a being would not seem to be the same as its
original germ in any sense which would permit us to regard its
bliss as a compensation *to it* for its previous sufferings. Here it
does seem probable that there must be some sacrifice of particular
individuals to the good of the whole. As we ascend the scale of
existence, the greater the worth of their life becomes, the greater
becomes the probability that no individual will be treated wholly
as a means. There we must leave the matter. It is perhaps too
dogmatic to assert that every individual will attain Immortality
even among human souls. It may, no doubt, be said that all
that we need for a rationalization of the Universe is a future,
and not an immortal, existence. That is quite true, but the
difficulty of believing in Immortality—either the real speculative
difficulty or the merely psychological difficulty of imagining or
envisaging it—is not greater than that presented by the idea of
a future but not unending existence (except perhaps for those
who regard all temporal existence as a mere delusive ' appearance '). The hypothesis of Immortality for all souls whose

actual or potential capacity reaches a certain level of value
is the one which most completely rationalizes the Universe.
Hence, upon the presuppositions already explained, it is the more
reasonable hope.

To deal with the difficulties presented by the antinomies
involved in the nature of time would carry us far beyond the
limits proper to an ethical treatise. From the point of view of
Ethics at all events human life is in time, and any completion of
the existing life which is to supply a meaning and justification
for the defects of the present must be represented as a continuance of the present life in the future. That all our ideas about
time are inadequate, and that from the point of view of a divine
knowledge the inadequacy must in some way disappear, may
be freely admitted. But that is a very different thing from
affirming that time belongs to the region of mere 'appearance'
and that the only Reality is one which is out of time. The idea
of an existence out of time is one which for us can possess no
meaning, unless it be taken in a merely negative sense as
implying an existence in which the difficulties inherent for an
intelligence in the idea of endless succession are 'somehow'
transcended, we know not how. These difficulties cannot be
here discussed. Suffice it to say that all our judgements of value,
and consequently all our moral ideas, presuppose that a good
which is not now real may by willing be made real. The fact
that that is so is by itself a sufficient reason for distrusting
theories of the Universe which tend to make all that is in time
a mere delusive 'Maia,' and to represent the real Universe as
one in which, as nothing really happens, inertia must be as
reasonable as action; or perhaps more reasonable, in so far as the
approach to inertia may be thought (however inconsistently) to
bring a man nearer to that timeless and changeless state from
which temporal existence is a lapse. For the Philosophies in
which that which becomes is mere appearance, values too should
be merely apparent and unreal[1]. The ethical theory which
insists on the vanity of all striving is the natural ally in the

[1] This will no doubt be denied. It may be said that timeless existence
may have value. But our judgements of value pronounce that there is
a real difference in value between a worse present and a better future : if

4 5

sphere of practice of the speculative theories which represent the world or God as an 'is' in whom and for whom there is no 'was' or 'will be' and therefore no becoming. That has been the general tendency of the great historical Religions which are based upon this conception : it would be the tendency of modern pantheistic philosophies if anybody ever thought of taking them seriously enough to attempt living by them. In so far as such theories have entered into the stream of the Western religious consciousness, they have frequently resulted in soul-destroying Quietism. Those who believe that Morality consists in striving, and that Morality is a good-in-itself, will find inspiration in a Theology which represents God too as striving, but as striving for an end which will hereafter be realized in such a measure as to make the striving reasonable.

That the view of Free-will which I have taken involves no difficulties is more than I shall assert. The man who declares that he has got a theory of the Universe which involves no difficulties is simply a man who does not think. I can only say that an idealistic Theism, rooted and grounded in Ethics and developed on the lines which I have endeavoured faintly to sketch, seems to me to involve enormously fewer difficulties than any other theory—constructive, destructive, or agnostic—with which I am acquainted. Nothing appears to be gained by the assumption of Indeterminism. That there is some further solution of the difficulties connected with Free-will and the existence of evil, that some further element of truth in Indeterminism unrecognized by determinist theories might reveal themselves to a more thorough examination, I think extremely probable. I hope that such a further solution of this supreme problem will in time be thought out. But I should myself be inclined to look for such a consummation in any direction rather than in any theory which could properly be called indeterministic.

Once more, I submit, Determinism of the kind I have suggested has nothing in it paralysing or depressing to the most strenuous

that is pronounced to be a delusion, it is difficult to see why any part of the judgement should be retained. At all events the value of the timeless cannot well supply a reason for change in the temporal.

moral effort. To my own mind it is far more inspiring than most Indeterminist theories of the Universe. It represents God as the ultimate source of all being in the Universe that has a beginning, and as directing the world-process towards the goal which shall attain as much of the highest ideally conceivable good as can become actual. He calls upon the higher spiritual beings who have derived their existence from Him to aid in this process. It is a real, and not a merely apparent, struggle to which their God-derived moral consciousness invites them. The evil is a real evil, though an evil destined to be more and more diminished. The rapidity with which and the extent to which the evil will be diminished and the good attained really does depend in part upon human effort. It is true doubtless that God knows how much each of us is capable of aiding towards the process, and how much he will aid; but we do not know, and no human being ever can know until he has acted. And there is nothing in these considerations to paralyse, but everything to quicken and reinforce, all those desires and aspirations which determine the extent and manner in which we shall actually be permitted to take part in the great process of world-redemption [1].

[1] The only modern writer fairly describable as an Indeterminist pure and simple who impresses me with the idea of thoroughly appreciating the question at issue is Lotze (*Microcosmus*, Eng. Trans., I. p. 256 sq.; *Practical Philosophy*, Chap. iii; *Phil. of Religion*, Chap. vii). I do not feel the same in reading Dr. Martineau (*Study of Religion*, II. p. 215 sq.). Nor can I quite understand whether Prof. Ward, whose vindication of the real causality of Will (in *Naturalism and Agnosticism*) seems to me of the highest importance, means to be an Indeterminist or not. The two most convincing arguments against Indeterminism which I know are to be found in Schopenhauer's treatise in *Die beiden Grundprobleme der Ethik*, and in Dr. McTaggart's *Some Dogmas of Religion* (Chap. v). The position which I have adopted is in the main that of Hegel and his followers, except (1) that their treatment of the subject (especially that of Green) seems to me often unsatisfactory on account of their vagueness as to the distinction between the particular and the universal Ego; and (2) that their theories of a timeless Reality and their views of Causation tend to reduce the causality of Will to be a mere seeming. I feel much in sympathy with Prof. A. E. Taylor's treatment of the subject in *Elements of Metaphysics*, Bk. IV, chap. iv. An admirable account of the real meaning of 'Free-will' (in the Self-determinist sense) is also given by Dr. Shadworth Hodgson (*The Philosophy of Experience*, Vol. IV. p. 118 sq.), though in connexion with a Metaphysic which I cannot accept.

CHAPTER IV

MORALITY AND EVOLUTION

I

I TRUST that the account already given of the nature of our moral judgements will by itself have dispelled the notion that there is anything in the position here advocated inconsistent with a frank and cordial acceptance either of the doctrine of Evolution in general or of the particular form given to it by the great discovery of Charles Darwin. The idea of Morality in general—which we have seen to be at bottom the idea of value—is an *a priori* idea in exactly the same sense as that in which the idea of Quantity or Cause or the laws of thought are *a priori*. And every particular moral judgement involves an *a priori* element just as every particular judgement about Quantity or Causality and every particular act of inference involves an *a priori* element. If the term *a priori* is open to objection, the term ' immediate ' will do as well. What is meant is that in these judgements there is an element of knowledge which cannot be explained as sensation or any generalization from sensation. It is undeniable of course that our ideas of Quantity and our powers of reasoning have developed gradually, nor are they equally developed in all races or all individuals. And yet no one thinks of doubting the truth of the multiplication table because there are some savages who (it is said) cannot count ten : nor does any one with a rudimentary training in Metaphysics think this any objection to their *a priori* character. Nor, again, are the varieties of individual judgement inconsistent with the authority that has been claimed for moral judgements as such.

In short, all that has been said as to the difference between the objectivity of the moral judgement and the infallibility of the individual Conscience, all that has been said in explanation of the variations in moral opinion even among individuals brought up in the same community and at the same stage of moral development, is applicable *a fortiori* to the differences between different races at various stages of moral and intellectual development. And it need hardly be pointed out that the development of the moral consciousness is not merely analogous to the general intellectual development, but is very closely connected therewith. Moral judgements and moral reasonings (though they do involve ideas which cannot be derived from or analysed into other ideas) do also involve every other kind of intellectual activity [1]. That power of abstracting and universalizing which forms to so large an extent the differentia of the human intelligence is eminently necessary in ethical thinking. In ethical matters, as in others, this capacity is gradually developed. Such abstract ideas as ' duty,' ' right,' ' good in general,' ' the duty of man to man as such,' can only be reached at all at a comparatively high stage, and in their most abstract and reflective form ,only at a very advanced stage, of intellectual development. In the present state of ethical thought it will be perhaps unnecessary further to labour the point that our moral ideas are gradually developed in exactly the same sense, and in exactly the same way, as any other of the capacities of the human soul, and that this forms no more reason for doubting their validity than in the parallel case of the multiplication table.

These considerations might be held to dispense us from any further treatment of the relation of Evolution to Ethics. The Moral Philosopher is no more bound to deal with the history of ethical development than the Geometrician is bound to preface a geometrical treatise with an anthropological or psychological discussion upon the genesis and development of the idea of space and its various determinations. The business of the Moral Philosopher is simply to analyse the contents of the moral consciousness as it is. No true account of what the moral consciousness actually is can possibly be vitiated by any true account of its genesis. No doubt accounts are sometimes given

---

[1] This point is well brought out by Mr. L. T. Hobhouse in his *Mind in Evolution*, Chap. xiii sq.

4 5 ★

of the genesis of Morality which do seem to be destructive of the authority claimed for the moral faculty. Where this is the case, it must be due to one of three causes: (1) Either the facts alleged are true as far as they go but they will not by themselves really explain the ideas which they are supposed to explain, or (2) the moral historian must be mistaken in the facts on which the theory is supposed to rest, or (3) what purports to be a mere statement of historical facts really implies already a theory about the actual nature of Morality and the developed moral consciousness which goes beyond the mere statement of historical or psychological facts.

An illustration or two may be desirable. It is asserted that 'Altruism' has grown out of 'Egoism.' But if I am right as a matter of psychological fact in asserting that I do now desire another's happiness, no history of the process by which a supposed primitive 'Egoism' passed into Altruism can possibly alter the fact that I am now altruistic, or require me to modify any ethical judgement which may be based upon the value of altruistic conduct. Any theory which purports to require such a modification must be one which at bottom implies that I do not now really desire another's good, but only appear to do so, while in fact I concern myself for my neighbour's good only as a means to my own : and that is a theory which can be refuted by mere introspection. Or take the attempts made to show that the idea of moral obligation is nothing but an inherited fear of the police. No demonstration that there were once people whose moral ideas were limited to a fear of the police, living or ancestral, human or ghostly, can alter the fact that I have now an idea of value which is quite different from a mere feeling or dread of some powerful being, visible or invisible. The theory either misrepresents what I now feel, or fails to account for it, or accounts for it in a way which implies (on the basis of some tacitly assumed metaphysical theory) that, even if I do now, as a matter of psychological fact, think an idea of rightness which is other than fear of an imaginary police, my belief is a delusion which has no basis or foundation in Reason or Reality. The psychological theory (with its ethical implications) does not really rest upon the history; the history rests either upon mistaken observation of present psychological fact or upon some mistaken metaphysical interpretation of it.

And that brings us to another reason against mixing up the question of what Morality is with theories about the process of its development. The sole data for any ethical theory are those supplied by the actual contents of the moral consciousness. And we know a great deal more about the moral consciousness as it is than we do about the moral consciousness or pre-moral consciousness of savages and animals. We are told by Spencer in regard to Ethics that 'as in other cases, so in this case, we must interpret the more developed by the less developed [1].' Within certain limits the statement no doubt holds to a large extent in the region of physical Science. Much light has no doubt been thrown on the actual nature of animals in the higher stages of Evolution by the study of the lower; but even here the converse statement would be at least equally true. That the undifferentiated protoplasm of the Amoeba discharges the function of nerve as well as of muscle is a fact which could scarcely have been discovered except by enquirers starting with the knowledge of what nerve is and what muscle is in their higher, more differentiated forms. And with regard to Morality and psychical life generally this is still more emphatically the case. For the minds of savages and of animals do not lie open to the direct observation which is possible in the case of their bodies. The simplest statements that we can make about them are arrived at only by inference from our own self-knowledge: and the difficulty of mentally picturing mental states lower than any that we know (to *know* them would at once make them different from what they are) is so great that there must be a considerable presumption against any method of ethical enquiry which pretends to explain the more developed by the less developed. No subject is more speculative than prehistoric (or even historical) Psychology. It is scarcely possible that any account of the genesis of Morality should not presuppose some view as to the actual nature of the developed moral consciousness. If that account is a false one, it must vitiate the whole

---

[1] *Data of Ethics*, p. 7. (This work now forms Part I of the *Principles of Morality*, Vol. I, but the pagination is unaltered.)

evolutionary history which is based upon it. A theory of Ethics which rests upon an evolutionary theory which presupposes it really rests upon nothing but itself.

Prima facie these considerations might be held to dispense us from touching upon the question of Evolution and Ethics, except so far as to point out its irrelevance to our present enquiry. The history of moral ideas is no doubt a most important and interesting, as well as a very difficult, subject. It belongs (from different points of view) to Anthropology, to Psychology, to Sociology, to general history, to the history of Philosophy, but not to Philosophy itself. For the present purpose the subject might very well be ignored altogether, and it is impossible to treat it otherwise than most inadequately. But for two reasons it seems better to make a few remarks on the subject than to pass it over altogether. In the first place it is alleged by some evolutionary writers that the doctrine of Evolution supplies us not merely with a history of moral ideas, but with an actual theory of conduct—actual information as to what ought now to be done or left undone—which could not otherwise have been arrived at : and these theories have attracted much attention both with Philosophers and with the general public. The reader may naturally expect that a writer who ignores such theories should at least give some reasons for his disregard of them. Secondly, while from the point of view here adopted it is inconceivable that a theory of Ethics resting upon a sound basis of introspection, with a sound Metaphysic behind it, should be fundamentally revolutionized by the facts of moral Evolution, it does not follow that these facts may not contain some instruction for the Moral Philosopher. All Philosophy must rest upon a comprehensive survey of the whole facts about the Universe as ascertained by Science and by History. Moral Philosophy must rest upon a survey of all the facts which concern the moral life : and among those facts the actual course of development in the moral ideas of mankind (and even of sub-human animals in so far as anything analogous to Morality can be detected in them) occupies an important place. There might well be supposed to be an *a priori* probability that a mental revolution so great as that involved in the general acceptance of the main principles of Darwinism should have some effect upon Ethics, as upon other departments of human thought. If we approach the speculations of the so-called evolutionary writers with less hope of instruction than we might otherwise do, it is not because the fact that moral ideas have developed, and the particular way in which they have developed, are not matters of profound significance for the Moral Philosopher, but rather because in the main the actual course of ethical development was fairly well known before. The doctrine of Evolution did not come into existence with Darwinism. Darwinism is itself only one particular application of this characteristic idea of all nineteenth-century speculation. The idea of development had been fully appreciated by Hegel, and had been abused by John Henry Newman, long before the appearance of *The Origin of Species.* These remarks are not made for the purpose of depreciating the influence which has been exercised upon thought by the distinctly Darwinian idea of development through natural selection, but merely to moderate our expectations as to the amount of instruction which the Moral Philosopher may expect to find in it.

II

Any discussion of the relation between Ethics and Evolution might be expected to begin with some account of the interesting chapter devoted to that subject by Charles Darwin himself in the *Development of Man.* But his remarks are of so simple and untechnical a character—so little directed to the solution of any definite question discussed by Moral Philosophers—that they hardly call for much remark from the point of view which we have adopted. Darwin's main object was to suggest that there was a complete continuity, in this as in other respects, between animal and human life, and so to prevent the moral capacity of human beings being employed as an argument against the hypothesis of their evolution by slow and gradual stages from a non-human ancestor. This continuity is in one sense of the term a fact which no Moralist, theoretical or practical, has the slightest interest in denying. The differences between man as he is in his developed state and animals as we know them become neither greater nor less because it is possible to trace a continuous development from the one to the other. It is only the absurd Psychology which supposes that a mental state which has grown out of another mental state or activity still is the state or activity which preceded it—that mental states can be resolved into antecedent states as chemical compounds can be resolved into their component elements—which can raise any prejudice against the admission that intellectually and morally as well as physically man has grown out of a mere animal. No difficulty is created for Ethics by the admission that the non-moral animal has become the moral man by passing through a number of intermediate stages, which has not always existed in the fact that the non-moral infant-in-arms grows into the imperfectly moral child, and the imperfectly moral child into the full-grown and moral adult. In the one case as in the other the difference between the two is in no way lessened by the fact that it is impossible to point to the exact moment at which the transition takes place. Nor is it only our defective knowledge which debars us from drawing the line at any definite point of development. For the difference between the moral and the non-moral is not a single, definite, and assignable difference. We may by abstraction talk of a 'moral faculty,' but the presence of that faculty makes everything else in consciousness different, or (from another point of view) it presupposes such differences in everything else—impulse, feeling, habit, intelligence, will. We might take particular aspects or features of the difference between the moral and the non-moral being and ask in detail when each begins; but even for perfect knowledge the germ of each would be so unlike the developed product that it is only in the light of what it may become that any common character could be discerned between them. It is enough therefore to say that this continuity between the man and the animal may be fully accepted without affecting anything that has been contended for or will be contended for in this book [1].

That there are germs of Morality—germs which, though not

---

[1] It is true also that all development is only intelligible as a continual series of absolutely new beginnings, and that at particular moments these new beginnings may be of fundamental significance and importance. But I do not profess to expound any theory as to the nature of mental Evolution.

Morality, supply the soil, as it were, in which Morality grows—in the higher animals is probable: it is certain that the lowest men are moral in a very imperfect and rudimentary sense. Their superiority to animals consists, indeed, largely in the fact that they possess a vastly greater capacity for moral education than any existing race of animals. It is only in the light of some practical purpose that there is any meaning in requiring us to say definitely and categorically where Morality begins. With children we shall always have to face the difficulty as best we can. We punish infants only as we punish animals, and at different ages we recognize different stages of 'responsibility' or moral capacity. Fortunately the disappearance of the 'missing links' between mere animal and full man renders the practical questions that arise in this connexion comparatively easy of solution. Even among existent races it is right to recognize their variable moral capacity. We do not give votes to Australian Aborigines, and for many purposes they are rightly treated as children. We may in the fullest degree assert the rights of all existing savages to the elementary rights of humanity—to life, to some measure of liberty and of property—without denying that, had various intermediate species survived, great difficulties might have been felt in deciding who were entitled to be regarded as 'men.' And it might well be that the answer would have been different for different purposes. We might quite reasonably have refused to recognize rights of property in those to whom we still accorded the right to life: we might have defended the enslavement of beings whom we should rightly have protected from arbitrary massacre, and whom we should have scrupled to eat.

Besides this plea for continuity there is little in Darwin's famous chapter which calls for remark here. It is true that he tends to look at Morality from a purely naturalistic point of view, but the treatment is so slight and so popular that the non-naturalistic aspects of Morality are rather ignored than denied. The greatest men of Science are, as a rule, those who know their own limitations best. The pretensions of Evolution to give us a substitute for the old ideas of 'Conscience,' authority, moral obligation, and the like, may therefore be more conveniently examined in the works of the writer who has usually been regarded as the prophet of Darwinism in the region of Philosophy. The task is not an easy one; for, though Herbert Spencer claimed, as his greater predecessor did not claim, to write Philosophy, he uses terms in so vague and popular a sense, he is so unacquainted with the previous history and real meaning of the ethical and metaphysical controversies on which he touches, he shows such a profound misconception of the theories which he criticizes, that the humblest student who has the advantage of an elementary training in Philosophy is apt to treat him as one would treat a writer on Geometry who had never read Euclid (or whatever may be his modern equivalent), or a book on Mechanics whose author showed an ignorance of the first law of motion.

Such an estimate of Herbert Spencer would, however, be a mistake. It is true that the Theology against which he girds is a Theology which, even in that writer's early life in a provincial town, could hardly have been preached even in the pulpit or the Sunday school without qualifications and reservations which he did not take the trouble to observe. The exaggerated 'Altruism' which he attacks is something which no Philosopher, Christian or other, has ever seriously taught [1]. The exhortations about the moral duty of preserving one's health, not going out on cold days without a great-coat, and the like were well-recognized ethical precepts even among such very unphilosophical characters as fill the pages of Miss Austen's novels, though the best of them might have given a somewhat lower place in their ethical ideal to mere Valetudinarianism. The 'Intuitionism' which he attacks is something which has never been maintained, though it is undoubtedly true that many intuitional writers have not always fairly faced even the elementary difficulties upon which Spencer harps. It will be unnecessary to examine elaborately this side of Spencer's teaching. But running through these 'glimpses of the obvious' there are two or three ideas which deserve serious attention

---

[1] Such Altruism was condemned even by mediaeval Councils. The proposition that one ought to love one's neighbour better than oneself has been treated as a definite heresy.

if only because, in more or less altered forms, they have commended themselves to writers of a higher intellectual stature than the author of the *Synthetic Philosophy*.

III

The ethical doctrine of Herbert Spencer may be said to contain three main elements : (*a*) the attempt to reduce the idea of moral authority or rightness in general to the inherited fear of social, regal, and divine or ancestral displeasure ; (*b*) the attempt to explain by evolutionary forces, and particularly by the doctrine of natural selection, why this idea of moral authority or rightness came to attach itself to particular kinds of conduct to such an extent that the individual regards the moral rules in question as 'self-evident' or '*a priori*'; (*c*) the attempt to substitute a 'scientific' moral criterion for the 'hedonistic calculus' of empirical Utilitarianism. A few words must be said on each of these.

The first point in Spencer's Ethics which it seems desirable to notice is, then, his explanation of the idea of moral authority in general or of the idea of duty. In so far as he refers the idea of obligation to the inherited effect of 'sanctions'—social, political, and religious—his doctrine is of course simply the doctrine of all sceptical Moralists from the time of Thrasymachus to that of Mandeville, with the addition that the idea is supposed to be impressed on the consciousness of the individual by heredity as well as by tradition. All that has been said in previous pages in defence of the idea that our judgements of value are rational judgements might be repeated here as an argument against the theory which makes the idea of duty or good into a merely subjective, emotional susceptibility. The theory, if it were true, is one which undermines the belief which it professes to explain. In so far as a man comes to believe that the feeling of awe with which he contemplates the idea of failure in duty is due *solely* to the inherited terror of now powerless chiefs or of ghosts which no longer walk the earth, that terror must tend to vanish. We know as a matter of fact that it persists in persons who are quite free from superstitious terrors about the dangers of ancestral displeasure. I know that my idea of Right is not such a merely subjective terror by immediate reflection, just as I know that my idea of Causality or Number is not a mere subjective tendency to expect the recurrence of sensations resembling those which have previously been associated in my experience, or to escape the penalties which failure to repeat the multiplication table correctly may at one time have incurred.

But the imaginary police theory is only one half of Spencer's doctrine. It is, after all only the 'compulsiveness' attaching to the ordinary idea of duty which is traced to what Mandeville would have called the 'political progeny of prejudice begat on pride.' The idea of authority is, it would appear, something distinct from the idea of 'compulsiveness,' and for this idea Spencer has no strictly evolutionary justification. The idea of duty in general is obtained by abstraction from particular feelings which carry with them the idea of authority. What these feelings are, may be best described in Herbert Spencer's own words :—

'We have seen that during the progress of animate existence, the later-evolved, more compound and more representative feelings, serving to adjust the conduct to more distant and general needs, have all along had an authority as guides superior to that of the earlier and simpler feelings—excluding cases in which these last are intense. This superior authority, unrecognizable by lower types of creatures which cannot generalize, and little recognizable by primitive men, who have but feeble powers of generalization, has become distinctly recognized as civilization and accompanying mental development have gone on. Accumulated experiences have produced the consciousness that guidance by feelings which refer to remote and general results, is usually more conducive to welfare than guidance by feelings to be immediately gratified. For what is the common character of the feelings that prompt honesty, truthfulness, diligence, providence, &c. which men habitually find to be better prompters than the appetites and simple impulses ? They are all complex, re-representative feelings, occupied with the future rather than the present. The idea of authoritativeness has therefore come to be connected with feelings having these traits : the implication being that the lower and simpler feelings are without authority. And this idea of authoritativeness is one element in the abstract consciousness of duty [1].'

---

[1] *Data of Ethics*, pp. 125-6.

The main difficulty which one feels in criticizing this account is the extreme uncertainty in which Spencer leaves us as to what he supposes 'authority' to mean. If he means by it anything like what ordinary people mean, one has only to say that he admits his opponent's case. The process by which we have come to attach the idea of authority to certain acts rather than to certain other acts is in a sense—not very lucidly or convincingly, it must be said—on Herbert Spencer's premisses explained. But the explanation is one which postulates the idea of authority already in the minds of those who feel it. For what after all is it that the course of Evolution has taught the human race? 'That guidance by feelings which refer to remote and general results, is usually more conducive to welfare than guidance by feelings to be immediately gratified.' 'Conducive to welfare'—but whose welfare? If one's own, it is clear, as is frequently admitted by Spencer, that, though an enlightened Ethic will recognize a moral obligation in the precepts of Prudence, it is specially to rules of conduct which conduce to other people's welfare that this idea of authority inherently attaches. And what is meant by saying that 'authority' attaches to such rules; that we think that they ought to be obeyed? It is true that the authority which is ascribed to these rules is not, according to Spencer, ultimate: it belongs to them as means to general welfare. General welfare, then, is recognized as something which *ought* to be promoted, as the rational *end* of action, as possessing ultimate *value*. But why should we be guided by feelings conducive to other people's welfare? From other parts of Spencer's writings, it would seem that the answer would be 'from sympathy.' This explanation may possibly explain the fact that some people do actually, in a greater or less degree, promote other people's welfare: it cannot explain why they should feel bound to do so, whether they feel naturally inclined to do so or not. It cannot explain why sympathy should be regarded as a 'better guide' than selfishness—which is the fact of consciousness which presumably Spencer set out to explain. If all that Spencer means is that this rational idea or category of Rightness has only gradually developed, and that social pressure of various kinds has been one of the conditions of its development (just as Arithmetic was developed under pressure of commercial necessities), there is nothing in his contention which any modern Idealist would wish to deny. With regard to all Spencer's explanations of the idea of duty in general, it is difficult to make out whether he himself thinks that he is explaining it or explaining it away—whether the explanation is put forth as a vindication or as a refutation of its validity.

There are, indeed, parts of Spencer's writings—especially the section of his *Principles of Ethics* styled *Justice*—in which he would seem almost prepared to admit the simple, *a priori* un-analysable character of the idea of Right. The treatment which he there bestows on that virtue would seem to suggest that he recognizes the rule of Justice—on account of its supreme conduciveness to pleasure, which is with him the ultimate end— as an *a priori* dictate of Reason. It is not easy to believe that the following passage can really have been written by the author of *The Data of Ethics*:—

'But what is the ultimate meaning of expediency? When it is proposed to guide ourselves empirically, towards what are we to guide ourselves? If our course must always be determined by the merits of the case, by what are the merits to be judged? "By conduciveness to the welfare of society, or the good of the community," will be the answer. It will not be replied that the merit to be estimated means increase of misery; it will not be replied that it means increase of a state of indifference, sensational and emotional; and it must therefore be replied that it means increase of happiness[1]. By implication, if not avowedly, greatest happiness is the thing to be achieved by public action, or private action, or both. But now whence comes this postulate? Is it an inductive truth? Then where and by whom has the induction been drawn? Is it a truth of experience derived from careful observations? Then what are the observations, and when was there generalized that vast mass of them on which all politics and morals should be built? Not only are there no such experiences, no such observations, no such induction, but it is impossible that any should be assigned. Even were the intuition universal, which it is not (for it has been denied by ascetics in all ages and places, and is demurred

---

[1] On the Logic of this argument I have commented below, p. 378.

to by an existing school of moralists), it would still have no better warrant than that of being an immediate *dictum* of consciousness [1].'

And Spencer goes on to show that the greatest happiness principle becomes meaningless without the *addendum* 'one person's happiness . . . is counted for exactly as much as another's.' 'Hence the Benthamite theory of morals and politics,' he admits, 'posits this as a fundamental self-evident truth [2].'

The passage is doubly inconsistent with the Spencer of the *Data*, for, in the first place, in *Justice* the ultimate end of conduct becomes, not as in the *Data*, that mere 'welfare' in general (no matter whose welfare it is) which the 're-representative feelings' promote, but the promotion of Justice, which is something quite other and possibly inconsistent with the promotion of general welfare—the rule that 'Every man is to do what he wills, provided he infringes not the freedom of any other man.' And secondly, it is not now mere 'feelings' to which ultimate moral authority attaches, but a dictate of Reason which, we may suppose, recognizes that these feelings have a preferential claim to respect. And this dictate of Reason implies a distinct and analysable idea of 'rightness' or 'goodness,' for 'consciousness' cannot tell us that it is right to be just unless we know what 'right' means. Such an idea of authority cannot be distilled by any process of abstraction from 're-representative feelings,' unless those feelings are already invested with this idea of authority by something which is not feeling. Here the great Evolutionist appears in the light of a rationalistic Moralist, and one feels for the moment tempted to see in the passage the influence of some deceased and deified ancestor whose ghost, still haunting his descendant, has compelled him to do sacrifice to the idols which the *Synthetic Philosophy* was, once for all, to have demolished.

But such an interpretation as I have suggested would probably be unjust. After all, it would seem that these *a priori* beliefs are not really *a priori*. They are *a priori* to the individual

---

[1] *Justice* (*Principles of Morality*, Vol. II. pt. iv), pp. 57, 58.
[2] Ib

4 6

but *a posteriori* to the race. They are due to accumulated experiences. But experiences of what ? The rightness or authority of any course of action cannot be 'experienced.' At most it would only be a belief in the conduciveness of this rule of Justice to tribal welfare which could be experienced, and so transmitted by inheritance and natural selection. We think we ought to speak the truth, we know not why : but the evolutionary philosopher is in a position to tell us that originally our ancestors discovered that truth-speaking was conducive to the preservation and welfare of the individual and the race, and natural selection has killed off those individuals and those races which were most incurably given to lying—a very bold hypothesis in view of the habits of some surviving races. This at least is the explanation which Spencer gives of the apparently *a priori* character of other axiomatic truths. The question whether two and two make four or five was to our remote ancestors an open question to be decided by experience ; but from constant familiarity with cases in which two and two were found to make four they eventually bequeathed to their posterity a physiological incapacity for supposing they made five, so that to us the idea that they make four has become a logical necessity of thought. Whether Spencer himself would have attempted to extend this doctrine as to the source of our belief in axioms to the fundamental moral truth that it is right to promote general welfare, and how he would have done it, it is impossible to say; but on the assumption that this attempt would have been made, a few remarks on the Spencerian theory of axioms may not be out of place.

A full examination of the theory would evolve an elaborate metaphysical discussion. It may be enough to point out that it is a theory which, though it holds out an attractive prospect of reconciling the empirical with the *a priori* School of Metaphysics, really undermines all our confidence in the validity of knowledge. Every inference that we make implies certain laws of thought or principles of reasoning. If these laws are really no necessities of thought but mere inherited results of accidental experiences, it is possible that they are untrustworthy. To believe in the law of contradiction may at one time, under a particular set of circumstances, have aided our ancestors in the struggle for existence; as on Spencer's view, and on any possible view, has undoubtedly been the case with many beliefs not objectively true. The more clear-sighted thinkers who discerned its falsity were, it is conceivable, killed off by natural selection: while, as to ourselves, we have now become physiologically incapable of discovering the ancestral mistake. That being so, we are compelled to accept Spencer's theory about ethical and other axioms (which professes to rest upon clear thinking); but if belief in the law of contradiction may really be false, all the arguments upon which Spencer's theory rests may likewise be untrustworthy and the theory may be false after all, no matter how little we can help believing in it. True, it is assumed that the beliefs were engendered by accumulated experiences of actual fact, but then these experiences were partial and local. Our race may have originated in parts of the world in which the law of contradiction happened to prevail, and which contained no circles with segments greater than their arcs. But the deep-sea regions revealed to modern explorers might teem with such circles, and yet the explorers would be *ex hypothesi* incapable of perceiving the fact[1]. Spencer's theory involves us in hopeless scepticism, as does every theory which attempts to account by experience for the principles of thought, which are implied in every step of the process by which experience itself is turned into knowledge.

A theory which leads to such results when applied to the ultimate bases of knowledge is equally incompetent to account for the ultimate basis of our moral beliefs. In this case no doubt the same easy *reductio ad absurdum* is not possible. It is not so easy to reduce to self-contradiction the theorist who professes to explain away the idea of duty as the theorist who explains away, while professing to explain, the law of contradiction. For we can argue without assuming the truth of moral principles, though we cannot argue without assuming the axioms of thought. But we can point out that the two kinds of axiomatic truth really rest upon the same basis. And it is, as

---

[1] I borrow this line of argument from Professor Cook Wilson's brilliant inaugural lecture on 'Mr. Spencer's Theory of Axioms.'

a rule, fairly easy to show that the critic who tries to explain away moral obligation has the idea, and more or less completely acts upon it, as much as the people whom he criticizes. Herbert Spencer himself is constantly using the terms 'higher' and 'lower,' 'ethically higher and lower' in a way which would be meaningless if he really meant them in the evolutionary sense—that is to say, more 'integrated,' more differentiated, more complex—and when he argues in support of his view that pleasure is the ultimate good or end, he shows how impossible it is to think without implying the idea of Value. His judgement that pleasure is the sole good is, in short, like all ultimate moral principles, an *a priori* judgement of value, true or false. At bottom it is probable that nothing was further from Herbert Spencer's intentions than to explain away the ultimate authority of the Moral Law. He did not see that what he offered as an explanation and vindication of that authority must really have the effect of undermining it.

IV

Considered as an attempt to explain the idea of validity or self-evidencing authority attaching to our intuitions in general and to every one of them, Spencer's theory must be treated as part and parcel of a metaphysical system which there are good metaphysical grounds for rejecting. But if the theory is put forward simply as an explanation of particular 'intuitions' in the popular sense of the word, of rules of conduct which have actually presented themselves to particular races and individuals as self-evidently binding, it may at once be admitted that there may be considerable truth in it. No accumulation of experiences, personal or ancestral, could ever generate the idea of 'good' or 'value' in a consciousness which did not possess it: but, given the existence of such a concept (which, of course, does not express itself in an abstract form prior to particular judgements of value but is implied in the simplest of them), the varying experience, environment, and intellectual development of races and individuals unquestionably does and must explain why the idea of value has come to attach itself to particular kinds of conduct rather than to others.   It is undoubtedly true, as Spencer has so exhaustively shown in his *Principles of Sociology*—a much more interesting and important work than the *Principles of Ethics*—that it is the necessity for military efficiency which accounts for the high estimate placed by some races upon such qualities as courage, endurance, and submissiveness to chiefs, and for their contempt for the more amiable and the more industrial virtues, while peaceful tribes have attached a high value to truth and a very low one to discipline or obedience.   The qualities were originally valued because they were felt to be conducive to tribal Well-being, and afterwards came to be valued for their own sake without any such conscious regard to tribal Well-being.   All this is undeniable, and there is little in it that can be claimed as the monopoly of 'evolutionary Ethics.'   Essentially it is the commonplace of all pre-evolutionary Utilitarianism, and will not now be denied by non-hedonistic Moralists who have recognized the slow development of Morality; though these last might insist that even very barbaric ideals of tribal Well-being contain an element which goes beyond the conception of a 'greatest quantum of pleasure' for the tribe. Only two elements in this explanation of apparently intuitive beliefs are new.   Firstly, the theory of natural selection is held to explain how the tendency to practise and approve conduct conducive to personal or tribal Well-being was strengthened by the dying-out of individuals or of tribes which did not accommodate themselves to the socially beneficial ideal.   And secondly, there is the idea that moral beliefs have been transmitted, not merely by education and the influence of a continuous social environment, but also by direct inheritance.

That there is some truth in both these new ideas is not impossible.   It is probable that some Evolutionists are disposed greatly to over-emphasize the influence of natural selection in accounting for the actual history of moral ideas, especially in the later stages of that history.   If Biology now finds that it cannot get on without the idea of 'quasi-purposive' behaviour in accounting for the growth of the individual organisms, still more must quasi-purposive action be admitted, even where we cannot think of directly and consciously purposive action, as an important factor in social Evolution [1]. Still it is, no doubt, true that Nature, in primitive stages of Evolution, has eliminated the exceptionally cowardly and, at a later period, the phenomenally idle and imprudent: and that in all ages Society has deliberately eliminated some few of those whose ideals were most conspicuously ill-adapted for social life. Still more important has been the influence of the struggle between tribes in promoting the survival of those whose ideals were most fitted in early times for conquest, and in later times for a combination of industrial with military efficiency: though nobody has pointed out more forcibly than Spencer himself in his eloquent diatribes against Militarism how little the code of conduct that promotes survival can be regarded as identical with a code of morals possessing permanent and absolute validity.

The other distinctively 'evolutionary' doctrine—the propagation of moral ideas by inheritance—involves much more difficult and debatable questions. The scientific world has not generally accepted Spencer's doctrine that acquired moral beliefs can be inherited. The question is really in large measure a physiological one, upon which it would ill become the layman in such matters to dogmatize. I may perhaps be allowed to remark that superficial observation of the facts would seem to suggest that, while certain moral capacities or incapacities can scarcely be separated from those physical and intellectual characteristics which are undoubtedly inherited, it is questionable whether the fully-developed moral belief or 'intuition' could be transmitted to offspring apart from the influence of education and environ-

[1] 'When we say that life consists of purposive action and development, we do not mean that there is a conscious and purposive application, *ab extra*, of mechanical force by some independent agency. Such a conclusion would only signify the reintroduction, under another form, of the old mechanical theory. We mean rather to record that we have observed phenomena which present no analogy to the mechanical or chemical action on each other of independent atoms, and which do present a certain but very limited resemblance to the action of a number of intelligent individuals working together to fulfil a common end.' Haldane, *The Pathway to Reality*, I. pp. 243, 244. The earlier chapters of Von Hartmann's *Philosophy of the Unconscious* may be referred to for a brilliant demonstration of the impossibility of accounting for the instincts of animals and the quasi-instructive ideas and habits of men by natural selection alone.

ment. Here, as in the matter of physical habits of various kinds
in the lower animals (even those most nearly approximating to
mere ' reflexes '), what is inherited is probably a capacity for
acquiring or being taught rather than any actual moral belief.
So far the Spencerian theory has contributed an element to the
explanation of moral evolution, though it is an element which
really adds very little beyond a change of phraseology to the
accounts of ethical development which might have been given,
and were given, before the publication of the Darwinian theory [1].

There is a constant disposition to forget that the ' struggle for
existence ' as a fact was a well-known element in human history
from the very earliest times. The originality of Darwin's theory
consisted in seeing its bearing upon the ' origin of species.' The
struggle for existence certainly does not explain the ' origin of
Morality ' in the sense in which it helps to explain the ' origin
of species.' At most it represents one of the complex forces
which go to explain the fact of moral progress. It contributes
an element to ethical history ; but does it add anything to
ethical theory ? To a very limited extent I think that it does.
It adds some shade of additional presumption to the other grounds
which may be given for assuming that a rule of conduct which
is *de facto* established in any society must have its origin in
some consideration of social convenience, and that its observance
must be in some way beneficial to that society. And, therefore,
when we find ourselves feeling a strong repugnance to certain
kinds of conduct, even though the repugnance be one which we
find it difficult to justify on any rational principle, it is reasonable
to assume that it probably possesses some utilitarian justification,
which should make us unwilling to act against such an instinctive
repugnance, unless we are very sure of our ground. Neither on
Spencer's principles nor on any other can it be contended that
this consideration compels us to acquiesce without question in
each and every apparently intuitive disposition to approve or to

---

[1] The question turns to some extent upon the view that is taken of
Weissmann's theory of the non-inheritance of acquired characteristics,
upon the truth of which I express no opinion. But of course the
inheritance of acquired physical modifications does not prove the inheritance of acquired beliefs.

condemn any kind of conduct. For, though the instinct may have had its justification in some supposed social utility, that utility may have been entirely imaginary. Many of the strongest ethical beliefs of savages are based upon the supposed connexion between various acts and divine favour or vengeance. Sometimes, no doubt, there may be a real utility in the custom or practice approved, although the utility may not be what the savage himself supposes; as for instance it is possible that the custom of Exogamy, resting upon a complex of totemistic ideas, has prevented the marriage of near kin and increased the vigour of the tribe [1]. But it would be a monstrous assumption, though it is one which some evolutionary writers go very near to countenancing, to lay it down that this must always be the case. Not all qualities or tendencies or inherited 'variations' of a species or group promote survival. A species may survive because some of its qualities promote survival in spite of qualities which, taken by themselves, would tend to its extinction. In the same way it is obvious that there are many of our inherited tendencies and traditional beliefs which have not promoted survival, or which have even tended to extinction without actually producing it. There can never have been the slightest social advantage in the practice of killing children who cut their lower teeth first rather than any other children. No belief could possibly have militated more against survival than the belief prevalent among Australian natives that every death, not due to obvious violence or accident, must be the result of witchcraft and must be avenged by the death of the bewitcher [2]. The presumption in favour of the established or transmitted belief may, therefore, be rebutted by sufficient evidence of its inutility. And it is fully admitted by Herbert Spencer himself that a

[1] It is true that it was at first only kin on the mother's side who were forbidden to intermarry, but it seems probable that, as the primitive clan-system broke down, the prohibition was extended to all kinsmen.

[2] Spencer and Gillan, *The Native Tribes of Central Australia*, pp. 46–8. The writers remark, 'It need hardly be pointed out what a potent element this custom has been in keeping down the numbers of the tribe.' I suppose there might be conditions under which a limitation of numbers might help the survival of a species in competition with other species. But this would be no argument for the general adoption of a custom tending to such limitation.

belief which once had a relative justification in real social utility may outlive its justification.   A large part of his voluminous writings are, in fact, devoted to the demonstration, with impressive if wearisome iteration, of the social inutility of the beliefs and ideas which modern industrial societies have inherited from societies accustomed to habitual militancy.   It cannot therefore be rational to regard these inherited 'intuitions' as final guides to conduct.   If Evolution has supplied us with a new moral criterion, it is not to be found in this doctrine of inherited intuitions.   The doctrine, in so far as it has a sound physiological basis, can at most only slightly reinforce that presumption in favour of established Morality from which the sane Moralist of any school sets out.   So far I have argued on Spencer's own hedonistic principles.   From the point of view taken up in previous chapters, we should further have to admit that a practice or inherited belief may promote survival, and so, ultimately, increase of pleasure, and still not be approved by the developed moral consciousness.   To us the quality of life and of pleasure is important and not merely its quantity.   If Morality did in a sense come into existence to promote life, it exists (as Aristotle would say) for good life, and good life does not mean merely pleasant life.

V

But Herbert Spencer is not content with giving a psychological explanation either of our moral ideas in general or of particular moral rules in detail.   His writings, at least his earlier ethical writings, represent that Evolution has actual guidance to bestow as to what Morality ought to be now.   The third and the most characteristic feature of Spencer's ethical system is the attempt to substitute a 'scientific' for an 'empirical' Utilitarianism—to substitute an appeal to rules which the course of Evolution has impressed upon us, and thereby proved to be conditions of Well-being, for the direct empirical calculation of pleasure and pain adopted by the older Utilitarians.

Spencer agrees with the Utilitarians in regarding pleasure as the ultimate end of human life.   A word must be said as to the method by which he thinks he has proved this fundamental tenet. He habitually assumes that the only alternative to accepting pleasure as the ultimate test of conduct is to treat pain as the ultimate end, or else a neutral state which is neither pleasurable nor painful. Ridiculing Carlyle's substitution of 'blessedness' for 'pleasure,' he says:

'Obviously, the implication is that blessedness is not a kind of happiness; and this implication at once suggests the question —What mode of feeling is it? If it is a state of consciousness at all, it is necessarily one of three states—painful, indifferent, or pleasurable. Does it leave the possessor at the zero point of sentiency? Then it leaves him just as he would be if he had not got it. Does it not leave him at the zero point? Then it must leave him below zero or above zero![1]'

It is really difficult to exhaust the logical fallacies of this reasoning. In the first place there is the assumption that 'a kind of happiness' is the same thing as 'happiness'; and that, if Carlyle had admitted that 'a kind of happiness' is good, he would have had to admit that all kinds of happiness (by which of course Spencer means pleasure) are good. Secondly, there is the assumption that there is nothing in consciousness but feeling, and that therefore it must be some characteristic of feeling—to the total exclusion of will and thought, which must possess intrinsic value. Thirdly, there is the assumption that feelings have no content—that they are simply pleasurable, painful, or neutral, and nothing else—so that, if 'blessedness' were admitted to be neither pleasurable nor painful, it would leave the possessor 'just as he would be if he had not got it.' The same naïve assumption—that pleasures have no content— prevents Spencer from recognizing the possible alternative that the intrinsically desirable state of consciousness might be differentiated from others by some criterion quite other than its pleasurableness or painfulness; so that either all the desirable states might be pleasurable and yet not preferred simply on account of their pleasurableness, or all might even (as a logical possibility) be painful or neutral, and yet not preferred because painful or neutral; or again the line between the desirable

[1] *The Data of Ethics*, p. 41.

and undesirable might wholly cut across the lines which divide the pleasant from the neutral and the neutral from the painful, and include some pleasurable, some painful, and some neutral states, or states in which there entered elements of pain as well as of pleasure. Elsewhere [1] he assumes that because he has shown the difficulty or unreasonableness of denying that 'pleasure somewhere, at some time, to some being or beings, is an inexpugnable element of the conception' of a desirable state of feeling, he has shown that pleasure is the good and the whole good, and that there is no other good but pleasure.

Except that his method of arguing in favour of it is rather worse than that of less 'scientific' Hedonists, Spencer's position is so far the same as theirs. But while the ordinary Utilitarian is contented to trust to experience—his own experience, the experience of others, the recorded experience of the race—for discovering how a maximum of pleasure is to be obtained, Spencer believes himself to have discovered in the laws of Evolution a scientific criterion of Morality, which will prove not only that such and such kinds of conduct will actually cause pleasure, but that they and no others *must* cause pleasure. What this criterion is had better be stated in Spencer's own words, lest the reader unacquainted with the *Synthetic Philosophy* should remain unconvinced of the accuracy of my representation:—

'If we substitute for the word Pleasure the equivalent phrase —a feeling which we seek to bring into consciousness and retain there, and if we substitute for the word Pain the equivalent phrase—a feeling which we seek to get out of consciousness and to keep out; we see at once that, if the states of consciousness which a creature endeavours to maintain are the correlatives of injurious actions, and if the states of consciousness which it endeavours to expel are the correlatives of beneficial actions, it must quickly disappear through persistence in the injurious and avoidance of the beneficial. In other words, those races of beings only can have survived in which, on the average, agreeable or desired feelings went along with activities conducive to the maintenance of life, while disagreeable and habitually-avoided feelings went along with activities directly or indirectly

[1] *The Data of Ethics*, p. 46.

destructive of life ; and there must ever have been, other things equal, the most numerous and long-continued survivals among races in which these adjustments of feelings to actions were the best, tending ever to bring about perfect adjustment [1].'

Instead, therefore, of consulting experience to find out what rules have actually promoted happiness, we must study the laws of human life, individual and social—physiological, psychological, sociological, and ascertain what are the conditions which have actually promoted survival, it being assumed that whatever produces survival will also produce a balance of pleasure. These laws being ascertained, we can feel sure that it is only by obedience to them that further progress can be secured. The course which calculations of Utility, Reason, common sense might prescribe as most likely to secure happiness must, it would appear, be resolutely set aside in favour of the principles resulting from the study of animal and human evolution. An exhaustive criticism of the theory would require a volume. The following may be briefly suggested as some of its chief difficulties :—

(1) In the first place a few preliminary remarks may be made with regard to Herbert Spencer's fundamental assumptions :

(a) The definition above given of pleasure would seem to commit the author to the hedonistic Psychology, which is elsewhere very decidedly repudiated. The possibility of real Altruism, when it conflicts with Egoism, is absolutely denied if we necessarily aim at expelling from consciousness every feeling but those which are pleasant, and seek to retain those only which are pleasant and in so far as they are pleasant. If sympathy with another's pain be painful, it would follow that we must necessarily seek to expel it from consciousness, as soon as it appears; and there are generally quicker ways of effecting that expulsion than the relief of the suffering which occasions it. The only way of escape is to say that sympathy with pain is always pleasant, but Spencer shows no disposition to adopt such a mode of bridging over the gulf between Altruism and Egoism.

(b) The principle here put forward is quite definitely a different principle from that of reliance upon inherited intuitions, which

---

[1] *Principles of Psychology*, § 124, repeated in *The Data of Ethics*, p. 79.

has already been explained and criticized. It cannot surely be
contended that the 'intuitions' of every ordinary society—even
the most advanced—are completely in harmony with the results
of the studies recommended by our author. Indeed, much of
Spencer's book is devoted to declamations against the ethical
code, commonly accepted on the basis of Intuition, which he
assumes to be that of his own society. When the excessive
Benevolence to which large numbers of persons feel intuitively
prompted (whether they act upon such promptings is not to the
point) comes into collision with the stern, and in the main
sensible, Charity Organization principles recommended by Spencer,
or the promptings of Loyalty with the theory of extremely limited
State-action which he supposes to result from the study of
Evolution, what principle is to arbitrate between them? Have
we not, on Spencerian principles, as much right to say that our
intuitions represent, and must represent, the true lines of social
health, imprinted on us by natural selection, as he has to appeal
to the results of his studies? As a matter of fact, Spencer
himself usually appeals to experience, private and historical, to
show that the societies which have obeyed the laws which he
recommends have been happy, and those which have disobeyed
them have been miserable. Here the appeal is after all made to
the much-decried hedonistic calculus.

(c) The alleged concomitance between tendency to survival
and pleasure is, in the extreme and absolute form given to it by
Spencer, a highly questionable doctrine. It is proved only by
his favourite logical expedient—treating contrary propositions
as contradictories, and assuming that a middle is excluded when
it is not excluded. Pleasure, it is argued, must be the invariable
concomitant of beneficial actions because, if pain were their
invariable concomitant, the race would perish. It may be
observed further that even so the proposition is only made out
by the assumption that men and animals always aim at pleasure,
which in the case of men is inconsistent with Spencer's own
admission of Altruism, and in the case of animals is inconsistent
with the existence of instinct. No doubt the performance of
instinctive actions gives the animal some pleasure, but it is not
proved that they are always pleasant on the whole. Some

instincts of animals, as Spencer himself has shown, lead them to self-sacrifice : and from a purely biological point of view it may be urged that the ' sociality ' of animals—their tendency to perform instinctive actions which do not give pleasure to the individual—is quite as important a factor in determining the survival of race or group as the instincts which give pleasure to the individual [1].

If Spencer contends that the pleasure which is necessarily the concomitant of beneficial actions need only be the pleasure of the race, the fact of such invariable concomitance is not proved by the Spencerian Psychology. If an action beneficial to the race may be performed though painful to the individual, we cannot assume that, even if the action produced more pain than pleasure to the race, it would cease to be performed by the individual. It might conceivably be productive of pain to the race, though conducive to survival [2]. Finally, to return to my main point, the fact that a concomitance between beneficial actions and painful ones would lead to extermination does not prove the *invariable* concomitance between pleasure and beneficial action. For, be it remembered, Spencer has to establish not merely that actions which produce survival produce some pleasure (on the whole, no doubt, with some reservations, a probable statement), but that they produce the greatest pleasure that is possible. Only if that is proved, can we accept the fact that a race has survived by the observance of certain rules as a proof that it has got in that way a maximum of possible pleasure, and should therefore be imitated by us. It is possible that with less survival (e. g. a smaller population or absorption in a conquering people) there might have been more pleasure. Or again there is the possibility that two sets of rules might have been equally conducive to survival, but the one which was not adopted might have produced the larger amount of pleasure.

(d) If we return once more to the individual and assume

---

[1] Cf. Giddings, *Principles of Sociology*, p. 79 sq.

[2] Von Hartmann has contended that this is actually the case with the human race as a whole, and he has certainly accumulated much evidence which should make us hesitate to assume that survival always implies predominance of pleasure over pain.

Spencer to mean that life-preserving actions are always pleasant to the individual, we are met with the obvious cases in which what is immediately pleasant is clearly not conducive to survival—poisons for instance. If it is said (as is pointed out sometimes by Spencer) that the pleasure is sooner or later followed by pain, the immediate pleasantness cannot be taken as any proof that the action is beneficial : for, however long we wait, the ill consequences may still lie in the future. Thus we are thrown back upon the empirical weighing of pains against pleasures before the Spencerian rule can yield any guidance— the very calculation which 'Scientific Utilitarianism' was to supersede. We cannot tell whether the taking of poison be good for welfare or not without an appeal to experience with all its uncertainties.

(2) If the dogma about the concomitance between pleasure and life-preserving action is not true wholly and without exception, or if it is true only in a sense which is nugatory, it can hardly be fitted to supply the basis of a strictly 'scientific' criterion which is to end the painful uncertainties of the hedonistic calculus. But let us provisionally assume its truth and ask whether it will work.

Spencer seeks to establish an equation between the two categories, 'pleasant actions' and 'actions conducive to the welfare of the organism.' But it is never quite apparent in which way he means us to apply his formula. Are we first to observe for ourselves what things are immediately pleasant, and then to infer that these must be in accordance with the laws of the organism ? Or are we first to discover the laws of the organism, and then assume that their observance will secure the greatest attainable pleasure ? If the first alternative be adopted, we have already indicated the difficulty. The doctrine, if true at all, can only be true on the understanding that 'pleasant' be understood to include remote as well as immediate consequences. And then we are reduced once more to that tedious process of accumulating experiences of pleasant and painful effects, and balancing the one against the other, from which the scientific clue to Utility promised deliverance. Are we then to shut our eyes to direct experience, to get at the general laws of the organism, and assume that whatever is in accordance with them will be conducive to a balance of pleasure on the whole? The theory can hardly be tested without recognizing a distinction between the laws of the individual and the social organism which in this connexion Spencer himself rarely makes. Let us deal with the individual organism first. We are then to assume that whatever is in accordance with the laws of the individual organism is conducive on the whole to the pleasure of that organism. It may, indeed, be asked how we are to ascertain what are the laws of the organism except by interrogating experience. It may be asked whether these 'laws of the organism' are not very largely the result of those calculations of pleasant and painful consequences which Spencer deprecates? But let us waive that point, and assume that we have arrived somehow at 'laws of the individual organism' which are independent of any empirical calculation of the greater pleasantness or painfulness on the whole of different courses of action.

Where are we to look for such laws? As far as I know, Spencer has only given us one single example of an ethical truth which results from the study of the laws of the individual organism, but which might otherwise have escaped the rude methods of empirical Utilitarianism. It is a law of the organism, we are told, that any unnatural or abnormal stimulation of an organ must be followed by a reaction. The stimulation is pleasant, but the subsequent reaction must bring with it in the long run, not merely pain, but pain (or loss of pleasure) which outweighs the pleasure. Here then at last we have reached a valuable practical conclusion. The mere empirical Utilitarian might have fallen into the mistake of supposing that, because the moderate use of wine, beer, spirits, tea, coffee, tobacco, and snuff seems to bring with it present pleasure and apparent gain in efficiency without any appreciable loss, or a loss apparently compensated by its beneficial effects, such moderate use may be permitted. But here the evolutionary Moralist, duly trained in biological and sociological studies, steps in and warns him of his fatal mistake. The bad effects may escape the observation not merely of the superficial observer, but of the scientific Physician; yet they must be there all the same, and must outweigh the good effects. Amid all our difficulties in discovering the actual precepts of the new 'scientific' Hedonism, here there is one solid, tangible result—evolutionary Ethics are teetotal, and they condemn tea, coffee, tobacco, and snuff.

But just at the moment at which we seem to have reached a result of practical value, we are suddenly confronted with another peculiar feature of the Spencerian system—the distinction between 'absolute' and 'relative' Ethics. Absolute Ethics prescribe the conduct which is conducive to life in circumstances of perfect adaptation—perfect adaptation of the individual to his environment. Relative Ethics deal with the conduct which is suitable to such and such an individual in a society at a given stage of imperfect adaptation. Nothing is absolutely right but what promotes pleasure pure and simple without any admixture whatever of pain. Relative Ethics often prescribe what is really only the less of two evils. It is only a perfect society that can observe the counsels of perfection enjoined by absolute Ethics. A single cup of the weakest tea administered to an individual in a state of perfect health in a perfectly adapted society dwelling in a perfectly adapted physical environment would necessarily disturb the delicately adjusted harmony, and involve a diminution of pleasure on the whole. But in our present state of imperfect adaptation, when we have to breathe contaminated air, to lead sedentary lives, to make unwholesomely exacting efforts physical and mental, and so on, the gain may often be greater than the loss. The Ethics adapted to our present imperfect state positively prescribe the moderate use of all the stimulants interdicted by 'scientific' Hedonism. What then, it may be asked, is the use of absolute Ethics, if after all we have to depend for practical guidance upon relative Ethics which are just as empirical as the much-decried 'empirical Utilitarianism'? Herbert Spencer's system of Moral Philosophy will be of use when we reach a social millennium—not till then. Nor do absolute Ethics throw a single ray of light upon the path by which that millennium is to be reached. I will not here examine the grounds of Spencer's optimistic assumption that we are tending to a state of things in which, with complete adaptation and adjustment, absolute Ethics will become available. Whether an adjustment so com-

plete that an animal might go from birth to death without
suffering a single pang is physiologically possible, even barring
those unpreventable accidents which, it is admitted, will still
occur in Spencer's evolutionary Paradise—whether birth, child-
bearing, or death, for instance, will be rendered painless by
increased 'adaptation'—may well be doubted. At all events,
such a state of things is so remote from the world that we know
that a code of Ethics appropriate to it must be completely
unavailable [1].

We have seen that neither of the two possible interpretations
of the Spencerian equation (pleasurable = healthful) can be got
to yield us real guidance. The truth is that Spencer himself
adopts whichever criterion happens to supply the best support
for the particular article of his own practical code on which he
is insisting for the moment—a code which he has really arrived
at by methods quite unconnected with the evolutionary principles
which he recommends. When he is protesting against the
excesses of 'Altruism' or of traditional Asceticism, we are told
that it is a mistake to look with suspicion upon the immediately
pleasant—to reserve, for instance, the pleasantest mouthful to the
last—because pleasure is the concomitant of healthy discharge of
function. On the other hand, when he wants to find weapons
against the short-sighted Utilitarianism which bases its ethical
or political teaching upon the human experience of a few
hundred or thousand years, we are told that this empirical
guidance by direct observation of immediate or even proximate
pleasures is worthless. However undeniable the immmediate
benefits resulting from factory inspection, free libraries, compulsory education, and the like, we are merely laying up for
ourselves a harvest of social misery in the remote future, when
Evolution will be justified of her children; and our descendants
will be punished for our disregard of laws of the social organism
only disclosed to those whose study of Sociology begins with an
investigation of the structure of the Amoeba and the strifes of

[1] That social Evolution leads to increased social differentiation, and so
multiplies occasions of conflict between the tendencies of individuals and
between classes and societies, has been maintained by Simmel, and he has
much to say in defence of his thesis.

the ant. It is true that, if the equation were really well
established, it would make no difference which side of it we
adopted as our working guide. But as any superiority which
the theory can possess over commonplace Utilitarianism must
lie in the fact that our judgements as to what is really pleasant
in the long run and as to what is really healthful are liable to
error, it may make a great difference in practice which side we
take as the index to the other. As to when we are to infer the
really beneficial from the apparently pleasant, and when we are
to infer the eventually pleasant from the laws of the organism,
the theory itself will supply us with no guidance.

VI

We have so far dealt mainly with the case of the individual
organism, and the physiological laws of health undoubtedly
supply the nearest approach to the kind of principles of which
the scientific Utilitarian is in search : since, though they do not
dispense us from the necessity of comparing pleasures and pains,
they do undoubtedly supply us at times with the means of
anticipating, and thereby of avoiding, pains which might not
have foretold their advent to mere empirical observation. But
what of the laws of the social organism ? There are two main
lines of thought running through Spencer's treatment of social
and political Ethics. They must be examined separately.

The first is the tendency to find a justification for Individualism
in the fact that among animals and men alike development has
taken place through a struggle for existence, and the resulting
survival of the fittest in accordance with the laws of natural
selection and inheritance. Man having so far progressed through
the operation of the struggle, it is inferred that the conditions
of future survival, health, and development will be the same as
they have been in the past ; hence any conduct, individual, social,
or political, which interferes with this tendency must be bad.
And thereupon follow impressive warnings against excessive
Altruism, misdirected charity, government interference, Socialism,
&c. A full examination of this individualistic tendency of
evolutionary Ethics in its bearing upon the question of State
interference would be only appropriate in a treatise on Politics.

The best way of dealing with it, so far as it is necessary for our present purpose, will be to admit Spencer's assumptions (large and unsupported as they often are), and insist upon his admissions. It may quite reasonably be contended that, even in dealing with purely animal evolution, Spencer has overlooked the importance of habits of co-operation or sociality in promoting the survival and progress of race or group. Still, he does at times admit that there are traces of co-operation in animal life, and that these have promoted survival. And when he comes to human history, it is conceded that the struggle has never been an unrestricted struggle. Militancy itself—which, in spite of the evolutionary importance of 'struggle,' is Spencer's bugbear —has brought with it increased 'integration,' co-operation, solidarity within the group; and though the growth of Altruism has been checked by the brutalities and cruelties inseparable from militancy, he has shown that, with increasing industrialism, co-operation more and more takes the place of aggression, and conduct becomes more and more altruistic. And, though, in the interests of Altruism itself, conduct can never cease to be largely egoistic, the element of Altruism is increasingly predominant and becomes increasingly compatible with and conducive to the Well-being of Society. Moreover, not only has Altruism gained upon Egoism, but there has been an increasing conciliation between Altruism and Egoism. With the progress of adaptation men have more and more come to take pleasure in things socially beneficial, and with improved social arrangements the welfare of Society has required less and less voluntary self-sacrifice upon the part of the individual, and less and less involuntary elimination of the unfit. Ultimately, there will be a complete coincidence between the precepts of ' Altruism ' and those of ' Egoism.' At present nothing is possible but a rough working compromise. Such is Spencer's position. But, at what point, in the present intermediate stage of development, is the compromise to be fixed ?

At times he would seem to argue that, because it was essential to wolves and hyenas to struggle for food (though as a matter of fact instinct sets decided limits to aggression on their own species, and the ' struggle' is not for the most part the direct, violent, and sanguinary struggle between individuals that the word is apt to suggest), therefore there must be no interference with such a struggle in the human species. But it is admitted that the socially beneficial proportion between Altruism and Egoism— the proper balance between co-operation and competition—is not the same at different stages of Evolution. How then can the study of pre-human Evolution tell us what is the proper proportion between the conflicting tendencies in human society, or the study of savage societies supply us with a clue to the solution of modern political and social problems ? Interferences with the struggle which were once bad may now be good. How can we tell at what moment interference becomes bad ? Is there any guide but empirical observation and calculation, aided by that historical study of countries and races not too unlike our own, which Spencer, by precept and practice, seems to regard as so much less important than the study of the Amazulus and the ' peaceful Arafuras' ? As we have had occasion to observe in dealing with other ethical systems, when once an exception is admitted to any ethical criterion, the principle upon which the exception rests really becomes our working criterion. The principle upon which Spencer determines when to obey his absolute Ethics, and when to take the more obvious Utilitarian road to his ultimate end, is really the Utilitarian principle itself. There is no difference in principle (though, of course, there may be wide differences in their empirical justifications) between the protection of life and property, together with the restricted voluntary ' beneficence' for which Spencer contends, and the interferences advocated on utilitarian grounds by the most advanced champions of Socialism. The real grounds of Spencer's objection to interference by individuals or States are derived from the experience which he believes himself to have accumulated in favour of his thesis that as a rule such interference does more harm than good. If he attaches peculiar importance to his studies of savage history, while Utilitarians who have suffered from the defects of an antiquated education believe themselves to have gained more instruction from the experience of ancient or modern civilizations, that is not a difference of principle. No Utilitarian, no Moralist of any school (except those whose

4 7 ★

ethical system consists in acting on the inspiration of the moment), denies that it is desirable in choosing the means to our ultimate ends to avail ourselves of wider inductions to check the conclusions to which we might be led by a more limited experience. At all events it is to such calculations that Spencer himself invariably appeals when faced with the question of the limits to which absolute Ethics are to be pushed. Take, for instance, the precept of Justice which assigns to each man the exact equivalent of the work he has done. He allows that the harsh operation of this law upon the sick, the feeble, and the old may be tempered by a considerable amount of voluntary beneficence. There is, so far as it is possible to gather, no warrant for such beneficence in the code of absolute Ethics. And yet Spencer himself allows it. Why? Because he thinks that, when duly restricted to cases of unavoidable misfortune, the immediate pleasure resulting from beneficence outweighs the indirect good which would result from following the teaching of absolute Ethics, and allowing the unrestricted struggle for existence to exterminate those whose extinction by natural law would prove them (under the conditions) unfit to live. It is obvious that exactly the same reasoning will justify any amount of interference with the evolutionary struggle, and with the laws which absolute Ethics derive from it, in all cases where the gain to Society, on the whole, may seem to outweigh any which may be expected to result from the unrestricted struggle.

Between Spencer's system of limited ' interferences ' with the struggle for existence and the Socialist's more extended interference there is, I repeat, no difference in principle. For the difference between interference with a code of absolute Ethics by the individual or a philanthropic society and interference by the compulsory action of the State is not a difference of principle but of detail. If the individual may rebel against absolute Ethics when the immediate advantage of doing so seems to outweigh the ultimate gain of obeying them, so may the State. It is idle to say that absolute Ethics forbid compulsory philanthropy ; for (if we have the right to rebel against absolute Ethics at all) we have just as much right to rebel against the prohibition of compulsion as we have to rebel against the interdiction of the beneficence itself, when once experience leads us to believe that the result will be beneficial. To discuss this question of State interference further would lead us too far away from the sphere of moral into that of political Philosophy. I content myself with remarking that the idea that 'compulsion' is avoided by the absence of State interference is a delusion arising from superficial insight into the meaning of words. The workman who is compelled to accept subsistence wages under penalty of starvation is just as much 'compelled' or 'interfered with' as if he were threatened with imprisonment by the State. To suppose that unrestricted freedom of contract can secure real 'equivalence' between work done and reward received is a belief too naïve to require serious refutation. If a Spencerian declares that it would do so in a completely 'adjusted' society, we can only once again remark on the uselessness of absolute Ethics for guidance in that world with which human Morality has to deal.

VII

I have already dwelt upon the number of unreconciled first principles which jostle one another in the Spencerian system. In the part of his *Principles of Morality* styled *Justice* we are introduced to a new one.   Here we are presented with an *a priori* principle of 'Justice' which does not claim to be the special product of evolutionary teaching ; here it is not even suggested that its self-evident or axiomatic character must ultimately have been produced by accumulated experiences of its beneficial results, though consistency might require that its origin should be thus accounted for. To my own mind the principle that 'every man is free to do that which he wills, provided he infringes not the equal freedom of any other man [1]' is as self-evidently absurd as to Herbert Spencer's it was self-evidently true. But a proposition may no doubt be really true and really self-evident though some people do not see it. As a criticism of Spencer it will be more to the purpose to point out that it is absolutely inconsistent with the line of thought last dwelt upon ;

[1] *Justice*, p. 46. The rule (as Spencer recognized) is identical with that formulated by Kant.

to insist that the fact of the observance of the above principle
having been the condition by which social progress has reached its
present point can hardly be alleged as establishing a binding
rule for our guidance in the future by a writer who is never
weary of complaining that it has never actually been observed,—
or anything approximating to it, except among a few of the
most primitive tribes, still (it may be supposed) in the gruesome
condition of ' unstable undifferentiated homogeneity,' such as
that which may be supposed to have prevailed among the
Pueblos and 'the amiable Ainos.' It might be open to Spencer
to contend that in proportion as nations have approximated to
this ideal, they have approximated to happiness, and that there has
been in the course of Evolution a progressive tendency towards
such a state of non-interference. It is doubtful whether, even
during the period which lends itself best to such a generalization,
the very recent period in which there really was some increasing
approximation towards the system of absolute non-interference
by one individual with another [1], such an account of the matter
would represent anything but a very partial and one-sided view
of social development. It is only by arbitrarily restricting
the idea of freedom to absence of *governmental* interference
that, even from the study of those palmy days of individualistic
Liberalism and Manchesterian Economics in which Spencer did
his thinking and formed the opinions now stereotyped in some
6,000 pages, something like a case can be made out for such an
interpretation of social progress.

And yet a comparative absence of State interference does not
really involve even an approximation to the idea of individual
freedom being limited solely by the like freedom in others.
It is only Spencer's failure to see that the most *laissez-faire*
Industrialism necessarily involves quite as much mutual interference as Militarism, though interference of a different kind,

---

[1] Such a period as this in England may perhaps be very roughly said to
have begun in 1688 and ended with the first Factory and Education Acts,
though in the economic region the period hardly began till Adam Smith's
Wealth of Nations produced a revolution in legislative methods. It is
doubtful whether any such tendency can be traced outside the United
Kingdom : elsewhere antiquated ' interferences ' have generally been
abolished only to make way for fresh interferences of another type.

which allows him to suppose that a freedom consistent with the like freedom for every one else can be obtained by leaving the struggle for existence to take its course. The very existence of Capital, as could be demonstrated out of Spencer's own works, involves a radical inequality—a perpetual interference with the rule of equal freedom [1] : for every private appropriation of the instruments of production is so much interference with the right—to Spencer the sacred *a priori* right—of the individual to use his labour to his own advantage. A labourer without Capital is about as free to appropriate the value of his labour as a lame man without crutches is free to walk. In so far as there has been any approximation to such equality of freedom, it has been won by a progressive interference with that law of Nature which, according to Spencer, requires that every individual should be allowed to take the full advantage of his superiority. Spencer's ideal of Justice is one which could only be carried out by pushing the principle not merely of interference, but of State interference, to the point of absolute Socialism. There is a profound truth in the statement that the extremest kind of Socialism is only Individualism run mad : it might with equal truth be added that extreme Individualism is Socialism run mad.

VIII

One can hardly take leave of Spencer's evolutionary Ethics without saying a word as to his optimistic assumption that human society is on the way towards that state of perfect 'adaptation' in which absolute Ethics will become practicable, and that that state is destined to be actually reached. The assumption appears to rest upon the great cardinal doctrine of the whole *Synthetic Philosophy*—the doctrine that throughout the history of the Universe there has been and must always be a progress 'from an indefinite, incoherent homogeneity to a definite, differentiated, coherent heterogeneity [2].' That such

---

[1] This was so clear to Spencer himself when he wrote *Social Statics* that he at that time condemned private property in land. He did not recognize that all capital rests upon the same principle, and that most of it has originally grown out of that earliest form of Capitalism.

[2] *First Principles*, p. 396.

a principle really applies not merely to the evolution of in-
organic Nature, but to the sphere of Biology and Sociology,
could only be proved by an induction based upon the whole of
our experience in each province of Science. The attempt to
prove such a conclusion in the case of human society is not
seriously attempted. How far the assertion that the physical
Universe is on the way to a state of absolutely definite, absolutely differentiated, absolutely coherent heterogeneity can be
made with any truth or even with any meaning, I leave it to
Physicists to say. But, however true or valuable the assertion
may be in the physical sphere, that certainly does not prove that
it must be true in the case of either the human or the social
organism. Nor, if we were to admit the application of this
extremely abstract formula to the course of organic and social
Evolution, does it seem clear that a 'definite, coherent heterogeneity' would necessarily imply that state of complete adaptation
in which pain shall be absent, and in which it will even become
possible to perform those absolutely moral actions which involve
no pain to any one, but only pleasure.

No animal has yet been evolved which exhibits such a state
of perfect adaptation, and, apart from the formula itself, there
is no evidence that it ever will do so, or that what is scarcely
physiologically conceivable in the case of the human organism
will ever be true of a society. If we grant that Evolution
shows a tendency in the direction indicated, there is no reason
to believe that the tendency will necessarily reach its ideal
limit ; or that the reverse process, the 'involution' or retrogressive dissolution, which is, according to Spencer, the ultimate
destiny of the Universe, may not begin long before that limit is
approached. It is impossible to say that the retrogressive tendency may not have already begun. And in the absence of this
assurance that Evolution is actually tending to this ideal goal,
all reason disappears for assuming that, if we could discern the
'laws' which social changes now exhibit, they would also be
the laws under which the human race will attain the best life
that is possible to it; such an assumption is unwarranted
even on Spencer's hedonistic view of the end. It is still more
unwarranted on any higher view.

Another fallacy which runs through Spencer's ethical and political writing is the idea that the course of human history, when it is 'left alone,' will supply us with a guide to human action. He admits that the course of social evolution represents a continuous predominance of purposeful action over unpurposeful. If the 'natural' course of things is to exclude that part of human action which is guided by Reason, we have no data for ascertaining what is the 'natural' course of things in human society, since the evolution of human society has habitually and increasingly been controlled by human Reason, 'interfering' at every turn, in pursuit of its purposes, with the operation of those forces by which Nature is governed in the absence of such interference. If the 'natural' course of things is to include the deliberate action of self-conscious beings in pursuit of the ends, then 'interference' with the course of Nature is a sheer impossibility. We are as much falling in with the 'laws of Evolution' when we interfere as when we abstain from interfering. In neither case can the idea of 'following Nature,' in the modern evolutionary form of that formula, supply us with any guidance in conduct. It must be admitted that Spencer has scarcely, in so many words, committed himself to such a way of expressing his ethical criterion, but the idea indicated by the precept 'thou shalt not interfere with Nature' seems to underlie much of his writing. And his disciples have not always been so circumspect.

The above criticisms are not intended as an adequate appreciation of Herbert Spencer's ethical, social, and political writings. His treatment of social and political problems, however little one may agree with it, is entitled to respectful consideration. Of all his encyclopaedic writings, next to those metaphysical portions in which there is really no Metaphysic, the least valuable element seems to me to be his attempted contribution to ethical theory. His practical teaching, however little it really flows from his evolutionary principles—however much, very often, it is opposed to what might seem logically to flow from such principles—is (if we make allowance for his too individualistic and rather 'bourgeois' point of view) unexceptionable enough ; and if it contains much less that is really new and

startling than he himself evidently supposed, he might plead
that the best ethical teaching must be largely a reassertion in
new forms of what no reflecting person denies.   As to the form
of it, tastes will differ ; but there are no doubt minds to which
the accumulation of biological metaphor and physical analogy
will prove more impressive than the traditional language of
Theology, Philosophy, or common sense.   And, if one is irritated
by the preaching of platitudes as if they were paradoxes, it
should be remembered that Spencer's works, though many of
them written and published quite recently, represent ideas which,
in the author's youth, though they could never have been as
shocking as it pleased him to think, were doubtless less commonplace than they have become now—partly, though only a little,
through the influence of his own earlier writings.   Unfortunately,
while the rest of the world was moving on, Spencer's thought
stood still, when it did not go back.   With all its faults, the
Synthetic Philosophy has a considerable place in the history of
human thought, if but a small place in the history of Philosophy
strictly so called.   What is denied in these pages is that it has
provided any new basis for Ethics, or that it has advanced
beyond the point of view of the old empirical Utilitarianism
which Spencer disparaged.   What is best in Spencer's excellent
sermonettes on the minor Ethics consists in various illustrations
and applications of the familiar Utilitarian maxim that we should
consider the consequences of one's actions.   We are not surprised
to find Spencer in the preface to the last instalment of his
Principles of Ethics confessing : ' The Doctrine of Evolution
has not furnished guidance to the extent I had hoped.   Most of
the conclusions, drawn empirically, are such as right feelings,
enlightened by cultivated intelligence, have already sufficed to
establish.   Beyond certain general sanctions indirectly referred
to in verification, there are only here and there, and more
especially in the closing chapters, conclusions evolutionary in
origin that are additional to, or different from, those which are
current [1].'   The value of these additions, and the logicality of
the process by which they are extracted out of the evolutionary
facts, remain then the only points of difference between Herbert

[1] *The Principles of Ethics*, Vol. II. Pref. to pts. v. and vi (1893).

Spencer and his critics. Considered as a new and original system of Ethics, the *Synthetic Philosophy* is a bubble which has been pricked by the hand of its creator.

The publication of Spencer's Autobiography has thrown much light upon the genesis of the *Synthetic Philosophy*. It has shown that the ethical, social, and political ideas commonly associated with the name of Herbert Spencer were not reached in his own mind by any induction or deduction from biological or sociological principles. They were fully formed in their author's mind long before he had become a disciple of Darwin, and were simply the result of the teaching of his uncle, the Rev. Thomas Spencer, a distinguished Poor Law Reformer and representative of the old Manchesterian Economics. In so far as they were founded on experience, they were based upon his experience of a Somersetshire village in 1834-6, and not upon any study of the habits either of the Amoeba or the 'peaceful Arafuras.' All the biological and sociological apparatus of the system was simply an afterthought, an attempt to invoke the supposed 'teaching of Science' in support of foregone conclusions.

IX

We started with the admission that an intellectual revolution so great as that which is associated with the name of Charles Darwin might reasonably be expected to have some bearing upon ethical thought. I go on then to ask what this bearing is. Just because it is a far-reaching and penetrating difference of intellectual tone and temper which it has introduced rather than definite theory or dogma, the change is one which may be pointed out in a few words.

(1) The fact that Morality has slowly evolved is no discovery of Darwinism or of any other theory of biological 'Evolution.' The Old and New Testaments, taken by themselves and read even without the light of modern criticism, were enough to show that men's moral ideas had not always been the same, and that there had been a growth in them. Still less excuse was there for any ignoring of this fact by educated men who could compare the ethical ideas of the Bible with those of Homer and Aristotle or with the tales of travellers about the life of savage tribes. Nor

were these differences unobserved. They form the usual stock-in-trade of the Utilitarian critics of *a priori* Morality in all its forms. The Morality of static, invariable, infallible 'innate ideas' is satirized by John Locke with much more insight and humour than is to be found in the corresponding polemics of Spencer. Nor did the constructive Moralists altogether ignore either the differences or the developments of actual Morality. But it must be admitted that they did so very inadequately. Moralists like Butler and Kant might no doubt have pleaded that they were only concerned with Morality in its fullest development; but they made scarcely any attempt to bring their doctrines into connexion with the moral history of the world, or to grapple with the *prima facie* difficulties suggested by the infinite variety of actual moral beliefs. There can be no doubt that the thoroughgoing application of the evolutionary idea to every department of human history has enormously emphasized facts which were known to, but too little regarded by, the Moralists of an earlier generation. And this characteristic category of our age reached its climax in the bridging over by Darwin and Wallace of the gulf which once seemed to divide the lowest of mankind from the highest of the animals. The disappearance of special creation theories, though from a high philosophical point of view it may have left matters very much where they were before, has stamped the idea of development upon the popular imagination, and (by its indirect effects) has transformed the older, or at least the cruder, forms of Intuitionism.

(2) Darwinism has not merely reinforced the evolutionary view of the world's history which was already making progress both in philosophical and in general thought long before Darwin; it has introduced new ideas as to the way in which that development, intellectual, moral, and physical, has taken place. The notion that the character of peoples and of individuals was to some extent affected by physical conditions was not indeed new. That idea found, indeed, its crudest and most startling expression in the pre-Darwinian Buckle[1]. But it is impossible

---

[1] This crudity was partly due to the attempt to account by immediate environment – especially food and climate – for variations of character and ideas really due to much more slowly acting forces.

to deny that the application of the 'survival of the fittest' doctrine to the growth of moral ideas has emphasized in a very startling way this dependence of character, and therefore of moral ideas, upon historical and partly physical circumstances. Considered simply as a history of the way in-which detailed moral beliefs have been moulded by social conditions, Spencer's sociological work undoubtedly has its value, though much of his Anthropology is already obsolete.   But this question of origin is not, as has been intimated, the task of Moral Philosophy proper. All that I can attempt is to suggest the importance that the results of such an enquiry have or may have for the Moral Philosopher.

Although, from the metaphysical point of view presupposed in this book, it is impossible to regard moral ideas as the mere products of physical forces, it is undoubtedly true that the moral development attained at any particular time and place is at every turn conditioned by physical facts.   Education does not 'produce' our geometrical ideas : they are only producible in a mind already potentially endowed with a capacity for apprehending them.   And so with moral ideas.   It would be as absurd to talk about the 'struggle for existence' and 'natural selection' as constituting by themselves the 'origin' of our moral ideas as it would be to treat the cane of the schoolmaster as being the 'origin' of our geometrical ideas, though there may be persons in whom these ideas would never have been developed without that instrument.   Moral ideas could have developed only in beings endowed with a capacity for Moral Reason : and the truths of which our Moral Reason assures us are not less true because we recognize that certain physical and biological facts and processes have been the condition of their discovery by this or that individual in this or that generation.   Certain physical processes are no doubt the conditions under which all mental development takes place in the individual; but for the Idealist all such processes are themselves ultimately spiritual, and the slow development of the psychical concomitants in the individual implies the previous existence of a Mind to which they are already present.   Moral ideas are no more 'produced' or 'generated' by physical events than any other of the axioms or categories

of human thought.   When this is recognized, there should be no
hesitation in admitting that all the biological and psychological
and sociological facts insisted upon by the evolutionary Moralists
have really been conditions of moral development.   They really
do help to explain why such a virtue was developed at such
a time and place and another virtue in different circumstances,
why this aspect of Morality was emphasized in one kind of
community, and another in another, and so on.   The social or
political pressure to which Spencer refers at least the element
of ' obligatoriness ' attending our moral ideas, has certainly been
a condition favouring the development of the moral ideas themselves, just as we recognize that the individual's sense of truth
owes much to the discipline of home or school, without being
forced to admit that the intellectual approbation and the corresponding emotions which attend the speaking of truth might
with equal ease have been transferred by a contrary education
to the idea that lying was a virtue, or that, even if that were
possible [1], it would prove that Truth is not intrinsically better
than lying.   The question remains for us ' what significance
these questions of origin have for deciding the question of truth
or validity ? '

On the one hand we have seen that the doctrine of natural
selection supplies no absolute guarantee that the moral belief is
conducive to the good of the Society, even on the hedonistic
view of ' good,' still less on an ideal view.   It does not supply
an absolute guarantee that the resulting rule of conduct was
socially beneficial even at the time.   At the most Evolution
supplies us, as has already been said, with a slight additional
reason (in addition to our general confidence that human Reason
never adopts beliefs without some ground) for assuming that
a moral rule actually accepted by a race once possessed more or
less social justification.   When it is inferred that an existing
belief still has that justification, the inference is far more precarious.   Yet until we can trace the history of the belief, and

[1] To some extent this may have been actually done by particular systems
of education, but only at the cost of keeping back the whole moral and
intellectual development which would necessarily have resulted in a
recognition of the value of truth.

explain to our satisfaction the causes to which the rule owes its real or supposed utility, the evolutionary history of Morality does supply us with an additional caution against tampering with deeply-seated moral convictions. I should myself be disposed to apply this caution to any attempts to tamper with the received morality about Suicide, even when a plausible case may be made out for supposing that some departure from it would be for the true (and not merely the hedonistic) good of Society.

Still, so long as some accepted moral belief is unexplained, the presumption in favour of the rule cannot be a very strong one. It supplies a caution against rash amendment of moral rules : it cannot forbid the amendment of a rule when we have sufficient experience to convince us that the rule introduced by the change will really conduce to our end, and when the end is one about the value of which our moral Reason is clear. But the chief advantage to be derived from the study of ethical history, and of the Darwinian contribution to ethical history, is to be found, as it seems to me, not so much in the presumption of a beneficial tendency in unexplained and unanalysed 'intuitions' as in the assistance which it gives us in explaining the growth of some particular moral belief, and so in determining how far the circumstances to which it owes its beneficial tendency are like or unlike our own. Morality essentially consists in the promotion of a good or ideal of life, the nature of which is discerned by our rational judgements of value. If my Reason tells me that such and such an end of action is good, I have a right to say that my judgements of value cannot be discredited by any account of the process by which I came to have such judgements. But, as we have constantly had occasion to remark, the supreme authority of Reason, and the claim that each of us possesses some share in that Reason, do not involve the claim to personal infallibility. All our knowledge rests ultimately in part upon self-evident truths, in part upon experience. And yet, both in the perceptions upon which experience rests and in the intellectual activities by which sensation becomes perception and perception knowledge, there is at every turn room for the distortion of our judgements by habit, tradition, prejudice, desire, passion. Even in doing a sum of multiplication we may make mistakes, and

these mistakes may be psychologically explained by a desire to
get a particular answer (as when a boy bona fide believes that
he has done a sum correctly because he has brought out what he
already knows to be the right answer) ; or by some idiosyncracy of
false association by which we may be in the habit of confusing (as
is related of an eminent Divine) eighteenpence with one and eight-
pence ; or by the lapses of that memory to which we really trust
when once the multiplicands become too big for a distinct immediate
envisagement of the process by which the result is reached.   It
is only where an *a priori* truth is very simple and abstract
that the general trustworthiness of Reason practically prevents
the possibility of thinking that which is false, or (if we choose
to say that false thinking is no thinking) from supposing that
we are thinking when we are not.   No habituation or prejudice
or desire could make a member of any nationality or party
accept the abstract proposition that a man is guilty of treason
because he is a Jew; but it is quite possible that a jury or a
court martial may actually come to believe him guilty because
they know that he is a Jew.   Now we have seen that it is only
where moral truths are reducible to a purely formal shape,
dealing with an abstract distribution of good, and involving no
judgement as to the content of good, that they possess the kind of
self-evidence which belongs to the axioms of Mathematics—the
self-evidence which makes it impossible for any sane man to
deny them except under the influence of a speculative opinion
which makes him distrust them just because they do seem self-
evident.   The judgement ' two men's good is greater than that
of one ' possesses this degree of self-evidence [1] ; but directly we
attempt to assign a content to the idea of ' good,' then we enter
upon a region in which our *a priori* judgements, as they may
still in a sense be called, are in a peculiar degree liable to be
influenced by prejudice, desire, emotion, character.   In fact, so

[1] I presume that those who say that goods are not commensurable
would say that the judgement is 'insignificant,' since goods are incommensurable.   The judgement may be said to involve the larger judgement
'Whatever is good has quantity, and the axioms of quantity can be applied
to it.'   The judgement 'Good has quantity,' which no doubt involves
a judgement not purely formal, is a judgement about the content of ' Good,'
and a judgement which some philosophers actually deny.   I should myself

much is this the case that a large class at least of them actually cannot be made at all without the presence of certain emotions. A judgement of value is a self-evident judgement ; and, so long as we really judge it, it is reasonable to trust to it and act upon it, for we have nothing else to trust to. But such a judgement may nevertheless be influenced by all the sources of error which we have mentioned, and it is possible sometimes to detect the source of the error. Either we may say that we are liable to mistake our mere inherited or acquired instinct or prejudice or desire for a real judgement of value ; or we may say that our apparent 'intuitions' are real judgements of value, but that they are wrong judgements, influenced by the causes of error above mentioned. When reflection convinces us that our judgement was influenced by passion or prejudice, then we alter it, and make another judgement. There is no infallible way of correcting these mistakes. The errors of thinking, in this as in other departments, can only be corrected by harder thinking.

There can be no appeal from the immediate moral judgement to any other standard, but the reconsideration of a moral judgement in the light of fresh facts may always result in its revision. And further knowledge of the circumstances under which we or others made our original judgements, and of the influences which swayed us in making them, is one of the most important of the 'new facts' which may lead to such a reversal. Now a knowledge of the history of moral beliefs may be a most important influence in revising the *prima facie* judgements of our own consciousness and of the society from which we have, with or without moral reflection of our own, absorbed them. And to this history of our moral judgements the facts and laws which have either been taught us, or have had their significance greatly enhanced, by Darwinism have undoubtedly contributed an element, though an element which has (as we have seen) disappointed even the protagonist of evolutionary Morality. Every child performs this process of ethical revision on a small scale when he learns gradually to distinguish the rules of his father's household or the idiosyncracies of his parent's ideal from the code

be disposed to trace their mistake to prejudices of psychological origin, usually some 'idol of the theatre.'

accepted by the world outside. The discovery of the difference
throws him back on his own moral judgement, and compels him
either to side with his father against the world or with the
world against his father. He may have been led to put smoking
on a level with drinking, and moderate drinking with excessive
drinking. When he discovers that the world in general thinks
otherwise, he may be compelled to find a reasonable ground for
continued belief in the parental tenets; or, if he do not do so,
he will be driven to abandon them. In the same way, on a more
extended scale, I have no doubt that to many Scotsmen a generation ago the sinfulness of whistling on the Sabbath presented
itself as a strictly self-evident judgement—self-evident at least
upon the assumption of certain facts for which it was believed
that there was a sufficient evidence in history. A further
knowledge of the process by which the Scotch Sunday was
evolved, of the way in which Sunday has been regarded at other
times and in other places, may gradually enable such a man to
disentangle the belief in the continued obligation of the Jewish
Sabbath from some idea as to the duty of worship or the value
of rest which may still commend itself to him as a self-evident
judgement of value. There is no appeal from a moral intuition,
but in the light of facts like these what seemed an intuition is
seen not to be so; or (what is really the same thing) the intuition
which the individual's moral consciousness once possessed has
disappeared altogether.

In the foregoing instances the facts of moral history which
lead to the reversal of apparently intuitive judgements are facts
upon which the Darwinian doctrines have no bearing. But
there are some on which they may have a bearing. It is not
very easy to find good illustrations, for the most obvious cases in
which ideas may have owed more or less of their apparent authority
to natural selection, but have partially outlived their social justification, are ideas which were discarded long before the appearance of
the Darwinian theories. Anthropology has certainly led us to see
that the high estimate in which courage is held by modern men
is a direct inheritance from a time in which courage was the one
paramount condition of tribal survival and of social usefulness
in individuals. Courage of the military sort is certainly less

useful to modern societies. In a distant future it might even cease to be socially useful at all. In that case, upon hedonistic grounds, cne would be compelled to say that it is a quality which might be dispensed with. From a non-hedonistic point of view, no account of the process by which the human race became possessed of its admiration for courage could prevent us from saying that we still regard the capacity for facing pain or danger as an essential quality of ideal manhood. But the discovery of its evolutionary history may reasonably lead us to treat this virtue as (in its ordinary forms) a very elementary one, to recognize that the grounds on which we admire courage should compel us to condemn various other kinds of moral turpitude as men now condemn cowardice, and to insist that our conception of the courage which may still claim to be in a sense the fundamental virtue must be expanded and elevated till it includes at least that willingness to face adverse opinion in the cause of Right which has received the name of moral courage, even if it does not include all kinds of defiance and endurance of pain or evil in the cause of Right.

The evolutionary explanation of Courage may prompt us to modify but not actually to reverse an accepted belief. Are there any cases in which the evolutionary origin of our moral judgements may compel an actual reversal? It is possible that cases in which the evolutionary explanation may at least inspire doubt and suggest reconsideration may be found in that class of moral intuitions which some Evolutionists explain by their influence upon the growth of population. The smaller importance attached by modern communities to such increase has already led to the abandonment of the rule which in many communities actually condemned celibacy. And among our actual moral intuitions there is probably none in which the influence of natural selection may be more plausibly traced than in the instinctive repugnance to the marriage of near blood-relations. It is a peculiarly good instance because it can hardly be supposed that the moral disapproval was originally or exclusively due to a reflective observation of its physiological consequences. And, though the condemnation may be owing primarily to a horror of contact with the tabooed blood of the

maternal clan—a horror closely connected with totemistic ideas [1]
—it is possible that the influence of natural selection may have
strengthened the tendency by the elimination of families or
tribes which did not share the beliefs which prohibited the
marriage of near kin [2]. This is a case where the evolutionary
explanation, if valid, does not destroy but rather reinforces the
code of Ethics which direct experience would establish ; for the
same considerations of physiological utility which explain the
rule justify its maintenance.　But, though this evolutionary
explanation cannot compel any abandonment of the rule against
intermarriage of close kin, the discovery of its true ground
may compel its rationalization.　Among primitive peoples,
if it was natural selection which established the barrier
against the marriage of near kin, natural selection certainly
overshot the mark and extended the prohibition much further
than was necessary to maintain the vigour of the race.　It
can hardly be pretended that the elaborate and arbitrary table
of prohibited degrees established in many tribes can ever have
had any social justification at all, except as being indirectly
connected with customs which had a social justification—a useful
reminder of the truth, so often forgotten by Evolutionists, that the
survival of a modification does not *prove* its social utility even in the
purely biological sphere.　And if the prohibition of the marriage
of kin was only secured in ancient times by codes which carried
with it the prohibition of many harmless unions and sanctioned
some harmful ones, it is conceivable that the feeling against the
marriage of the deceased wife's sister, to which the physiological
objection does not apply, may really be an instance of a moral
prejudice not based on any real social convenience or genuinely
moral consideration.　A case in which it is still more conceivable that the recognition of origin may tend to modify our

---

[1] M. Durkheim (*Le Prohibition de l'Inceste* in *L'Année Sociologique*, 1898)
has attempted to show that the horror of incest was originally connected
with the custom of exogamy, which in turn arose from the horror of contact
with blood, especially menstrual blood, and particularly the blood of the
maternal clan, i. e. the blood of the totem-god incarnate in each member
of it.

[2] The physiological ill effects of such marriages have, however, been much
disputed.

judgement as to validity is supplied by a great ethical question on which I have already touched.   It is probable that the once strong disposition to condemn the restriction of families may be traced either to a more or less consciously accepted theory that everything which checked population made against tribal efficiency, or perhaps simply to a natural disposition to accept the usual or 'natural' as the moral [1].   The probability of such an origin may naturally weaken the authority of such a feeling for those who think that an unlimited increase of population is not to be desired.   But the most that such theories of origin can do, even when they are well founded, is to clear away prejudice, and leave the question to be decided on its own merits—that is to say, mainly upon the answer we give to the question how far a continuous increase of population is desirable and conducive to the greatest quantity of the best and highest life.   It is quite conceivable that this may still be the case, though for different reasons from those which made it conducive to survival in a primitive tribe [2].

The instances just adduced may, however, suggest an important caution, which sets a very rigid limit to the expectation of any very extensive practical guidance in Ethics from the study of moral evolution.   It is of paramount importance to remark that the cause which has originally dictated a moral rule may be very different from the causes which explain, and which justify, its continued enforcement.   Obliviousness of this fact enormously impairs the value of Herbert Spencer's speculations on the early history of Religion, and it is sometimes forgotten in his ethical speculation also.   It is possible (I express no opinion) that the

[1] This very powerful factor in the production of actual ethical codes has been much emphasized by Simmel.   A curious instance of its operation in the sphere of elementary economic Justice is the fact that in primitive societies it was not always recognized that everything could be exchanged for everything.   If you want slaves, you must buy them with guns; if you want ivory, you must buy it with guns and powder; no quantity of tobacco will buy the smallest piece of ivory, though it will buy many other things.   See an article in the *Economic Review* (Vol. XII, Ap., 1902) on 'The Relation of Economics to Ethnology,' by Mr. W. W. Carlile.

[2] See the important articles of Mr. Sidney Webb in *The Times* of Oct. 9 and Oct. 16, 1906.

worship of the Sun may, at least in this or that particular instance, have originated in the childish mistake which took an ancestor called 'Sun' for the heavenly body itself. But it is obvious, to minds not preoccupied with the desire to trace religious ideas to some one single principle, that this belief could hardly have imposed itself even upon the savage mind, still less have survived among civilized races, unless it has satisfied deeper intellectual or emotional needs than were satisfied by ancestor worship. If a mistaken etymology may in this or that tribe have led to the development of a deified ancestor into a Sun-god, it was because the tribe had reached a stage of intellectual and religious development in which a Sun-god seemed a more proper object of worship than an ancestor. In the same way, proof that some moral belief originated in a mistake, an accident, in what we should regard as an immoral tendency, or in natural selection depending on considerations of social utility no longer applicable, is in no way inconsistent with the belief that it has perpetuated itself, and commends itself to us, on account of its true or objective validity. Thus it is held by Professor Westermarck that clothes originated neither in an innate sense of decency nor in the desire for warmth, but in the love of ornament and particularly of immodest ornament [1]. It was the habit of wearing clothes which produced the sense of decency, not the sense of decency which led to the use of clothes. Modesty is thereby proved to have originated in indecency. But the fact, if accepted, would by no means prove that, had men never worn clothes, they would have attained to as high a standard of thought and feeling about sexual matters as they have actually done—still less that the tone of feeling about such matters would now be improved by the abandonment or relaxation of the existing practice. Nor does the fact that the primitive horror of bloodshed was partly due to ideas connected with Totemism and Taboo [2] show that an enlightened people should abandon its prejudices against murder and man-slaughter. The feeling against impurity before marriage may conceivably have originated mainly in the social utility of an

[1] *History of Human Marriage*, Ed. iii, p. 191 sq.
[2] L. R. Farnell, *The Evolution of Religion*, p. 125 sq.

increased population and the due maintenance of offspring; or (according to another school) it may have been connected in its origin (like the feeling against Incest) with ideas about Totemism and Taboo, Exogamy and the maternal clan, which have long since been abandoned; or again, it may have resulted simply from a transference, by association or mistaken analogy, to all extra-matrimonial intercourse of feelings originally directed against such intercourse within the limits of family or clan. But such facts of moral history (if facts they be) cannot compel us to conclude that the prohibition of such impurity should be relaxed, on the ground that universal marriage is not now socially necessary, or that general immorality is possible without the appearance of illegitimate children, or that the reasons which originally dictated the prohibition are now known to be baseless superstitions. Our approval of a moral judgement *may* be altered by the discovery of its history; but, where it persists, we are no more bound to distrust it than we are called upon to give up some mathematical principle which may have originally been discovered and valued for astrological purposes. It cannot be too emphatically stated that the present value of modes of conduct or modes of feeling, of emotions or likings or dislikings, does not depend upon their origin.

The evolutionary history of Ethics may then supply us with some help—chiefly negative help—towards (as it were) purging our value-judgements of irrelevant matter due to mere inheritance or tradition or prejudice and the like. Unfortunately it can supply us with no absolute specific for distinguishing our own real judgements of value from those apparent judgements which are really explainable by merely psychological causes—still less for ensuring the absolute or objective validity of the judgements.

There is a third way in which the Darwinian doctrine of Evolution touches the province of Ethics—through the simple physiological doctrine that race-maintenance requires the elimination of the unfit and still more the prevention of that 'inverted selection' which promotes the survival of the unfit. Of course, when we bring this doctrine into connexion with human and civilized society, we must extend the idea of 'fitness' and 'unfitness' beyond that mere adaptation to conditions which produces physical survival in animals. It must be so extended as to include fitness for the kind of life which we judge to be ethically desirable. We have seen reasons for rejecting the crude and coarse application of the doctrine advocated by those who would revive among us the infanticide which the higher moral sentiment even of the Greeks condemned. Such artificial imitation of natural selection could at most secure physical fitness, and as even physical fitness in human beings depends quite as much upon education as upon birth, even this could not be effectual unless the ethics of our neo-Paganism (unlike the older Paganism) allowed a periodic elimination to extend much beyond the period of infancy. It is not necessary for the present purpose to determine the difficult question how far moral and intellectual qualities are inherited, and how far the undoubted transmission to their offspring of the qualities which have made parents social failures is due mainly to their incapacity for educating their children. The success of such work as that of Dr. Barnardo certainly seems to suggest that comparatively little is due to inheritance and very much to environment. But, however this may be, there can be no doubt that legislatures and social reformers ought to endeavour to secure that the physically, intellectually, or morally incapable (up to a certain point of course the three kinds of incapacity are apt to coincide) shall have less chance of leaving offspring than the more capable, or that at all events they shall not have more chance of doing so. This last possibility is well within the reach of injudicious charity, private or public. We have approached to such a state of things in some places quite nearly enough to illustrate the enormity of the social peril. How to deal with it is one of the great practical problems of our age, but the discussion belongs rather to social and political than to purely ethical Philosophy. And there is the less need to insist upon it inasmuch as the subject has been admirably dealt with by Professor Bosanquet[1]. This danger may no doubt be used as

---

[1] See his Essay on *Socialism and Natural Selection* in *Aspects of the Social Problem*. It will be seen from the text that I do not regard the considerations very properly dwelt upon by Professor Bosanquet as a final refutation of Socialism.

a warning against the wilder forms of Socialism, and still more against some of the wilder socialistic experiments in a non-socialistic society. But it must be remembered that the competitive régime—in the form which it assumes in a modern industrial society—secures such selection to a very inadequate extent. Failure in the economic struggle has to be so very complete before it prevents marriage and the production of children. It is those who have the lowest standard of comfort who marry earliest. Any social reorganization which tends to raise the standard of comfort tends, as far as it goes, to decrease rather than to promote the production of unfit children. In this way Darwinism has certainly emphasized a social law of vast importance, which it was quite within the reach of the most empirical observation to discover. But this is merely an instance of the application of a new scientific discovery to a particular ethical question. Such a contribution to ethical doctrine is merely the kind of contribution which every scientific discovery may incidentally make. Every new discovery, even of some quite isolated scientific fact—every improvement in drainage, every new drug, every new economic law must obviously modify the details of individual or social duty, and involve the abandonment of practices or rules of action in which our forefathers believed. There is no question here of any new ethical principle or of any general improvement of ethical methods unknown to pre-Darwinian thinkers.

We have seen then that the doctrine of Evolution in its Darwinian form has strengthened and emphasized the already sufficient evidence of moral evolution, and warned us against the cruder forms of Intuitionism; that it has supplied us with an additional ground for a *prima facie* confidence in apparently intuitive moral beliefs, while at the same time it has enforced the necessity of asking whether such beliefs have or have not outlived their justification. In so far as it has thrown light upon the causes which have determined the growth of particular moral beliefs at particular times and places, it has helped to facilitate the process of discriminating between mere inherited instincts and deliberate deliverances of our present moral consciousness. Finally, the doctrine of survival through natural

selection has an important social application.. Most of this
teaching springs rather from facts of moral history and laws of
social development which were quite well known before Darwin.
Here as elsewhere the distinctly Darwinian element in the
general doctrine of Evolution has played directly but a small
part in producing that general tendency of modern thought
which finds the explanation of things in a history of origins.
Yet the impetus which the epoch-making discovery of the
'origin of species' has given to that tendency cannot be considered a small thing. That the doctrines of the evolutionary
Moralists also illustrate the erroneous modern tendency to think
that the *mere* study of the historical development of anything—
of an institution, of a Religion, of the human mind—is by itself
a sufficient explanation of it and a sufficient basis for the understanding of it, I have also attempted to show in the course of
this chapter [1].

[1] The popularity of Spencer's writings has made it desirable to examine
the claims of Evolutionary Ethics in the form which he has given to them.
Otherwise a study of Sir Leslie Stephen's *Science of Ethics* (1882) or Professor
Alexander's *Moral Order and Progress* (1889) might have been better worth
making. There is much in Sir Leslie Stephen's ethical writing the value
of which is quite independent of Evolution; but in so far as there is anything 'evolutionary' in his views, he differs from Spencer chiefly (1) by
omitting much that is open to criticism in Spencer, and substantially
reducing the evolutionary element to the doctrine that traditional or
inherited rules or tendencies of conduct may be presumed to have originated
(through natural selection or otherwise) in considerations of social Well-
being; (2) substituting the very vague idea of 'social health' for pleasure
as the ethical end. Professor Alexander, whose book also contains much
excellent writing which has no particular connexion with evolutionary
theories, has attempted to apply the idea of struggle for existence, not to
societies or individuals, but to the strife between conflicting ideals. He
assumes that the ideal which has *de facto* survived is shown *ipso facto* to be
fittest for this or that particular society at this or that particular time.
Substantially, Professor Alexander's thesis is simply a revival of Hume's
doctrine that Morality is nothing but dominant public opinion in combination
with the assumption (on evolutionary grounds) that public opinion is
always right—an assumption which has been incidentally criticized in the
course of this chapter. Later writers who exhibit the same tendencies seem
to have abandoned the attempt to find a new basis for Ethics in the fact or
theory of Evolution, and may be simply described as 'naturalistic' rather
than in any distinctive sense 'evolutionary' Moralists. Had the first volume

of Professor Westermarck's *Origin and Development of the Moral Ideas* come into my hands earlier, I might more frequently have referred to it.   But after all, though it is impossible to exaggerate its interest and importance as an historical or anthropological work, it contains nothing particularly new in the department of ethical theory.   His view of Ethics is substantially the Moral Sense view of Ethics, and there is nothing in the introductory chapter devoted to ethical theory which demands any addition to, or modification of, the treatment which I have given to the subject in my chapter on Reason and Feeling in Book I.   In spite of his great learning in all that relates to Moral Philosophy (it may be doubted whether he has the same acquaintance with Metaphysic), Professor Westermarck does not seem to appreciate the existence of any form of rationalistic Ethics except the crude Intuitionism which supposes that a consciousness without feeling or emotion, without experience of life or experience of consequences, could lay down *a priori* detailed rules of conduct which would be actually coincident with the generally acknowledged Morality.   In spite of having reduced Morality to subjective feeling, Professor Westermarck from one end of the book to the other constantly assumes that some one mode of moral feeling is intrinsically truer and higher than another.   His position is, in short, that of Hume without Hume's clear consciousness of the speculative and practical consequences of such a theory.

CHAPTER V

CASUISTRY, ITS POSSIBILITY AND LIMITATIONS

I

THIS work began without any formal enquiry into the scope or character of the Science with which it deals. And by this time the author's view of it has, it is hoped, become sufficiently plain to make a formal discussion of the matter unnecessary. There remain, however, some controverted questions about the sphere and scope of Moral Philosophy which it seems desirable to clear up. The most important of these is the question, ' What, if any, is the practical use of Moral Philosophy ? '

Primarily, no doubt, Moral Philosophy must be looked upon as a branch of speculative Philosophy, and therefore as not intended to have any practical use. The justification for its study is so far just the same as the justification for the study of Metaphysics or the higher Mathematics. If either actual knowledge or the exercise of the intellectual faculties in the effort to know is of any intrinsic value, no knowledge can have a higher value than that knowledge of things in general—of the Universe as a whole—which is the aim of Philosophy in contradistinction to that of the special or departmental Sciences. And Moral Philosophy, though concerned with a particular aspect of Reality, deals with an aspect of it so fundamental and comprehensive, that many of its problems cannot be sharply distinguished from the problem of Reality in general; and it therefore takes its place by the side of Logic, Aesthetic, and Metaphysic as one of the branches of Philosophy rather than among the special Sciences[1]. But though there would be ample justification for

[1] Logic, Aesthetic, and Ethic are sometimes spoken of as normative Sciences, i. e. Sciences which set up standards, or which deal not simply with what is, but with what ought to be. They determine the principles upon which we distinguish between true and false, right and wrong judgements about the true, the beautiful, and the good. As I have no particular

the study of Moral Philosophy even though it were in the ordinary sense of the word useless, it does not follow that it does, as a matter of fact, serve no purpose beyond that of satisfying the desire to know, and supplying scope for the mental activities involved in the effort to satisfy that desire. We do not study Astronomy merely as an aid to Navigation, but it is a fact that Astronomy does aid Navigation. A Science is not degraded when it is shown to be useful; and in considering the particular persons who are to study a particular Science, and to what point they are to study it, the question of its utility is of fundamental importance. No Science contributes more to a scientific conception of Nature as a whole than Astronomy: but (in so far as it can be distinguished from general Physics) it has comparatively few students, because its practical applications are smaller than those of Chemistry or Physiology; and the only considerable class of persons who actually study more than its elements are those who learn it not for the general improvement of their minds, but as the theoretical basis of the art of Navigation. It is possible then that besides its importance in the construction of an ultimate theory of the Universe, Moral Philosophy may have, like some special Sciences, a practical value of its own which may constitute a reason for its study. Nor, even when looked on from the purely speculative point of view as a branch of Philosophy, is it necessarily useless. It must not be assumed that the importance of speculation itself is purely speculative. Although Metaphysic is in a sense of all Sciences the most useless, it is in another sense the most useful on account of its intimate connexion with questions of vital importance to the spiritual interests of Humanity.

It may be doubted whether the tendency to emphasize the supposed uselessness of Metaphysic, which is now somewhat in fashion, is really conducive to the interests of the Science simply as a Science [1]. While no doubt the desire for immediate edifica-

affection for the term, I do not care to discuss the objections which have been urged against its use.

[1] There are no doubt now traces of an extreme reaction against this tendency. The present writer has no sympathy with the 'Pragmatism' which not merely denies the value of Truth but seeks to break down the distinction between the true and the useful or the good.

tion—the desire to get a sanction for rules of life regarded as of practical importance or to bolster up some political or ecclesiastical system—has often interfered with the thoroughness and honesty of philosophical enquiry (even in systems ostensibly of the most purely speculative character), it still remains true that the greatest steps of philosophical progress have been taken by the men in whom the desire to find guidance for life has been at least as prominent as the desire to satisfy a purely intellectual curiosity. No one is really without practical interests; no one is really beyond reach of the temptation to allow his theoretical judgement to be swayed by his social aspirations, his inherited religious convictions, his personal likings and dislikings. And the interests of Truth are best served by a candid admission of the fact. The men who have pursued Philosophy in most ostensible detachment from all practical aims have possibly not been the least swayed by the passions which militate against the attainment of Truth. To be without ethical feeling is to be anti-ethical; to be without social feeling is really to be anti-social; to be without the desire to justify, or at least to discover, a religious creed is almost invariably to adopt an attitude of hostility to all religious creeds. The desire to find a sure basis for aspiration and conduct is not in the least incompatible with the desire that that basis should be a sound one. To be indifferent to the results of enquiry is not really a love of Truth. A strong sense of the practical importance of Truth for purposes of life is possibly less injurious to calmness and clearness of judgement than the love of paradox, the childish desire to shock, or the mere parade of intellectual force. There need be no collision between the love of Truth and the love of Good: if good be really good, to be without the love of it cannot be a. necessary condition of intellectual sanity. Nor is a predisposition to find some measure of Truth in the beliefs of the past a disqualification for their impartial examination. No man is really without desires: the idea of making the mind a *tabula rasa*, in the sense of getting rid of all practical interest in the consequences of our thinking, is an *ignis fatuus* as foolish as the mystic's attempt to rid himself of desire—an aspiration which is itself a desire. Desire cannot be extinguished: one desire can only be balanced, controlled, or in time supplanted, by other desires. The true security for intellectual open-mindedness is not the extinction of other desires, but the presence in due proportion of the love of Truth, based upon the conviction both of its essential value for its own sake, and of a faith (for which no *complete* speculative justification can be given) that in the long run it must be best even for the most severely practical of human interests to know the truth, and that so at the last Wisdom will be justified of her children. This is a faith which might no doubt conceivably have to be given up if growing knowledge failed to justify it: it is enough to say here that in the present writer's view it represents a presumption which the whole of our experience up to this point in the world's history tends to confirm.

If then there is nothing unbefitting the dignity, or injurious to the interests, of even the most speculative Philosophy in the admission that we pursue it partly on account of its value for life, still less is there anything injurious in such an admission in the case of Moral Philosophy. It would be natural to suppose that, besides its value as a branch of the speculative Science of Reality, Moral Philosophy should have a peculiar value of its own, inasmuch as the element which it contributes to the total theory of Reality is that which has the most direct bearing upon the conduct of life, whatever be the nature of that bearing. Even when regarded on its more speculative side, Moral Philosophy may reasonably claim a special practical importance on account of the element which it contributes to Theology and so to Religion, or to that ultimate theory of and attitude towards the Universe at large which takes the place of Theology and Religion from the point of view of those who do not accept the beliefs usually covered by those terms. In this sense its practical value will hardly be questioned even by those who most delight in exhibiting its unpractical character[1]. But Moral

---

[1] If it should turn out, as the result of enquiry, that a theory of things in general is not an assistance in the conduct of life, this would itself be a conclusion of direct practical value. To get rid of illusions (for those who on whatever ground believe that it is best to know the truth) must by itself throw some light upon the path of life.

Philosophy is not merely the Science of conduct in general but
of conduct in particular. If the view taken of it in these pages
be well founded, its special problem (to which all others are,
from the point of view of pure Ethics, subordinate) is to determine what it is right to do [1]. And such an enquiry might
reasonably be expected to throw some light upon the practical
questions of life.

It would be almost a contradiction in terms to assert that
a scientific enquiry into the question what it is right to do has
no bearing whatever upon the question what it is right to do.
Upon a purely sceptical theory which would deny the possibility of a scientific answer to the problems which the Science
cannot but ask, such a result might no doubt be barely thinkable, though (as in the case of still more ultimate problems) even
sceptical or negative conclusions may have a very important
bearing upon life. Moral Philosophy would have some bearing
upon life even if its only verdict should be 'So far as Science is
concerned, you may do just whatever you like,' or 'The best
way to do right is not to think at all about what it is right to
do.' Such a view as to the actual content of our Science is not
the one which has been taken in these pages; and from the
point of view of a constructive Moral Philosophy Ethical Science
might be clearly expected to have a more positive bearing upon
detailed problems of duty. The nature and amount of such
practical utility we have, however, yet to examine. It may
well turn out that the amount of guidance to be practically
obtained from the scientific study of Morality may be much
smaller than our view of its theoretical scope might naturally
lead us to expect. If the view of Ethics which we take is
a true one, Casuistry is undoubtedly the goal of Ethics, but it
must not be assumed that the goal is one which has yet been, or
even which is ever destined to be, fully attained [2].

[1] On the view we have taken that enquiry merges in the enquiry 'what is
the good?' but it is desirable to state the aim of a Science in terms of its
problem rather than of a conclusion which would not be universally admitted.

[2] 'So far as Ethics allows itself to give lists of virtues or even to name
constituents of the Ideal, it is indistinguishable from Casuistry. . . . Casuistry
is the goal of ethical investigation. It cannot be safely attempted at the

If it is the goal of Ethics scientifically to discover what ought to be done, it is not so much the practical utility of the Science as its limitations which will require to be insisted upon. *Prima facie*, we might expect Moral Philosophy to possess a practical importance which, by almost universal admission, it does not actually possess. *A priori* it might be supposed that the Science of Life ought to be as important to right living as the Science of Hygienics is to the production of physical health, and that the whole lives of those who do not possess the Science themselves ought to be at least as completely regulated by those who do, as it would be ideally desirable that the physical side of life should be controlled by expert medical advice. By almost universal admission this is far from being the case. And that being so, my task will practically consist as much in explaining why the Science of Morals does not possess this immense utility as in asking what usefulness remains to it when chimerical aspirations have been laid aside.

In so far as it succeeds in its aims, the bearing of Moral Philosophy upon life is obvious; the usefulness of a Science which should really enable us to pronounce with accuracy and certainty what each one of us ought to do at every particular moment of his life needs no demonstration. It is more necessary, and more difficult, to explain why it is not likely—perhaps ever, certainly not for an indefinite period in the future—to achieve even an approximate realization of those aims. And the first limitation to the probabilities of its practical usefulness is constituted by the fact that its ultimate data are simply those deliverances of the moral consciousness which the Moral Philosopher shares with the rest of mankind. Its business is to analyse the way in which we actually judge about conduct, just as the business of Logic is to analyse the way in which we actually think. As the Logician does not necessarily think more logically than other men, so the Moral Philosopher does not necessarily judge about conduct better than other men. A trained Logician may be a very poor reasoner, and a very good reasoner may know nothing of logical Science. So a competent

beginning of our studies, but only at the end.' Moore, *Principia Ethica*, pp. 4, 5.

Moral Philosopher may be a bad adviser in matters of conduct,
while the best and practically wisest of men may be quite innocent
of an ethical system. This comparison of Moral Philosophy to
Logic has been made by Mr. Bradley, one of whose most violent
explosions is directed against the whole idea of Casuistry,
whether of the old priestly and authoritative or of the modern
Utilitarian sort. It is worth while therefore to ask firstly,
whether, in so far as the scope of Moral Philosophy can be
compared to that of Logic, the acceptance of the parallel necessarily forbids us to look for any practical Utility in the Science,
and secondly whether the parallel is a complete one.

As this chapter is largely an examination of the view taken
by Mr. Bradley, I give the whole passage :—

'There is another false science more unlovely in life and more
unpleasant in decay, from which I myself should be loath to
divide it. Just as Logic has been perverted into the art of
reasoning, so Ethics has been perverted into the art of morality.
They are twin delusions we shall consign, if we are wise, to
a common grave.

'But I would not grudge Casuistry a Christian burial. I should
be glad to see it dead and done with on any terms ; and then, if
all the truth must be spoken, in its later years it has suffered
much wrong. That it became odious beyond parallel and in
parts most filthy, is not to be denied ; but it ill becomes the
parents of a monster, who have begotten it and nourished it, to
cry out when it follows the laws of its nature. And, if I am to
say what I think, I must express my conviction that it is not
only the Catholic priest, but it also is our utilitarian moralist,
who embraces the delusion which has borne such a progeny. If
you believe, as our Utilitarian believes, that the philosopher
should know the reason why each action is to be judged moral
or immoral ; if you believe that he at least should guide his
action reflectively by an ethical code, which provides an universal rule and canon for every possible case, and should enlighten his more uninitiated fellows, then it seems to me you
have wedded the mistake from which this offensive offspring has
issued. It may be true that the office of professional confessor
has made necessary a completer codification of offences, and has
joined doctrinal vagaries to ethical blunders. We may allow
that it was the lust for spiritual tyranny which choked the last
whisper of the unsanctified conscience. It may be true that, in
his effort theoretically to exhaust the possibilities of human

depravity, the celibate priest dwelt with curious refinement on the morbid subject of sexual transgression. But unless his principle is wholly unsound I confess that I can hardly find fault with his practice; for if there is to be an art and a code of morality, I do not see how we can narrow its scope beforehand. The field is not limited by our dislikes, and whoever works at the disgusting parts, is surely deserving not of blame but of gratitude. Hence if the Utilitarian has declined to follow the priest, he has also declined to follow his own principles; he has stopped short not from logical reasons but from psychological causes [1].'

But in the first place I should submit that Logic is not wholly useless. Mr. Bradley has no doubt done good service by insisting upon the impossibility of reducing all valid reasoning to the syllogistic form. He is perhaps right even in holding that it is for ever impossible to construct any completely adequate Grammar (as it were) of correct reasoning—any complete enumeration of the types of inference to one or other of which all valid arguments can be reduced. It is quite true that primarily Logic is a speculative Science, that there is no art of correct reasoning, and that the idea that the business of Logic is to teach people how to argue a good or even a bad case has led to grave misunderstandings as to the nature and content of the Science. But all the same it may quite reasonably be urged that Logic does in some measure help people to think correctly. Logic is thinking about Thought: and though people may in practice think very well about other things without having thought abstractly about thinking itself, and may think very badly about other things when they have spent their lives in thinking about Thought, it is nevertheless true to say that *ceteris paribus* a man is the more likely to think well about other things when he has bestowed some study upon the conditions of valid inference, the ultimate grounds of our ordinary and our scientific beliefs, and so on. Teachers of Physical Science are often desirous that their pupils should go through the discipline of elementary Logic, and find that even a very elementary course of Logic [2] is of some practical value to

[1] *Principles of Logic*, pp. 247-8.
[2] Mr. Bradley would probably insist that much of what is ordinarily

students of Physical Science. To have their attention called to the ultimate grounds of all belief, to the most usual types of conception, judgement, and inference, to the most ordinary forms of incorrect reasoning and the most common sources of error, has a tendency to help the student in following actual concrete reasoning, to guard him against error in such reasoning, and still more perhaps to aid him in distinguishing between the various degrees of certainty, probability, and possibility with which scientific propositions may be affirmed. No doubt it remains true that the detailed methods of enquiry and reasoning employed in each Science are part of the business of that Science. Logic must follow, and cannot anticipate, the methods of Science. Each man judges best about the matters with which he is familiar, and the fact that to minds properly trained in a particular Science arguments may often appeal which strike persons unfamiliar with them as precarious enough is not necessarily a final condemnation of such arguments. Criticism of the methods of a Science from the outside has no doubt a very restricted value, at least so long as the man of Science really confines himself to the proper scope of his particular Science. But this the scientific man is not always willing to do. He may not always estimate correctly the degree of probability attained even by his own Science within its proper limits. Still more often he may inadequately appreciate the abstract character of its results, and the limitations within which alone they are really applicable. When there is a question of collision between the apparent conclusions of different Sciences, or of the co-ordination of their results, then logical training, and indeed philosophical training in general, may not be without a very direct bearing even upon matters which are usually considered to belong exclusively to the Physical Sciences pure and simple. That some consideration of

taught under the title of elementary Logic is really very bad Logic or not Logic at all. Such an admission would only strengthen my case. If the Logic commonly expected in elementary Examinations were in closer touch with the actual procedure of the scientific intellect, the results might be better, though after all it is probably familiarity with the difficulties and problems of Logic, rather than with any particular solution of them, that makes Logic a good propaedeutic for Science.

the nature of proof in general might be a useful propaedeutic for the votaries of many other branches of knowledge besides Physical Science is a conclusion suggested by the perusal of critical and historical arguments both of the ultra-conservative and of the ultra-speculative schools. I should not hesitate to say that *ceteris paribus* a man who had studied Logic would be likely to make a better theological or historical critic than one who had not. Value of this restricted and pedagogic kind might well be claimed for Moral Philosophy, even if we accepted the parallel of Logic as expressing the whole truth about the matter. But, when all is said, it must be admitted that the value of Logic as an aid to correct reasoning is comparatively slight and indirect: the main problem is how far the parallel between Logic and Moral Philosophy is an exact one.

The reason why the utility of Logic for the Sciences is of this very restricted character is that Logic can do nothing but make abstract generalizations about the actual methods employed in thinking about something else. It has, therefore, no object-matter except what is common to it and all the Sciences. It studies from a particular point of view the very thinking by which the other Sciences are made. Moral Philosophy, on the other hand, has a special object-matter which is not the object-matter of the other Sciences. Its business is not with Thought abstracted from its contents, but with a particular object of Thought—that is to say, human conduct. It is true that the Science of Ethics has no instrument but the moral Reason and the ordinary intellectual faculties which are common to the scientific Moralist and the ordinary individual. But that fact is, as far as it goes, a reason for retaining, and not for surrendering, the expectation that the Science might prove practically useful. It is equally true with regard to the other Sciences that their professors only employ the same methods of thinking which other men employ, and employ them upon matter which falls also to some extent within the experience of ordinary men. Each Science is the attempt to study some particular department or aspect of human experience, but to study it more thoroughly and systematically than ordinary men study it. Every Science starts with the experience of common life and with the methods

of common life, though it ultimately reaches conclusions which
go beyond common knowledge. And that is exactly the position
of Moral Science. It aims at thinking about those matters
of conduct about which all men think to some extent, but at
thinking more thoroughly, consistently, and systematically than
most ordinary men habitually do think. It might be expected
that the result of such scientific thought would supply a better,
truer, more valid guide to conduct than the ordinary, confused,
and often self-contradictory thinking of ordinary persons in
ordinary life. It is true that Moral Philosophy deals with these
problems in general, and in a highly abstract way ; but, after all,
that is the case with all Sciences, and yet that does not prevent
their having various practical applications. It may be that the
exceptionally general and abstract character of Moral Science
as compared with the exceptional concreteness, particularity,
and complexity of practical problems will set some limits to this
usefulness. But though the Science is abstract, it is not so
abstract as Logic. Logic, as we have seen, is a thinking about
Thought in abstraction (in so far as such an abstraction can be
made) from any special object of thought. Moral Philosophy
is a thinking about an object-matter which, though a wide and
general one, is something distinguishable from the object of
Thought in general.

To this line of argument Mr. Bradley has a reply. Ethical
thinking is not 'discursive.' It is a delusion to suppose that we
can 'know the reason why each action is to be judged moral or
immoral,' or that to 'guide his action reflectively by an ethical
code' is even an ideal to be aimed at. Such declarations may
mean a good many different things. But, if we are to follow
out the line of thought suggested by the furious diatribe against
Casuistry quoted above and by the whole tenor of his *Ethical
Studies*, we must suppose Mr. Bradley to mean that there is
actually no such thing as arguing or reasoning about conduct.
Consistency is not a demand of the ethical consciousness, or
of the ordinary Reason and Understanding when applied to this
particular subject-matter. Ethical judgements are simply isolated, incoherent, particular, *ad hoc* pronouncements of an inward
oracle. No attempt to systematize or rationalize them, in the

way in which we attempt to systematize and rationalize other
elements of crude, immediate experience, is likely to make the
resulting judgements more valid. We can never argue that,
if a certain action is right in one particular case, another course
of conduct cannot also be right in another case which resembles
the former in all relevant particulars. I cannot argue that,
if it is wrong to murder white men, it must be wrong to murder
black men, unless I can point to some difference between white
men and black men which the moral consciousness can recognize
as a ground for this differential treatment. We cannot call upon
a man who sends people to prison for stealing and yet steals
himself to admit that one part or other of his conduct must lack
ethical justification. On the contrary, to think about conduct,
it would seem to be suggested, is already the first step to moral
downfall[1]. The moral judgements of the educated and reflective
person are not more, but, if anything, less likely to be true than
those of the uneducated[2]. If this is seriously Mr. Bradley's meaning, I need not repeat the arguments against it which the first
two books of this work were largely occupied in setting forth.
I need only say that it is a view of which, in the whole course of
ethical speculation, Mr. Bradley and Bishop Butler in some of his
more irrational moments are, so far as I am aware, almost the
only supporters. I cannot, of course, seriously suppose that
Mr. Bradley intends consequences so absurd, but such would
seem to be the natural meaning of his often repeated assertions.
I will only suggest two other lines of reflection.

In the first place, Mr. Bradley is hardly likely to deny that
our particular, immediate, instinctive moral judgements are
in their actual content largely the result of custom, tradition,
extraneous influence of one kind or another. If these instinctive
judgements are not to be critically sifted and made consistent

---

[1] *Ethical Studies*, p. 180.

[2] I should of course admit that there are cases where 'instinct' is more
likely to go right than reflection, but then there are as many or more cases
where 'instinct' without reflection is a cause of immoral conduct, e. g.
indiscriminate almsgiving. The reasons which explain the value of
'instinct' have been dwelt on partly in the chapter on the relation between
Feeling and Reason in Book I, and partly in the chapter on Authority in
Book II.

with themselves, and brought into connexion with a wider range
of experience than that with which each individual begins life,
not only is there an end to all prospect of moral progress, but
there is an end to all possibility of moral ' autonomy,' for the
' instinctive' judgements of the average man clearly owe
much to his education.   That there is a limit to the extent to
which it is desirable that each individual should attempt to
think himself clear of the traditional beliefs of his society,
I have fully admitted.   But, if this criticism of moral beliefs is
never to be attempted, I fail to see how the progress which
has undoubtedly taken place in the ethical beliefs of the past
is to be accounted for ; unless Mr. Bradley should fall back
upon the somewhat startling paradox that all moral progress
has come from the actions of wicked persons who had the
presumption to question the crude and unanalysed intuitions of
themselves and their society, and by trying to be more moral
than their neighbours became *ipso facto* actually less so.   I can
hardly believe that a Morality entirely heteronomous could be
deliberately accepted by Mr. Bradley as his ideal, though there
are certainly passages in Mr. Bradley's writings which seem to
point in that direction.   The second criticism which I would
make upon Mr. Bradley's attack upon Casuistry is that he entirely
fails to carry out his own principles.   In a paper upon Punishment [1] he observes that, though the Darwinian doctrine of
Evolution throws no light upon the end of moral conduct, it
may have much to say about the means : and he proceeds to
defend a system of wholesale infanticide upon similar grounds
to those which commended themselves to Plato (though apparently upon a much vaster scale), reinforced by the physiological
doctrine of the necessity for selection, natural or artificial, to
keep up the efficiency of the race.   The advocacy of such an
ethical revolution upon such grounds seems to imply that the
proper method of Ethics is to form a conception of the social end
which we wish to attain, and then to consider (in the light of
all available experience) by what action on our part that end is
to be reached.   Such a method seems totally inconsistent with

[1] ' Some Remarks on Punishment' in the *International Journal of Ethics*
(April, 1894).

the doctrine of immediate and unimpeachable oracles, in each man's breast or in the general consciousness of a given time and place, about the details of conduct. It is true that our ethical judgements are not discursive, if by that is meant that our ultimate moral judgements are immediate.   But because immediate, they are not necessarily final, nor is the demand for consistency in these judgements necessarily excluded. Where (as is often the case with all facts of apparently immediate experience) two particular judgements seem to contradict one another, we feel compelled to give up or modify one or both; and the progressive effort to remove these contradictions leads to the formation of a general moral ideal, however imperfectly this ideal may reflect itself in the ' general rules ' which we necessarily formulate as the result of such reflection.   Even, then, in forming our conception of the end there is room for the critical, universalizing, harmonizing action of reflection.   Still more obvious is it that for ascertaining the means best fitted in any particular complication of circumstances for the attainment of our end, there may be room for a modification of the instinctive judgements of ' common sense ' by all the experience to which the individual can get access, and by all the processes of the reflective understanding by which the results of that experience can be generalized and applied to particular cases.   Little as I agree with his conclusion, Mr. Bradley's argument for infanticide supplies an admirable example of the inevitableness of Casuistry, and a very fair illustration of its proper methods.

II

If the method of Ethics adopted throughout this book, and (as we have seen) by Mr. Bradley in one of his moods, be accepted, that scientific discussion of particular cases of conduct which is called Casuistry is certainly possible ; and, if the difficulties of such a scientific determination are such as to make it impossible for every individual to undertake to guide his own conduct by such a reflective clearing-up of the ethical end and such an empirical ascertainment of the means as I have just sketched, that would only seem to point to the need for a body of ethical experts who would undertake to issue general instructions for the guidance of the untrained public, and to assist them in the application of those instructions to the detailed difficulties of particular lives. If we have no great confidence in the practicability or desirability of such a scientific regulation of life, we must ask once more ' why are there in practice such strict limits to the practical usefulness of a Science, the possibility and indeed the actual existence of which we are theoretically bound to admit ? '

Many of the objections commonly urged against the possibility of Casuistry seem, indeed, to turn upon easily demonstrated mistakes, confusions, or exaggerations. It is urged that the complexity of life is so great that no two cases of conduct resemble one another, and that therefore each case must be considered on its own merits. If this means that there are no general principles in Ethics at all, the objection is one which has been already dealt with, and which is not open to those who have accepted our ethical method. If it means merely that, besides features which the case has in common with other cases, it has features peculiar to itself, that is true ; and it is true equally of every medical case—a consideration which does not prevent Medical Science and medical books from being of the utmost utility. No two cases are exactly alike, but they may be alike in all relevant particulars ; or if not alike, the difference can be allowed for in the treatment of the particular case— an allowance which may itself be covered by some more or less definable general principle. The existence of Medical Science and medical books does not dispense with the need for the trained tact of the Physician, or even (in some cases) with the exercise of common sense by the patient. The argument would only tend to show that the trained Casuist must be as important as his Science. Then it is urged that, though the detailed consideration of ethical questions is possible, it is morally unwholesome and undesirable. The objection seems to be largely based upon the concentration of attention upon one or two particular departments of Morality, in which no doubt the objection has some force ; though the medical analogy might still allow the apologist of Casuistry to plead that the task, though disagreeable and not without moral peril, has to be faced

on certain occasions and by certain persons. But the most
serious misconception which seems to be at the bottom of the
objection lies in the assumption that Casuistry necessarily deals
with detailed particular cases—either cases which have actually
occurred or which may occur, envisaged in all the wealth and
variety of circumstance which belongs to actual life. This
is a complete misunderstanding. Casuistry deals with classes of
cases. And there is no difference in principle between such discussions as we find in the pages of so comparatively uncasuistical
a Moralist as Green—discussions, for instance, as to the grounds
for asserting the principle of monogamous marriage or as to the
conditions under which political rebellion is justifiable—and
the kind of cases which fill the pages of the professed theological Casuists, Roman Catholic, Puritan, or Anglican. At
most the difference is merely one in the degree of particularity
to which the discussion is carried. Even if we admitted that
objections exist to the detailed anticipation of those strange and
abnormal difficulties which seldom occur, and in which the true
solution depends upon such a delicate estimate of circumstances
that the actual case will never be exactly the anticipated case,
there would still be room for a Casuistry which should deal with
the difficulties which do arise every day—the question when
if ever it is right to tell a lie, what constitutes a just price
or a just wage, what constitutes commercial Morality, the
morality of gambling, the legitimacy of field sports or of Vivisection, and the like. And in these questions there would seem
to be room both for the casuistical writer and for the trained
judgement of the expert in that Science.

The bare mention of the casuistical expert is at once apt to
suggest the Jesuit Confessor, and all the justifiable antagonisms as
well as the traditional prejudices which are apt to be awakened by
the mention either of Jesuits or Confessors. Few Protestant
Moralists who have touched upon the subject have been able to
avoid the idea that the very existence of Casuistry necessarily involves the system of private Confession, the quite distinct system of
'direction,' the tyranny over Consciences, the superstitious and
immoral belief in the efficacy of priestly absolution, the authoritative and external Morality which, if they have not been wholly

confined to the Roman Church, have found their most conspicuous illustrations in the history of that communion. And yet it is obvious that the existence of Casuistry, and even of trained advisers in conduct, no more involves any of these things than the existence of medical and legal Science with the corresponding bodies of practitioners imply a tyranny of the Physicians or of the Lawyers, or a belief in the infallibility or the divine right of either. I am convinced that the prejudice against systematic and detailed Casuistry which is perhaps at bottom wholesome, and the misconception as to the nature of Moral Philosophy which that prejudice has brought with it, are for the most part due simply to the fact that the most elaborate and conspicuous attempt to construct and apply a system of Casuistry has been made by Priests of the Roman Catholic Church, and especially of the Society of Jesus. It may be well, therefore, very briefly to point out what are the features of the system which have brought Casuistry of this type into not undeserved discredit, in order that it may be seen how little a condemnation of such Casuistry necessarily carries with it the idea that there is anything either absurd or pernicious in the scientific consideration of cases of conduct.

In the first place, there is the association of the Science with the whole system of confession, penance, priestly absolution, priestly direction, authoritative Ethics which need not be further insisted on. Such an association, however, while it might easily account for the resulting system of Casuistry being in many ways out of harmony with modern ideals, would not by itself seem specially likely to result in a system of extreme laxity. To understand that feature of the Jesuit system, it is necessary to remember the historical circumstances under which the Jesuit Order grew up. It was the object of that Order to bring back to the Roman Church a Europe which had almost thrown off its yoke. To effect that object in an age of nearly universal Absolutism the Jesuits made it their special business to render the Roman system acceptable to Kings, Princes, nobles, and men of the world. One way of acquiring that influence was to show that the Roman creed offered cheaper as well as more secure 'terms of salvation' than Protestantism. Hence everything

was done to attenuate the discrepancy between the ordinary
pleasures and practices of the world and the requirements of
Christianity, to offer the man of the world the maximum of
indulgence which was compatible with submission to the
minimum requirements of the Church and with the use of his
influence and authority in its service.   This was effected chiefly
by the doctrine of Probabilism, which laid it down that a man
might safely and unblamably take the course recommended by
any 'probable' (or approved) authority, even if in fact and in
the judgement of the agent there was a greater weight of Reason
and Authority on the other side.   A host of learned Theologians
set themselves to manufacture the authority which *ipso facto*
established the safety of the less thorny path to heaven.   To
effect this object, valuable assistance was given by the intrinsically immoral doctrine of a fundamental distinction between
two classes of sins—mortal and venial—a distinction depending
upon the nature of the external act and not upon the degree of
moral guilt which it implies.   Mortal sins alone entailed dam-
nation in the event of death without absolution.   The old
patristic list of mortal sins certainly represented an austere
Morality enough, but by a system of ingenious distinctions mortal
sins could be reduced to venial ones.   Mortal sins could be
reduced to venial ones by 'venial accidents'—among others, a lack
of 'perfection' in the sin.   Drunkenness, for instance, was
mortal, but only perfect drunkenness.   Drunkenness which did
not involve the total loss of Reason for a space of an hour was
venial [1].   Theft was a mortal sin, but if a servant thought himself insufficiently paid by his master, he could then, under
certain conditions, rob his master to a corresponding amount
without committing even venial sin [2].   Christianity required men
to give alms of their 'superfluities,' but superfluity was dependent
upon the rank and circumstances of the person, and no wealth
could be superfluous for a man of position [3].   And so on.   Men
were taught how, if they wished to sin, they could nearly
always—so long as they recognized the authority of the Church

[1] St. Alphonso Liguori, *Theol. Moralis* (Parisiis, 1845), L. II, c. 3, Art. ii.
[2] See Lea, *History of Auricular Confession*, II. pp. 395-8.
[3] Pascal, *Les Provinciales*, Lettre xii sq.

and complied with certain ecclesiastical regulations—ensure that
their sins should be only venial, even where the Casuist's
ingenuity failed to remove even this barrier to inclination.
And no accumulation of venial sins or deliberateness in their
perpetration could ever amount to a mortal sin. The demoralizing
tendency of the whole system is obvious enough. It is fair to
remember that the problem of the Roman Casuist was not what
conduct Preachers or Confessors should recommend, but what
was the minimum of good behaviour by which the penitent
could escape the Church's censure, with the temporal and eternal
penalties attaching thereto. But this very attempt to fix a minimum of conformity with detailed and prescribed regulations,
and practically to acquit of all blame, to rid of all serious anxiety
or moral condemnation by themselves or others those who
complied with it, was by itself quite as immoral as any of the
detailed machinery by which the art of evading obvious duties
was taught. This slight sketch of the more objectionable ideas
and practices involved in the Probabilist Casuistry of modern
Romanism may perhaps be sufficient to suggest how little these
features necessarily attach to all Casuistry as such. The business
of the Jesuit Moral Theology was not to help people to be as
good as possible, but to show how they could be as bad as
possible without suffering for it[1]. The immoral tendencies of
such a system supply no argument against a Casuistry which
should aim at showing what ought to be done by people who
seriously want to do what they ought.

III

Having thus, it is hoped, removed some of the prejudices
which stand in the way of a dispassionate discussion of the
subject, I proceed to ask 'Within what limits is it possible that

[1] By authoritative decisions the Probabilist Casuistry, long vehemently
disputed within the pale of the Roman Church, has now become, in its
main principles, formally binding on Confessors, though there are, I believe,
many who practically ignore it. I do not of course attempt to say how far
this system, secretly disliked by the more progressive Roman Catholic
clergy, really exercises in modern communities the demoralizing effects
which might naturally be expected from it.

a scientific system of Casuistry can be built up?' And here it becomes important to bear in mind the distinction between the apprehension of ends and the apprehension of means. So far as the right course of action turns upon a correct apprehension of the ethical end, it is based upon an immediate intuitive judgement or system of judgements. And the Moral Philosopher as such has no greater power of making such judgements correctly than other men. No doubt, inasmuch as he has specially directed his attention to the subject, he may perhaps claim that his faculty of moral judgement, if naturally of normal strength, is likely to be better trained than that of other men. For, if he is not merely a Moral Philosopher but a good Moral Philosopher, he must at least not be altogether without the normal capacity for judging conduct (just as a good art critic, though he need not be himself an artist, must at least have some capacity for aesthetic feeling); so that, even if his natural appreciation of the moral value of particular ends in human life be not exceptionally acute, he will at least have exercised his mind more than other men upon the comparative value of different elements in human life, and will thus be less likely to be unduly swayed by an exclusive enthusiasm for some particular form or kind of good life than other men, especially perhaps those men of exceptionally intense moral conviction whose very devotion to one kind of good often makes them underrate the value of others, and whose very enthusiasm for the best often leads them to undervalue the good. All these pleas might, I think, be truly urged; but the fact remains that the Philosopher's power of judging values depends ultimately upon his qualities as a man and not upon his acuteness as a Philosopher, though his superior power of analysing and expressing them may not be without practical usefulness.

Moreover, it must be borne in mind that these judgements as to the relative value of ends rarely admit of exact formulation. It is easy to say that Culture is good and is in the abstract better than ordinary social intercourse, but the whole practical difficulty lies in saying how much of one's life should be devoted to one end and how much to the other. And here we can only admit with Aristotle that the judgement must take the form of 'feeling' or 'immediate perception.' Hence, though the advice

of persons who have thought about the subject is valuable, there
are strict limits to the extent to which their generalizations
can be stored up, so to speak, and applied to the regulation of
other lives than their own. And, in so far as it can be so formulated and communicated, it is rather to the men of intuitive
moral genius—to the prophets and the sages—that we should go
for advice as to the ultimate purpose and meaning of life than
to academic Philosophers. We must remember too what has
already been said as to the influence upon moral judgement
both of emotional capacity and of actual goodwill. Hence it is
in many matters not so much to those who have exceptional powers
of thinking or talking about Morality that we should go for
guidance as to the moral ideal, as to the men of exceptional moral
performance. The complexity of the ethical end is so great that
it can often be best represented by a concrete example. Hence
we often turn for guidance not even to the prophets or sages
so much as to the moral heroes, or to the men who unite both
characters. The biography of the best and wisest of such men
teaches the nature of the end better than formal discourses. Or
if in some matters we feel that the greater ethical minds, just
because they have been completely dominated by the importance
of the highest things in life, have not explicitly taught or
have positively underrated the value of goods less than the
highest—if we wanted, for instance, a just estimate of the place
of Culture in life—we should turn not so much to the formal
ethical treatise as to the writings of Goethe or Ruskin or
Matthew Arnold. Finally, it must be remembered that, when
we get beyond some very general principles, there is no consensus, either among the experts of any kind or sort or among
the general public, as to these questions of value; and that
consequently judgements about conduct based upon one man's
ideal of life can only be valid for those whose own moral consciousness recognizes and accepts that ideal, at least sufficiently
to be willing to regard the other's judgement as more or less
authoritative. And, if we regard it as an important part of the
moral ideal that (within the limits which have already been
dwelt upon) the ethically mature mind should regulate its life
by its own and not by other people's ideals, it will not seem

desirable that this reverence for the judgement of others should be pushed beyond a certain point. Within certain limits we should prefer that a man should act wrongly on his own judgement than do what was objectively right on another's. These considerations might easily be expanded, but they will be sufficient to indicate why it is that a Science of Conduct cannot be formulated which should command the sort and degree of general acceptance which are conceded to the laws of health as formulated and taught by medical practitioners and to the detailed precepts based upon them.

So far we have been dealing with ends of action; but there might still be much room for a scientific treatment of the means to the ultimate end, which should have validity for those who share the ideal upon which it is based. The first limitation which suggests itself is that so large a part of conduct directed towards the realization of the ethical end demands, and depends for its effectiveness upon, the co-operation of others, that it is only within small limits that the individual can with advantage attempt the task of considering for himself the means by which this end may most effectively be realized. Nine-tenths of life (so to express it) is already regulated by the rules either of law or custom, rules which in most cases it would do more harm than good to transgress even when they are not intrinsically the best adapted to this end. No doubt the critical examination of these rules is (within certain limits) a very desirable thing, and this constitutes one of the most useful tasks to which the Moral Philosopher can apply himself. And such criticism may in time lead to an alteration of the rules. Formal Moral Philosophy may thus contribute something to that general criticism and remoulding of accepted ethical rules and ideals which is always going on in the general consciousness of every progressive community. But, when the attempt is made by the Moral Philosopher to push his formulation of the rules best adapted to realize the good of Society beyond a certain very modest point, he finds that the task soon requires a knowledge and experience which no one man can possibly possess. Here the objection is not that there is no room for the specialist, but that we want fifty specialisms rather than one. It is not that Casuistry is impossible, but that Casuistry, when we come to details of conduct, becomes too vast a subject for any one man or any special class of men to profess. Even if we put aside the arts and the trades which (in so far as they can be morally justified) are engaged in making or doing the things conducive to the ideal life, all the professions and specialized callings, all the professors of the separate branches and departments of social Science or Philosophy, represent so many specialists in the Science which determines the means to the good. In practice, and to some extent inevitably, the members of these professions make abstraction of what would ordinarily be called the ethical question. The Physician advises his patient as to the means to one particular end—health— without undertaking to advise him as to the extent to which, under particular circumstances, it is right for him to pursue health; the Lawyer helps his client to win his case—not indeed by all means, but by all means which a certain accepted professional code has recognized—without raising the question whether the client is morally justified in insisting upon a legal right or availing himself of a technical defence [1]. But still it remains true that the professional man is an expert in some particular kind of means to the good. And there are very numerous kinds of such expert knowledge outside the recognized professions. In so far as the means of social good can be attained by legislation, it is the practical Statesman or the theoretical writer on Politics who is the expert; in so far as they can be promoted by the regulation of Charity, the trained charity organizer; in so far as they can be attained by Education, the teacher or the man who has made a study of Education.

There remains, no doubt, for the expert in Ethics pure and simple the task of discussing those questions as to the means to the good with which the professions as such do not occupy themselves—that is, either the more general ethical questions the answer to which is presupposed by the specialists (how far health is to be preferred to other ends, whether and when it is

---

[1] Of course in each of these cases the professional man often does and ought to give ethical advice to his client, but then the value of his advice depends upon his qualities as a man, though no doubt his special experience has a value in determining even the ethical question.

right to go to law, &c.), or those details of conduct which do not
form the province of any recognized office or profession. But
even here the knowledge required is so vast that it is hopeless
for any one to go beyond very general precepts which often leave
the real problems unsolved. Thus, for instance, the question
what constitutes commercial Morality is a question to which
a professed Moralist might very well apply himself. And I distinctly hold that some training in theoretical Ethics would be
a very valuable qualification for any one who undertook such a
task. But he would soon find that the knowledge of facts—the
actual usages of business, the economic effects of these usages or
of any change in them, the possibility of introducing such and
such a change, and so on—is so great that only an experienced
Moralist who was also an experienced man of business, or at
least one who had devoted much time to enquiry into the subject,
could satisfactorily undertake the scientific discussion of these
casuistical questions which constantly present themselves to
every man engaged in trade, from the manager of a great concern
down to the salesman who wants to know where legitimate
' puffing ' ends and downright misrepresentation begins. Moreover, should the Moralist chance to have had some business
experience, or try to avail himself of the experience of others,
he would soon discover how very little even business men usually
know about the usages, and consequently about the ethical
difficulties, of any branch of commerce except their own; and
that the wider question how particular practices affect not this
or that individual or this or that trade but the community at
large is one which the business man has very little considered
and is not specially qualified to consider. He would find that
the solution of very many ethical problems would demand
a considerable knowledge of technical Economics. Thus, as the
enquiry extended from one department of life to another, the
would-be constructor of a universal Casuistry would soon discover that one kind of practical knowledge after another, one
theoretical Science after another, would have to be mastered—
that, in short, if the enquiry as to what it is right to do is to
descend to the actual particular problems of conduct, even in
so far as these could be anticipated and brought under definite

heads or categories—the universal Casuist would require something not far short of universal knowledge. That that is so was one of the precious truths enshrined (amid many ideas of less permanence) in Plato's doctrine that the knowledge of the good involves a knowledge of all Reality.

IV

Are we then to give up altogether the notion that Moral Philosophy may be practically useful in deciding cases of Conscience? By no means. We may indeed dismiss as a baseless dream the idea that there will ever be produced some vast, many-volumed Encyclopaedia of Casuistry by a reference to which either the layman or the casuistic expert may settle a disputed case as a lawyer ascertains the law by reference to his code or his cases, or as the medical practitioner, as soon as he has diagnosed the case, copies his prescription out of a form-book. And, if a Moral Philosopher be a good guide in practical difficulties, it will be rather his qualities as a man—his practical insight, his experience of life, the character which in conjunction with knowledge and experience brings wisdom with it—than his scientific training that will make his opinion valuable. The scientific training by itself will be of very little practical value. But that is a very different thing from denying that, in conjunction with other influences, Moral Philosophy may offer valuable assistance in training the practical judgement. There are a number of mistakes due to mere prejudice, or confusion of thought, or want of reflection, which, in spite of the wide differences of opinion on ethical subjects found among Moral Philosophers as among other people, are almost certain to disappear as the result of that thoughtful consideration of ethical problems which we call Moral Philosophy. There are a certain number of ethical problems about which ordinary people are divided, but about which even now we might confidently appeal to a jury of Moral Philosophers, and expect a nearly unanimous verdict or at least a far smaller range of variation. At all events there are certain opinions which they are pretty sure not to share; and still more confidently it may be said that, though a Moral Philosopher may conceivably hold on many questions almost any conceivable ethical opinion, he will not urge in favour of it arguments which are often used by those who have not made a scientific study of the subject. It is a great misfortune that in this country (it is otherwise in Germany) we have no word to express the idea of 'Science' which does not suggest the certainty and precision which we are accustomed to associate with the Physical Sciences alone. That is a prejudice which appears to have influenced even philosophical declaimers against the pretensions of Casuistry. In Germany it is recognized that every subject may be treated 'scientifically,' whatever the degree of accurate conclusion it may admit of. When that prejudice is removed, it ought, I think, to be admitted that the scientific treatment of ethical questions may reasonably be expected to aid the development of right ideas about Morality and life in general, to assist in the formation of sound opinions about the still disputed questions of detail, and to assist in the application of those principles to the particular problems of individual or of social life.

In asking more positively what help the Moral Philosopher can contribute to the solution of ethical problems, we must once more revert to the distinction between ends and means. The Moral Philosopher may have no more power of discerning the true end of human life than the normal educated and moral person: and the ideal that he recognizes, in so far as it can be traced to particular minds, will largely be an ideal created for him by the great ethical thinkers who have not always been, though sometimes they have been, systematic Philosophers. But the analysis and systematic exposition of the moral ideal may help to make that ideal clearer, and so to clear up ethical difficulties which arise simply from the want of intellectual lucidity about that ideal of a supreme good which analysis discovers to underlie the ordinary moral judgements of practical people. And the attempt to analyse involves also the attempt at greater consistency; and to get this greater consistency some amendment in the received conception of the end may often be required. And the greater consistency, coherence, and connected-ness which the Moral Philosopher finds it necessary to introduce into his own beliefs may spread in time firstly to the actual students of his works, and then (through the ordinary channels of literature and social influence) to a wider public. So again, when we turn to the question of means, the Moral Philosopher may not be a better judge than other men of the way to secure a given social end. But he must at least have accustomed himself to consider the relation of means to ends, to ask the ground of the received rules of conduct, to bear in mind both the importance of general rules and the limitations to their application, to think of remote consequences as well as immediate ones, and finally to recognize when the solution of the problem depends upon a question of fact or some matter of technical knowledge upon which other experience than his own must be consulted. We have been obliged for the sake of clearness to distinguish the question of means from the question of ends, and yet I have already insisted on the impossibility in practice of so separating them. Every means, as we have seen, has its own positive or negative value; the ethical end is not something over and above all the means, since it consists very largely of activities which, though directed towards an end, are themselves of as much value as the ends which they realize or even of more value. The question of the means to the end is thus also a question of elements in the end. Hence there is no possibility of breaking up each ethical problem so completely into two distinct problems, and handing the solution of each over to a different person: we cannot once for all get the question of the end settled by the spiritual genius, and hand questions of means over to the man of experience and practical skill. Sometimes, indeed, such a separation is possible, but very often the ethical problems will involve both the due appreciation of comparative values and the adaptation of means to ends. In fact, very often the breaking up of the problem into a question of ends and a question of means almost carries with it the solution of it; at least this is just the contribution towards the solution which the Moral Philosopher as such is especially qualified to make.

In ways like these it may reasonably be contended that the study of Moral Philosophy—the labours of the professed Moral Philosopher, the direct study of Moral Philosophy as an element of education, and the indirect influence of its ideas on the

community generally—may contribute a valuable element to
the solution of moral problems, to that gradual clearing up of
the moral ideal, that gradual decision of disputed questions, that
gradual advance to higher ideals, or that fuller application and
realization of ideals already accepted, in which moral progress
consists.   But to say that he may contribute to the solution is
a very different thing from supposing that the solution of them
can be handed over to the ethical expert as such.   The value of
a man's opinions upon particular questions of general conduct
or individual duty, whether he is a Moral Philosopher or not,
will depend no doubt mainly upon his natural capacity for moral
insight, upon the training which that capacity has received, upon
character, upon general intellectual training, upon experience of
life in general or of the particular department and aspect of
life in question.   But the great difference between the Moral
Philosopher and the 'plain man' or the professor of some
specialized practical Science is this:—that the Moral Philosopher
knows, or ought to know, distinctly what he is aiming at, and
the practical man often does not.   It is not so much that the
Moral Philosopher can answer ethical questions better than other
people, but that he knows how to put them better than other
people.   Take, for instance, the case of Vivisection.   As one
reads the utterances of Judges, Physiologists, Physicians, Eccle-
siastics, Politicians, and Journalists upon the question, one is
struck by the fact that not one in fifty of them seems to know
what he has got to prove.   The Physiologist often shows that
he has but a very confused idea of what a moral question is.
He labours to prove that Vivisection advances knowledge or
saves pain without seeming to be aware that some people might
quite intelligibly hold that knowledge ought not to be obtained
or pain saved by such and such means or in such and such
circumstances, and that the question whether they are right or
not cannot be settled by Physiology.   On the other hand, the
Anti-vivisectionist rails at the immorality of doing evil that
good may come without asking how on such a principle he is to
justify a surgical operation or a judicial punishment.   In the
present state of opinion, Moralists are not likely to be in entire
agreement about Vivisection more than other people.   Even

among Moralists of the same school there is still room for different applications of accepted principles. But even so, it would probably be found that the extremes of opinion would rarely be discovered among competent students of Moral Philosophy. If anybody doubts whether the conscious and deliberate application of theory to moral questions is not capable of enormously reducing the debatable area, he should read Edmund Gurney's Essays on the subject in *Tertium Quid*. That very earnest and independent thinker argued the question on hedonistic-utilitarian grounds, and decided in favour of Vivisection severely limited and regulated; and this is just one of the cases where the decision is not likely to be very much affected by the adoption of an ideal in place of a hedonistic Utilitarianism, though the non-hedonist is likely to give greater weight than the Hedonist to the effect of the thing upon the character of those who practise or witness it.

I may put what I have been saying in another form by saying that the function of the Moral Philosopher in the decision of ethical questions is rather that of the Judge than that of the jury. Consulted as to what a man ought to do under such and such circumstances, he will not, *qua* Moral Philosopher, say, 'You should do this or that,' but rather he will explain the relevant ethical principles, apply them to the facts of the case, and then say, 'If you think that this action will produce such and such results, or if you think such and such an end more important than this or that other end, then do so-and-so; if not, don't. If you think, for instance, that these experiments have such and such a chance of saving pain; if you think that the pain they may save is equivalent to what they must cost; if you think that the good to humanity which they may effect is morally more than equivalent to any hardening of the heart which they may possibly bring with them, then perform these experiments; if not, don't.' Such is the way that the Moral Philosopher will sum up the case, whether to his own Conscience or to somebody else. The Moral Philosopher is the Judge, the Conscience and judgement of the individual (whether the philosopher himself or his client) are the jury.

V

I may add one further remark. Most of the objections brought against Casuistry, whether in its theological or its purely philosophical form, affect mainly the scientific consideration of individual, and especially of abnormal and exceptional, problems in conduct. The most, it seems to me, that Moral Philosophy can do for such cases is to produce, in conjunction with other studies and influences, a habit of mind favourable to their reasonable consideration. We may quite well deprecate the discussion of such abnormal cases by anticipation, and may even admit that when they do occur in actual practice a healthy instinct will decide them better than theoretical subtlety. But the assailant of Casuistry usually talks as if on the general questions of conduct—on those general questions of which each man has to settle a good many for himself one way or another every day between the time he gets up in the morning and the time he goes to bed at night—he talks (I say) as if on such questions as these there was a general consensus, at least among sensible and well-meaning people. Such an assumption seems to me the very shallowest of delusions. Directly we leave words and come to things, the consensus disappears. It is merely the vagueness of language that seems to sanction its existence. People are agreed, no doubt, as to the wrongness of murder. But that is only because murder means killing, except where killing is justifiable. As to the immorality of killing in war, or by means of punishment, or to reduce population, or by way of Euthanasia, there is no consensus at all. No doubt, in these questions of merely negative Morality there is an approximate consensus among the great majority. But come to positive precepts. There, again, we find a consensus as to copy-book headings, such as ' Be truthful, be honest, be charitable, be temperate.' There is a consensus as to virtues; there is none as to duties. ' Be temperate.' Yes. But there are many ways of being temperate. It is possible to eat and drink wealth equivalent to one pound, or even five pounds, a day without positively injuring one's constitution; and it is possible also to live on a shilling a day, or with practice on a great deal less.

Which course am I to adopt, my income and position being so-
and-so? I ought to give money to Charity; but how much?
I ought to provide for the future; but how much? I ought to
devote myself to my profession; but how much time should
I give to my pupils? I ought to research; but how ought I to
divide my time between research, teaching, and amusement, or
more general social duties? It is no use to say that an exact
determination of such questions is impossible. There is scarcely
a consensus as to the barest outline of an answer. It is on these
general questions of conduct, which can never be escaped, rather
than in the discussion of abnormal complications of individual
circumstance, that the practical application of clearly thought
out ethical principles seems likely to be most fruitful.

VI

The question what in detail are the methods by which Moral
Philosophy solves these questions of means to the ideal end
for individual and community is one which it does not lie
within the scope of this work to discuss. There is no conceivable
branch of knowledge which may not at this or that point have
a bearing upon some question of conduct. Every Science has or
may have its social applications. It may no doubt be contended
that the Science which has the most direct and immediate
bearing upon questions of conduct is the Science of Society in
general. It has recently been contended that the place of Moral
Philosophy, as it has hitherto been understood, is hereafter to be
taken by a 'rational moral Art' based upon a comprehensive
Sociology. It is not even suggested that such a Science can give
us a new method of discovering the true end at which Society
ought to aim—the criterion by which to judge whether one state
of society is better than another. And, so long as the suggestion
relates merely to the mode of discovering what kinds of conduct
are best suited to attain a given end, it cannot be denied that
the understanding of Society and the ways in which it evolves
is the Science of all others which would be most calculated to
throw light upon the means of social improvement, and consequently upon problems of individual conduct. It is hardly
alleged that such a comprehensive Science exists in a form which

is at present competent to supply much information as to the means of social improvement. Sociology, in the form which it has hitherto assumed, consists for the most part of generalizations which, even if well founded, are far too vague and abstract to be fruitful of practical applications. Such attempts at rapid and immediate application as have hitherto been made are too often vitiated by assumptions and confusions of the kind which we have already examined in connexion with the Ethics of Herbert Spencer. It is a good feature of the more recent sociological teaching that the idea of a complete Sociology, resting for the most part on more or less distant physiological analogies and more or less irrelevant generalizations from Anthropology, seems to be in process of being superseded by the idea of a group of sociological Sciences, each of them dealing with some particular aspect of social phenomena—religious, economic, political, hygienic, and the like—or of careful enquiries, by way of statistics or otherwise, into the causes of particular social tendencies and the remedies for particular social diseases. There is really nothing particularly novel in the idea that the accepted codes of ethical behaviour have been, are being, and must be, criticized and remoulded in the light of advancing knowledge, and that such knowledge must be based upon the study of past and present social facts. The changes that have taken place in the general attitude towards the problem of poverty, for instance, have been profoundly modified by the teaching first of the older political economy and then of the more socialistic tendencies of recent economic thought. Our ideas as to the duties of parents and educators have been revolutionized by a change of sentiment based in part upon experience of the effects of different kinds of treatment, which we may, if we like, call an advance of pedagogic Science. Of Sociology so understood it may fairly be said that there is nothing new about it except the name.

It is no doubt possible to speculate about a future Science of Society which will hereafter sum up and co-ordinate all the results of the separate lines of sociological enquiry. But it may be doubted whether the idea of a single Science of Society does not really represent too vast a programme to be treated with

much success by any special body of experts. The professor of
any particular branch of Social Science ought, no doubt, to know
something about Society in general and about the Science of
Society in general, in so far as such knowledge admits of being
reduced to the form of a Science: but when it comes to practical
applications it is probable that the opinions of the 'Educationist'
(if indeed his opinion is to be preferred to that of the experienced
teacher) on a question of education, or of an Economist on
a question of financial policy, or of the political thinker on
a question of Legislation or Administration will not always be of
more value than the opinion of an expert in so comprehensive
a science as the Science of Society in general.

Even if we look forward to the gradual building up of
a Sociology of a kind which, it is admitted, does not now exist,
it will be impossible to admit that ethical Science will ever be
wholly swallowed up in that of Sociology. The moral nature of
man, though undoubtedly in very close connexion with other
aspects of his nature, will always remain a distinct aspect of it,
and an aspect quite as much worthy of separate study as the
physical or economic aspects of individual or society. It is true,
again, that this moral nature can—sometimes, from some points
of view, for some purposes—be studied as exhibited on a large
scale in the actions, characteristics, and conduct of whole societies,
but after all those larger phenomena only admit of being understood in the light of a close study and appreciation of the
individual man. Even in studying Society at large, it must be
remembered that moral progress, though closely connected with
other kinds of progress, is not the same thing as any other kind
of progress. It must further be insisted that no possible study
of the facts of past history will ever by itself supply a solution
of present moral difficulties. The moral ideal grows and
developes; its growth is affected doubtless by environment and
by history, but we can never construct a moral ideal merely out
of the study of the past. It is the tendency of the Sociologist to
insist upon the influence which history and circumstance have
exercised upon ideals without remembering the equally important influence which ideals—ideals which from their very nature
are new and unpredictable—are continually exercising upon

history. The ideals are always growing, and for that very reason it is never possible that the mere study of the past, or even the discovery of sociological laws, can form a complete guide even as to the means to what presents itself to us as the true ideal—still less as to the value of the ideals themselves. It is no doubt well to emphasize the fact that individual conduct often depends upon the answer that is given to large problems of social and political policy which can only be solved by the study of social facts, and cannot be determined off-hand by the intuitions of the average man or even of the moral genius. But there will always remain the question of the individual's duty in the face of a given social situation and of ascertained social laws[1]. And the question what that duty is will always be a question which, in so far as it admits of scientific study and solution at all, must remain the problem of Moral Philosophy, the methods of which, for reasons which have already appeared in the course of our enquiry, can never be precisely the same as those of any other Science.

We might no doubt, if we pleased, break up Moral Philosophy into a Science of ends which is a branch of Metaphysic, and a Science of means which is a branch of general Social Science, but in each case the branch which deals with the question of individual duty is so distinctive a one that it will always demand separate treatment, while the fact that from the ethical point of view the means are part of the end will always forbid a too sharp separation between the two problems. The close connexion between Moral Science and the particular social Sciences which exist or the more comprehensive Social Science which is little more than an aspiration, may be admitted. It is only the patronizing and superior tone which such writers as M. Lévy-Bruhl adopt towards the whole conception of a Moral Science which compels us to insist that it is only by ignoring the real problems of the moral life that that Science can be

[1] I pass over the question of the sense in which we can speak of 'laws' in social matters as a problem belonging in part to Logic, in part to Sociology itself, merely protesting against the idea that such laws are to be identified with mechanical 'uniformities.' The limitations which must always exist to the discovery of such laws have been insisted on in the chapter on Free-will.

treated as already superseded by a positive Science of Society.
The distinction between what is and what ought to be, between
what is and what is good, must always be an important one
except for those who believe that they have abolished the latter
category altogether. For those who believe in the distinction
there must always remain a Science of the good and of the
means thereto [1].

VII

It is no doubt extremely important that the ethical enquirer
should not make immediate edification his primary object. His
business is to examine, to test, and to criticize existing moral
ideas; and, if he is to perform that task, he must avoid the
temptation to become the mere apologist of the actually received
Morality. But, if the primary object of every Science is simply
knowledge for its own sake, it is unreasonable to assume that
any Science will exercise no influence upon practical life, and
that assumption is peculiarly gratuitous when we have to do
with the Science whose very object-matter is practice. And

---

[1] These remarks are suggested by M. L. Lévy-Bruhl's *La Morale et la
Science des Mœurs* (Ed. ii., 1904). The real difference between the author's
position and that taken up in the present work lies not so much in what
the author actually contends with regard to the relations between Sociology
and Morality as in the whole conception of the Universe, of Man, and of
Society implied by his book—a conception which is rather assumed than
established by any attempt to grapple with its difficulties. On these ultimate
questions this clever writer does not appear to have advanced much beyond
the position of Comte and Herbert Spencer, though he has no doubt
avoided many of their crudities; but at bottom he traces the idea of moral
obligation exclusively to the operation of external social sanctions. M. Rauh,
in his *L'Expérience morale*, seems to me to have a much juster ideal of the
true relations between the individual and the social Conscience, and again
between the place of Science and the individual moral judgement. 'Entre
l'art de vivre et la philosophie de la morale il y a place pour une science de
la vie (ib., p. 237).' This seems to be just the modern equivalent of the old
Casuistry which I desiderate—the attempt to bring the actual, growing
Conscience of mankind into contact with the real problems of life and
Society in general in the light of full scientific knowledge of Man and of
Society; though the author seems to me somewhat unduly to disparage the
importance of Metaphysic as a basis (though not a substitute) for the
theoretical study of Morals, and even its practical value in helping to
a proper appreciation of the idea of Morality in general and consequently
of duties in particular.

the practical value of ethical Science does not consist, I believe, entirely in the discussion and settlement of particular disputed questions of conduct.   I am prepared to contend that the study of the general principles of Moral Philosophy is not only an important element in general intellectual education, but that it is likely (if conducted in the right way) to exert a stimulating influence upon character and life.   'To the attainment of the virtues knowledge conduces little or nothing,'[1] said Aristotle. That is quite true ; and it is no less true that 'knowledge puffeth up, but love edifieth.'   But it is true, also, that very often 'more harm is done from want of thought than want of will.'   To produce the habit of reflection about conduct, or what Thomas Arnold used to call 'moral thoughtfulness,' is one of the chief objects of moral education.   After all, it would really be strange if the thinking about duty should be found, as a rule, to have a demoralizing tendency.   Moral Philosophy will not make a good man any more than Theology will make a religious man. But it has usually been considered that a certain amount of religious or theological teaching is helpful in that direction, when conjoined with that personal influence by which alone, as it has been well said, Virtue is really teachable.   It is a modest plea to urge that good effects may, likewise in due subordination to the living influence of personal character and other emotional forces, spring from the thoughtful consideration of moral prin- ciples carried to whatever point of theoretical abstraction is demanded by the general level of the individual's education and culture.

   Such study is likely to be beneficial in two ways—in a directly ethical way and in another way which may be called ethico-religious.   The mere clearing up of difficulties and per- plexities of personal conduct is likely to be the least conspicuous effect which the study of Moral Philosophy may have upon those who study it in a right spirit.   First, as regards the directly ethical way—there are, as we have discovered, strict limits to the extent to which even professed students of Moral Philosophy are likely to be the better able to clear up such difficulties owing to their theoretical training.   But exceptional

----

[1] *Eth. Nic.* II, cap. iv, 3 (p. 1105 *b*).

5 1

difficulties are not the greatest difficulties of practical life.
Apart altogether from the abnormal crises which supply
problems for the Casuist and plots for the literary Artist, most
people find it hard enough, or would find it hard enough if they
thought more, to deal with the difficulties that occur in every
life and at all periods of that life. It is by giving men a clearer
conception of the end of life and of their particular duty in it
that Moral Philosophy is, I think, likely to be of most practical
use. And this influence, be it observed, is to a large extent
independent of the particular system which the man learns and
the particular books or living teachers whom he chances to fall
in with. To some extent every one must build up his own
ideal of life for himself: but he may be powerfully aided in
building it up by having his attention directed to the theoretical
aspects of the subject, and by being forced to give a definite
answer to the questions which men are tempted to postpone till
the answer to them is useless. Intellectual clearness is not the
chief prerequisite of a good life. In the infancy of speculation
men were disposed to exaggerate its influence. Socrates and the
great Stoics, though even they were quite as much ethical
prophets as speculative philosophers, have been less successful
ethical teachers than the Saints and the heroes who have cared
little for ethical theory. But Socrates was not wrong in
believing that intellectual clearness about the ideal of life is one
of the influences that make for Morality, at least by taking
away some of the obstacles to it in characters not wanting in
the desires and emotions from which right action must spring.
It will very likely be objected that I am confusing the functions
of the moral teacher with that of the Moral Philosopher. But
I should submit that no absolute line can be drawn between
the provinces of the two. There is some theory even in the
Catechism; and there is much practical teaching, good or bad,
to be found in the writings of Plato and Aristotle, of Kant and
Hegel, of Spinoza and Schopenhauer. The higher the intellectual level of the moral teaching, the larger may be the
amount of theory introduced into it, or at least the larger may
be the influence which a sound moral theory may exercise upon it.
All ethical teaching should be, as far as possible, consistent with

a sound ethical Philosophy, though the practical teacher may himself be very little of a Philosopher.   When the object of the teaching is mainly practical, the element of theory will naturally be kept very much in the background.   In the teaching of Moral Philosophy as a branch of intellectual study the intellectual side—the desire to get theoretical truth—should be uppermost : and no desire for immediate edification should prevent difficulties being probed to the bottom.   It is otherwise in the practical teaching of the School, or the newspaper, or the pulpit.   But the man who thinks and the man who acts are, after all, one and the same person : and at a high level of Culture the theoretical study of Ethics may often be a means of awakening interest in the practical problems of life, and of stimulating the sense of duty—particularly in minds in which the break-up of traditional religious or ethical systems has involved a confusion or a reaction which does not always stop at the merely intellectual form under which moral ideals have been presented to them.   There is no reason why Moral Philosophers, or persons not uninfluenced by the systematic study of Moral Philosophy, should not also to some extent be moral teachers, as they were (with admirable results) in the days of Seneca and Marcus Aurelius.

The second way in which Moral Philosophy is likely to be practically useful is through its connexion with Religion. A reasonable Theology must be based upon a sound ethical system : or, to put it in a more concrete way, it must be based upon the evidence and the contents of the moral consciousness [1]. That does not of course mean that the individual must have consciously gone through the intellectual process by which the reflective Philosopher arrives at his speculative system.   Even for the highly intellectual man (as I have fully explained) Religion may at times be perfectly rational and yet largely ' unconscious '—in the sense that its intellectual basis is not fully analysed.   But, in the present state of religious thought, it is but too obvious that for many besides persons of the highest education this 'unconscious' Religion often gives way through

---

[1] This must be understood in the sense and with the qualifications set forth in the first and second chapters of this book.

the breaking-down of the historical and dogmatic traditions with which it has been associated. I believe the study of Moral Philosophy to be one of the means by which for such minds Religion may be purified and its influence restored. No doubt the speculative basis of Religion must be sought not in Ethics taken by itself but in Ethics taken in connexion with that general theory of the Universe which we call Philosophy. But of all branches of Philosophy Ethics is the one which has the closest connexion with religious belief; and, if its province be extended so as to cover the connexion between the idea of an objective Morality and a religious view of the Universe, it is, I think, not impossible for Ethics to be studied with advantage even by persons who have hardly the leisure or capacity for any very thorough study of pure Logic or pure Metaphysics. There is no hard and fast line between Moral Philosophy and a sound practical teaching of Ethics; just as there is none, or ought to be none, between the highest Religious Philosophy and the Religion which may be taught to a child. There may be teaching and writing and study at every level of theoretical thoroughness and completeness. The reading of formal books of Moral Philosophy must necessarily be confined to a comparatively small class; but the larger that class can become, the more it is likely that the general teaching of Religion and Morality will be pervaded by the influence of a sound religious and ethical Philosophy [1].

[1] It may be objected, perhaps, that I am assuming that the Philosophy which will be taught is the particular system expounded in these pages (or some other system favourable to a theistic Religion based on Morality); and that the teaching of Moral Philosophy may result, either through the influence of particular teachers and books or through the working of the readers' and pupils' own minds, in a sceptical attitude towards both Religion and Morality. This is of course true, but such results have been known to follow from the teaching of the most rigidly conservative systems of Ethics and Theology. Of course there are limits to the extent to which it is desirable that speculative questions should be presented to untrained or very immature minds. But I freely confess that I know of no way of teaching people to think without their sometimes taking the liberty to think differently from their teacher. For all that, I am prepared to maintain that to make people think is both a good thing in itself and on the whole likely to have good results in the more narrowly ethical sense.

These remarks are made from the point of one who personally believes that the idea of an objective Morality logically involves the theistic view of the Universe, and is most effectively taught in connexion with that view. But I do not limit the value of this teaching of Moral Philosophy to the influence of persons and books in harmony with these views. I should expect some good effects to flow from the teaching of any Philosophy which recognizes the objectivity of the Moral Law ; and much of what I have said of the practical effects of ethical teaching might even be applicable to the teaching of systems of a sceptical or destructive tendency ; since the moral consciousness exists even in those who deny its authority or misunderstand its nature, and its influence may be increased even by inadequate attempts at the explanation of it. Still it is impossible for one who admits the influence of theory upon practical life to deny that the tendency of false or one-sided or sceptical theoretical influences may, and must in the long run, have a destructive and injurious practical influence. But it is not for those who believe in the ultimate rationality of the Universe to attempt to counteract the influence of such theories by the suppression or discouragement of serious thinking.

Moral Philosophy must be looked upon primarily as a speculative Science. Its study requires no other justification than the fact that it is the study of one of the most fundamental of our intellectual ideas, of one most important department or aspect of Reality. But in considering the question by whom and to what extent Moral Philosophy should be studied, the question of its practical bearing upon life is not irrelevant. Even the purely speculative Science should have its group of special students, but it need not necessarily have a place in ordinary non-specialist Education. A few words may be said on this latter topic.

VIII

The place of Moral Philosophy in Education must depend in part, of course, upon the place which we assign to Philosophy in general : and it is impossible here to attempt an adequate defence of the position that Philosophy is the ideal culmination

5 1 *

and goal of all non-specialist Education. The reason for that conclusion is simply the fact that Philosophy is the Science of the Universe at large : some thought and some ideas about the Universe at large do seem almost obviously to form part of an ideal education. And in that Science of the Universe at large the Science which deals with the ends of human life and the means by which they are to be attained must naturally occupy a peculiarly prominent place. It is possible, of course, to impart ideas about the true end of human life in other ways than by the theoretical study of Morality—by literature, by history, by systematic religious and moral teaching of the hortative, authoritative, or emotional kind. But when that questioning spirit which it is the business of the highest Education to evoke has once been aroused, it will not be content with a moral instruction which rests wholly upon Authority or appeals only to the emotions. Some knowledge of the nature and grounds of moral obligation should indeed form part of all Education, even the most elementary—some teaching about the existence and authority of Conscience, and about the general rules of action. When this kind of Education is carried up as it were to the highest intellectual level, it becomes Moral Philosophy. There is no absolutely sharp line of distinction between those general ideas about the Universe which actually do form part of all Education, even as it is, and that systematic and reasoned enquiry which we call Philosophy. When and in proportion as the attempt to think about things in general becomes systematic and thoroughgoing, it becomes Philosophy. In the same way there is no absolute line of distinction between simple moral instruction when once it attempts to give a reason—when it says 'don't do this *because* Conscience forbids you' or 'don't do that *because* it gives pain or has such and such other bad results'— and the most scientific Ethics. Just as an ideal intellectual education would culminate in Philosophy, so the ideal moral education would culminate in Moral Philosophy. It is true that when we reach the intellectual level which we call systematic Philosophy, it is an essential part of the intellectual discipline that we should not be too narrowly or immediately eager about practical results. While we are actually engaged in speculation, the mind must be opened not only to the question 'what is duty' or 'what is moral obligation,' but also to the question whether there be such things as duty and moral obligation or not.   But that does not prevent our holding that in the long run, at a certain level of intellectual development, for minds and characters duly prepared, it is to the interest of practical Morality that such questions should be raised; and that the attempt to answer them is an instrument not only of intellectual but of moral Education.   And, if Religion be, in the sense which has been explained in previous chapters, founded upon the testimony of the moral consciousness, it will be a means of religious Education also.   In an age in which authoritative Religion often loses its hold over cultivated minds in consequence of the discovery of the inadequate views of History and Theology with which it has been associated, the study of Philosophy, and especially the ethical and religious side of it, may be a peculiarly valuable means of strengthening or restoring the beliefs which are essential or most favourable to the highest kind of life.   These remarks are of course made from the point of view of those who believe that such questions as 'what is duty?' 'what is the end of the Universe?' and the like admit of a constructive answer.   What is the best means of moral Education from the point of view of those who do not believe that there is in our sense of the word any such thing as Morality or moral obligation, is a question which I do not profess to answer.

I will not here enlarge upon the practical reasons which make our ideal of an education culminating in Philosophy an ideal which cannot actually be carried out even in the case of all those who receive what is, in the ordinary sense of the word, the highest education.   The ideal education must remain an ideal: those who are best trained in Science or History, in Literature or Philology, must often in practice learn very little about that philosophic view of the Universe as a whole which is the ideal culmination of all knowledge: those who busy themselves with ultimate questions about the Universe must too often remain ignorant enough of the particular branches of knowledge upon which ideally a true Philosophy of the Universe should rest.   All we can do is to aim at the ideal in so far as practical needs and circumstances permit. I will only make two further remarks which directly concern the place of Moral Philosophy in Education. The first is that Moral Philosophy seems peculiarly well adapted for the study of those who can only study Philosophy a little. It is less technical, and in its earliest stages less difficult than Logic or Metaphysic : and, though it is not (I think) desirable that it should be taught in entire disconnexion from the metaphysical or theological problems to which it ultimately leads, these problems are here approached from their most practical and least technical side. The other point on which I should insist is that it would seem especially desirable as an element in the education of all whose sphere of work is man or human society in general, rather than the dealing with material things or even with any highly specialized department of human affairs. It would seem specially important for the clergyman (on account both of its theoretical connexion with Theology and of its practical bearings upon life) ; for the teacher, who can have no theoretical idea of the object of Education without it ; for the writer on public affairs—I hope it will not be thought to involve too Aristotelian a view of the State if I add the practical politician or civil servant. If from one point of view Moral Philosophy connects itself with Metaphysic or speculative Philosophy, there is another point of view from which it is closely connected with the theoretical study of Politics, of Law, and of Social Philosophy in all its branches. These can hardly be dealt with scientifically at all without some previous study (however general and elementary) of that ideal of human life which, as Aristotle held, is the same for the man and for the citizen, and of that moral nature of man which makes such an ideal possible. Moral Philosophy is the essential basis of any Political Philosophy that has any claim to be called Philosophy at all. Political Philosophy is generally regarded as concerned chiefly with the means to the end of human life in so far as it can be promoted by State action. There is indeed so much consensus as to what is good in human life, in that broad and rough way in which the good can be promoted by State action, that for the most part political discussion, whether theoretical or practical, is concerned chiefly with the question of means. But still no true theory of the State, or of

its functions and limitations, is possible without some preliminary
clearing up of the ideas of right and wrong, justice and injustice,
good and evil.   And there are a large class of questions relating
to State interference in various departments of life—Punishment, Liberty, Coercion, Toleration, and the like—which lie on
the borderland between Moral and Political Philosophy, and
which cannot be satisfactorily dealt with without some consideration of purely ethical problems.   In no department of life
is it easier to show that the most important practical results
have followed from the view which people have consciously or
unconsciously taken of what may seem very theoretical and
speculative questions.   I have explained already that in questions
of practical action the Moral Philosopher as such is a man who
knows how to put the question better than other people rather
than the man who knows how to answer it better than other
people.   But very often to put the question rightly goes a long
way towards giving a satisfactory answer to it.   In their attitude towards social problems, in their dealings with crime, in
their relations with lower races, in their religious and educational
policy, modern States have been and obviously are at.this moment
dominated by all kinds of theories of the kind which it is the
business of Moral Philosophy to test.   It is a modest claim for
Moral Philosophy to contend that some acquaintance with these
questions in their speculative form may conduce to clearness of
view in dealing with them on their practical side.

The mention of Political Philosophy may, I trust, be valuable
as an indication of the kind of practical usefulness which we
may expect from Moral Philosophy.   As regards Political Philosophy the prejudices which have stood in the way of a reasonable
view of the relation between theory and practice are largely
absent.   Nobody supposes that the political thinker as such is
necessarily well qualified for any one of the branches of practical Statesmanship or administration.   Everybody is aware
that many of the very greatest Statesmen have been entirely
ignorant of, or very little influenced by, political theories in anything like a speculative form.   And yet there is no shallower
view of History than to suppose that in the political sphere
theories have not profoundly influenced life—theories which

have often had their origin in the brains of purely speculative or academic thinkers. Plato's mistake about the Philosopher-King consisted only in the assumption (so far as we take him literally) that the person who excogitates and expounds the theories must be also the person to give them practical effect as legislator or administrator. The influence which the Moral Philosopher has exercised, and with advantage might exercise to a still greater extent, over practical life is, I believe, of the same kind as the influence of the theoretical writer on Politics : and to a very large extent that influence will be exercised in the same sphere, for it is (as I have already contended) in respect of large questions of public or social policy that there is most room for the theoretical discussion of questions of duty, and that the dangers and limitations which attach to the attempt theoretically to discuss details of personal conduct have the least application. To discuss some large question of social duty or policy—the uses of wealth, the limits of personal expenditure, the way to deal with poverty, the treatment of the unemployed, the problem of religious and moral education, the treatment of crime, the organization of industry, the morality of Vivisection, the duty of the higher races to the lower—with due reference to first principles would seem to be the proper sphere for such applied Moral Philosophy or Casuistry as is possible and desirable under the conditions of modern life. The Moral Philosopher as such has of course only to do with the principles, not with the particular applications, and to discuss any one of these subjects in any detail involves many kinds of knowledge and experience which the Philosopher as such is very far from possessing. To make himself master of the knowledge required for the solution of some one practical problem or group of problems, and to discuss it in the light of a reasonable theory of life and of Society, would be enough to absorb the energies of a Moral Philosopher who wished to become a Casuist of the kind that the modern world requires.

In the present work the discussion of even the most general problems of conduct has been smaller perhaps than is usual in formal treatises upon Moral Philosophy. I have touched upon such questions sufficiently, I trust, to indicate the lines on which they should be dealt with, and to avoid the imputation of having

shirked the real difficulties of our subject.   Even for the purely
theoretical interests of Moral Philosophy it is essential, I believe,
at every turn to take practical examples.   Whatever may be
thought of its claims as a definite Science, Casuistry is essential
for the illustration of Moral Philosophy even in its most abstract
form.   In the present work the treatment of particular virtues
or duties has hardly gone beyond the limits of illustration.   To
give a more detailed account of the ideal of life—of the chief
goods of life, their relative importance or their place in *the* good,
and the main rules of action which conduce to the attainment of
these goods, is, I believe, a task which falls strictly within the
province of Moral Philosophy.   It might even be contended that
the very general discussions with which this work has been
chiefly occupied are the mere Prolegomena to an ideal 'System
of Moral Philosophy.'   But in the present state of ethical Science,
there is no consensus even as to the Prolegomena.   It is here
that the purely theoretical or strictly philosophical difficulties of
the subject lie, though it is after these Prolegomena are settled
that the real difficulties for the practical ethical judgement begin.
Perhaps I shall some day be tempted to essay some fuller account
of the practical ideal which to my own mind would seem to result
from the principles which I have endeavoured to indicate.   Why
a more detailed application of the ideal to the concrete difficulties
of individual and social life is a task which is not likely to be
attempted with success by persons much better qualified for the
task than the present writer, I have already tried to explain.
Such a task is not the proper task of Moral Philosophy, not
because Casuistry is impossible or immoral, but because it is too
extensive a Science to be professed, and too difficult an Art to be
practised, by any one person or any particular class of academical
or professional persons.   The Science and **Art** of Casuistry merge
in that Science and Art of Life which all branches of theoretical
knowledge, all branches of enquiry or literature, all professions
and callings are or ought to be in various manners and degrees
engaged in constructing and in practising.   It is enough for the
Moral Philosopher and his Science if, by the discussion of the more
general principles upon which such questions should be decided,
they may make a not unimportant contribution to their solution.

INDEX

It is hoped that the Analytical Table of Contents prefixed to each volume will dispense with the necessity of a fuller index.